Also by Frank J. Donner

The Un-Americans

THE Age OF
Surveillance

THE Age OF Surveillance

The Aims and Methods
of America's
Political Intelligence System

BY Frank J. Donner

ALFRED A. KNOPF   NEW YORK   1980

THIS IS A BORZOI BOOK
PUBLISHED BY ALFRED A. KNOPF, INC.

Copyright © 1980 by Frank J. Donner

All rights reserved under International and Pan-American Copyright Conventions. Published in the United States by Alfred A. Knopf, Inc., New York, and simultaneously in Canada by Random House of Canada Limited, Toronto. Distributed by Random House, Inc., New York.

Grateful acknowledgment is made to Norma Millay Ellis for permission to reprint an excerpt from Sonnet CXL, "Upon This Gifted Age" by Edna St. Vincent Millay. From *Collected Poems*, Harper & Row. Copyright 1939, 1967 by Edna St. Vincent Millay and Norma Millay Ellis.

Library of Congress Cataloging in Publication Data

Donner, Frank J.
The age of surveillance.

Bibliography: p.
Includes index.
1. Intelligence service—United States.
I. Title.
JK468.16D65   1980   353.0074   79-3479
ISBN 0-394-40298-7

Manufactured in the United States of America

FIRST EDITION

To

My wife, Madeline ("Through all our earthly seasons true")

and children, Eleanor and Daniel

Contents

Acknowledgments

This book is the product of my work as Director of the American Civil Liberties Union Project on Political Surveillance. I owe a great debt to Aryeh Neier, who, as Executive Director of the A.C.L.U., conceived the project, worked to ensure its funding, authorized reprinting and dissemination of my articles on surveillance themes, and provided useful counsel. A.C.L.U. lawyers and affiliate heads, most notably John H. F. Shattuck, Jack Novik, and Melvin Wulf, generously responded to my numerous requests for help. Grants from the Stern Fund and the Rabinowitz Foundation in the early years of the project contributed costs of field trips, document reproduction, and research aid. The Yale Law School provided office space, student researchers, and library resources. The Center for National Securities Studies (and in particular Monica Andres, its librarian), the Law Center for Constitutional Rights, the Constitutional Litigation Clinic at Rutgers University, the Committee for Public Justice, the Tax Reform Research Group (especially Louise Brown), and the American Friends Service Committee provided vital assistance in the form of documents and other source material. The Field Foundation funded my final research.

For research help I am grateful to Kathe Fox Winn, Emily Soltanoff, Ann Fabian, and Leslie Engel. To Emily Oprea I owe a special debt. This extraordinary woman significantly aided my research, expertly administered a document acquisition program, organized and indexed my file collection, and typed original and revised versions of most of the book's chapters. For guidance and encouragement I am deeply indebted to Carey McWilliams. As always, lawyers were more than generous, particularly Richard Lavine, Eugene Cerruti, William Bender, Douglass Cassel, Kenneth Tilsen, Richard Gutman, Marshall Perlin, Doris Petersen, Flint Taylor, George Corsetti, Ramsey Clark, Burton Weinstein, Doris Walker, David Kairys, David Rudovsky, Robin Yeamans, and Jerry Berman. Professors Thomas Emerson, H. H. Wilson, Vern Countryman,

Frank Askin, Norman Dorsen, and Herman Schwartz contributed both advice and research assistance. Among the many journalists who shared with me the fruits of their investigations I owe special thanks to Jack Anderson, Les Whitten, Joseph Spear, Paul Altmeyer, Jason Berry, Victor Navasky, and Marc Weiss. For information about various aspects of intelligence, both operational and institutional, I am indebted to Nancy Miller, Joseph Burton, Barbara Stocking, Christopher Pyle, Donna Allen, John Elliff, Harvey Kahn, Sheila O'Donnell, Esther Herst, Syd Stapleton, William Florence, Paul Mayer, Raye Matthews, Richard Criley, Jon Frappier, Lee Hertzenberg, Louise Halper, Don Donner, Michael Wright, Daniel Ellsberg, Robert Wall, David Sannes, and Lillian Albertson. My hunt for source material was aided by a number of legislators and officials, especially Senator Abraham Ribicoff, Congressmen Don Edwards, Robert Drinan, Robert Kastenmeier, and staff members of committees with which they are associated. For expert manuscript typing and secretarial assistance I owe much to Mary van Sante, Pauline Stow, Joan Welch, Arlene Fields, and Victoria Markoe.

Introduction

This book, together with a companion volume now in preparation on urban political intelligence, marks the end of a long journey. In the late forties I began collecting materials from a wide range of sources—press clippings, legal documents and court records, pamphlets, interviews, reports, government publications, to name the salient ones—dealing with official attacks on nonconformity. The intensification of repression in the fifties led to an obsession (no other word will do) with the collection and filing of such data. To ensure more complete coverage, I enlisted a nationwide network of friends, colleagues, victims, and libertarian activists who regularly monitored local follies and cruelties for me. My file library itself in turn became a source for civil liberties lawyers and writers and (later, in the seventies) for congressional investigative committees. The accumulation and filing of such material served a deep personal need. The files and each item in them became for me a form of remonstrance, a private protest against betrayal by the government of its democratic premises. Beyond this lay the vague hope that someday I might wrest time from my law practice to present my final accounting in a book. My work as a civil liberties lawyer not only provided fresh material for my files but sharpened my desire to put it all down in a grand reckoning. As a trial consultant and later as an appellate brief writer in a series of sedition cases under the Smith Act, I became professionally concerned more directly with surveillance questions, since the government's case in all of these trials was uniformly based on an assortment of secret political intelligence practices. Similarly, my responsibilities as counsel to witnesses subpoenaed by congressional countersubversive committees and the preparation of appeals from contempt convictions of defiant witnesses illuminated in a new perspective the underpinnings of repression in our political culture. The conviction that surveillance, people watching, and similar activities unrelated to law enforcement constituted a serious and largely ignored threat to political freedom led to my acceptance of a post in 1971 as director of the American Civil Liberties Union Project on Political Surveillance. The hearings and reports of Senate and House committees investigating intelligence abuses in the early and mid-seventies produced disclosures which confirmed what I had been urging in articles and legal briefs for the preceding two decades: that an ever-growing domestic political espionage system had become an institutionalized response to dissent.

No aspect of our common life has been so battered by misconduct and betrayal as our commitment to the fullest measure of political freedom. And none of the manifold excesses of the past can compare in scope and intensity with the secret war waged continuously for over fifty years against all shades of dissenting politics by the domestic intelligence community, a virtually autonomous network of executive agencies dominated by the Federal Bureau of Investigation and supported and protected by a powerful congressional constituency. The documentation that has emerged as a result of legislation providing access to government records, congressional investigations, litigation, and journalistic enterprise tells the intelligence story with unique completeness and detail. The material used in this book to illustrate and document the treatment of such subjects as intelligence targets (virtually the entire gamut of political dissent), operational techniques (for example, informers, wiretaps, break-ins, photography), file compilation and dissemination, and aggressive ("covert") actions hardly exhausts the available supply—a supply that is continually augmented by new file releases and discovery procedures in the course of litigation. (The embarrassment occasioned by this stream of information during a period when the intelligence establishment is closing its ranks and campaigning for a restoration of its power has resulted both in a growing effort to reduce the scope of the relevant legislation, the Freedom of Information and Privacy acts, through congressional action and in the over-broad interpretation of exemptions, together with administrative curtailment of the duration of file retention.)

The enormous range and volume of these disclosures—their documentation of practices that continued unchecked without regard to the changing coloration of particular administrations—confirm beyond challenge that the surveillance of dissent is an institutional pillar of our political order, a mode of governance. At the same time, they renew the perception that judicial proceedings not only deny protection against intelligence abuses but block an understanding of the true role of intelligence in American statecraft. Intelligence activities that involve an abuse of power or an invasion of constitutional protections of individual victims are, in theory, subject to judicial restraint. But such relief has, in practice, been rarely forthcoming. To begin with, the clandestine character of intelligence operations, the difficulty of identifying the source of a claimed abuse, handicaps the pursuit of a judicial remedy. And the ambiguity of the injury suffered by the target, contrasted with the importance of the interest (the security of the nation itself) asserted in defense of the challenged conduct, increases a complainant's burdens. Moreover, even when such obstacles are surmounted, the successful outcome of a particular lawsuit is powerless to reduce the intimidating impact of surveillance programs: judicial remedies are typically limited to individuals and, in any event, delayed until long after the conduct complained of. As Professor Jerold Auerbach has put it, the operation may ultimately succeed—that is, the charges of rights violation may be vindicated —but the patient dies.

Only with the recent disclosure of the scope and impact of political intelligence abuses in years gone by has it been possible for its victims to seek judicial relief. Yet at this late date the courts can only order the wrongdoer to pay damages—in taxpayers' dollars, of course—for past injuries inflicted on the rights of political dissenters, and to sin no more in the future. Such relief cannot restore to bloom in the political desert of our time the movements and groups that were destructively targeted by the intelligence community in the past. Belated redress for the invasion of individual rights is, indeed, a cheap price for the protection of the status quo and the neutralization of change movements.

Despite its dubious efficacy, the availability of a courtroom remedy has protected intelligence from more basic institutional challenges. In effect, our court structure has served as a shield for political intelligence by offering deceptive relief from its excesses without disturbing its power. For this reason, this study focuses on the politics of intelligence, on the institutional usurpation and abuse of power, rather than on the violation of individual rights.

The style and tactics of adversarial intelligence systems are largely shaped by the perception of risk. The value of the intelligence product must be weighed against the safety and security risks of exposure or failure. In contrast to the sophisticated and deceptive style of high-risk intelligence employed in foreign intelligence operations, domestic intelligence has been minimally risk-conscious —and not only because of the limited role of the courts in curbing intelligence. Bureaucratic, power-and-publicity seeking, internal intelligence operations are typically marked by a crude, homespun style. To be sure, one finds cautions about the need for discretion, but even these are expressed in multi-copied memos routed to an assortment of files and possibly disseminated to other agencies or leaked to friendly press outlets. This discounting of risks reflects a confidence that no serious consequences are threatened by exposure—as, for example, a rebuke or criticism by a higher branch of government. More basically, intelligence institutions have in the past acquired strength and invulnerability because of their links to two powerful constituencies: a nativist, anti-radical political culture and an ideological anti-communism, identified with Congress and the executive branch respectively.

Allied with the political conservatism that dominates American political institutions, a nativist anti-radicalism has survived and flourished not merely as an offering in the political marketplace but as a destructive Manichean demonology. Echoing larger themes in American society, nativism is fear-centered, nourished by the twin myths (versions of reality that require no proof) of an all-powerful internal subversive enemy and a permanently endangered national security, which deny vitality to the protected freedoms. In contrast to more prominent individual rights, the court-oriented tradition associated with mainstream liberalism, it has been sustained by a passionate tribal constituency, which seeks to implement its suppressive commitment at the decision- and policy-making levels of government. From this political culture have emerged a steady stream of powerholders—elected and appointed—eager to implement its assumptions. This layer of officialdom is supported by nativist cadres, an old-boy bureaucratic net that keeps the flame burning in those periods, like the present, when the excesses of countersubversion stir the winds of criticism. The nativist suppressive syndrome also supplies private-sector recruits (individuals, organizations, and a media support structure) which have historically collaborated with official intelligence in the pursuit and harassment of targets.

American liberalism has failed to curb the repressive thrust of nativism—and not only because it has chosen to take a stand at the wrong point (the courtroom) in the governmental structure. Its commitment to the libertarian tradition has been deeply flawed (I refer here to its dominant sectors) by anticommunism and by subservience to the corporate sector. And, since the New Deal, liberal standard-bearers—intellectuals, academics, and lawyers outside of the political mainstream—have been all too ready to compromise a professed commitment to full freedom of political expression as a demonstration of political realism, the price the idealistic outsider must pay to enter the corridors of power in an insider's role. In its retreat, liberalism has historically acquiesced in substantive limitations on political expression in exchange for procedural, "due process" palliatives. In the same spirit, and until recently, it embraced clandestine countersubversive domestic intelligence sponsored by the executive as a libertarian alternative to such cruder repressive modes as legislation and exposé-style congressional investigation.

Like other dubious enterprises, intelligence has resorted to a claimed professionalism—and in particular, a cosmetic vocabulary—as a badge of legitimacy. Language has become an integral part of the subject of intelligence. Not because its terminology is particularly arcane or technical, but rather because it uses what George Steiner has called the "complex energies of language" as a shield against the constitutional, political, and ethical attacks to which it is highly vulnerable. (The same defensive need explains the proliferation of euphemisms and pseudo-professional jargon in the Vietnam War era.)

Verbal deception is itself an intelligence practice. The root term "intelligence" is adapted from military and diplomatic usage. Standing alone or in conjunction with "political," the word echoes with overtones of consequence and gravity. Spying may be objectionable, but who could object to "gathering intelligence"? The following exchange between a spy for the Committee to Re-Elect the President (CREEP) and the Watergate investigating committee counsel Samuel Dash illustrates the way in which the word "intelligence" itself masks reality:

> MR. DASH: But you were there as an infiltrator and to gather information. Therefore you were doing political espionage, were you not?
>
> MR. MCMINOWEY: I was doing political intelligence gathering.*

After World War I, the vocabulary of military intelligence was absorbed by law enforcement. The subject came to be viewed as a specialized branch of a broader general investigative function: the advance collection of information to

---

*Watergate Hearings, Bk. II, p. 4498. For a similar effort to distinguish between espionage and acceptable intelligence gathering, see the testimony of John "Fat Jack" Buckley, another CREEP operative. "I make a distinction," Mr. Buckley explained, "between deception and deceit"—Bk. II, pp. 4435–4475.

prevent and detect crime. This demilitarization of the context of intelligence stimulated in turn its assimilation to other forms of information gathering by nonpolice agencies. In this broader setting, intelligence simply means "information acquired or communicated," or in a more particularized definition, "evaluated information." In considering the role of intelligence in the governmental process, a Hoover Commission task force broadly defined it as "dealing with all the things that should be done in advance of initiating a decision." The underlying activities that produce such intelligence have been described in this way: "Gathering, processing, interpreting and communicating the technical and political information needed in the decision making process." The lumping of an essentially adversarial process of secret surveillance with acquiring information through investigative research techniques for use in planning and decision-making gave political intelligence a social science cachet as a branch of "information," or "decision" theory.

In addition to supplying a functional rationale, both military conflict and social science have contributed cosmetic language and images to disguise the realities of investigative purpose and conduct. Thus, for example, sociology contributed the term "data collection" to describe, inter alia, surveillance, wiretapping, and the use of informers. The FBI uses "domestic" or "internal security" intelligence to designate what I here call political intelligence. It staunchly rejects "political intelligence" as a suitable usage because that includes mainstream politics. However, the terms "political intelligence" or "domestic political intelligence" accurately describe what the Bureau does: it collects information about the politics of domestic targets. "Internal security," "national security," and "subversion" are the master terms of political intelligence, the principal conceptual actors on its stage. Their meaning has been ravaged, reduced to disembodied buzz words* with overtones but no core meaning. This transformation is the most telling documentation in our time of Tocqueville's observation that mass politics inflates language and devalues meaning. Domestic intelligence is our shield against threats to "internal security," while foreign intelligence is supposed to provide the same protection for "national security," the interest threatened by hostile external activity. The distinction between the two concepts and their cognate intelligence programs is filmy at best. "National (or internal) security" and "subversion" form the rhetorical path by which intelligence entered the political process and became institutionalized. Although it has from time to time been questioned by the courts as lacking in precision, "national security" has only in recent years encountered broad skepticism. "Subversion" was judicially challenged long ago. In 1940 Attorney General (later Supreme Court Justice) Robert H. Jackson wrote:

> Activities which seem helpful or benevolent to wage earners, persons on relief, or those who are disadvantaged in the struggle for existence, may be regarded as "subversive" by those whose property interests might be affected thereby; those who are in office are apt to regard as "subversive" the activities of any of those who would

*So called "because they make a pleasant buzzing sound in your ears but convey little meaning, yet have a conscious or unconscious purpose"—Mario Pei, *Double Speak in America* (Hawthorn Books, 1973), p. 2.

bring about a change of administration. Some of our soundest constitutional doctrines were once punished as "subversive."*

The survival of these terms, not merely as intelligence usages but in the broader realm of political discourse, reflects the power of a myth system in which intelligence rescues a permanently endangered national security from the never-ending machinations of subversion. They have become so deeply rooted in our political culture, in intelligence documents, in court decisions, in legislation, and in scholarly studies that it would be impossible, if not misleading, to offer substitutes. They are used throughout this book in an intelligence context and are therefore to be read as though in quotation marks.†

The protective climate in which intelligence flourished over so many decades left it unprepared for a possible future challenge or accounting—perhaps the most revealing clue to its abandonment of professional concerns. Its recklessness and scorn for risks in its response to the unrest of the sixties brought a shocked public awareness of its role as a control instrument. The post-Vietnam, post-Watergate disclosures of such massive government intervention have made possible for the first time a full exploration of its scope and threat to the democratic process. In a changing time, the long-deferred retracing of the road we have traveled has become an imperative. Only through a nationally shared understanding of the reasons for our aberrations can we hope to prevent their recurrence.

---

*Robert H. Jackson, "The Federal Prosecutor," *Journal of the American Judicature Society,* June 1940.

†Intelligence terminology is discussed further in Appendix I.

THE Age OF
Surveillance

1 The Theory and Practice of Domestic Political Intelligence

The Politics of Deferred Reckoning

The twentieth century has been marked by a succession of different forms of restraint on political expression: criminal anarchy statutes, sedition laws, denaturalization and deportation, injunctions, security checks, loyalty oaths, enforced registration. Many of these measures have been rendered unenforceable or invalidated altogether by court decisions because of conflicts with constitutionally protected freedoms. While restraints such as these have come and gone over the past half century, a more formidable and enduring body of curbs on political and social movements in opposition to the status quo has flourished in the form of a system of political intelligence immune to changes in political climate, judicial scrutiny, executive or congressional control. Largely extralegal, autonomous, and clandestine, this political police system has monitored dissent with ever-increasing intensity since the end of World War I.

"Intelligence" is best understood as a sequential process, which embraces the selection of the subject (an organization or individual) for surveillance, the techniques, both overt and clandestine, used in monitoring the subject or target, the processing and retention of the information collected (files and dossiers), and its evaluation in the light of a strategic purpose (the intelligence mission). Intelligence also includes an activist or aggressive aspect, specifically designed to damage or harass the target. But whether formally classified as passive data collection or aggressive intelligence, the intelligence function is dominated by a punitive or proscriptive purpose. Even the selection of a target embodies a judgment of deviance from the dominant political culture.

Intelligence in the United States serves as the instrument for resolving a major contradiction in the American political system: how to protect the status quo while maintaining the forms of liberal political democracy. To a far greater extent than in other Western democracies, capitalism in this country has asserted superiority over socialism by insisting that it alone can guarantee political

3

freedom. But the political freedom that legitimates the economic system poses a threat to the stability of the political order, indeed, a mounting threat in view of the ever-increasing dependence of capitalism on state intervention and subsidy. Given such an alliance between the government and the wealthy and powerful, how can the government enjoy mass support and the loyalty of all classes? How can it avoid the emergence of political options that offer alternatives to capitalism? The need for political socialization within the confines of the economic system—a need once served by the media, the family, schools, and private associations—has become a major responsibility of the government, and in particular its political intelligence institutions.

The effectiveness of this system of controls can be measured by the extraordinary weakness of movements for basic change in the United States. Certainly the failure of these movements, their inability to attract mass support, cannot be ascribed to the success of the free enterprise system. Other capitalist countries have been more responsive to the needs of their citizens. And while it may be true that Socialist and Communist movements have failed to adapt themselves to American realities, and that they have been handicapped by the absence of an attractive model for an alternative system, still in assessing the reason for the failure of such movements, we cannot ignore the repressive impact of intelligence. And this impact is due in important part to the fact that intelligence is the steward of American anti-communism, long an intransigent reality of our political culture. Anti-communism has so conditioned our thoughtways and politics that Americans are hardly aware of its impact, as reflected for example in the gradual restriction over the past four decades of political programs, common enough in the thirties, for redistributing wealth; the discrediting of even central planning ("creeping socialism") as a legitimate responsibility of government; and—on the basic level of communication—the elimination from popular discourse of subversive words such as "capitalist," "working class," "class struggle." American anti-communism has become institutionalized through the intelligence function of the Federal Bureau of Investigation, which authoritatively interprets and implements the anti-Communist ideology. An independent organ of state administration operating to monitor, punish, and frustrate extra-judicially the political activities of a country's nationals is the classic embodiment of a political police force and, indeed, a benchmark of a police state. Certainly we are far from a police state; but it would be a semantic quibble to deny that the FBI is a political police force with a counterrevolutionary mission typical of such units in nondemocratic societies.

The Bureau's primary intelligence targets are various Marxist persuasions and their adherents. The basis for this priority is ideology not behavior, theory not practice. They are considered dangerous both because of an assumed strategic commitment to violence and a claimed subservience to foreign influence and control. The selection of targets for surveillance, operations such as informer infiltration and wiretapping, and file storage practices reflect what may be called the politics of deferred reckoning, the need to know all about the enemy in preparation for a life or death showdown between capitalism and communism. Domestic countersubversive intelligence is, in theory, future-oriented: "subversive" activities are, in the language of the Bureau, those "aimed at" future overthrow, destruction, or undermining of the government, regardless of how legitimate these activities might currently be or how tenuous the link between present intentions and ultimate action.

To this "subversive" classification of intelligence targets was added in 1959 an "extremist" category ultimately embracing such groups as the Black Panthers, the American Indian Movement, the Students for a Democratic Society, the Weathermen, and the Ku Klux Klan, considered dangerous because of a commitment to tactical violence in the pursuit of political change. In both classifications, advance intervention through surveillance is justified on preventive grounds. The coverage of subversive targets is more comprehensive because of an assumed ideological guilt by association; in the case of extremism, such coverage depends on Bureau estimates (frequently exaggerated) of the potential for violence of the group or of particular individuals associated with it. But distinctions in standards for target selection and coverage tend to be bureaucratic rather than substantive; what is important to bear in mind is that political intelligence is highly expansive and hostile to distinctions that would reduce its scope.

The nature of the interest protected by intelligence, the very life of the nation, encourages and justifies repressive overkill. Why take chances when so much is at stake? This rationale is used to justify not only the extraordinarily intensive surveillance of primary targets but of a wide spectrum of dissident groups and individuals. The search for Communist influence, the establishment of degrees of consanguinity to a subversive parent stock, enormously multiplies the target population and handicaps movements for even modest changes. In 1975, at a time when the FBI sought to reduce criticism, it admittedly targeted no less than 1100 organizations suspected of being Communist-infiltrated, Communist-dominated, Communist fronts, and so on—all designated in the Bureau's files as "COMINFIL." Intelligence institutions have extended the boundaries of subversion, first by the application of notions of vicarious, imputed, and derived guilt; second, by a process of cross-fertilization, which proscribes an organization through the individuals associated with it and the individuals through their relationship to the organization; third, by increasing the number of condemned organizations because of parallel programs, mutual objectives, or overlapping leadership; and fourth, by treating subversion as permanent, irreversible, and indeed hereditary.*

The nature of the intelligence enterprise itself ensures overkill and at the same time protects it from criticism on the ground of excess or failure to validate its investigative assumptions. Targeting, surveillance, and related activities are,

---

*This technique was ingeniously applied in a document, a Report on the SDS Riots, Oct. 8–11, 1969, issued by the Illinois Crime Investigation Commission, April 1970, and reprinted in June 1970 by the Senate Internal Security Subcommittee. Pivoting on the SDS demonstration ("Days of Rage"), this 400-page report is a virtual encyclopedia of radicalism among youth, replete with dossiers, photographs, personal letters, diaries, and documents relating to the SDS figures with whom it purports to be primarily concerned, and as well to a host of other individuals and organizations about whom the Commission had collected intelligence information linked in the most tortured fashion to the subject matter of the Commission's report. This information, much of it highly inaccurate, was made public for the immediate purpose of punitive exposure of intelligence targets and as part of a nationwide intelligence mobilization against young radicals.

it is pointed out, stages in an investigative process: why object to the search for even a single subversive nugget simply because tons of ore are unearthed in the process? And especially since, as it is typically claimed, the investigation is only preliminary: one must investigate in order to determine whether there is a need to investigate. It was this rationale that served as a justification for the Bureau's infiltration of the anti-Communist National Association for the Advancement of Colored People (NAACP) for a twenty-one-year period. Nor is the investigator ever embarrassed by seemingly barren results, for an innocent fact may turn out to be a clue to a sinister, yet-to-be revealed conspiracy. Here is FBI Director Hoover's version of this thesis: "An isolated instance in the Middle West may be of little significance, but when fitted into a national pattern of similar incidents, it may lead to an important revelation of subversive activity." Then, too, the very fact that the coast is clear of subversives in itself proves the effectiveness of intelligence. How can one be certain that the investigation itself did not drive the plotters out of range?* The very failure of the subversive prey to show his hand becomes proof of his cunning and of the need for a more determined pursuit. And, far from confining and disciplining the intelligence enterprise, constitutional norms tend to stimulate it. Since only urgent necessity justifies invasion of First Amendment freedoms, the intelligence establishment, in ironic deference to the need for a justification, consistently exaggerates the threat of revolution and violence. Thus a permanently endangered national security is the illegitimate child of the First Amendment.

Political intelligence is a by-product of diplomatic and military conflict, and despite its domestic provenance, is marked by a similar hostility toward the intelligence target (itself a revealingly hostile term of art). Like its military model, political intelligence reductively divides the world into patriots and traitors, friends and enemies, us and them. Even though the target is an American national, engaged in lawful political activities in his own country, he is viewed in an adversary context. Life in a relatively open society, which boasts of its freedom, makes the target enormously vulnerable when his politics come under hostile investigation by a secret police unit with an anti-subversive mission. Nowhere else in our society is the private life of unprotected individuals subjected to such intensive scrutiny by an agency of the government, and for reasons unrelated to any familiar and recognized government function such as law enforcement. The individual's vulnerability is intensified by the secrecy of the probe and the knowledge that even if no "derogatory" information is developed, he or she will become a permanent file subject. Inevitably, surveillance and even the fear of surveillance on the part of those not actually monitored produce a pervasive self-censorship.

The search for actual or potential enemies of the government necessarily embraces masses of people and a huge area of their private lives—far more extensive than formal political associations and activities. In order to make a judgment about a subject's politics, an investigator may find it necessary to

---

*A report of the General Accounting Office in 1976 glossed its conclusion that the Bureau's domestic intelligence activities yielded puny results with the comment: "Who is to say that the Bureau's continuous coverage of such groups and their leaders has not prevented them to date from achieving their ultimate subversive and extremist goals?"

probe his habits, visitors, sex life, reading preferences, use of leisure time, views on topics of the day, lifestyle, educational background, the books in his library, the identity of his correspondents—the list is not a short one.

Political investigations and surveillance typically invade a subject's privacy. But it would be misleading to view such surveillance simply as an especially grave violation of the right to privacy. Conventional privacy invasions associated with technology and bureaucracy are alienating and even dehumanizing, but still leave the individual with a means of altering the governmental decisions and policies that have victimized him. Political surveillance tampers with the very process by which political change is brought about.

We live in a society which, as the social psychologist Jules Henry has observed, is programmed for fear. Just as fear is packaged to stimulate consumption, it is marketed to promote conformity. The impact of surveillance on the individual's sense of freedom is enormous, and for this reason it yields the greatest return of repression for the smallest investment of power. Because it is so efficient, surveillance has transformed itself from a means into an end: an ongoing attack on nonconformity. The intimidation of dissent (in order to prepare for an ultimate reckoning with violent revolutionaries) has made political intelligence a vital asset of conservatism in the struggle for mainstream political power.

A Government of Men—Not of Laws

The history of intelligence in this country is dominated by a systematic invention, usurpation, and abuse of the power to engage in it. In American public life we almost invariably reduce power conflicts to issues of due process, of individual rights; the one is typically abstract, and the other more accessible because it is specific and "human." A need for stability, a desperate dependence on institutional order and continuity, makes us reluctant to confront claims of usurpation of power, as though the very recognition of its possibility would deny meaning to the American experience.

But one can hardly sweep under the rug the wealth of evidence that intelligence in this country has emerged and spread into a formidable instrument of control simply as the result of a series of power grabs. For more than three decades J. Edgar Hoover claimed that the FBI had been entrusted by a presidential directive of September 1939 with an open-ended intelligence mission unrelated to law enforcement. When Director Clarence M. Kelley took over in 1973, this alleged Magna Carta for domestic political intelligence was all but abandoned. Similarly, the Bureau's political filing practices were justified by this spurious intelligence mandate until the Congress, by a 1974 statute, required a law enforcement justification. Despite the austere language of the Constitution limiting the Army's role in civilian affairs, military intelligence developed a vast civilian anti-subversive surveillance capability, wholly unrelated to its narrow function of responding to a call-out when, in the judgment of the President, such action was warranted. The Internal Revenue Service likewise diverted its revenue collection resources into a wholly unauthorized system for identifying and punishing political dissidents. By even cruder deceptions, congressional committees have used legislative mandates as a pretext for such nonlegislative practices as identifying alleged subversives, indexing their political affiliations, and developing huge dossier collections. Federal grand juries, judicial bodies limited under our legal system to an accusatory role, were in the same way taken over by the executive branch in the Nixon years and converted into intelligence instruments.

The case of the CIA is perhaps the most arresting. A 1947 statute creating the Agency bars it from "internal security" functions, language intended to proscribe secret political intelligence practices on our shores. Yet the Agency has systematically engaged in these prohibited practices. Similarly, the same statute was intended by Congress to confine the Agency primarily to passive data collection, worlds away from the aggressive covert practices that subsequently became the CIA's trademark.

This pattern of improvisation and abuse of power has emerged in a political system that jealously guards the exercise of power and insists on an explicit definition of its scope and the terms of its delegation, in order to ensure a "government of laws and not of men." Congress, our lawmaking body and the arm of government charged with responsibility for checking the improper exercise of power by the executive, has been virtually excluded from the intelligence area. In the case of both the FBI and the CIA, where Congress did act, the claimed authority for challenged intelligence activities was based on executive order, not on a statutory charter. Although the Supreme Court has repeatedly insisted that the Constitution makes special demands for precision in the delegation of power involving a threat to First Amendment rights of freedom of expression and association, no guidelines or effective restraints have, until recent years,* limited the conduct of intelligence agencies in the political sphere. Neither the FBI nor the CIA has regarded itself as subject to legal or constitutional restraints; the agents who conceived or participated in 2370 aggressive actions (counterintelligence programs—COINTELPROS), or the attack on Martin Luther King, Jr., or law violations resulting from "black bag jobs" felt outraged that their conduct should have been questioned. As for the authority to engage in such practices, the CIA counterintelligence staff chief James Angleton put it quite simply; he found it "inconceivable that a secret intelligence arm of the government has to comply with all the overt orders of the government."

But it would be misleading to suggest that the record would have been different if Congress had played a significant role as overseer. House and Senate have in the past rejected opportunities for genuine investigation, either because of their approval of challenged practices or their unwillingness to confront power abuses, out of fear of political reprisal by the anti-Communist constituency and the power of FBI Director Hoover.† In the case of the CIA, the

---

*Modest restraints, discussed below, were imposed by Attorney General Edward H. Levi in 1976.

†Prior to the House and Senate Committee special investigations of political intelligence in 1975–76, three major congressional inquiries dealt with intelligence-related issues. A special inquiry was authorized in 1964 by the House Committee on Government Operations on "The Investigative Activities of Federal Civilian Agencies." Hearings were held on a wide variety of subjects in 1965 and 1966 by a subcommittee chaired by former New Jersey Congressman Cornelius E. Gallagher,

congressional role has been even more remote, a result of the intelligence mystique of *raison d'état,* the protection of a secret élite, and a surrender of responsibility to the executive.

The Bureau's charmed life and vigorous growth despite its gross abuse of power dramatizes the extraordinary achievement of its Director, and validates for our own time the simple insight of the founding fathers that the alternative to the rule of law is personal despotism. The conquest of unchecked power was —literally, not metaphorically—Hoover's prime mission and most successful intelligence coup. The Director succeeded in freeing himself of restraints despite the checks-and-balances mechanism structured into our system of government. This feat was accomplished by the use of the intelligence arts of propaganda, deception, infiltration (he had access to all the sources of power with a threat potential), wiretapping, and media leaks. In addition, it is no longer possible to deny that the Director used congressional blackmail and the fear of blackmail as weapons to achieve his mission, an updating of practices associated with many spymasters in the past.

Nor did functional considerations stand in the way. The need for intelligence, that is, information, arises out of some authorized, substantive official function. The scope and duration of the investigation are supposedly shaped by the particular problem under investigation. After the probe is completed, the agency seeking the data must first evaluate its meaning and importance and then decide how to use the final product. Such is the textbook teaching. But, in fact, neither the White House nor any government agency, not even the Department of Justice, made important use of the Bureau's intelligence product in policy formation or decision-making. On the contrary, the Bureau was not only the producer of intelligence but its primary consumer—at once collector, interpreter, and disseminator.

The Menace

"What," to borrow from Marianne Moore, "went through that thin thread to make the cherry red?" More prosaically, what accounts for this institutional and operational growth in the unpromising soil of a democratic system? The key reason for the emergence of domestic intelligence as a system of repression is

but no attempt was made to probe the Bureau's countersubversive investigative practices. In 1965, a Senate subcommittee of the Committee on the Judiciary, headed by former Missouri Senator Edward V. Long, launched a probe continued until March 1967 into privacy invasions, including wiretapping, mail opening, informer penetration, and dossier compilation, by a score of federal agencies—but not the FBI. Both Gallagher and Long were faced with serious legal charges, a circumstance that may explain their tenderness toward the Bureau. But no such circumstance can explain a similar inconsistency in the conduct of the 1971–74 inquiry by former Senator Sam J. Ervin, Jr.'s, Subcommittee on Constitutional Rights. These hearings thoroughly probed a number of countersubversive areas; their investigation of the domestic intelligence abuses by the Army is a model. Further, Ervin was not unaware of the serious issues raised by the Bureau's investigative practices; but he chose to bypass this area, out of a combination of personal reluctance and a sense that the full Senate would not support the subcommittee's entry into such hallowed ground. There was no question that Mississippi Senator James O. Eastland, the conservative chairman of the full Judiciary Committee, would have vigorously opposed the use of the power of his committee to call the Hoover agency to account.

the depth and pervasiveness of the fear of communism. I refer here not to a conventional civic and political opposition to communism, domestic or foreign, but to a mania that mobilizes the entire society in a comprehensive *Kulturkampf.* The American obsession with subversive conspiracies of all kinds is deeply rooted in our history. Especially in times of stress, exaggerated febrile explanations of an unwelcome reality come to the surface of American life and attract support. These recurrent countersubversive movements illuminate a striking contrast between our claims to superiority, indeed our mission as a redeemer nation to bring a new order to the world, and the extraordinary fragility of our confidence in our institutions. This contrast has led some observers to conclude that we are, subconsciously, quite insecure about the value and permanence of our society. More specifically, that American mobility detaches individuals from traditional sources of strength and identity—family, class, private associations—and leaves only economic status as a measure of worth. A resultant isolation and insecurity force a quest for selfhood in the national state, anxiety about an imperiled heritage, and aggression against those who reject or question it.

Like other countersubversive movements, anti-communism is a projection of Richard Hofstadter's "paranoid style," an "all but ineradicable part of the American political tradition," marked by "the qualities of heated exaggeration, suspiciousness and conspiratorial tendencies." Movements in the paranoid style perceive a hostile world as threatening, not merely this or that individual or institution, but a "nation, a culture, a way of life." Unlike "normal" behavior, the paranoid style regards conspiracy—huge, all-embracing conspiracies—as the *motive force* in historical events. The paranoid style finds a comfortable place for itself in a larger society with an insatiable gothic appetite for gore and grotesquerie.

Traditional countersubversion is marked by a distinct pathology: conspiracy theory, moralism, nativism, and suppressiveness. Some of these elements in the countersubversive syndrome are found in other movements, but they are all prominent in anti-communism. Indeed, anti-communism is not only an identifiable movement; it influences and binds all the other extremist movements of our time. But in contrast to the others, anti-communism is not confined to a narrow sector of society. It brings together élites that feel threatened by change and the masses who might gain from it. Thus, élitist opposition based on predictable charges of statism and collectivism fuses with the demotic objections listed above to form a patriotic consensus, which equates corporate enterprise with the national interest, freedom, patriotism, and virtue, and its opponents with repression, treason, evil, and immorality. Of the long train of "menaces" that have ignited discontents and anxieties in the past, none can match the Communist Menace in its duration, scope, impact on social and cultural values and on voting behavior.

Anti-communism is further distinguished from its predecessors in that it is at once an ideology (in the sense that it rationalizes the specific interests of a particular, capitalist class) and a myth system dominating the entire society. The disappearance of shared values, which give identity and exclusivity to a society, has left us with their antithesis, a common agreement on the "stigma of unworth," communism. Anti-communism has thus become an indispensable nourishment for our ethnocentric hungers, the means by which we define and differentiate ourselves. It is this role of communism as the "other," the "enemy," the answer to the need for chosenness, which has molded it into a negative myth, a means of fantasizing the evil of the enemy without having to document it in reality. Moreover, the myth is self-perpetuating: attacks on its validity merely confirm the power of the enemy. In a period of social and economic change during which traditional institutions are under the greatest strain, the need for the myth is especially strong as a means of transferring blame, an outlet for the despair men face when normal channels of protest and change are closed. Indeed, it is not too much to say that if there were no Menace—that is, no system of active and moving images of an all-powerful Communist enemy—the stability of the capitalist order would be threatened. Domestic intelligence is thus charged with a dual mission: to develop mass fear of the Menace and to implement the aggression which such fear fosters. In some respects it plays a role similar to that of the armed services externally.

The Hunt for Subversives

The fear of conspiracy has traditionally been abstract or metaphorical. Indeed, the unparticularized insistence on the role of unseen and powerful forces has plagued such movements, reducing their appeal and credibility. But anti-communism posits a conspiracy of real, identifiable, evil individuals, "the Communist conspiracy" as it was explicitly called in the fifties.* This modern adaptation of conspiracy theories corporealizes the conspiracy, while at the same time pressing the older thesis of sinister, hidden forces whose concealment is itself proof of the conspiracy's power.

In adapting traditional conspiracy theories to anti-capitalist movements such as Marxian communism, intelligence is undeterred by the fact that revolutions on the Marxist model cannot succeed in the absence of the requisite objective conditions. In the past, it dismissed this difficulty by inviting an equation of pre-revolutionary czarist Russia with the United States. Intelligence continues to take for granted the existence of a favorable climate for revolution in this, the most powerful capitalist country. However, the weakness of the Communist movement in the United States haunts both intelligence and its constituency. "I am not willing to accept the idea," Senator Barry Goldwater said in 1959, "that there are no Communists left in this country; I think that if we lift enough rocks we will find some."

The need to produce and expose live Communists has made identification the most pressing mission of American intelligence operations; it dominates the

*Congress in the Internal Security Act of 1950 made findings of fact that gave official expression to the Communist conspiracy theory. Section I of those findings states: "There exists a world Communist movement which, in its origins, its development, and its present practice, is a worldwide revolutionary movement whose purpose it is, by treachery, deceit, infiltration into other groups (governmental and otherwise), espionage, sabotage, terrorism, and any other means deemed necessary, to establish a Communist totalitarian dictatorship in the countries throughout the world through the medium of a world-wide Communist organization."

work, not only of the Bureau but of other intelligence institutions such as the congressional countersubversive committees, domestic military intelligence, and the Nixon era countersubversive grand juries. Without a free-flowing supply of actually identified Communists, anti-communism would suffer the fate of other extremist movements. In the same way, identification enhances the professional role of intelligence as a precise, factual pursuit, far removed from the irresponsible, unsupported charges of zealots. Because a mass society, and ours in particular, is ridden by voyeurism and a lively curiosity about the secret lives of its members, identification, invariably highly publicized, is a highly efficient means of exploiting fears of conspiracy. (Think of it—those nice people next door!) Beyond this, identification is the prime tool in the already described process of expanding the boundaries of subversion; it is much easier to condemn an organization or cause as subversive for reasons of personality than politics. Finally, identification makes possible the harassment or punishment that is the ultimate objective of the intelligence system. This obsession with individuals is reflected in the General Accounting Office (GAO) audit, which estimates that such intelligence activities as wiretapping and informing, the compilation of dossiers, the vast file collections (over 500,000 domestic intelligence files in Washington alone and an even greater number in the field offices), the retention of stale data —all are best understood when viewed as interrelated aspects of a process for connecting particular individuals to subversion. Similarly, highly developed computerized systems of identification, data retrieval, and retention have been shaped by this stress on individuals. A 1966 memorandum from William C. Sullivan, longtime Bureau intelligence chief, extols "black bag" burglaries as a unique means of ferreting out "materials held highly secret and closely guarded by subversive groups and organizations which consisted of membership lists and mailing lists of these organizations."

In responding to the challenge of identification, the process of lifting as many rocks as possible, intelligence begins with a deeply ingrained preconception: that subversion lurks everywhere. The job is to unmask it. E. M. Forster's adjuration "Only connect" might well be inscribed as the working credo of American intelligence. And for the subversive-hunter, there is always a connection to be made once the web of deception is pierced. In a society that attacks and stigmatizes radicals through private as well as public sanctions, all movements for basic change are bound to have a subsurface, or semi-concealed, dimension. But in our intelligence system, the secrecy and caution bred by repression in turn become proof of subversion. Ironically, those with the most fragile, abstract, or theoretical commitment are frequently viewed as the truly dangerous conspirators, as opposed to those who have assumed the risk of exposure.* These supporters and followers, operating behind the scenes, camouflaged in various ways, are seen as the principals of the open activists. This seeming inversion of priorities, as I have indicated, is a way of exaggerating the threat of subversion by adding to the modest number of known activists invisible hosts of reinforcements. Lurking in positions of power, they are ready at a given

_____

*The thesis that subversive groups are dominated and directed by hidden principals was first developed by the Pinkerton Detective Agency. See Chapter 2.

signal to raise their visors and reveal their subversive commitment. This concept of the enemy within the gates was expressed initially by the metaphors of the Trojan horse, the tip of the iceberg, and during the cold war by that of the fifth column.

Since politically involved individuals frequently make an ideological journey from the left rightward, the intelligence assumption is that many subjects harbor dirty little secrets—youthful lapses that need but be aired to establish the subversive character of the target and his or her associations. A striking example of the Bureau's readiness to exploit the past in the hunt for names is found in the 1975 testimony of Charles Brennan before a Senate committee (the Church Committee). A longtime chief of the Internal Security Section of the FBI's Domestic Intelligence Division, and in 1970–71 head of the Division, Brennan justified the Bureau's dragnet investigative programs in the seventies against opponents of the Vietnam War who had no prior record of involvement in violence on the basis of future need. Such programs were set up, he said, in order to avoid the "tragic mistakes" of the thirties, when college students, moved by the depression, "became involved with Communist activities . . . [and] were subsequently employed in sensitive positions of Government and the Government had no records of their previous Communist involvement. I did not want a repetition of that sort of circumstance to come about." The Bureau had the responsibility, Brennan insisted, to develop dossiers on even nominal members of the New Left to enable the government in the future to judge their qualifications for employment.

The most prized form of subversive identification is current membership in the Communist Party. But given the Party's limited appeal, intelligence must frequently settle for less—though wherever possible making it sound like more. Past membership is the more fruitful intelligence pursuit, since membership is typically transient. The remoteness in time of the involvement is overcome in a variety of ways: subsequent failure to recant, suggestions that the Party was more revolutionary when the subject joined and that he left because its line moderated, or that the abandonment was for tactical, not principled, reasons. A key purpose of all countersubversive surveillance is to preserve the subject's political past by compiling a dossier for future reference. Moreover, in the view of intelligence, subversion is a disease that is hereditary, chronic, incurable— and contagious. The subject, however remote his original subversive connection, taints all the groups and causes to which he subsequently becomes attached.

A classic problem is to attribute subversion to an individual in the absence of proof of membership in a subversive organization. The solution: correspondence between the subject's views and those considered subversive makes him an "objective" Communist or subversive. Dr. Owen Lattimore, an authority on the Far East, was condemned as a Communist, not because he was a provable Party member but rather because he was "under discipline," a more dangerous-sounding relationship than mere membership and almost impossible to disprove. Dr. Martin Luther King, Jr., was wiretapped by the Bureau because of his alleged associations with a "Communist agent." This alleged subversive associate was not called a Party member—no evidence of his membership could be found. But a careless reading of the Bureau's request for tapping authorization might lead to the conclusion that the alleged associate was someone far more sinister than a mere rank-and-file member, an "agent" or spy. The same formula of making a semantic virtue out of factual necessity is also used to characterize groups—as in a "Communist-infiltrated organization" to designate an organization not controlled by the Communists but with Communist members.

But individual or group characterizations, even with the help of semantic deceptions, false criteria, unwarranted inferences, and stale data, cannot generate the truly large numbers needed to portray subversion as a threatening movement. To be sure, the Russian Revolution is considered a useful precedent here too: only a handful of Bolsheviks, Director Hoover was wont to remind us, pulled it off. Indeed, crude arithmetical juggling led him to the triumphant conclusion that American communism in 1947 was relatively stronger than Bolshevism in 1917 (speech, May 1947). Yet the problem was not to make plausible the threat of revolution but to create a nurturing environment for countersubversion as a force in mainstream politics and to ensure intelligence power and funding. The commitment to identification was a gamble: the credibility won through identification of live subversives would be lost by unimpressive total numbers. Thus the padding of the population of subversives became the most important mission of intelligence assessment, a counterpart of the identification mission assigned to intelligence operations. This was a daunting task in view of the initial small number of Party members and the steady decline both in membership and influence beginning with the cold war. The Director's contribution was to end the practice of publicizing membership figures, to insist that the decline was proof of strength, not of weakness, and to warn of armies of secret adherents, "members of the conspiracy."

The emphasis on individuals—*cherchez la personne!*—plays another quite separate role in the intelligence schema. It personalizes unrest and thus detaches it from social and economic causes. Under this view the people are a contented lot, not given to making trouble until an "agitator" stirs them up. As soon as he or she is exposed or neutralized, all will be well again. The agitator is an "outsider," who comes on the scene with a sinister arsenal of rhetoric and slogans to make trouble. The agitator's giveaway, the most revealing clue to his role, is not his views or his actions but his persistence. A subject who belongs to a number of organizations and keeps going to meetings or rallies or is repeatedly involved in "incidents" is soon marked as an agitator (more sophisticated terms call him "militant" or "activist," sometimes preceded by "hardcore"). The outside agitator is a descendant of the "foreign agitator" or "agent of a foreign power."* In fact, all agitators act in the name of foreign principals even if their ties are not readily apparent. Readers may recognize in the intelligence version of the agitator a familiar figure from the American past, the fast-talking confidence man with a concealed identity, who comes from another milieu and preys on what is most precious: the hunger of his audience for frankness and authenticity.† Like his counterpart from the past, the agitator's

---

*A still current usage dating from World War I.
†Another forebear is the "ringleader," long used in England to characterize a chief instigator or organizer of reprehensible activity such as a riot or mutiny.

followers or constituents are victims, not genuinely convinced, but "dupes" seduced by promises or carried away by rhetoric.*

Because a key purpose of intelligence is to neutralize and punish the agitator, identification cannot be left to chance. Beginning in the Palmer era and continuing from 1939 to the present, the Bureau developed lists of especially dangerous subversives for reference when the showdown comes. These lists of proscribed individuals and groups include the Security Index, the Communist or Reserve Index, the Administrative Index, and the Rabble Rouser or Agitator Index. In addition, the Bureau developed the Key Activist and Key Extremist programs, beginning in the late sixties, as internal investigative guides. The agitator thesis is a suggestive clue to the political conservatism embedded in intelligence: it echoes the conservative rejection of environmental, economic, and social causes to account for unrest, attributing it instead to malcontents who are unwilling to accept the sacrifice and discipline indispensable to an ordered society.

The Myth of Violence— "Reckless of Human Life"

When the Menace first emerged in the twenties, the reds were attacked as godless, bestial, dirty, and depraved practitioners of "free love," lusting to "nationalize" American womanhood like their Bolshevik counterparts in Russia. This moral condemnation of the enemy was reinforced by a crusade to purify the national consciousness: the standard of the "American way of life" was raised to resist the onrushing Asiatic hordes as we confronted their materialism and atheism with our idealism and spirituality. Those who were unfit for the "American way of life" were, of course, "un-American"†—a term replaced in the forties by the equally foggy "subversive." While this purely moral assault gave way to a more directly political attack, it was never wholly abandoned. The dichotomies of depravity and innocence, atheism and religious faith, were renewed in the fifties, most notably in the political sermons of John Foster Dulles. Both godlessness and moral depravity continued to be heard as battle-

---

*"Agitation" is a pejorative label for speech that would otherwise lay claim to constitutional protection. It connotes verbal coercion in the same way that "propaganda," another intelligence favorite, connotes verbal deception. Speech can be stripped of its constitutional protection and turned into agitation when the speaker is an outsider. Thus the report of the United States Coal Commission, appointed in September 1922, assures us that "Men have, of course, the inalienable American right to go into strange communities and diagnose the evils under which the community suffers and offer remedies for a cure. But many times it is not expedient to exercise this right. Men not connected with the industry have no right to make inflammatory speeches leading to the use of violence"—U.S. Congress, Senate, *Report of the United States Coal Commission,* 68th Cong., 2d sess., Sen. Doc. 195, Part 1 (Washington, D.C., 1925), pp. 176, 179.

†Derived from "Americanism" or "100% Americanism," usages that were the product of our early search for positive communal values and self-definition with which to confront Bolshevism. The term "100% Americanism" first appeared in the 1919 preamble to the constitution of the American Legion—see Raymond Moley, Jr., *The American Legion Story* (Duell, Sloan & Pierce, 1966), pp 71–72, and foreword by J. Edgar Hoover, pp. vii–viii. While the use of "un-" for "anti-" Americanism is (as Mario Pei states) semantically inaccurate, it faithfully echoes the nativist totalism that equates the two.

cries in the speeches of J. Edgar Hoover, and not only in the speeches; the documents of the late sixties dealing with counterintelligence programs (COIN-TELPROS) assume that immorality is a handmaiden of radicalism. In an angry memo on student radicals sent to all field offices in October 1968, Hoover chastised field agents for ignoring the "mounting evidence of [the radicals'] moral depravity," and instructed them to be particularly alert to "the depraved nature and moral looseness" of student radicals.*

But the most common charge was and remains that of violence. As in other areas, we begin in the twenties with images of blood-dripping Bolshevik murderers and assassins, "reckless of human life," wiping out first the Romanovs and then the rest of their political opposition. By the late twenties and thereafter, the charge was politicized: the use of violence to attain power was a cardinal Marxist doctrine. The attribution to Marxist communism of revolutionary violence became the foundation of the deportation frenzy of the twenties, the ground for the subsequent denial of recognition of the Soviet Union, and the justification for the passage of a sedition act in 1940 (the Smith Act). Here, as in the case of identification, the absence of objective evidence of the use of violent tactics, visible to the naked eye as it were, was circumvented by sinister gloss and strained inference. The Director's favorite formulation was that the Communists were prepared to engage in bloody violence on a signal from their Attila-like masters. Even when prosecutions under the Smith Act foundered because of the inability of the government to establish incitement to violence on the part of the defendants, the Director stuck to his guns. Invited to testify in 1968 before the National Commission of the Causes and Prevention of Violence (the "Eisenhower Commission"), Hoover awarded the palm for violence to the Communists because they "inculcate hatred and bigotry," which in turn "breed violence." Despite public disavowal, Hoover said secret internal evidence showed that "the use of violence is—as it has always been—the primary technique for the Communist seizure of power." Anyway, he continued, "they lead demonstrations many of which become disorderly."

The strained quality of this charge—far removed from the assassinations, street violence, and vigilantism under investigation—emphasizes the strength of the link in the intelligence mind between communism (and indeed all forms of radicalism) and violence. Like the image of thousands of visible and invisible conspirators, violence is an intelligence assumption that is not open to challenge. Even if there is no foreseeable threat of a violent takeover and the history of the past half century has entirely obliterated the Russian Revolution as a model for the transition to socialism, the intelligence equation of Marxism to violence is not likely to yield to reality. Most of the other elements of the anti-Communist

*Not only does sexual misbehavior accompany subversion, but subversion itself is a form of sexual gratification. This notion was conveyed in congressional testimony presented in October 1970 by Michael A. Amico, sheriff of Erie County, New York, who organized an informer-and-surveillance system in the Buffalo area. Referring to the groups under surveillance, he testified: "Many of these organizations start their meetings clandestinely by burning the American flag before they go into their rituals. It is difficult to get young undercover agents to remain disciplined to withstand, if you know the reaction, what does happen upon the burning of the flag. These are the rituals and different practices and, as said by the undercover man, orgasms are obtained by the different activities that follow because of the burning of the flag."

syndrome (conspiracy, immorality, deception) are threatened by the passage of time and generational change. Moreover, appeals relating to collectivism and statism have little power to stir mass response. But the charge of violence, however mythic it has become, is the rock upon which the intelligence church is built. It accommodates repression to democratic norms that exclude violent methods, is most efficient in generating fear and renewing it by attributing to communism the politically motivated violence of others, and finally, makes a special contribution to conservative politics. The violence stereotype does not apply to ultra right-wing political groups, and for this reason in contrast to the left, their influence is not regarded as a source of danger or as a justification for the surveillance of politically related groups. When in fact violence-prone—as in the case of the Ku Klux Klan and Minutemen—they are monitored primarily for crime prevention purposes.

The lack of proof of present or planned violence by Communists has in more recent years been ascribed to their cunning and conspiratorial machinations. By concealing their intentions and biding their time, they have deceived the authorities and sapped their vigilance. Why should they take by force what was being freely given them?* It was not that they had rejected violence—the acceptance of such a view (by pseudo-liberals and bleeding hearts) was in itself a tribute to their guile—but that advance surrender had made it unnecessary. Today the future of the violence charge as a countersubversive weapon depends on the ability of American intelligence to link historical Marxist-style revolutionary and radical movements to terrorism, a subject to which I will return.

The reader should be reminded here, however, that the explanation for the nonoccurrence of predicted violence as a triumph of subversive trickery is an example of a continuing countersubversive phenomenon (found in varying measures in all ideologies): the rationalization of a negative circumstance into proof of its opposite. A most illuminating example is the interpretation of the seeming decline in Communist numerical strength over the years as a calculated shedding of the timid summer soldiers to clear the arena for the showdown gladiators. Thus, far from being reassured by such evidence of loss of mass appeal, we should be terrified as we are confronted by a "steeled," "fanatic," "disciplined" "hard core."

Foreign Influence— The Quintessential Subversion

A tradition of nativist xenophobia has from the beginning fueled war on radicalism. Countersubversive movements have historically singled out the alien as the enemy because of his foreign birth, his espousal of foreign ideas ("isms"), and his asserted allegiance to a foreign country. At the end of the eighteenth century, domestic criticism and unrest were condemned as unwelcome old

*One of the more vigilant of the nation's guardians against subversive deception was Richard M. Nixon who, as Vice-President, warned his countrymen that the Communists had called an organization the DuBois Clubs (in honor of the black leader W. E. B. DuBois) for the deliberate purpose of inviting confusion with a patriotic youth organization, the Boys Clubs of America.

world discontents, and linked to the French Revolution. In the nineteenth, Socialist thought and ideas were stigmatized as foreign, as were their immigrant adherents. The Haymarket trials and the Palmer Raids flamed with this nativist fury. The foreign radicals had unforgivably rejected a government and society that were man's highest achievements, the treasured fruits of a divinely guided historical experience. Barbarians because they had spurned an opportunity to become Romans, they were not merely political "undesirables" but a threat to civilization itself.

This rage against rejection, capsulized in the equation of dissent with disloyalty, echoes in the bitterness of the frequent complaint: "Can't you people ever think of anything good to say about this country?" Nor are native-born radicals spared: unnatural children, they have befouled their precious American heritage. Those who have done well or have inherited wealth are particularly excoriated as betrayers, biters of the feeding hand. The "foreignness" of radicalism, whether through the person of a radical or a rejection of Americanism, explains the extraordinary hold of anti-communism over provincial America, where left politics have always been weakest. One can hear this political xenophobia in the taunt of the thirties addressed to dissenters, whether aliens or not: "Why don't you go back where you came from?" Another version appears on bumper stickers today: "America—Love It or Leave It."

The charge that radicals, whatever their national origin, harbor a secret allegiance to foreign countries also boasts a long history. All spymasters— Walsingham, Fouché, and Sidmouth, to name just three—have exploited the foreign-influence theme to serve their ends. Familiar American examples of such suspected foreign-sponsored conspiracies are the Jeffersonian Republicans, the Illuminati, Roman Catholics, Freemasons, abolitionists, slaveholders, and the "international Jewish bankers." The claim of foreign influence is the dominant American response to domestic unrest. The World War I fear of German spies and saboteurs shaped the modern stereotype of the foreigner not merely as a troublemaker but as something far more sinister. In the twenties the Bolsheviks and their American disciples were portrayed as "Asiatic hordes," descendants of Genghis Khan and almost unimaginably foreign. World War II and its cold war aftermath popularized the image of the radical—again, whether native-born or alien—as a crafty foreign agent. In the case of the Japanese, racial stereotypes of Oriental wiliness and betrayal, fortified by Pearl Harbor, further popularized this spy image. Such endemic suspicion of the foreigner is reflected all too clearly in the prominent role of the alien in almost all of the federal measures to curb movements for change, beginning with the Alien and Sedition Acts and including a series of deportation acts from 1903 to 1920, followed by the Foreign Agents Registration Act, the Alien Registration Act with its sedition provisions, and the Internal Security Act.

The need for an ever vigilant intelligence capability to monitor domestic communism rests basically on the claim that it is part of a worldwide movement, controlled and directed from Moscow. In the event of war with the Soviet Union, so the argument goes, the Communists in this country would become a traitorous fifth column. This, too, is an unchallengeable "given," an assumption impervious to such considerations as the break-up of monolithic world communism, polycentrism, and the hazards of an atomic war. The worldwide rivalry between the two superpowers is as important to domestic intelligence as it is to the military. The role of intelligence as the nation's domestic defender is expanded and operations become more aggressive during periods of tension in Soviet-American relationships. But the assumption of a long twilight struggle between the two remains constant and is perhaps most clearly projected in the persistence of the lists of potential detainees for a round-up when the hour strikes. Domestic radical and revolutionary sects that have emerged from the New Left of the sixties rarely, it should be added, protest the foreign-influence charge. Their very inability to attract a mass following leads them to seek a "movement identity" by proclaiming their adherence to this or that international movement, whether Chinese (a current favorite), Soviet, or "third world." Far from validating an assumption of special danger, this ritualistic identification with larger world movements is a symptom of the pathology of powerlessness that afflicts all movements for systemic change in this country.

Like the agitator concept, the claim of foreign influence is a means of discounting domestic unrest. Indeed, the agitator was classically a "foreign agitator." The need to discredit the anti-Vietnam War movement of the sixties and early seventies, as well as campus and ghetto unrest, reinvigorated the foreign-influence and Moscow-gold theories of the past, despite the fact that these movements were manifestly indigenous and indeed typically quite opposed to Soviet communism as well as its domestic (Old Left) supporters on the grounds of bureaucracy, "revisionism," and repressiveness. The unpromising reality did not, as I will show, deter the intelligence evaluators, although their efforts were of little value in discrediting their targets.

A second reason for externalizing the motivation and impetus of dissent is that it enables intelligence to justify its efforts as defensive, a necessary and temperate response to enemies gnawing away at the nation's entrails. The psychological phenomenon of projection plays a key role in American countersubversive practice. As a people, we feel compelled to insist that all our swords are shields. European intelligence experts are amused at the readiness of their American counterparts to justify domestic practices as defensive "counterintelligence." This has become apparent in the justifications for wiretapping. One can see it clearly in the report of the Saxbe Committee on the FBI's counterintelligence programs. This document, released in November 1974, justified the most aggressive forms of counterintelligence, deployed in a program conducted for some fifteen years against nominal Communists, on the ground that it "was conceived as a 'counter-intelligence' effort in the purest sense." The targets, the report argued, were really foreign spies and saboteurs.

A super-secret FBI counterintelligence program was designated "Special Operations." The full details of this program were withheld when facts about the other counterintelligence programs were made public on the ground that it dealt with the activities of the intelligence service of a "hostile foreign power." But the three documents that were released bearing the file caption of this program deal with the Black Panthers, hardly—whatever one may say about them—the intelligence agents of a foreign country. Operation CHAOS, the CIA's project for monitoring domestic groups, was entrusted to its counterintelligence branch. It need only be added that there is a huge irony in our obsession with foreign influence in view of the fact that for three decades the CIA has played the foreign agent's role *par excellence* on political stages all over the world. In the same way, the Army's enormous computerized domestic intelligence filing operation at Fort Holabird with its 100,000 subjects was called the "Counterintelligence Analysis Branch," on the theory that it was merely monitoring the activities of foreign intelligence agents.

In order to give these defensive pleas a color of plausibility, it becomes necessary to exaggerate the intentions and strength of the external enemy. "It is a universal truth," James Madison wrote to Thomas Jefferson in 1798, "that the loss of liberty at home is to be charged to provisions against danger, real or pretended, from abroad." It is this "invented terror," to use Aristotle's term, that has historically served as a justification for repression against domestic radicals. As A. Mitchell Palmer put it, in justifying the 1920 illegal mass deportations, "There could be no nice distinction drawn between the theoretical ideas of the radicals and their actual violation of any national laws." The country had to be cleansed of these "criminal aliens," this "alien filth." Thus the mass deportations were both a physical removal of such aliens, with a "misshapen caste [sic] of mind and indecencies of character," and a rite of purification. And barely in time! For the "Government was in jeopardy. . . . Confidential information and confidential intelligence removed all doubt." As for the Constitution, the anti-Communist canon denies that the enemy has a right to a stall in the marketplace of ideas. To tolerate his dissent, to recognize his claims to the protections of the First Amendment, would be to yield to a proven un-American a status he does not deserve and has not earned. Has he not spurned our heritage? His intent to use power for immoral purposes in itself shows that he is not our kind.

Akin to the practices of ostracism, outlawry, and banishment made familiar by primitive legal systems, the tribal impulse to expel—to purge the "enemy within our midst"—has a strong grip on countersubversive thoughtways. Hence the popularity in the twenties and thirties of expulsion of reds from the community as a police weapon, and the resort, then and later, to such cleansing and purifying measures as denaturalization, deportation, the Japanese relocation centers, and the emergency detention camps created by the Internal Security Act.

The thrust to render illegitimate the target's status as an American is also reflected in the readiness of powerholders to move directly against subversives, as in the case of the punitive, personalized exposure practices of the congressional antisubversive committees used for over a quarter of a century. The impulse to punish found a more direct outlet in the FBI's counterintelligence programs (COINTELPROS), which for a fifteen-year period (1956–71) were deployed as weapons against dissidents and their organizations. This version of attainder, a form of punishment for past actions without trial, is directed at specific individuals or readily identifiable groups. Attainder in medieval law entailed an extinction of the civil rights and capacity of the condemned person; its modern counterpart punishes and stigmatizes an individual without trial for political acts committed in the past.

Intelligence and Law Enforcement

If the goals of countersubversive intelligence are really punitive, the reader may well ask, why not prosecute under a criminal statute such as the sedition provisions of the Alien Registration Act of 1940 (the Smith Act), which punish the advocacy by citizens and aliens alike of the violent overthrow of the government, as well as membership in organizations engaged in such advocacy? There are distinct intelligence advantages in countersubversive law enforcement. Domestic intelligence practice, detached from law enforcement, is difficult to justify in a democratic system. Statutory measures directed at countersubversion supply a vital pretext for conducting surveillance for intelligence purposes alone. Besides, a criminal trial is a useful forum for the public identification of nondefendants, of hidden subversives. In addition, a criminal trial frequently propels the intelligence functionary onto the public stage. For a publicity-hungry J. Edgar Hoover, this was no small inducement.

But there are also serious difficulties. A criminal prosecution against radicals may fail because of conflicts with the First Amendment, at the same time legitimizing the defendant's politics and confirming his status as an American, entitled to the protections of the Constitution. Then, too, a prosecution condemned on broad constitutional grounds jeopardizes the future use of the contested statute as a law enforcement justification for intelligence purposes.

After the constitutionality of the Smith Act was upheld by the Supreme Court in 1951, the Court in 1957 narrowed the construction of the statute by ruling that it could not be applied to mere advocacy of the forceable overthrow of the government or the discussion of abstract doctrine, but only to incitement to action or preparation for overthrow. No reading of Communist literature could, without an expansive gloss ("Aesopian language"), supply such evidence of incitement. In order to obtain a conviction after the 1957 Yates case, the government would have to rely on the testimony of informers pliant enough to link a particular defendant with the language of incitement at a given time and place. This would not have been an insuperable obstacle but for one circumstance: two weeks after the Yates decision, the Supreme Court ruled, in the Jencks case, that a defendant in a criminal case was entitled to inspect all the reports made by the informer witness concerning matters about which he had testified. It was all but certain that these contemporary accounts now subject to a defendant's scrutiny would not jibe with the subsequent courtroom testimony attributing incitement to the defendant. The game was hardly worth the candle. Even before the 1957 decision, many of the convictions were reversed on procedural or substantive constitutional grounds. Of the 130 defendants indicted under the advocacy provisions of the Smith Act, 28 were ultimately jailed; similarly, the membership provisions had yielded only one jail term after 15 indictments. Another anti-Communist measure, the Internal Security Act of 1950—a by-product of the Korean War as the Smith Act had been of World War II—is directed against organizations designated as Communist action, Communist front, or (after 1954) Communist-infiltrated, and their members. In addition to registration, the statute requires the labeling of literature distributed in the mail, the denial of employment in defense facilities, and other crippling sanctions. But after court decisions had invalidated its key provisions, it too was wholly abandoned as unenforceable.

There were other reasons for rejecting law enforcement, besides the constitutional barriers. Despite the meager results, sophisticated intelligence theorists came to realize that the entire countersubversive system depended upon the existence of an identifiable subversive movement, "in place," as it were. Statutory outlawry might kill the goose that had laid so many golden eggs. (In fact, the 1954 statute criminalizing Communist Party membership was never enforced.) Further, law enforcement required the surfacing of scores of informers, a price the Bureau was increasingly reluctant to pay. In any event, it was more effective to strike directly at the targets in secret; injury would be assured, constitutional problems eliminated, and the supply of informers left intact. These considerations led in 1956 to the targeting of the Communist Party in the first of a series of COINTELPROS, and in the same year to the exploitation of the resources of the Internal Revenue Service (raids, seizure of assets, and membership lists) to harass the Party and its official publication, the *Daily Worker*.

Although legislation, such as the Smith Act, directed at political expression and association is no longer considered enforceable, the Bureau has from time to time (see Chapter 3) responded to challenges to its authority to engage in political intelligence, the open-ended monitoring of First Amendment activities, by claiming a law enforcement purpose, a function clearly within its authority. But this claim, that the agency in its political surveillance activities is merely collecting evidence of law violations, must be viewed as a pretext. Indeed, the distinguishing characteristic of political intelligence as it has evolved in this country is its separation from—and in many cases, as we shall see, inconsistency with—the law enforcement investigation. Law enforcement involves a finite investigative procedure with a clearly identifiable goal: the collection of evidence of criminal conduct, leading to indictment, trial, and conviction. But political surveillance is a continuous process of people watching conducted in many cases for years, in order to develop information for use at some time in the indefinite future. Moreover, a criminal suspect is investigated when evidence links him or her in some rational way to a crime (probable cause), but the selection of a target for political surveillance is typically governed by ideological considerations. Then, too, the interest protected by political intelligence, "national security" or "internal security," is broad and amorphous. In contrast to criminal statutes, its meaning and scope cannot be defined or derived from language dealing with specific conduct. Further, the scope of a criminal investigation is determined by the nature of the offense, its *modus operandi*, possible motivation, the physical evidence, and the suspect's milieu; but political intelligence operations are typically shaped by subjective judgments and evaluations. Political intelligence has an expansive aspect that is *sui generis.* Conventional criminal behavior—transporting a stolen car, embezzlement, bank robbery—may be engaged in by a single individual or a few confederates; but behavior that generates political surveillance almost invariably has a group dimension, which requires surveillance of leaders, members, and followers. The former sifts a body of unconfirmed information about potential suspects in order to pinpoint an offender and his accomplices, while the latter expands available data as broadly as possible. For this reason, the role of files is more central in political intelligence than in law enforcement. The new FBI headquarters building in Washington devotes 35,000 linear feet to domestic intelligence files, while the remaining matters under the Bureau's jurisdiction are served by 23,000 square feet of file space.

An intelligence investigation may sometimes yield evidence that a law has been violated; but continuing coverage, as the Bureau itself has conceded, is frequently considered more valuable than prosecution. It may become desirable to try to "turn" the subject, to feed him false information, or simply to watch him for leads to his confederates. And when pressures to prosecute overcome intelligence considerations, the criminal case, as will be shown, is frequently compromised by the necessity of using evidence obtained in violation of the defendant's constitutional rights.*

The defenders of political intelligence both within and outside the Bureau have largely abandoned the view that authority to engage in political intelligence may be spelled out of the agency's law enforcement mandate, and have even recognized that prosecution is not a primary intelligence aim. Yet using a crime prevention analogy—the conventional investigation of conspiracy, inchoate, or planned crime—they have urged that political activities be surveilled to anticipate and prevent future politically motivated violence such as terrorism and sabotage. But, as will be argued later, the protective potential of such an intelligence program is outweighed by its predictably disruptive impact on political dissent.

Security and Its Offspring—Secrecy and Deception

The growth of the FBI's power as a political police force despite its questionable authority, operational improprieties, and targeting overkill is explained in part by the protective environment of secrecy characteristic of the intelligence enterprise. Secrecy is an operational imperative arising from the need to keep the target in the dark. Electronic surveillance and informer penetration, for example, must be concealed to avert exposure, which would, of course, render them useless. Similarly, the fruits of intelligence—files, evaluations, dossiers—cannot be divulged without risking exposure of the surveillance itself and thus ending its usefulness.

All intelligence practice balances the value of the information against the risk of obtaining it. When the risks are minimized by secrecy, intelligence tactics become bolder. Although we generally view with suspicion activities conducted in secret, the clandestine character of intelligence process tends, ironically, to legitimate it. Information derived from clandestine sources is assumed to be

*For these reasons, the British internal political intelligence unit, MI5, has no arrest or law enforcement powers. These are entrusted exclusively to Scotland Yard's Special Branch.

intrinsically valuable—else why go to so much trouble to obtain it? In the same way, the fact that the information is obtained secretly invites the inference that it is accurate—in the nature of an admission because obtained without the subject's knowledge. Further, the use of undercover methods in itself confirms suspicion: the targets are so cunning that stealth alone can contain them.

As Edward Shils has observed, Americans are sometimes cross-pressured into an ambivalence in which fear of divulging secrets competes with an insistence on openness and publicity. Many have come to believe that secret operations are purely defensive measures, necessary protection against dangerous conspiratorial enemies, and, indeed, frequently suspect critics of secrecy as members of the conspiracy. (Why should they object if they have nothing to hide?) But secret *power* (not isolated practices) invisibly exercised—especially domestically and in peacetime—finds few defenders in a democratic society. Long ago the Bureau adapted secret operational practices, used to thwart discovery by a target, to political uses for bypassing accountability to the Congress, the President, the Attorney General, and the courts. The need for secrecy, the ritualistic identification of disclosure of even petty operational details with an endangered national security, not only blocked the path to effective judicial review of particular abuses but shielded the agency from congressional inquiry. Such secrecy also frustrated an effective judicial review of challenged intelligence practices by preventing identification of the source of a claimed injury. Similarly, allegations of danger to the national security frustrated the litigant's efforts to obtain judicial relief. Information secretly acquired can also become a means of courting powerholders by making them insiders. So it was that Congressman John Rooney, long-term head of the House Appropriations Subcommittee dealing with the Bureau's budget and a close Hoover ally, knew more about the Bureau's gamier practices than either Attorneys General or Presidents.

In addition, intelligence routinely resorts to lying, deception, plausible denial, and related arts to escape detection, or, on higher levels, responsibility. Hoover's right-hand man, Cartha DeLoach, thus falsely assured Attorney General Nicholas de B. Katzenbach that the Bureau tapes of Martin Luther King, Jr., wiretaps which he had offered to play for a *Newsweek* reporter, were made by a Georgia police unit and not by the FBI. Director Hoover frustrated Attorney General Francis Biddle's order in 1943 to terminate a detention list merely by changing its name. Richard Helms lied to a Senate committee about CIA involvement in "de-stabilizing" the Allende régime in Chile as well as its role in attacking domestic dissidents. Director Hoover regularly understated in congressional testimony the number of electronic surveillances maintained during the previous year by excluding figures relating to microphone surveillances and by shutting down some of the wiretap installations on the eve of his testimony, only to resume them later. In 1966, the Bureau prepared a statement for the use of Senator Long of Missouri which it knew to be false and misleading. Neither Attorneys General nor Presidents were ever informed about the massive COINTELPROs or the Bureau's involvement in mail openings and the electronic monitoring of international communications. The Director's deception and circumvention of the sixteen Attorneys General under whom he served—or, as the witticism has it, who "served under him"—were routine: whenever he sensed a possible adverse repercussion, Hoover covered himself through the use of cryptic language in a memorandum and continued on his way. Bureau officials not only denied access to files to congressionally authorized General Accounting Office investigators but attempted to sabotage the investigation through secret instructions to field agents.

Because intelligence breeds secrets on every level, it becomes necessary to devise a governmental function to prevent their divulgence to the enemy. This function is security: the safeguarding of secrets, the prevention of leaks, the control of access to "sensitive" materials. Although, technically speaking, security protection is not an intelligence function but a police responsibility, it has become a major intelligence concern. The most familiar form of defensive intelligence, as it is sometimes called, is the safeguarding of intelligence secrets themselves. The divulgence of such materials by an employee who also works for the enemy—the best-known case is that of Kim Philby, who while serving Russian intelligence occupied a key post in the British SIS (Secret Intelligence Service)—is the great intelligence nightmare. Such a double agent is well placed to frustrate intelligence programs of all kinds, mislead his nominal employer by feeding him false information, and learn the identity of informers.

But secrets that require security precautions are not limited to the narrow field of intelligence, nor, for that matter, to traditional nineteenth-century areas of diplomacy and statecraft. The cold war threw a security net over vast new areas of government operations and transactions. As the nation tooled up for a showdown struggle with an expansive Soviet Union for world hegemony, it revived the suppressive thrust of anti-communism, held in check during the war. The Menace—its power to stir response weakened in the aftermath of war—was renewed in the waters of crisis indoctrination, war mobilization, and the threat of an atomic holocaust. Since communism was a threat to freedom, anti-communism became a badge of libertarianism. The conflict between domestic anti-communism and freedom was eliminated simply by ignoring the evidence of repression, ideologizing the meaning of freedom, and a process of role reversal (they were repressing *us*).* The instrument for the achievement of world liberation was intelligence, domestic and foreign, in all its modes, passive and active, overt and clandestine. This role of intelligence is symbolically reflected in the convergence of the two meanings of "mission": national destiny and intelligence objective, the end and the means of attaining it. And it was not ideology alone, but history, the shared experience of yesterday, that hastened this process.

All wars glamorize and popularize intelligence and at the same time release into a postwar society cadres trained in intelligence practice. But this process was not, as in the past, merely a by-product of World War II. The master themes of this war were betrayal and deception (one need only recall Pearl Harbor, Munich, and the fifth column), replayed in the conflict itself through an intelligence battle of wits between the enemy's crafty and ruthless spies and our brave

*The practice of ideologizing norms and ignoring inconsistent data so as to exclude the enemy is common in our history. See David Brion Davis, *The Slave Power and the Paranoid Style* (Louisiana State University Press, 1969), pp. 58–59; and Ole Holsti, "Cognitive Dynamics and Images of the Enemy," *Journal of International Affairs*, Vol. 21 (1967), p. 17.

and resourceful counterspies. Espionage, double agents, "dirty tricks," electronic eavesdropping, behind-the-lines deceptions, disguises and altered identity, daring radio operators, secret transmitters—all forms of spycraft were absorbed and romanticized by the popular culture.

The spy thriller, whether cut to James Bond's swaggering cloak-and-dagger pattern or John le Carré's bleak figures of loneliness, sacrifice, and commitment, invaded the media from the late forties on and became an identifiable genre in TV, comic strips, films, as well as in the more serious form of novels, memoirs, biographies, and autobiographies. An outlet for fantasies of freedom and power (not to speak of sexual gratification), the spy thriller, especially in its popular version, symbolically reenacted the triumph of "us" over "them."*

Intelligence thus served as the catalyst for transforming politics into culture. In the years that followed, it became difficult to determine whether life was imitating art or the reverse. There is a straight line from a James Bond, licensed to kill in the name of freedom and democracy, to the COINTELPROS. Acceptance of this transcendent goal left little room for challenge of the means. And those who did question this benign view were quickly told one had to fight fire with fire. In fact, their spies were swarming all over our country, penetrating our most secluded conference chambers, stealing our secrets, yes—even the secrets we had stolen from them. To guard against the enemy and his ruthless spies, secrecy was institutionalized through a classification system. Originating in limited World War II directives, this system was expanded first by President Truman in 1950 to include nonmilitary agencies and later by his successors.

Although declassification procedures were ordered over the years, the documentary birth rate far exceeded the death rate. Today, an estimated 100 million documents are classified "Top Secret," "Secret," and "Confidential"—a grim tribute to the national security mystique. The justification of national security served to bar both Congress and the public from the relatively small number of documents that were in fact sensitive, such as materials dealing with military plans or diplomacy, as well as from great quantities of information wholly unrelated to national security. The classification process—like secret operations themselves—ultimately becomes self-justifying. If the information is secret, it must be too sensitive to bear public exposure.

The first line of defense against the compromise of secrets was a trustworthy bureaucracy. The highest security priority were the employees with access to classified documents or empowered to classify them. These employees or applicants for employment, if cleared, became insiders, an army of converts to the intelligence mystique. But even applicants for nonsensitive employment were required to qualify both on security and loyalty grounds.† Employees of defense

---

*Simply by making 007 a black man pitted against a repulsive white adversary, the spy film also became a popular revenge fantasy among black audiences. See Pauline Kael, "Notes on Black Movies," *New Yorker,* Dec. 2, 1972. A measure of the impact of espionage on the popular imagination is supplied by the emergence of the sophisticated spy spoof. Thus, a *New Yorker* advertisement for Wyborowa Vodka depicts a glamorous beturbaned *femme fatale* smiling behind a bottle of vodka as she recalls, "In Vienna we imagined everyone was a spy. Remember the clerk's face when we drank to his 'mission' with Wyborowa Vodka?"

†The standard ultimately adopted requires a conclusion that there is no "reasonable doubt as to the loyalty of the persons involved."

contractors were likewise subject to employment clearance investigations. It has been estimated that by 1953, 13.5 million persons—one out of every five in the work force—were subject to loyalty-security requirements. Of the 4,756,705 persons checked for government employment, the Bureau made 26,000 field investigations, most of which involved alleged associations* with organizations on the Attorney General's list, authorized by the Truman executive order, of "totalitarian, fascist, Communist or subversive" groups. Originally covering 82 organizations, the list by 1950 proscribed some 197, including 132 alleged Communist and Communist front entries. The list served not only as a yardstick for measuring fitness for government employment but as a pretextual justification for Bureau intelligence activities, even after 1972 when it was abandoned.

The Intelligence Surge of the Sixties

Both the cold war and the McCarthy eras stimulated the growth of American intelligence practice. But, beginning in the early sixties and as the decade progressed, political intelligence emerged as the major instrument for containing the exploding protest movements of the time. Established institutions were challenged on three fronts, all of them areas of historic intelligence concern. The first, the anti-Vietnam movement, brought into play the traditional intelligence mobilization against domestic opponents—by putative traitors or foreign agents —of military conflict with other nations. The second, racially related unrest, is also a historic source of intelligence concern, rooted in century-old fears of a black insurrection. And the third, the youth and campus revolt, began as an intelligence concentration in the late thirties, when youth and intellectuals replaced workers as an intelligence group priority.

But the challenges far outran the available intelligence capabilities. The intelligence agencies, especially the FBI, were powerless to cope with the escalating unrest. Their techniques were as outmoded as their notions of subversion dominated by an Old Left composed of "Communists," "fellow travelers," and "fronts." Intelligence files were choked with millions of dossiers on aging or dead radicals. Policymakers and officers of intelligence agencies were faced with the need to identify and control new actors on a new political stage—no easy matter in view of the anarchic radical milieu, characterized by highly mobile and anonymous young people generally hostile to formal organization and leadership. The social remoteness of the new radicals concentrated in tribal, self-contained groups made it all the more difficult to identify them.† No less frustrating were the problems posed by ghetto disturbances. The challenge was not merely an operational one—keeping track of dissidents and monitoring their activities—but that of linking such dissidents with revolution or a related goal which would justify surveilling them at all. In short, to reinvigorate the Menace with a new "communism." Inevitably, this effort came to naught; and as the

*The proscribed degree of association ranges from "membership" to "sympathetic associations."

†In the late sixties the Bureau's intelligence high command decided that the national security required it to open an investigative file on every individual who lived in a commune.

decade progressed, dissidents of every hue were indiscriminately targeted and surveilled. This ecumenicism is reflected in the emergence of a new intelligence classification: "persons of interest" as a description of surveillance and file subjects without negatively classifiable affiliations.

Agencies with primary intelligence jurisdiction, such as the FBI, as well as units with intelligence resources ancillary to some other function, such as the Internal Revenue Service, expanded and developed political intelligence coverage. This process was in turn supplemented by the launching of new units both for operational and coordination purposes. By the end of the decade the Bureau had become an intelligence Leviathan with an ever-growing caseload of investigative targets, a conservatively estimated budget of $40 million, and a staff of more than 1000 agents on internal security assignment.* In addition to the Bureau, some twenty separate units attached to ten agencies were, by the end of the decade, engaged in domestic intelligence activities.

These new or revitalized programs reflected to an important extent a mounting concern by the Johnson and Nixon administrations over the scope and intensity of domestic protest. The role of the executive in monitoring dissent through intelligence—manifested in the employee security and classification programs discussed in the preceding section—became unmistakable in the sixties. At the same time, congressional anti-subversive committees with similar containment objectives became involved in operational surveillance as well as in the coordination of efforts of state and local intelligence units. These nonfederal forces, which had been eclipsed by the Bureau for two decades, also became highly active in the sixties. A major stimulus was the formation in the late fifties by state attorneys general in the South of an intelligence network in an effort to curb the integrationist efforts of students and activists. In the early sixties state intelligence police, North and South, focused on publicly supported universities, particularly on campuses removed from large urban centers where intelligence needs were served by local police departments.

The sixties brought roses to the cheeks of urban political intelligence units ("red squads"). Already a standard operation in every large American city, the existing forces expanded while new units were formed even in smaller cities and towns. They operated under a variety of names (Anti-Subversive Squad, Intelligence Unit, Civil Disobedience Unit), and in some cases used a "human relations" or "community relations" cover. Similarly, during the sixties a campus constabulary spread throughout the country's higher education community. Its functions included both overt and clandestine intelligence activities such as undercover work and wiretapping and were meshed with the operations of other intelligence agencies, federal and local.

While agencies with a foreign intelligence mission are part of an "intelligence community," sharing information and dividing their functions, their domestic counterparts have in the past managed only an informal and unstructured cooperation. But the pressures of the sixties produced considerable

*The total investigative budget for fiscal year 1975 was about $82.5 million, an amount that includes nonpolitical investigation. The Bureau refused to supply more detailed itemization on national security grounds. In November 1972 an estimated 1265 Bureau agents were assigned to political intelligence; 1034 in April 1973; and 861 in March 1974 (GAO Report, pp. 131–132).

interagency collaboration. For example, a Cook County grand jury reported in November 1975 that the Chicago Police Department's Security Section "routinely funneled [intelligence data] to the Federal Bureau of Investigation," and that "from 1969 to 1971 [it] was in almost daily contact with the United States Army 113th Military Intelligence Group . . . [and] during this time the 113th Military Group planned and conducted intelligence gathering operations in direct cooperation with the Chicago Police Department's Security Section."

Surveillance and the compilation of dossiers by private detective agencies and conservative political groups—historically an important component of the domestic intelligence system—also were adrenalized by the unrest of the sixties. In a period like the present, when government agencies fall under attack, these private efforts have continued to play an important role, collecting, storing, and disseminating file material until a changed climate of opinion permits the reemergence of officially sponsored government surveillance.

The disclosures in recent years, through an assortment of channels, of illegal intelligence activities by government agencies have reinforced the perception that hidden power structures have exercised an effective veto over the political process. This awareness was heightened by the Watergate scandals, which laid bare the functioning of a covert vigilante state centering on the Presidency, targeting threats to its sovereignty and policies. For some, the public airing of official misconduct—the train of admissions, defensive pleas, resignations, exposés, and court trials—have scrubbed away the stains on our escutcheon and restored the political honor of the state. But confession and the pledge to sin no more cannot alter the hard reality that our democratic commitment is threatened by a vigilante political culture deeply rooted in our past.

2 The Emergence of the American Political Intelligence System

The Slow Beginning

Intelligence served as a means of repressing dissent and neutralizing potential threats to powerholders long before the emergence of the modern state. And history, ancient and modern, has also made us familiar with the repressive role of clandestine surveillance practices, especially political espionage. The use by governments of political spies was regarded with revulsion by the founders of the Republic, long familiar with such abuses both in antiquity and in the contemporary practices of George III. The planting of informers in protest groups and movements was associated in the minds of the founders with the offense of seditious libel, the key instrument of repression in eighteenth-century England.

From 1761 until the adoption of the First Amendment in 1791, England was the theater of more than seventy seditious libel prosecutions and some fifty convictions.[1]* The Crown typically relied on the testimony of political informers; the defendants in two notorious cases, John Horne Tooke and John Wilkes, were idolized in this country as freedom fighters.[2] When the Sedition Act of 1798 was proposed, Edward Livingston warned:

> The country will swarm with informers, spies, delators and all the odious reptile tribe that breed in the sunshine of despotic power. . . . The hours of the most unsuspected confidence, the intimacies of friendship, or the recesses of domestic retirement, afford no security. The companion whom you must trust, the friend in whom you must confide, the domestic who waits in your chamber, are all tempted to betray your imprudent or unguarded follies, to misrepresent your words; to convey them, distorted by calumny, to the secret tribunal where jealousy presides —where fear officiates as accuser, and suspicion is the only evidence that is heard. . . . Do not let us be told that we are to excite fervor against a foreign aggression

*Notes to chapters can be found on p. 484.

30

to establish a tyranny at home . . . and that we are absurd enough to call ourselves free and enlightened while we advocate principles that would have disgraced the age of Gothic barbarity.[3]

And the repression in England in the wake of the French Revolution and thereafter throughout the Continent made informing and political espionage anathema to Americans, not merely a violation of the protected freedoms but a betrayal of the American idea. If at the beginning of the nineteenth century they knew that sedition meant spies, at its end they knew that spies meant a secret police. For by the turn of the century every European state, as well as Great Britain, was served by a national secret political police corps.[4]

In contrast to European experience, intelligence in the United States was not a direct response to threats to the safety and stability of the state but to interests of a lesser magnitude. Unique, too, was the role of private detectives in the service of nongovernmental clients. During the Civil War, the Pinkerton Detective Agency was recruited for military espionage by the War Department and was used by employers in subsequent years as a weapon against labor unions and their activities. The Pinkertons achieved their greatest triumph in their successful campaign in the late 1870s on behalf of the Reading Railroad to smash the Molly Maguires.[5] In the course of tracking and exposing the Mollies, the Pinkerton Agency developed a *modus operandi* that would become the model for intelligence infiltration of political organizations. Every group was assumed to be led by a tight inner circle of conspirators whose program and tactics were closely held secrets. These insiders were, in theory, surrounded by an outer ring of followers, many of them unaware of the criminal purposes of the leaders. In order to unmask these purposes and apprehend the leaders, it was necessary first to join the outer ring, and then, through craft and daring, to gain access to the leaders. Such penetration had a single aim: the arrest and conviction of the members of the inner group on conspiracy charges.[6]

From intervention in labor strife, it was a short step to the recruitment of private detectives as a means of aborting unionism. Labor espionage was thus institutionalized as a tactic in class warfare. This enlarged role was accompanied by an expansion of the agency's mission to include not only evidence collection for law enforcement purposes but infiltration and penetration purely for intelligence gathering unrelated to law enforcement. In effect, private detectives became secret auxiliaries of employers, charged with waging guerrilla warfare by any means necessary against labor organization.

Since, in many instances, the movement for labor organization was influenced by political and ideological currents, it was inevitable that surveillance of union organization and activity would also embrace political targets. And this was particularly so because it was easier to discredit and discourage labor unionism and strikes by association with violence, conspiracy, and revolution. The merger of the two forms of surveillance did not flow only from an overlapping subject matter: they both typically involve the same kind of behavior—speech, association, organization, voluntarism, and mutual aid. The techniques required to gather intelligence were the same in both cases: physical surveillance, infiltration, informers, provocateurs, the recruitment of defectors, the identification of leaders, and the development of files and dossiers. In both cases the information was used to influence public opinion through a distinctive fear-mongering rhetoric to discredit unionism and radicalism, and also to generate private sanctions against targets: black list, ostracism, denial of use of facilities, and so on.

The use of agents provocateurs became a hallmark of this private intelligence-gathering system. Employers were reluctant to spend money for surveillance in the absence of "labor trouble." The agency's provocateurs produced such trouble and, at the same time, enmeshed unionists, especially strikers and their leaders, in framed charges of law violation. Other forms of aggressive intelligence were developed to wreck unions and to sabotage their activities. Labor spies were also used to control unions and direct their policies and activities into paths favored by the employer. This entire process of surveillance, propaganda, provocative and aggressive tactics, and control inevitably created a self-perpetuating momentum in the drive to retain and expand the market for anti-union services.

By the end of the first decade of this century political detective units in the public sector had emerged in most American cities, first in response to the anarchist movement (they were frequently called "bomb squads"), and subsequently to labor organization and strikes. By the outbreak of World War I a network of police and private detective agencies girdled urban America, joined together in a unique collaboration, sharing the same objectives and surveillance methods. This collaboration in the labor field continued until the mid-thirties, when labor espionage both by private and police agencies succumbed to New Deal attack. Radical political activities, labor unions, and industrial conflict were monitored by traditional law enforcement measures: unlawful assembly, disorderly conduct, conspiracy, incitement to riot. But an equally important source of urban intelligence was the routine police peacekeeping function—the control of crowds, parades, and demonstrations to prevent disturbance or violence. The requirement of permits for meetings and the use of public facilities was also a pathway to police intelligence involvement. The urban police thus became line officers in the intelligence war, specializing in the continued surveillance of agitators and troublemakers. A more ideological role fell to the states. By 1920, many states had enacted laws creating such political crimes as criminal syndicalism, sedition, and criminal anarchy. This statutory arsenal provided state police with a justification for the initiation and development of European-style political espionage and file systems, systems that persisted long after the statutes became dormant.[7]

The Federalization of Intelligence

If labor strife and political anarchism were the parents of nonfederal intelligence, World War I and the Russian Revolution played the same role in the federalization of intelligence. Prior to World War I, the Secret Service and the Justice Department's Bureau of Investigation conducted limited intelligence-style investigations without a clear law enforcement purpose. The problems created by the resistance to World War I—opposition to the draft, in particular —along with the registration and surveillance of enemy aliens as a check on espionage and sabotage, brought the Department of Justice into confrontation with dissenters, radicals, aliens, and pacifists. The Department's Bureau of Investigation worked closely during the war years with private patrioteering groups, principally the American Protective League (APL), officially designed as a Bureau auxiliary for ferreting out spies, slackers, and saboteurs.* The collaboration between the Bureau and the APL crested in a series of nationwide draft raids, conducted in September 1918 over a three-day period, which resulted in the arrest of tens of thousands of men who could not establish their right to be walking around in civilian dress. Only a tiny fraction of those arrested were found to be draft evaders.[8]

If World War I created a climate favorable to the federalization of intelligence, the 1917 Bolshevik Revolution gave it a permanent *raison d'être,* constituency, and mission. As war-borne hatred of the "Huns" was transferred to the reds, the defenders of America closed ranks in a new countersubversive consensus that dwarfed similar movements of the past.[9] The great American nightmare of a foreign-hatched conspiracy had become a reality. The twin traumas of war and revolution at once consolidated a nationwide countersubversive constituency and made intelligence its spokesman. This wartime collaboration between intelligence and grass-roots nativism permanently influenced the growth and direction of political intelligence—its structure, priorities, and style.

The catalyst of the federalization of intelligence was the bomb scare of 1919. In May and June of 1919 a series of bombs exploded in American cities; one explosion, on June 2, 1919, damaged the front of the Washington home of Attorney General A. Mitchell Palmer. Palmer responded by reorganizing the anti-radical operations of the Bureau. He appointed Francis P. Garvan as Assistant Attorney General in charge of anti-radical activities, and to lead the Bureau he selected William J. Flynn, formerly chief of the Secret Service (hailed by Palmer as "the greatest anarchist expert in the United States"), assisted by Frank Burke, also a former Secret Service operative.

In the latter part of June 1919 Palmer persuaded Congress to appropriate $500,000 supplementary to the $1.5 million already appropriated for fiscal year 1920 to subsidize the Department's anti-radical drive. Palmer's House Appropriations Committee testimony warned that "on a certain day, which we have been advised of, there will be [an attempt] to rise up and destroy the Government at one fell swoop." According to Palmer, July 4, 1919, was the day set by the radicals for a wave of bombings and terror.[10] Garvan gave equally hairraising testimony before the Senate Appropriations Committee. Palmer needed the money to fund a new departmental unit, the General Intelligence Division (the GID or Radical Division, as it came to be called).[11] Launched in August,

---

*In his Annual Report for 1917 (p. 83) the Attorney General noted that ". . . the American Protective League has proven to be invaluable and constitutes a most important auxiliary and reserve force for the Bureau of Investigation. Its membership, which is carefully guarded, included leading men in various localities who have volunteered their services for the purpose of being on the lookout for and reporting to this department information of value to the Government, and for the further purpose of endeavoring to secure information regarding any matters about which it may be requested to make inquiry." See also Attorney General's Annual Report, 1918, pp. 14–15.

the Division was conceived as a source of information for "a thorough-going understanding of the situation as a whole."[12]

The Government Is Watching

The newly appointed Flynn promptly launched an expanded intelligence program. In a memorandum dated August 12, 1919, to "all special agents and employees" (this last a designation of undercover operatives), he issued orders to launch "a vigorous and comprehensive investigation of anarchistic and similar classes, Bolshevism and kindred agitations advocating change in the present form of government by force and violence, the promotion of sedition and revolution, bomb throwers and similar activities." To implement the deportation statutes the agents were instructed to concentrate on aliens, but not to ignore citizens' activities, "with a view to securing evidence which may be of use in prosecutions under the existing state or federal laws or under legislation of that nature which may hereinafter be enacted." The agents and informers were further instructed to report "all information of every nature whether hearsay or otherwise. . . ."[13]

Garvan, already a countersubversive zealot, viscerally hostile to foreigners, sponsored J. Edgar Hoover, then twenty-four years old, to head the GID.[14] Like Attorney General A. Mitchell Palmer himself, both Garvan and Hoover had backgrounds in the enemy alien field dating back to 1917, Garvan as Palmer's chief investigator in the Alien Property Custodian's office and Hoover as a clerk in the Enemy Alien Registration Unit, headed by John Lord O'Brian, which he joined after a short stint as a cataloguer in the Library of Congress. Ambitious and energetic,[15] young Hoover tore into his first assignment: to learn all there was to know about revolutionary and radical movements.[16] Utilizing his library experience, he set up in the GID an index of radicals, their organizations and publications.

The initial collection of 150,000 names climbed to 450,000 a few years later. The index and file system contributed importantly to Hoover's rise in the Department. The young ex-cataloguer had not only broken down domestic radicalism into detailed categories; he had also annotated the files with entries dealing with special local conditions. To deal with the migratory character of agitators, the cards were so classified that references to particular cities could be produced on demand.[17] Hoover also organized the preparation of biographies of radically inclined individuals "showing any connection with an ultra radical body or movement." By February 1920 this political rogues gallery contained more than 70,000 biographies, including "oral and written" statements of the subjects, with a view to "determining the extent of the danger which may be anticipated from their activities and the kind of legislation which will be sufficient to protect the government against such of them as are really dangerous." In addition, "stenographic reports of speeches made by individuals prominent in the various movements [were] filed, and together with articles in the newspapers or publications [were] digested or briefed and made available for immediate reference."[18] The biographies included such prominent liberals as Jane Addams and Fiorello La Guardia.

Radical literature of all kinds—books, newspapers, and pamphlets, entire libraries seized in raids—was systematically collected, "almost say by the bale," as Palmer put it. A grand total of 625 newspapers and periodicals was filed and indexed, of which 251 were classified as "ultra-radical"; 325 of them were in 25 foreign languages and were translated by a corps of 40 multi-lingual translators, who prepared daily reports for the GID on "radical articles" as they appeared in the press. Special projects were organized to study the Negro press and the publications of the IWW. By the end of 1919, Attorney General Palmer could boast that the GID's anti-radical resources probably constituted "a greater mass of data on this subject than is anywhere else available."[19] Many of Palmer's claims were challenged by his critics, but not this one.

For Palmer, eager to justify his anti-radical pursuits, the files were a godsend. The sheer accumulation of index cards, literature, biographies, and newspapers justified his crusade, diverted attention from his abuses and failures, and won congressional support and funding. A society and its Congress conditioned to view government investigation as a handmaiden of law enforcement had to be led into new ways of thinking. The files—tangible, physical objects, full of information—were highly efficient for this purpose. Besides, how could one answer Palmer's insistent claims that they were a necessary protection against predictable eruptions of revolutionary violence in the future? True, the bombings remained unsolved. But was it not clear that other bombers would be deterred by the Bureau's files and its intelligence activities generally? Anti-radical intelligence work, the Attorney General insisted, "does not always show in arrests . . . but it does show in a remarkable collection of facts, available for future use . . . and it shows also in the knowledge that it imparts to these persons of revolutionary design, that the government is watching."[20]

The Palmer Raids

Still, it was the claimed need for the GID as a law enforcement aid in the solution of the bombings that won it congressional approval and funding. Indeed, after the initial funding, Congress was persuaded in December 1919 to grant a deficiency appropriation of $1 million on Palmer's assurance "that the money would be expended largely in prosecution of the red element in this country, and running down the reds. . . ."[21]

With the termination of hostilities, the wartime espionage and sedition acts directed against citizens and aliens had lapsed. Aliens were a prime target: "90% of the Communist and radical agitation is traceable to aliens," Palmer reported. Existing legislation was amended in 1918 to provide for the deportation of aliens who were "anarchists" or "members of, or affiliated with any organization that entertains a belief in, teaches, or advocates the overthrow by force and violence of the government of the United States." But Justice Department appropriations were limited to expenditures for the "prosecution and detection of crimes against the United States." Deportation was not a criminal proceeding. A highly restricted authority to investigate noncriminal matters enacted in 1916 required a prior State Department request and, in any event, was confined to "official matters under the control" of the Justice or State departments. But jurisdiction over the deportation of aliens was exclusively within the province of the Department of Labor. Besides, deportation required a prior proscription of the organizations covered by the 1918 statute and the identification of those members who were aliens. But these, too, were matters solely for the Secretary of Labor. Despite these difficulties, Palmer and his aides decided, in June 1919, that a mass round-up for the deportation of alien radicals was the most promising means of saving the country. The Attorney General made no bones about this deliberate lawlessness: "The administration of this [deportation] law is entirely within the jurisdiction of the Department of Labor. However, under existing conditions of our laws, it seemed to be the only means at my disposal of attacking the radical movement. . . ." It had to be a mass sweep, he explained, because "the individual agitators were so migratory in their habits and so cautious in their oral utterances that it was quite difficult, if not impossible, to pick them off one by one."[22]

The mass raid deportation strategy that Hoover had helped formulate was first put into effect on November 7, 1919, when Bureau operatives in collaboration with the Immigration Service of the Labor Department staged simultaneous raids on twelve cities and arrested hundreds of members of the Federation of the Union of Russian Workers (URW), of whom only forty-three were found to be deportable aliens. This group, together with over 200 others found deportable as anarchists (including Emma Goldman and Alexander Berkman), were deported on December 21, 1919, on the ship *Buford* (dubbed the "Soviet Ark").[23]

Hoover, who together with Flynn supervised the departure of the *Buford,* was jubilant over the size of the haul and the speed of the deportation process.[24] True, the raid resulted in charges of brutality against aliens and even casual visitors at URW halls, not to speak of the destruction of property and files. Hoover not only refused to investigate the charges but indignantly urged that the lawyer for the complainants "ought to be disbarred from further practice before the immigration authorities." The anarchists represented only one section of the radical movement. Hoover also tried to proceed against the Industrial Workers of the World (IWW), but his plea was rebuffed by Secretary of Labor William B. Wilson.[25] There remained a third grouping: the newly formed Communist and Communist Labor parties.

The November raids were a dry run for a crackdown on the Communists. A joint meeting of the Immigration Bureau and Justice Department officials, including young Hoover, agreed on a plan for simultaneous raids throughout the country designed to sweep in several thousand Communists on warrants issued in blank by the Department of Labor. The seized aliens were to be held in custody under the warrants, filled in with their names as soon as they were identified. When the raids took place in cities all over the country early in January 1920, Bureau agents, frequently with the assistance of local "red squads," rounded up from 5000 to an estimated 10,000 suspected radicals, holding most incommunicado and subjecting many to extreme brutality. Hundreds were incarcerated for long periods of time without arrest warrants, and warrantless searches were common.[26]

Despite his denials in later years, Hoover played an important and responsible role in planning these raids and also in supervising the details of their execution. The secret confidential instructions sent to the field on December 27, 1919, in preparation for the raids, directed the local agents to "communicate by long distance to Mr. Hoover any matters of vital interest or importance which may arise during the course of the arrests." And, the instructions continued, on the morning subsequent to the arrests, the participating agents were to mail to him by special delivery a list of those arrested and whether they were arrested without a warrant. At the same time, Hoover was to be notified by wire of "the results of the arrests made . . . the total number of persons of each organization taken into custody, together with a statement of any interesting evidence secured."[27]

When Attorney General Palmer appeared before the House Rules Committee in June 1920 to defend himself against charges of misconduct and abuse of power, levied by Assistant Secretary of Labor Louis F. Post, Hoover sat at his side as the expert with full knowledge of the facts.[28] And in the spring of 1921 when the Senate Judiciary Committee, headed by Senator Thomas J. Walsh, initiated an investigation to explore the charges of twelve eminent members of the bar, set forth in a *Report Upon the Illegal Practices of the Department of Justice,* it was again Hoover who was designated by Palmer as the functionary responsible for the execution of the raids. As Palmer himself put it when asked by Senator Walsh about the number of search warrants that had been issued prior to the January 2, 1920, raid: "I cannot tell you Senator, personally. If you would like to ask Mr. Hoover, who was in charge of the matters, he can tell you."[29] Moreover, Hoover was well aware that his GID was illegally meddling in deportation matters. On February 20, 1920, in an interdepartmental memo to his superior, Frank Burke, he had himself observed that there was "no authority under law permitting this Department to take any action in deportation proceedings relative to radical activities."[30]

Hoover argued vigorously against the imposition of bail and, where bail was allowed, recommended a prohibitively large amount or opposed reduction, on the ground that release would simply permit agitators to spread their propaganda. He also requested the Immigration Bureau to deny bail to any person who refused to answer questions put by his agents. He thought that it virtually "defeats the ends of justice" if the agents could not get from the aliens themselves the evidence that would justify deportation.[31] Hoover objected to the presence of lawyers until after his agents had finished their interrogation, and even argued that aliens against whom there was no proof of deportability should be detained on the chance that such evidence might be unearthed later and that, if they were released for lack of proof, they should be placed under conditional parole as a curb on future radical activity.

But Hoover's draconian position on bail and the right to counsel reflected Bureau policy. Informers, then actual employees of the agency, had played a key role in the raids*—and not merely as identifiers and fingermen. They were instructed to arrange for the holding of meetings on the night the raids were scheduled. Indeed, it was the availability of the Bureau's huge corps of informers that was the principal inducement for the Immigration Bureau's acceptance of the Department's organizing role in the raids. Bureau chief Flynn, from the beginning, insisted on the protection of the identity of his informers, a policy that barred their appearance on the witness stand. The most promising alternative source of evidence was the alien himself, provided he could be detained and isolated from his lawyer long enough. The strategy failed, and the subsequent wholesale release of the detainees dramatized the conflict between intelligence needs and law enforcement, a conflict that has since haunted countersubversive prosecutions and other legal proceedings.

While the November raids produced only limited protest—mostly from lawyers on behalf of their clients—the January ones stirred waves of criticism all over the country. The response of Palmer, Garvan, and Hoover to their critics initiated a technique highly favored in subsequent years. Hoover attacked lawyers who charged Bureau agents with brutality against their clients, questioned their patriotism, and had a search made of military intelligence files for evidence linking his critics to subversion. Liberal and even conservative defenders of dissent were themselves denounced as agents and supporters of Bolshevism. The following passage from a memo (apparently prepared by Francis P. Garvan) distils the flavor of the Bureau's response to its critics:

> There was in the situation of the apprehended reds a certain specious appearance of martyrdom which touched the American heart. But there would have been no vicious and hurtful criticism of the administration, but rather free praise from all responsible sides for its promptness and good effect, had it not been that the press agents of the reds and their hallucinated friends among the parlor bolsheviks, and even a certain class of liberal writers, from whom better discretion might have been expected, drenched the newspapers and magazines with malicious or false descriptions of the raids, of the deportations, and the policy of the administration.

Hoover even had a search made of the records of the IWW for evidence of a secret tie between the Wobblies and the Bureau's arch-critic and accuser, Assistant Secretary of Labor Louis F. Post.[32]

Post had taken over his duties, which included supervision of the Immigration Bureau, in March 1920. By that time Labor Secretary William B. Wilson had ruled that the target of the November raid, the Union of Russian Workers, was a proscribed organization under the 1918 statute and had reluctantly authorized the issuance of arrest warrants in the January raids. It was not until the end of January that he found the Communist Party to fall within the 1918 law. After Post took over, matters changed considerably. In May the Communist Labor Party was specifically held to be beyond the reach of the 1918 statute—

*The cornerstone of the raid strategy was a network of undercover agents planted in target groups long before the raids. According to the New York Times of Jan. 3, 1920: "For months Department of Justice men, dropping all other work, had concentrated on the Reds. Agents quietly infiltrated into the radical ranks, slipped casually into centers of agitation, and went to work, sometimes as cooks in remote mining colonies, sometimes as miners, again as steel workers, and where the opportunity presented itself, as 'agitators' of the wildest type" (reprinted in Walsh, p. 319).

a ruling that infuriated Hoover. Post charged in subsequent testimony that the Department had been taken in by Palmer's representation that a nationwide plot had been hatched "to overthrow our Government by means of a physical force Revolution," and that "the danger was both extreme and imminent." Under Post's influence, the Department now insisted on conformity with due process and factual proof of illegal advocacy as a prerequisite of adverse rulings under the 1918 statute. Most important, Post rejected Hoover's contention that mere paper membership in a revolutionary group was ground for deportation without proof that the alien either was aware that he was a member or had any knowledge of the organization's platform or goals. Immigration Bureau chief Anthony Caminetti was forced to abide by the decisions of his superiors, but Hoover sought and received the aid of the Attorney General in a vendetta against his Labor Department adversaries that raged in Congress for a long time.[33] It was this clash that taught the young bureaucrat the vital importance of developing a congressional base.

Palmer vigorously defended the raids on nation-saving grounds—the term "national security" had not yet entered the intelligence lexicon. (What Palmer could have done with it!) He initiated a "public relations" campaign to rally and broaden his countersubversive support and wooed the press with the materials fed him by Hoover and edited by Garvan. A prize item was *Red Radicalism,* a pamphlet that served as a showcase for the most lurid items extracted from the GID files. Denying that his efforts constituted "propaganda," as his critics had claimed, he insisted that they were merely intended as a "convenience" to magazine editors by supplying them with "documentary proof to show what these people were doing. . . ."

Further enlightenment came from photographs, news stories, and cartoons designed to spur "patriotic support of all true Americans in its fight to protect their homes, religion and property from the spreading menace of Bolshevism. . . ." In addition to material of this sort—transmitted to newspapers free of charge on plates for easy reproduction—the Attorney General sent a form letter to magazine editors throughout the United States with exhibits drawn from the GID files. The purpose of the mailing was to demonstrate that the radical movement "is a dishonest and criminal one . . . an organized campaign to acquire the wealth and power of all countries for the few agitators and their criminal associates."[34]

Although the chief legal officer of the United States, Palmer preferred to ignore the impact of these exertions on the many pending cases. The Lawyers' Report already referred to went even further and charged that the publicity was "patently designed to affect public opinion in advance of court decisions and prepared in the manner of an advertising campaign in favor of repression." The report added: "If a private lawyer were to try his cases in the press in this manner, he would be in danger of disbarment."

A Star Is Born

Hoover's role in the Justice Department's holy war against the reds is frequently obscured by the fact that at the time he was overshadowed by more important figures, especially the redoubtable Attorney General, and outranked by superiors like Flynn, Garvan, and Burke, who made more headlines. As head of the Intelligence Unit, Hoover was entrusted with the evaluation of the strength and purpose of domestic radicalism. Instead of a professional estimate of the true strength of the radicals, extraordinarily weak at the time,[35] he quickened the pursuit and collaborated in the misconduct that accompanied it. Hoover's subsequent career as the nation's number one red hunter runs in a straight line from his first seven years in government devoted almost exclusively to countersubversion. Moreover, there can be little doubt that, in the twenties, as historian Paul Murphy has observed, the exploitation of anti-Communist hysteria opened a new pathway to power and advancement.[36] For the ambitious Hoover, countersubversion became a career choice, a professional specialty. That the young man "found himself" in countersubversive intelligence is quite clear from his initial report on the work of the GID submitted in October 1920. Stressing the need for protection of the national safety against aliens and citizens, he cited the GID's services in the deportation and state sedition cases. He had extended the unit's work "to cover more general intelligence work, including not only the radical activities in the United States and abroad, but also the studying of matters of an international nature, as well as economic and industrial disturbances incident thereto." Anticipating later formulations, he described radical groups and individuals in fearsome rhetoric but said little about the detection or prevention of criminal acts. Both the deportation and state prosecutions had slowed up the course of radicalism, he reported, but he offered no comfort for the future. The young unit chief also worked out liaison arrangements with military intelligence that provided MI with investigative aid in exchange for its foreign-source information, which had been denied Hoover by the State Department.

On the basis of Marxist-Leninist texts, the revolutionary literature of the old world together with the radical printed matter and reports of agents and informers that poured into his office, he prepared a number of briefs that were intended to justify the issuance of arrest warrants by the Department of Labor.[37] These were widely circulated to agents in the field for use in the post-raid legal proceedings, presented to congressional committees in support of proposed sedition legislation and anti-radical appropriations, and fed to the press.[38]

Although Hoover remained proud of these briefs all his life (and indeed they are the foundation of his reputation as an expert on communism), they are little more than sloganizing tracts that echo the conspiratorial clichés of the time. (Judge Anderson, who presided in the case of *Collyer* v. *Skeffington,* termed them "so-called briefs.") The basic argument of the briefs, that revolutionary theory was a blueprint for immediate violent overthrow of the United States, rested upon quotations extracted from their documentary context and the overheated rhetoric of the newly formed Communist parties. In the same way, he argued that formal paper membership in a proscribed organization was in itself sufficient to warrant deportation. In his brief on the Communist Party, he denounced early European communism as the brainchild of "a few intellectual perverts blinded by the thought of achievement of a utopian political commonwealth."[39] In his unsuccessful brief on the Communist Labor Party, his peroration characterized Communist doctrine as the "very essence of the principles of immorality, of lawlessness, and of ruthless government, as has nowhere else been found at any time in the history of the world."[40] The ferocity of young Hoover's response to communism comes through in this passage from the same brief:

> The ignorant primarily, but also the vicious, criminal element, which in Russia has murdered all who stood in their way and has robbed all who had any wealth, have accepted the doctrines of Communism. No right minded person can countenance such revolutionary propaganda as the Communists are spreading.

In conclusion we are told that the doctrines of communism "threaten the happiness of the community, the safety of every individual and the continuance of every home and fireside. They would destroy the peace of the country and thrust it into a condition of anarchy and lawlessness and immorality that pass imagination."[41] In Labor Department testimony he stated his case more bluntly, testifying that the Communist Labor Party was "a gang of cutthroat aliens who have come to this country to overthrow the government by force."

The virulence and intellectual crudity of Hoover's efforts are only in small part explained by the dogmatism of an auto-didact and the polemical passions of a young lawyer who overidentifies with his client. Hoover was a child of his time, a countersubversive fanatic. Radicalism was something demonic and unclean—an infection that threatened not only American political institutions but civilization itself. Our way of life, the purity of our women and the innocence of our children, were being befouled by the bearded foreigners, godless and filthy, cunning and bloodthirsty, in alliance with parlor Bolsheviks and intellectual perverts. What mattered details like due process or lack of jurisdiction when the beast was poised to spring at the nation's throat? It is this extraordinary absorption of the cause by the self that made the child of the twenties the father of the man of the forties, fifties, and sixties. The inner voice, which sounds in the early writings, would remain unchanged for the next half century, echoing with its pristine, nativist horror. Hoover permanently captured the countersubversive imagination, and at the same time won respect in more enlightened circles. In 1923 he was requested to consult with the State Department concerning the recognition of the Soviet Union. Don Whitehead, in his semi-official account, asserts that the brief submitted by Hoover persuaded Secretary of State Charles Evan Hughes that the Soviet Union should not be recognized because of its advocacy "of the use of force and violence to obtain communist ends."[42]

Looking for Business

After the raids, the Bureau was all dressed up but had nowhere to go. Left without even a color of anti-radical jurisdiction, its resources continued to be used to support pleas for new countersubversive legislation. Desperate for a legal justification, it persisted in the claim that radical hunting was a prudent preparation for this yet unenacted legislation. By default, the enforcement of state sedition laws became its greatest operational priority. This work expanded under the guidance of a new Bureau chief, William J. Burns, who replaced Flynn in March 1921. Like Flynn, Burns had served as chief of the Secret Service, retiring in 1909 to form a private detective agency with his son.[43] In a few years the newly formed agency rivaled Pinkerton's in its coverage of the radical, foreign-born, and labor worlds, its success spurred by Burns's reputation as the nemesis of the alleged Los Angeles *Times* dynamite conspirators, the McNamara brothers.[44] Before the entry of the United States into World War I, Burns had served as an investigator of British activities for the Germans, and of German activities for the British. His detective agency, like others, had openly collaborated with the Bureau in anti-radical and anti-labor cases, and would continue to do so on an even more favorable basis after he became Bureau chief. A boyhood friend of President Harding's Attorney General, Harry M. Daugherty, a master blackmailer and close ally of leading patrioteers and witch hunters, he was hardly the man to impose long-overdue standards of professionalism on the Bureau.

With the aid of young Hoover, whom he had promoted to the post of Assistant Bureau Director, Burns converted the Bureau into an expanded version of his own detective agency. But involvement in state prosecutions, improper on the face of it,[45] reflected departmental policy. As Attorney General Daugherty explained in his 1921 Annual Report:

> These [state] statutes reach the citizen as well as the alien. As the only remedy available to the Federal Government is by deportation of such agitators as are aliens, this department frequently not only cooperates with the State and city officials, but in many instances has furnished information upon which individuals have been successfully prosecuted.[46]

The outstanding example of this form of Bureau involvement in countersubversion was the raid in August 1922 in Bridgman, Michigan, on a Communist convention. Conceived and executed by Bureau agents, it was supplemented in its final stages by the local sheriff and a posse of about twenty private citizens. The order to place the convention under surveillance came from Burns himself, who received a tip about the gathering from a Bureau undercover man. A number of the arrested Communists were prosecuted under the Michigan criminal syndicalist law. The chief witness for the state was a Bureau undercover agent, one Francis Morrow, a Camden, New Jersey, shipfitter.[47] The Bureau's involvement could hardly have been more blatant. But after it fell under criticism, Burns, in his appropriations subcommittee testimony in 1924 for the next year's budget, not only belittled the role of the Bureau but invented a justification for its involvement, the alleged presence at the convention of representatives of the Communist International and of fugitives—from what, he neglected to say. Having made the stock complaint that "we have not now a law on the books that enables us to suppress these people when they advocate force and violence," he nevertheless objected that "when our men aided the authorities at Bridgman, Michigan, the Civil Liberties Union of New York promptly demanded to know what authority we had for sending our agents there. They insisted on knowing specifically under what law we did it."[48]

Burns suppressed other facts in his appropriations subcommittee testimony about the Bureau's role in the Bridgman case. Michigan authorities were reluctant to spend the considerable amounts needed for a mass trial of the Bridgman defendants. Burns's good friend, super-patriot Ralph Easley of the National Civic Federation, came to the rescue and supplied him with the funds needed for preparing the case. In addition, Burns cooperated with R. M. Whitney of the American Defense Society in publishing the material seized in the Michigan raid. Though held by the government under a search warrant, it was turned over to Whitney for use before the trial in paid newspaper articles. In the same way, the GID's files were made available to groups such as the National Security League and the National Civic Federation. In contrast to this generosity, Burns declined to furnish to the National Council for the Prevention of War material in the Bureau's files used as the basis for charges against it by Burns. In response to its request, he wrote: "I must advise you that it has long been the practice of the Bureau to hold its files confidential and available for confidential use only. . . ."[49]

In collaboration with an assortment of private groups, local police, and military intelligence, the Bureau launched a major drive against the legitimacy of postwar labor strife. The Bureau's prime labor target was the IWW; but it achieved its greatest success in its assault on the steel strike of 1919. Consistently exaggerating the radical views of strike leaders, it treated strikes generally as part of a planned revolutionary takeover. In April 1920 Hoover went so far as to claim in congressional testimony that at least 50 percent of the strikes then erupting were inspired by Communist groups—a conclusion wholly unsupported by the evidence.[50] And in his 1924 Appropriations Committee testimony, Bureau chief Burns insisted that "the proof is very conclusive . . . overwhelming —that in all strikes in the United States this radical propaganda enters into the situation. These radicals . . . take advantage of the ordinary strikes that occur throughout the country, intensify them and create a great deal of trouble and disorder."[51]

In the same way, racial unrest was consistently ascribed to alien agitators. As Burns explained it, "social activities" were considered by the Bureau as a matter "of a general intelligence nature," along with radical and anarchistic activities. The Department regarded calls for labor organization among unskilled blacks as especially sinister.[52] In a document prepared in 1920 by the Department based on intelligence sources, we are told:

The reds have done a vast amount of evil damage by carrying doctrine of race revolt and the poison of Bolshevism to the Negroes. In New York and Chicago . . . and wherever there exists [sic] conceivable numbers of colored workmen in the towns, the damage done by these incitations and by the well subsidized Negro propaganda press which has been aiding them, has been most serious. This business has perhaps been the most contemptible and wicked performance of our American revolutionary fanatics.

And in Hoover's Communist Party brief a similar equation is made between organizing black workers and subversion.[53]

Comes the Revolution

Neither at the time of the organization of the GID nor at any time thereafter had the Attorney General received a countersubversive intelligence assignment from the President or Congress. The lack of an authorized function beyond the "detection and prosecution of crimes" was overcome through the process of budgetary review. As long as congressional appropriations committees could be persuaded to grant money for intelligence activities, that was all that mattered. Congress could either be deceived about the real purpose of the expenditures, co-opted as a partner, or frightened into silence by predictions of revolution. Palmer had obtained his initial huge appropriations by insisting that it was necessary to prepare for an immediate revolutionary disturbance. The failure of the predicted July 4, 1919, outbreak to materialize did not change the febrile quality of his appeals nor impair their success. After the December 1919 deficiency appropriation, Palmer appeared in March 1920 for an equally generous renewal for the following fiscal year. Shortly before his March appearance, Palmer flooded the country with GID predictions of a violent series of radical demonstrations for May 1, 1920, which, like the previous year's warnings, came to nothing.[54] When he appeared before the Congress in March, he promised that of the entire sum requested, at least 40 percent would be used "in the campaign against alien radicals and anarchists in this country."

In his annual report for that year he commented that, alas, "a renewal of this radical agitation was noted in May, and the same has been growing constantly since that time." It became quite clear to Palmer that by playing on fears of revolution he could extract generous appropriations for the entire Department, and at the same time, build up the Bureau and the GID to positions of power and importance. As Robert Murray has written: "Certainly, the hunt for radicals during the 1919–1920 period 'made' the Bureau of Investigation and started it on the road to becoming the famous FBI of the present day."[55]

The effectiveness of the Palmer formula is reflected in the Bureau's budgetary history. In the decade between 1913 and 1923 the expenditures of the Bureau of Investigation rose from $415,452 in 1913 to $2,166,197 in 1923, although this period saw only a nominal increase in the number of criminal prosecutions. Indeed, the number of convictions declined from 11,474 in 1913 to 11,205 in 1923. In 1918, demands of wartime investigation and litigation resulted in almost tripling of the level of expenditures over the previous year—from $617,534 in

1917 to $1,748,226 in 1918.[56] The anticipated decline in funding seemingly made inevitable by the ending of the war never materialized because of the exploitation of the fears of radicalism.

The pattern is evident from the appropriations testimony and the Attorney General's report in the years that followed. In the 1922 hearing on the next year's appropriations bill, Burns testified that "radical activities have increased wonderfully . . . over a year or two years ago." The very absence of overt disturbances was ominous: "They have not been blowing up yards and ammunition places, but the underground system by which they are carrying this on at the present time is stronger now than it ever was, this shop propaganda, and the underground propaganda everywhere; in other words, the radicals have almost revolutionized their methods . . . today it is all underground work and a great deal of it is going on."[57] When asked a final question as to whether "radical activities are particularly dangerous or of a violent character at the present time," Burns responded: "I cannot impress upon you too much how dangerous they are at the present moment."[58]

By 1924 Burns's recital of the achievements of the GID included the fact that it had received (presumably from agents or informers) some 27,436 reports about "ultra-radical activities," and that its current surveillance coverage embraced 2724 individuals, groups, and organizations. He reported a large increase in "radical propaganda," which was being disseminated "in the churches, schools and colleges throughout the country." When asked by a skeptical congressman to explain the nature of the propaganda and its dangers, Burns replied that it

> principally consists of urging the working man to strike, with the ultimate purpose of bringing about a revolution in this country. . . . Radicalism is becoming stronger every day in this country. They are going about it in a very subtle manner. For instance, they had schools all over the country where they are teaching children 4 and 5 years old, and they are organizing athletic clubs through the country. I dare say that unless the country becomes thoroughly aroused concerning the danger of this radical element in this country, we will have a very serious situation.[59]

Burns also played variations on earlier themes of foreign influence. There was constant communication between Moscow and American Communists (1921); the Soviet government was responsible for most of the radicalism in the country (1922): "The Communist International at Moscow is directing activities in this country among . . . Negroes, labor unions and various social organizations including women's clubs and famine scouts . . . to undermine these organizations with the end in view of overthrowing the Government of the United States and the establishment of the dictatorship of the proletariat." But there was no cause for alarm; "we are in very close touch with . . . this shop propaganda and the underground propaganda." The Bureau's and the nation's stoutest shield was the undercover informer. As Burns explained to the committee: "Nobody but that class of man can go in. You can imagine the great difficulty we have in getting men who can do that character of work whom we can trust, and, of course, we check them out very, very closely."[60]

Burns had good reason to be touchy on the subject of Bureau informers.

One of them, Wolfe Lindenfeld, had "confessed" in 1921 that the Third International had perpetrated the Wall Street bombing. When this turned out to be a hoax, Lindenfeld was denounced as a double agent.[61] More serious problems were presented by one Albert Bailin or Balanow, a former operative for the Department of Justice, military intelligence, the Burns Agency, and a number of other detective agencies engaged in political and labor surveillance. On assignment from his employers, Bailin had infiltrated a cluster of radical organizations. In a deposition taken in 1923 for use in the Bridgman trial, Bailin implicated the Burns Agency in an assortment of provocations, thefts, and forgeries, including the purchase of a secret file of the Bureau's former chief, William J. Flynn. According to Bailin, the head of the Burns Agency's radical department had instructed him to write a threatening letter on the typewriter of a rival agency where Bailin had been employed, purportedly from an anarchist group threatening to kill the Postmaster General and blow up the Woolworth Building. Bailin's story was denounced by Burns as an attempt to frame him, while the current head of his agency charged that Bailin had been planted by the Soviets to discredit government and private surveillance of radicals.[62]

These charges were uncorroborated, but the proof was indisputable that Burns had permitted the Bureau to engage in a variety of squalid practices, including the use of agents and informers to frame critics of the Harding administration and collaboration with private detective agencies, especially his own, in anti-radical and anti-labor matters.[63] The Bureau served as a secret police force for the equally corrupt Department of Justice, the operating base for the Ohio gang of Harding administration boodlers.[64] Forced to resign, Attorney General Harry Daugherty, like his predecessor, insisted that he was a victim of a red plot to hound him out of office.

In March 1924 President Coolidge named Harlan F. Stone as Daugherty's successor. The former Columbia Law School dean was not only familiar with the Bureau's intelligence abuses but had himself publicly attacked the agency on these grounds. Voicing the fear that "a secret police may become a menace to free government and free institutions because it carries with it the possibility of abuses of power which are not always quickly apprehended or understood," the new Attorney General insisted: "The Bureau of Investigation is not concerned with political or other opinions of individuals. It is concerned only with their conduct and then only with such conduct as is forbidden by the laws of the United States." Hoover followed with a circular to Bureau personnel to the same effect, and in May he reassured a Senate investigating committee particularly concerned with avoiding a repetition of the Palmer-Daugherty era abuses that "instructions have been sent to officers in the field to limit their investigations in the field to violations of the statutes." But neither Senate nor House could be persuaded to approve then-pending bills that would have reinforced such voluntary restraints with legal sanctions for Bureau misconduct.

In October, two months before he became Director, Hoover submitted a memorandum to his superior, Assistant Attorney General William J. Donovan, stating: "It is, of course, to be remembered that the activities of Communists and other ultra-radicals have not up to the present time constituted a violation of the Federal statutes, and consequently, the Department of Justice, theoretically, has no right to investigate such activities as there has been no violation of the Federal laws."[65] These belated admissions that the Bureau's entire course of anti-radical investigations, surveillance, propaganda, and harassment was without legal foundation are a counterpart of the Director's private statement some five years earlier that the deportation raids were lawless and beyond the authority of the Department. But, as we shall see, the problem of its intelligence jurisdiction has continued to plague the Bureau until the present time.

In early August 1924 a representative of the American Civil Liberties Union, Roger N. Baldwin, conferred privately with Attorney General Stone and Hoover about the future conduct of the Bureau. Reassurances were offered. The GID was abolished and its intelligence functions terminated. Bureau agents were no longer permitted to work up cases under state sedition laws, nor would there be any repetition of cases such as had been filed in Michigan and Pennsylvania against radicals at the instigation of Bureau agents. As to provocateurs, there were none then operating in radical groups or labor unions—but any agent found acting in such a role would be promptly discharged. There was to be no future collaboration with private detective agencies, and the practice of giving out confidential information in the Bureau's files to private detective agencies and patriotic groups had been wholly discontinued. The Attorney General added that he could not destroy the files and cards without an act of Congress, but he insisted that all propaganda about radicals had been definitely discontinued. And Hoover promised that neither he nor anyone else in the Department, except the Attorney General, would make any more speeches dealing with the Bureau or its work.[66]

In the Beginning Was the Word

The forced retirement of the Bureau had no impact on radical hunting beyond leaving the field open to the wilder practitioners of the art. The hunt quickened, in fact, with the consolidation of the veterans movement, unrelenting pressure on labor organizations, and the revitalization of nativism in response to growing urbanization. The availability of countersubversive intelligence as a tool of government repression as well as private self-help gave this enlarged consensus new perspectives for action. World War I, to a much larger extent than any war in the past, produced an intelligence capability: it trained large numbers of men in the arts of intelligence, which were then readily adaptable to other uses. At the same time, it created a pervasive awareness of the potential effectiveness of intelligence as a weapon against domestic enemies. The end of the war thus made available the services of soldiers, ex-officers, reservists, as well as patriotic amateur detectives, all thirsting for peacetime assignments. Those who had served first as wartime spy hunters and then, in the postwar years, as countersubversive snoopers and spies, inevitably embraced intelligence as the answer to subversion.

The root anti-subversive impulse was fed by the Menace. Its power strengthened with the passage of time, by the late twenties its influence had become more pervasive and folkish. Bolshevism came to be identified over wide areas of the country by God-fearing Americans as the Antichrist come to do eschatological battle with the children of light. A slightly secularized version, widely shared in rural and small-town America, postulated a doomsday conflict between decent upright folk and radicalism—alien, satanic, immorality incarnate. The enemy was perceived with the kind of retching horror evoked by the biblical cry "Unclean!" In the thirties this secular religion evolved into present-day anti-communism, and, influenced by populist politics, it retained a highly personalized conception of radicals and dissenters, not as advocates of programs for legitimate political ends but as individuals, evil men plotting in dark corners, heretics who mocked the truth that we are a uniquely created nation. Although formally identified with politics, the Menace became a cultural stigma, the embodiment of the "other," a negative definition of our national being.

In this atmosphere, the nonfederal institutional radical hunters flourished as a network of urban, state, and county operations expanded. Police intelligence became an élite function, an assignment especially coveted for ideological reasons. Its chief frequently emerged as an important public figure, far more important than his conventional law enforcement counterparts, even those with higher rank. This role is typified by Captain William F. Hynes, who in 1922 began as an undercover agent for the Los Angeles Police Department after wartime service in military intelligence, and by the end of the decade became the nationally known head of its intelligence bureau. In Chicago, Lieutenant Make Mills, while not such an imposing figure, was widely respected in the anti-Communist movement, both for his encyclopedic file collection and his knowledge of Russian. Similarly, in every large city local political saviors moved center-stage, seized the headlines, and traveled the luncheon circuits.

Despite the Bureau's withdrawal from the field, Hoover remained a leader of the nation's countersubversive constituency. In 1930 the Bureau persuaded the House to authorize a special committee (the "Fish Committee") to investigate "communist propaganda" in the United States. In June of that year Hoover appeared before the committee and testified in a confidential session. Introduced by the chairman as "perhaps as well informed as any Government official on the activities and propaganda in connection with the Communists," he read from documents seized in raids or acquired from informers prior to 1924, as well as later material supplied to him unofficially, to show the extent of subversion. In addition to his oral testimony, Hoover introduced into the record a variety of leftist publications. Anticipating what later became a favorite technique as a witness, he illuminated his subject matter with "a chart that I would like to submit confidentially to the committee. . . ." He also provided the committee with the principal briefs he had drafted during the pre-1924 period, including his 1923 presentation urging nonrecognition of the Soviet Union. With a shrewd feel for his audience, he called particular attention—here, too, anticipating his later style—to the racial issue ("there is nothing more dangerous than to preach and talk about class consciousness and to stir up racial enmity") and the sinister Communist designs on youth. To demonstrate the unspeakable evil of the reds, he read Joe Hill's song, "The Preacher and the Slave" ("long-haired preachers come out every night"), and commented, "It is that sort of thing they teach these little children."

Hoover pointed out to the committee that the Bureau's earlier anti-radical forays had relied on the deportation laws or cooperation with state prosecutions, but he opposed legislation that would extend the Bureau's authority beyond federal criminal investigations. (Later, in a memorandum to the Attorney General dated January 1932, he made clear the reasons for his position. The abuses of 1919–24 were too fresh in his mind. All his work to clean up the Bureau would be threatened by a resumption of undercover intelligence activities. Once again the Bureau would become subject to criticism.)

To the Fish Committee he pressed for more direct attacks on radicalism. Reminding the committee that "self-preservation of the Nation is the first law of patriotic duty," Hoover urged the passage of a statute punishing advocacy of the violent overthrow of the government through speech or publication. Words alone, short of action or even incitement to action, were properly punishable, he insisted, because they constituted "propaganda." An obsession with propaganda as an evil beyond the protection of the First Amendment's freedoms had, since 1919, dominated the thinking of the anti-radical establishment and became the most favored argument for a sedition statute. It is no accident that, beginning with Senate Resolution 439 in 1919 extending the authority of the Overman Committee, the congressional anti-subversive committees had uniformly singled out "propaganda" as their target.

This view of propaganda as a threat to the safety of the Republic emerged in the course of World War I and its aftermath, when new techniques of persuasion were employed by the combatants to gain American support. The resort to similar practices to build support for the war and to suppress dissent were defended as legitimate "educational" or "public relations" efforts to arm the populace against well-nigh irresistible appeals. The literature of political minorities in particular was regarded as a fearful and coercive tool for transmitting pressure on behalf of sinister, unseen principals. It was associated with foreign plots to subvert the democratically determined national interest through a rape of the mind. The spoken and written word thus became a prime intelligence target, a priority reflected in the fact that the publications and archives of American intelligence units are the best documentary sources for a history of radicalism in this country.[67]

Raids to seize radical literature became standard federal and local counter-subversive practice: "Words were captured . . . in raids and then publicly exhibited, just as an enemy might be captured and exhibited."[68] This booty was circulated, cited, and filed as though the words themselves were evil, like obscenity or blasphemy. The revolutionary literature of the twenties and the thirties was a perfect foil for this fear of propaganda. Much of it was strident and bombastic ("Arise!") and was premised on the theory that stentorian exhortation without organization or the presence of appropriate objective conditions could, by itself, produce a Bolshevik-style revolution.

"Propaganda" served another important purpose. Intelligence had regularly jeopardized its credibility by making false predictions of red-inspired violence—the boy-who-cried-wolf dilemma. This problem is largely eliminated when the evil becomes the word itself rather than its materialization. The mass of literature was also used to support the thesis that unrest and "class hatred"

were not caused by legitimate grievances but by the lure of propaganda—
especially among Negroes, unskilled workers, aliens, and youth. Indeed, it was
the power of these radical Pied Pipers ("agitators") to seduce the innocent, the
ignorant, and the unwary that made them so loathsome—a theme that Hoover
repeatedly stressed. This subversive role of propaganda is well described in the
1920 Lusk Committee Report:

> The Socialist, Communist, and anarchist movements in this country, as well as the
> industrial organizations which are the out-growth of their propaganda, are not
> spontaneous expressions of unrest brought about by critical economic conditions in
> this country, but are the results of systematic and energetic propaganda, spread by
> representatives of European revolutionary bodies. The agitation was begun many
> years ago largely among the elements of foreign workmen who had come to this
> country, and was carried out almost exclusively by the alien agitators. But with the
> increasing number of aliens and the renewed activity of agitators the propaganda
> has spread from alien groups, so that today it permeates all classes of society in this
> country.*[69]

For Hoover, the potency of propaganda was sufficient reason for making
words of advocacy the gravamen of a crime. He explained to the committee that
overt acts, the actual resort to force and violence, were no longer indispensable
to the accomplishment of revolutionary objectives; the war had demonstrated
that.

> I think the authorities of the War Department and the Navy Department would
> confirm the statement that some of the defeats on the Italian front were accom-
> plished by the dissemination of propaganda literature or leaflets, demoralizing the
> morale of the troops. We are now facing another, new instrument of warfare never
> before recognized in any war in which this country was ever engaged, so far as force
> and violence are concerned. My contention is that it is just as possible to accomplish
> this end by propaganda. In fact it is leading up to an armed conflict by a program
> and campaigning among the workers.[70]

While the committee made legislative recommendations even more stringent than those proposed by Hoover, its main proposal was for the restoration
to the Bureau of an intelligence mission with authority to engage in surveillance
over "revolutionary propaganda and activities" and to develop surveillance
specialists. These recommendations bore no immediate fruit, even though the
political intelligence proposal was echoed in the committee's minority report.

In the early thirties mass response to the depression revived demands to
investigate radicalism. Outside of Congress, pressure continued for a renewal of
the pre-1924 anti-radical role of the Bureau. In November 1934 the United States
Chamber of Commerce issued a report ("Combatting Subversive Activities in
the United States") blueprinting a legislative and intelligence program against
the left that would become a reality in the late forties and fifties. Calling for an

---

*This classic version insisted that the agitator's duped victims would revert to a contented state
as soon as he was neutralized—either by invented criminal charges or by enforced departure, tactics
in which intelligence specialized. A later, more conciliatory version concedes the existence of
genuine grievances; but these are exploited by the agitator for his own illegitimate ends, a political
concession intended at once to make the charge more credible and the role of the agitator more
cunning.

aroused public opinion to combat "the spread of propaganda and activity by numerous subversive groups," the report demanded the passage of anti-subversive legislation, including a sedition law, and urged that a "special agency within the Department of Justice be created to investigate subversive activities, with particular attention to the Communist Party and its members. . . ." But by this time the prospects were more promising. Countersubversion, historically a marginal, transient movement, had finally entered the political process.

3 The Bureau's Spurious Intelligence Authority

The August 1936 Curtain Raiser

Of the many controversies centering on American domestic intelligence in the post-Hoover years, the least publicized, but the most important, is the challenge to the legitimacy of the authority of the FBI to conduct political intelligence operations at all. What is the source of this authority: statutes, presidential orders, departmental regulations? Or was this vast power center permitted to come into being and flourish in disregard of the requirements of authorization and accountability prescribed by the political system and constitutional norms? It would be startling enough if it turned out that, say, the Federal Aeronautics Authority, the National Labor Relations Board, or the Interstate Commerce Commission had simply emerged from behind the political arras as it were, without debate, approval, supervision, or even the knowledge of a responsible branch of government. But what if such conjury produced an intelligence agency whose activities, many of them now condemned as illegal, had powerfully influenced vital areas of political expression for three decades? Verification of the claims of Bureau intelligence operations to a valid source of authority was thwarted in the past by invocation of prerogatives of secrecy; disclosure, it was claimed, might imperil our security. The Freedom of Information and Privacy acts (FOIPA), the hearings of congressional committees, and an investigation by the General Accounting Office (GAO) helped open the tangled trail.[1] And the Bureau, too, finally came forward with a defense—not one, but several—of its legal authority to conduct domestic intelligence operations. The story begins in the thirties.

The Communist Party's post-depression activism, revolutionary rhetoric, and proclaimed allegiance to the Soviet Union spurred demands in the early thirties for a renewal of countersubversive intelligence. In the tradition of World War I, volunteer red hunters kept the Bureau posted and updated its file collection. The nativism that in the twenties had found an outlet in the Ku Klux Klan now entered the larger political stage, with a proliferation of fronts, legions, mobilizations, and crusades, unified by a shared conviction that the showdown with the Menace was at hand. The rise of Nazism gave the struggling movement an ideological impetus and reinforced its anti-Semitic constituents. Anti-communism drew strength from another source: the search by employers for hidden links between labor organizations and communism ("Join the CIO and Build a Soviet America"). The trade union movement in time served as the laboratory in the development of intelligence standards for measuring Communist influence and infiltration. But the first officially sponsored intelligence investigation in the thirties was directed at the German-American Bund. The Bureau, in 1934, along with the Secret Service and the Immigration Bureau, was assigned to investigate the Nazi domestic movement with particular reference to activities "having any possible connection with official representatives of the German Government in the United States. . . ."[2]

In August 1936 President Roosevelt met with FBI Director Hoover to explore a proposed investigation of domestic communism and fascism. In briefing the President, the Director spent little time on the burgeoning ultra-right movement, but gave him an earful about the threat of communism, impressing Roosevelt with the fact that the Communists were in a position to paralyze vital areas of the economy as a result of their infiltration and control of key labor unions. The nature of Hoover's disclosures leaves no room for doubt that, while he lacked authority to conduct countersubversive investigations, he was busily collecting material from private sources. The President's requested investigation stirred a reminder of Attorney General Stone's warning in 1924 against noncriminal investigations. Beyond this, a related dilemma was posed—the appropriations statute, which confined the Bureau to "the detection and prosecution of crimes." But the Director had the answer: Still on the books was the 1916 statute, already referred to, authorizing expenditures for the investigation of matters referred to the Bureau by the Secretary of State. Why not have the State Department request such an investigation, which could be acted on under the authority of the statute and funded through the already approved Bureau appropriation? The President, Secretary of State Cordell Hull, and Hoover met the next day and arranged for such a request after the President had pointed out to Hull that the international dimensions of the problem justified it. Apart from Hoover's memoranda reporting on the two conferences, no formal record was made, in accordance with the President's desire for confidentiality. Hoover's memorandum does not indicate that Hull objected or requested details about the nature and scope of the proposed investigation. He may well have been troubled by the fact that the 1916 measure contemplated limited, closed-end investigations related to foreign affairs (the dynamiting of a consulate, the suspicious movements of a diplomatic attaché), not the extended domestic political probe that the President apparently had in mind.[3] The only tenable conclusion from Hoover's account of the conference is that the President, Hull, and Hoover deceived Congress for what the President regarded as a justifiable end—and, on another front, Hoover betrayed his own 1924 commitment to Stone.[4]

In the history of legitimacy struggle, the intended scope of the Roosevelt

1936 assignment is a key issue. It has been argued—on the basis of the State Department's sponsorship and the President's expressed concern in the conference with Hoover about the domestic activities of a Russian diplomat—that the investigation was to be confined to foreign-directed activities against the national interest, as was the case with the 1934 Bund investigation. But Hoover's account of the meeting states that the President desired "a broad picture of the general movement and its activities as [they] may affect the economic and political life of the country as a whole."[5] A 1972 Bureau report champions this foreign-influence interpretation, and points out that "the concern for national security was related to two international movements" and not to "indigenous anarchists or other groups designing to overthrow the Government." However, a later Bureau analysis (October 28, 1975) rejects the 1972 view in favor of the contention that the involvement of the Secretary of State was merely a device for overcoming the limitations of the Bureau's basic appropriations statute and did not set "jurisdictional limits or serve in some way to limit the scope of investigation to foreign or foreign controlled activities to the exclusion of domestic."[6]

The significance of the 1936 oral assignment lies both in its breadth and in its secrecy. Congress was doubly deceived: the launching of the probe was kept secret, and its funding authority deliberately misused. The assignment reflected President Roosevelt's spacious view of his powers as chief executive, a natural affinity for the intelligence process, a sometimes gossipy and voyeuristic delight in the insider's role, and a callousness to the claims alike of privacy and free expression.* But for all of its authenticity as an expression of the man and the President, the 1936 assignment is, ironically enough, feeble precedent for a claimed inherent executive power to conduct domestic intelligence activities. After all, it had been formally requested by a Secretary of State pursuant to a law enacted by Congress. Nor could an assignment under this law contemplating closed-end, ad hoc investigations with an espionage or foreign intelligence focus[7] be clothed with permanent vitality. No one could persuasively claim—although the Bureau has not hesitated to do so—that Secretary Hull requested an investigation in 1936 which permanently empowered it to conduct domestic intelligence investigations.

A question of coverage is also posed by the fact that Hoover's initial memorandum clearly indicates that the investigation was to be confined to communism and fascism—not to other purely domestic organizations or movements. Further, it is quite clear that the President wanted "general intelligence information" about the two movements—not dossiers, identifications, hidden linkages requiring penetrative surveillance. The intelligence product, commissioned by the President, would seem to have called for research, analysis, and evaluation by trained professionals. Was Hoover, a stationhouse mind steeped in the Menace, really expected to furnish the President with a broad picture of

---

*The President's record as a social reformer has obscured his anti-libertarian tendencies, reflected not only in his policies on such issues as wiretapping and Japanese relocation but in his prior career in public life. One need only recall his praise, in his 1920 campaign for the vice-presidency, of the raid the previous year by American Legionnaires on the Centralia, Washington, headquarters of the IWW as a "high form of red-blooded patriotism."

the impact of communism and fascism "on the economic and political life of the country as a whole"? If this was the expectation, the assignment was grotesquely misconceived, the prototype of a series of intelligence pleas for the bread of enlightenment to be answered with the stone of countersubversion. The President surely knew what to expect from the efforts of the Director—if from no other source than his report on the earlier Bund investigation and his contribution to the two conferences. To ensure that the project would serve his professed informational needs, should he not have insisted on the presence of Attorney General Homer S. Cummings at the briefing sessions and on his continuing supervision and guidance? Yet Hoover was permitted to represent the absent Attorney General, who thereafter acted merely as a conduit between the Director and the President. This striking discordance between professed ends and means is a hallmark of intelligence developments in the Roosevelt era.

For the Director there was no discordance at all. He treated the assignment as carte blanche for a countersubversive probe in the style of the twenties and advised the Attorney General that the Bureau had been requested to "have investigation made of the subversive activities in this country, including communism and fascism." Once again acknowledging, as he had belatedly in 1924, that being a Communist violated no law, Hoover confidentially instructed his agents in September of 1936 that: "The Bureau desires to obtain from all possible sources information concerning subversive activities being conducted in the United States by Communists, Fascists and representatives or advocates of other organizations advocating the overthrow or replacement of the Government of the United States by illegal methods."[8] Hoover proceeded to do what came naturally: a broad informer program was commenced (the Secret Service had already planted informers in "every Communist group" to ferret out plots against the life of the President) and a reporting system organized to provide daily memoranda on "major developments in every field" of subversive activities. The Bureau rapidly developed a file classification system, a dossier collection on "persons whose names appear prominently at the present time in the subversive circles," an index of names, and a library fed by newspapers, periodicals, and pamphlets and research activities.[9] The Director simply resumed where Attorney General Stone had forced him to leave off in 1924.

Hoover also used his assignment to renew and strengthen his ties with his constituency. The openly Fascist movement then flourishing apparently failed to stir his juices; it was merely an outgrowth of communism. On September 19, 1938, he made a speech before an American Legion audience that rings with the patriotic rhetoric of the twenties. He praised the Legion as a safeguard of American ideals and institutions, then went on to say: "Fascism has always grown in the slimy wastes of Communism. Our democratic institutions cannot exist half American and half alien in spirit. We are proud of our American form of government. If we want to improve it, we will do it in our way and in our own time." And a month later, before the Detroit Economic Club: "Subversive alien theories and isms are not only a drastic contrast to American ways of thinking, feeling and acting, but they stand for a complete overthrow of established ideals of American life and philosophy of government to which America is dedicated."

In the fall of 1938 the President requested a review of what he called the "espionage situation." Attorney General Cummings reported that the FBI was harmoniously collaborating with the Military Intelligence Division (MID) and the Office of Naval Intelligence (ONI) on domestic intelligence matters. His recommended authorizations for appropriations for the service agencies to continue this cooperation presented no problem since the surveillance operations of these agencies were primarily confined to their own personnel. But the Bureau situation remained sticky. In a memorandum dated October 10, 1938, the Director recommended continued use of the State Department request device:

> In considering the steps to be taken for the expansion of the present structure of intelligence work, it is believed imperative that it be proceeded with, with the utmost degree of secrecy in order to avoid criticism or objections which might be raised to such an expansion by either ill-informed persons or individuals having some ulterior motive. The word "espionage" has long been a word that has been repugnant to the American people and it is believed that the structure which is already in existence is much broader than espionage or counterespionage, but covers in a true sense real intelligence values to the three services interested, namely, the Navy, the Army, and Justice. Consequently, it would seem undesirable to seek any special legislation which would draw attention to the fact that it was proposed to develop a special counter-espionage drive of any great magnitude.[10]

What the Director was proposing was the expansion of an unauthorized domestic intelligence program "already in existence" through a continuing deception of Congress by means of a State Department counterintelligence cover.

In reporting on his accomplishments during the previous two-year period, the Director informed the President that he had organized a General Intelligence Section to investigate "activities of either a subversive or so-called intelligence type." Striving to improve its input, the Section had developed through field offices "contacts with various persons in professional, business and law enforcement fields," as well as liaison arrangements with the MID and the ONI. The Director was off and running: a $300,000 appropriation would permit expanded intelligence coverage and "specialized training in intelligence work." The President approved the program for what he called "counter-espionage activities," cut the requested Bureau intelligence appropriation in half, and adopted Hoover's suggestion for a continuing use of the State Department to circumvent congressional obstacles.[11]

The Counterfeit Magna Carta

The 1938 program for exclusive control of domestic intelligence by an FBI-MID-ONI troika was hampered from the beginning. Other federal agencies, especially the Secret Service, reached for pieces of the intelligence action. Even worse, the State Department—whose invented needs were the foundation for the entire federal domestic intelligence structure—rebelled. The tail of operations was wagging the dog of jurisdiction, a not uncommon phenomenon in the evolution of intelligence structures. Under pressure from Hoover to end this muddle, the new Attorney General, Frank Murphy, wrote to the President in

June 1939 that investigation "of all espionage, counterespionage and sabotage matters" must be concentrated in the FBI and the two armed services units. As in the past, the Bureau's primacy over other domestic intelligence units was stressed by reason of its investigative capability, and even more important, its file holdings (identification data relating to "more than ten million persons, including a very large number of individuals of foreign extraction").[12]

On June 26, 1939, the President, in a confidential directive drafted by the Department of Justice and addressed to all federal agency heads, vested the FBI, MID, and ONI with sole responsibility for "the investigation of all espionage, counterespionage, and sabotage matters." The instruction continues:

> No investigations should be conducted by any investigative agency of the Government into matters involving actually or potentially any espionage, counterespionage, or sabotage, except by the three agencies mentioned above.
>
> I shall be glad if you will instruct the heads of all other investigative agencies than the three named, to refer immediately to the nearest office of the Federal Bureau of Investigations any data, information, or material that may come to their notice bearing directly or indirectly on espionage, counterespionage, or sabotage.

While the use of the terms "potentially" and "directly or indirectly" reflected an expansive view of the troika's intelligence assignment, it cannot be construed, as it subsequently was by the Bureau, as "an unquestionable delegation of investigative authority" over wholesale domestic radical watching. It merely reflected the Director's insistence that competitors be barred from the turf to which he had been already been (illegally) assigned. And, most important, there was no reference to "subversion" or "subversive activities" either in the Hoover memorandum urging Murphy to act, Murphy's recommendation, or the June presidential directive.

The June directive was secret, as were all the intelligence authorizations of the five-year period 1934–39. (The only Bureau investigations in the counter-subversive area that were matters of record were the investigations of alleged violations of the Foreign Agents Registration Act of 1938.) But the outbreak of war in September forced federal intelligence out of the closet. It also invited the expansion of urban police units. Bureaucracies, it has been frequently observed, are inherently expansive and tend to collide with one another. Such conflicts dominate intelligence in a special way. Personal ambition, funding needs, institutional loyalties, claims of superior resources and skills, along with a vast scorn for rival claims, contribute to the creation of jealous intelligence fiefdoms frequently as much in conflict with one another as with their targets. In many nations, World War I set the stage for such a rivalry between domestic civilian and military intelligence, and World War II between domestic and foreign. In the United States, in addition, the urban units were formidable entries in the intelligence sweepstakes. This drive to monopolize the intelligence field strongly influenced the growth of the Bureau and the conduct of its chief. On September 6, Attorney General Murphy, again in response to Hoover's urgings, wrote a letter to the President stressing his concern that "matters relating to espionage and sabotage be handled in an effective, comprehensive and unified manner. To this end it is extremely desirable informally to correlate any information regarding these subjects that might be received or secured by state and local law enforcement agencies." On the same day the President signed a document, headed "Formal Statement," a proposed draft of which had been enclosed in Murphy's letter:

> The Attorney General has been requested by me to instruct the Federal Bureau of Investigation of the Department of Justice to take charge of investigative work in matters relating to espionage, sabotage, and violations of the neutrality regulations.
>
> This task must be conducted in a comprehensive and effective manner on a national basis, and all information must be carefully sifted out and correlated in order to avoid confusion and irresponsibility.
>
> To this end I request all police officers, sheriffs, and other law enforcement officers in the United States promptly to turn over to the nearest representative of the Federal Bureau of Investigation any information obtained by them relating to espionage, counterespionage, sabotage, subversive activities and violations of the neutrality laws.[13]

Although issued in the form of a press release or public notice, this document has been repeatedly referred to as a "presidential directive" and the Magna Carta of the Bureau's intelligence mission. According to Don Whitehead's semi-official *The FBI Story,* this directive made the FBI "not only a crime-fighting organization, but also an intelligence agency. . . . In contrast to intelligence work in the past, which had been limited to specific, short-term assignments, President Roosevelt made the FBI's responsibility a continuing one, involving a broad new front." In reality, this alleged intelligence birth certificate simply reaffirmed the fact that war-related investigative matters were entrusted to the FBI. The only reason for the communication was to ensure an unimpeded flow of information to the Bureau from local law enforcement authorities already in the field. In this respect, it paralleled the June directive, which performed the same function in a more formal way on the federal level.

The September 6 document assumed a fundamental importance in the legitimation of intelligence because of its reference to subversive activities. But this language, contained in a paragraph requesting cooperation by local authorities, could hardly expand the authority conferred on the Bureau in the initial paragraph to investigate war-connected matters. On the face of it, the first paragraph defines the investigative responsibility of the Bureau, while the "subversive activities" portion deals with the collection of materials developed by others. In effect, the Bureau claimed that its investigative authority was defined by the kind of information local police officials were requested (in the third paragraph) to transmit, and not by the language of the first paragraph explicitly referring to the Bureau. Besides, if a reading of the document leaves doubts about its meaning, the formal order of June 26, which it implements, establishes the intended scope and limitations of the Bureau's authority.

The only other relevant official document is an executive order made on September 8, 1939, authorizing the Attorney General to increase the personnel of the FBI by 150 agents. The order justifies a need for the added manpower by referring first to an emergency proclamation issued on the same day, which stresses the necessity for safeguarding neutrality and strengthening the national defense. A second "whereas" refers to the FBI's "additional and important duties in connection with such national emergency."

The subsequent distortion of the September 6 document is especially ironic in view of the explanation by Attorney General Murphy of its meaning and intended purpose. On the day the President's statement was released, Murphy announced to the press: "Foreign agents and those engaged in espionage will no longer find this country a happy hunting ground for their activities. . . . At the same time . . . it must not turn into a witch hunt. We must do no wrong to any man." And in a subsequent address to the National Police Academy, Murphy reemphasized that the country was prepared to run down spies, "But we will not act on the basis of hysteria. We are just as anxious to protect the rights of our own citizens as to see to it that those who attack the United States do not go unwhipped of justice. Twenty years ago inhuman and cruel things were done in the name of justice; sometimes vigilantes and others took over the work. We do not want such things done today for the work has now been localized in the FBI." Director Hoover followed with a speech in which he warned against hysteria and witch hunts. But he did not neglect the "termites" undermining the nation's foundations: "It is known that many foreign agents roam at will in a nation which loves peace and hates war. At this moment lecherous enemies of the American society are seeking to pollute our atmosphere of freedom and liberty . . . there are even native-born American citizens as well as aliens who have sold their birthrights for the proverbial 'mess of pottage.' "[14]

On November 30, 1939, Hoover appeared before the House Appropriations Committee to justify a supplemental emergency appropriation of about $1.5 million to fund "intelligence work which has been initiated during this year." Besides the expenditures for new personnel, the supplemental estimate also included an additional $100,000 for the "confidential fund," a reference to the fund used for the payment of informers. The extraordinary character of this commitment can be gleaned from the fact that only $20,000 in all had been previously appropriated for this purpose for the entire fiscal year 1940.

A second, newly inaugurated program also required funding. "In September of 1939 we found it necessary," Hoover explained, "to organize a General Intelligence Division in Washington. . . . This division now has compiled extensive indices of individuals, groups and organizations engaged in these subversive activities, in espionage activities, or any activities that are possibly detrimental to the internal security of the United States." As in the 1920s, the system was tailored to the mobility of the subjects: "The indexes have been arranged not only alphabetically but also geographically, so that any time should we enter into conflict, we would be able to go into any of these communities and identify individuals or groups who might be a source of grave danger to the security of this country. Their backgrounds and activities are known to the Bureau."

In a special spy pitch, Hoover testified that, in contrast to fiscal 1938, when a total of only 250 complaints were received involving violations of national defense statutes, during the fiscal year ending June 30, 1939, 1651 such complaints were received; and since that time, Hoover reported, an average of 214 such complaints was being received daily, with the result that for the entire fiscal year the total number could be expected to soar to "about 78,000." This, he said, was a conservative estimate; the outbreak of war would drive sky-high the number of spy reports that would have to be investigated.

These figures raised some eyebrows among congressmen. "About what percentage were you able to dispose of as preposterous on their face? . . . What percentage of the complaints have not any substance?" one congressman asked. Hoover insisted that none of the 214 daily complaints was preposterous on its face. And, he solemnly added, "only a small percentage turned out after investigation to lack substance." Only the vigilance of the General Intelligence Division (GID) could save the country from these swarms of spies. But there was no cause for congressional concern. After all, the entire intelligence operation was to be of limited, emergency duration. "Will these additional people be kept on through the next fiscal year if the emergency continues?" asked Congressman Clifton A. Woodrum. "If the emergency continues," Mr. Hoover responded. "But," Congressman Woodrum persisted, "if the emergency does not continue, you anticipate that the force will be reduced?" Hoover agreed, while at the same time pointing out that he had established "ten new field offices to conduct this work in various parts of the country." This apparent commitment to permanence led Congressman Woodrum to ask for the third time, "And if the emergency ceases, the need for the additional force will cease?" "Yes," Mr. Hoover again replied. World War II would come and go, but not the "emergency."[15]

The Director had invited trouble because his budgetary request was tied to the President's September 8 "Emergency" proclamation. When, in early January 1940, he reappeared for a deficiency appropriation, he shifted to the September 6 statement, which he falsely, but without challenge, described as "directing that there be coordinated under the Federal Bureau of Investigation all the matters of investigative work relating to espionage, sabotage and violations of the neutrality regulations, and any other subversive activities." In support of a Bureau budget request that included an additional $100,000 for the confidential fund, he testified that he was staggering under a backlog of 311 treason cases and 1307 espionage cases. But that was nothing; he again reminded the committee members that he anticipated a probable total of 78,000 espionage cases for fiscal 1939 as he had indicated in November. To make the situation even more frightening, 41 percent of the pending national defense matters were unassigned because of lack of manpower. But the GID was standing guard. It included a supervisory staff of nine, a code section as well as a translation section "to keep in touch with any foreign-language communications, documents, or papers obtained by us in the course of our investigations." A program of "special investigations of persons reported upon as being active in any subversive activity in movements detrimental to the internal security" could readily be enlarged to pinpoint targets who "may need further investigation by Federal authorities."[16] The subsequent June 1940 Appropriations Committee Hearings left little doubt about the drift of the Director's intelligence efforts. The "general intelligence index," he told the panel, "includes the names of persons who may become potential enemies to our security."[17]

The Quest for Libertarian Modes of Repression

The August 1939 signing of the German-Soviet Pact and the subsequent invasion of Finland by the Soviet Union left domestic communism naked to its enemies. In a shift reminiscent of the twenties, the images of savagery and ruthlessness associated with the Nazis were absorbed into the Menace. As anti-communism mounted, it became an increasingly powerful weapon against administration policies. In the spring of 1939, hearings began on legislative bills that ultimately became the Alien Registration Act of 1940. The debate writhed with a virulent xenophobia: no less than thirty-nine anti-alien bills were pending in Congress, many of them directed at West Coast labor leader Harry Bridges. Some measure of the intensity of the anti-alien feeling is provided by these remarks of Representative Thomas F. Ford during the debate: "There is no use arguing against this bill. It will pass. I am satisfied in my own mind that the mood of this House is such that if you brought in the Ten Commandments today and asked for their repeal and attached that request to an alien law, you could get it."[18]

When the legislation was finally passed in June 1940, it included an entirely unrelated seditious advocacy measure—punishing, inter alia, the teaching or advocacy of the "duty, necessity, desirability or propriety" of overthrowing the government by force or violence. Hoover now had both statutory and intelligence assignments. Characterized by Professor Zechariah Chafee, Jr., the nation's foremost authority on the law of free speech, as "the most drastic restriction on freedom of speech ever enacted in the United States during peace,"[19] the statute was passed without serious administration opposition. The Department of Justice did not testify at all, while the armed services were permitted to urge its passage. Only Secretary of Labor Frances Perkins was heard in opposition to the alien registration requirements. President Roosevelt refused to veto the bill, insisting that its advocacy provisions could "hardly be considered to constitute an improper encroachment on civil liberties in the light of present world conditions."

This concern for "present world conditions" coincided with a fear of a damaging political clash with a powerful bipartisan anti-Communist congressional bloc. Some way had to be found to divert this red-baiting thrust, so threatening to administration programs, without alienating liberals. This search for a moderate alternative, a "right way" to counter "the wrong way to fight Communism" (in the phrase of the time), inevitably stressed the role of intelligence. The sense that countersubversive intelligence offered something to everybody is reflected in Murphy's praise of the initial grant of intelligence powers to the Bureau as a salutary alternative to vigilantism and private initiatives. It was not only that intelligence was cast in a benign role: the hope was that the Director, with his already substantial following, could become Exhibit A in the administration's "right way" strategy, the professional expertly accommodating the nation's defense needs to the claims of the First Amendment. But, from the start, Hoover refused to follow the script; his instincts bound him tightly to the forces he was expected to defuse. The risks were minimal. The administration could not afford to tangle with the Director. If he would not serve as a shield against domestic red hunters, he was indispensable as a protection against fifth columnists, potential collaborators, and foreign invaders. Such a rationale would not have seemed strange by early June 1940, when France had fallen, Paris was occupied, and Dunkirk evacuated.

The administration's vulnerability and caution are both reflected in its struggles with the Special Committee to Investigate Un-American Activities and Propaganda in the United States (the "Dies Committee"). Organized in 1938, the committee soon was locked in conflict with the administration over its intervention in the election campaign of Michigan Governor Frank Murphy. In 1939 the rift widened as the committee denounced the American League Against War and Fascism and the American Youth Congress as subversive sanctuaries for government employees, a poorly concealed assault on the administration and, in the latter case, Mrs. Roosevelt. In the same year, the committee renewed its attack on Murphy (then Attorney General) for his failure to prosecute alleged subversive groups. The President characterized its procedures as "squalid," but refused to engage it in a head-on conflict.

In March 1939 Murphy, in his reply to Congressman Martin Dies's request for a Bureau report on the Bund, turned over the document but insisted that investigations in such matters should be handled exclusively by the Bureau. In a committee hearing in June 1939 California Representative Jerry Voorhis, an administration congressional spokesman, asked a witness:

> General, don't you feel, as a matter of fact, that the Department of Justice and the Federal Bureau of Investigation is [sic] the proper agency to get information of this kind; weren't they the people that we have set up in our government to do that?

Republican committee member J. Parnell Thomas interjected:

> Right on that point, I have a letter signed by Mr. Hoover, which I received within the past three months, to the effect that the Department of Justice has not made any investigation of Communism . . . since 1924. . . .[20]

This representation was of course false—and a clue to Hoover's rejection of his assigned role of foil for the Dies Committee.

While intelligence offered a "responsible" alternative to wild and unsubstantiated congressional charges, it gained support for more positive reasons. To many liberals, the notion of dealing with Communists by measures short of outright repression held a strong appeal. It would be wrong to jail them, but to identify and watch them seemed unobjectionable. The notion of identification and surveillance, originally conceived as a defense against foreign-inspired subversion, acquired domestic political significance because the Communists had committed themselves to a united front policy of subordinating revolutionary objectives to a joint struggle with democratic, non-Communist forces against Fascism. This tactic made it easy to denounce liberal reforms as collectivist and their sponsors as concealed agents of Stalin or dupes. Identification and registration would stop such demagoguery and, liberals thought, strengthen the democratic process. The marketplace of public discourse would be improved and cleansed, so the argument ran, if its offerings were properly labeled. If securities had to be registered and labeled under the Securities and Exchange Act, why not an "SEC of ideas"? The 1938 Foreign Agents Registration Act to prevent the deception of innocents by the propaganda of foreign-sponsored agitators, and the alien registration requirements of the 1940 statute, were followed by the Voorhis Act. Sponsored by the same congressman who, as the colloquy already quoted shows, urged Bureau surveillance as the enlightened alternative to committee harassment, it required registration under criminal penalties of subversive organizations with foreign ties.

But statutory sanctions could reach only aliens or those linked in an agency relationship with foreign principals; and even here, the evasion risks were enormous. What about supporters or latent sympathizers? The commitment to self-registration was inevitably stretched to approval of surveillance by others to determine concealed allegiance. Although such concealment was typically a defensive response to hostility and repression, it was viewed as a sinister tactic requiring continuing adversarial surveillance, which, in turn, fostered even more widespread concealment. More than any one single circumstance, the acceptance of political identification by a substantial consensus as a necessary governmental function eliminated challenge to the Bureau's emergence as a political police force. Even those in positions of power who had reservations did not dare oppose this development—if for no other reason than to demonstrate that they were not "soft" and could be as realistic as their adversaries.

The rapidity of the retreat from libertarianism is mirrored in the observations of Attorney General Robert H. Jackson. In March 1940 Jackson wrote to Senator George Norris of Nebraska in answer to a complaint concerning the alleged abuses of Bureau agents. The growth of war hysteria required, he said, a professional, nonpolitical investigative unit, to prevent private vigilantism as well as to reduce the danger that "the legitimate protection of the Government might be perverted toward such activities as the suppression of free speech and press. . . ." He had conferred with the Director and, as a result:

> Mr. Hoover is in agreement with me that the principles which Attorney General Stone laid down in 1924 when the Federal Bureau of Investigation was reorganized and Mr. Hoover appointed as Director are sound, and that the usefulness of the Bureau depends upon a faithful adherence to those limitations.
>
> The Federal Bureau of Investigation will confine its activities to the investigation of violation of Federal statutes, the collecting of evidence in cases in which the United States is or may be a party in interest, and the service of process issued by the courts. . . .
>
> As one long interested in civil liberties, I can readily understand your concern in this matter, and if my confidence that the work of the Department can be handled without infringements upon civil liberties proves unfounded, I hope that I shall be the first to admit it, so that remedies can be applied by the Congress.

A month after this exchange, on April 1, 1940, Jackson, in an address to federal prosecutors, warned against prosecution of offenses based on "subversive activities" and, in a passage already quoted, stressed the dangerous vagueness of this phrase. Cases involving "subversive activities" must be handled courageously and dispassionately to protect civil liberty, "because the prosecutor has no definite standards to determine what constitutes a subversive activity such as we have for murder or larceny." But by August 1940, in the wake of the devastating triumph of German arms, Jackson had changed his tune. He told a law enforcement conference on national defense problems that the Bureau's intelligence responsibilities required "steady surveillance over individuals and groups within the United States who are so sympathetic with the system or designs of foreign dictators as to make them a likely source of federal law violations." The concern for threats to civil liberties posed by overzealous prosecutions of subversive activities vanishes when the same standards are used for the selection of targets for "steady surveillance." Jackson, who had a strong distaste for the nitty-gritty of radical hunting, left it to the Director to determine the relationship between a subject's sympathies and future law violation. And Hoover's contribution to the same conference left no doubt that "subversive activities" were in the intelligence saddle. Supporters of foreign isms, he told the conference, had "succeeded in boring into every phase of American life masquerading behind front organizations."[21]

Although Jackson had condemned "subversive activities" as a criminal investigative standard, he had no difficulty with Hoover's adoption of it in intelligence practice. Minds less fastidious than Jackson's, especially lawyers disciplined in precise expression, shunned the term because of its vagueness. It was especially repellent to liberals, familiar with it as an epithet prominent in the right-wing rhetoric of the time. Until the late thirties it is rarely encountered in the formal documents dealing with intelligence.* But the formulations that were used ("espionage," "sabotage," "counterespionage") were virtually automatically translated into "subversive activities." The record is barren of official complaint that the Director had gone too far. One can only conclude that liberals chose to ignore the gap between word and deed, clinging instead to verbiage that insulated them from the reality of countersubversion.

Although the language of the September 6 statement precluded it, the Bureau was permitted to monitor and harass individuals solely because of their opinions, expressions, and associations, even though they were fully protected by the First Amendment and light-years removed from espionage, sabotage, and law violations of any kind. Thus, at the very outset, we are confronted with the "particular fault"—officially condoned usurpation and abuse of power—from which the entire intelligence system takes corruption. Administration supporters fully endorsed Attorney General Stone's warning of May 1924 that "a secret police system may become a menace to free government and free institutions because it carries with it the possibility of abuses of power which are not always quickly apprehended or understood." But they failed to perceive or understand those abuses as they unfolded before their eyes—which they preferred to keep closed.

---

*The term "subversive activity" was used by President Roosevelt in a directive of May 21, 1940, to Jackson authorizing wiretapping under limited circumstances (see below, Chapter 7). In a press conference at the time of announcing the September 8 executive order, the President characterized hostile activities on behalf of a foreign country as "subversive"—Church, Book III, p. 405.

Doctoring the Record

The published regulations of the Attorney General's office assign the Bureau the duty, under the supervision and direction of the Attorney General, to:

Carry out the Presidential directive of September 6, 1939, as reaffirmed by Presidential directives of January 8, 1943, July 24, 1950 and December 15, 1953, designating the Federal Bureau of Investigation to take charge of investigative work in matters relating to espionage, sabotage, subversive activities and related matters.[22]

The three post-1939 directives referred to suggest that the entire corpus of presidential orders supports the expanded ("subversive activities") authority claimed by the Bureau. Surely the Attorney General would not have said so without sound reason. Or would he?

On January 8, 1943, the President issued a statement revealingly captioned "Police Cooperation," reaffirming the September 6 release with an explanatory gloss:

I am again calling the attention of all enforcement officers to the request that they report all such information [relating to espionage, sabotage and violations of the neutrality regulations] promptly to the nearest field representative of the Federal Bureau of Investigation, which is charged with the responsibility of correlating this material and referring matters which are under the jurisdiction of any other Federal agency with responsibilities in this field to the appropriate agency.

I suggest that all patriotic organizations and individuals likewise report all such information *relating to espionage and related matters* to the Federal Bureau of Investigation in the same manner.

I am confident that all law enforcement officers, who are now rendering such an invaluable assistance towards the success of the internal safety of our country will cooperate in this matter. [Italics in original][23]

This addition discourages an expanded interpretation of the original document beyond a war-connected context. It again refers to "espionage, sabotage and violations of the neutrality regulations" and, in the President's copy, the key phrase, "relating to espionage and related matters," is written in what is apparently the President's hand and underlined by a pen stroke. Nor is this all. The final paragraph refers not to a threatened "internal security" (the ritualistically invoked danger justifying a curb on "subversive activities") but to the more specific "internal safety of our country," a logical predicate for "sabotage, espionage and related matters."

On July 24, 1950, a month after the outbreak of the Korean War, President Truman approved a directive drafted by Attorney General J. Howard McGrath purporting to renew the earlier grants of authority to the Bureau. It describes the September 6, 1939, and January 8, 1943, documents as "Presidential directives," which authorized the FBI to "take charge of investigative work in matters relating to espionage, sabotage, subversive activities and related matters."

The background of this bit of document fakery is illuminating. In 1948

Attorney General Tom Clark had drafted a similarly worded proposed directive misstating the contents of the earlier documents. The Bureau urged the President to sign quickly, "to spike vigilante activity in the internal security field by private organizations and persons"—yet another attempt to legitimize the Bureau's domestic intelligence authority on libertarian grounds. But wary advisers warned the President off.*[24] The outbreak of the Korean War two years later created a fresh opportunity to legitimize the Bureau's subversive activities intelligence authority. A committee of the National Security Agency, headed by Director Hoover, recommended that "a Presidential Statement be issued to bring up to date and clarify prior Presidential Directives . . . outlining the responsibilities of the Federal Bureau of Investigation in connection with espionage, sabotage, subversive activities and related matters." The President's men once again smelled a rat, but this time were powerless to overcome the force of a National Security Council recommendation.[25]

Why, it may be asked, was President Truman not simply requested to issue a directive on his own giving Hoover what he had long craved, instead of an order faking the contents of the earlier document? The answer is that a fresh "subversive activities" authorization would have quickly called attention to the fact that the Director had misused the September 6 statement, while renewing what had been previously granted by President Roosevelt would provide a favorable cachet. How could President Truman be attacked on libertarian grounds for reaffirming what had been done by his illustrious predecessor? This bid for approval of the enlightened was, it should be added, an extension of a Bureau strategy reflected in the earlier "spike vigilante activity" appeal. The same lip service to libertarianism is projected in a statement by Hoover issued at the time of the signing of the Truman directive denouncing "hysteria, witch-hunting and vigilantes," and assuring his countrymen of his concern for "protecting the innocent as well as . . . identifying the enemies within our midst." (This identification problem, he went on to explain, was brutal: the deceitful Communists, "enemies of the American way of life," utilized "cleverly camouflaged . . . peace groups and civil rights organizations to achieve their sinister purposes.")[26]

The Bureau's expectations that the Truman document would cure its jurisdictional infirmities—not only for the future but retroactively—is hard to understand. McGrath's draft purported to give the Bureau the same investigative authority it had previously been granted, and no more. He could hardly enlarge the scope of the earlier document, by falsifying its contents. But the text of the Truman document gave the Bureau something more solid to work with than the embarrassing Roosevelt statement. In 1953 the Bureau invited the Eisenhower administration to legitimate its jurisdictional claims in a memorandum to which it attached the Truman directive but not the original Roosevelt statement. This new lobbying effort pointed out that the Bureau's "internal security responsibility" was broader than its statutory authority. In December of that year, President Eisenhower referred inaccurately to the three earlier directives as back-

---

*Clark was more successful in persuading President Truman to "reaffirm" and broaden earlier wiretap authorizations by similar misrepresentations of their scope.

ground for an informal statement requesting cooperation by law enforcement personnel as well as "patriotic organizations and individuals" in reporting violations of the Atomic Energy Act to the FBI.[27]

Thus the Bureau twisted history's arm to force a permanent grant of authority to engage in subversive activities intelligence—in the face of the fact that both the claimed delegation and its scope are unsupported by the documents on which it relied.[28] Moreover, as the table in Appendix III shows, the Bureau had no difficulty persuading the nation's highest law enforcement officers, its Attorneys General, to adopt its distorted interpretation. In turn, this systematic misrepresentation of what had been a narrow, transient assignment became, with the active collaboration of the Attorneys General, the source of the Bureau's institutional transformation into (to use the language of a Bureau report) "the civilian intelligence agency having primary responsibility for protecting the Nation's internal security."

But what of the role of Congress—clearly deceived by the executive directive fiction? After all, it was Congress that had confined the Bureau to the "detection and prosecution of crimes." If the Bureau's responsibilities were to be expanded, surely that was a job for the legislature. Again, the 1919–24 precedent comes into play: there was no need to run the legislative gamut. All that was required was to win over the appropriations subcommittee, manned by the Director's ardent supporters committed to a flourishing internal security intelligence capability shielded from the intrusions of congressional outsiders. Attorney General Jackson, it will be recalled, in the first flush of his short-lived libertarianism, thought that Congress should rein in the Bureau if the necessity arose. But the Attorneys General for the most part embraced the Director's co-optation of the appropriations subcommittee. And why not?—the panel's enthusiasm for the Bureau's internal security role helped the fiscal aspirations of the entire Department.

Hoover's repeated efforts to "clarify" retroactively the Roosevelt precedent indicates that he knew very well that his house rested on a shaky foundation. How could he not have known? His Palmer-Daugherty apprenticeship was one long jurisdictional crisis in which he himself had twice acknowledged usurpations of authority. The Stone warning to the Director to stick to his law enforcement last and the bypassing of Congress in the 1936 Roosevelt-State Department maneuver reflected his awareness of the problem of authority. The record indicates more affirmatively that he knew the 1939 precedent was questionable even in the relatively uncontroversial area of foreign intelligence. In 1953 Hoover gave highly important testimony before a Senate committee in support of charges by Republican Attorney General Herbert Brownell that former President Truman had knowingly harbored and indeed promoted Harry Dexter White, charged with being a member of a Communist spy ring. The situation was not only politically touchy but personally embarrassing for Hoover. If White's espionage role became known in 1945, as Brownell charged, why had the Director not acted or at least developed corroborating evidence? The explanation is illuminating. It was difficult to develop the full facts, Hoover explained, because the acts charged to White took place during peacetime. "The responsibilities for internal security assigned the FBI in 1939 by Presidential directive were directed towards the times of emergency rather than periods of peace. That is the situation today." It would seem that the Director took an expansive view of the 1939 statement—except when it was personally embarrassing.[29]

The Bureau's stake in the forged Roosevelt precedent was enormous, not only because it legitimized current intelligence investigative authority but because of its scope—"subversive activities," a hunting license for all seasons. For example, in its Annual Report for 1965, the Bureau stated that it "seeks to identify individuals working against the United States, determine their objectives and nullify their effectiveness." Who were these people? What was there about their activities that justified their surveillance? All we are told is that they are "the Nation's domestic enemies." The executive rationale did more than liberate the Bureau from the confines of law enforcement. It was read not merely as a grant of power, an authorization to conduct investigations should the need arise, but as a "responsibility," an affirmative duty. And who was to be charged with this duty? The President, in discharge of the awesome undertaking solemnized in his oath of office to "preserve and defend the Constitution of the United States," had appealed directly to the Bureau, not to the Attorney General, for help. This mission, with its resonance of defense against a foreign threat, transcended hierarchical niceties as well as congressional accountability. It can hardly be doubted that this executive format laid the basis for the Director's close ties to the White House, the development of the Bureau's autonomy, and its transformation into an instrument of presidential royalism. The Nixon years brought the ironic payoff: if the Director was a servant of the White House, he could be summoned directly without the involvement of the Attorney General, as in the case of the Huston Plan (described in Chapter 7). His successor, L. Patrick Gray III, could be directed to limit and obstruct the Watergate investigation, dramatizing a clear conflict of interest between the Bureau's criminal investigative work and its domestic security assignment, the former requiring independence and the latter subject to White House direction and control.*

The Rejected Magna Carta—Back to the Statute Books

Although the Ervin Committee did not undertake an investigation of the Bureau's intelligence jurisdiction, its hearings—begun in 1971—touched sensitive Bureau nerves, especially when the North Carolina senator proposed to introduce a bill barring a noncriminal Bureau investigation of any individual without his consent. The death of Hoover in May 1972 released pent-up demands for an inquiry into FBI intelligence activities and at the same time created the opportunity for one: the 1968 Omnibus Crime Bill specifically pro-

*In July 1970, Charles Brennan, then head of the Bureau's Intelligence Division, testified before the Scranton Commission on Campus Unrest that the Sept. 6, 1939, Roosevelt directive had conferred on the FBI authority to investigate "subversive activities," and that it was "within the framework of this executive order that basically the FBI over the years has tried to fulfill these responsibilities."

vided that future nominees to the post of FBI Director had to be approved by the Senate.

After serving as Acting Director from May 1972, to February 1973, L. Patrick Gray III was nominated to the post by President Nixon. The appointment drew a damp response: Gray had no law enforcement experience and had obviously been chosen as a reward for his enthusiastic political support of the President. In fact, during his stint as Acting Director, he had exploited the Bureau's prestige by making a number of political speeches at the request of the White House. The Senate Judiciary Committee used the confirmation hearing to explore the FBI's intelligence jurisdiction. It was hardly necessary to force any doors open to get into this subject. At the beginning of the hearing Gray told the panel that in his very first weekend in office, in May 1972, he had assigned a series of key problems for intensive research and reports by senior officials of the Bureau, including, under the heading "Subversion," a position paper setting forth a "detailed analysis and justification for our current policy with regard to the investigation of individuals where there has been no specific violation of Federal law. Is additional legislation needed in this area?"[30] But his doubts on the subject did not prevent him from assuring a crime control conference shortly thereafter that the FBI, "under Executive Directives" and laws of Congress, "will continue to investigate acts by individuals and organizations that threaten the security of the nation and the rights and freedoms of American citizens. This is an area which I expect to draw the heaviest salvos of protest and complaint because those who would alter drastically our form of government must . . . and will . . . remain vehemently opposed to the work of the FBI on behalf of all of the American people." Still, these subversive critics might have a point. In a speech in October 1972,[31] he reminded a Chicago audience that the question of jurisdiction was basic: "Are we commanded by Federal law or Executive Order to act? If not, we will not act . . . we will not move . . . and we will not investigate!"

In response to a request at the confirmation hearings for the source of internal security intelligence, Gray submitted a document citing some twenty-two laws alleged to authorize "intelligence type national security investigations" —but not the September 6 document and its progeny.[32]

Yet for more than thirty years the Bureau had insisted that it wore two separate and quite different hats: a general investigative hat for probing violations of law and, far more important, an internal security intelligence hat. This vital internal security responsibility was not measurable, the Attorneys General repeatedly insisted, by such workaday law enforcement yardsticks as arrests and convictions.* Now (in 1973) the Senate committee was told that the primary source for the Bureau's internal security function was the authority conferred on a piecemeal basis to obtain evidence of violation of particular laws, passed by Congress over the years, and involving speech or conduct touching on internal security.

When Gray testified in March 1973, the Bureau had already drafted a

---

*See, for example, Attorney General's Annual Report (1953), p. 24: " . . . [S]ince this work of domestic intelligence is primarily preventive in nature, its successes cannot be measured in terms of arrests and convictions."

proposed set of revised guidelines for incorporation in its *Manual of Instructions,* with a far narrower statutory base than that reflected in his testimony. These guidelines, ultimately adopted in June and made public as the result of the pressure of Senator Edward M. Kennedy, stated that "subversive activities" investigations were to be confined to "specific statutory jurisdiction and Departmental Instructions."[33] The *Manual* states that "investigations conducted under this section [Section 87, Subversive Organizations and Individuals] are to be directed to the gathering of material pertinent to a determination whether or not the subject has violated, or is engaged in activities which may result in a violation of, the statutes enumerated below; or in fulfillment of Departmental Instructions."* The statutes enumerated are limited to three—dealing with Rebellion and Insurrection (18 U.S.C., Section 2383), Seditious Conspiracy (Section 2384), and Seditious Advocacy (the Smith Act, Section 2385). Conduct linked to violations of these statutes is alone to be considered "subversive" or "subversive activities." In addition, a supplementary investigative authority is derived from policing the registration requirements of the Internal Security Act of 1950 (U.S.C., Sections 781–810).

This change in 1973 from an executive to a legislative justification had no discernible impact on the Bureau's actual investigative practices, which remained as sweeping as before. The revised guidelines simply replaced one deception with another. No student of the record would seriously believe that the post-1973 Intelligence Division confined itself to collecting evidence of possible violations of dormant Civil War statutes dealing with physical force rebellion and insurrection, along with the unenforceable Smith and Internal Security acts. The claim was even more strained than the one made in the earlier 1919–24 period—that intelligence collection was justified on the basis of still anticipated legislation.

In testimony presented to the House Internal Security Committee (HISC) in the spring of 1974, Assistant Bureau Director in charge of the Intelligence Division W. Raymond Wannall stated that the Roosevelt document was not "a grant of new or additional authority" but merely ordered the Bureau to "sift out and correlate security investigative matters" for the purpose of assigning them to other executive agencies with jurisdiction, retaining only those matters for investigation clearly within its own already existing jurisdiction. The view that the September 6 statement—trumpeted for three decades as the wellspring of the Bureau's internal security authority—was merely a procedural instruction was echoed in the same hearing by the Department of Justice specialist in internal security investigations, Kevin Maroney, who testified that the presidential directives were only "requests for coordination by the FBI of domestic intelligence information. . . ."[34]

But the new champions of congressional authority admittedly did not propose to tailor the Bureau's investigative practices to a law enforcement model. The testimony of intelligence chief Wannall made it quite clear that if, in the Division's judgment, activities "could be in violation" or "lead toward" a viola-

*Section 122 of the *Manual,* dealing with "Extremist Matters and Civil Unrest," uses the same language in connection with investigations of "extremists."

tion of a security-related statute at some indefinite time in the future, an investigation would be justified. Nor, Wannall explained, did the revised guidelines reduce or limit the Bureau's historic identification mission; the Division would continue under the guidelines to monitor and identify "individuals who are actually supporting . . . subversive goals . . ." as well as "front organization[s]" and the "activist types" associated with them.[35]

What the Bureau contemplated was a continuation—on the pretext of law enforcement and evidence collection—of its traditional open-ended political investigations, without regard to the prosecutive realities. And what made all this particularly ironic was its purported deference to congressional authority. After all, it was Congress which in its appropriation statute had defined the law enforcement function as the "detection and prosecution of crime," well-established procedures that focus on the collection of evidence, not for use at some remote future time but in order to determine whether or not a crime has probably been committed warranting present prosecutive action. The law enforcement justification suffered a heavy blow when the General Accounting Office reported in 1976 that out of 797 domestic security case files sampled, only 24 cases resulted in prosecutive referrals, in which 10 were prosecuted and 8 convicted.[36]

The new line did not abandon the theory of inherent executive power to conduct intelligence activities, nor deny continuing vitality to the September 6 document to conduct intelligence activities; but it did soft-pedal its first paragraph, dealing restrictively with the scope of delegated investigative power, and stressed instead the third ("subversive activities") paragraph concerned with the processing of data collected by others. In the same way, the Bureau's *Manual of Instructions* states that the Bureau has a broad responsibility "to coordinate and collect all information relating to the internal security of the United States," which, however, "is not to be confused with our jurisdictional authority for conducting active investigations . . ." based exclusively on statutes. This strategy thus reduced the Bureau's reliance on inherent executive power and its formal implementation as a source of intelligence authority without abandoning it altogether. But the law enforcement rationale that replaced it is hardly credible: it postulated an investigative penumbra, surrounding each statute, so extensive as to permit a continuation of the free-floating intelligence operations of the past. The more things changed in theory, the more they remained the same in investigative practice—as reflected, for example, in the undiminished caseloads under the new guidelines.

Prevention—With So Much at Stake, Why Take Chances?

When Clarence M. Kelley, then the Director-designate of the FBI, made his appearance in June 1973 at the confirmation hearings before the Senate Judiciary Committee, Senate Majority Leader Robert C. Byrd observed that a "different atmosphere" had prevailed during Hoover's directorship, and that the time had come for Congress to deal with the question of the authority for the Bureau's domestic intelligence gathering. In his confirmation testimony, Kelley seemed receptive to a proposed fresh look at the problem of intelligence authority. Subsequently, he was called to confer with the newly appointed Attorney General, Elliot Richardson and his deputy, William Ruckelshaus, who had himself done a three-month stint as acting Bureau chief. Richardson and Ruckelshaus explored with Kelley sweeping changes in the Bureau's operations, especially in the field of intelligence. One of the agenda items was the possible need for an explicit statutory basis for the Bureau's intelligence function.[37]

Before further action could be taken, however, Richardson resigned and Ruckelshaus was fired in the "Saturday night massacre." In August, Kelley directed to the new Attorney General, Edward H. Levi, a memo embodying the Bureau's conclusion that "had there never been a single one of the Presidential directives in question," an "umbrella of legislative enactments" authorized "intelligence type investigations." Still, Kelley recognized that the umbrella was leaky; two of the statutes "were designed for the Civil War era and not the Twentieth Century." New anti-subversive legislation was required to serve as a more realistic basis for the Bureau's investigative authority, as well as a new executive order to authorize investigations "not normally associated with the enforcement of the statutes."[38]

Just two weeks after the departure of Richardson and Ruckelshaus, Kelley attacked the Bureau's internal security critics. In a speech on November 4, he presented the traditional version of the we-must-get-them-before-they-get-us formula, highlighted by the following:

> On occasions we hear complaints that the FBI has investigated people who have merely been involved in non-violent, peaceful demonstrations. . . . Experience, however, has taught that all too often violence-prone subversive groups attempt to exploit the activities of these legitimate organizations . . . the legitimate group is infiltrated, if not completely taken over by extremists. Adherents of the original and worthy group simply drop out. The extremists, those persons who do not respect the law and refuse to accept restraints, become dominant. Within the group a transition has occurred from a peaceful and lawful posture to one of potential or actual violence.[39]

In the same speech Kelley presented the approved, standard version of the Bureau's intelligence jurisdiction: legislative authority flowing from specific enactments and "Presidential Directives dating from 1939. . . ." The Bureau's Annual Report, released on December 14, 1973, stressed the Bureau's dual investigative functions: gathering evidence for prosecution and "intelligence type data."

After considerable waffling, Director Kelley (and Attorney General Levi) finally came to rest on preventive law enforcement as the basis for internal security jurisdiction. Intelligence investigations are, of course, a familiar tool of crime prevention. The government is not required to wait until a kidnapping or a bank robbery takes place; it may acquire information that would permit it to thwart the planned crime. But in the case of alleged subversive activities, the inference of threatened law violation from present conduct is typically remote and subjective. The stakes, it is argued, are too high to wait for the emergence of evidence. Here is Kelley's version:

> Unlike certain crimes against persons and property, the consequences of a violation concerned with the Nation's welfare are too grave to wait for the offense to occur before taking action. It is an inescapable fact that this Nation houses persons who seek to disrupt the orderly processes of the law, persons who would willingly use violence to achieve their goals, and still others who would foment anarchy. Indeed, there are those who would even subvert the country for profit or by misguided zeal. We are determined that they shall not succeed.

And who are these disrupters, fomenters of anarchy, subverters for profit, and misguided zealots? We are somewhat enlightened by a speech of November 29, 1973, which marks Kelley's complete abandonment of his earlier concessions to the need for a new look at intelligence. In it he warned:

> We must gather intelligence type information, for example about groups and individuals who may outwardly appear innocuous and law-abiding but who are liable to undertake serious acts of violence as part of an effort to interfere with or destroy our democratic form of Government.[40]

The prevention formula thus weaves together a number of strands of deception: first, that open-ended political surveillance is really the collection of evidence of potential criminal conduct; second, that the seeming innocence of the surveillance subjects masks a criminal purpose; third, that the government is too weak to permit the constitutionally protected activities of these subjects to go unmonitored; and fourth, that the evidence typically collected through surveillance could in any event ultimately support a successful prosecution. Whether labeled law enforcement or crime prevention, subversive activities remained the name of the game. Consider the December 1974 convention of the Young Socialist Alliance (YSA), which the Bureau proposed to infiltrate with informers instructed to identify the participants and to report what was said. When challenged in court by the YSA lawyers, the Bureau claimed that it was merely collecting evidence for law enforcement purposes. This was a reasonable precaution, the Bureau insisted, because the YSA's parent body, the Socialist Workers' Party (SWP), was a Marxist party and a member of the Fourth International. The Bureau and the Justice Department thought this circumstance overrode the fact that the thirteen prior YSA conventions had been peaceful and that a primary purpose of the convention was to launch the group's presidential candidate. When, in the course of litigation, the Department's continuing failure to produce evidence of the SWP's threat to the national security became embarrassing, surveillance was not ended, but instead transferred from the Internal Security to the General Investigation Division.

In 1975, Attorney General Levi ordered an end to this "preventive" law enforcement. Some time later, in March 1976, he established investigative guidelines for domestic internal security. The guidelines, subsequently retained by the Carter Administration, specified a three-tiered investigative system (preliminary, limited, and full); purport to limit the grounds for opening an investigation; and provide review mechanisms for such practices as informer infiltration, mail covers, and electronic surveillance.

But the resort to a law enforcement justification for intelligence-style surveillance continued even after establishment of the Levi guidelines. In January 1978, in a lawsuit involving the Institute for Policy Studies (IPS), the Bureau was asked in a pretrial proceeding to "state the factual and legal basis for the continuation of the investigation of plaintiff Institute for Policy Studies (IPS) from 1968 through 1974." The Bureau responded by insisting that the six-year IPS investigation was conducted to gather evidence of violation of statutes dealing with rebellion, insurrection, seditious conspiracy, advocacy of the overthrow of the government, nonregistration of persons trained in foreign espionage systems, passport and visa violations, espionage, and concealing of fugitives. But the trifling evidence which the Bureau cited, such as the fact (most heavily relied on) that the IPS was, according to an informer's report, visited by a Weather Underground fugitive, provided no credible support for the Bureau's six-year surveillance, which included the use of over fifty informers, trash covers, wiretaps, and similar tactics.

Equally curious is the Bureau's response to a request for the reason for the discontinuance of the surveillance on February 28, 1974. The investigation was ended, it was claimed, "after the FBI made a careful analysis of the facts developed in the investigation and concluded that there was insufficient evidence to support prosecution of the IPS leaders or members under existing Federal statutes." By a suspicious coincidence, the investigation was terminated two weeks after the IPS commenced its lawsuit. Like the straight law enforcement rationale, crime prevention—advance intervention to abort a criminal scheme —was discredited as an intelligence justification by the GAO report already cited, which concluded that in only 2 percent of the total sample did an investigation develop advance information of planned subversive or illegal activities. And the 1977 follow-up report confirmed the earlier findings that "only a few cases produced advance information of planned violent activities or information useful in solving related criminal investigations."[41] The uniformly negative results in both conventional law enforcement and crime prevention reflect an institutional commitment to large-scale investigative activity that outweighs compliance with guidelines. And, in any event, requirements for justifying a criminal investigative standard—such as "probable cause"—could always be met (as in the IPS case) by reliance on questionable informers' reports.*

The embrace of legislative authority has also raised the issue of the Bureau's power to engage in file compilation and storage. Authority to develop and store political files was the subject of the Privacy Act of 1974. The committee version barred all executive agencies, "unless expressly authorized by statute," from maintaining files about the political beliefs or activities of any individual. Con-

---

*Testifying in a 1976 trial of two Indians for the murder of two FBI agents, Kelley admitted that a nationwide alert about possible violence by Indians over the July 4 weekend—including the blowing up of buildings by militant armed native Americans, the shooting of policemen and tourists, and the assassination of the governor of South Dakota—was based on no evidence other than a (wholly false, as it turned out) report by an informer, characterized in the alert memorandum as a "source with insufficient contact made to determine reliability, but in a position to have information." Kelley justified the dissemination of the memorandum as a means of preventing violence.

gressman Richard Ichord, noting that there was no statute "which expressly and generally authorizes any particular agency to maintain the records of political . . . activities of subversive groups,"* proposed an amendment, adopted by the Congress, which exempts from the prohibition on political record-keeping data "pertinent to and within the scope of a duly authorized law enforcement activity." Thus not only intelligence investigations but the filing and storage of the intelligence product turns on the validity of the Bureau's law enforcement rationale.

Inherent Executive Authority—*Redivivus*

Although the post-Hoover Bureau and departmental spokesmen retreated from earlier reliance on presidential directives, especially in dealing with Congress, they clung to the view that intelligence is peculiarly and appropriately an executive function. And, indeed, this claim to an exclusive intelligence power, beyond the reach of congressional control, was a hallmark of the Nixon administration. Its reliance on inherent executive power as a source of intelligence authority first came under congressional scrutiny in the Ervin Committee hearings. In response to questioning by Senator Ervin, William H. Rehnquist, then Assistant Attorney General and legal adviser to the President and now a Justice of the Supreme Court, testified that the executive possessed an inherent power to engage in domestic intelligence on the authority of Article II, Section 3, of the Constitution requiring the President to "take care that the laws be faithfully executed . . ." and Article IV, Section 4, which guarantees to every state "a republican form of government. . . ." No judicial review of possible executive abuse was necessary: the President's "self-restraint" was sufficient to guarantee a benign use of this inherent power. Besides, Rehnquist went on, the targets of surveillance suffered no real injury; no constitutional right protects the citizen against political surveillance by the executive.[42] (This wide-open view is reflected most clearly in the Nixon administration's defense of warrantless electronic surveillance, discussed in Chapter 7.)

*Ichord correctly summarized the state of the law. The applicable legislation deals with "identification records" and authorizes exchange with other governmental units (federal and local) of "identification, criminal identification, crime and other records." The current legislation is mainly a codified version of a law passed in 1930. When the House Judiciary Committee in January 1930 reported the proposed legislation to Congress, it appended the phrase "other records" with this explanation: "There are two classes of information. One is criminal records, and another is the information that is gathered about criminals that is not a matter of record. These they do not give out, but the criminal records they do give out." In view of this explanation, Congressman LaGuardia proposed that the committee amendment be enlarged to read "and other criminal records"; the amendment was accepted by the committee and passed. Thus, this legislative history makes it plain that the filing authority was intended to be confined to law enforcement—no great surprise since the Bureau was not operating in the intelligence field in 1930. When the law was codified in 1966, the statutory housecleaning resulted in excision of the term "criminal," but the codifiers made it clear that no substantive change was intended. This view was endorsed in a 1971 federal court decision by Judge Gerhart Gesell in the case of *Menard* v. *Mitchell,* 328 F. Supp. 718, 726 (D.C.D.C.), on remand, 430 F. 2d. 486 (C.A.D.C., 1970). The floor debate referred to appears in CR, Vol. 72, pp. 1989–2199. The 1966 codification provision (80 Stat. 631, Section 7 (a)) states the legislative purpose to "restate without substantive change" the statutory antecedent of the codified measure, 28 U.S.C., Section 534.

In addition to the exploitation of the Bureau's investigative power for immediate political purposes on internal security pretexts, the Nixon administration tried to revive intelligence-related structures and to provide the FBI with a fresh investigative authority through an executive order dealing with loyalty and security qualifications for governmental employment. Under prior executive orders, the Bureau was requested to make a "full field investigation" in cases referred to it. Apart from the fact that such duties could furnish no basis for a claim of general intelligence powers, the Bureau's functions in this area have been sharply cut over the past decade. The Civil Service Commission, together with the federal employing agency, has come to play a more active role in applicant screening and has sharply reduced full field investigative referrals.

The Nixon order, No. 11605, purported to amend an Eisenhower directive by more broadly defining the classes of organizations whose members or supporters could be barred from federal employment. The "Attorney General's list" of subversive organizations, authorized by Truman, had long since fallen under constitutional attack. A Supreme Court decision in 1951 required notice and hearing before the listing of an organization. After a total listing of 283, no more organizations were added after 1955. By the early 1970's only thirteen of the listed groups survived. The Nixon order was intended to meet the Supreme Court's objections to the unilateral listing by giving the moribund Subversive Activities Control Board (SACB) the responsibility for conducting hearings on petition of the Department of Justice to determine whether an organization should be listed and thus rescue the agency from total idleness. At the same time the order was designed to give a new lease on life to the languishing Internal Security Division (ISD) of the Department of Justice, once busy preparing "front," "infiltration," and "membership" charges under the Internal Security Act of 1950 and its 1954 amendment for presentation to the SACB. Most important, the FBI would be empowered under the order to investigate potential organizational listees in order to develop data for processing by the ISD.

Executive Order 11605 was really a master stroke. But it contemplated a revision or an amendment of the Internal Security Act, clothing the SACB with powers never granted by Congress. Since the President had no power to legislate, the order was killed by a congressional appropriations rider in October 1972. The SACB, thus denied vital sustenance and left "swinging slowly, slowly in the wind," was abolished on March 27, 1973, simply by dropping it from the budget. This left the ISD totally without any important functions and it too was abolished at the same time—by a simple order of the Attorney General.*

The Bureau, despite its earlier embrace of legislative enactments as the primary source of intelligence authority, began to look with favor on the presidential directives as precedents. In February 1976 it disputed the conclusion of the General Accounting Office, which rejected the series of directives as a source of intelligence authority and insisted on the August 1936 assignment as a legiti-

---

*The Bureau's law enforcement defense was thus even more vulnerable than formerly. The ISD had in the past reviewed Bureau investigative reports to determine whether they contained evidence of law violations. In addition, another source of investigative authority was cut off by an executive order abolishing the Attorney General's list.

mate warrant for its subversive activities intelligence authority. A memorandum, written by the same assistant Bureau chief for intelligence, Raymond Wannall, who had in 1974 stressed the statutes as the principal source of intelligence authority, now insisted that "the intelligence-gathering activities of the FBI have had as their basis the intention of the President to delegate his constitutional authority," as well as the statutes "pertaining to the national security."[43]

The renewed reliance on executive precedent is explained by the collapse of law enforcement as a defense against the disclosures of intelligence abuses by congressional committees. There was, on the face of it, something absurd about the claim that thousands of Nixon era dissidents were surveilled, harassed, wiretapped, and bugged to forestall a seditious conspiracy or because of a fear that they were falling under the influence of Communists suspected of advocating the violent overthrow of the government in possible violation of the Smith Act even though the Constitution forbade their prosecution. Then, too, executive power seemed a welcome sanctuary from mounting congressional attacks on electronic eavesdropping and surreptitious entries. Besides, the earlier shift to legislation as the sole trigger of political investigation had encountered considerable resistance within the Intelligence Division.[44] Even the most deft rationalization could not overcome the difference between an intelligence investigation purely for the purposes of identification and file-feeding and the collection of evidence for prosecutive purposes.

Besides, it was the claim of an executive mandate that had made possible the Bureau's unique institutional status. The presidential directive thesis gave Hoover a free hand in the selection of targets and operational techniques. But investigation, surveillance, and identification are essentially police functions—in themselves not the building materials for an important governmental structure. For the power-hungry Director, a policeman's lot was indeed not a happy one; he remedied matters by branching out into noninvestigative fields, beginning with propaganda and publicity programs in direct conflict with the anonymity and discretion functionally required by intelligence work. To authenticate his propaganda, he moved into a self-serving style of evaluative ("pure") intelligence and trend assessment associated with policy and decision-making; invented the authority to circulate his intelligence product to agency and department heads; and, less openly, supplied investigative materials to his legislative allies. Thus, the vertical core of his power was buttressed by a horizontal, government-wide structure, again developed through an unchallenged assumption of authority.

The death of Hoover, followed by a post-Watergate rebellion against executive abuse of power, exposed the flimsy foundations of the entire political intelligence edifice. As its defenders lurched from an executive to a congressional and back to an executive warrant, it finally became apparent that the Bureau's intelligence powers were indeed themselves the result of an intelligence coup, a mission that had succeeded for thirty years. The record does not show whether the Director ever contemplated a shift from executive to legislative power as a source of his agency's intelligence authority. His own frustrating experience of the twenties with the justification of legislative enactment—anticipated federally* and in the meantime borrowed from the states—would undoubtedly have barred such a venture. But there was no need even to contemplate it. Through his power, persistence, and plain flim-flam he held off challenges from every quarter for more than thirty years—unquestionably his greatest achievement. What a long, triumphant road he had traveled from 1938, when he cautioned against openly seeking a legislative authorization because of the popular repugnance to "espionage"!

---

*Of interest is the formulation, reminiscent of the twenties, offered in Church Committee testimony by former Bureau intelligence chief Charles Brennan: "I think that . . . intelligence investigations are designed not specifically for prosecutive intent, but basically to develop intelligence information which will be provided to officials of the United States Government to enable them to possibly consider new types of legislation which may be affecting the security of the country"—Church, Vol. 2, p. 51.

4 The Lengthened Shadow of a Man

A Giant Passes

It has been said of J. Edgar Hoover that in his prime he had more admirers than any other American, and that he was the most popular unelected official in our history. Not only did he wield greater power for a longer period of time than any comparable figure in public life but he held on to it to a more advanced age. The first act of President-elect John F. Kennedy, on the day after his 1960 victory, was to announce Hoover's reappointment. It was then thought that the Director would bow out at the mandatory retirement age of seventy, which would fall on New Year's Day 1965. But President Johnson, as early as May 1964, waived this requirement. The next obvious milestone was his seventy-fifth birthday, but again he survived despite mounting criticism and indications of senility. On May 2, 1972, when he was seventy-seven, death finally pried the reins from his grip. In the days following, some 158 representatives and senators paid their respects in lavish tribute, subsequently collected along with laudatory articles and editorials in a special memorial volume. On May 25, Congress passed a bill designating the FBI headquarters building, then under construction in Washington, as the J. Edgar Hoover Building. As Hoover's body lay in state in the Capitol rotunda, an honor ordinarily reserved for the greatest leaders and heroes, 25,000 mourners filed by in a 21-hour period. The Chief Justice of the Supreme Court delivered the eulogy, and President Nixon outdid himself in his homage: ". . . it can truly be said of him that he was a legend in his own time. For millions he was a symbol of the values he cherished most: courage, patriotism, dedication to the country, and a granite-like honesty and integrity." At the funeral service he eulogized Hoover as a "giant who stands head and shoulders above [his] countrymen, setting a high and noble standard for us all."[1]

This was not ritualistic, graveside *nil nisi bonum* praise. The Director's entire forty-eight-year career as Bureau chief was a long glory road. The tributes flowed unceasingly: honorary degrees from nineteen colleges, universities, and law schools; formal commendations, certificates, awards, and resolutions from an adoring Congress, the armed services, and private groups for "distinguished service," "service in the battle for civil rights and liberties," "integrity and devotion to justice," and "selfless devotion to country and God." President Truman, in 1946, awarded him the Medal of Merit, and President Eisenhower honored him twice, first in 1955 with the National Security Medal and again in 1958 with a medal for Distinguished Federal Civilian Service.[2] These honors reflected only in part the enormous popularity of the Director and the Bureau. A 1953 Gallup Poll, conducted after Hoover's testimony in the Harry Dexter White case, which was criticized as partisan, showed a 78 percent favorable vote with only 2 percent recording an unfavorable opinion of the Director (20 percent expressed no opinion). A 1965 poll of the FBI's standing revealed an 84 percent "highly favorable" rating, which in 1970 dropped to 71 percent. Despite this decline, the pollsters found that the Bureau was more highly regarded than any other governmental agency. A Gallup Poll published in May 1971, when the Bureau was under strong attack, showed that 70 percent of those interviewed rated Hoover's performance as either "excellent" or "good."[3]

This approving consensus, reflecting the Bureau's carefully cultivated reputation for achievement, efficiency, rectitude, and incorruptibility, enfolded a cult of personal devotees. Men may fear power, but they also worship it. Hoover fed on the needs of the powerless and the insecure to merge themselves with a strong personality. By basking in the power of an authoritarian figure, by unconditionally surrendering to him, the individual feels the security, strength, and courage he finds lacking in his own life. The Director gloried in this role; his narcissism and cocksureness ("the infectiousness of the unconflicted personality")[4] invited transference, the submission to his "truth." While offering an opportunity for an escape from freedom (in Erich Fromm's formulation), he conveyed to his followers his own need for their support, his powerlessness in isolation. They responded with cascades of letters of support and denunciation of his critics, along with requests for his views on suspect organizations and individuals.

Hoover's celibacy and close relationship with Clyde Tolson, his principal aide, stirred persistent talk that he was homosexual, attributed by the Director to "degenerative pseudo-intellectuals" and their ilk.[5] But to his followers, his bachelor status confirmed his virile Americanism in dealing with subversive enemies and his consuming devotion to the nation—a patriotic monkhood that left no room for sexual involvement, romantic diversion, or family responsibility.

Hoover's specialness, the unique role he played in American life, is most tellingly revealed in the many thousands of adulatory personal letters conveying concern about his health, anger and anxiety over his rumored replacement, requests for spiritual guidance and advice. The letter writers begged for his views on education, child raising, sexual permissiveness, and Bingo. What was the Director's favorite food, reading, relaxation, hymn; how did he like his steak; what kinds of suits, shoes, and ties did he wear, and what was his recipe for popovers? May 10 marked a special day for his devotees: the anniversary of his appointment. For his fortieth anniversary in 1964, Hoover was showered with telegrams, gifts, and celebratory tributes—114 plaques, scrolls, and resolutions.[6]

The dependence created by psychic need was strengthened existentially by Hoover's intelligence functions. The nativist fear of a demonic and conspiratorial force seeks reassurance in a protector who alone can provide a shield against the power of an unseen enemy. The Director, himself a blood-and-bones child of this tradition, became a sort of shaman, in touch with the evil spirits seeking our destruction.[7] When he wrote or testified that there were precisely 22,623 reds in the country—not one more or less—he conjured up in the minds of his followers a patient midnight review and evaluation of untold numbers of reports by informers scuttling at his bidding through the catacombs of subversion. Like his counterpart in many primitive societies, Hoover constantly renewed the fear required to validate his magical power and to further the prestige demanded by his preoccupation with self.[8] This exploitation of fear as a source of power is well described by Norman Ollestad, a former agent who flavorfully records the observation of a fellow agent:

> Why do you think the Director has a large personal following in America? Because of his reputation as a crime fighter? Hell, no, crime has increased tremendously during his career. It's because he has convinced people that he stands between them and a Commie take-over in the U.S.[9]

A sense of the protective role of both the Director and the Bureau comes through in the letters protesting a television program, "First Tuesday," presented on June 1, 1971, by NBC's Garrick Utley, a segment of which dealt with the Bureau's political surveillance activities. The letters,[10] which may well have been inspired by the FBI's propaganda apparatus (see discussion below), charged that Utley and critics of the Bureau appearing on the TV screen themselves required surveillance: only those with something to hide would object to the Bureau's intelligence work. "Law-abiding citizens have nothing to fear from the FBI." In the same vein, the correspondents condemned the program for giving comfort to subversive forces, coddling "creeps," and slandering the "greatest," "most wonderful" American. The fear for our security that threads the letters is revealed in these sample extracts:

> The FBI has been the image of right—the protector of right and I fear our position without it. I recognize that the left want a change. Personally, I want left organizations and extreme right infiltrated.

> I'm in favor of the FBI and wish they would investigate more of the radical, Communist-inspired organizations and individuals.

> If your program . . . about the FBI was an effort to console the enemies of the U.S.A. and the breakdown of the security the FBI gives to the *law-abiding* citizens, you have certainly succeeded.

> God help our Country if we lose the FBI. Your biased program will add to its demise. *Shame.*

> The Reds have already infiltrated our law courts, our institutions of learning, even Congress and corrupted many of our youth. Never forget that Russia has never faltered in her One [sic] aim in life—and that is to destroy America.

Mr. Pogorney [sic] of Russia loves your kind. Who pays you for such as this propaganda? The leader of the Hanoi government loves you too. Why don't you go over there and live? America has too many of your kind, worker for Satan.

You look like a female with your curly flip. . . . Why don't you go to Russia? I am sure you would come back knowing that the 2 creeps you dug out of the gutter to condemn the FBI would have been shot along with you right after your program.

What kind of a news man are you? For me you stink. Try to run our FBI down. If we did not have it our country would be lost. Just take a look at the people who are against it. *Radicals* & that is all.

The safety of the people of the United States is what the FBI is all about. Decent people are not against the FBI just anarchists—and other S.O.B.'s. . . .

There are only three giant steps left before a Communist takeover can be carried out, here in America: 1. Destroy the FBI, 2. Destroy the local police, and 3. Disarm the American people. I just hope most American people can see through this.

The FBI one of the pillars of our society does not have to be taken to task for doing its job of defending us from subversive groups who want to burn, bomb, riot, kidnap, assassinate to name a few. . . . If the FBI ever stops infiltrating leftist groups I will scream to my congressmen. In fact I would like to see it investigate NBC.

It is not the Bureau alone, but the Director who stands as the bulwark of our national security:

If we didn't have *Mr. Hoover* and the *FBI*, I would like to know how you and I would exist.

Thank God for J. Edgar Hoover. Thank God someone realizes that there is a Communist conspiracy in the United States—a conspiracy which at times masks itself under different names and in defense of popular causes, a conspiracy which reaches into high places. Some of our Congressmen sound as if they were representing Moscow. When will the media realize this????

Thank God for the FBI and an *honest* person like Mr. J. Edgar Hoover. The *U.S.A.* is lucky to have him.

It is repugnant to every loyal citizen to watch ambitious political leaders adopt the "technique of the great lie" in attacking J. Edgar Hoover, who for so many years has been the bulwark between anarchist planning to destroy our country and you and me.

The News media seems to be playing up all the "left wingers" in this country who for one reason or another have had their wings clipped by Mr. Hoover—I say God save Mr. Hoover and the FBI.

Do you honestly think that some creep that looks & acts like you should judge J. Edgar Hoover? What have you ever contributed to this country besides encouraging those that wish to destroy us?

I just think Mr. Hoover is the greatest & hope he lives to be 100+ is still head of the FBI. Take hope & pray he keeps watching everybody he want too [sic].

Finally, the spirit of dependence on the Director is distilled in a response to a critical *Life* magazine article: "You will not succeed in destroying J. Edgar

Hoover. He is to us, to *America,* a Rock of Gibraltar, the one man in an insane world who is determined to save America. We honor him. We love him. We place complete trust in him."[11]

How did a career civil servant instill in his fellow citizens such a passionate conviction that our survival as a nation depended on him alone?

Minister of Internal Security

In Sir Isaiah Berlin's metaphor of the hedgehog who knows one big thing and the fox who knows many, the Director was the supreme hedgehog: anti-communism was both a lifelong crusade and a personal obsession. For Hoover, Communists were more dangerous than criminals: they were godless, violent, immoral, deceitful, dirty, and unpatriotic. Neither the nation's constitutional commitment to the protection of dissent, nor the formidable strength of capitalism, nor the perennially feeble state of the Communist movement curbed his zealotry. The Director's anti-communism was total in its scope and depth, combining ideology, psychically rooted aggressions, and authoritarian character traits. Because of his usefulness as a champion of capitalism with a mass following, he was permitted, if not encouraged, to reshape and enlarge his limited intelligence duties to implement his manic anti-communism and stake out an autonomous fiefdom. Ambition and power hunger accelerated this success formula, to place the Director in command of what may be accurately called a ministry of internal security, the conversion of a dark strain in the American tradition into a government function.

This ministry came to surpass the Bureau's more important law enforcement responsibilities and so tilted the agency's priorities that in the sixties, no less than nine of the individuals on the "Sixteen Most Wanted" list were student radicals. As a government function, radical watching could, in contrast to law enforcement, justify itself without pointing to measurable results. And the importance of the interest protected by this function, the security of the nation itself, was used to justify more penetrative political surveillance techniques than those permitted in the law enforcement area. Greater secrecy, indiscriminate targeting, open-ended marathon investigations, and more comprehensive filing practices uniquely strengthened this ministry. In addition, it was buttressed by Bureau prerogatives already acquired when the ministry was formed: the bypassing of civil service requirements for personnel recruitment, promotion, and discharge; use of unorthodox budgetary procedures; and the molding of the Bureau's corps of special agents into a body with all of the hallmarks, described by Georg Simmel, of secret societies—the substitution of internal bureaucratic rituals and norms for those of the larger society, seclusion from the social environment, a tight solidifying central authority, and a requirement of subjection, of "de-selfing," by the individual members.

The Director knew all too well that his bread was buttered on the side of countersubversion, not law enforcement. As we have seen, he fabricated the Bureau's internal security authority out of the most unpromising materials. But if he was a glutton for political intelligence authority, he was a finicky gourmet about more conventional jurisdiction. When pressed to enter a case that was distasteful to him, he would deliver a lecture about the dangers of a "national police force . . . with a roving commission." He justified his foot-dragging in the fields of civil rights and police malfeasance on jurisdictional grounds and resisted entering the field of organized crime, denying for a long time its very existence, and later citing image concern, the reluctance to expose his agents to the "temptations of corruption and big money." Closer to the mark was the Director's realization that organized crime was interwoven with legitimate business, and that part of its income was used to buy protection from police and leading politicians with whom he identified.[12] In contrast to countersubversion, the political risks were great and, given the difficulties, the ballyhoo potential remote, especially in provincial America, the heartland of his constituency.

But no such conflicts burdened his intelligence strivings. In the fall of 1944, the director of the Office of Security Services (OSS), General William J. Donovan, submitted a secret memorandum proposing a permanent American foreign intelligence service reporting directly to the President. Adoption of the proposal would mean the replacement of the Bureau's Secret Intelligence Service (SIS), commissioned at the outset of the war for intelligence work in Latin America. The Director acquired a copy of the memorandum and leaked it to the Chicago *Tribune,* though it was classified Top Secret. When Hoover's maneuvers— including leaked charges that the OSS was Communist-infiltrated and the proposed Central Intelligence Agency would become an American Gestapo—failed to block the launching of the CIA, FBI agents were instructed to destroy their files rather than turn them over to their replacements.[13]

Hoover also tried to expand the overseas coverage of his "legal attachés" ("legats"). In addition to conventional criminal matters, such as the apprehension of fugitives, these agents engaged in security work involving American citizens or residents. In 1970 and 1971 Hoover proposed enlarging his network from ten to another dozen foreign capitals, formalizing and enlarging the legats' duties to include the collection of general political intelligence—a traditional State Department function—for transmission in code directly to the White House without clearance of the State Department or the CIA.*[14] Approval of this expansion became an item in the Director's White House courtship, and when he managed to extract authorization for new legal assignments, he told his aides (who were strongly opposed to the expansion) that the White House had insisted on it.[15] (The Director may have been encouraged by earlier White House pressures for evidence of foreign involvement in the domestic anti-war movement. And, as early as May 1965, at President Johnson's request, Bureau agents were dispatched to the Dominican Republic to supplement the CIA and make certain that the government installed by American arms was free of subversives.)

The Director continued his campaign to expand his foreign operations by

---

*One of the less glamorous assignments of the Bureau's legats was described in March 1974 at the conspiracy trial of John Mitchell and Maurice Stans. According to a witness, Mark Felt, former second in command of the FBI, Mitchell when serving as Attorney General used the FBI's overseas personnel to intercede on behalf of financier Robert L. Vesco, then in a Swiss jail— "Witness Rebuts Mitchell Account," *New York Times,* March 6, 1974.

extravagant claims in his March 1971 House Appropriations Subcommittee testimony:

> The FBI conducts considerable research in all phases of communism and the intelligence operations of the Soviets, their satellites and other communist nations in order to determine their tactics. Many of the various studies prepared in this field are furnished to other intelligence agencies which have on a number of occasions, commented favorably concerning the value of these research studies to their own agencies.

But these claims ignored the fact that the National Security Act of 1947 had clothed the CIA with exclusive responsibility for such intelligence evaluations. One can only marvel at the dreams of power that led the aged Director, then seventy-six years old, to raid the foreign intelligence field in an attempt to undercut both the State Department and the CIA. His motivation becomes all too clear when we note that in February 1970, at the very time he began lobbying for an expansion of the Bureau's foreign intelligence assignment, he broke off domestic liaison with the CIA because of the Agency's refusal to furnish him the name of a Bureau agent who had supplied them with information. In May of 1970 he terminated liaison with all other federal intelligence agencies.[16]

While the Bureau's intelligence functions abroad—whether as a collector or as a spy watcher—after World War II never amounted to more than a gleam in the Director's eye, its domestic counterintelligence responsibilities were both unambiguous and exclusive. It is, indeed, the Bureau's spy-catching mission in this country which has served to justify the Bureau's repressive surveillance of domestic dissidents. But the Director's success formula, with its stress on publicity and propaganda, had no place for the discreet requirements of successful counterespionage, demonstrated all too clearly by his disastrous wartime relationship with British intelligence in the United States. The British, for whom reticence in intelligence work was a religion, were reluctant to share information with the headline-hunting Director and were forced to wheedle his help by promises that the FBI would be given credit at the proper time. Finally, desperate for a more productive relationship, the British succeeded in 1941 in developing active liaison with William Donovan's newly organized OSS. Hoover was predictably enraged, and sulked when the British asked him to cooperate in a special program to "turn" German intelligence networks in this country so as to transmit misleading information. Although the Bureau was responsible for some limited achievements in this area, it was not the Director's cup of tea, since it offered no opportunity for claiming credit. According to Ewen Montague, a master of this "double-cross" technique, Hoover was an unreliable collaborator: "He wanted to publicize everything to enhance the FBI's reputation. We dared not confide to him certain plans for fear of leaks. Our methods depended on concealment. This made Hoover more distrustful."[17]

Hoover's sabotage of the double-cross system as well as other intelligence obstructions is chronicled in an account, virtually all of it corroborated, by Dusko Popov, a daring Yugoslav said to be the model for Ian Fleming's James Bond. Popov, or Tricycle, as he was code-named, was a double agent; after earning the confidence of the Germans, he became a British master spy, performing services that won their gratitude and awe. Not the least of his exploits was his readiness, whenever necessary, to reestablish his German Secret Service cover at enormous personal risk. In 1941, the Germans sent him to the United States to reorganize and run an intelligence network. This was an opportunity to deceive the Germans on a grand scale, providing that Hoover approved. The Director, however, was turned off by Popov from the beginning. He was a Balkan playboy, a double agent, sexually loose, living in a Park Avenue penthouse—why, he had even taken a trip to Florida with a girlfriend with whom he stayed as man and wife, in plain violation of the Mann Act. The fact that his swinging lifestyle was an ideal cover hardly impressed Hoover. His personal disgust with Tricycle's moral standards led to a rejection of British pleas to help preserve his cover with the German spy service by cooperating in feeding it false information through captured German transmitters.

Tricycle brought with him highly important intelligence: he had learned through German intelligence that the Japanese were interested in Pearl Harbor's fortifications and defenses. After letting him cool his heels, Hoover received the information four months before the attack on Pearl Harbor and buried it. He was hardly equipped to evaluate its importance—and besides, it had no publicity value. Popov also brought with him a valuable secret of German intelligence communication, the microdot. This did have publicity potential and, subsequently, in April 1946, *Reader's Digest* published an article under Hoover's by-line claiming credit for capturing the secret of the microdot from an enemy spy. (Understandably, the reader is never told what happened to this villain, invented to conceal the fact that the microdot secret had been handed to him by Popov.) The article was accompanied by an illustration that blew the cover of Popov's source, a Brazilian diplomat. When an enraged Popov threatened to expose the Director's fabrication, he agreed to try to repair the damage by stopping the publication of the article in the South American edition of *Reader's Digest*. [18]

Hoover's intelligence efforts were handicapped in another way. Ever the hedgehog, he regarded the Russians as the main enemy even when they entered the war as American allies. Hoover apparently saw nothing wrong with Nazism on either political or humanitarian grounds. Long after Hitler came to power, he maintained contact with top Nazi police officials, exchanging requests for information. W. Fleischer, counsellor to the Reich criminal police bureau, wrote the Director on June 26, 1939: "In my office I have pictures of various foreign criminal authorities with whom I am in constant contact. I should be very happy if I might complete my collection with your picture." Hoover provided an autographed photo. The Bureau also cooperated with the International Police Commission, now known as Interpol, despite warnings that it was German-dominated. It was not until December 4, 1941, three days before Pearl Harbor, that Hoover broke Bureau ties with it—and then as the result of urging by a conference of top FBI executives.*

*According to Harold A. R. ("Kim") Philby, the Soviet double agent who fled his British intelligence post to Moscow in 1956, his cover as a Fascist sympathizer won him the high regard of both the wartime OSS's Allen Dulles and D. Milton Ladd, who until his retirement in 1954 was the FBI's top intelligence officer and a Deputy Director. Ladd, Philby recalled (in an interview in

Hoover pestered the British for information in British intelligence files about communism, pulled strings to block the proposed sharing of intelligence information by the OSS with the Russians, and himself refused to exchange intelligence secrets with American allies out of fear of leaks to the Russians. At the same time, domestically, his anti-Communist vigilance continued as his agents and informers monitored wartime activities to promote Soviet-American relations—on the assumption that Russian sympathizers were embryonic spies. The Director did not neglect Nazi spies; but there had to be captures, and even better, arrests and trials with appropriate credit to make the game worthwhile.[19] The wartime Nazi spy trials brought warming headlines—and even material for magazine articles. But these trials were, for the most part, the products not of skillful counterespionage work but of volunteered evidence, defections, and information acquired by other agencies—a circumstance frequently suppressed for the greater glory of the Bureau.[20] The postwar Rosenberg-Sobell and Colonel Rudolf Abel cases were developed in the same way, although publicized by the Bureau as stupendous counterintelligence coups: the Rosenberg case became the subject of an exhibit in the FBI guided tour, as well as of the Director's *Reader's Digest* article "The Crime of the Century."

According to insiders, at least since the early sixties the Bureau's counteres-pionage operations directed at hostile intelligence services operating in this country have been sharply reduced—but not because of the abandonment of foreign espionage programs. Attempts to milk publicity out of the work brought conflict with the State Department;[21] besides, it required image-threatening techniques and skills (deception, impersonation, adaptability) conspicuously lacking in the Bureau's well-scrubbed, bureaucratically programmed staff of agents. Similarly, the Director could never be persuaded that agents' sedans, spotlessly polished according to regulations, were not the best vehicles for trailing spies, or that a stress on quantifiable results is fatal to the intelligence enterprise. (How many indictments, dollars saved, stolen cars recovered, over-time hours worked, etc.) Nor could any surveillance activity, whether of a law enforcement or intelligence variety, survive a conflict with the Director's ego needs—as witness his performance in the Berrigan-Capitol bombing affair.

On November 27, 1970, Hoover appeared before a subcommittee of the Senate Appropriations Committee in support of a supplemental appropriation for the FBI. The very fact of his appearance was curious. Hoover had for a long time limited his congressional committee appearances to the House Appropria-tions Committee, which invariably granted his budget requests, and had consis-tently rebuffed all attempts to lure him to the Senate side. He had already made his pitch before the House committee on November 19, and, as usual, it was sympathetically received. Why not? Hoover had merely asked for a routine supplementary appropriation—all of which had been already mandated by statute and approved by the Budget Bureau.

His unprecedented and gratuitous appearance—all the more notable be-

---

Izvestia reprinted in the *New York Times* for Dec. 14, 1967), "made an indelible impression" because "this astonishingly dense personage tried to convince me in all seriousness that Franklin Roosevelt was a Comintern agent."

cause it was before a subcommittee of two senators—was staged to exploit a sensational charge of a plot by a group of anti-war Catholic activists, headed by Philip and Daniel Berrigan, Catholic priests then imprisoned for anti-draft activities, to kidnap Henry Kissinger and to blow up underground electrical conduits and steam pipes in the Capitol area. No one who has investigated the matter seriously believed, then or subsequently, that the "plot" was more than rhetoric. The government itself—reliable evidence shows—thought little of it. In September, when Hoover briefed both the Attorney General and President Nixon about the details of the "plot," it was already manifest that it was a fantasy never intended to be acted on, despite the efforts of Boyd F. Douglas, Jr., an FBI prison informer, to breathe life into it. In the following weeks, lawyers in the Justice Department's Internal Security Division discussed the possibility of prosecution but made no move to present evidence or even to convene a grand jury. Instead, they told Hoover that the case was insufficient to warrant presentation to a grand jury and that he should continue surveillance to get more evidence. But Hoover had other ideas. After his November 19 House committee testimony, which was given in executive session, he arranged for a Senate replay; but this time, at his insistence, to be made public, despite the fact that it was to be presented in executive session for release only at the discretion of the committee. When he appeared, Hoover brought with him forty-five copies of a prepared statement that consisted of a "scrubbed" version (off-the-record comments deleted) of his earlier House testimony for distribution to the press as soon as he began to testify. The testimony—in no way relevant to Hoover's appropriation request—created a storm all over the country. The Berrigans, Daniel in Danbury and Philip in Lewisburg, strongly denied complicity in the charged plot, and others listed as co-conspirators also denied Hoover's charges.

Department of Justice officials who had reached the decision to hold off on prosecution demanded that Hoover be retired, but this was vetoed by President Nixon. Attorney General John Mitchell, talking off the record to reporters, admitted that he had been unaware that Hoover intended to make public charges and that he was surprised to hear them. Representative William Anderson of Tennessee asserted his belief in the two priests' innocence, and in a letter to the Director, as well as a statement on the House floor, said that due process had been gravely violated by Hoover's public accusations before any formal charges had been made. Anderson subsequently wrote to a constituent:

> It has been a long-cherished policy of the FBI that this government agency "only collects facts—never judges them." The mimeographed testimony of Mr. Hoover suggested the statement was not an inadvertent off-the-cuff opinion of the Director, but a carefully considered opinion which must have been internally reviewed by FBI administrative staff which the FBI Director has available to prepare reports to the Senate Appropriations Committee. . . . Mr. Hoover's statement was a declarative statement that prejudiced guilt. It did not presume innocence until guilt was proven in a court of law in due process.

Hoover himself gave no explanation for his usurpation of the grand jury's combined function as accuser and shield against unfounded or malicious prosecution. Instead, he went on to compound his impropriety in a series of press interviews, insisting that the "incipient plot" was still operative despite "intensive investigation," that it had not been abandoned even though its alleged leaders were in jail, and that he had substantial supporting evidence he was prepared to present to a grand jury. He added, on another not wholly unrelated theme, that he had no intention of retiring "as long as my health remains excellent," and that he had recently passed a physical examination "with flying colors."

Hoover may have hoped to force a reluctant Department of Justice to seek an indictment to vindicate his charges. Certainly the subsequent media campaign points in this direction; a measure of its intensity is supplied by the release to the press—prior to the handing down of an indictment in January 1971—of correspondence between Sister Elizabeth McAlister, one of the alleged conspirators, and Father Philip Berrigan, copied by the Bureau's informer. What is glaringly clear is that the seventy-six-year-old Hoover was motivated by a need to reestablish his authority and prestige, now at the end of his long career seriously threatened. To Hoover, the plot with its Capitol setting, underground tunnels, high government officials, priests and nuns, must have presented itself as a heaven-sent opportunity—here was a real threat to the "national security," and right in the government's front yard. Once again he could claim the gratitude of a rescued nation and confound his critics. And this vision of glorious new acclaim might well have been fed by the hope of finally erasing the failure of half a century earlier to catch the Wall Street bombers.

The history of nineteenth-century autocracies teaches that every spymaster seeks to restore a faltering grip by inventing or exaggerating subversive plots, and even by using provocateurs to help them along. P. F. Réal, Fouché's right-hand man, writes of an ambitious prefect seeking to supplant him that he "never went to bed without praying for a small conspiracy on which to demonstrate his rare ability."[22] But few recognized in Hoover's exposé a latter-day example of this practice—in itself a tribute to his extraordinary hold on the American imagination. The Director's reckless passion for the redeemer's role found its most revealing expression in his release on December 11, under FBI sponsorship, of his House committee testimony containing the plot charges, for national distribution in blown-up, easy-to-read format. This particularly shocked Justice Department lawyers because it was timed a scant week before the convening of a grand jury in Harrisburg, Pennsylvania, to hear evidence as to whether a crime had been committed at all.

Of course, Hoover depended on widespread publication of his charges to achieve his objective; but intelligence authorities must frequently elect between silence and continuing surveillance on the one hand, and disclosure on the other. Where important interests are potentially involved, the choice necessarily falls on the side of continuing surveillance so that the full scope of the danger and the identity of all the principals can be established. One hardly needs to be an intelligence expert to recognize that public testimony is a foolish, counterproductive response to a half-baked plot. Here even legal prosecution, with its inevitable public disclosures, is considered a last resort—either to forestall imminent criminal acts or to block the flight of an important conspirator.* And the folly was compounded by the puny legal return. The initial vindicating indictment (intended, as Mitchell put it, "to get Hoover off the hook") was superseded in April by a new, easier-to-prove indictment centering on anti-draft activities that had nothing to do with the Hoover disclosures. In addition, Daniel Berrigan, named by Hoover as a ringleader and included in the earlier indictment, was dropped from the superseding charges. Despite all this insurance against an outcome discrediting to the Director, the trial jury, in April 1972 after an eleven-week trial, deadlocked 10–2 for acquittal on the principal charges against the seven defendants and convicted Sister Elizabeth McAlister and Father Philip Berrigan on a minor charge of smuggling contraband letters. The government abandoned the entire case in July 1972.

Minister of Propaganda

Long before the 1939 intelligence assignment, Hoover had developed publicity into a major Bureau priority. Its well-staffed public relations machine fed the highly receptive media streams of copy exalting the triumphs of the fearless G-men over their gangster adversaries, the "Public Enemies." The FBI's corporate image glittered, but the Director got the credit. Arrests were announced in his name while the agents were forbidden to talk to the press. Between 1933 and 1940, twenty flattering portraits of the Director and his achievements appeared in nationally circulated publications. Even the lowliest pulp magazine could expect a letter of commendation from the Director himself for a favorable article. His exploitation of the Bureau as a vehicle of self-promotion was unmistakable in the articles that began appearing under his by-line—no less than sixteen of them in *American Magazine* alone between February 1934 and August 1936. Firmly convinced that nothing succeeds like excess, he gave his blessings to book projects that glamorized the Bureau, wrote introductions for pet authors, and even, in one case, had one of them (Courtney Ryley Cooper) introduce his own maiden effort *(Persons in Hiding),* which is a preachy rewrite of one of Cooper's earlier books.

But it was the assumption of the intelligence mantle that offered unique satisfaction for Hoover's self-promotional cravings. Who would be content with catching a nation's criminals when he could save its very soul from subversion? The Director had learned the utility and techniques of public relations in the Palmer era, when he played an active role in the press campaign to counter attacks on Attorney General Palmer's anti-radical crusade. In the process of rallying countersubversive support, the GID developed propaganda functions that drew fire from reformers. In the August 1924 interview previously referred to, Acting Director Hoover and Attorney General Stone promised ACLU's Roger Baldwin that in the future only the Attorney General would speak for

---

*Premature disclosure, of course, also jeopardizes conventional, nonpolitical law enforcement, a risk the Director stressed when it suited his purpose. In feuding with Attorney General Robert F. Kennedy, he opposed Kennedy's proposal to publicize the revelations of Mafioso informant Joe Valachi: "By making his story public, you will only destroy the value of whatever leads he has given us"—Quoted in de Toledano, p. 19.

the Bureau. But that was in another country. The absence of objective standards in the post-1940 assignment gave free play to the Director's personal values and formidable media skills in promoting them.*

Secret police chiefs are tempted to exploit the feeling of awe aroused by their penetration of private plots and knowledge of hidden mysteries. But historically, they have used their resources behind the scenes to win the support of a minister or sovereign or to blackmail critics and political enemies of their patrons or sponsors; it was too risky to bid for power directly. Besides, the requirements of secrecy and (in a democracy) neutrality would seem to eliminate political intelligence practice as raw material for a mass appeal. The intervention of the state in the competition of ideas by officially promoting some and attacking others was a totalitarian practice, "propaganda," in the Director's indignantly pejorative designation. Nevertheless, he converted his intelligence role and resources into a power base through what is surely the most elaborate propaganda apparatus ever developed by a government agency in this country. In a real, if unacknowledged, sense, he became our first minister of propaganda, an American Goebbels. And the hallmark of his ministry was the interplay between the process of opinion formation and the Director's self-promotion, reflected most clearly in the mass of material published under his signature but, for the most part, ghost-written by employees recruited and trained for that purpose.

In 1940 alone he "wrote" at least eight articles and made seven speeches on a mix of themes: the Menace, espionage, Americanism, precepts for raising children, and crime. From 1940 until shortly before his death, Hoover's output of speeches, articles, interviews, and pamphlets on these and related subjects was prodigious: according to incomplete records,† his published oeuvre totaled at least 400 major items, including articles (263), speeches (66), interviews in nationally circulated magazines, reports, pamphlets, testimony, and statements. His published articles, editorials, and speeches appeared in seventy-four different publications, ranging from the *Harvard Business Review* to *Scholastic,* from *Human Events* to *Popular Mechanics,* and in scores of newspapers. In addition, the Director's signature graced some sixty articles in law reviews and professional journals, from the obscure *Title News* to the prestigious American Bar Association *Journal,* on the subjects of law enforcement, civil liberties, and the

---

*Hoover's lifelong cultivation of the media, obsession with publicity, versatile command of *kitsch* solemnities, punchy style, and addiction to "wise-cracks" all link him to the twenties. The snappy putdown, the fleering twenties-style phrase, became Hoover's rhetorical trademark (as in "mental halitosis," "intellectual pervert"), sometimes sharpened by alliteration ("sabotage by semantics," "totalitarian tricksters," "Moscow monsters of mirage"), an outlet for his suppressed aggression and vengefulness. The influence of American advertising and press agentry, an offspring of the twenties, is apparent in his calculated exaggeration of the power of the enemy (as in his "crime wave" publicity) to gain respect, stimulation of fear to overcome doubt and, more generally, in his perception that the public had to be "sold" on himself and his achievements through the techniques used to sell merchandise and services—See Preston Slosson, *The Great Crusade and After* (Macmillan, 1931), p. 362.

†Many of Hoover's writings, as well as some interviews, appeared in small daily newspapers and obscure, unindexed periodicals—*The Airman, Future, Collegiate Challenge, The Lion, Retired Officer, Signs of the Time,* and *Ave Maria*—and come to our notice only when reprinted in the *Congressional Record.* His traceable articles, speeches, interviews, and other works are listed in Appendix II.

Menace. Specially prepared, officially sponsored pamphlets on civic and patriotic themes appeared regularly under his signature, as well as literature directed at special audiences—teenagers,* trade unionists, and (under State Department sponsorship) residents of foreign countries. In a more transient journalistic category, one finds guest editorials and columns prepared as a favor for his journalistic collaborators and admirers, as well as interviews.

Many of the works signed by the Director suffer from a potted quality, the mark of the tired ghost writer. For a livelier treatment of Hooverian views on government, politics, and society, one must turn to the FBI's *Law Enforcement Bulletin,* a house organ distributed to the entire national law enforcement community on every government level. Hoover contributed a monthly "message," as well as articles, editorials, and addresses that were channeled to the press and Congress. Also bearing a more personal stamp are Hoover's speeches delivered to conventions (the American Legion was a favorite host, with the DAR second) or in response to citations and honorary degrees. These were frequently reprinted verbatim, as pamphlets, or in condensed format for mass circulation at government expense with the official imprimatur of the Department of Justice and the FBI seal. In the same way, the Director's articles, interviews, testimony, and specially commissioned reports were reprinted by the Government Printing Office or privately by patriotic groups and fraternal orders.

Some 43 of Hoover's 66 speeches, 108 of his articles, and many of his editorials, interviews, and pamphlets were inserted into the *Congressional Record* and, reproduced in this impressive format, recirculated for the benefit of a wider audience. The Bureau's promotional pamphlet, *The Story of the Federal Bureau of Investigation,* is included in a packet of documents made available to visitors on a guided tour of the FBI headquarters. During the fifties and sixties as many as a half-million copies of this item were distributed annually.

Communists and spies stirred Hoover's muse far more than, say, Mafiosi. Of the four books appearing under his signature, only the first, *Persons in Hiding,* a dud, dealt with crime. His magnum opus, *Masters of Deceit* (1958), sold a quarter-of-a-million copies and was hailed as a stupendous contribution to an understanding of communism. A soft-cover edition sold an additional 2 million copies, in part the result of the efforts of Bureau personnel assigned by the Director to organize promotional projects among right-wing groups. *A Study of Communism,* published in 1962 as a high school text on communism, sold about 125,000 copies, and *On Communism,* an anthology of quotations from his writings and speeches, which came out in 1964, sold 40,000 copies. A second, more comprehensive compilation (324 pages), *J. Edgar Hoover Speaks Concerning Communism,* appeared in 1970. The two latter collections are the Director's "thoughts," the closest we have come to a capitalist version of an answer to Mao.

In addition to the Director's efforts, the Bureau's official reports and accounts of quotidian activities were processed and fed to the press in a never-ending pursuit of a well-burnished image by the Bureau's Crime Records Divi-

*"What Young People Should Know About Communism" (1965).

sion.* A modest noncontroversial function, record-keeping and analysis, thus provided a camouflaged shelter for a public relations enterprise larger than the entire Department's, enabling the Bureau to deny that it engaged in such activity altogether and deceiving would-be budget cutters. In the post-Hoover era it emerged from the closet as the External Affairs Division. To supplement this institutional apparatus, Hoover and his close aides developed a network of insiders, a journalistic claque ("leak men"), who were offered file information and direct quotes in return for a flattering product or for "kiting" a Bureau story.† Friendly newspapers and periodicals were used to plant or launder attacks on the Director's critics and to discredit or punish intelligence targets. Thus, the practice of recruiting reporters and photographers to moonlight as informers was a natural extension of the agency's exploitation of the press as both a publicity and an operational asset.[23]

Public relations became integral to the Bureau's functioning not only on the national level through the Bureau's publicity arm but in the field as well. Field agents exhorted "to carry on a very extensive program of . . . good public relations" were required to monitor the local press for material dealing with the Director and the Bureau. While favorable stories and editorials brought an appreciative note, critical items could generate surveillance, pressure, and discreet blackmailing attempts, as reflected in the 150-page released portion of a file on the Charleston (W.Va.) *Gazette.* The newspaper's criticisms resulted in intensive Bureau surveillance. Its editorial attacks on the Bureau or Hoover were transmitted to the Director, marked "Urgent." Individual editors were investigated; one was characterized as a "scurrilous character," and publisher W. E. Chilton III was accused of writing editorials "in praise of Red China" and "highly critical of the American Legion and the FBI." The paper was punished by removal from the FBI mailing list, and when one of its investigative reporters sought information for articles on police brutality in the South against blacks, Hoover instructed the Atlanta field office to "furnish no information or assistance" in view of the fact that the *Gazette* had been "consistently hostile" to the Bureau over the years.

Propaganda and image-making were not confined to the printed word. The radio program "The FBI Story" gave way after the success of *Masters of Deceit* to a television series, which the Bureau actively supervised, supplying plots and furnishing on-the-set technical advice; it starred Efrem Zimbalist, Jr., portraying an FBI agent as the very embodiment of fearlessness and patriotism. The Bureau also inspired and, in some cases, virtually produced films dealing with its achievements. The early *G-Men* (1935), starring James Cagney, was followed by films with countersubversive and spy themes such as *The House on 92nd Street* (1945), *Walk a Crooked Mile* (1948), *I Was a Communist for the FBI* (1951), *Walk East on Beacon* (1952), and *The FBI Story* (1959).

---

*The glorification of the Director was an institutional priority: it was a standing requirement that every press release mention the Director at least once in its lead paragraph.

†Most prominent in an insiders' circle of Hoover legend-builders was Walter Winchell, newspaper columnist and radio commentator. Introduced to Hoover in the Stork Club, Winchell became, in the mid-thirties, Hoover's personal friend and drum-beating courtier. The Director showed his gratitude through news tips which in turn stimulated ever more unctuous responses from Winchell.

As in the pre-1940 period, these promotional endeavors had the effect of superimposing the Director's persona on the Bureau's public image. The "brave men and women of the FBI" performed faceless parts in a scenario in which the Director was the real protagonist, pitted against unspeakably foul forces of subversion and crime. The Director received credit for the Bureau's achievements, but if an agent goofed, the hapless culprit would be disciplined—usually by a transfer to an undesirable post.

Hoover's own writings attacked the Menace with stupefying repetitiveness, endlessly warning of the danger and the folly of relaxed concern. In 1954, when the Communist Party was outlawed by an amendment to the Internal Security Act, Hoover published no less than ten articles (one appeared in two publications) stressing the continuing peril. In the two-year period 1961–62, when his tenure appeared precarious, he published over thirty articles, a record even for the prolific Director.

As the McCarthy era reduced the number and influence of the Communists, cunning and duplicity replaced violence as master themes. This transition was formalized by *Masters of Deceit.* The book's popular success was due not to its exposition of Communist theory—a "Dick and Jane" treatment— but to its exposé appeal. The Director, the supreme expert, "revealed," according to a cover blurb, "the facts that have taken more than forty years to uncover" about the "inside story of Communist strategy and tactics." And these bared mysteries (based on a selective account of informers' reports in Bureau files) were especially titillating because they had been wrested from diabolically crafty plotters. The substitution of deception for violence skillfully exploited the surefire American theme of innocence betrayed, explained away the seeming ineffectiveness of communism as a trick to reduce our vigilance, and justified surveillance of a wide variety of non-Communist movements and organizations as necessary to ferret out the hidden influence of the "masters of deceit." *A Study of Communism,* prepared for the high school market, developed a more sober theme, the conflict between Communist slavery and democratic freedom.

Intelligence officials who, like the Director, aspire to play more important roles than mere policemen are forced to involve themselves in policy matters. When unrest begins to threaten the established order, they must consider the possibility of recommending concessions as a means of restoring stability and thus lightening their burdens. Given his sermonizing proclivities, the Director very early in his career addressed himself to the problem "How to Beat Communism." It was simple. All that was required was a rededication to the verities of capitalism. Over and over again he pleaded for a reaffirmation of religious faith, a commitment to strict standards of personal conduct, and a rejection of collectivism. Most important of all, "Our best defense in the United States against the menace of Communism is our own American way of life." In his articles, editorials, and speeches he elaborated a model of capitalist man: law-abiding, God-fearing, individualistic, honest, moral, obedient, disciplined, patriotic, anti-intellectual, ambitious, neat, achievement- and property-oriented. Nor was this an abstract ideal; these and related virtues are mirrored in the qualifications for admission to the brotherhood of agents—many of whom, after their

Bureau apprenticeship, entered all levels of the corporate world—from high executive posts to personnel security.[24]

Like other ideological fanatics, Hoover did not bother to practice what he preached. The huge corpus of ghost-written publications presented as his is a tribute to a "master of deceit." Indeed, *Masters of Deceit* itself was written exclusively by Bureau personnel[25] and falsely presented as another product of the Director's busy pen, an updating of his 1920 briefs.* No acknowledgment is made in the self-preening preface of the contributions of others, beyond the "editorial guidance and advice" of the editor of *Look* magazine. American youth might not have been inspired to a more fervent commitment to the American way of life had they been told that Hoover and his two close associates pocketed the lion's share of the royalties while the principal author, a Bureau clerk, received an "incentive award" of $250, and this only after considerable pressure on the Director.[26] Nor would the Director's exhortations to spurn Communist materialism in favor of the rewards of the spirit have been so well received were it known that he sold Warner Brothers the movie rights to the book for $75,000, which he pocketed—an alleged bribe for permission to use the Bureau as the subject of a television series. Similarly, the high school students invited to believe that the Director wrote the *Study* himself in response to the urgings of educators, might have been distressed to learn that the freedoms they were urged to revere included plagiarism, self-enrichment at the expense of others, and misrepresentation.

It must be added that Hoover had accomplices in his deception: the editors and publishers of his ghost-written productions. True, the ghost writers of the journalism had managed to fashion an acceptable version of Hoover's charged-up style, diluted for popular consumption while still retaining its aggressive vigor. But the dominant expository tone of both *Masters of Deceit* and the *Study* was quite foreign to the Director's pitch. And the professional quality of the style was a dead giveaway. Of the two, the *Study* was an even more obvious counterfeit—and not solely because of its restrained didactic tone and smooth style. The Director, anti-intellectual, a confirmed reader of the New York *Daily News* (he abhorred impartially the *New York Times* and the Washington *Post*), whose recreation was typified by horse racing and the Lawrence Welk show, had no qualifications for dealing with concepts on even a rudimentary level. Not theory, but people, identifiable evil men, plotters with a "savage plan for the liquidation of a vanquished America," fueled his anti-communism. Praised in the publisher's blurb as "eminently qualified as an authority on communism" on the basis of "long first-hand experience," Hoover in fact knew little or nothing about the post-revolutionary Communist movement abroad, basic Communist doctrines, Communist expansion, its consolidation of power, and similar subjects considered in the *Study.* To be sure, he might have given himself

---

*Hoover was persuaded to write *Masters* while wintering at a La Jolla vacation retreat where he annually enjoyed the (free) hospitality of its owners, Texas millionaires Clint W. Murchison and Sid Richardson, and the diversions of the nearby Del Mar racetrack. Murchison, a patron of Senator Joseph R. McCarthy who was also a frequent guest, had acquired the financially ailing publishers Henry Holt & Co. and saw in an anti-Communist book by the Director both financial and political rewards—Robert Lubar, "Henry Holt and the Man from Koon Kreek," *Fortune* (December 1959).

a cram course as he had in his 1919 apprenticeship. But a curious editor might have wondered how the head of a huge government bureaucracy (with a staff then in excess of 13,000) could have written the numerous articles attributed to him in this 1961–62 period (including four in professional journals), prepared testimony, speeches, and reports and, in his spare time, whipped up a treatise on communism. Hoover's magic name with its assurance of a large circulation was enough to warrant the authenticity of any work to which he chose to attach his signature. Nor did critics and reviewers wonder about the authorship of *Masters of Deceit*. One reviewer of the later anthology *On Communism* did contrast the thoughtful quality of its introductory essay with the "rather simplistic clichés (like 'paganistic barbarism')" in the quotations from the Director's earlier works, and further observed that, although described as "the authoritative appraisal of the Communist menace" in this country, the book nowhere mentioned the numerical strength of the Party.[27]

The White House Connection

The Director had grafted his two ministries onto a subordinate agency of the Justice Department. But his warrant bore a White House stamp, the Roosevelt presidency's assumption of inherent executive power to engage in internal security intelligence activities. The circumstances that further contributed have already been mentioned: President Roosevelt's view of intelligence as an instrument of personal government, the defensiveness of New Deal liberalism, the war background, and the war itself. During the Roosevelt era, Hoover was encouraged to run the Bureau as an adjunct of the White House and to take the initiative in performing investigative services that might be useful. Thus, he instructed Bureau agents in London to spy on Harry Hopkins, assigned in 1941 to a special mission to Great Britain. Thereafter, in a letter to a presidential aide, he asked that the President be informed that his agents, planted at a dinner at Claridge's given by Lord Beaverbrook, had overheard nothing but praise of Hopkins. The President was delighted. Hoover also cemented White House ties by performing security assignments, consisting principally of tracking down suspected press leaks, an area in which the wiretapping of White House aides became self-justifying. In 1945 Hoover was assigned to conduct an investigation of leaks to the press of telegrams from Harry Hopkins reporting on his conversations with Stalin in Moscow.[28]

It was President Roosevelt's personal interest and support that made the relationship a heady one. FDR viewed the Bureau as his eyes and ears, an in-house detective agency. He also appreciated the thoughtful special amenities provided by Bureau agents on Hoover's instructions, supplementing the Secret Service's more routine duties. In some ways, the Bureau played a role similar to that of the contingent of state troopers made available to Roosevelt when he was governor of New York State.

The aggrandizement of presidential power, through hot and cold war, tightened the White House bond into a shared responsibility for national security. For all of President Truman's personal coolness to the Director, intimate ties were maintained both by means of a permanently assigned Bureau White House liaison agent and with the Director himself through Major Harry Vaughan.[29] The politicization of internal security, especially the issue of subversives in government employment, made the Director a vital White House asset in the Eisenhower years. Although his direct entree was limited, his goodwill was eagerly sought. The newly elected President himself, even before he was installed, assured the Director of his respect and support as long as he remained in office.[30]

Members of the Kennedy circle made threatening noises about retiring the Director. But the administration, fearful of the consequences, tried to control and appease him at the same time, principally through White House luncheons arranged by Robert F. Kennedy. At these get-togethers Hoover retailed his gossipy wares, and on one occasion he blew the whistle on the President's relationship with a girlfriend, Judith Campbell Exner, allegedly shared with two Mafiosi.[31] Nor did the Kennedys hesitate to use the Bureau for special White House political assignments such as tapping sugar lobbyists and intimidating press opponents of the administration's confrontation with the steel industry over a price freeze.[32]

President Johnson's official relationship with Hoover was strengthened by personal friendship, and a shared hatred of the Kennedys which found expression in a variety of ways. No chief executive praised the Director so warmly.[33] As majority leader, Johnson already had been receiving a steady stream of reports and dossiers from the Director, then his neighbor, which he prized both as a means of controlling difficult senators and as a gratification of earthier instincts. For President Johnson, secrets were in themselves perquisites of power, and whispered-in-the-ear disclosures (even of bogus secrets) a means of buying favor. But the Director had a special line of merchandise for Presidents: secrets about their own conduct (as in the case of Kennedy) or associations that might prove embarrassing if brought to light. These were offered ostensibly out of protective concern for preserving the dignity and image of the nation's chief executive, but with a barely suppressed blackmail threat. The Director had a jittery, semi-paranoid Johnson eating out of his hand after warning him off his protégé, Bobby Baker, because wiretaps had revealed that Baker was involved in deals with Las Vegas gamblers. According to H. R. Haldeman,* Hoover visited the newly elected Nixon and briefed him on the extent of Johnson's wiretapping of political targets, including Nixon himself.†

*In *The Ends of Power* (Times Books, 1978), pp. 4, 8.

†President Nixon's *Memoirs* (Grosset and Dunlap, 1978) are replete with his recollections of LBJ's alleged praise of Hoover for his contribution to Johnson's election victory (see pp. 308, 358, 596, and 598). The Nixon version is capsulized in the following passage (p. 596):

> It was under Lyndon Johnson that Hoover became a presidential confidant. Lyndon Johnson's admiration for Hoover was almost unbounded. I remember his telling me in 1968 that if it hadn't been for Edgar Hoover, he could have not been President. Johnson's fascination with information and gossip was as insatiable as Hoover's own. In many ways the relationship was not a healthy one because, as subsequent Senate investigations have shown, it was under Johnson that Hoover allowed the FBI to reach its peak of political involvement.

This account is marked by a familiar self-exculpatory bias. As will be shown, the Nixon White House pressed for the total politicization of the FBI and became embittered when Hoover balked because of the risks.

The grim hatchetmen of the Nixon White House had a pressing agenda and little patience with the old man's worn-out pitch—all those political enemies whose files had to be checked, hostile reporters like Jack Anderson and former CBS TV reporter Daniel Schorr to be taken care of, suspected aides to be tapped, Ellsberg to be nailed. It wasn't that the Director didn't try his best; but he was too old and fearful of the judgment of history to keep in step with the new breed.

When Nixon appointee L. Patrick Gray III became Acting Director, the White House takeover of the Bureau was completed. The White House did not hesitate to ask Gray to develop material on how it might handle campaign issues relating to criminal justice. Gray permitted the Bureau to become part of the Watergate cover-up, supplied information to the White House upon request, and even coached Deputy Attorney General Richard Kleindienst to prepare for his testimony before the Senate Judiciary Committee on the charge that the Department had compromised its case against the International Telephone and Telegraph Company (ITT) in return for promised contributions and favors.

The Director's need to be close to the throne—a subject to which I shall return—dominated his professional life. It was an element in the "retirement" of three high-placed Bureau functionaries: Cartha DeLoach; Courtney Evans; and William C. Sullivan, who enjoyed relationships with the Johnson, Kennedy, and Nixon administrations, respectively, that were possibly closer than the Director's. More important, it explains the Director's systematic bypassing of his nominal superior, the Attorney General. The escape from bureaucratic control was made relatively simple by the fact that the office of Attorney General, more than any other cabinet level post, has become an extension of the presidency, a circumstance reflected in the fact that many Attorneys General were selected primarily for their political qualifications and could always console themselves over Hoover's direct White House relationship with the reflection that they both worked for the same boss.

Although he consulted with the Roosevelt era Attorneys General more frequently than in later years, Hoover encountered little if any resistance from them to his autonomy. A close associate of Attorney General Francis Biddle, Edward J. Ennis, recalls in an interview with the author:

> Once Hoover developed this personal relationship with President Roosevelt, there was no stopping him. The Attorney General—whether it was Murphy, Jackson, or Biddle—had neither the guts nor the inclination to tangle with the man they were supposed to supervise and control. After all Hoover was only a Bureau chief in a large department, but he was allowed to write his own ticket. All three abdicated their responsibilities. There was also a feeling that he was tapping his critics and potential critics and even deeper fear that he had files on everybody.

One telling clue to this abdication was the fact that no attempt was made to limit or control Hoover's headline-hunting and propaganda activities. Before the very eyes of his superiors, Hoover distorted a routine bureaucratic publicity function into a vast system of opinion formation. From 1940 until 1945 he was responsible for some fifty articles and speeches on communism, spies, and crime, many of them bursting with contempt for the values of his superiors. And even the crude self-promotion that offended many Roosevelt supporters in Congress drew no rebuke from the Attorney General's office. While the Justice Department's responsibilities forced the Director into a measure of accommodation, in the internal security field it was he alone who called the tune.

His surface deference and compliance with liaison formalities concealed both personal contempt and power strivings. Only weeks after Frank Murphy was named Attorney General in late December 1938, Hoover opened a secret file on him that ultimately covered a ten-year period and contained derogatory items about his private life. He clashed with his successor, Robert H. Jackson, and carried his case to the White House. Attorney General Biddle did rein Hoover in on one occasion, ordering him to terminate a list of candidates for custodial detention—many of them prominent and far from radical. But Hoover faked compliance with this directive and continued the listing under another name.

In the sixteen-year period between the Truman and Kennedy presidencies, Hoover consolidated his power, established bureaucratic autonomy, and developed a political base, not with the mere acquiescence of his superiors (Attorneys General Tom Clark, J. Howard McGrath, J. P. McGranery, Herbert Brownell, and William P. Rogers) but with their complete approval. The process by which Hoover came to dominate the Department in the internal security area may be traced in the annual reports of the Attorneys General (Appendix III). In the forties these reports refer modestly to the Bureau's "national defense" responsibilities. But by 1950 we hear suggestions of a broader internal security mission, and in the 1951 report it has fully emerged:

> The advent of World War II . . . served to focus public opinion upon a lesser known but more vitally important responsibility of the Bureau, the maintenance of the country's internal security. The manner in which this wartime task was performed earned the gratitude and respect of all citizens. Its present domestic intelligence work is, in a sense, a continuation of that security program. . . . The spread of Communism and the subversive activities of its adherents represent the greatest and most immediate threat to that security, and it is in the counter-subversive field that the Bureau has achieved its most spectacular success.

As the fifties progress, the Director's style and tone overpower the Attorney General's. The Bureau takes over the section of the Attorney General's report dealing with its achievements, first as ghost and then openly. Ever more clearly, in both Bureau and Department reports, we hear the true voice, performing in muscular rhetoric, reciting the familiar Hooverian medley: the Bureau's supremely important internal security intelligence jurisdiction, delegated by the September 1939 document; the growing danger from Communist front and infiltrated groups; the heroism of informers ("these dedicated men and women") and the debt we owe them; the attacks by subversive critics on our internal security bulwarks; the agents' inhuman internal security workload; their spectacular achievements, which cannot be measured by arrests and convictions; and the never-ending struggle between the indestructible Communists, whose dwindling numbers belie their strength, and their relentless Bureau stalkers.

The Director, beginning with the early fifties, viewed himself as internal security czar, not a subordinate of Attorneys General but their consultant and adviser. They promoted this autonomous role primarily because it was politically useful. The high point of this collaboration was Hoover's 1953 testimony (cited in chapter 3) supporting the charges of President Eisenhower's Attorney General, Herbert Brownell, that ex-President Truman in 1946 had named Harry Dexter White as the U.S. executive director of the International Monetary Fund despite suspicions that he was a Soviet agent. Hoover's eager testimony at a time when Brownell (then Republican Party chairman) was making communism in government a central issue in the 1954 election campaign blemished his nonpolitical, nonpartisan image.

Attorney General Robert F. Kennedy was the first Department head to attempt to take over responsibility for the Bureau's operations—but only in such areas as organized crime and civil rights, not internal security.* He defended the Director from attacks by liberal critics, insisting on his importance both as a spy-catcher and as a check against McCarthyite excesses.[34] In the Johnson era, Hoover reinforced his established institutional autonomy through a personal relationship with LBJ. Attorney General Nicholas Katzenbach inherited the challenge to Hoover's power but fled from a showdown.[35] His successor, Ramsey Clark, made no attempt to limit the FBI's internal security activities, greatly expanded with the encouragement of the Johnson White House, but rejected many of the Director's wiretapping requests. On one occasion Hoover's freewheeling operations led to embarrassing results. In 1967, without the knowledge or approval of the Attorney General, Hoover sent a letter to his good friend, Republican Senator Karl Mundt of South Dakota, stating that Senate ratification of a Soviet-American consular convention which had been negotiated by the State Department would increase the threat of espionage. In the course of the testimony of Secretary of State Dean Rusk in support of ratification, Senator Mundt flashed the letter on an astonished Rusk, who thought he had Hoover's tacit support. In 1965 the Director had himself testified against the treaty and triggered a successful right-wing campaign to prevent ratification. But this time, despite a renewal of the torrent of hate mail from Hoover's followers, the Senate ratified—not, however, before Hoover had been induced to back off by assurances of increased appropriations to enable him to cope with the claimed new espionage problems.[36]

The Director was eager to please Nixon's Attorney General, John Mitchell. At the beginning of the administration he obliged Mitchell by furnishing Bureau file material for use by Congressman Gerald Ford in an attempt to have Supreme Court Justice Douglas impeached. But one freelance effort got him into trouble. In 1971 the Bureau displayed posters in Chinese throughout the Chinatowns of American cities inviting informants to report suspicious activities by Maoist agitators in accordance with a program to combat Chinese "intelligence-gathering and revolution-inspiring activities." Shortly thereafter, President Nixon announced plans for a diplomatic visit to the People's Republic of China —too late to head off the publication of the Director's article in the June 1971

---

*Kennedy did try to control the Bureau's publicity operations by channeling its output through the Departmental Office of Press Information. But it was a paper victory: having asserted the right to review, the Attorney General and his press officers drew back from censoring content, especially in the case of the most controversial materials, the Director's articles and speeches.

Veterans of Foreign Wars magazine warning of the dangers of Maoist subversion. The article was not reprinted as a Bureau pamphlet, as previously promised, for what were given as "budgetary reasons."[37]

Master of the House

Although the White House fathered the Director's career, it was Congress that offered him consistently staunch backing; more, Congress became his real home, the abode of his political family. For the conservative coalition of Republicans and Democrats that dominated the Congress for almost a quarter of a century, Hoover was an indispensable asset. As the authoritative voice of anticommunism he contributed to the political debate on basic issues—racial equality, peace, urban and campus unrest—in a context that equated change with subversion. Dissenters, if not themselves subversive, were the victims of agitators; their protest weakened the nation's unity and cohesion and thus invited the aggression of reds waiting in the wings for just such an opening. In the sixties he discovered what he called "opinion subversion . . . developed with such diabolical skill that . . . a surprising number of victims are transformed into the active promotion of causes which advance communist aims and ideas, blind to the basic communist strategy to further communist aims with non-communist hands. . . ."[38]

Duplicating the structure of Hoover's national constituency, a smaller, more committed group of legislators served as a sort of palace guard, composed of personal admirers, former agents—between 1950 and 1971, some seventy-five of them served in the House—and legislative spokesmen for nativism and racism. While a number of conservative senators held fast as his unwavering champions and collaborators, the House furnished a more numerous and enthusiastic claque. Fulsome tributes (frequently composed and prepared for delivery by the Bureau) rang through the House on his birthday and the anniversaries of his appointment to the Directorship; its contribution to his fortieth anniversary celebration in May 1964 was a unanimous vote of congratulations, gratitude, and hope for his continuance in office. His articles, speeches, reports, testimony, favorable reviews of his books, editorials, laudatory resolutions by local groups, interviews, news items, and feature stories all found their way—many more than once—into the *Congressional Record.* Equally extraordinary, as I will show in the next section, was the exploitation of the *Record* by his legislative supporters to attack the Director's critics. From 1940 until his death, the volume of *Record* speeches and insertions on the subject of the Director (overwhelmingly laudatory) dwarfs the coverage of any other single figure in American life.

The Director's allies on the Hill knew that they could count on him in a pinch—whether personal or political. Consider the case of Connecticut Senator Thomas J. Dodd. An ex-special agent, Dodd had for years stood out as a Bureau champion in the Senate both in floor speeches and in closed committee hearings. Hoover showed his gratitude by extending to Dodd the use of Bureau facilities for an investigation of a staff member. When Dodd himself was charged with corruption, the Director tried desperately to bail him out. Hoover's agents trailed the Dodd aide who had accused the senator in order to find some compromising evidence to discredit him, and treated him as though he was the accused rather than the accuser.[39] According to Drew Pearson and Jack Anderson, who aired the corruption charges against Dodd, Bureau agents after photographing relevant file documents about the case turned the investigation around into an inquiry concerning their sources. The Director expressed his gratitude to a later Bureau champion, ex-agent Congressman Lawrence Hogan, by presenting him with a plaque with the FBI seal "for his outstanding support of law enforcement and the FBI."[40]

As Hoover's prestige rose, congressmen and senators alike, far from seeking to exercise oversight, became clients eager for his patronage. He responded only to congenial legislative requests, ignoring potentially hostile ones. Congressional anti-subversive committees—heavily staffed by former Bureau agents—also served as the Director's champions and defenders, a legislative extension of his ministry.* There were functional as well as ideological ties: the committees were given secret access to Bureau files; subjects who refused to talk to Bureau agents found themselves faced with committee subpoenas; Bureau agents arranged for their informers to surface in committee hearings in order to publicize information and identifications.[41] The more prestigious Director regularly provided the committees with endorsements and reports when under attack—sometimes in the form of a signed letter.

Hoover also earned the gratitude of these panels through substantive contributions. In addition to testimony before the Senate Internal Security Subcommittee (SISS), he periodically gave it a "statement," usually dealing with a subject such as "The Communist Party Line" or an analysis of an event such as a Communist Party convention. In 1959 the subcommittee attached to one of its hearings, as an appendix, a Hoover magazine article entitled "Communist Illusion and Democratic Reality," in order to give it wider circulation. He testified more frequently before the House Internal Security Committee (HISC) and at its request prepared a report, *Communist Target—Youth,* defending the committee in the wake of a turbulent two-day hearing in San Francisco in May of 1960. Both committees gushed over his wisdom. Here is a sample from a House committee document about a Hoover speech: "[O]ne of the most significant and informative statements ever made on . . . subversive activities in the United States. . . . Because of its prodigious importance, the entire address . . . is reprinted here in full."[42]

Hoover's collaboration with Senator Joseph R. McCarthy's Government

---

*A striking example of this collaboration turned up in documents in the released FBI files of the National Committee Against Repressive Legislation (NCARL), the foremost critic of the anti-subversive committees. Bureau agents surveilled and harassed the group's Executive Director, Frank Wilkinson, disrupted its meetings, planted false reports about its activities in the press, shared its NCARL files with private groups such as the American Legion, disseminated anonymous "poison-pen" letters; sabotaged fund-raising efforts, infiltrated the leadership with provocateurs, resorted to burglaries, warrantless wiretaps, and examination of bank records, and sought to discredit its lobbying efforts. It turned over to the House Un-American Activities Committee and its successor, the House Internal Security Committee (HUAC/HISC) materials such as petitions to abolish the committee or cut its appropriation which were then used by the committee and its spokesmen to denounce NCARL as subversive.

Operations Subcommittee was equally tight, though more discreet (he was also a personal friend and admirer of the Wisconsin senator).

In turn, as the heat began to rise around the Director, the committees came to the rescue, attacking his critics as subversive. On the eve of a conference on the FBI in the fall of 1971, sponsored by the Committee for Public Justice (CPJ), HISC Chairman Richard Ichord released dossiers of CPJ members in an attempt to discredit the conference.

Not only were his potential critics intimidated by fear of the political consequences and personal blackmail (a subject dealt with later); he was shielded, too, by a phalanx of allies. For example, Warren Commission member Gerald Ford became a trusted Bureau informant within the panel, transmitting reports of secret testimony and deliberations.[43] And Southern legislators who shared Hoover's racism and political conservatism generally guarded his interests zealously. The Director's most important, though not most vocal, ally was Mississippi Senator James Eastland, chairman both of the Senate Internal Security Subcommittee and of the parent Judiciary Committee, charged until 1976 with exclusive responsibility—both legislative and investigative—for Bureau affairs. Eastland used his formidable powers to protect the Bureau from hostile investigation.* Eastland's colleague, the late Mississippi Senator John Stennis, returned and marked "Unread" a report on the FBI's involvement in Watergate that was submitted to him, as chairman of an FBI oversight subcommittee, by Senator Howard Baker.[44] Through a network of agents on leave or special assignment to grateful committee chairmen, the Director was informed of developments of interest to the agency (such as Bureau criticism by witnesses or legislators), as well as more personal matters.†

But the heart of the legislative machine was the subcommittee of the House Appropriations Committee assigned to provide funding for the Department of Justice, and chaired for twenty-five years by Congressman John J. Rooney, Hoover's worshipful admirer. The Director made the panel his exclusive congressional forum, pandered to the prejudices of its Southern members (no great effort was required), and to the eagerness of all of them to share his secrets. Transformed by Hoover from outsiders to insiders, they placed an approving imprimatur on his performance on behalf of the entire Congress (House as well as Senate), shielding him from more critical inquiry by congressional doubters and providing the timid with a justification for their silence. Hoover's testimony before the subcommittee was prepared and presented as a piece of theater with ritualistic concern for effect. Questions were planted in advance to produce answers to meet the political needs of committee members—such as the response to a question by a racist congressman that a black government aide had been hired without a security clearance. Juicy morsels of information were periodically thrown to the delighted committee members and intermittently the whole performance went off the record, as the congressmen were initiated by their revered hierophant into the sacred mysteries of anti-subversion. His budge-

*His counterpart in the House for twenty-two years, until he retired, was New York Congressman Emanuel Celler, also a Hoover ally.

†The congressional permanent investigative corps also included former agents, who performed similar services to demonstrate their continued loyalty.

tary requests were rarely denied, possibly a tribute not only to his appeal but to the fact that they were processed by Bureau agents assigned to the subcommittee.[45] Respect for the Director permeates the hearing record:

> We are delighted that you have dealt so successfully with the Communist menace. I do not know what we would have done in this country if it had not been for the FBI. Your foresightedness and efforts certainly reflect upon you and the personnel of your agency who have been persistent in combating those elements that would undermine or threaten our internal security. In the absence of your Bureau, the goal sought by these subversive elements could have well been achieved in this Nation. (1957)

> MR. FLYNT: Mr. Director, it is always gratifying to have you appear before us as a witness, someone who is as forthright as you are.. . . At the same time, someone who has the most comprehensive grasp of the statements that you make to us of any witness with whom I have any knowledge or with whom I have had any experience. . . . I would like to ask you if you are training your Associate Director and your Assistant Director in this fine art that you have mastered, to develop a sense of communication with Members of Congress, members of this Committee and with the public generally in such a way as to naturally instill the confidence that you seem to? (1966)

Representative John J. Flynt, Jr., a Georgia Democrat, did not quite reach the heights attained by Representative Lipscomb, a Republican, who at the end of the 1968 hearings told the Director:

> Mr. Director, it is a real privilege to listen to your testimony. It is always an outstanding presentation. The fact that you disclose in your budget the accomplishments of the FBI and also candidly report the problems in crime enforcement and espionage is always worthwhile. The public is able to get this information through this record. . . . The high regard that the American people have for the FBI and its integrity and the job it is doing is certainly a credit to your leadership and your associates' dedicated efforts.
> HOOVER: Thank you very much.
> LIPSCOMB: It is always a privilege to listen to you.
> HOOVER: Thank you, indeed.

Hoover's testimony—edited, spruced up, and printed by the subcommittee —was reproduced by the Director in a special blown-up edition for distribution to his national constituency, thus providing a flattering forum both for the Director and his committee acolytes.* In addition, portions of his testimony dealing with internal security were reprinted in the *Congressional Record,* sometimes more than once. The entire testimony, as well as official Bureau and Departmental reports, rings with self-congratulation in describing the Bureau's law enforcement triumphs: "new levels of achievement," "outstanding advances," "new all-time highs," "FBI soared to new heights." But the countersubversive testimony and reports claim no "new all-time highs" or "outstanding advances." A more sober tone is heard here, the result not of a selective modesty

---

*The full membership of the appropriations subcommittee was also listed in another, even more widely circulated Bureau publication, *The Story of the Federal Bureau of Investigation,* which, a preface states, was inspired by the subcommittee in order "to acquaint the youth of America with the work of the FBI."

but of a need to keep the Menace alive. Communism was, in Walter Karp's phrase, the Director's "indispensable enemy." No Communist, however committed, could have hoped more ardently for the Party's success. All of his countersubversive pronouncements and writings are unified and explained by a symbiotic formula of alarm and containment. He unremittingly warned his legislative and mass constituency of the undiminished perils of subversion. Yet it would hardly do to create such deep fear as to cast doubt on the Bureau's ability to cope with the situation. As combined arsonist and fire chief, Hoover regularly allayed the fears he had inspired with assurances that his vigilance had frustrated the subversives and prevented them from making their move. But the escape was always a narrow one. He could not cope with the danger by himself —everyone must join in fighting the Menace. His grateful followers applauded his grim warnings and girded themselves anew for the inevitable apocalyptic showdown with the "masters of mirage," "the many-faced monster," "the cancerous growth," "the Moscow masters of deceit" (to dip into the Director's rhetoric), as well as with the "pseudo-liberals" whose challenge to the myth was itself proof of its power. This formula dominated the appropriations hearings for a special reason; as in the twenties, fear-mongering loosened congressional purse strings.

While communism declined in the fifties, Hoover worked harder to maximize the Menace, drawing heavily on his considerable advertising skills. Charts served as a stock means of concealing and exaggerating the reality that words alone might betray. Three or four of them were *de rigueur;* but however graphic or blood-chilling, they could not obscure the numerical decline of the Communists. The Director, however, was never at a loss for an explanation. In 1952 he explained the persistence of the Communist danger in the face of a numerical decline by the fact that they had infiltrated key industries. This concentration among workers "shows the harm they can do notwithstanding the decrease in membership." No less than five charts were submitted to demonstrate more clearly the extent of the peril. And what made it all even more frightening were the "fronts": "There are about 165 such organizations in the country over which we maintain investigative scrutiny. Those organizations try to exploit the masses. They indulge in 'phony' peace fronts; they endeavor to penetrate into such fields as civil rights causes."

Hoover's 1955 testimony conceded that communism had suffered a further numerical decline. But, he tells us, it would be folly to rely on this fact as a measure of the danger to our security. Something new had been added: the reds had gone underground, with the result that "subversive activity today overshadows [what] we experienced during the peak of World War II when we were dealing largely with Nazi and Fascist elements." Where formerly one agent was needed, as many as ten were now required to cover Communist subversives "by reason of their intensive revolutionary training for years." The reduced Communist membership "represents a Trojan horse of rigidly disciplined fanatics unalterably committed to the ideological purposes of worldwide Communism." To make it all clear, the Director quoted from a book by a Communist leader, threw in six charts, and further enlightened the committee with off-the-record inside information.

In the next year the continued loss of membership was again minimized by charts and off-the-record explanations. Besides, this was the "hard core, a fifth-column potential . . . aided by a reservoir of concealed members." But they would not elude the Director: "We have been able to keep abreast of those efforts and are aware of their activities." Particularly trying were "the so-called pseudo-liberals" (doubly condemned, they were not even genuine fakes), who rejected the "menace of communism" as a "mere myth or hysteria." Communist fronts magnified the Communist Menace because Communist leaders themselves had estimated that they outnumbered the actual Party membership by ten to one. And, frightening to contemplate, since 1919, "some 625 groups and organizations" had at one time or another been placed in this class by various governmental agencies. (Left unmentioned was the fact that virtually all of them were defunct.)

The 1957 testimony predictably insists that the Bureau's domestic intelligence responsibilities have "increased in magnitude throughout recent years." A 14 percent drop (to 17,360, itself a highly inflated figure)* in Party membership over the previous year was deceptive: "I must warn that numbers mean nothing in this instance, for there are those nations which have attempted to assess the threat of communism on the basis of numerical strength alone and they are eating the bitter fruit of Communist slavery for their short-sightedness." In 1958 Hoover stopped supplying the subcommittee with figures, but assured its members that "It cannot be emphasized too strongly that the numerical strength of the Communist Party means nothing." Although he subsequently ascribed his discontinuance of numerical estimates to "national security," there was a more prosaic reason: in 1958, *Masters of Deceit* came out. It would have undercut the book's scary message had the true strength of the Communist Party been revealed. The book itself was, for the same reason, silent about the strength of the Communist Party.

Thereafter he stressed the "hard-core," "Trojan horse," "rigidly disciplined fanatics," "part of the predatory empire of the international Communist conspiracy" themes and, always, the invisible and sinister Communist influence on other organizations. In the sixties the thesis of Communist influence, the fall-back position to which Hoover had been forced to retreat when the numbers argument became implausible, was in turn discredited by the emergence of vigorous, broad-based protest movements, manifestly unplanned, offering few agitator scapegoats or links to communism. The Director, particularly anxious to make a contribution to the congressional civil rights debate, chose the appropriation hearings in 1964 to warn that the racial integration struggle was tainted by subversion: the efforts of Communists through propaganda and agitation to expand their influence among blacks. Once again he warned that numbers were unimportant.

In the face of a continuing decline both in Party membership and influence, the Director was increasingly driven to suppress the facts and to rely on Communist hopes, enthusiasm, and optimism—however unfounded and self-serving.

*By 1957 Communist Party membership totaled about 10,000, down from about 43,000 at the beginning of the decade and from 60–80,000 at the height of its popularity in the World War II period.

So in 1965 he testified: "It would be difficult to single out any period since the passage of the Internal Security Act of 1950 in which the optimism of the Communist Party, U.S.A. surpasses that exhibited in 1964." In 1967 he reported that "the Communist Party, U.S.A. is riding the crest of a wave of optimism . . . based on the belief that the political climate in this country is ripe for 'radicalism' and, consequently, the Party can reap substantial benefits from the changing times." By 1969 he was forced to acknowledge "the militancy of the New Left and racial disorders," but while these developments had overshadowed the Old Left, "the threat of Communism has certainly not diminished." In his 1971 testimony he reviewed the activities of a number of groups under surveillance (Panthers, SDS, Weathermen), but continued to dwell on the Party, its menace and its "crest of optimism" ("They visualize many opportunities to exploit the current unsettled conditions in this country"). In the late sixties and early seventies Communist strength faded to an estimated 3000–5000 members in this country, only a fraction of whom could be called activists. But to the end the Director insisted on formulations* that gave Communist subversion eternal life, protected his role of political savior, nourished the conservatism of his constituency in Congress and in the nation, and assured appropriations approval. Increasingly, he vented his bitterness not at history but at the "pseudoliberals" whose challenge to the strength of the Menace was threatening his life's work.

We know all too little about the dynamics by which accumulated social and political pressures finally explode. But the time did arrive when the Director's protective magic failed him. The long congressional slumber may have been initially disturbed by the controversy in the mid-sixties over the wiretapping of Martin Luther King, Jr., and finally broken by the Director's denunciation in a Washington *Post* interview on November 16, 1970, of Attorney General Robert F. Kennedy, for attempting to debase Bureau personnel standards through his insistence on nondiscriminatory recruiting practices, and of a successor, Ramsey Clark, for being a "jellyfish."[46] In the same interview Hoover compounded what seemed to many a reckless partisanship by giving then Attorney General John M. Mitchell the highest marks of any Justice Department head in his long career. On November 30, 1970, Representative William F. Anderson sharply criticized the Director for his Berrigan testimony three days earlier. In the spring of 1971 Senator Edmund S. Muskie told the Senate that FBI agents had spied on peaceful Earth Day rallies the previous year, including one gathering at which he was the principal speaker. "There is not justification," he told his colleagues, "for any part of the federal intelligence community surreptitiously observing and reporting on legitimate political events which do not affect our national security or which do not involve a potential crime."[47] On the House floor, Majority Leader Hale Boggs, Jr., delivered a blast (first in preliminary charges and then, on April 22, in a sixty-minute speech) that his home telephone had been tapped and demanded Hoover's resignation. This was the first major attack on the Director by a politically important figure.[48] While Boggs's evi-

---

*The introduction to *On Communism,* Hoover's final effort to rescue the Menace, warned of the dangers of "becoming ideologically disarmed" (p. 54) and assured readers that the Party's frustrations were merely the result of transient tactical problems that would ultimately be resolved.

dence seemed to some unpersuasive,* documentary proof came to light at the same time in a court case that FBI agents had tapped telephone conversations between Texas Representative John Dowdy and a Bureau informer, casting doubt on Deputy Attorney General Richard Kleindienst's prior denial that FBI agents had "used electronic surveillance" on congressmen. The Department explained that a tap was considered "surveillance" only if used without the knowledge of both parties to a conversation. Kleindienst also stated that he welcomed a congressional investigation of the entire issue, but he thought better of it the very next day, an unsurprising reversal in view of the many illegal administration wiretaps then in operation.[49]

There were undeniable elements of self-protection and personal motivation in the Boggs attack and in the support of a few of his colleagues, but the Louisiana congressman had almost singlehandedly placed the FBI and its sacrosanct chief on the agenda of serious congressional concern. In April and May of 1971 batches of intelligence documents stolen from the Media, Pennsylvania, Bureau office were released to the press and made available to a few congressmen. On their face, they invited criticism both of the Bureau's operational techniques and of its target selection. One congressman, Representative Henry S. Reuss, tried unsuccessfully to obtain Bureau files about his daughter, the subject of some of the released documents, and called for an investigation. The Bureau's embarrassment was compounded by its failure to catch the culprits. (And because the Director thought the Xerox Corporation had been uncooperative in the investigation, he ordered a Bureau-wide switch to IBM machines.)

But the most detailed attack on the Director and the Bureau came from Senator George McGovern. The South Dakota senator admitted to a certain bias: on the eve of the South Dakota senatorial election in 1960, Hoover had saluted McGovern's successful opponent, Karl Mundt, in full-page advertisements published statewide, which, it was widely thought, influenced the outcome of the race.† The senator's bill of particulars was substantial,[50] beginning with the disciplinary transfer, for "atrocious judgment," of a Bureau agent, John F. Shaw, who criticized the Director in a letter (filched from discarded copies in a typing pool and rushed to Hoover) written to a professor giving a course at John Jay College in New York. Hoover also ordered fifteen agents who were enrolled in the course to drop out. When a TWA pilot accused Bureau agents of mishandling a hijacking, McGovern told Congress, Hoover attempted to

*What is clear is that Boggs's conversations with Speaker McCormack's office were overheard in the course of an investigation of McCormack's confidential assistant Martin Sweig and a suspected influence peddler, Nathan Voloshen. What especially infuriated Boggs was an FBI derogatory rundown that included allegations of heavy drinking; but this blind report could well have been a standard Crime Records Division memorandum based on material obtained from sources other than wiretaps.

†To preserve the appearance of evenhandedness, Hoover named, along with Mundt, Congressman John Rooney of New York; Speaker John McCormack of Massachusetts, both Democrats, and Senator Styles Bridges of New Hampshire, a Republican like Mundt. The Director proclaimed them all "outstanding members . . . fearless men," braving "the scorn and abuse that would be heaped upon them by the Communist pseudo-liberals and others of like ilk. . . ." Of the South Dakota senator, Hoover said, "The Communists both here and abroad have long felt the heel of Senator Karl Mundt . . . as the author of a number of anti-Communist bills and as an active, courageous member of several committees seeking to expose and fight this menace—he has truly combined experience, knowledge and far sightedness."

destroy the pilot's career on the basis of an item dug out of his Air Force record. When this failed, he decreed a Bureau boycott of the airline and forbade agents from acting as air marshals on TWA flights. This move, like the Xerox decree, was finally abandoned. During this period Hoover forced the resignations of three Bureau clerks who had volunteered to stuff envelopes for a peace group, and ordered eleven others to drop an American University course because of a derogatory remark by the instructor. (Five reenrolled after the university president apologized.)[51]

The administration, itself unhappy with the Director but unwilling, as it prepared its reelection bid, to appear to yield to Democratic critics, rallied to his support. Attorney General Mitchell unctuously reproved Hale Boggs: "He should recant at once and apologize to a great man." Nixon said that he had been "maligned unfairly" and that "the great majority of Americans back Mr. Hoover."[52] The Director responded in kind; he hailed President Nixon as he presented him with a set of gold cufflinks with the Bureau seal as the guardian of "the destiny of the free world," and Attorney General Mitchell, the recipient of a gold special agent's badge, as the inspiration of a confidence in law enforcement "which we didn't have before your administration."[53]

To deal with Bureau defectors and congressional critics, Hoover now brought out his heavy artillery. He circulated through Bureau channels a long anonymous memorandum, "The FBI: Target of KGB Department of Disinformation," reinforced by ten bulky exhibits which charged, among other things, that an unsigned letter supporting McGovern, assertedly on behalf of Bureau agents and written on Bureau stationery, was a KGB concoction. Twenty-one upper-echelon administrators, led by Clyde Tolson, who orchestrated the response, rebuked the senator in the vituperative prose that had become a trademark of the Director's replies to critics.* These letters, inserted by the senator into the *Record,* were followed by what he called "an avalanche of mail from lower-level FBI employees" protesting McGovern's attack.

Yet amidst the *Sturm und Drang,* the ranks held firm as the *Record* sprouted posies for the Director and weeds for his critics. The fight-back crested in a planned congressional oratorical round robin on May 10, 1971, the forty-

---

*Thus Tolson wrote, "I term you an opportunist because it is no small coincidence that you have singled out a man of Mr. Hoover's national stature for attack at a time when waves of publicity are urgently needed to buoy your political career." Assistant to the Director John Mohr told McGovern, "In thirty-seven years of government service, I have never witnessed any act so grossly irresponsible or so transparently self-serving as your reprehensible actions in issuing a press release attacking Director Hoover and calling for an inquiry into his administration of the FBI." The other letters are only slightly less intemperate: "an attempt to mislead the people," "extraordinarily reprehensible," "gullible," "an attempt to raise [your] stature at the expense of others," "your motives are . . . suspect," "a new low in the campaign to malign J. Edgar Hoover," "demagogue."

A somewhat milder letter was belatedly sent by Assistant Director William C. Sullivan, calling the Senator's attention to the Director's "unique record" and complaining of the "undisciplined attack" on the Director and the "obvious ill-will motivating it." When the letter was written, Sullivan himself was in the Director's doghouse for an address which had offended Hoover by denying that domestic communism was responsible for the unrest of the sixties. Thereafter, in August, Sullivan himself wrote the Director a letter highly critical of Bureau policies; and in late September the Director abruptly terminated Sullivan's thirty-year Bureau service by replacing his office locks. Sullivan subsequently emerged as a critic harsher in some respects than McGovern himself. See Sullivan, pp. 242–243, 265–277.

seventh anniversary of Hoover's appointment. Some seventy-one House members and five senators swore fealty; twenty-seven pages of the *Record* were filled with House speeches alone.[54] Only after the Director had departed would an investigation become politically feasible; the old lion's domination of Congress had freed him from meaningful oversight for the entire period of his tenure, an eloquent contrast to the pre-1924 investigations that had exposed the abuses of the GID under Palmer and Daugherty. The 1972 Senate hearing (already referred to) on Hoover's proposed successor finally pierced the protective dike. That it was this hearing that served as an initial outlet for long-suppressed criticism was ironic, for it was conducted pursuant to a 1968 statutory provision for Senate approval of future Bureau directors, a measure sponsored by conservative Republicans and favored by Hoover, certain that his Senate allies would block any appointment not to his liking in the event of his retirement.[55]

Knowledge Is Power

In his articles, speeches, pamphlets, and testimony, Hoover triumphantly confronted godless communism with Christianity and democratic freedom. But his neo-fundamentalism allowed no room for the forgiveness of his enemies; nor did his sloganized version of freedom extend to his critics and opponents. Presidents, legislators, and Supreme Court Justices might be legitimate targets of criticism and even of impeachment drives, but not the Director. Like the classic tyrant, his absolutism in the exercise of power was matched by his ruthlessness in suppressing criticism. In Hoover's case, this response is the master symptom of a pathological syndrome (discussed below) rooted in an obsession with power. Even before he took on his internal security assignment, Hoover seems to have convinced himself of his greatness. This megalomania was suggested by the life-size bronze bust of himself that greeted visitors in the foyer of his home and the framed text in his office, which read in part: "In every field of human endeavor, he that is first must perpetually live in the white light of publicity. . . . When a man's work becomes a standard for the whole world, it also becomes a target for the shafts of the envious few."[56]

Radical-hunting gave the Director far more effective ammunition for dealing with criticism: it was all part of a red plot. This response, implemented by attacks on the motivations and backgrounds of individual critics, was soon politicized by treating all criticism as evidence of subversion, proof of the power of the Menace, and a vindication of the Director's contribution to the national security. Every knock became a boost. The Director's periodic announcements that his undercover agents had brought him fresh evidence of a plot to destroy him renewed gratitude for his vigilance and made spicy copy. "Communists at a meeting yesterday in New York," he told a *Time* magazine interviewer in 1940, "have instructed two of their best writers to portray me as a Broadway glamor-boy and particularly to inquire into my affairs with women in New York." Later, the KGB replaced the domestic Communists as the snake in the Director's grass.

As his power grew, his counterattacks became bolder. After an unsuccessful attempt to block the publication, in 1950, of Max Lowenthal's critical book on the Bureau, Hoover launched a campaign to discredit and even suppress it. Agents were assigned to prepare material for use in answering the book's charges, savage book reviews were made available to Hoover's media friends, and booksellers were pressured by agents in the field not to stock the book. The fact that its author was a prominent lawyer in the field of railroad reorganization and a former close aide of President Truman did not prevent the Director from attacking him as a subversive. In an anticipation of later practice, a House committee was induced to interrogate the author in executive session in an effort to discredit him, and a Hoover ally attacked Lowenthal on the House floor. Similar drives by specially assigned teams of agents were initiated against four other authors of critical books on the Bureau: William W. Turner, Fred J. Cook, Bernard Conner, and Norman Ollestad.* In response to a Fund for the Republic study, which concluded that the FBI had inflated the extent and influence of domestic communism, the Director ordered a Bureau counterattack on both the Fund and its head, Dr. Robert M. Hutchins. An initial report, based on the Bureau's files, did not satisfy the vengeful Director, and he ordered a harsher treatment, which was then leaked to the press. When W. H. Ferry, an officer of the Fund, lambasted the Bureau in 1962, a Bureau compilation of background file material (including Ferry's years in high school) was circulated to Hoover's friends on Capitol Hill and leaked to the press. Henry Steele Commager, a distinguished American scholar and Bureau critic, also became a target: field agents were instructed to attack him by leaking material to local media. Hutchins, Commager, and many other prominent critics were entered on a no-contact list of people who were to be denied Bureau information. Inclusion on the list, ultimately extending to 332 entries, was triggered by a "name check" report on the subject.

The defections of former agents particularly enraged the Director.† After former agent Jack Levine published an article attacking the Director, Hoover succeeded in barring him from other employment in the Justice Department, and tried to prevent his admission to the Arizona bar. Hoover charged that Los Angeles *Times* reporter Jack Nelson had been assigned to write derogatory articles about him and spent three hours with a top executive of the newspaper

---

*Lyle Stuart, publisher of Ollestad's book, *Inside the FBI,* was first placed under surveillance in 1951 after publishing an article critical of Hoover's friend, Walter Winchell. Ollestad's book, with its attack on the Director, led to the standard pattern of harassment used against writer-critics (planted hecklers in TV studios where interviews were conducted, teams of agents assigned to write protest letters and make abusive telephone calls to studio executives, and the dissemination of hostile Bureau-drafted book reviews). In addition, the field was instructed, as in the case of other critics, to develop discrediting materials about Stuart—a mission which produced a series of false reports, including charges that he was "an articulate member of a Soviet apparatus," a friend of Lowenthal's son (whom he had never met) and a "known homosexual who frequents midtown bars." This last (wholly invented) tidbit so delighted Hoover ("Good stuff!") that he chose to ignore an accompanying caution that its source was an informer "whose reliability has yet to be tested"—Lyle Stuart, "The FBI and Me," *Seven Days,* July 1978.

†The Society of Former FBI Agents expelled Richard Schott and Norman Ollestad for writing books critical of the Director and the Bureau. Hoover's vendetta against ex-agent William W. Turner included confrontations by agents assigned to silence him, and instructions to deny assistance or information to a magazine that published one of his articles. "FBI Harasses Its Critics," *Freedom,* October 1979.

urging Nelson's discharge. Investigative files were maintained on critical journalists such as Harry Hoffman, editor of the Charleston *Gazette,* and James Wechsler, *New York Post* columnist. After monitoring the planning in 1959 of a *Post* series on the Bureau through an informer, Bureau agents gained access to the Washington hotel room of its investigative team in a search for material to discredit the reporter.[57] The Director mobilized his congressional allies to discredit critics through a device that became standard practice: the author's file was made available to friendly journalists, whose product was then reproduced in the *Congressional Record* with an introductory denunciation by a congressional ally. Washington lawyer Joseph Rauh, a leader of the Americans for Democratic Action, and Alan Barth, Washington *Post* editorial writer, both received this treatment. The Director's obliging proxies were, in Rauh's case, Senator Hickenlooper, and in Barth's case, Senator Goldwater. An article by the author on campus FBI spies inspired two newspaper stories by Edward J. Mowery, based on Bureau files, which were then introduced into the *Record* by Senator Mundt.[58] Mowery's journalism was also used to implement the Director's counterattack against a long article by Fred J. Cook, critical of the Bureau, which appeared in the *Nation* magazine. Secretly fed Bureau materials, he published a series of newspaper stories dealing with an alleged Communist plot to "get" Hoover and the FBI. In the spring of 1959 the entire series was reprinted as a Senate document at the request of Republican Senator Roman Hruska of Nebraska and distributed by the Government Printing Office.*

When the subversive treatment was inappropriate, critics were charged with seeking to "undermine confidence in law enforcement" or with political motivations. The fact that the Director was increasingly using the Bureau for political ends—his own and his allies'—seemed only to lend added vehemence to his claim that he alone stood guard against the political corruption of the Bureau. Had he not consented to assume leadership of the agency in 1924 only on Stone's reassurance that he would be allowed to keep it free of politics? A self-righteous response was, especially in the later years, matched by an abusive tone. Hoover's answer to a rather restrained factual piece in the conservative *National Observer* in 1971 states that it was "slanted, unfair, distorted, fantasy, sensationalized, an outright lie . . . a blatant attempt to set forth a string of innuendoes, inaccuracies and plain outright distortions in such a manner [that] they give the appearance of representing true facts which they do not."

But it was the *potential* critics that the Director handled most efficiently— through intimidation and the fear of possible blackmail. When in the Kennedy years he felt threatened by rumors of replacement, he warned that his files could be used by a successor for evil ends. One of his closest journalistic collaborators, the syndicated columnist Paul Harvey, wrote (April 25, 1963) that the Director

*Perhaps the most striking illustration of press criticism as a triggering mechanism for bizarre behavior is the Director's investigation in the mid-fifties of the late Walt Kelly, cartoonist of the comic strip *Pogo,* which featured a recognizable caricature of Hoover. The Director ordered a cryptanalysis by Bureau experts of the dialogue of sample strips to determine whether its humor concealed further disparagement—in code. According to released FOIA documents, the report concludes: "Efforts were made to interpret specimens Q 1–Q 10 according to purported meaning supplied [but] examination did not reveal any technical basis to establish validity of interpretations of the submitted 'Pogo' cartoons."

was "keeper of the keys to the closet where our considerable conglomeration of skeletons are stored." The FBI files, Harvey explained, were so complete as to threaten almost every appointed or elected official. Only the Director "stands as a sentinel" to protect us from "persons who would use them for political blackmail."[59] The Harvey column does not explain how Hoover acquired such potentially damaging files, but the present threat is unmistakable: If you dump the Director, you won't have anyone to protect your dirty little secrets. The use of intelligence for private blackmail, a long-established abuse, had been a prominent aspect of the corruption in the Burns Bureau which had led to the appointment of the Director. But here, as elsewhere, the doctor contracted the disease: the collection and use of information about the private lives of subjects—sexual activities, drinking habits, gambling proclivities, and similar items—became a vital asset in the Director's climb to power. Beyond this Hoover took a voyeuristic delight, bordering on the kinky, in the boudoir exploits and "sexual hang-ups" of public figures. While not squarely in the line of duty, monitoring the passions of the powerful and their possibly compromising pillow talk could be justified as a protection of the national security. Immorality and subversion, in the Director's book, were closely linked. A politician's girlfriend might be a Mata Hari,[60] an agent of the KGB. Active investigation of public figures yielded a substantial flow of such private information not only about the subject, as in the case of Dr. Martin Luther King, Jr., but about others not under investigation, especially where electronic surveillance was employed. An even more fertile source was the data, largely rumor and gossip, volunteered by neighbors, associates, relatives, enemies, and opponents of the subject. Secret Service dossiers on the personal and private lives of thousands of prominent Americans in all spheres (theater, politics, sports) were also duplicated for Bureau use, as were the files of urban police departments. It was widely known in the field that an agent could earn the Director's gratitude by routing all such material to him.[61]

An offering of personal information was, in the beginning, Hoover's own way of ingratiating himself with his superiors. Attorney General Francis Biddle recalled that:

> I sought to invite [Hoover's] confidence and before long, lunching alone with me in a room adjoining my office, he began to reciprocate by sharing some of his extraordinary broad knowledge of the intimate details of what my associates in the Cabinet did and said, of their likes and dislikes, their weaknesses, and their associations.[62]

All Presidents, from Roosevelt to Nixon, were regaled with spicy tidbits about political opponents, critical journalists, and celebrities. For at least one of them, Lyndon B. Johnson, it became favorite bedtime reading. According to Benjamin C. Bradlee, a close friend, President Kennedy said of these offerings: "Boy, the dirt [Hoover] has on these senators. You wouldn't believe it." The Director, Bradlee recalled, even brought Kennedy a picture of a Capitol Hill prostitute plying her trade. H. R. Haldeman told TV newscaster Mike Wallace in an interview that such offerings were made to President Nixon as a form of "lobbying for the FBI . . . [the Director] was [not only] trying to provide information . . . of non-official interest to the President, but also trying to pique the President's curiosity and his respect for the FBI's ability to find things out and stay on top of things, as a means of . . . fighting . . . for his agency in terms of Presidential support."

As advancing age threatened Hoover's tenure and placed it at the mercy of the President, Hoover's scandal-mongering became more ardent, both as a bid for favor and as an expression of gratitude for his retention. When the Director turned seventy-six, on January 1, 1971, he institutionalized the transmission of scandal to the White House through a program called Code Inlet. A memorandum entitled FBI INTELLIGENCE LETTER FOR THE PRESIDENT states that "the Bureau during 1969 initiated captioned program of furnishing high-level intelligence data in the security field to the President and the Attorney General on a continuing basis. The material to be furnished is not of a routine nature but rather that which has the qualities of importance and timeliness necessary to secure the President's interest and to provide him with meaningful intelligence for his guidance." One category of information is described as "Items of an unusual twist or concerning prominent personalities which may be of special interest to the President or the Attorney General." The meaning of this item is explained by a special gloss: "It is to be noted that the type of information desired . . . may be obtained through investigations, not wholly related to the security field."

This voyeuristic intelligence was not confined to Presidents, but was shared with others as an offering of friendship, payment for a favor, a bid for support —and a covert threat. In our moralizing society a private scandal can be the nemesis of the most promising career, and the fear, however unsubstantiated, that the Director was privy to personal secrets was enough to silence potential critics. No one knew this better than the Director; he tried to convey to Presidents and legislators alike that he knew more about them than he actually did, that, in Nixon's phrase, "He had files on everybody." When the subject was classified a subversive or a Bureau critic, the exposure was predictably broader, as in the case of the circulation of the Martin Luther King, Jr., wiretap tapes and transcripts. These were made available to Presidents Johnson and Nixon, to congressmen and senators, personal friends and editors (of *Reader's Digest* and *Newsweek*), and were offered to the news press as well. When the Warren Commission investigation into President Kennedy's assassination was attacked, Hoover leaked file material to a Commission member, Hale Boggs, about the personal lives of the critics, including photographs of sexual activities, the fruits of surveillance programs authorized by President Johnson.[63]

Investigative files on the subject of racial unrest are particularly rich in scandalous material. Black leaders who were prominent targets included Walter Fauntroy, congressional representative (nonvoting) for the District of Columbia, Martin Luther King, Jr., Coretta King, his widow, Ralph Abernathy, Jesse Jackson, Floyd McKissick, Roy Wilkins, and Bayard Rustin. Many of these files contain the fruits of bedroom electronic surveillance, including details about the sex lives of the subjects.

Watergate Committee testimony by H. R. Haldeman and others indicates that the White House freely obtained Bureau file material for "background information." The Bureau contends that its collection of celebrity files was based on public record information, but the folders are full of personal details supplied to investigators by sources hostile to the subject, "informants," landlords, taxi drivers, waiters, and the like, reporting, for example, the fact that a famous novelist is a homosexual; or that a prominent conductor was a friend of a priest actively opposed to the war. The file subjects include football stars Lance Rentzel and Joe Namath; actors Marlon Brando, Paul Newman, Rock Hudson, Tony Randall, Donald Sutherland, Harry Belafonte, and Zero Mostel; actresses Jane Fonda and Eartha Kitt, boxers Joe Louis and Muhammad Ali; entertainer Dick Gregory and atheist Madalyn Murray O'Hair.

While the files deal in part with the politics of the subjects, we find in almost all of them a heavy concentration of personal items. Here is one wholly unrelated to politics:

> "X" [name deleted here] has not been the subject of an FBI investigation. During 1965, however, a confidential informant reported that several years ago while he was in New York he had an "affair" with movie star "X." The informant stated that from personal knowledge he knew that "X" was a homosexual. The belief was expressed that by "personal knowledge" the informant meant he had personally indulged in homosexual acts with "X" or had witnessed or received the information from individuals who had done so.
>
> On another occasion, information was received by the Los Angeles Office of the FBI that it was common knowledge in the motion picture industry that "X" was suspected of having homosexual tendencies.
>
> It is to be noted in May, 1961, a confidential source in New York also stated that "X" definitely was a homosexual.
>
> Our files contain no additional pertinent information identifiable with "X."
>
> The fingerprint files of the Identification Division of the FBI contain no arrest data identifiable with "X" based upon background information submitted in connection with this name check request.

A prime source of personal data was the Crime Records Division which, in accordance with Bureau policy, routinely prepared "name check" memoranda on congressmen, public officials, and prominent individuals in private life considered of interest to the Director. These dossiers, many of which were ultimately stored in the Director's private "Official and Confidential" (OC) file collection, include for example memoranda on all the members of Senator Edward V. Long's subcommittee, which threatened (in 1966–67) to investigate the Bureau.[64] Of the 164 folders in the Director's OC collection, some 48 contain derogatory information about prominent persons, including members of Congress, and in one case a memorandum that the Director had disseminated derogatory information about a congressional critic. The files reflect a strong preoccupation with the rumored homosexuality of various politicians and government officials, including Hoover himself.[65]

Material on congressmen was also collected in Bureau investigative files,* begun, in some cases, before they took office. The Director denied Hale Boggs's

---

*Information about the private lives of legislators served a variety of purposes besides blackmail. Documents reveal, for example, that details about the private life of Congressman Daniel Rostenkowski were fed to a Chicago informer in order to bolster his cover as a double agent assigned by the Polish government to monitor Chicago's Polish-American community.

charges that House members had been wiretapped and bugged, but could not deny that details about the lives of congressmen were overheard over tapped lines. Two outstanding examples of such inputs into the phone conversations of congressmen are the bugging of the phone of lobbyist Fred Black in 1966 and the subsequent tapping of phones in the Voloshen-Sweig investigation. On February 28, 1974, Congressman Bertram Podell, under criminal indictment, charged that his phone had been tapped. An affidavit by Attorney General William B. Saxbe stated that "one of the defendants" in the Podell case had, in the congressman's words, "been electronically surveilled on numerous occasions in the interests of national security as the result of an order of the President of the United States, Richard Nixon." Embassy taps also provided a useful input, not only to legislators but to Executive Department officials as well. According to reliable accounts, Bureau agents lent to congressional investigative staffs—a common practice— were instructed to report back "personal derogatory information" about members of Congress, either orally or in "Do Not File" memos for the Director's perusal. When the Director acquired a possibly damaging item of information from any source, he discreetly conveyed his reassurances to the legislator that it would be forever locked in his bosom. As Sullivan put it in describing this practice, "From that time on [he] would be right in Hoover's pocket."[66]

Beginning in 1950, the Bureau commenced a program of gathering and filing information on nonincumbent candidates for Congress, the Congressional Relations Service, another Crime Records Division operation. In the summer of 1972 this practice came to light as the result of the investigative inquiries of a Lorain, Ohio, FBI agent into the background of the democratic candidate for Congress in Ohio's 13th District. Acting Director L. Patrick Gray, in a press release terminating the program, explained:

> The information was gathered for our own internal use and not in response to any regulation or statute. At first, information was sought only on nonincumbent candidates for Congress. In 1960, the requests were expanded to include nonincumbent candidates for Governorships, since FBI officials also felt their contacts with Governors could be enhanced by some prior knowledge of the individual's background.

As with the celebrity files, Gray contended that these files were noninvestigative public record compilations. Yet, according to an FBI source, "We ran a hell of a clipping operation, but it went far beyond that." Gray himself admitted that the publicly available material was:

> . . . augmented by a summary of any data (already in the files) of the field office. This might include correspondence exchanged with the candidate; memoranda concerning personal contacts; results of investigations involving the candidate, either as a subject, a victim, a witness, or a reference; or information voluntarily submitted to the FBI.

What Gray did not say is that the Bureau fed the Congressional Relations Service information to friendly incumbents and initiated special investigations of challengers to help a friendly incumbent.

The House Appropriations Committee members and its chairman, John Rooney, in particular—or rather, his political opponents—received special treatment for reasons hardly inscrutable. In 1972 the Bureau, on Hoover's orders, investigated Rooney's opponent Allard K. Lowenstein and, according to a Bureau source, gave Rooney "everything we knew" about the challenger. In 1968 Rooney had been unsuccessfully challenged for the Democratic congressional nomination by a young civil rights lawyer, Peter Eikenberry. Eikenberry claimed that Rooney made use of two smear items against him: that as an undergraduate, fourteen years earlier, he had been arrested on a minor charge, and that he had been dismissed from an ROTC unit—information which, Eikenberry claimed, could only have come from the Bureau. A document subsequently released in a federal court suit revealed that, pursuant to a request by Rooney relayed through a former agent in the appropriations committee staff, Hoover approved a recommendation that some material be furnished in a "blind" memorandum. The memorandum describes an innocuous incident of a "public record" type in Eikenberry's past, and also the fact that Hoover vetoed a suggestion for a "discreet check" of Eikenberry.[67]

In the same way, Hoover did not hesitate to use the investigative resources of the Bureau to "get" a congressman or senator who had offended him. As, for example, Tennessee Congressman William Anderson, whose attack (see p. 88) on the Director's Harrisburg testimony inspired an intensive Bureau probe. When the report of the assigned Nashville agents yielded no usable information, Hoover ordered a second round. A call girl was interrogated, but she denied ever meeting the congressman. Finally, the madam of a local house of prostitution said she thought, on the basis of a photograph shown her by the agents, that the congressman had been a client some years earlier. Hoover wrote "whoremonger" on the agents' reports and passed them on to the White House. Anderson vigorously denied the claimed involvement. It obviously required a special order of courage, not a conspicuous congressional trait, to bring to the open legislative forum the fears and whispers that festered in cloakrooms. And a legislator ready to brave the *corrida* of personal embarrassment, planted media attacks, and constituency disapproval had to bear in mind that a consolatory executive or judicial appointment in the event of a defeat at the polls would entail a Bureau investigation of his background. The Director's effectiveness in mastering the House was eloquently recorded by Congressman Boggs in his April 22 speech:

> Our apathy in this Congress, our silence in this House, our very fear of speaking out in other forums has watered the roots and hastened the growth of a vine of tyranny which is ensnaring that Constitution and Bill of Rights which we are sworn to uphold.

"The Real Me"

Since men are not angels, as Madison reminds us in *The Federalist*, No. 51, we must protect ourselves against the threat of arbitrary or oppressive conduct through laws precisely defining and policing the powers of those who govern us. In the case of the Bureau, we are dealing, not with a "government of men" but of one man, not in a conventional, regulatory area but in the sensitive sphere of dissent, and not for a brief moment in the sunshine of power but for the longest period of one-man rule in our history. For more than three decades the Director's political values and assumptions dominated official conceptions of our internal security and of the conduct that might endanger it. As with Watergate, the Director's career offers disturbing proof of the vulnerability of the democratic process to personalized power drives. Our more narrow concern here, however, is with the political intelligence system, shaped as it was by the values and assumptions of the man who brought it into being.

Hoover's public image as the quintessential anti-Communist served, in varying measure, two purposes for each successive administration: proof to its opponents of its all-out anti-Communist commitment, and reassurance to liberals of its moderation. But the Director's first role as anti-Communist scourge and symbol completely submerged the second as buffer against irresponsibility and vigilantism. Throughout his entire internal security ministry, beginning with the 1939 reassuring statement of Attorney General Murphy, the Director's role as the foil of extremists paid rich dividends. McCarthyism renewed his prestige as a professional and moderate. In the Stouffer study of popular attitudes toward communism and civil liberties, published in 1955, most respondents voted for Hoover and Eisenhower—27 percent and 24 percent, respectively —as the persons whose views on how to deal with communism they trusted most (McCarthy ran third, with 8 percent). Asked whether this trust was based on their confidence in the individual, or because they knew his opinions quite well, they responded as follows:[68]

	Opinions %	Person %
Hoover	33	55
Eisenhower	19	65
McCarthy	58	31

Although this image of Hoover's moderation and integrity reflected his role of a reassuring, counter-vigilante professional, his performance gave the show away: a stream of public notices, sponsored not only by the Justice but on occasion by the Defense Department, warning about the need for continuing anti-Communist vigilance, urging self-education in the Communist danger and the means of combating it, and requesting that suspicious individuals and incidents be reported to the nearest Bureau office. These appeals, justified as an antidote to "self-help" and hysteria, simply renewed the fears and stereotypes of nativism, stimulated a flow of private accusations for investigation and filing, and invited dependence upon the Director as the protector of the nation.

The Director's most open political ties were with the respectable, super-patriotic conservative subculture represented by the veterans' organizations, the Daughters of the American Revolution, the American Security Council, and the Freedom Foundation. Another important institutional link was with the right-wing Christian churches, which welcomed his fervent outcries against Communist godlessness and calls for Christian regeneration in defense of the existing order.

With the publication of *Masters of Deceit* in 1958, Hoover became the idol of the entire right, from the conservative political sector to the lunatic fringe. Nor did he discourage this idolatry: he was personally flattered by letters of commendation from the extremists as well as by their use of his writings in "documented exposés" (see Chapter 12). The ultras had further proved their friendship by attacking the OSS and CIA as hotbeds of communism and, though hostile to the political process, thought that Hoover alone conformed to their image of a suitable president. The Director's popularity in crackpot circles, plus the fact that the Bureau's informer coverage was almost entirely confined to the left, generated pressures on him by the Kennedy administration for greater evenhandedness. Enraged at this White House meddling, Hoover made his trip to Canossa by publishing an article (plainly ghost-written) in the American Bar Association *Journal* for February 1962 denouncing "vigilante methods" and complaining that "extravagant name-calling, gross exaggeration hinder our efforts." But this appeal, like its successors, was pure ritual: he admonished the ultras in a whisper, but attacked their enemies the "pseudo-liberals" in a roar. The Director managed to convey to his ultraist supporters that they had nothing to fear from him, despite the pressures of the Kennedys. They knew that he was, as Joseph Conrad wrote of Lord Jim, "one of us." The native Fascist demagogue Gerald L. K. Smith spoke for them when he wrote of the Director in February 1962 (the month of the publication in the ABA *Journal*) that "he is one of the most valuable citizens America has ever had—a brilliant strategist in the campaign against Communists" *(The Cross and the Flag)*.

The pressure on the Director to do something about the far right coincided with rumors that he would be forced to retire at the end of the first Kennedy term. Most prominently mentioned as a prospective successor was an aide to Secretary of Defense Robert S. McNamara, Adam Yarmolinsky, whose original appointment in 1961 Hoover had tried to block with the support of the ultras. The rumor that Yarmolinsky (a Jew!) might replace the Director himself, leaked through a friendly newsman, was like a trumpet blast summoning the faithful to battle. Letters from far-right groups begged the Director to say it wasn't so. He responded warmly, assuring them that he had no intention of retiring and answering requests from even the most far-out groups for materials for use in exposés, which were then reprinted as supporting documentation.[69]

Hoover's nativist identity is most clearly established in his perception of the relative threat posed by foreign and domestic communism. The nativist countersubversive tradition has always, as I have tried to show, seized on a foreign-inspired conspiracy as the fountainhead of subversion. But such external plots have merely served as a rhetorical setting, a metaphor for the evil threatened by domestic movements which, it is claimed, pose the real danger. In this tradition, modern nativists have stressed domestic communism, not the international movement, as the enemy.

Like his nativist counterparts, the Director did not neglect the doom-laden rhetoric of foreign conspiracy ("the international Communist conspiracy is clearly the greatest menace free civilization has ever known," he told the appropriations subcommittee in 1959) but only for the purpose of magnifying and making credible the "danger from within." Thus when President Kennedy, in the fall of 1961, opened his administration's attack on the far right in a speech blasting the "danger from within" thesis, the Director, shortly thereafter, in a nationally televised speech ("The Faith to Be Free") insisted that "the threat from without must not blind us to the threat from within," which is "reaching into the very heart of America." Confined all his adult life to a tight bureaucratic regimen, isolated by his intellectual limitations from the springs of political behavior, self-removed from affective social or family influence, Hoover was a captive of the nativist stereotypes of the Palmer era. Like the latter-day ultras, his anti-communism was at root a form of bigotry, a prejudice; he hated Communists as the anti-Semite hates the Jew, the racist the black. Hofstadter's paranoid style, the Manichean conviction that a subversive conspiratorial enemy seeks the destruction of our heritage, dominates his writing and speeches. Hatred for this enemy defines his politics.

What we know of Hoover's career and the huge published corpus of his views provide material for a closer, more personal assessment of his politics. "I have often thought," wrote William James, "that the best way to define a man's character would be to seek out the particular mental or moral attitude in which, when it came upon him, he felt himself most intensely active and alive. At such moments there is a voice inside which speaks and says, 'This is the real me.' " As we have seen, Hoover used an assortment of voices, but it is not too difficult to recognize the voice of the "real me." One hears it in the verbal thuggery that throbs in his diatribes against subversives and critics alike, the howl of the embattled self.[70] Hoover's performance as a young government lawyer was already marred by his barely leashed invective. His climb to power and importance decades later, far from softening his language, intensified its ferocity; it became clear that the rhetoric was the uncontrollable projection of an inner aggression. This style made him a great favorite of American Legion conventions, and among others it won him respect for his "forthrightness" and "sincerity." It is a symptom of a pathology best described by T. W. Adorno and his collaborators, who urge that "the anti-democratic individual, because he has had to accept numerous externally imposed restrictions in the satisfaction of his needs, harbors strong, underlying aggressive impulses. . . . [O]ne outlet for this aggression is through displacement onto outgroups leading to moral indignation and authoritarian aggression."[71]

Behavioral scientists, such as Adorno and others, concerned with anti-democratic and Fascist political movements, persuasively argue that the need to find an outlet for aggressive impulses generates an authoritarian or anti-democratic syndrome, reproduced with significant fidelity in the life and career of the Director. Before dealing with the constitutive aspects of the authoritarian pattern, one is struck at the outset by the authoritarian subtraits prominent in Hoover's character and thoughtways: his passion for neatness (his lawn was made of astro-turf—a synthetic material); stereotyped and oversimplified perceptions of the world; hostility to intellectuals, the subjective, and tender-minded;* social and moral conventionalism; preoccupation with strength, viril-

---

*The Director's classic statement on this question was made at the American Legion's convention in 1939: "Intellectual license and debauchery is un-American. In righteous indignation it is time to drive the debauchers of America out into the open."

ity, and toughness; and a puritanical concern with sex and "sexual goings on,"* alongside a punitive attitude toward violations of sexual mores.

Like the classic authoritarian, Hoover scored high on the scale of ethnocentricism; he was both racist and anti-Semitic.† One senses further that he felt threatened, as do authoritarians generally, by the permissiveness of democratic norms and by the complexity of political pluralism. Particularly revealing was his attraction to the role of lawgiver and rulemaker. This authoritarian trait, a bid for submission to his protective power, dominates his countersubversive writings. As the FBI agent already quoted told Norman Ollestad:

> [Countersubversion] allows him to make comments and speak about subjects that otherwise would be out of his field. Now he can talk all about the Commie movement in civil rights, the Supreme Court decisions, the Communist speakers on U.S. college campuses, the moral, religious, political undertones of Communism. He speaks on foreign affairs. He even commented on a trade agreement with iron curtain countries . . . and a possible wheat sale to Russia.[72]

Hoover's authoritarian need to lecture, scold, and moralize finds expression almost from the beginning of his emergence as a public figure. Like subversion, crime was an early prey to his homiletic passions. While he boasted of his triumphs over the criminal enemy, he took more pleasure in explaining the rise in the crime rate because it gave him an opportunity to inveigh against moral failings and permissiveness, leading an observer to comment that "Hoover gets more credit every time the crime rate rises."

The use of his office and authority as a pulpit is further seen in his warning women against the dangers of baby-sitters and bridge playing,** campaigning against child molesters and smut salesmen, deploring television violence, denouncing juvenile delinquents as "teenage brigands," and circulating coloring cartoons to arm children against kidnappers.‡ The preacher regularly gave way to the prophet, excoriating political and cultural pharisees for their "self-indulgence, neglect of duty, and public lethargy in a nation of free men."[73]

All of his adult life Hoover exhibited in a revealing way the paired qualities of dominance and submissiveness that form the psychological core of the au-

---

*Prominent among many examples is the Director's denunciation, in an August 1941 magazine article, of roadside cabins (the precursors of motels) as "a new home of disease, bribery, corruption, crookedness, rape, white slavery, thievery and murder," which in the bargain lewdly provided innocent married couples with mattresses previously used in "illicit relations."

†Hoover's racism ("one of those states' righters," he called himself) is now too well established to require elaboration. Not only were Jews shunned as agent material but anti-Semitism flourished, especially in the core of functionaries surrounding Hoover. A true Archie Bunker, Hoover's bigotry was so deep-rooted that he rarely felt the need to conceal it. ("A Lebanese Jew" was his contemptuous putdown of Robert Mardian of the Nixon Justice Department when Mardian attempted to assert departmental authority over the Bureau). Fifty years earlier he had ordered an investigation of Eamon de Valera, President of the Irish Republic—then in the United States to raise money for the cause of Irish independence—to check on reports that De Valera was a "Spanish Jew."

**Hoover's denunciation of maternal indulgence reflected not only his authoritarianism but his profound hatred of women. In a 1944 article, "Mothers, Our Only Hope," he described Ma Barker, the mother of gangster sons, as a "monument to the evils of parental indulgence . . . an animal mother of the she-wolf type" who had turned into "a veritable beast of prey."

‡"Boys and girls—Color the pictures and memorize the rules. Turn down gifts from strangers. Avoid dark and lonely streets. Know your local Policeman. J. Edgar Hoover"—Quoted by John Crosby in "The FBI's Commercial," *New York Herald Tribune,* Oct. 2, 1961.

thoritarian personality. No public official fought so tenaciously to eliminate competition or feuded with so many rivals and critics in his own field—federal and urban.[74] In his long career, he never once found it possible to admit a personal mistake or a Bureau failure. This obsession with power and authority explains the vengeful character of his response to criticism by those seen as inferiors. Martin Luther King, Jr.'s, race, his leadership in the integrationist movement, and his alleged affair with a white woman all mobilized Hoover's authoritarian prejudices; but it was King's criticism of the Bureau and the Director that explains the reckless, personalized quality of his pursuit, expressed ultimately in an invitation to commit suicide, and defamation after King's death. The destructiveness of the pursuer contrasts with the sentimentality and graciousness of the wooer of the powerful, the important figures the Director boasted he had been "close to" (a favorite usage) and whose inscribed photos lined the walls of his home. The ardor of the Director's courtship of the influential was legendary: letters conveying "my deepest esteem," congratulatory notes, messages of support to his patrons and potential allies, cards for every occasion, flowers, and gossip. The entire staff of agents was mobilized as a resource to be used in providing comforts and conveniences for the influential and powerful.* Former Attorney General Francis Biddle recalled: "He knew how to flatter his superiors, and had the means of making them comfortable. The Attorney General, when he was traveling, could count on an agent to meet him at the station, to settle him on his plane with an armful of newspapers, to take him in an FBI car wherever he wished to go." The legats were especially useful as the Director's surrogates in smoothing the path and earning the gratitude of dignitaries traveling abroad. (The Director was particularly anxious for legat coverage in Switzerland for the convenience of winter vacationers.)

On at least one occasion, a courtship backfired. In October 1964, after Walter Jenkins, a White House associate of President Johnson's, was arrested for a second time on a "morals charge" (homosexual solicitation), the Director sent him flowers at the hospital where he was a patient with a card inscribed "J. Edgar Hoover and Associates." Hoover's right-wing supporters were shocked—not on the claimed ground of partisanship, but . . . flowers! And from an idol whose rumored homosexuality they had repeatedly and indignantly denied. One of them, Representative Walter Judd, demanded to know if the Director had been "involved in such a way that [he] fears being hurt by some revelation Jenkins would make."[75] The Director charged that the KGB's disinformation arm subsequently exploited the incident in its never-ending plot to discredit him.

As already suggested, Hoover's access to the White House without submission to the Attorney General crowned his authoritarian strivings. Those who ignored this symbolic prerogative could expect hostility, as the Huston planners learned too late. Attorney General Robert F. Kennedy's efforts to assert his

---

*Hoover was awed as much by great wealth as by political power and reveled in the company of conservative millionaires. The wealthy toy manufacturer Louis Marx was not an intimate, but he supplied Hoover with annual shipments of toys for Christmas gift-giving. Outraged by the fact that Marx, Daniel Ellsberg's father-in-law, had been interviewed without his permission, he demoted and disciplined the responsible functionary, Charles D. Brennan.

authority quickly ended with the assassination of President Kennedy. Department of Justice press chief Edwin Guthman recalled that President Kennedy's body was barely cold when Hoover moved to reestablish a direct relationship with the White House.[76]

Hoover's scorn for his immediate superiors seems inconsistent with the submissiveness attributed to authoritarian personalities. But as Erich Fromm has pointed out, the authoritarian's submissiveness is sometimes deceptive: superior authority is recognized only when exercised harshly. (The same man who called the departed Ramsey Clark a "jellyfish" toed the mark for his successor, the brusque strongman John Mitchell—even to the extent of voluntarily sending Mitchell an accounting of his fees for books and movies when damaging press reports began to appear.) An authoritarian in the Director's mold may be outwardly servile to those seen as superiors, but subconsciously hostile, bending over backwards in formal praise and repressing his hostile impulses, which are directed against subordinates and the powerless generally.

The Director had a genuine, psychic need to submit to a higher, superordinate level of authority, and to identify with it. But only the nation itself, the supreme power, could claim such submission. This grandiose identification gave him a sense of invulnerability, based on a genuine conviction that *quod licet Jovi non licet bovi*. This assumed immunity from the normal consequences of aberrant behavior explains his routine use of Bureau personnel and property for residential improvements, the vehemence of his denials of documented charges, his lies and pretexts such as the fiction that Clyde Tolson's services were needed beyond his compulsory retirement age to complete an unfinished project despite the fact that he had suffered a series of disabling strokes, his readiness to claim credit and royalties for the work of others, and his self-righteously arrogant inconsistencies. One example of the last must suffice. In his mid-November 1964 press conference, he intemperately denounced Martin Luther King, Jr., as the "most notorious liar in the country," the Supreme Court Justices as "bleeding hearts," and the Warren Commission as unfairly critical of the Bureau. A week later he addressed a Loyola University award dinner: "It is a great misfortune that the zealots or pressure groups [spearheaded at times by Communists and moral degenerates]* always think with their emotions, seldom with reason. They have no compunction in lying and exaggerating with the fiercest passion."[77]

The rage which the Director suppressed in dealing with authority figures made him a martinet in the administration of the Bureau. Agents were required to submit unquestioningly to weird rules and regulations, to conform totally to the Director's standards of dress, conduct, and morality, and to demonstrate an unwavering commitment to the Director's infallibility. An agent or associate might risk his future merely by disagreeing with the chief. The Director pronounced "pseudo" (indissolubly linked to "liberals") as "sway-do." But not even his closest aides dared correct him. Similarly, the term "Mafia" was taboo, because the Director had denied that such an organization existed; "La Cosa

---

*The bracketed phrase, an apparent reference to King, was added to the formal text on delivery, an instinctive indulgence in the zealotry that the Director condemned in his critics.

Nostra" (or the abbreviation "LCN") became the official usage when reality forced a retreat. Like the true autocrat, the Director's rage was not assuaged by an offender's benign motive or intent. To "embarrass the Bureau" (meaning the Director) was a capital offense for which there was no acceptable plea in mitigation.

The Director pushed the *Fuehrerprinzip* to its outermost limits: he kept a record, according to Senator McGovern, of all agents who had neglected to request his autographed picture or to demonstrate their gratitude by appropriate birthday and Christmas gifts. Sycophancy was both job insurance and the key to advancement. One Bureau insider recalled:

> Let's say you're an agent. Go in there and tell him he looks better than ever, that you are inspired by his leadership, that he's saving America and you hope he lives forever. As soon as you leave there will be a memo from the director saying, "This man has executive ability." A lot of agents have caught on.[78]

Glorification of the Director was institutionalized; Bureau personnel were regularly assigned to draft resolutions gushing over the Director for adoption, after his prior approval, at the annual meeting of the International Association of Police Chiefs. Such flattery and extorted tribute, however fulsome, traditionally leaves the autocrat hungry for more authentic offerings, personal reassurances of his supreme worth from a source not obviously motivated by fear or ambition. Clyde Tolson played this classic role of the king's personal attendant and alter ego, celebrating verbally and by exemplary deference his glory as "the greatest man of the century" and, in the king's name, ferreting out suspected disloyalty. But Tolson merely expressed the Director's self-estimate, constantly renewed in the waves of adulation and gratitude endlessly flowing from his devotees.

Madison could hardly have found a more eloquent vindication of his fears about the un-angelic proclivities of powerholders—nor Shakespeare's Claudius of his warning that "Madness in great ones must not unwatched go." Something chilling happened to the Director in the course of the last decade of his life. The patriarch was overtaken by an autumn crowded with reckless, cruel, and arbitrary actions, caricatures of his "normal" authoritarian behavior and typically motivated by threats to his authority and power found lurking in criticism and even disagreement. One need only recall the severance of relationships first with the CIA and then with all other federal intelligence units, the Shaw, American University, TWA, and Xerox incidents, the earlier outburst against King, and his enraged ukase (subsequently revoked) against any dealings with the Washington *Post,* the *New York Times,* Los Angeles *Times,* CBS, and NBC.[79] It was not merely the aging process but the terror of death itself that explained the Director's autumnal madness. The fear that death might rob him of the power he had successfully defended against so many other threats is suggested by his obsession with physical fitness, the concealment of illness and decline, a phobia about agents stepping on his shadow, a finicky suspicion of particular food or modes of preparing it, efforts to learn through agents abroad of Swiss medical experiments in life prolongation, and such bizarre precautions for his physical safety as the installation of violet-ray toilet lamps to kill infectious germs, the reservation of five bullet-proofed limousines for his personal use alone (one each in New York, Los Angeles, and Miami, and two in Washington),* the ukase to avoid left turns after a minor accident in which his chauffeur-driven car had been struck from behind while making a left turn, the refusal, a result of the same accident, to sit behind the driver on the left side of the car ("the death seat"), and the practice of propping a decoy hat in his car to foil a would-be assassin.[80]

Like Stalin, the Director equated power with life itself. The elimination of imagined threats to one became a way of staving off the real threat of the other. And, if all else failed, the Director, like Marquez's patriarch, looked to a surrogate, Tolson, to do his dying for him. Since supreme power claimed its ultimate reward, survival, the Director saw no need to prepare for his replacement and, although he had expressed a preference for an in-house successor, systematically eliminated all prospective Bureau candidates for the post. But power raged in vain against the dying of the light. And as the Director's confidence in his biological survival ebbed, his already paranoid behavior took ever more bizarre turns, mirroring Dr. Robert J. Lifton's description of an aging despot who, at the ultimate stage of death fear, "requires the death or defeat of a never-ending series of 'enemies' in order to reactivate his own life and revive an ever-faltering sense of immortality."†[81] In the "mad king" tradition, his glory is preserved by the immense J. Edgar Hoover Building, the preoccupation of his last years, which symbolically dwarfs the Justice Department headquarters building and dominates the inaugural route between the Capitol and the White House.

But Hoover's true legacy was not memorialized in stone and mortar alone. Out of nativism, anti-communism, super-patriotism, religious and political conservatism, he forged an ideology of capitalism in the American grain, a blueprint for an American fascism. And in his own career he demonstrated how this ideology could be exploited to obtain power, despite structural and normative barriers. The intelligence function nourished both ideology and power quest, which in turn expanded its assumptions and operational scope.

---

*In Bureau records they were inventoried as "trucks, light" for the same purpose as the "crime records" dodge to deceive potential critics and economizers. The cover explanation for this fakery was that their heavy armor-plating required truck-type engines.

†This is not to say that Hoover was possessed by a drive for personal immortality. His antagonist was not so much death itself as its imminence. Nor did he cling to anti-communism and its preservation as a form of symbolic immortality, a reactionary counterpart of Mao's revolutionary immortality, described by Dr. Lifton in the work from which the quoted passage is taken. Anti-communism was simply a source of the power with which he combated the threat of physical extinction.

5 The Bureau in Action— Target Selection, Operations, Files

Subversion and Extremism

The dominant role of the Director—his personality, assumptions, and values—in the evolution of federal intelligence is not altogether *sui generis.* Historically, the intelligence function has often been strongly influenced by the personal views of a bureaucratic chief or minister. But, however subjective his style, his agenda is determined by broader, objective circumstances. The political intelligence system of every modern state is the product of its history and stage of development; its mission is to protect the established order against adversary challenges that have emerged from the national political culture: separatism, nationalism, the replacement or restoration of monarchy, colonial liberation, anarchism, syndicalism, anti-totalitarianism, socialism, communism. In the United States it is communism that has, from the beginning, served as the chief justification for the federal intelligence enterprise, and professedly not out of resistance to systemic change as such, but to imputed violence and foreign manipulation. In no country in the West are the fears and vulnerabilities that nourish intelligence so removed from political reality as in our own. All Marxist ("Old Left") groups are monitored under the subversive rubric to prevent assumed violence, even those that reject it as a means of achieving the ultimate transition to socialism. Neither the remoteness of the possibility of a revolutionary attempt, nor the limited numbers and powerlessness of the target—its lack of mass support and manifest inability to bring about a revolution at any foreseeable future time—shield it from surveillance. Despite (or perhaps because of) its purely ideological character, the violence thesis has important operational consequences: it is considered such a prominent, unambiguous tenet of Marxist groups that surveillance is more penetrative, continuing, and comprehensive than in the case of other targets. Every member is conclusively presumed both to be aware of and to approve of the group's violent intentions, and therefore is considered an appropriate subject for surveillance and for priority arrest and detention in the event of an emergency. Personal nonviolent convictions and a record of peaceful activity are considered irrelevant in determining the dangerousness of a subject who is a member of a Marxist group.[1]

Over the years, a reluctant recognition of reality has forced the Bureau to subordinate the violence thesis to the claim of foreign influence and control, which in turn serves as a justification for monitoring Communists as potential spies and hence targets of the Counterintelligence Branch of the Intelligence Division.

The violence charge has played a contrastingly more prominent role in the second core classification, that of extremism, and the scope of the coverage is in theory at least[2] more flexible, depending on Bureau estimates (frequently exaggerated) of the degree of commitment to violence of the group itself, its leaders, members, and supporters. The organizations targeted for claimed extremism can more plausibly, if not by the record of their activities then by their rhetoric, be tied to violence and law violations. But the FBI prefers to deal with them as political, internal security threats rather than criminal suspects. Where, as is typically the case, the alleged extremist activities involve no violations of federal law, the Bureau circumvents the absence of primary investigative jurisdiction by relying on its claimed "subversive activities" authority, attributing to the alleged extremists strategies of governmental overthrow.[3] Such formulations, which insist that the Black Panthers or the Native American Movement, for example, are plotting the destruction of the existing political system, are even more strained than the subversion-violence equation applied to Marxists.

While subversive and extremist groups are subjected to extensive probes, such investigations account for only a small part of the Bureau's coverage. In 1974 the Bureau investigated 157 organizations in both categories. But this figure is quite misleading. Despite widespread criticism of over-targeting, as late as 1975 the agency was conducting surveillance of 1100 organizations and their subdivisions. But this is only the tip of the iceberg. Thousands of individuals fall under intelligence scrutiny, either as primary targets or as the subject of an "investigative matter" as a result of their suspected or confirmed involvement in group activities. Thus, the GAO Report already referred to (at page 71) concludes that in 1974, out of a sample of some 19,659 domestic intelligence case files, about 90 percent (17,528) involved individual targets investigated because of a suspected relationship (membership, support) to a target group or, in a relatively small number of cases, because of a suspected personal involvement in an activity, such as a demonstration. This concentration on individuals accounts for the enormous number, 930,000 in all, of investigations conducted by the Bureau from 1955 to 1978. In a single year, 1972, the Bureau opened some 65,000 domestic files with an internal or national security classification.[4]

Sources and Methods

The investigative process, whether preliminary (a ninety-day vetting) or full-scale, is sparked by information linking an individual or organization to subversion/extremism. This evidence, ranging from suspicion of active involvement to the license plate number of a car parked at the site of a demonstration, comes to a field office through a functioning Bureau political informer in about half (48 percent) of the investigations undertaken. The informer—a term rejected by the FBI, because of its pejorative connotations, in favor of "informant" —is defined in the FBI *Manual* as "an individual actively engaged in obtaining and furnishing information on security or intelligence matters. . . ." In a small number of cases, a lead comes from a true informant or tipster who furnishes information on a casual, nonrecurrent basis and, in contrast to the informer, is typically unpaid. A related category, the "confidential source," triggers 8 percent of the investigations and includes bankers, landlords, educational and public utility personnel—individuals who transmit information already in their possession on the assurance that their identities will not be disclosed. In almost a third of the cases, investigative leads are supplied by professional agencies such as the police or Bureau agents attached to offices in other areas.

The field investigation itself relies on a variety of overlapping sources and techniques, as indicated by the following chart:[5]

Bureau Intelligence Collection Techniques

	%
Informers	83
State and local police	77
State Motor Vehicles Division	52
Confidential sources in utilities, educational institutions, and state employment agencies	54
One or more interviews with informants	42
Subject interviewed	22
Physical surveillance	19
Pretext contacts	20
Electronic surveillance	8
Surreptitious entry	1
Mail covers	1

Motor vehicle records are useful because they include data that provide leads to Social Security records; in addition, they provide photographs of subjects. Direct photographic surveillance is employed in an estimated 4 percent of the caseload. Subject interviews are encouraged because they furnish an opportunity to develop informers or, short of this, to warn the subject of the dangers of involvement in political activities that the Bureau finds objectionable. Interviewed sources other than the subject include friends, relatives, neighbors, teachers, merchants, bartenders, cab drivers, and, in many cases, politically hostile snoopers. Physical surveillance—either fixed, mobile, or periodic—is routinely used to identify a target and to monitor his or her participation in political activities. A pretext contact is one in which the agent impersonates someone else (a lawyer, jury clerk, insurance agent, building inspector) or, in a passive version, refrains from revealing his identity. Electronic surveillance techniques are, like informers and surreptitious entry, especially useful because information is yielded not only about the primary target but about others not already under surveillance. Thus the GAO Report concludes that in sixty-seven of sixty-nine sample case files containing information derived from electronic surveillance, leads were obtained as the result of "overhears" in the course of surveillance targeted against subjects not included in the investigative sample.

The Bureau draws heavily on the resources of federal and state agencies such as, in the former case, the Postal, Customs, and Immigration and Naturalization services, and in the latter, voter registration and prison records. These are supplemented by private record sources such as credit agencies, banks, insurance companies, and car rental agencies. Newspapers and periodicals are also staple sources, combed to identify potential targets or to obtain information about those already under investigation. Agents also, when the need arises, obtain prints or photographs of demonstrations from newspapers and consult their morgues for background data. Newspapermen are sometimes asked for information about individuals they have interviewed. A more fruitful source is the left press: newspapers (both news stories and letters to the editor), periodicals, and leaflets. The first two are obtained on a systematic basis through blind subscriptions sent to a post office box. Informers supply leaflets and pamphlets as well as documents such as petitions (especially to place radical candidates on ballots) and legal briefs such as those filed *amici curiae* in leftist court cases, prized, along with newspaper advertisements, because they contain names of potential subjects. Other sources include applications for employment, records of court trials, automobile registrations, and copies of materials—literature, address books, check stubs, membership lists, minutes—seized in raids by local police. This and related data are described, sometimes inaccurately, as "public record" material and are supposed to be used exclusively in monitoring subjects to determine whether more intensive surveillance is warranted. In addition, the Bureau circulates such "public record" compilations, usually in a "blind" (sans identifying letterhead) format, about prominent individuals or agency critics whom it seeks to discredit. The "public record" character of the information shields the Bureau from the charge that it has conducted surveillance against subjects or that it has breached file confidentiality should its role in disseminating the material become known. But the "public record" designation is not infrequently merely a label to cover all information, whether or not in the public record, that is not developed through the Bureau's own investigative efforts. In some cases, it creates a "public" source by laundering surveillance-derived data through a planted press story, and in others it uses the fruits of surveillance by other agencies.

Investigative techniques also include mail covers (copying return addresses to identify subjects corresponding with a targeted organization),* mail openings

---

*The surveillance process is triggered by the slightest contact with a subversive group. Lori Paton, as a fifteen-year-old high school student, wrote a letter in 1973 to the Socialist Labor Party (inadvertently addressed to the Socialist Workers' Party) requesting information about its program as part of a class assignment in a social studies course, "From Left to Right." Presumably on the basis of information on the envelope, the Bureau swung into action and launched a "subversive activities" investigation. It sought information from a local credit bureau and the chief of police about Ms. Paton as well as her parents. An agent appeared at her high school and told the principal that she was under investigation on the basis of her contact with the Socialist Workers' Party. Her

(chamfering), warrantless electronic surveillance, and surreptitious entries, a euphemism that blankets both entries without resort to force or patently illegal methods and burglary-related break-ins.

The record establishes that agents have been trained for surreptitious entries by formal instruction in lock-picking and related techniques and rewarded with bonuses for successful assignments to compensate them for the risks, since, if caught, they are required to assume full personal responsibility.[6] In 1966 the Director banned, as "clearly illegal," "black bag jobs," that is, entries by force to steal documents, membership lists, handwriting samples, and the like. The ban, reissued the following year, undoubtedly had some effect on the frequency but did not end the practice.* Both microphone installations (which, even when performed by forcible or illegal means, were not placed in the "black bag" category and thus not prohibited) and burglaries continued, though on a reduced scale, until the Director's death in 1972—and thereafter. In January 1976 the FBI reported in a memo to the Church Committee that it had carried out "at least 238" burglaries against fifteen unidentified domestic organizations from 1942 until 1968. In addition, the memo refers to "three domestic subversive targets [which] were the subject of numerous entries from October 1952 to June 1966," as well as "one white hate group."[7] Although the FBI covered itself against possible charges of deception by noting that its list was "incomplete," one can only conclude that the intent to deceive the Church Committee—both about the total number of entries and targets and the date of termination of the burglary practice—was deliberate. Nothing suggests a purpose to mislead so clearly as the fact that the unit which collected the data for submission to the Church Committee in 1972 was in charge of a course of instruction in burglary

---

local high school paper learned about the investigation and wrote an article about it. A subsequent successful lawsuit to expunge Ms. Paton's record revealed that her name had been acquired as the result of a Bureau mail cover of the SWP headquarters, authorized in 1973 by the Post Office. (A mail cover permits the agency authorized to conduct it to copy all data on the outside of first class letters and to examine the contents of second, third, and fourth class mail forwarded to the surveillance target.) In November 1978 a federal district court ruled in the Paton case that the postal regulation allowing mail covers in national security investigative matters is an unconstitutional invasion of the First Amendment because of the vagueness of the term "national security" as a predicate for the scrutiny of citizens' mail. In the same month, a federal court of appeals affirmed an award of damages to three individuals whose mail to the Soviet Union had been opened by the CIA in violation of the Agency's charter.

*The Nixon administration's Huston Plan (1970) refers to the prohibition in justifying the need to reinstitute the practice. The 1966 stop order overrode the protests of William C. Sullivan, who was the architect of the Huston Plan. Sullivan subsequently provided the Nixon White House with a list of precedents of surreptitious entries against domestic targets in prior administrations. President Johnson's Attorneys General Katzenbach and Clark denied knowledge of such practices. In 1975, in a changed climate, Sullivan—a veritable chameleon—did a turn-about and insisted that it was Clark's repeated rejection of Hoover's requests to burglarize a diplomatic site that led to the 1966 ukase. The record suggests, however, that such foreign intelligence break-ins were reduced in frequency but not entirely abandoned. The reasons for the slowdown stemmed from the fact that modern coding machines had made the easy-to-steal code books obsolete, from Hoover's resentment at incurring risks to acquire information for the benefit of other agencies, and a mounting image concern. Sullivan's last word on this subject was his grand jury testimony in August 1977 that Hoover had authorized burglaries in the early seventies as a desperate measure to apprehend the Weather Underground fugitives—"Burglaries Laid to Agents of FBI in 30-Year Period," New York Times, Aug. 24, 1973; "The FBI's 'Black-Bag Boys,' " Newsweek, July 28, 1975; William C. Sullivan, Letter to the Editor, "The 'Black-Bag' Memo," Newsweek, Nov. 10, 1975.

techniques at Bureau headquarters in Quantico, Virginia.[8] While Do Not File procedures for destroying records of burglaries as well as cover-ups of field data preclude an accurate compilation, a more realistic estimate of burglaries to steal information and forcible entries to install microphones from the early forties until the early seventies against domestic targets is close to 7500.*

One of the three domestic targets admittedly the subject of surreptitious entries is the Socialist Workers' Party (SWP) and its affiliate, whose offices in New York City were burglarized at five different sites at least ninety-two times from 1960 to 1966—once every three weeks for a six-and-a-half-year period—yielding a total of about 10,000 photographs of documents such as correspondence, records, minutes, letters, and other materials. (In all but a few cases, the material obtained was not removed but photographed on the spot.) At least two other related burglaries were conducted at private homes, and in a number of cases the burglaries supplied information for use in disruptive (COINTELPRO) operations. Moreover, as late as 1975, at a time when the FBI was under active investigation by congressional committees, documents described as having been "removed" or "stolen" from the SWP's headquarters on at least eight occasions in the first half of that year turned up in FBI files.[9]

In the early seventies the New York City FBI office regularly used burglaries and similar techniques to enter the homes of friends and relatives of the Weather Underground fugitives, both to forage for clues to their whereabouts and to plant microphones. In August 1976, after he had reassured the public that, except for a handful of embassy break-ins, burglaries had been effectively banned since 1966, FBI Director Kelley admitted that he had been deliberately deceived by aides who had suppressed information about the Weather Underground break-ins.[10] (He said nothing about the deception in the memo submitted to the Church Committee in January 1976.) Kelley was forced to reverse himself by a pending grand jury probe of FBI misconduct, which in April 1977 returned an indictment against retired agent John J. Kearney, who had headed Squad 47, a special unit assigned to the apprehension of Weather Underground fugitives. The indictment charged only wiretapping and letter opening—not burglary. However, a year later the Kearney indictment was dropped and replaced by a new indictment. Though presumably brought in response to complaints that Kearney was "only following orders" of his superiors, the charge against these officials, L. Patrick Gray III, Mark Felt, and Edward Miller, alleged a different offense altogether—namely, that the defendants had authorized and approved illegal break-ins and burglaries against friends and relatives of the fugitives, conduct which Miller and Felt had admitted in their grand jury testimony.†

*It is, of course, possible to steal information and to plant microphones by a variety of methods that do not require forcible entry by an agent, such as obtaining a key, using an informer in place of an agent, wiring an informer or, in the case of hotels, renting an adjoining room—an optimal choice since it does not require trespass. Foreign embassies with their security safeguards are typically penetrated by illegal methods. Illegal investigative techniques would, if discovered, taint a subsequent prosecution and for this reason are used less frequently against criminal suspects than against intelligence targets.

†The Gray-Felt-Miller indictments do not even mention wiretapping and mail opening, the offenses charged to Kearney. The implausibility of the claim that the purpose of the substituted indictments was, as the Justice Department alleged, to reach "the highest levels of authority and responsibility" is underscored by the fact that the Kearney case charged a conspiracy between late

What is quite clear is that Attorney General Griffin Bell, yielding to outcries of damaged agent morale, substituted the new indictment of retired officials as a convenient escape from a bureaucratic squeeze and as a containment device to prevent damaging pretrial disclosures of the widespread scope of illegal practices on the operational level. But long before the trial began, the Bureau's illegal break-in activities and its cover-ups were suggested in allegations transmitted to the Justice Department prosecutors by M. Wesley Swearingen. A retired agent with twenty-five years' Bureau service, Swearingen contradicted the break-in figure submitted by the Bureau to the Church Committee: "I myself actually participated in more than 238 while assigned to the Chicago office. . . . The Chicago office conducted thousands of bag jobs. I have numerous letters of commendation and one cash award in the amount of $150, in recognition [of these break-ins]." He stated that in Chicago alone two dozen agents were assigned full-time to the burglarizing of homes of Communist Party members. Swearingen charged that Bureau agents had lied to the General Accounting Office as well as to a Washington grand jury about the number, locations (not only in New York, as the Bureau agents had represented, but in Chicago, Los Angeles, Washington, D.C., Portland, Oregon, Newark, New Jersey, and San Francisco), and duration of the illegal practices in pursuit of Weather Underground fugitives. In addition, he attacked as "absolute nonsense" the contention of one of the indicted FBI defendants, W. Mark Felt, that the break-ins were authorized under the Nixon administration's abortive program for expanded intelligence operations (the Huston Plan), pointing out that during the seven years (1970–77) he served as Los Angeles coordinator of the Weather Underground case, no presidential authority had ever been cited for conducting break-ins.

Warrantless wiretaps (discussed in Chapter 7) and forcible or deceptive entries by government agents are not only criminal, but constitute violations of the search-and-seizure provisions of the Fourth Amendment to the Constitution. However, the use of political informers (or "security informants," as the Bureau calls them), a far more widespread practice, has not yet been held constitutionally impermissible.[11] The Supreme Court has held (in the Hoffa case) that the use of informers in criminal cases is not subject to the warrant require-

---

1970 and April 1972, while the offenses charged in the new indictments cover the period between May 1972 and May 1973 when Gray served as Acting Director. Gray denied the charges altogether. Miller and Felt have argued that the break-ins were connected to a foreign intelligence operation, which made it a legitimate concern of the Executive, and thus exempt from the warrant requirements of the Fourth Amendment.

Subsequent to these indictments, FBI Director William Webster announced that he would prefer administrative charges against 6 of a total of 68 agents referred to him by the Justice Department as participants in illegal break-ins, mail openings, and wiretaps. Ultimately, a supervisor was discharged, another demoted, and two street agents censored. The head of the FBI's New York office, J. Wallace La Prade, was also disciplined for authorizing the illegal operations including wiretaps and "black bag jobs." In defense of his own and his agents' conduct, the outraged La Prade charged in April 1978 that such practices were "still in use." The Bureau, however, claimed that these techniques were authorized only in cases involving "agents of foreign powers" or "foreign terrorists." But Justice Department sources in a leak to the press asserted that the condemned practices continue to be employed against U.S. citizens whom the Bureau intentionally mislabels as foreign agents or terrorists—"Five Incidents Spotlight Need for FBI Curbs," Chicago *Sun-Times,* July 30, 1979.

ments of the Fourth Amendment. But the Court has suggested that expectations of associational privacy, not present when an informer is planted in a suspected criminal setting, might require a warrant in the case of the infiltration of a group engaged in activity that is itself protected under the First Amendment, especially since the warrant requirements of the Fourth ("unreasonable search and seizure") Amendment are historically intertwined with the First Amendment's protection of political dissent. And beyond the Fourth Amendment warrant issue, a further question looms: whether the infiltration for intelligence purposes alone of groups engaged in political activity violates per se the guarantees of the First Amendment.

Informers have been denounced since biblical times on ethical grounds as betrayers of trusting associates, and as unreliable sources;* perhaps most important, informing as an institution has been widely condemned because it compromises our democratic commitment. The classic weapon against political and religious dissidents, informers were used against the Jews and Christians in Roman times, non-Catholics in the Inquisition, Catholics in seventeenth-century England, the colonists in eighteenth-century America, slaves seeking emancipation in the nineteenth century, British reformers in the England of Pitt and Castlereagh, the British Chartist and trade union movements of the nineteenth century, the Continental Socialist and Communist movements of the same era, the struggle for Irish independence, by Czarist regimes in Russia, and more recently by the Soviet Union against dissidents of all kinds. In America, informers have dominated the response to domestic dissent in the course of this century up to the present.

There are four basic types of intelligence informers apart from casual informants and tipsters. The most common category is the planted infiltrator, "somebody," in the words of an ex-agent, "completely unconnected with the organization . . . young enough to fit in with the group . . . and willing to cooperate." Old Left groups are typically monitored by "deep penetration," informer-spies who have operated in an organization for years, many of them recruited "in place," that is, while functioning as bona fide members or officers. Because of their value as continuing sources of high-level information, such penetration agents are rarely required to take risks that might result in exposure. Related to the in-place informer is the defector. If the prospective recruit is merely a lapsed member, the contacting agent may seek to induce a resumption of activity as a spy. The renegade or turncoat who has burnt his bridges—the true informer of the Judas legend—"cooperates with the FBI," in the classic euphemism,

---

*The theme of informer betrayal echoes through a vast literature. See, for example, Ecclesiasticus, XXI, 31. Here is a modern example from an interview with an ex-agent in which he recalled his relationships with his informers:

> I had an informant in the Nation of Islam, a Black Muslim group. He was sick for quite a while and sent in reports that were completely useless; but we continued to pay him. Finally he had to be hospitalized. While he was in the hospital, he was visited by some of the Brothers. They left him a get well card which they all signed. He sent me the card and asked me to accept it as a substitute for a regular report and pay him his monthly reimbursement for services because he needed the money very badly.

The objections to informers on credibility grounds are equally substantial and deep-rooted, beginning at least with the delators of Tiberius described by Tacitus.

through a process of debriefing and makes himself available to answer questions as they arise. The Bureau is reluctant to waste its functioning informers in law enforcement proceedings; thus the defector who has no future as a source is the preferred candidate for the witness stand. Indeed, the need to economize on the use of informers and at the same time to provide a steady source of income for the defector witness not infrequently results in the "professional witness" phenomenon, the use of the same paid witness over and over again, and in a number of court trials. (The late Elmer Davis referred to such a professional as a "seven-shot repeating witness.") When such an informer-witness exhausts his capital of information, he is tempted to renew it by recalling new and fresh evidence of subversion previously overlooked, or by developing inputs of his own to the target. Similarly, the witness role may pave the way to a career as writer or lecturer.

A fourth category consists of individuals not committed to a continuing relationship, paid on an ad hoc basis to attend and report on meetings, usually of a public or semi-public character, participate in debriefing sessions, and identify subjects from photographs. In this unstructured grouping can also be included "confidential sources," apprentices, "potential" security, racial and extremist informants, who after a trial period are signed on for regular service.

Planted and in-place informers, in contrast to the ad hoc and probationary variety and defectors, are linked to the Bureau in a continuing relationship and are paid either a fixed stipend (sometimes supplemented by special rewards or bonuses) or in accordance with the value and volume of the information reported. But, whatever the arrangement or mode of payment, the FBI informer is required to sign a statement that he is not a Bureau employee and promises not to hold himself out as such. While the agency determines the informer's pay scale, whether fixed or bounty-style, and has the power to hire and fire, it is not an employer because, it argues, it does not control the way the spy does his work —for legal purposes, he is an independent contractor. "We pay," the Bureau claims, "only for the information produced and not the services" of the spy. The Bureau's insistence on the spy's independent role thus enables it to have things both ways: to claim the fruits of his work while disclaiming responsibility for the manner in which he performs it—or even for his performing it at all. Its reluctance to assume the role of employer of political spies is also evident in its policy against the use of its regular agents in undercover political work, although agents do sometimes play an undercover role in conventional criminal investigations.* This strained rejection of the employment relationship is not primarily based on the fear of legal responsibility for the informer's conduct, but rather on political and image considerations. An important ground of attack on the GID's radical-hunting excesses of the twenties was its use of its own agents as informers and *agents provocateurs*. The record shows that Hoover feared a resumption of the practice would make the reconstituted agency vulnerable to renewed attack on this score. The problem was overcome with a "right way"

---

*In a few cases—such as the Chicago convention—agents were used to infiltrate the New Left. But because long hair and related disguises were required, the assignments were kept secret from the fastidious Director—Sullivan, pp. 158–159. In the seventies, agents were used to infiltrate West Coast groups—Payne, *passim;* "Infiltrating the Underground," *Time,* Jan. 9, 1978.

solution: the informer would not be the "confidential employee" of the twenties but an outsider, a patriotic volunteer in his country's service. This formula shielded the agency from possible criticism for requiring agents to dissemble their loyalties in order to become accomplices in subversion; and it averted what in Hoover's view would have been a serious blemish on the agent's image if he had been forced to wade through the muck of radicalism, even in the line of duty. And in any event, the straight-arrow types considered the most suitable agent material were hardly equipped for the impersonation, deception, and role-playing demanded in the intense and protracted involvement of the success-ful infiltrator. In the same way, the agent's lack of "feel" for the infiltrated milieu typically limits his scope as control-handler to bureaucratic and bookkeeping functions, far removed from the healing, supportive ministrations ascribed to such figures in fiction and occasionally in life. (The fact that the handler's primary concern is with enhancing his own performance record sometimes induces in the informer the feeling that he is a pawn, distilled in the bitter question put to me by one of them: "Who gets the bird, the hunter or the dog?")

In order to erase the stigma of spymaster and to resist constitutional chal-lenges, the FBI and the Justice Department try to assimilate political intelli-gence-gathering informers to the conventional law enforcement variety. How-ever, they are a breed apart and come to us through a separate historical route. Political informers, like their law enforcement counterparts, may turn up evi-dence that a crime is being planned or has been committed, but such a function is only incidental to a broader, basic assignment. The political informer is charged with reporting not on a particular activity but on an unrestricted range —everything the target individual or organization does is grist for his mill, whether public or private, criminal or constitutionally protected, including such information as the organization's members and officers, factions, meeting times and places, copies of all literature, financial contributors, addresses of individu-als and organizations. The highest priority is the identification of individuals; thus, a plant who acquires access to names—by, for example, getting himself elected secretary of the group—is not infrequently rewarded by a bonus. Even more helpful is an informer who becomes a security officer charged with pre-venting infiltration and ferreting out already functioning informers. Also highly prized and rewarded are informers with special skills or resources, such as access to explosives.*

The informer performs other chores as well, such as stealing keys, furnish-ing diagrams and office layout drawings for use in break-ins; identifying photo-graphs; interpreting cryptic communications overheard by tappers; alerting his control agent to a scheduled telephone conversation considered important

---

*For example, Louis Salzburg, a New York photographer, received about $10,000 in the two years he served as an FBI informer. With these payments he financed a studio, sold pictures to left publications, and procured negatives for the FBI. After surfacing at the Chicago conspiracy trial, he testified before the House Internal Security Committee (HISC) and furnished the committee with negatives as well as documents and correspondence taken from the files of Veterans for Peace and the Fifth Avenue Peace Parade Committee. In the same way, informers with the requisite skills and equipment are routinely instructed to attend meetings of target groups where speeches are electroni-cally amplified or recorded, and to add a microphone to those already surrounding the speaker in order to tape his remarks.

enough to spot-tap; and—a highly important service—supplying information to be used as a basis for a "reliable informant" affidavit to legitimate electronic eavesdropping or other forms of surveillance.

Even without special instructions from his handler, the informer involves himself in the group's activities as prominently as possible, both to protect his cover and, by his militancy, to qualify for a higher post that will enhance his value (and his compensation). Similarly, a spy may, either out of political animus or personal hostility,* engage in a course of destructive conduct directed against the target, confident that his relationship with the Bureau will protect him from any adverse legal consequences. Aggression sometimes takes the form of provocation: the instigation of criminal acts or the provision of matériel and skills in order to create a justification for criminal sanctions against the targets. The FBI has disclaimed responsibility for law-breaking by informers by pointing to the cautionary instructions that agents are required to convey to their charges. But evidence is abundant of informer violence and provocation under circumstances in which knowledge or approval is clear.[12]

During the period of the COINTELPROS, informers under instructions or with the knowledge and approval of higher-ups engaged in a variety of harassments and "dirty tricks." The very first of these programs (against the Communists) instructed field offices to direct their informers to "seize every opportunity to carry out the disruptive activity not only at meetings, conventions, et cetera, but also during social and other contacts with CP members and leaders." All later COINTELPRO were modeled on this one.

The relatively open character of our society is psychologically disarming and makes the average subject highly vulnerable to fear when his or her politics are secretly monitored by the FBI—the national symbol of our identification of dissent with subversion. The undercover character of the investigation, the benighted standards of the informer, the assumed guilt of the subject, the denial of an opportunity to answer any charges and confront the accuser, can all be shattering. Because it is such an efficient instrument of repression, the informer system has been transformed from a mere investigative means into an end in itself. It is not the information furnished by the spy that makes him a prized Bureau asset but the fact that he is there: a concealed hostile presence to instill fear.

This goal of intimidation explains why informers are kept in organizations for years, turning in tedious and repetitious reports of no substantive value, and why, within the same infiltrated organization, informers frequently inform on each other and are paid for similar reports about precisely the same meetings. It is this coercive aim, too, that accounts for the curious dualism in American infiltration practice: while the identity of the individual informer is concealed, the fact that there is a widespread network of informers in the American left is widely publicized.

The use of informers as an instrument of repression necessarily requires an abundant supply. Until the early seventies, agents were taxed with informer

---

*Psychotics, thrill seekers, and correspondence school hawkshaws are common informer types. A notable example of a flaky informer is Sara Jane Moore, an informer for both the FBI and the ATF, who in September 1975 attempted to assassinate President Gerald R. Ford.

quotas that not only forced the retention of redundant and gamy spies but induced the faking of recruitments. In an interview in 1971, ex-agent Robert Wall described how he and others in the Bureau "recruited" fictitious informers by selecting names out of the telephone book and fabricated their "reports" for the file in accordance with prescribed Bureau procedures. The payment of informers has traditionally fostered graft and corruption because of the limited accountability dictated by security requirements. In the case of the FBI's bogus informers, the opportunities for abuse were especially lush. Agents could plausibly claim that their fictitious recruits insisted on cash stipends (as a protection against exposure), then pocket the payments. A portion of the cash outlays to genuine informers could easily be "skimmed" without their knowledge—a common practice, according to retired agent Swearingen.

The demands of blanket coverage suggested by the GAO Report figures on the relative prominence of informers as a surveillance tool are corroborated by subsequent government submissions in the course of litigation: from 1940 until April 1978, the FBI deployed some 37,000 informers—29,166 in classification 134 (security) and 7893 in 170 (racial and extremist). (These, it should be added, are quite conservative totals. Excluded are informers with a "criminal informant" classification, 137-S [code designation for "security"], an "administrative" category [62], those grouped with their targets under the listing "subversive activities" [100], and others with a counterintelligence designation.) Between 1966 and 1976 the Chicago field office alone paid out $2.5 million to 5145 informers in the process of investigating or developing files on 27,900 organizations and individuals. Similarly, over a sixteen-year period, the coverage of the Socialist Workers' Party and its youth affiliate, with a combined membership of no more than 2500, cost $1,683,000. This sum was paid to 301 informers who joined the two groups, and does not include additional remuneration for 1000 others who supplied information but did not join.* The saturation of the New Left and other Vietnam era dissident groups is reflected in the special recruitment drive to increase coverage of "collectives, communes and staffs of underground newspapers" as "listening posts." Even as late as 1976, in the face of mounting criticism, the FBI fiscal year budget allocated $7,401,000 for its political informer programs, more than twice the budget for organized crime informers. In May 1978 FBI Director William H. Webster announced a cutback from 535 (itself a sharply reduced figure) to 42 informers in the field of "internal security and terrorism." But this figure too is deceptive;† it excludes a large number in the fourth category (probationary and ad hoc) described above, as well as an estimated 250 Communist Party informers who were reclassified out of the "domestic intelligence" ranks when, in 1976, Communist Party surveillance was removed from a domes-

---

*Not all of these were of the casual informant variety. In the late sixties the Bureau established fixed relationships with situational informers who reported on the entire radical scene rather than a single target.

†This is not to say that the FBI's political informer ranks have not been sharply reduced in recent years. The shrinkage can in part be attributed to the elimination of the quota system and the screening out of invented informers. See "Ex-Agent Alleges Fraud in FBI, Says Many Informers Are Bogus," *New York Times,* Dec. 6, 1978; "Ex-Agent Accuses FBI Executive of Perjury in Suit over Informants," *New York Times,* Jan. 16, 1979; and "Former Agent Tells the True Story," *Freedom,* Dec. 1978 and Feb. 1979.

tic to a "foreign intelligence" classification.[13] Subsequent to announcing his tally, Webster (in March 1979) refused to permit a congressional audit of the Bureau's use of informers.

The FBI and the Justice Department have also resisted disclosure of the identity of political informers in a number of cases brought by the victims of FBI surveillance, on the ground that such disclosure would expose the identified informers to serious risk. This contention—its legal name is "informers' privilege"—as in the case of the First and Fourth Amendments, blurs the distinction between the two classes of informers. Unquestionably, an exposed *criminal* informer may well face harsh reprisals and even death, and there is a valid basis in such a case for invoking the informers' privilege. But in the intelligence sphere the reaction of the spy's victim is typically confined to a shocked resentment, and only rarely finds an outlet stronger than ostracism or abusive telephone calls. (See the discussion of the Albertson case in Chapter 6.) Far from fearing retaliation, many internal security informers insist on surfacing, out of fear of the stigma of subversion as a career handicap, the hope of using their experience as book or lecture material, or guilt for betraying people they have come to admire.

In any event, the privilege of confidentiality as traditionally invoked is not absolute but turns on a balancing of the competing interests of the government and its courtroom adversary. In the case of the *Socialist Workers' Party* v. *Attorney General* (S.D.N.Y.), Judge Thomas Griesa, without ruling on the constitutionality of the use of political informers, nevertheless ordered eighteen FBI informer files turned over to the plaintiff's attorneys, pointing out that on the one hand, admittedly no evidence of wrongdoing by the plaintiff had been uncovered over four decades of informer infiltration while, on the other, evidence had accumulated in the course of the lawsuit that infiltrators had engaged in illegal activities severely damaging to the plaintiff and its members.

Attorney General Griffin Bell defied Judge Griesa's disclosure order and was found in contempt of court. Bell was relying on the sworn testimony of FBI Associate Director James Adams that surrender of the files would violate the FBI's "pledge of confidentiality" to its informers. But at the time he testified, in 1976, the Bureau's *Manual of Instructions* made no reference to such a pledge and, during the period covered by the lawsuit, Bureau policy with respect to domestic intelligence informers was expressed in a 1968 memorandum from the Director to the field stipulating that: "As a general rule all of our security informers are considered available for interview by Department attorneys and for testimony if needed." In March 1979, a federal appellate court reversed the contempt order as too severe, but withheld approval of the Justice Department's confidentiality plea.

Building Communism with Non-Communist Hands

Beginning with its initial 1936–38 investigations, the FBI targeted alleged Communist fronts. The concept of the "front" and its role as an intelligence priority emerged from the Communist Party's post-1935 shift from a line of Socialist revolution to a "united front" tactic to promote reforms and strictly limited aims while retaining allegiance to the Soviet Union. This rejection of revolutionary change ironically led to an expansion of surveillance as the Bureau's 1939 subversive activities assignment was interpreted to authorize surveillance of a broad range of non-Communist groups, either because of claimed secret Communist domination or to determine whether in fact the target was dominated or controlled by the Party. This concern rose to the top of the intelligence agenda in the forties, presaged in Hoover's August 1940 speech charging that advocates of foreign "isms" had "succeeded in boring into every phase of American life masquerading behind front organizations." The congressional anti-subversive committees, too, as well as state and urban intelligence units, concentrated on a wide range of non-Communist associations. This expansion was facilitated by the replacement of violence as the key ingredient of subversion with cunning and deception, tactics that peculiarly justified the role of intelligence.

It was difficult, however, to establish that an organization with non-Communist objectives and membership was in fact a creature of the Communist Party, and the charge became little more than an epithet to discredit unpopular groups and causes. The difficulty was compounded by the repression of the fifties: Smith Act prosecutions, the activities of the McCarthy and other anti-subversive congressional committees, deportation and denaturalization proceedings—all these left the Communist Party in ruins, its cadres depleted, its leaders in hiding, and its supporters largely confined to a small libertarian constituency protesting its suppression. The supply of front targets simply dried up; the Party was powerless to maintain itself, let alone fronts. Thus the Subversive Activities Control Board, mandated by the Internal Security Act of 1950 to register Communist fronts, issued rulings against only twenty-two organizations, many of them already moribund and others destroyed by the registration proceedings. But despite the puny haul of registration orders, the Internal Security Act deepened people's fears of joining public interest organizations and discouraged the entire process of group formation and activity. Tocqueville's tribute to the importance of the role of voluntary associations in American public life mocked the grim reality. Intelligence was confronted with a familiar dilemma: its zeal had deprived it of a *raison d'être*.

The Bureau came to the rescue with the discovery of a fresh subversive peril. In order to foil its pursuers, overcome its isolation, and restore its influence, the Party, according to the Bureau, had devised a cunning plot "to infiltrate unsuspecting legitimate organizations" which "have the best interests of the American people at heart." This infiltration tactic, the Bureau charged, would enable the Party to hide its face while "it strives to contaminate respectable individuals and organizations with its creed," thus creating new burdens in "identifying and exposing not only the Communists, but also the groups through which they promote their objectives." And both tactics were based on deception: in the former case, the controlling leadership deceived the innocent members (remedied by the front registration requirements of the Internal Security Act, which were justified as a "consumer protection" measure),* while in the latter, the well-intentioned leadership was deceived by the sinister infiltrators. The infiltration concept was an immense intelligence triumph. "Infiltration" itself suggested a conspiratorial takeover plan, a vast masked invasion. The Bureau not only rescued the languishing Menace but transformed it into a slimy predator; its innocent victims for that reason alone became part of a vast new intelligence subject matter. One would suppose that only the infiltrators would be "identified and exposed" and not the victimized organization, which would be presumably alerted to the danger. Not so: the group itself was placed under surveillance, usually through informer plants.

Under the warrant of protecting the democratic process from disruption and violence, the Bureau seriously jeopardized it. The Bureau protested that it was concerned only with the subversive, and not with the legitimate activities of COMINFIL (as the infiltration program is code-named) targets. And further, that agents were instructed to direct their informers to pay no attention to collective bargaining activities of labor organizations and, in the case of campus informers, classroom matters. "Sure, those were our instructions," ex-agent Robert Wall has stated in an interview. "But informants shovelled everything into us and our reports covered all of the activities in their reports."

Despite the scope of infiltration coverage, the evidentiary requirements for launching such probes were minimal. To begin with, the objective of the intelligence hunt, influence, is a filmy notion, virtually impossible to measure. Unlike the surveillance of fronts, vicarious instruments already in being, the predicate for surveillance was not actual infiltration, let alone demonstrable influence on the target's policies and programs, but a Communist decision, resolve, or rhetorical exhortation which, in the nativist countersubversive canon, is readily transformed into evidence of a sinister takeover conspiracy.

The Bureau stretched the influence rationale by inferring a takeover plot from the mere presence or activities—however innocuous—of suspected infiltrators. These Typhoid Marys (the Bureau viewed them almost literally as defilers, carriers of communicable disease against which there was no defense) were frequently far removed from the infection's source. A former Communist, out of the Party for years and in disagreement with its tenets but seeking an outlet for his views on issues of the day, could play the infiltrator's role and, *faute de mieux,* a spouse or other relative of someone with a Party record could provide infiltrator credentials. Indeed, a seeming remoteness from the Party might itself be grounds for suspicion. As the Bureau explained, many important Communist functionaries had been deliberately instructed to hide their allegiance and shed all indications of membership in order to function more effectively as infiltrators.

---

*In filing a registration petition against the W. E. B. DuBois Clubs as a Communist front in March 1966, Attorney General Katzenbach said: "Historically Americans have the freedom to organize in dissent. At the same time, in accordance with the law, young people who might consider joining this organization are entitled to know its nature and sponsorship. This is a disclosure, not a criminal action. Registration does not imply illegality and does not curtail an organization's activities. . . ." In fact, under the statute, registration *did* imply illegality and was intended to stigmatize and punish organizations through a variety of crippling sanctions. Hearings on the DuBois Clubs' petition came to a close before the issuance of a final order because of the administration's reluctance to disclose wiretapping details.

Besides, there were thousands of ex-members who left the Party "for one reason or another, but . . . still feel themselves Communists. . . ."

But as in the case of the Smith Act, the provisions of the Internal Security Act of 1950 and its 1954 Amendment, which had supplied a predicate for the investigation of non-Communist organizations, became casualties by the closing years of the fifties of court decisions and a slowly changing political climate.* Then, too, the justification for investigating groups to determine whether they should be entered on the Attorney General's list of proscribed organizations became questionable when the listing was halted as a result of a Supreme Court decision in 1955 that affected organizations were entitled to a hearing before they could be listed. But these developments did not curtail the ever-widening investigative quest for Communist influence. The Bureau continued to rely on unenforceable measures as its authority and also moved to higher ground, a version of "pure intelligence": the duty to inform the executive branch about the Communists' hidden role ("subversive pressures," as Attorney General Herbert Brownell put it) in political life. The rationale that assigns surveillance a role in policy formation became, as we shall see, an all-purpose sanction in the Vietnam era. But it originated in the Eisenhower administration's need for a reason to avoid dealing with the mounting discontents of the fifties. The monitoring of suspected infiltrated groups extended, in the language of Attorney General Brownell, to "the entire spectrum of the social and labor movement in the country." The hunt for Communist influence ranged from political and legislative, racial and youth matters, to the activities of women, farmers, veterans, youth, religion, education, and industry. Members of "respectable bodies" were specifically warned to be on guard against the insidious infiltrators, instructed to influence and subvert church groups, parent-teacher associations, welfare councils, and labor unions.

COMINFIL was especially useful as a justification for monitoring the movement for racial equality, quickened by the 1954 *Brown* decision. As the battlelines formed around the civil rights issue and the enactment of civil rights legislation in the early Kennedy years, the Bureau was faced with intensified pressures from its Southern constituency to discredit the movement by linking it with subversion. For almost a decade racist politicians, both in the states and Congress, had fought the freedom movement with the weapon of countersubversion. Now they looked to the Director to give his official blessing to their outcries that the Communists were seeking to exploit the civil rights issue for subversive ends.

But Hoover's racist passions and desire to please his political constituency

---

*The 1954 Amendment to the Internal Security Act of 1950 denied the benefits of the National Labor Relations Act to labor unions found by the Subversive Activities Control Board to be in fact infiltrated. Only one union (International Union of Mine, Mill and Smelter Workers) was ruled by the Board to be infiltrated, but an order directed against it in 1955 was vacated in June 1966 when the Justice Department admitted it lacked evidence to support such a claim of infiltration within the time period specified by the statute—"U.S. Stops Trying to Prove a Union Red Infiltrated," *New York Times,* June 15, 1966. Although in 1962 the Attorney General was still charging that "Party members have intensified their efforts to infiltrate various legitimate organizations. They are especially anxious to control, influence or undermine the affairs of unions, peace movements, and minority, youth, veteran's and women's cultural, educational, civil rights and similar groups," we are never told whether in fact these efforts and anxieties bore fruit.

were in themselves insufficient to overcome court decisions, a national reawakening of conscience, and the sheer thrust and scope of the freedom movement among blacks. There was the further obstacle that Communists, as Hoover well knew from the Bureau's own COMINFIL investigations of civil rights movements in the fifties, were far from prominent in the development and leadership of the movement. In the summer of 1963 Senator A. S. Monroney, an Oklahoma Democrat, wrote to Hoover seeking verification of charges—attributed to the agency by its Southern allies on the Hill—of Communist influence in the civil rights movement. The Director referred the inquiry to Attorney General Kennedy, who on July 23 wrote:

> Based on all available information from the F.B.I. and other sources, we have no evidence that any of the top leaders of the major civil rights groups are Communists, or Communist-controlled.
>
> It is natural and inevitable that Communists have made efforts to infiltrate the civil rights groups and to exploit the current racial situation. In view of the real injustices that exist and the resentments against them, these efforts have been remarkably unsuccessful.[14]

The Attorney General's answer was based on data and conclusions of intelligence chief William C. Sullivan, incorporated in a detailed seventy-page analysis presented a month later and prepared in response to the Director's request in connection with the August 28, 1963, March on Washington. Despite the Kennedy letter, Hoover scornfully rejected the report's conclusion that the Communists had failed to make an impact on the civil rights movement. Nor was he impressed by the fact that less than 200 out of an estimated 250,000 participants in the March were identified as Party members. In a memo composed on the day after the March for transmission to the Director, Sullivan wrote: "The Director is correct. . . . We greatly regret that the memorandum did not measure up to what the Director has a right to expect from our analysis." The repentant intelligence chief pointed out that there was no yardstick for measuring Communist influence; but this difficulty could be overcome: "There are many Negroes who are fellow travellers, sympathizers who aid the Party knowingly or unknowingly, but do not qualify as members. These we must not ignore. The old Communist principle still holds: 'Communism must be built with non-Communist hands.' "

A subsequent memo of September 16, 1963, from the still abject Sullivan proposed a major program, Communist Influence in Radical Matters (CIRM), using "all possible investigative techniques," including offensive counterintelligence practices, to neutralize such influence. After initially rejecting the proposal with a sarcastic comment ("No. I can't understand how you can agilely switch your thinking and evaluation"), Hoover relented when Sullivan once again humbled himself and begged for an opportunity to "do everything that is humanly possible to develop all facts nationwide relative to the communist penetration and influence over Negro leaders and their organizations." The Director noted: "I am glad that you recognize at last that there is such an influence," and in a subsequent memorandum proposing an aggressive counterintelligence program (COINTELPRO), he wrote: "I am glad to see that light has finally, though dismally delayed, come to the Domestic Int. Div. I struggled for months to get over the fact that the Communists were taking over the racial movement. But [illegible]* couldn't or wouldn't see it."

The key target of this intensified drive was the Southern Christian Leadership Conference (SCLC) and its leader, Dr. Martin Luther King, Jr. It was King and his movement which had organized the August March. Even before the March, the Georgia minister had emerged as the best hope of his people in the peaceful struggle for racial equality and the foremost administration ally in the drive for civil rights legislation. The payoff for establishing a linkage between King's movement and communism could hardly have been greater. King himself was the primary target. Since King had demonstrated his outstanding role in the movement, Sullivan wrote, "We must mark him now, if we have not done so before, as the most dangerous Negro of the future in this Nation from the standpoint of Communism, the Negro and national security."

Initially, the King group was targeted under a program headed "Racial Matters," which comprehensively mandated the collection of "all pertinent information" in the public record about activities "in the racial field, whether or not linked to communism or violence." In November 1961 the Atlanta office advised Washington that "there was no information on which to base a security matter inquiry." In October 1962 the Bureau opened a COMINFIL case despite the SCLC's commitment to nonviolence and the absence of evidence of the kind called for by *Manual* requirements then in effect of a "Communist Party program to infiltrate [the] organization and influence its policy." Nor did the Bureau ever claim that it had evidence of specific instructions to infiltrate, let alone of infiltrators "in sufficient strength to influence or control the organization." One of King's advisers, Stanley Levison, was vaguely charged in Bureau documents with Communist Party ties; the Bureau searched in vain for proof, and even instigated an *in camera* Internal Security Subcommittee probe to get the goods on him. (Levison repeatedly denied that he was a Communist Party member or a "Communist agent," as he was characterized in FBI documents.) Another adviser, Hunter Pitts ("Jack") Odell, had formerly associated with Communists, but had broken with them early in 1963 because of their foot-dragging on civil rights issues. A third associate, Bayard Rustin, the director of the King-sponsored March on Washington in August 1963, had journeyed from youthful membership in the Young Communist League to a vigorously anti-Communist position. The desperate quality of the search for a surveillance justification is reflected in a memorandum from the Director concerning Rustin in response to the New York SAC's report that Rustin was unsympathetic to the Party's cause. The Director noted, "While there may not be

---

*The context indicates that the illegible name is Sullivan's. Hoover's repeated needling of Sullivan is explained by something more than his "normal" sadism in dealing with aberrant subordinates. Rumors of his displacement had made Hoover especially dependent on the support of Southern allies on the Hill whom he had already disappointed by the July 1963 memo to Senator Monroney. Faced with a conflict between their overdue IOUs and critics of his performance in protecting civil rights demonstrators, Hoover desperately needed intelligence material to establish the subversive character of the integration movement both to vindicate himself and to help his allies. Sullivan was thus not merely misguided but (far, far worse) "disloyal."

any direct evidence that Rustin is a communist, neither is there any substantial evidence that he is anti-communist."*

Despite the Bureau's futile investigative efforts and the Sullivan report of the previous August, Hoover's testimony before the appropriations committee in January 1964 (already referred to) finally delivered the goods his Southern allies had so eagerly sought. Echoing Sullivan's recantation, he reminded the legislators of the "old Communist principle" that "Communism must be built with non-Communist hands," and added: "We do know that Communist influence does exist in the Negro movement and it is this influence which is vitally important. It can be the means through which large masses are caused to lose perspective on the issues involved and, without realizing it, succumb to the Party's propaganda lures." To bolster this charge, Sullivan's newly launched CIRM project was instructed to step up the identification of all black members of the Communist Party.

The desperation of this campaign to discredit the civil rights movement is perhaps most dramatically illustrated by the Bureau's pursuit of the National Association for the Advancement of Colored People (NAACP). Under Bureau scrutiny since 1941, the NAACP offered slim pickings for a COMINFIL program. Moderate in goals and tactics and hostile to communism, its principal contribution to the civil rights struggle was a highly effective program of litigation. Yet, in 1965, the Bureau intensified its marathon probe in a special nationwide drive. Bureau field offices were exhorted to find evidence of Communist influence and to reexamine earlier reports clearing the group of subversive taint. Confidential sources and informers (151 in all, including 6 in Detroit, 16 in New York City, and 11 in St. Louis) were mobilized to "follow and report all efforts by the Communist Party to infiltrate the NAACP" both nationally and locally. Ancient dossiers of leaders were dusted off; pretext telephone calls were utilized to compile membership figures and Party plans to try to influence the organization's policies were reported. The reports summarizing this new hunt were, on orders from Washington, prepared in a format suitable for dissemination to other executive agencies as well as military intelligence.

Another prominent non-Communist target was the American Civil Liberties Union (ACLU). Directed against all offices of the ACLU, both national and local, the pursuit was begun in the twenties and lasted until the mid-seventies, utilizing a wide range of investigative techniques: confidential sources, informers both casual and planted, volunteer and solicited, wiretaps, file searches, credit and bank account checks. ACLU meetings of all kinds, open or closed, board and committee sessions on the national and affiliate level, were monitored. Its members, supporters, activists, and officers were surveilled, harassed, and dossiered. Ultimately, the FBI's files on the national ACLU and its field affiliates totaled 40–50,000 pages.

Beginning in 1941, the FBI also mounted an intensive surveillance drive against the National Lawyers Guild, a left-wing organization of lawyers formed

---

*The bogus charge of Communist infiltration of King's organization, based on the evidence summarized here, was used to extract approval by Attorney General Robert F. Kennedy of Hoover's request for electronic eavesdropping authorization. In turn, the tapes of the overheard King conversations were used to discredit him. (See Chapter 6.)

in 1937. The group was infiltrated, its meetings monitored, its offices wiretapped and burglarized. The Guild's opposition to the Truman government employee loyalty program and foreign policy initiatives such as the Marshall Plan resulted in intensified surveillance and persistent but unsuccessful lobbying by Hoover that the Guild be included in the Attorney General's list of proscribed organizations. At Hoover's direction, memoranda summarizing the agency's files of "subversive derogatory information" on the Guild and individual members were circulated to discredit the group's criticism of the Bureau. To further this campaign, the FBI collaborated with the House Committee on Un-American Activities (HUAC) in the preparation and dissemination of a report denouncing the Guild as the "Legal Bulwark of the Communist Party."

Another prominent organization surveilled for more than fifty years is the American Friends Service Committee (AFSC), a Quaker service organization that received the Nobel Peace Prize in 1947. Here, too, the principal focus of this protracted pursuit was a claimed concern with subversive influence. Although detailed FBI memoranda beginning in 1942 repeatedly concluded on the basis of informal reports that the AFSC was a "sincere pacifist group" and that it was free of subversive taint, the surveillance continued and, as in the case of most other non-Communist dissident targets, was augmented by activities of other federal (CIA, military intelligence, IRS) and local countersubversive units. Although not formally a target of a disruptive project, its office files in Philadelphia, Miami, Cambridge, and Des Moines were stolen or set on fire in a mysterious series of fire-bombings, break-ins, and thefts.*

The surveillance of these quite different groups was spurred in each instance by some special perceived threat. In the case of the ACLU, the fear was that the organization might resume the role it had played so effectively prior to 1924 as the leading critic of the Bureau. And this self-protective concern is clearly visible through the agency's countersubversive cover, a transparent pretext in view of the ACLU's ban, in effect between 1940 and 1967, on Communist board members. Hoover himself stated that there was no evidence that the ACLU was subversive, but the Bureau files internally characterize the ACLU as, for example, "nothing but a front for the Communists." This flim-flam is reflected in Hoover's personal authorization of a search of ACLU files at a time when he was repeatedly denying to ACLU organizer and long-time director Roger Baldwin that the ACLU was under investigation. These deceptions were the progeny of Hoover's grand deception of 1924 (see p. 47 above) when his libertarian reassurances that he would in the future confine the agency to law enforcement investigations led to Baldwin's approval of his appointment. Although objective evidence is lacking, it would have been a miracle had Hoover's personal vengefulness not influenced both the initial targeting in the twenties (marked by crudely chauvinist characterizations) and subsequent surveillance of the ACLU.

---

*The files show that while the AFSC was not a primary infiltration target, there was a considerable amount of low-level coverage by informers and the transmission of internal documents. The AFSC itself was not made a COMINFIL target only because "it could conceivably embarrass the Bureau." Instead, individual activists were surveilled, harassed, and tapped for the purpose of discrediting the organization and (during the Nixon years) "stifling criticism of the President's policies within his own church."

Having bent the knee to Baldwin as the price for power, he was not the man to forget such humiliation when power came to him.*

The record of the National Lawyers Guild surveillance also makes the FBI's protective concern quite clear. The Guild became a high-priority target when it attacked the Bureau and its methods. In addition, the prominent role of Guild lawyers in the defense of victims of political repression revived resentments reminiscent of the twenties. In the case of the AFSC, its peace and disarmament agendas provided a continuing spur to investigations that invariably yielded little more than the conclusion that the group's policies, especially those opposing the Vietnam War, paralleled those of groups considered subversive.

By the fifties the FBI's role as an authoritarian guardian of acceptable political and cultural values had become a reality of American life. Defenders of the status quo turned to it for help in combating what they considered subversion in private associations, both secular and religious. Members of organizations as well as critics on the outside emerged as a corps of "informants," voluntary unpaid sources of information about these groups' personnel and policies. It became routine for opposition forces in liberal associations and labor organizations to seek the aid of field offices in discrediting rivals and their policies. In the next phase, higher officials of such groups visited Washington headquarters, where they engaged in soul-baring sessions with Bureau officials. These "confidential sources" and "informants" received little or nothing in return beyond an outlet for hostility, compliments for their patriotism, and a gratified sense of power and importance.

In the case of the AFSC, this collaboration was minimal—letters to the Director urging investigation or seeking reassurance that the group was not subversive. In addition, the agency appears to have acquired access to an internal document written by insiders critical of the AFSC, commenting on the propriety of its involvement in political affairs, its alleged anti-Americanism, its feeble support of capitalism, and failure to attack Communist régimes. In the case of the National Lawyers Guild, the Bureau was buttressed by private support of another kind. In the sixties, American Bar Association president-elect John C. Satterfield met with Hoover and requested background information for use in reinstituting a ban on Guild membership and the adoption of a policy expelling Guild attorneys who were already ABA members. The Bureau obliged with a twenty-four-page report comparing Guild positions with those of the Communist Party. But the ABA nevertheless refused, as a result of the resistance of its younger members, to adopt the proposed disqualification. Similarly, private groups professedly liberal (CORE, American Jewish Congress, and American Jewish Committee) which had become active in the civil rights field organized a meeting in the early sixties with a Bureau functionary, Cartha DeLoach, to explore methods of preventing the involvement of Guild lawyers in a project organized to provide legal aid to Southern civil rights demonstrators.

A network of collaborative arrangements between ACLU insiders in field affiliates and the FBI flourished from the mid-forties on. During a seven-year

*In a revealing memo to the Attorney General in December 1925, Hoover recalled that the ACLU had "viciously attacked the Department [of Justice] for what it considered to be unwarranted activities infringing on . . . freedom of speech . . . and press."

period in the fifties national ACLU officials and staff members fed the FBI on a continuing basis internal reports, memoranda, files, minutes, and other material and documents dealing with the ACLU's policies, plans, and activities. They provided the FBI with information on the politics and private lives of individuals, informed it of pending actions, divulged internal conversations and discussions. In return, they sought Bureau assistance in identifying or clearing suspected Communists and solicited the agency's help both to influence ACLU policy and to implement its ban on Communist board members. This ironic collaboration between professed libertarians in positions of trust and an agency not merely hostile to free political expression generally but to the ACLU itself, was promoted by ideological considerations that are made especially clear by documents dealing with the activities of Irving Ferman, the director of the ACLU's Washington office from 1952 to 1954, and Morris L. Ernst, for many years the ACLU's general counsel and board member. Both Ferman and Ernst, in implementation of a militant anti-communism, cultivated Bureau bigwigs and took an insider's pleasure in this special relationship. Ferman subsequently justified his activities on "right way" grounds: that his influence with the FBI enabled him to prevent the publication of a report by the House Un-American Activities Committee critical of the ACLU. Ernst shared internal communications with Bureau officials and became in effect its agent in ACLU councils.

Ernst's courtship took the form of "My dear Edgar . . . for your eyes alone" letters to Hoover about internal ACLU matters and an article (in *Reader's Digest,* December 1950) entitled "Why I No Longer Fear the FBI." Ernst gloated over his intimacy with the powerful Director (not unlike Hoover's own boasts of his closeness to those *he* numbered among the mighty). But in 1964, after twenty years of personal correspondence with Hoover, Ernst was dropped from the special correspondence list on orders of Clyde Tolson, because he had referred to Hoover as "a treasured friend" during a closed session of a Senate subcommittee. "Any correspondence to him [Ernst] over the Director's signature may bring about repetition of his referring to the Director as a close, personal friend," the memorandum said. Thereafter, despite a generation of personal correspondence with Hoover, Ernst received only "in absence" replies from the FBI—letters written on behalf of Hoover by an aide.

On the Trail of Subversive Individuals

As already noted, the FBI's investigation of individuals absorbs most of the time and energy of its field agents. The subjects of individual investigative files released under the FOIA are not only members, past and present, of Marxist or violence-prone ("extremist") groups but thousands of individuals targeted solely because of their involvement in controversial causes and dissident organizations.* These records reflect common patterns: intensive investigation, highly

---

*The distinguished American educator Helen Keller, blind and deaf, was the subject of a dossier covering at least a decade of her life. The range of targets is vast—from Felix Frankfurter to Bertolt Brecht to Garry Wills to Henry Steele Commager to Robert Hutchins and many thousands of others less prominent.

detailed accounts of the subject's political and private life, a negative bias that finds clues to subversion in everything the subject does, a high factual error quotient, endless repetition occasioned by periodic updating of stale memoranda, a wide range of penetrative and privacy-invading surveillance techniques, a blind acceptance of informers' reports no matter how implausible or lacking in corroboration, and in some cases conversion of the passive collection of information into aggressive attempts to do injury. Beyond this, one is struck by the absence in the bulky files—in a great many cases reflecting decades-long pursuit—of procedures for terminating surveillance because the trail leads nowhere. There is no mechanism for breaking the bureaucratic momentum, for asking and answering the question: Why are we doing this? The only decision the investigative process seems to have addressed itself to is an internal bureaucratic determination: Should the subject be placed on a list for custodial detention in the event of future emergency (discussed below), and if so precisely what classification of dangerousness does he or she fall into? Grave discussions result in decisions to initiate, remove, or restore a listing, to raise or lower a subject's dangerousness ranking. Two case histories typify these patterns.

Dr. Quentin D. Young, Chief of Medicine at the world's largest hospital, Cook County (Chicago) Hospital, since 1972, was surveilled for nearly thirty years. His file, which begins when he graduated from medical school in 1948, extends to more than 3200 pages and includes, in addition to informers' reports, bank records, vacation itineraries, private correspondence, and medical information about some of his patients. His involvement in civil rights, civil liberties, and anti-war movements, and the fact that he treated radicals, all fueled the suspicions of the Chicago field office, which falsely listed him as a "prominent Communist." ("Absolute drivel," Young said when he read this entry.) The FBI found confirmation of Young's subversiveness in the fact that he helped organize the Chicago Medical Committee for Human Rights to oppose discrimination in health care. (In time the committee itself became a target because, according to a 1972 memo, "Some individuals in the organization in the past have taken positions contrary to policies of the U.S. government.") In March 1966 the Bureau sought to entrap Young in a sedition charge by sending a decoy posing as a draftee for a physical examination in the hope that Young would falsify his medical condition. The plan backfired when it turned out that the decoy, whom Young had referred to an orthopedist, suffered from a serious knee condition requiring his draft deferment. Nevertheless, the Chicago SAC pushed for authorization for a more intensive probe of the Medical Committee for purposes of building a sedition case. Young's patients, correspondents, and associates, including individuals who used his name as a reference on job or apartment applications, were subjected to background checks. The office of a group in which he, along with other prominent Chicagoans, was actively involved, the Chicago Committee to Defend the Bill of Rights, was burglarized by Bureau agents seeking a list of the committee's financial supporters.

Nor was his private life spared. A 1964 holiday trip with his daughter and a friend to the Shakespeare Festival at Stratford, Ontario, and a European tour in 1967 both became investigative magnets. In the latter case, agents took the trouble to obtain his itinerary and passport application and periodically made pretext calls to his office to learn whether he had returned. The agents also made investigative reports about his divorce and the background of a girlfriend. In July 1970 Young was raised from the lowest classification of dangerousness in the emergency detention listing to the highest, only after a reconsideration to be reclassified back to his original status. One never learns from the record the reasons for these evaluative shifts, or indeed why Young was put on the list at all.

Thomas I. Emerson, a recently retired professor at the Yale Law School, is the country's outstanding authority on the First Amendment. As he put it, "I always thought of myself as an unreconstructed New Dealer, a constitutional liberal." But Emerson's file, over 1500 pages thick and covering three decades, reflects an altogether different view of the professor's politics and values. Emerson's is a classic instance of the built-in hostility and operational intensity that mark the investigation of subjects critical of the Bureau and its Director. Emerson was a leader of the National Lawyers Guild and himself an effective libertarian critic of Bureau operations. In June 1948 the Bureau learned from a tap on the Guild's Washington phone that someone from Yale had requested the Guild office to obtain for his use a transcript of Hoover's congressional testimony on the subject of wiretapping. ("After such knowledge, what forgiveness?") The Bureau, suspecting that it was Emerson, directed its New Haven field agents to make a discreet inquiry into Emerson's planned use of the statement, "so as to preclude the possibility of Professor Emerson learning of the Bureau's interest in the matter." Months later New Haven transmitted to headquarters a copy, reproduced on eight rolls of microfilm, of a draft of an article by the Yale professor on the government employee loyalty program critical of the Bureau's wiretapping and mail interception practices. Ironically, the draft itself was almost certainly obtained by a surreptitious entry into Emerson's office, filmed, and then returned to its original location—a standard practice in documentary theft and reproduction. (On an earlier occasion in 1941 the Bureau acquired an address book with frequently called telephone numbers under circumstances that also point to a break-in.)

Hoover's special interest in Emerson festered. A May 1953 memo indicates that the Director had actively lobbied to have Emerson subpoenaed by the House and Senate anti-subversive committees. Shortly thereafter, on June 16, Emerson pursuant to subpoena testified before SISS, and though the testimony was taken in executive session and presumably secret, the transcript was promptly transmitted to the FBI's Domestic Intelligence Division for review, followed by a memo summarizing a report to the Bureau by SISS counsel Robert Morris, who confided that Emerson "had been a keen disappointment" because of the ease with which he had handled the questions. But all was not lost: in January 1954 a Bureau contact on the SISS staff offered the tip that Emerson was then in Europe, allegedly to attend a conference of Communist lawyers in Vienna. The SISS staffer was watching this with particular interest since such a tie-in might provide a justification for recalling the Yale professor and assuaging the disappointment occasioned by his original testimony. This report and its buttressing detail, such as a statement that Emerson's trip to Europe was rumored to have been sponsored and paid for by the Guild, was an invention.

Emerson was in Europe on a sabbatical study program at the London School of Economics and knew nothing about a meeting of lawyers in Vienna or anywhere else. The Bureau, eager for some sustenance, nevertheless enlisted the State Department in investigating the matter.

Meanwhile, Emerson's domestic activities were being internally monitored through an informer network. His friends and associates—including prominent figures in public life—were characterized in an informer's report as "definitely pro-Communist in their activities and associations." For over a decade he is reported in the file as a member of a Communist cell on the University of Washington campus in Seattle, although he had never been on that campus (or in the state of Washington for that matter) during the period in question, and so informed an agent-interviewer. Because the file reflected uniform tributes from students to his objectivity as a teacher, the Bureau concluded that he was "under deep cover" and was possibly "a secret high level member of the Communist Party." Aggressive initiatives included a planted media attack and briefing, and an abortive inquiry by the Immigration and Naturalization Service into his deportability. Like Dr. Young, he was placed in various categories of custodial detention listees, periodically altered in accordance with changing calibrations of his dangerousness. In anticipation of the possibility that the professor might resist custodial detention by filing a habeas corpus petition, an agent prepared a twelve-page memorandum for use in such a proceeding.

Monitoring the Movement

Between 1965 and 1972 the FBI's intelligence caseload mounted sharply, in response first to the civil rights and anti-war movements, and thereafter, beginning in 1970, to the emergence of the New Left. By the end of fiscal year 1972 the Domestic Intelligence Division workload had risen to approximately 62,000 investigative matters,* from an estimated 45,000 in 1965. In fiscal year 1972, 45 percent more subversive investigations were initiated than in 1970. Extremist investigations rose even more sharply: by 1971 the investigative caseload increased by 161 percent over fiscal year 1965, principally as the result of the Bureau's intensive monitoring of militant black groups, especially the Panthers. Initially, the Bureau strove to develop an anti-Communist internal security rationale for these investigations. But by the mid-sixties Communists had become an endangered species, ravaged by the very agency now in desperate need of a fresh supply with which to taint the proliferating dissidence of the era. Not only numerical decline but lack of influence made the gambit forbidding. The aging Party cadres did not speak the same language as the Vietnam era dissenters. The Party's stress on working-class primacy, its insensitivity to the status revolt (women, youth, students, soldiers, etc.) and to cultural discontent, its blind allegiance to the Soviet Union, bureaucratic rigidity, "straight" rhetoric,

*An "investigative matter"—a Bureau internal usage to measure workload—embraces any major investigation generated by a particular case, such as a referral to a field office from the office originating the investigation.

and ideological stereotypes all repelled the new rebels, as did the sectarianism and the solemnity of the emerging Maoist sects. Just as infiltration/influence replaced fronts, so new, even more tenuous standards of subversion were brought to the fore. The field offices were endlessly exhorted to match the aims and objectives of proposed targets with those of the Communist Party, to focus on organizations "likely to be susceptible to Communist influence" or with goals that "served the Communist cause." "This necessarily includes," a headquarters memorandum points out, "anti-war and pacifist groups, civil rights and other radical groups which advocate civil disobedience and oppose the exercise of authority by duly constituted Government officials."[15]

The strained quality of the hunt for an internal security predicate comes through in the documentation of the 1969–73 surveillance program of women's rights groups, designated as the Women's Liberation Movement (WLM) in Bureau files.*[16] A number of field offices advised Washington headquarters that there was no ground for a countersubversive probe of women's liberation activities and requested permission to close their files. The San Francisco SAC added in an August 1969 report:

> The Women's Liberation Movement may be considered as subversive to the New Left and revolutionary movements as they have proven to be a divisive and factionalizing factor. . . . It could be well recommended as a counterintelligence movement to weaken the revolutionary movement.

But the Director knew better; though loosely structured, the WLM, he insisted, was a nationwide movement, with a demonstrated proclivity for violence and a willingness to support and accept support from subversive groups. It was therefore "absolutely essential that we conduct sufficient investigation to clearly establish subversive ramifications of the WLM and to determine the potential for violence presented by the various groups connected with their movement as well as any possible threat they may represent to the internal security of the United States." In the extremist category, too, the linkage problem, as already noted, was tricky: the Bureau recognized that most of the violence which could be ascribed to a political source involved local law violations not within its primary investigative jurisdiction. In order to justify Bureau involvement, the agents were instructed to find a connection between the violence and "subversive elements" already under investigation by the Bureau.[17]

The simplest way to overcome jurisdictional problems, however, was to label such investigations "exploratory," initiated for the purpose of determining whether in fact the target was subversive or extremist. Investigations opened as "discreet preliminary" inquiries wore on for months and years. The monitoring of the "WLM" on a discreet preliminary basis continued for more than three years. Beginning in August of 1972, the Bureau instituted a "discreet preliminary inquiry" into a radical political-theory study group organized by three college

---

*A directive to target the "WLM" on the assumption that it was an identifiable organization brought back a bewildered reply from a field office that its informers "had no information concerning a group or organization called 'Women's Liberation Movement.' . . . It would seem an abortive attempt may have been made to organize or affiliate all women into an organization, but it never materialized."

professors by penetrating it to determine whether it was a subversive front. It was not until June 1975 that the investigation was finally abandoned because of the subject's inactivity.[18]

In the drive to expand organizational coverage of the growing anti-war movement, the COMINFIL requirements of some expression of takeover purpose by a Communist group was abandoned in favor of the head-count formula already developed in the civil rights field. This stress on individuals was also dictated by the unstructured tribal character of the new radicalism, its rejection of traditional organizational norms and hierarchy, and its scorn for formally stated goals. Significantly, 90 percent of the Vietnam/civil rights era caseload represented investigations of individuals based largely on the fiction invoked to justify investigation of Communist Party members: No one could join (whatever that meant) a New Left group without accepting the necessity and desirability of violence as a tactic. But even a tenuous group relationship cannot explain the growth of individual investigations, an estimated 47 percent of which involved subjects not affiliated with any group. This expansion, in large part stimulated by White House pressure, is reflected in a decision in the fall of 1970 to open some 10,500 new cases: an estimated 2500 on each member of the SDS, 4000 more on members of other New Left campus groups, and the same number on black student activists and leaders (see Chapter 7).

The monitoring of individuals in turn created a justification for the surveillance of an immense range of protest activities—meetings, conferences, lectures, rallies—simply because of the presence or participation of an individual target. For example, the Bureau's intelligence operations against "black nationalists" in Chicago resulted in the monitoring of all black leaders who were seen from time to time with these suspected militants at public meetings. The product of this sweeping surveillance, much of it collected by informers, was stored in extensive secret files on hundreds of black civic business and political leaders in Chicago, including Congressman Ralph Metcalfe ("File 137"). The pretextual quality of the claim that broad, unfocused surveillance was required to keep track of particular subjects comes through in the controversy that emerged around the Earth Day rallies. In the spring of 1971, on assignment from the Nixon White House, the Domestic Intelligence Division monitored a nationwide series of Earth Day rallies (National Environmental Teach-Ins) sponsored by an environmental protection coalition, including a bloc of interested congressmen. A letterhead memorandum (LHM) on the Washington area rally, one of more than forty surveilled nationwide, at which Senator Edmund Muskie was the principal speaker, was disseminated to a number of executive agencies. The memorandum covers every phase of the affair, beginning with the application for the use of a park as the site of a demonstration, and including summaries of press accounts of the planned meeting, the slogans on picket signs, the literature distributed, and the speeches. It also identifies the sponsors of the press conferences, the participating organizations, their leaders, and publications, together with background reports. Thus the memo states that the publicity director of one of the sponsoring groups "has been publicly identified as a Communist Party leader" (in fact, he had been a mere member, who had left the Party years earlier). It further notes that the list of speakers included Rennie

Davis, one of the convicted defendants in the Chicago conspiracy trial, whose participation in the meeting was subsequently used as the reason for the surveillance. Two appendices summarize the dossiers of the SDS (because one of the participants had formerly been associated with it as an undergraduate) and of the Progressive Labor Party (because of its involvement in a factional dispute within SDS).

In response to an attack by Senator Muskie on the surveillance and the disseminated memorandum, Robert Mardian, head of the Internal Security Division, claimed that it had been initiated by the Bureau as a precaution against the possible assassination of the senator, suppressing the fact that it was instigated by the White House for less benign reasons.[19]

In order to process the ever-expanding coverage, droves of informers were needed. Not primarily to infiltrate a particular organization—that was easy enough: one simply went to a meeting or a demonstration—but to swim in the sea of the "movement," the amorphous, shifting, overlapping complex of organizations, committees, communes, vigils, collectives, coalitions, publications, etc., etc. in which the "activists" functioned at large. The ecumenicism of informer surveillance in the late sixties is indicated by the following list of organizations covered by Robert Merritt, an FBI and D.C. metropolitan police informer:

> The Academy of Political Science
> Action Resources Collective
> American Civil Liberties Union
> *The Advocate,* a publication of the National Law Center at Washington University
> American Friends Service Committee
> Anti-War Union
> Attica Brigade
> Black Peoples' Party
> Clear Creek
> Children's March for Survival
> Coalition of National Priorities and Military Policy
> Committee for Study of Incarceration and D.C. Corrections
> Common Cause
> *The Furies,* a radical feminist publication
> Md.-D.C. Committee to Oppose Political Repression
> Community Bookshop
> D.C. Statehood Party
> Gay Activist Alliance
> Howard University Committee to Free Angela Davis
> Institute for Policy Studies
> Middle East Research and Information Project
> National Organization for Reform of Marijuana Laws
> *Off Our Backs,* a woman's monthly feminist magazine
> People's Coalition for Peace and Justice
> RAP, Inc., a local drug rehabilitation program
> Tenants' Rights Workshop
> Runaway House
> The Union of Radical Political Economists at American University[20]

The strained dialectic by which the dissidence of the sixties replaced communism as the touchstone of subversion is capsulized in the 1968–74 investigation of the anti-war Institute for Policy Studies (IPS). We begin with a mid-sixties Communist influence investigation of the Students for a Democratic Society (SDS), ordered by President Johnson for ultimate propaganda use against his anti-war opponents.* By 1968 the SDS itself, along with its leaders and activists, is being thoroughly surveilled by a network of informers and wiretaps; two years later every member becomes a target. In June 1968 a research fellow of the IPS, Arthur Waskow, approached a New York SDS activist (who subsequently became a Weather Underground fugitive) and advised him that he was one of "50 young intelligent leftist militants recommended to attend a three-day meeting of the Foreign Policy Association" in New York that summer. According to the Bureau, it was then decided to probe the relationship between the SDS and IPS, ostensibly to determine on the basis of this single exchange between two individuals, neither of whom was alleged to be a Communist, whether a CP-SDS taint then being investigated extended to the IPS. In addition, in October 1968, Washington received a report via a field informer that an IPS fellow had offered "some apparent cooperation" to *Ramparts* magazine in the preparation of an article on a trip to Cuba by SDS members that year. Now, according to the Bureau, the plot thickens. Could there be "a relationship between 'Ramparts' and the IPS, inasmuch as both had demonstrated an interest in SDS"? For six years the IPS was infiltrated by scores of informers; its premises were burglarized, its trash scrutinized, its fellows' phones wiretapped, its publications and brochures channeled into swollen files. Not only the Bureau, but the CIA, military intelligence, the Office of Naval Intelligence, a federal grand jury investigating the Pentagon Papers affair, and the D.C. metropolitan police got into the act. Ultimately, as we have seen, a law enforcement pretext was improvised as a retroactive justification.

It was not until the end of the Vietnam War and the exhaustion of the social movements it stimulated that the investigative tide receded. By that time the toll of targets had run the gamut of dissent—from the Quakers and Methodists to SANE and the War Resisters League, from the NAACP to the Panthers, from environmentalism to the Native American Movement. The number of individual files, not only of leaders but of lowly participants, soared to record heights. While "Communist influence" lost its credibility as an investigative rationale, the materials for fashioning a new Menace accumulated in the polarized confrontation between "the movement" and "the system." Opposition to the war and compassion for its victims went hand in hand with a demand for new domestic priorities. Beyond this, the new politics were largely congruent with

---

*After a conference with President Johnson in April 1965, Hoover instructed his subordinates to prepare a memorandum linking SDS with communism:

> While I realize that we may not be able technically to state that it is an actual communist organization, certainly we do know that there are communists in it. It is somewhat similar to the situation that we found in the Selma-Birmingham march in which we were able to identify 75 communists in New York City as being in that march even though there were many others in the march who were not communists and we could not be certain that it was a communist demonstration. What I want to get to the President is a background with emphasis upon the communist influence therein so that he will know exactly what the picture is.

the rejection of establishment culture and morality, resembling the Menace as it emerged in the twenties—scornful of capitalism's offerings and intentions, immoral, dirty, and disloyal. For the Bureau, imbued with the Director's self-righteous moralizing zeal, the challenge could hardly have been greater. How could the intelligence sword be permitted to rust in its scabbard when not merely capitalism and its institutions but civilization itself was at stake?

This zeal found an outlet in aggressive covert action (discussed below) and in collaboration with private groups. In another throwback to the twenties, the Bureau, in 1969, met with private employers in the New York area to plan a defense against a threatened (but never actually consummated) infiltration by SDS members of industrial plants to radicalize the work force. An even closer collaboration between the Honeywell Corporation and the Minneapolis FBI field office stretched over the period 1969–72. According to an internal Bureau memorandum and corroborating data, the Minneapolis SAC was authorized to furnish file information, obtained from informers, "to a confidential source in the company's management" in order to frustrate an anti-war group, the "Honeywell Project," and its supporters, who were protesting the company's manufacture of cluster (anti-personnel) bombs for use in the Vietnam War. Honeywell's director of security, a former FBI agent, told the press that he was "not aware of any special liaison between the Bureau and the company," although the specific goal of the field office was "to prevent any attempt to obtain publicity or embarrass the corporate officials."*

Nor was the mobilization against the movement confined to the Bureau. A constellation of agencies—the Internal Revenue (IRS), the CIA, military intelligence, the Office of Naval Intelligence, the National Security Agency, grand juries, and other federal agencies—complemented by a nationwide urban intelligence structure, joined in the pursuit with the objective of harassing, discrediting, and containing the multi-faceted protests of the time. It was repressive warfare with new weapons and against an entire milieu, seen as threatening the very foundations of the state. Total intelligence, implemented by a coalescing intelligence community, emerged as an instrument of social and political control. The intensity and scope of this assault are most revealingly illustrated by the intelligence activities that focused on the college and university campus.

Intelligence Goes to College

The 1970 Huston Plan recommended increased intelligence coverage of "violence prone campus and student related groups" through illegal operational methods. The reason for the recommendation was ascribed in the memorandum to the fact that the "campus is the battle ground of the revolutionary protest movement." Tom Charles Huston, the author of the plan, himself a former

---

*A lawsuit filed by the American Civil Liberties Union charged that, in addition to informer penetrations, the Bureau resorted to illegal wiretaps and covert action such as spreading false information about the plaintiffs, encouraging violence, and promoting dissension—*Davidov et al.* v. *Honeywell et al.* (U.S. District Court of Minnesota); "ACLU Suit Charges Honeywell Conspired with the FBI to Infiltrate Activist Groups"—*New York Times,* April 21, 1977.

conservative campus leader, surely exaggerated the lack of campus intelligence coverage. Since the 1950s the college and university campus had been the most important single concentration area of American intelligence units, both federal and local. The anti-war movement and the youth rebellion of the late sixties generated even more intensive intelligence activities.[21]

Quite apart from the college setting, American political intelligence has always placed a heavy emphasis on youth as a surveillance target. A monitoring of the involvements of youthful subjects is indispensable in the politics of deferred reckoning; the struggle is as much for the future as for the present. The agent or investigator, to use the language of one of them, wants to "save" the subject "from mistakes [he] may regret later on"—an expression of a neo-Freudian thesis cherished by the intelligence community, that the political preferences of one's youth are fixed, and unless a subject defects or informs he will bear watching for the rest of his life.

The FBI's role in campus surveillance is rooted in the loyalty-security program for screening applicants for government employment. Such investigations gave the Bureau an official campus entree and, indeed, institutionalized its relationship to the college. Bureau agents who specialized in loyalty background investigations in the fifties and early sixties became familiar with the academic establishment and developed a friendly relationship with even the starchiest deans, registrars, secretaries, and professors. A key purpose of campus surveillance is the identification of organizations engaged in suspect activities, their members and supporters. Since these are not infrequently recorded in an administrative office, the cordial relationship paid off. Agents had no difficulty in persuading college personnel to turn over files, even though access might be formally barred by regulations. But identification is only part of the Bureau's campus mission. Applicant screening served as a useful pretext for a full-scale investigation of individuals. Universities seeking to cooperate in applicant screening, but not in countersubversive investigations of nonapplicants, freely accepted the agent's explanation of the reasons for the investigation. In this more comprehensive investigative process the Bureau also relied on covert campus sources, such as paid student informers, switchboard operators, postal employees, landladies, dormitory maids, and maintenance people. Nor did the principles of academic freedom hamper Bureau agents in the development of "confidential sources" among cooperative faculty members, ready to inform on colleagues and students. This occurred principally in connection with field investigations of employment applicants or appointees (as in the case of John Kenneth Galbraith). Ideologically committed faculty members also volunteered as informers. For example, in July 1953, Dr. Henry A. Kissinger, then a teacher at Harvard, opened a letter sent to a participant in a seminar on international relations he was conducting, and communicated its contents to the Boston FBI office, which then dispatched an agent to interview him.*

*The documents, released under the FOIA, were published by a Columbia professor of sociology—Sigmund Diamond, "Kissinger and the F.B.I.," *Nation*, Nov. 10, 1979. Kissinger also supplied the Bureau with suggestions as to the identity of the letter's author. It is unclear whether Kissinger became a "confidential source" on a continuing basis, as a Bureau memo recommended in reporting the matter to Washington. However, there is no doubt that Kissinger played an

As the sixties progressed, the Bureau encountered growing hostility and was forced into greater reliance on its covert campus sources. In the spring of 1966, following a Students for a Democratic Society peace demonstration at Wesleyan College, two FBI agents demanded that the college authorities submit the names of all members of the SDS. College Dean Stanley Idzerda refused, on the ground that the college kept no lists, and issued a statement that:

"We consider the student's activity his own affair. At the same time, it is unfortunate that a climate of suspicion can be created by such activities that might lead some students to be more circumspect than the situation requires. Things like this can be a danger to a free and open community if men change their behavior because of it." The resultant furor brought forth first a denial by the FBI New Haven office and then a claim that there had been a "misunderstanding." No probe of the group as such had been contemplated, but only "possible infiltration of the SDS Chapter by Communist influence." The agent added that the FBI "makes inquiries every day on campuses throughout the country—we inspect 175 types of files, security as well as criminal." In response to a protest to J. Edgar Hoover that the investigation constituted an infringement on academic freedom, the Director replied that the charge was "not only utterly false, but also is so irresponsible as to cast serious doubts on the quality of academic reasoning or the motivations behind it." In a subsequent letter to the *Connecticut Bar Journal,* Hoover admitted that the visit took place and insisted that it was an authorized investigation to determine the extent of Communist infiltration of the SDS—a reference to the Johnson assignment.[22]

The disclosure in 1967 of CIA involvement in student-related matters resulted in a White House instruction to the Bureau to reduce its campus presence. Agents were cautioned to restrict their physical appearances on campus, to obtain authorization for on-campus interviews, to make known to the individual interviewed the purpose of the inquiry, and to avoid contact with faculty members critical of the Bureau. But these restraints simply resulted in increasing reliance upon established sources on the campus and the deployment of more campus spies.

The importance of campus "established sources" in the surveillance process, and the use of a variety of other surveillance techniques, are well illustrated by the Media papers, a haul of over 1000 documents removed in March 1971 from an FBI resident agency at Media, Pennsylvania. One of these documents refers to "educators and administrators who are established sources," while others mention such sources as a Swarthmore College switchboard operator "(conceal identity due to position at school)," a registrar at an Eastern women's college "(protect identity at school)," an administrative employee at the University of California at Berkeley who transmitted file material to a Bureau agent, the Swarthmore College campus police chief, and a file custodian at Swarthmore "who requests that her identity be protected."

One of these established sources tipped off the Bureau about an anti-war

important role in the initial authorization of wiretaps by the Nixon administration (discussed in Chapter 7) to monitor alleged national security leaks: the taps were installed following a conference between Kissinger and Director Hoover on May 5, 1969—*Impeachment Hearings,* Bk. VII, pp. 55–120.

Conference of War Resisters scheduled at Haverford College in the fall of 1969. The memo instructs fourteen resident agents in the Philadelphia division of the Bureau as well as field agents who served as contacts to mobilize their informers, some twenty-two in number, for the upcoming conference for the purpose of determining whether the conference "will generate any anti-U.S. propaganda (be most *discreet* in handling this matter)." The most detailed of the Media campus surveillance documents concerns a Bureau student anti-subversive program, STAG ("Student Agitation"), launched on August 28, 1970. One document was addressed a month later to some 18 agents assigned to monitor Philadelphia area colleges with a total enrollment of some 140,000 students. It indicates that files had already been opened on student activities at twenty-two area institutions, including community colleges and seminaries. Each resident agent was required to report to a coordinating special agent in Philadelphia in charge of the "New Left desk" the following information:

(1) current number of university or college sources on the academic or administrative staff including security officers broken down under these categories;

(2) number of current student security informants or PSI's [i.e., "potential security informants"];

(3) any other current sources for information re student agitation (by position or agency);

(4) identity (i.e., professor, police officer, student) of any of the above who can provide you with *advanced* [sic] information on student agitation;

(5) listing of what information of Bureau interest cannot be obtained from the university or college (not limited to STAG);

In a scrawled, home-made shorthand, there are listed the following possible sources for the information requested for the STAG program: infiltration, subscriptions to college newspapers through a Philadelphia post office box, and more frequent liaison with the college secretary's office.

The operational consequence of the decision to concentrate on black student organizations is reflected in a document—an urgent directive dated November 4, 1970, from Washington, with a deadline—inaugurating a stepped-up drive to recruit black student informers. The Director explained: "Black Student Unions (BSU) and similar groups . . . are targets for influence and control by the violence-prone Black Panther Party (BPP) and other extremists." Although the Director acknowledged that the BPP had not yet succeeded,* he called his agents' attention to the fact that "the distribution of the BPP newspaper on college campuses and speakers of the BPP and other black extremist groups on campuses clearly indicates that campuses are targets of extremists." This tenuous justification for the surveillance of black students in no way limits the intensity of the planned coverage. All campus groups, "organized to project the demands of black students," that are not already being watched are to be made surveillance targets, "carefully conducted to avoid criticism," but still thorough

---

*The Bureau was apparently uninformed of (or preferred to ignore) a fact widely known in integrationist circles: that at no time in the history of the black protest movement did the Panthers gain a foothold on the college campus. Black students and their organizations were overwhelmingly influenced by black nationalism, a form of commitment deeply hostile to the Panther program.

enough to identify "leadership, key activists" on whom dossiers are to be compiled with a view to determining the necessity of further surveillance of these leaders. In the meantime, the results of the preliminary surveillance are to be widely disseminated, together with recommendations for further action. The program is to include not only four-year colleges but junior and two-year colleges as well.

On December 2, two days before the deadline, Philadelphia's SAC reports to the Director on the steps he has taken to carry out the November 4 instructions. Investigative coverage has been expanded from an initial two targets; files have been opened on black student groups on thirteen area campuses. The list includes the Black Student Union of Pennsylvania State University, Students for an Afro-American Society at the University of Pennsylvania, and the Association of Blacks for Progress at Bucknell. Attached to the memorandum is a list dated May 1, 1969, of black students at Swarthmore prepared by the secretary to Swarthmore's registrar, a woman whose name recurs throughout the Media papers ("an established source who requests that her identity be protected").

If the Director's November memo generated an investigation of thirteen colleges in the Philadelphia area alone, it seems apparent that the resultant nationwide surveillance, including as it did two-year and junior colleges, must have been tremendous in scope. Moreover, these were merely preliminary inquiries; leaders and key activists were to be targeted for further investigation and dossier compilation, a process that would generate subsequent surveillance not only of these persons but of other organizations with which they might become associated. Beginning with a 1960 report, commissioned by the House Committee on Un-American Activities, denouncing San Francisco student demonstrations protesting the committee's hearing as "communist-inspired," Hoover throughout the rest of the decade launched a fiery, the-Communists-are-after-our-youth campaign based on the Bureau's campus surveillance efforts. In 1963 he called for a ban on Communist campus speakers on the grounds that their propaganda was too insidious for the unwary students and that the honoraria paid them was a sinister subsidy. The "communist conspiracy," he warned, was craftily laying traps for youth, to "coax them into the communist movement itself or at least agitate them into serving the communist cause." By the end of the decade his apocalyptic rhetoric had reached new heights: campus radicalism was a "specter haunting the western world," threatening "the orderly process of education as the forerunner of a more determined effort to destroy our economic, social and political structures."

Hoover's campaign, augmented and supported by the congressional anti-subversive committees, bore fruit. In the fall of 1970 Congress approved a measure for 1000 additional FBI agents to deal with campus bombings and aerial hijacking. The legislation passed despite the urgings of college administrators, local police chiefs, and student leaders that the Bureau agents be barred from the campus unless invited in by local authorities. More strikingly, the legislation was wholly gratuitous: the Bureau never lacked manpower to deal with campus bombings. As the *New York Times* noted editorially on September 25, the proposal was "so patently redundant that its motives, as well as its defects, raise some serious questions." Despite this legislation and the media disclosures the

following year of a campus network of Bureau confidential sources and informers, the Director denied shortly before his death in May 1972 that the Bureau
was active on college campuses. What could not be denied was that the Bureau
was ineffective in containing campus violence or in identifying perpetrators of
bombings. For example, it failed even to anticipate the bombing of a laboratory
on a Wisconsin campus in 1970 or to apprehend the culprits. And, despite
massive surveillance of the SDS, it neither anticipated the emergence of the
Weather Underground nor succeeded in apprehending those involved in its
underground activities.

Beginning in the fifties, the CIA also developed campus ties via secret
subsidies of academic research and the funding, through a maze of foundations
and dummy conduits, of a number of groups, most notably the National Student
Association, a nationwide organization of college students, to ensure support for
the official U.S. foreign policy line at international conferences.* Other beneficiaries of the program included the Independent Research Service, the International Student Conference, Policy Research Inc., the American Society for
African Cultures, and the International Development Foundation.

Investigation turned up other forms of CIA involvement in the domestic
academic community. CIA agents routinely approached professors and students who received grants for foreign travel or research with requests to
moonlight as intelligence agents during their study abroad. Not infrequently,
the student or professor was first interviewed on his return and invited to
report, or to answer questions of interest to the CIA, or even to supply copies
of photographs. Cooperation was stimulated by a generous "consultation fee,"
as well as the hope of a new grant. Veterans of these sessions routinely
stopped by a CIA office for a "debriefing" after a sojourn in such places as
Africa, Indonesia, or India. A related practice involved the use of foreign
study or travel grants as a cover for spying abroad by CIA agents with domestic academic credentials. In addition, foreign exchange students disclosed that
the CIA had infiltrated their delegations with "politically reliable" students
from their home countries to spy on them, some of whom were also trained
here by the Agency for espionage in their home countries. Student members of
such delegations sometimes found that their visas were mysteriously canceled.
The CIA also recruited students and faculty spies as an investment protection
measure—to check the loyalty of academics working on CIA contract projects
in American universities and the reliability of students and professors subsidized for foreign intelligence work.

A comprehensive report published in January 1967 by the American Anthropological Association's Committee on Research Problems and Ethics stated
that in many parts of the world, American anthropologists were suspected or
believed to be engaged in intelligence activities, that "there is some basis for

*The CIA's involvement in campus and student affairs was initially revealed in an article in
the March 1967 *Ramparts* magazine, which in turn led to a series of broader disclosures of CIA
intrusions in the academic as well as other spheres. But the critical response to the disclosures flared
only briefly before the establishment closed ranks. The CIA withdrew from the funding program
that had ignited the flare-up but continued uninterruptedly its involvement in certain key university-
based activities.

these suspicions and beliefs," and that as a result legitimate anthropological research had been severely handicapped. The Association's knowledgeable members reported that CIA agents had posed as anthropologists or used anthropological research as a cover, and that qualified anthropologists were hired by the CIA for intelligence work either directly or through certain CIA fronts. "In some cases," the report said, "such persons have falsely represented themselves as still being associated with universities, although their prior academic affiliations no longer existed." In addition, anthropologists denied funds for legitimate research "have been approached by obscure foundations or have been offered supplementary support from such sources only to discover later that they were expected to provide intelligence information, usually to the Central Intelligence Agency."

Campus surveillance was also a priority concern of military intelligence.[23] Surveillance was conducted by military agents overtly, as well as through agents planted undercover in college classes. In addition to general political surveillance by personnel assigned for that purpose, campuses were monitored by agents more narrowly charged with responsibility for personnel security investigations. These investigators, who had legitimate reason for entering the campus, were instructed when visiting local colleges and universities to moonlight and in the words of one such investigator, in congressional testimony,

> to be alert in connection with personnel security investigations for notices of any marches, rallies, meetings or demonstrations. We were instructed to collect any and all newspapers, flyers, pamphlets, or notices relevant to any student political activity. Agents were urged to visit especially the larger schools such as the University of Chicago, Northwestern University, Loyola University, and the University of Illinois at Chicago Circle, regularly for this purpose.

Students and faculty members were surveilled, photographed, and dossiered by hundreds of military intelligence agents, who enjoyed the cooperation of campus security police and college authorities. The most detailed account of campus surveillance came from ex-Sergeant Richard Kasson, one of ten military intelligence agents working out of Region V of the 113th Military Intelligence Group at Fort Snelling, Minnesota, for about a year beginning in February 1969. Kasson's duties on the University of Minnesota campus consisted primarily of notetaking at speeches, photography, identifying speakers, and estimating the size and mood of the crowd. At the time of Kasson's surveillance assignment, a University of Minnesota policy permitted public disclosure, without written authorization, only of a student's address, degree earned, and date of enrollment. While most of Kasson's investigations consisted of personnel security inquiries for which the student subject presumably gave permission, Kasson recalled that he and others had "easy access" to confidential files:

> I just gave them a 3×5 card with a name on it and they gave me the whole file. We knew the people and we'd go ahead and give them a list of names that we wanted, get their files, and could review all their information, any correspondence that they had with the university, their transcripts and so forth. Once the military [liaison] is established with the university, you have pretty much free run of the place.

These charges were subsequently verified by the findings of an administration official. At Minnesota, as at virtually every other large university, the campus police removed obstacles and became gung-ho collaborators of the military intelligence agents. As the university's President, Malcolm Moos, testified: "The agents of military intelligence made regular visits to our university police department to develop personal relationships with officers in the department." These liaison visits resulted in an exchange of data and photographs with the military agents on a regular basis, and ultimately developed into a weekly joint session in which events would be reviewed and activists identified. The director of the university police, in turn, submitted a weekly intelligence summary to the governor's office, which summarized information from a variety of local police agencies and the Military Intelligence Group.

The extraordinary scope and intensity of campus surveillance by the military are typical of a style of excess I shall discuss later (in Chapter 8). But beyond this, the operation involves an irony: President Johnson, in the wake of the 1967 disclosures of CIA in academia, ordered the FBI to reduce its campus presence. But the abandoned territory was simply reoccupied by the Army, in response to requests by the Johnson administration for greater coverage of areas of potential disruption and violence!

Custodial Detention Programs—Listing
Candidates for Concentration Camps

The perennial wolf cry of an endangered internal security has, over the years, lost much of its power to validate intelligence. Apart from a relatively small group of true believers in the Menace, for the mass of Americans the trajectory spanning currently monitored activities and a future violent revolution disappears over the horizon of political reality. Domestic intelligence has, however, retained an alternative mission and a cognate operational program based on a different danger. That danger is sabotage and betrayal in the event of war with a Communist enemy. The intelligence mission is the investigation and listing of these potential traitors for forced detention when a war situation emerges. This concern about the potential enemies in our midst dominated American intelligence during World War I; both military intelligence and Hoover's GID compiled lists of potential traitors and saboteurs. On the eve of World War II, Hoover restored it to its former importance, and in the decades that followed, it dominated the monitoring of individual targets. The core of this preventive intelligence mode is the classification of identified targets into categories constructed to reflect their potential threat. The notion of custodial detention is an expression of the fears rooted in the countersubversive tradition: the obsession with ultimate treachery and betrayal by secret agents of foreign principals, the stress on identifiable evil individuals as prime movers (agitators), and the tribal resort to ostracism, isolation, and purge to protect the loyal citizenry.

Immediately after the Roosevelt announcement of September 1939, Hoover initiated a program for "custodial detention of individuals" with "strong communist [or Nazi] tendencies, whose presence at liberty in this country in time of war or national emergency, would constitute a menace to the public peace and safety of the United States Government."[24] The criteria for listing were broadly interpreted to include distributors of propaganda favorable to foreign interests and hostile to "the American way of life," as well as agitators of "internal strife" and "hatreds." Candidates for listing were selected on the basis of public as well as surveillance-derived information, and divided into immediate internment and close surveillance categories. In addition to the file listings, an index card system detailed the basis for the listings and the classification of dangerousness to which the subject was assigned. To keep the program secret, Bureau agents were instructed to use the Foreign Agents Registration Act as an investigative cover and to conduct investigations if required to supplement the available information. In July 1943 Attorney General Biddle ordered Hoover to end the program, pointing out that it lacked specific statutory authority and was not an exercise of the Bureau's "proper function," the investigation of law violations. Besides, Biddle noted that the evidence used for classifying subjects was inadequate, the applicable standards defective, and the underlying assumption that a classification could be made in the abstract without regard to particular circumstances "impractical . . . and dangerous."

A month after this instruction to terminate the listing and to cancel the classifications, Hoover nevertheless continued the program under a changed name. Field agents were ordered in a strictly confidential memorandum that the rechristened "Security Index" (SI) and cards should be kept secret, not mentioned in investigative reports or discussed with agencies or individuals outside the Bureau other than the representatives of naval and military intelligence services. The SI program, briefly cut back when the war ended, was expanded after its existence was made known to Attorney General Tom Clark in March 1946. In 1948 Clark directed the Bureau to prepare an Emergency Detention Program pursuant to a departmental master plan (the "Attorney General's Portfolio"), which contemplated detention of the individuals on the Security Index, the suspension of the writ of habeas corpus, and wholesale summary arrests without court review pursuant to a master warrant signed by the Attorney General. In addition to a mass arrest warrant, the program also contemplated wholesale raids through a master search warrant procedure (see Appendix IV). In 1950 Congress passed, over President Truman's veto, the Internal Security Act, providing formally for an emergency detention system with less repressive standards of apprehension than the Attorney General's program, retaining the writ of habeas corpus and providing for individual warrants based on probable cause and for evidentiary court hearings within forty-eight hours. Not only Clark but his two immediate successors, Attorneys General McGranery and Brownell, instructed the Bureau to ignore the more limited statute—itself the subject of widespread criticism*—in favor of the departmental program.

---

*This extraordinary measure was the contribution not of conservatives but of Senate liberals led by Hubert Humphrey and Paul Douglas, and was drafted by members of Senator Douglas's staff in consultation with ACLU attorneys. It was conceived as a "right way" strategy to replace the deportation and registration provisions of the McCarran bill with a "tough" substitute, at once proving the anti-Communist commitment of its sponsors, shaming their conservative opponents by

Those listed on the Security Index were subject to more penetrative investigation than run-of-the-mill subversives, including such areas as their private lives, financial resources, and day-to-day activities. In addition, field officers were required to verify the whereabouts of the high-priority listees every three months, and of subjects lower on the list every year. Annual reports were required on the eligibility of marginal listees for continuing inclusion. The criteria for listing broadened over the years to include such indicators as "formal or informal leadership in a front group," "anarchistical revolutionary beliefs," indications of a "willingness to interfere with a war," and the fact that a subject had relied on the Fifth Amendment to the Constitution, the privilege against self-incrimination, in testimony before a government body when questioned concerning present or past membership in a subversive organization. Beginning in 1948, a second index was developed, known as the "Communist Index," a listing of individuals unable to qualify for the Security Index and its summary procedures but considered sufficiently dangerous to watch with special care in the event of an emergency. The nucleus of the Communist Index consisted of some 14,000 individuals removed from the Security Index when it was reduced from 26,174 to 12,870 in the mid-fifties. This back-up compilation, along with internal FBI priority arrest lists (COMSAB and DETCOM), was by explicit instruction to the field kept secret from the Justice Department.

The listing programs brought harassing confrontations between agents and individual subjects and, indeed, such confrontations were a key objective. Interviews were conducted with subjects both to confirm that they were dangerous and to determine whether they should be dropped from the Security Index. A "refusal to cooperate" was considered an indicator of dangerousness. Subjects transferred from the Security Index to the Communist Index could redeem themselves altogether by agreeing to inform or otherwise "indicate complete defection from subversive groups." These enticements may have succeeded: by 1959 the Communist Index with its 17,783 names was cut back to 12,784. The investigative activities required to implement the listing programs—keeping track of subjects, interviews, confrontations, bids to recant and inform—required enormous outlays of money and manpower. The thick files generated by these pursuits (I have examined the files of ten custodial detention subjects, including my own) are a weird blend of Keystone Kops and Kafka. An individual tracked from one field

---

their realism and, according to their lights, striking a blow for freedom. But the plan backfired when the proposal, instead of replacing the McCarran bill, was added to it. Nor could the sponsors of the measure—most of whom ultimately voted for the entire package—justify it on the ground that it was less stringent than the detention program already adopted by the Justice Department and the FBI, since the existence of that program had been kept secret from Congress.

At the time of Douglas's legislative activity to promote the adoption of a custodial detention measure, he was himself the subject of detailed FBI files opened in the early forties and maintained through 1964, two years before he was defeated for reelection. No ordinary surveillance target, he was specially listed for arrest and custodial detention as a potential threat to national security, "believed to be engaged in espionage activities for the Russian government." A perhaps even more biting irony: Douglas had enlisted for Marine combat service in World War II at the age of fifty, risen to the rank of lieutenant colonel, and won a Bronze Star for heroism. He subsequently became known as an unreconstructed anti-Communist and a supporter of the Vietnam War. But the Bureau was more impressed by his one-time membership in the Socialist Party, his involvement with the NAACP, and informers' reports in the forties of his association with Communists.

office to another for over five years turns out to be a case of mistaken identity. After repeatedly losing jobs as a result of agent pressure, a subject changes her name and is thereupon interviewed by another agent for possible information as to her whereabouts. Interviews and physical surveillance ("fisur") are recurrently used to portray subjects falsely as "wanted" and in flight, and thus to ensure their discharge. An entry misspelling a subject's name is subsequently converted into an "alias"; a characterization of a subject as an international spy suspect is retroactively altered to read "reliable (protect)," an indication that he may have been a spy of quite a different sort.

The "Reserve Index," which replaced the Communist Index in 1960, was intended to pinpoint special groups of individual targets, "who should receive priority consideration with respect to investigation and other action following the apprehension of our SI subjects." Individuals not considered dangerous enough for the Security Index were relegated to Section B of the new Reserve Index, while Section A's coverage included:

> those individuals whose subversive activities do not bring them within the SI criteria but who, in a time of national emergency, are in a position to influence others against the national interests or are likely to furnish financial or other material aid to subversive elements due to their subversive associations and ideology. Included therein would be individuals falling within the following categories: (1) Professors, teachers and educators; (2) Labor Union organizers and leaders; (3) Writers, lecturers, newsmen and others in the mass media field;* (4) Lawyers, doctors and scientists; (5) Other potentially influential persons on a local or national level; (6) Individuals who could potentially furnish financial or material aid.

In 1962 Dr. Martin Luther King, Jr., was placed in the Section A listing.

The Security Index itself was expanded by new categories of dangerousness such as, in the early sixties, persons identified with "pro-Castro Cuban activities." The absence of Lee Harvey Oswald from the list proved to be an embarrassment, subsequently remedied by new "dangerousness" criteria such as repatriated Soviet bloc defectors, and "a history of emotional instability or irrational behavior" of a subject with a subversive background, reflecting "a propensity for violence and hatred against organized government." In the late sixties, the already discussed personalization of countersurveillance investigations strongly influenced the criteria of dangerousness. Field offices were instructed not to neglect investigations of individuals for Security Index listing simply because "no membership in a basic revolutionary organization could be established," to investigate for index listing first all SDS regional office personnel, then *all* members of SDS and other "pro-Communist New Left-type groups," and (in April 1970) all members of every "commune" (individuals communally residing in one location who "share income and adhere to the philosophy of a Marxist-Leninist-Maoist oriented violent revolution").†

*Prominent journalists, especially Bureau critics, had been included in lists before, but never on such a scale. See James Wechsler, "Inside an FBI File," New York *Post,* Jan. 4 and 5, 1977.

†These constantly expanding guidelines merely served as a predicate for enlarging the population of surveillance subjects without protecting any legitimate governmental interest. Thus, as in the case of Oswald, the Security Index did not list Lynne Alice (Squeaky) Fromme, who in September 1975 attempted to murder President Ford.

In a parallel development, the former priority arrest listings (COMSAB and DETCOM) merged in 1969 into a Priority Apprehension Program with three levels: top leaders, secondary leadership, and a catch-all compilation of the entries on the master custodial detention list. The implementation of the program required checks by agents, in order to be certain that potential arrestees could be promptly located, and to verify their home and business addresses—every three months in the case of top leaders, and annually for the remainder, which by 1970 totaled 10,640 persons. The "Rabble Rouser Index" or "Agitator Index" was authorized in August 1967, after the Kerner Commission had inquired of the Director whether the Bureau could identify individuals prominent in stirring up civil disorders, but was abandoned in April 1971 as redundant.

The listing of individuals, whether for ultimate detention in the event of war or for clues to the source of civil disorders, masked an underlying tension between passive monitoring and barely suppressed aggression. Why wait for the future showdown? What can be done to get at these people now? This tension found an outlet in special programs directed at "key figures" and "top functionaries," singled out for close penetrative and continuous surveillance. Operational aggression also marked the Key Activist and Key Extremist (originally Black Extremist) programs in effect from the late sixties until February 1975. These programs mandated specially intensive surveillance (informer and electronic coverage, photographs, handwriting specimens), and was directed at travel plans, personal finances, foreign contacts, and income tax returns. The hostility latent in these programs was finally formalized in the COINTELPRO operations, which concentrated on these targets.

In the fall of 1971 Congress awoke from a long slumber and repealed the emergency detention provisions of the Internal Security Act of 1950. The wording and background of this 1971 statute demonstrate that Congress intended not only to wipe out custodial detention but to terminate all incidental authority to compile lists of potential detainees, to conduct surveillance of such individuals, or to engage in any other activities addressed to the forced mass detention contemplated by the repealed 1950 statute. The 1971 measure on its face broadly bars detention "except pursuant to an Act of Congress," and its legislative history further indicates that the statute was intended to abolish the authority of the executive in this field altogether. As in the case of the original 1950 statute, the Bureau and the Department proceeded to circumvent the 1971 repealer. Indeed, according to a Bureau theorist, the fact of repeal itself made circumvention urgent. The Security Index had to be retained, "since the potential dangerousness of subversives is probably even greater now than before the repeal of the Act since they no doubt feel safer now to conspire in the destruction of this country."[25] Confident that somehow, despite the language and purpose of the law, a reliance on inherent executive power could justify a continuation of past practices, Bureau and departmental officials were nevertheless worried about charges of flouting the will of Congress, and devised the familiar rationale that continued listing was a provident measure to prepare for possible future legislative enactment. In response to a Bureau request for authorization to continue the indexing practice as well as to conduct countersubversive investigations generally, Attorney General John Mitchell wrote on October 22, 1971, that the repeal did not affect the Bureau's authority to compile lists of dangerous subjects or to conduct investigations of subversive activities. On the basis of this reassurance, the Bureau initiated the Administrative Index (ADEX), which continued the SI and Reserve Index listings in the event of national emergency.* The ADEX included the standard classifications of revolutionary leaders and individuals with a claimed propensity for violence, but also lesser figures as well: activists, rank-and-file members of proscribed organizations, and individuals "who are likely to seize upon the opportunity presented by a national emergency." A lower priority (Category III) embraces those considered dangerous despite their limited activity in objectionable groups or causes. Category IV incorporates the old Section A of the Reserve Index, including teachers, lawyers, writers, intellectuals who might influence others, and those who are likely to furnish financial aid.[26] As in the case of other lists, the ADEX was trimmed in 1972 after the death of the Director from 15,259 to 4786, and then in 1976 to approximately 1250 individuals. In 1973, to conform the ADEX to the new deference to enacted legislation, the field was informed that the ADEX was not to be regarded as a guide to "investigative decisions or policies"—that was to be found in statutes—but as "strictly an administrative device," a feeble attempt to provide a mantle of legitimacy for a practice expressly condemned by Congress. Despite the reduced number of listees, the ADEX was marked by the same overkill as its predecessors. In December 1975 a Bureau official testified that the ADEX listed 110 members of the Socialist Workers' Party, notwithstanding the fact that the organization itself had been removed from the Bureau's surveillance agenda on the basis of testimony that it had never engaged in violence.

Like the domestic intelligence system as a whole, the fabric of custodial detention investigation and listing is woven on the loom of foreign intelligence, the monitoring and apprehension of individuals considered actual or potential agents of foreign countries. Apart from wartime spy-catching, discussed in Chapter 4, the Bureau's day-to-day foreign intelligence operations are not the stuff of which best sellers are made. Here the Media papers are again a useful guide. One document describes a Bureau program addressed to individuals (students, professors, scientists) returning to this country from a visit to the Soviet Union of more than one month's duration. They are interviewed by an FBI agent assigned by the Bureau office in the subject's home area, who is required to ascertain if any attempts have been made by the Soviet intelligence services to recruit the subject for intelligence work either in the USSR or, after his return, in the United States. Discretion is required: the subject should not be made to feel that the Bureau's intervention threatens academic or intellectual freedom. A second document deals with the DESECO ("development of selected contacts") program and is designed to recruit spies for our side. A memorandum

---

*Although Attorney General Mitchell did not formally authorize the ADEX as a continuation of the Security Index detention lists, the documentation reflects an assumption that the Bureau could proceed on that basis and that ADEX was a means of circumventing the repeal of the Emergency Detention Act. Bureau Chief Kelley assured an inquiring congressman in 1975 that the Security Index had been abandoned and destroyed in October 1971, but Bureau sources indicated in press leaks that those cards not absorbed by ADEX were kept in a reserve file—"FBI Is Said to Retain File of Most on Detention List," *New York Times*, Oct. 25, 1975.

of November 1970 requests all industrial security officers in private industry to report planned travel to or through a Sino-Soviet bloc country or to attend an international meeting where its nationals might be in attendance. The local Bureau field office is required to conduct a "sounding out" interview to determine whether the individual has "potential for possible development as an informant" under the DESECO program. A list of potential interviewees—scientists, consultants, and other technical personnel planning trips abroad—is attached to enable the field office to identify possible area recruits. Such delicate interviews are not to be undertaken without Bureau permission where the DESECO candidate is employed in the news media, entertainment, religion, education, or is a labor leader, public official, or "prominent person."

Association with nationals of Soviet bloc countries automatically invites Bureau investigation. In February 1966 a Quaker couple invited the chairman of the Institute of Ethnography and Folklore of the Czechoslovakian Academy of Sciences to visit them in the United States and to lecture here. What subversive plans did this invitation mask? It seems that in 1961, an undercover agent had reported that among the names and addresses on addressograph plates of the Fair Play for Cuba Committee was that of Mrs. H————. A "characterization" of this committee is appended to the memorandum. A 1957 investigation of the H————s had produced many testimonials of their loyalty. In a personnel clearance investigation, Mr. H———— had denied membership in any organization on the Attorney General's list and had suggested that his attendance at public meetings sponsored by such groups may have led to his receipt of their literature in the mail. As for Mrs. H————, investigation disclosed that in 1956 she wrote to the director of the Yugoslav Tourist office on Madison Avenue in New York City. This was no small matter. A Bureau "legat" in Rio de Janeiro, Brazil ("protect identity"), had been told by a self-confessed former Yugoslav intelligence agent that the tourist office director with whom Mrs. H———— had corresponded was a representative of the Yugoslav intelligence service. Further investigation is recommended.

A related document deals with an investigation of a thirty-two-year-old Boy Scout leader who was an associate professor of physics at the University of Idaho. On the stationery of the university, he had written a letter to the Soviet Embassy seeking assistance in connection with a planned camping trip to the Soviet Union by six Explorer Scouts. There is nothing in the letter that could conceivably lead to suspicion of the writer's politics or of the trip's purposes, even by the Bureau's far-out standards. The young visitors want to meet their counterparts in the Soviet Union and, as for the writer, "I personally think such contacts are by far the best way to promote peace and understanding between our peoples. . . ." The Soviet Embassy turned the letter over to a Philadelphia travel agency, which handles many such inquiries. But the agency's owner could not explain how a referred inquiry of this kind had reached the files of the FBI. (That the agency's five employees included a Bureau informer is a virtual certainty.)

In monitoring Soviet bloc embassies and consulates the Bureau employs physical surveillance, in addition to mail opening and wiretapping. This surveillance program turns up an unusually rich haul of subjects prominent in public life: congressmen, senators, and high government officials. When in the fall of 1970 former Attorney General Ramsey Clark called the Soviet Embassy in an effort to make arrangements for his participation in the trial of Soviet dissidents, his conversation was overheard by the Bureau and reported to the Nixon White House, which leaked it to the press. Identification of visitors is usually made through license plate numbers and covert photography. From one Media document we learn that a couple from a Pennsylvania town allegedly visited a Soviet consular office in July 1970, in a car identified by make, year, and license plates. However, the identification remains unsubstantiated until a neighbor identifies their photograph; the file is completed with this verification.

Files and Dissemination

The Media documents reflect, in a resident agency's microcosm, the importance of files and record keeping in the intelligence process.[27] A large proportion of Bureau files deal with criminal investigations, but—for reasons already suggested—political intelligence files are relatively more numerous and comprehensive. "The world's largest file cabinet," as it has been called, the new FBI headquarters building, contains some 7500 six-drawer file cabinets spreading over half a square block and housing, according to a 1974 estimate, some 6.5 million files and 58 million index cards, covering both primary subjects and references to others mentioned in the files. This general index collection, growing at an estimated 900,000 entries a year with an estimated 1.3 million new entries and 400,000 deletions annually, is, in reality, a mini-file collection intended to cover gaps in the files. For example, the index lists those attending a meeting of a group that is the subject of a file but who are not themselves under investigation. The index is crammed with substantive information such as the "associates and relatives of the subject; members of organizations under investigation . . . individuals contributing funds to subversive type activities; subversive or seditious publications; writers of articles for subversive and seditious publications; bookstores specializing in subversive-type publications and related types of information." Even unsolicited charges involving matters of a personal nature that do not result in an investigation are indexed.

The files contain information of two different kinds: raw data—photographs, memoranda, accounts of interviews and physical surveillance, transcripts and summaries of electronic eavesdropping, informers' reports—and the materials describing and summarizing this data. The latter, typically, consists of reports from agents about the results of an investigation or, more usually, an aspect of an investigation, frequently in the form of a Bureau letterhead and hence called a "letterhead memorandum" (LHM). The Washington file and index card collection covers both investigative files, which deal with current investigations, and general files, which store information of no current operational value. These general files are considered a resource of "strategic" (as opposed to "line") intelligence, and are "warehoused" for long-range use in the politics of deferred reckoning. They are also valuable for "name checks." Unlike criminal investigative files, headquarters' subversive and extremist files are retained indefinitely, even after a case is closed in the formal sense that no agent is currently assigned to it. Moreover, information acquired even after an investigation is formally ended is placed in the "closed" file. The file collections stored in the field offices are far more extensive than the headquarters' collection. Each field office retains files of cases never referred to headquarters, including those in which investigations were not actively pursued, were dropped, or not referred to Washington. File material is routinely sent to Washington when the subject is considered important, an investigation has turned up information considered useful, an extensive investigation has been terminated, the subject is recommended for custodial detention, or advice and assistance are sought. In only a fraction of the cases processed by the field is the raw investigative data transmitted to Washington; in the remainder of the cases this material, collected during an investigation, is retained in the field and usually only summarized in Washington transmittals.

Because much of the pertinent data in outstanding cases is summarized or duplicated in Washington, field officers are permitted to destroy files ten years after the matter has been closed, but only after a determination that the file no longer has potential value. But so tenacious is the filing mystique that even material that is slated for destruction—because it is embarrassing or inadvisable to retain it—is filed pursuant to a "Do Not File" procedure and retained until Washington authorizes its destruction.*

The filing procedures mirror the investigative process as it expands from an initial focus on an organization to its leaders, members, and supporters. Here is a description by a former Bureau agent:

> In D.C. we have an individual file and an organizational file. . . . We start out by investigating an organization; then when we had compiled a big file on the organization itself, we'd start investigating all of the officers in the organization on an individual basis and then prominent members of the organization, also on an individual basis. Each one of these people would have a separate file on them and into that file would go, first of all, all the background information we could dig up on a guy—from whatever source we could get it from. Then we'd go into all of the informant's statements that identified him at a given meeting or at a given demonstration or rally. Then also we would go into the reports from other agencies that this guy had done such and such.

In the next stage, the ex-agent recalled, individuals not connected with an organization became individual file subjects simply because they "were going to be around or were in a prominent position."

Files are the cornerstone of all domestic political intelligence systems. The mere fact that information appears in a file in itself becomes a warrant of its

---

*To shield itself from the embarrassments of file disclosures mandated by the Freedom of Information and Privacy acts (FOIPA) the FBI in October 1977 limited the retention period of field files to five years, on the grounds that the Washington central office file summaries adequately preserved all significant information. At the same time, auxiliary office files (information stored in an office other than the office of case origin) were ordered destroyed after six months. In 1978 the FBI asked the U.S. archivist for permission to destroy even the central files in criminal cases more than ten years old. The fate of Washington noncriminal internal security-extremism files, now a source of considerable embarrassment, will ultimately be determined by the outcome of the attack on FOIPA by the congressional countersubversive bloc.

truth and accuracy, automatically raising it above the level of its source, however dubious it might otherwise be. The reduction of a mass of material into subversive classifications, of events into a chronological sequence, of names into alphabetical order, can somehow clothe a body of questionable data, assembled by the most arbitrary and unreliable standards, with a special aura of objectivity and professionalism. In short, the process by which material is organized overcomes its lack of relevance or probative value. The serried ranks of file cabinets join the microscope, camera, and electronic transmitter as valuable intelligence instruments.

By assembling evidence of transient political involvement and activity into an ideological mosaic, the Bureau's filing procedures help solve its key problem: how to make credible the threat of domestic subversion. The sheer accumulation of items—a signature on a peace petition, presence at a demonstration, receipt of left-wing literature, a speech at a conference on police brutality—each innocuous in itself, invites the inference that the subject is subversive. Quantity is transformed into quality; the end result is greater than the sum of its parts. In the same way, the file system maximizes the population of subjects by preserving a usable past of "derogatory information." When a former executive of the Bureau's Domestic Intelligence Division, Charles Brennan, was asked by a member of the Church Committee why the Bureau decided to target some 6500 young people who had "no experience in violence and . . . no activity that would suggest that they have been involved in violence," Brennan replied that it was important to have them "on public record . . . recorded for future reference in FBI files." He reminded his interrogator that in the thirties many individuals who had been Communists at college subsequently sought government employment and that the government had no records of their previous involvement. "I did not want to see a repetition of that sort of circumstances [sic] come about."[28]

Because political files have always had a powerful impact on the American imagination, they have been exploited to nourish the Menace, and in the fifties became an asset of right-wing political movements. The mere existence of such files, no matter how limited their access, inspires fear. They "document" the intelligence thesis that dissent is a form of political original sin, permanent, incurable, and contagious, and impose on the political life of the individual a "record" that he cannot change; they make him a "subject," tied forever to political views and associations he may have long since abandoned. Moreover, a single FBI file is a midden of details about the subject's personal life—divorce, love affairs, children, parents, financial problems, neighbors' gossip—and for this reason is a source of potential blackmail.

Files are the sinews that bind the intelligence community together, the standard means of disseminating information. Reports and memoranda from the Bureau's file collection pour in a torrent to other members of the intelligence community. Bureau reports and investigative summaries are directly transmitted to the Department of Justice for prosecutive review. In addition, pursuing the self-assumed function of alerting interested agencies to subversion, the Bureau transmits what it considers relevant data to such intelligence agencies as the Secret Service, the armed forces intelligence, and some twenty-three other federal agencies, as well as a chain of state and local law enforcement units. The disseminated material has been criticized as quantitatively very burdensome and inaccurate.* Not infrequently such reports are made at preliminary stages of a Bureau inquiry that may ultimately turn out to be warrantless. Here too, as in so many areas, the subjects of the disseminated memoranda are identified with subversion in highly tenuous ways: in most cases such people are neither violence-prone nor leaders in extremist or subversive groups.

To a measurably greater extent than investigations, political files are condemned by a large segment of the American public, even when not in basic disagreement with intelligence objectives. The Bureau's focus on individuals—rather than associations and groups—invites subjective identification. This initial vulnerability in filing procedures is intensified by suspicions of the motives of the compiler. The fear response, so deeply rooted in our thoughtways and, indeed, the foundation of the political intelligence system, has, especially in recent years, bred popular mistrust of the intentions of government itself. Such mistrust in part reflects an increasing awareness of manipulation, of governmental strategies to gain support by exploiting fear through falsehood. For a growing number of Americans, agents of government, especially those operating anonymously or in secret, are "they," nameless pursuing Eumenides. A secret political file serves up a banquet of fears. Do "they" have a file on me? What could "they" possibly have found out about my past? Is there any derogatory information in my record? And these fears are fueled by periodic disclosures that the Bureau keeps files on numberless individuals who are not remotely threatening to any legitimate government interest. To these subjective sources of criticism must be added a fairly widespread recognition that the entire political filing cycle—recording, dissemination, accumulation, and retention—is the hallmark and symbol of a police state. These fears and objections might have remained unfocused and inchoate without the catalysts of the release, first, of the Pentagon Papers and later of the Watergate documents, and, finally, by the hardening of a conviction in Congress that secret files threaten the legislators personally. The convergence of these considerations led to the passage, in the fall of 1974, of the Privacy Act, which banned the maintenance by federal agencies of any records concerning the political and religious beliefs of individuals unless authorized by the subject or in connection with a bona fide criminal investigation, as well as an amendment to the Freedom of Information Act broadening access to government files theretofore protected from disclosure by arbitrary and pretextual claims of "national security."

The Bureau's efforts to overcome the police state image associated with political files have been alternately deceptive and ludicrous. Shortly after his appointment as Acting FBI Director, L. Patrick Gray III told reporters, "None of you guys are going to believe this—and I don't know how to make you believe it—but there are no dossiers or secret files."[29] Gray did not restore his credibility

---

*A revealing critique of the Bureau's data transmittals appears in James F. Ahern's *Police in Trouble* (Hawthorn, 1972), pp. 44–55. The author, a former chief of the New Haven, Connecticut, Police Department, dealing with Bureau reports furnished him on the eve of a planned demonstration in New Haven, complained of the Bureau's exaggeration of the violence potential as a result of its reliance on unverified rumors.

by subsequent insistence that the Bureau's materials dealing with the politics of individual subjects were "files," not "dossiers."*

In a 1954 article in the *Northwestern University Law Review* on the Federal Employee Security Program, the Director reassured his readers: "Information in FBI reports is available only to individuals specifically authorized by law. This safeguards the data, preventing it from falling into the hands of unauthorized individuals who might attempt to subvert it for unscrupulous ends." At the very time the article appeared, Senator Joseph McCarthy was facing charges that he had used classified Bureau file information, reproduced in an Army intelligence document. In an article two years later entitled "The Confidential Nature of FBI Reports," the Director repeated his earlier assurances of confidentiality. At the time of the publication of this article, the Vice-President, Richard M. Nixon, attacked a Democratic California congressman as a subversive on the basis of data almost certainly derived from FBI files.[30]

Executive orders by Presidents Truman and Eisenhower designed to preserve the confidentiality of the files had no impact on the flow of file information to the Director's congressional allies. Disseminated file materials have been regularly leaked by receiving agencies, which are rarely punished by a denial of further access as required by Bureau regulations. The Director himself violated the secrecy canon whenever it suited his political purposes, as in the 1953 White Hearings where file material freely circulated. Memoranda summarizing file material have not infrequently been made available to state and federal antisubversive committees and investigations. And the House Appropriations Subcommittee was regularly favored with summaries and tidbits from the files. The following colloquy between NBC telecaster Garrick Utley and Appropriations Subcommittee Chairman Congressman John Rooney tells its own story ("First Tuesday," June 1, 1971):

UTLEY: At times the F.B.I. has leaked information about people in this country, like the wiretaps on Martin Luther King. Is this right?
ROONEY: Now you talk about the F.B.I. leaking something about Martin Luther King. I happen to know all about Martin Luther King, but I have never told anybody.

---

*The following colloquy occurred during Gray's confirmation hearing:

SENATOR TUNNEY: Do you know how many names you have in the files that you have dossiers on?

MR. GRAY: I don't use that word "dossier." You know, every time you use it I am going to respectfully reserve the right to say—.

SENATOR TUNNEY: I will not use it.

MR. GRAY: I don't use the term "dossier." I know what the dictionary definition is but we don't talk about it in terms of "dossier." We talk in terms of "files."

SENATOR TUNNEY: Fine. [Laughter]

Intelligence functionary James B. Adams likewise suffers from a "dossier" hang-up and prefers "files" because it has no "sinister connotation." Similarly, John W. Marshall, the Bureau's assistant director in charge of the Files and Communications Division, told a reporter in 1974 that "We do not have dossiers on people. This is a myth that has grown up over the years." The Bureau, of course, keeps thousands and thousands of "dossiers on people"—Church, Vol. 6, pp. 90–91; "Those Mysterious Files," Washington *Star-News,* March 15, 1974.

UTLEY: How do you know everything about Martin Luther King?

ROONEY: From the Federal Bureau of Investigation.

UTLEY: They've told you—gave you information based on taps or other sources about Martin Luther King?

ROONEY: They did.

UTLEY: Is that proper?

ROONEY: Why not?

Similarly, file material was regularly offered as insider's bait to stimulate readership for the Director's books and articles. Both Presidents Johnson and Nixon were, as we have seen, personally courted with file tidbits. For the Nixon White House, access to Bureau files and their contents was considered a perquisite of executive power; not only could they be used to attack enemies but also destroyed to divert suspicion. James McCord, security chief of the Committee for the Re-election of the President (CREEP), himself a former FBI and CIA agent, was "plugged in" to the FBI and a recipient of file materials. Although charged with responsibility for preventing violence to CREEP headquarters, he received at least one document in LHM form ("A confidential source of known reliability has advised, etc.") dealing not with CREEP security at all but with the Vietnam Veterans Against the War (VVAW) and a planned support arrangement between the VVAW and the McGovern campaign headquarters. CREEP also received oral reports on target groups and individuals from a Bureau agent assigned for that purpose.

File confidentiality was systematically compromised by the Bureau's collaboration with the media. File materials—memoranda, summaries, reports—were channeled to the Bureau's press allies in a variety of ways: blind releases, files conveniently left lying at an abandoned desk accessible to a reporter, anonymous messages, and telephoned answers to prearranged inquiries. Beginning in the late sixties, the Bureau was plagued by involuntary leaks through employees, "whistle blowers" seeking a press outlet. (We have yet to comprehend the ramified impact of reproduction technology on attempts to preserve documentary confidentiality or limited access.)

The already discussed use of files to punish critics of the Director, the Bureau, or its allies also embraced a broad spectrum of doghouse targets, ranging from high-level bureaucrats to labor union officers. Similarly, file secrecy was regularly violated in the field. A Bureau field agent channeled investigative leads and evidence to Congressman Richard Nixon, then in charge of the congressional investigation of Alger Hiss, through Father John F. Cronin, who served as a liaison between the Nixon probe and the Bureau field office.* In the fall of 1973 a former University of Oregon student body president obtained money damages and a retraction in settlement of a lawsuit based on the release

---

*Cronin, who in the forties was assistant director of the Social Action Department of the National Catholic Welfare Conference (NCWC), became an authority on communism with the help of file material supplied by friendly Bureau agents and in return fed them information on his specialty, communism in unions. Secretly retained by the Chamber of Commerce, Cronin wrote three widely circulated pamphlets for the Chamber on communism, based in part on Bureau file material. One of them, *Communists Within the Labor Movement* (1947), was particularly effective in the drive for legislation requiring labor union officers to execute non-Communist affidavits.

by a field office of his file to the news director of a local radio station.

File secrecy plays an important role in protecting the Bureau from embarrassment. The Bureau's selective use of confidentiality in the post-Hoover era is perhaps best illustrated by its refusal in 1974 to make available to the General Accounting Office (GAO), commissioned by Congress to make an investigation of Bureau intelligence operations, the raw investigative material or summary reports from its files. Instead, the Bureau prepared its own summaries and rejected a proposal for verifying them by random selection of original file materials. The reasons for this refusal are illuminated by the grand jury testimony of a Bureau clerk in the New York field office who helped prepare the summaries, to the effect that the chief of the New York office Intelligence Division directed him to suppress file information in preparing his summaries dealing with the illegal Weather Underground break-ins.[31] The Bureau gave the Church Committee a more favorable response to its requests in May 1975 for files, including those containing "raw data." But, despite assurances that all relevant material had been turned over, the Bureau did not even bother to review its secret field files, thus once again concealing its burglary program, which was documented by files in the New York field office subsequently unearthed as a result of a court-ordered search. In the same way, self-protective evasions have been used to frustrate requests under the Freedom of Information and Privacy Acts.

The "No Evaluation" Fiction

The Bureau's defense against filing abuses is confined to a perfunctory caution in the *Manual* and an insistence that "unverified raw data" in the files is carefully sifted before it is used in an investigative report. Beginning with the 1946 Coplon case, however, publicly disclosed documents clearly show that Bureau agents do incorporate this material into investigative reports without further verification. But, the Bureau argues, what harm is there in that? Do not the LHM's and similar materials, which are concededly circulated and recirculated in channels wholly beyond the Bureau's control, expressly state that they "contain neither recommendations nor conclusions of the FBI"? This disclaimer is purely ritualistic. In fact, these summaries and reports are heavily biased, suppressing unwelcome facts and inviting misleading conclusions. Hoover's testimony in the Harry Dexter White case illustrates the limitations of the no-evaluation gambit. At the outset, the Director gave the standard Bureau position on evaluation:

> As the members of this committee know, the Federal Bureau of Investigation is a service agency. It does not make policy; it does not evaluate; it secures facts upon which determination can be made by those officials of the United States Government who have the responsibility for taking whatever action is indicated. We do not inject ourselves into legislative matters. We do not express opinions or draw conclusions in our investigative reports. We have well-defined channels of official distribution through which we direct the results of our investigations.
>
> Since we are not an agency for decision as to action, we are legally, morally,

and in good conscience obligated to relay all information and facts we secure to the responsible officials and agencies of government.

Two sentences later, he testified:

> Our American way of life, which has flourished under our Republic and has nurtured the blessings of a democracy, has been brought into conflict with the godless forces of communism. These Red Fascists distort, conceal, misrepresent, and lie to gain their point. Deceit is their very essence. This can never be understood until we face the realization that to a Communist there are no morals. . . .

Presumably on the basis of what he learned as a collector of the facts, Hoover expressed opinions and drew conclusions. Indeed, the Director's publications and speeches are a mass of evaluations intended to influence policy determination and political decisions. To be sure, the Bureau has never assumed a formal, functional responsibility for evaluating the data it collects. As the GAO noted, it lacks an "evaluation and analysis capability"—but this failure to develop a formal evaluation capability is deliberate, enabling it to claim credit for its restraint and at the same time permitting indulgence in ideological bias wholly removed from investigative reality. Facts rigorously sifted and weighed —the foundation of sound intelligence practice—would embarrass the Bureau and frustrate its mission.

"Evaluation" has been the Bureau's trademark. The investigative operations themselves feed into a mechanism that systematically processes the intelligence product into warnings, denunciations, prophecies, preachments—a steady stream of evaluations. Evaluation dominates and shapes the rationale for target selection as well as the entire surveillance process and product, including the choice of operational modes, the opening and retention of files, the circulation of partisan "studies,"* the invitation to draw an inference of subversion from such evidence as, for example, a speech on world government; the heavy concentration on black targets; the Senate committee testimony in the Berrigan case; and the decisions to close or continue an investigation, to include, retain, or drop a custodial detention subject. Evaluation is not a casual or sporadic deviation from an otherwise observed norm of neutrality, but the principal source of the Bureau's growth and power, itself a dramatic demonstration of the dangers of entrusting to an intelligence agency autonomous authority to evaluate the intelligence product. But the most illuminating commentary on the Bureau's claimed role as a conduit of information for the use of others and nothing more (as well as on the asserted confidentiality of its files) is the resort to covert aggressive action, directed toward an assortment of targets—a subject to which we must now turn.

*For an example, see Appendix V.

6 Aggressive Intelligence

From Investigation to Injury— The Flowering of the Seed

The FBI's assertedly modest intelligence function as an early warning alert for prosecutors and a decision-making resource masks its true role as a weapon against threats to the existing order. Planned injury, implemented by an illegal autonomous system of power, explains domestic intelligence far more convincingly than either the "pure" or "preventive" intelligence thesis. Investigation and accumulation of information are at root merely the means to the ends of punishment, intimidation, frustration, and defeat of movements for change of any kind. Quite apart from the formal programs of aggressive action discussed below, hostility and confrontation are rooted in domestic intelligence. The field agent, initially recruited on the basis of his social and political conformity, is rapidly developed by the bureaucratic climate into a full-fledged ideological zealot. Like the Director, the model and inspiration of the Bureau's countersubversive mission, he too comes to view himself as a nation-savior, a front-line defender of the patriotic faith. Inevitably, countersubversive investigation becomes a highly personalized function, unfettered by professionalism or, for that matter, the norms of legality and accountability. This dualism is distilled in the term "responsibility," which regularly emerges as an "anything goes" justification for countersubversive abuses. The agent has a routine duty, based on statutes, to collect evidence of law violations. But countersubversive investigations involve something more awesome and grandiose, the discharge of a "responsibility" for the nation's security. Denver agent Theodore Rosack in 1976 told a federal grand jury investigating the Bureau's acquisition of documents stolen from the Socialist Workers' Party by one of its informers, that "it is our responsibility . . . to investigate . . . [an] organization which does not have the best interest of this country at heart"—as though this somehow was a defense of the agency's complicity in the burglary.

Inevitably, the agent's ideological hostility is reinforced by a personal animus and a self-righteous zeal. Ironically, this anger is intensified by typically barren surveillance returns; sheer frustration—if only these plotters could be exposed!—dissolves the tattered remnants of detachment. The acting out of the agent's personal antagonism provokes the subject's resentment and defiance, spiraling into harsher countermeasures. The most common form of pressure is the personal interview; the subject is typically requested to acknowledge his or her membership in an organization or to identify others or to "cooperate" more broadly by turning informer. Where the subject is uncooperative or such a confrontation is considered futile, harassment follows to force the subject to reduce or abandon his involvement. The individual harassment of subjects, which began in the forties, escalated in the fifties in a variety of forms: twenty-four-hour watches, tailgating, verbal abuse, insulting telephone calls, invented summonses to jury duty, and intrusive photography. In the sixties these "intensive" investigative practices abandoned all pretense of professionalism. According to the late Saul Alinsky—a pioneering technician of community organizing and a perennial Bureau target—a Bureau agent took pictures of him during a field trip leaving a young woman's cottage early in the morning and later presented the photos to him on his arrival at the Washington, D.C., airport. The intimidating potentialities of the physical interview itself were not lost on the Bureau. In one of the Media documents, "New Left Notes," the Philadelphia SAC instructs his agents that more interviews are "in order . . . for plenty of reasons, chief of which are it will enhance the paranoia endemic in these circles and will further serve to get the point across that there is an FBI agent behind every mailbox. In addition, some will be overcome by the overwhelming personalities of the contacting agents and will volunteer to tell all—perhaps on a continuing basis."[1]

The pursuit not infrequently culminated in job pressure, and attempts to induce the subject's eviction from his home or nonrenewal of his lease. These forms of punishment emerged from the sympathetic response by third parties (employers, landlords) to initial attempts to locate a subject by representatives of a government agency more widely revered than any other. In the hostile climate of the fifties, Bureau agents found that privately communicated suggestions, suspicions, or charges of subversion could do wonders to deprive an uncooperative subject (or one considered too committed to interview) of a livelihood, a place to live, an outlet for his or her views, an expectation of physical safety or police protection. In the same way, sympathetic media response forged a powerful weapon against organizations, especially the Communist Party.

The transformation of sporadic and ad hoc aggressive intelligence into Bureau programs began in 1956 with the program known as "COINTELPRO-Communist Party USA" (COINTELPRO-CPUSA) and was followed in 1961 by the "SWP Disruption Program." These programs served as precedents for three others: "White Hate Groups" (1964), "Black Nationalist-Hate Groups" (1967), and "New Left" (1968).*[2] These aggressive ("covert action") projects were

*The existence of the programs was first revealed in a series of documents turned over in December 1973 and March 1974 to Carl Stern, an NBC newsman, after a long legal battle commenced under the Freedom of Information Act. Stern's curiosity about the programs was stirred

uniformly designated "counterintelligence"—a flimsy pretext. The unglamor-
ous reality is that they extended and normalized preexisting modes of aggression. External harassment was supplemented by internal disruption, overt hostility by deception. Under the new dispensation, the Bureau could finally use its
richest asset, informers, for something more than channeling dreary organizational details into the files: the latest party fund-raiser, disputes over dogma, and
similar excitements. The army of informers—by 1956 there were an estimated
1500 of them in the Communist Party—could now be deployed on new fronts,
reporting to control agents opportunities and vulnerabilities for dirty tricks, and
subsequently relaying reports of their effectiveness and impact. In contrast to
the casual, unplanned earlier practices, the informer could himself now be
programmed for an aggressive role in scenarios worked out with his agent to
ensure a maximum of damage not only to organizations but to individuals as
well.

All too aware that planned injury to people—as opposed to actions against
groups and their activities—was the least defensible of all its COINTELPRO
initiatives, Bureau witnesses have insisted that individuals were targeted not to
do them harm but as a means of disrupting the group. But the systematic attack
on people, the unprecedented commitment of a law enforcement agency systematically to do injury to others outside of the legal system, was deliberate.
When the first program began in 1956, criminal prosecution under the Smith Act
still offered a weapon—although increasingly inefficient—for dealing with Communists. But the 1957 judicial developments already described finally closed the
door on the possibility of prosecutions. Field practice had already pointed the
way to a third option in addition to passive surveillance and law enforcement:
covert action to "neutralize" the subject; and in contrast to open legal proceedings with their extravagant expenditures of informers, the concealed role of the
Bureau and its spies generated fear, which intensified and expanded the impact
of the action itself.

The destructive targeting of specific identifiable individuals through expulsion or status rejection is, as we have seen, embedded in American nativism. We
are once more summoned to the twenties and the spirit of vigilantism and
self-help that dominated the repression of that era. The COINTELPRO concept
brings to mind Attorney General A. Mitchell Palmer's defense of his lawless

---

by one of the Media documents, a memorandum designated "COINTELPRO—New Left." Attached
to this memo was a reprint of an article from *Barron's,* a conservative magazine, which charged
that the seizure of buildings at Columbia University in the spring of 1968 was the initial stage of
a revolutionary plot to take over the industrial power of America. The routing slip suggested that
the reprint should be mailed anonymously to other educators and administrators "who have shown
a reluctance to take decisive action against the 'New Left.' "

In addition to the five programs, released documents give us a glimpse of two others purportedly dealing with foreign intelligence activities: "Special Operations" (discussed below) and "Soviet-
Satellite Intelligence." These records clearly show that the Bureau engaged in intelligence activities
abroad through informers and cooperative sources. Still another program, instituted in 1960, was
directed at the movement for Puerto Rican independence and although designed to disrupt only
violence-prone organizations, in fact consistently harassed groups committed to peaceful methods
—Church, Bk III, p. 14, n. 59; Saxbe Report in Hearings of Civil and Constitutional Rights
Subcommittee of the House Judiciary Committee, Nov. 20, 1974, pp. 10, 15; "Documents Show FBI
Harassed Puerto Rico Independence Group," *New York Times,* Nov. 22, 1977.

deportation raids on the ground that no "nice distinctions" could be drawn between the beliefs of the raid victims and "their actual violation of our national laws." The fact that Congress had denied him authority to act was unfortunate, but, Palmer insisted, the "rights of common citizenship" required prompt action. While the Palmer Raids are a shameful record of official misconduct, they were carried out in public, were of limited duration, and were redressed—at least in part—in the courts. But the COINTELPROs reflect a deliberate intent to punish targets who were concededly neither suspected nor convicted of crime; they were conducted by government representatives over a period of years, and in secret. The entire COINTELPRO experience is a nativist version of the English judgment of outlawry: "It is the right and duty of every man to pursue him, to ravage his lands, to hunt him down like a wild beast and slay him; for a wild beast he is; not merely is he a 'friendless man,' he is a wolf. . . . *Caput gerat lupinum*—In these words the courts decreed outlawry."[3] The FBI treated the subject as though he or she wore a wolf's head; but, while the label of outlawry was the execution of a decree by a tribunal, here the Bureau constituted itself the secret instrument of a tribal system of justice directed against people it had itself defined as enemies and outcasts.

Yet the Bureau did not act in a social vacuum. As Tocqueville has written, "To commit violent and unjust acts, it is not enough for a government to have the will or even the power; the habits, ideas, and passions of the times must lend themselves to their committal." Director Clarence Kelley echoed these sentiments when, in defense of the program, he cited "the personal encouragement of myriads of citizens both within and without the government." And William C. Sullivan, the FBI functionary who was the architect of the later programs, defended them on the ground that they saved the taxpayers money.[4] The constituency for which these Bureau functionaries spoke included President Eisenhower, who, after rebuking the late Chief Justice Warren for the Supreme Court's decisions protecting the constitutional rights of Communists, was asked by Warren how he would deal with Communists in America. Eisenhower's reply: "I would kill the S.O.B.s."*[5]

---

*To the same effect are such grass-roots sentiments as the following, expressed in letters to James Earl Ray when confined in a Memphis, Tennessee, jail charged with the murder of Martin Luther King, Jr.:

God answered my prayers when Communist Rev. Martin King (nigger) was shot. He had it coming.

I'm praying for you, for you are not guilty of murder. You killed a Communist.

Every day the leaders of our country proudly announce that good American soldiers have killed hundreds of Communists in Vietnam. And we honor the Americans who kill Communists. But when you killed a Communist, the United States spent a million dollars to track you down. You should be freed, honored, and rewarded.

One correspondent congratulated Ray and pointed out that since "the FBI classed him [King] as a 'trouble-maker' . . . he had it coming to him"—William Bradford Huie, *He Slew the Dreamer* (Delacorte Press, 1970), pp. 207–212.

A Profile of the COINTELPROS

The COINTELPRO operation was formally ended in April 1971, not because of any internal recognition of its impropriety but out of a prophetic fear of exposure through the recently released Media papers.* The entire series of projects processed a total of 2679 action proposals, of which 2340 were implemented. Some 715 approved actions were designed to cause disruption within a group or between two groups.† Informers had established their effectiveness in implementing this tactic in the first (Communist Party) aggressive program. Its success led to its subsequent popularity in Bureau field offices throughout the country. For example, a 1971 "airtel" from the Chicago SAC to Washington reported:

> The current split in the above two National Socialist groups continues in Chicago. The faction loyal to the NSWPP (National Socialist White People's Party) headquarters has raided the NSPA (National Socialist Party of America) faction's headquarters at 2519 West 75th Street, Chicago, breaking windows and beating up several persons. NSPA members have filed court suits against the NSWPP and have sworn out warrants of arrest on several of them. The NSWPP is attempting to wrest control of the building at 2519 West 75th Street through legal means. *Chicago is encouraging all of the above through its informants.* [Emphasis added.]

The techniques for promoting such disruption, which sometimes bore violent fruit, included anonymous or fictitious letters attacking an ally, a membership sector, or a leader through false, defamatory, or threatening information; forging signatures, letterheads, membership cards, press credentials, or other items of identification for the purpose of disruption; instructing informers to spread false rumors, or promote factionalism or mistrust, and creating bogus organizations ("notionals") to attack or disrupt a bona fide group. Another script, "putting a snitch jacket" on an individual (raising the charge of informer), was designed to eliminate or discredit a subject and to disrupt his organization. Only slightly less common (about 695 cases) was the practice of using the media in collaborative arrangements or through anonymous communications to attack individuals and groups. Attempts to prevent targets from

---

*The memo closing down the program is loaded with euphemistic intelligence rhetoric: "To afford additional security to our sensitive techniques and operations, it is recommended the COINTELPRO'S . . . be discontinued . . . although successful over the years." Future counterintelligence actions are not precluded but "will be considered on a highly selective, individual basis with tight procedures to insure absolute security." Another stimulus to the discontinuance of the COINTELPROS may have been the attack by House Majority Leader Boggs on the Bureau's secret police practices on April 22, 1971, five days prior to the date of the termination memo.

†These figures and those that follow in the text are based on FBI data submitted to the Church Committee. They are almost certainly understated. Moreover, they are misleading for another reason: they do not include disruptive and aggressive actions undertaken without requests for approval (maverick operations) such as car burnings and assaults, programs not formally captioned COINTELPRO, and the disruptive burglaries, provocations, and "dirty tricks" of informers committed in the normal course of their services—See, for example, Roger Rapoport, "Meet America's Meanest Dirty Trickster," *Mother Jones,* April 1977; Ron Wolf, Doug Vaughan, and Rosemary Cowes, "The Redfearn File," *Straight Creek Journal,* March 24, March 31, April 7, April 21, 1977 and Ch. 5, note 12.

speaking, meeting, or engaging in political expression account for some 350 of the actions and are typified by approaches—usually through anonymous letters —to operators of hotels or meeting halls to persuade them to deny space to particular groups. About 260 cases involved employment and related pressures, including questioning at the job site, letters to employers, and requests, usually anonymous ("A Concerned Citizen"), to foundations, civic groups, and public figures that a target be denied recognition, money, or support. A fifth category (an estimated 210 cases) consists of attempts to abuse government processes as, for example, by sending bogus letters purportedly from constituents to elected officials, or encouraging inspectors or administrators in areas such as health, safety, building regulations, welfare, unemployment insurance, alcohol tax, and licensing to harass a particular group; instigating tax audits and intervening in the judicial process by furnishing confidential information concerning an individual's arrest record to unauthorized recipients, including employers; informing a defense attorney falsely that one of his clients as well as other individuals with whom he has been professionally associated were Bureau informers. Two remaining tactics account for 110 of the COINTELPROs: the instigation of hostile actions through a third party (such as the American Legion* or the Catholic War Veterans) and the discrediting of organizations as Communist-infiltrated through anonymous mailings and releases. With the exception of this last tactic, all of the other techniques were used in the five programs, the frequency of use depending on effectiveness in a particular setting. Factionalization and propaganda were heavy favorites, exceeded only in popularity in the New Left program by attempted suppression of speech, writing, and meeting.

Newly confirmed FBI Director Clarence M. Kelley in July 1973 lauded the COINTELPRO operation, insisting that it had done more good than harm, and calling for legislation to authorize its reactivation in the event of an emergency. Further legitimization efforts included an attempt to obtain the approval of the Senate Judiciary Committee. But conferences with the committee's elders— Chairman James Eastland and ranking Republican member Roman Hruska— to arrange for protective committee hearings yielded only the advice to lie low until the whole matter blew over.[6] Instead, Attorney General William B. Saxbe took the initiative and ordered an investigation by a special committee, headed by Assistant Attorney General Henry Peterson and consisting of four Justice Department and three FBI representatives. It was clear from the start that the underlying aim of the probe was a whitewash to discourage further inquiry, whether by journalists, scholars, or congressional committees. The choice of Peterson was not reassuring: it was he who saw nothing wrong in sharing grand jury secrets with President Nixon. Instead of examining the original documents, the panel accepted selected Bureau summaries.[7] Its final report[8] stressed that many of the actions "were entirely proper and appropriate law enforcement procedures," and excluded from the application of its limp standards of propriety the mass of actions targeted against the Communist Party USA (CPUSA). Violence prevention was advanced as a justification both by the Peterson probers

---

*Collaboration with the American Legion stemmed from a long-standing separate operation, "American Legion Contact Program."

and by the FBI itself.*[9] The principal targets, however, were for the most part not violence-prone, and the Bureau was unable to pinpoint a single instance in which its counterintelligence operations prevented violence. A last-ditch defense is the claim that its aggressive tactics limited the effectiveness of New Left groups that might in the future turn to violence.[10] Evidence collection and law enforcement were thus admittedly scrapped in favor of an all-out vigilante warfare undertaken, to use the language of radical philosopher Herbert Marcuse, "to prevent hostile ideas and organizations from forming as an alternative to repressing them politically once they have already formed."[11]

The blunderbuss means were, on the grossest functional test, not justified by any violence-prevention end. The tightly knit, security-conscious units committed to bombing and violence as a political tactic are virtually impervious to informer penetration, "snitch-jacketing," internal disruption, and discrediting propaganda ploys that produce results only when directed against targets functioning within the political process or dependent on popular support. The ironic reality is that these programs, far from preventing violence, promoted it, as we shall see. Moreover, the militant sectors of radical groups were quick to attribute such hostile action, however concealed their source, to police agencies. Thus, the Bureau strengthened the very groups and tendencies it sought to discourage by providing a ratification of their politics.

But the true justification for this extraordinary police state program, an embryonic version of officially instigated terrorism, is not to be found in these clumsy post hoc apologetics but rather in a nation-saving afflatus in which the Director had enveloped the agency and which persisted after his death. The Bureau took these actions in pursuance, as Kelley put it, of its "on-going responsibilities," not to the Congress, the Attorney General, or even the President, but to the "American people."[12] This self-assumed mission of preserving the existing order in direct response to the voice of the people is revealingly mirrored in the rhetoric of the Bureau's internal memoranda. These documents reflect a totalistic concern over challenges to the prevailing order, ranging from morality to foreign policy.† The programs reveal an agency aflame with self-righteousness and a sense of mission, a secular church in full cry against desecrations of the American way of life by those "unappreciative of their heritage." Small wonder that it did not feel bound by the standards it applied to its victims. Reminding its field agents that a "civilized society cannot survive without law and order," it proceeded to violate the law.‡ It bitterly denounced targets for

*Despite the high incidence of civil unrest between 1963 and 1968, violence claimed no more than 220 lives and the victims were not the objects of protest but the protesters themselves: 20 civil rights workers and most of the rest ghetto-dwellers. During this period the civil strife death rate was 1.1 per million in this country, compared to a European rate of 2.4 per million—*Violence in America: Historical and Comparative Perspectives,* National Commission on the Causes and Prevention of Violence (GPO, 1969).

†To help agents meet their "increased responsibilities relating to communist-inspired student agitational activities," the Bureau showed them a film depicting the subversive influences on "student agitational demonstrations in opposition to the United States' position in Vietnam."

‡William C. Sullivan told the Church Committee, "Never once did I hear anybody, including myself, raise the question: 'Is this course of action legal, is it ethical or moral.' We never gave any thought to this line of reasoning because we were naturally pragmatic." Similarly, a senior Bureau official in charge of the counterintelligence program against blacks replied, when asked whether he

their "deviousness" as it devised ever more cunning tricks to disrupt them.*
Shuddering in horror over the immorality of its targets, it wallowed in porno-
graphic fantasy, and did not hesitate to authorize its own informers to engage
in sexual conduct it considered immoral.

Did Hoover's superiors approve of or know about these programs? Internally, within the Bureau, they were kept secret and disclosed only on a "need
to know" basis. In a public statement accompanying the Saxbe Report, Director
Kelley referred to communications by the Director to five Attorneys General
"furnishing . . . information" about disruptive activities. Two of them, Clark and
Katzenbach, thereafter repeated earlier denials of knowledge of such programs;
Clark pointed out that the Director may have slipped into a memorandum an
ambiguous reference for later use as a cover. Indeed, Kelley conceded in an
interview that the memos to which he had referred were typically vague
("Hooveresque"), quite incomplete, and possibly deceptive.[13] The record indicates that Hoover could not resist bragging, and on various occasions Attorneys
General, presidential advisers, cabinet members, and members of the House
Appropriations Subcommittee were apprised of the existence of the CPUSA and
White Hate Group COINTELPROs, but not about the other three programs,
presumably because no objections could be anticipated even to extra-legal attacks on Communists and Klansmen.[14] But no claim was made that the destructive tactics used against even these unpopular targets were formally made
known or submitted for approval to higher authority, although it is questionable
whether, with the exception of Attorney General Ramsey Clark, approval
would have been withheld had it been requested.

COINTELPRO-CPUSA—"Counterintelligence in the Purest Sense"[15]

COINTELPRO-CPUSA, launched in August 1956, was the oldest program,
with the greatest number of approved actions—1338, more than half the total
of all actions approved. The Saxbe Report outdid itself in justifying COINTEL-
PRO-CPUSA. The Communists were, perhaps, victims of "McCarthyist sentiments" but, the report insisted, "they were, in varying degrees, *effective* in such
areas as sabotage and espionage" (italics in original). The attempts to injure
them and to disrupt their activities were therefore clearly justified as "counterintelligence in the purest sense." These actions were, the report concluded,
"clearly legitimate and proper undertakings, within the scope of the FBI's
ongoing responsibilities, and are listed as 'COINTELPRO' activities only because
they were reported as such."[16] Even the Bureau's ultimate defense of this program made no such extravagant claim but confined itself to the classic thesis that

had ever discussed the constitutionality of the program or its legal authority, "No, we never gave
it a thought."

*It was not merely that the actions relied heavily on lies and trickery. The overriding require-
ment of every action—the precondition for its approval—was that the Bureau's role be concealed.
While the ostensible purpose of this stricture was to ensure operational success, a deeper concern
was to conceal the Bureau's responsibility for illegal acts.

actions against Communists, however illegal and unauthorized, were self-justi-fying, regardless of the policies and conduct of the targets. Thus an intelligence functionary, James B. Adams, suggested that Congress was unduly disturbed about the Bureau's aggressive intelligence since, after all, "59% of [all the actions] were directed against the Communist Party."*[17] What is indisputable is that the Bureau considered the program a huge success and used it as the model for those that followed.

This operation and its successors charged field agents with submitting proposed actions to Washington for approval by the Director himself† after processing by a specially designated "COINTEL Coordinator," who was required to submit to Washington ninety-day "status reports" covering proposed and pending actions and evaluating the results of completed ones.

The normalization of aggression against Communists was inevitable, given the virulence of the Bureau's anti-communism, the emerging role of CIA covert action abroad in the struggle with the Soviets for hegemony (in 1954, the Hoover Commission concluded that in the future there could be no holds barred in the foreign intelligence game), the opportunities presented by the Khrushchev reve-lations at the 20th Communist Party Congress in the Soviet Union, and the invasion of Hungary. There were also cultural and professional craft pressures. Agents with a cloak-and-dagger itch knew all too well that their endless investi-gative rounds and bureaucratic routines to determine whether a subject was a Communist or to trace his whereabouts were far removed from professional intelligence practices made familiar by the cold war, the popular culture, and their experiences in the shooting war. Besides, such pallid chores denied the action-hungry agent a powerful psychic need, the pleasure of really hurting the enemy. For the times had further contributed to the vulnerability of the Com-munist target the notion that he was a combat adversary as unprotected by the rule of law as an enemy soldier. Counterintelligence also spurred conventional investigative intelligence by creating new uses for its products.

All of the techniques already described, from cancellation of meeting hall

*This view that "internal security" immunizes the Bureau from accountability for what it does to Communists is reflected in the Attorney General's initial denial of requests for documents relating to the program. Beyond conceding its existence, the Attorney General refused, in the course of the Stern litigation, to disclose the relevant documents dealing with its launching and operation, claiming it had been abandoned. But this was hardly a persuasive reason for denying access to the documents in view of the release of documents relating to all the other programs also abandoned. In addition, the Attorney General relied on the "Secret" classification of the documents, again an unimpressive argument in view of the fact that they have been so classified for reasons of "internal security" only after the request for their release. It was not until November 1977 that some CPUSA-COINTELPRO documents were made public and included in a release of over 50,000 pages of COINTELPRO files. Apart from the fact that 12,000 pages of documents were withheld entirely, the released materials are so heavily censored as to conceal basic operational details. Clues to practices the Bureau prefers to keep buried are excised on a variety of pretexts, such as the need to protect "sensitive techniques," "sources and methods," and the identity of informers. And always, the ritualized claim that disclosure—even of material twenty years old—would endanger the nation's security.

†It seems clear that the Washington transmittals were actually drafted by subordinates, frequently in a remarkably accurate imitation of the Director's style, including his grammatical lapses. Indeed, nothing so graphically illustrates the cult of personality that gripped the agency as the bureaucratization of the Director's modes of expression. The Director came close to achieving the ventriloquist's dream: the unaided projection of his voice by "talking dummies."

arrangements to instigated raids, were used to frustrate and rout the Communists. Propaganda, the cultivation of news media, originally institutionalized through the Crime Records Office for image-building, inevitably expanded into a weapon of countersubversive warfare. Under this new program, information obtained from Bureau spies but far more particularized than formerly was systematically distributed to a network of press outlets and, in a new development, documents drafted by Bureau personnel in the Crime Records Office were channeled to the media with the cover sponsorship of a group such as the Catholic War Veterans. File information or stories unacceptable to standard press outlets were leaked to obscure far right anti-Communist sheets, newsletters, and bulletins, laundered, and then recirculated as "public source" material along with stale and fabricated exposés, congressional committee materials, and arrest records.[18] Other propaganda techniques included planting embarrassing questions with friendly reporters for use in interviews with Communists, arranging for press photographers to take pictures of Communist leaders appearing in public with officials of the Soviet Union, and tipping off television cameramen about secret Party schools, meetings, and conferences. CP members and supporters were bombarded with mass mailings of pamphlets and reprints of articles drafted by Bureau personnel attacking policies, prominent leaders, and Communist subgroups. Such mailings were also pinpointed to influence hostile action, such as the cancellation of a speaking engagement, or to promote factionalism. The Chicago SAC was especially proud of having arranged for a friendly reporter to publish articles attacking Illinois CP leader Claude Lightfoot as a "slumlord," which the reporter then had reprinted in a catchy format and mailed to other Party figures.

A support network of private groups was invaluable for staging crowd scenes, demonstrations, and counterdemonstrations, and as a source of hostile claques to disrupt meetings through planted questions and provocations. The historic collaboration between the Bureau and the IRS became more intimate. In the late fifties, IRS audits were instigated on a large scale by the FBI against Communists who had gone underground. In turn, information obtained from the IRS served the field as a basis for aggressive action. In the early sixties, the IRS was persuaded to revive a crushing tax assessment against the Communist Party that had been dormant for five years. (It was ultimately abandoned as a result of an adverse court decision.) Job pressures against Communists had become a priority long before the formal launching of the program. The Bureau justified such attacks on the livelihood of its targets by a variety of rationales: the subject was not just an employee but an infiltrator bent on subversion of the employing enterprise; his income contributed to the Party treasury, and if deprived of employment he could pay no dues; even if the reasons for termination were withheld, repeated job loss would bring home the message and force the subject's retreat; his unhappy experience would weaken and demoralize the entire group. The case of Mary Blair is illustrative.

In June 1960, the Milwaukee field office was horrified to learn that Mary Blair, the wife of Fred Blair, state chairman of the Wisconsin Communist Party, had, on the recommendation of a school principal and a parent-teachers' group, been appointed a den mother of a local Cub Scout troop and, even worse, "had held a meeting of her pack at her residence." The office won Washington approval for a project to squelch this abomination: the circulation of a newspaper article identifying her and accompanying a letter "expressing alarm at the possibility of indoctrinating the Cub Scouts in Un-American ideas." To eliminate this threat, her employer was also to be notified through a mailing purportedly from a fellow employee. The den mother post was duly cleansed; but the Milwaukee office remained unhappy. Ms. Blair's job and income, a memorandum points out, gave her both the "peace of mind" and money "vital . . . to her activities in the CP." As a result of a nudge to fire her from an anonymous letter drafted by the Bureau, her employer, the Olson Publishing Company, contacted the Milwaukee SAC, the anonymous author of the letter, to verify the fact that Ms. Blair was a Communist. The firm assured the SAC that it would discharge the subject as soon as economically possible, "preferring to wait for a slack season." A memo dated April 1961, ten months later, impatiently noted that the subject was still employed; "in view of the current business recession this is the opportune time for Olson to discharge Mary Blair." Approval was requested for another anonymous pressure note, pointing to the adverse publicity risk in retaining Ms. Blair. The second letter was duly sent, but again the passage of time brought disappointment. By June the jig was up on the second try. A Bureau contact in the company reported that the letters were dismissed as the work of a crank.

But the Milwaukee office refused to accept defeat. In September 1961 a new opportunity emerged for another crack at Ms. Blair's livelihood. An article by CP secretary Gus Hall, along with two enclosures, had been mailed to a list compiled by the local Communist Party. The Milwaukee Bureau office accumulated about fifteen such packets and, with Washington approval, sent them in envelopes similar to those used in the original mailings to the entire Olson Company staff, already incensed at the subject as a result of the Bureau's prior efforts. On November 13, 1961, the Milwaukee office triumphantly reported:

> This is to advise that Mary Blair, Secretary-Treasurer of the Communist Party of Wisconsin and an employee of the Olson Publishing Company, Milwaukee, has been discharged from her employment. . . . The mailing of Communist Party literature to 17 employees of the Olson Publishing Co. had its desired effect upon the employees and executives of the Olson Publishing Co.

It took three tries, but the Bureau finally got its woman. The record does not show whether the Milwaukee office received the bonus usually awarded to agents for outstanding performance. But in May 1979, Ms. Blair was awarded $48,000 by a court in settlement of her claims for damages against the Bureau.

While retaining the cruder weapons of the past, COINTELPRO-USA, in the early sixties, borrowed more artful techniques from the bag of tricks developed by the CIA in foreign intelligence. This refinement in tactics was the contribution of William C. Sullivan, who ascended to the leadership of the Domestic Intelligence Division in 1961. Sullivan's twenty-year Bureau career prior to that time had uniquely equipped him for the role of intelligence innovator. An intellectual, familiar with the world of contemporary intelligence and its utility as an extra-legal weapon, he had served during World War II with the Bureau's foreign intelligence arm (Secret Intelligence Service) both domestically and in a confidential foreign assignment. His 1961 appointment embraced, in addition to domestic intelligence, responsibility for all of the Bureau's intelligence operations in Latin America, Canada, Asia, and Europe; and for a decade prior to his departure from the agency in October 1971, he had served as a Bureau representative on the United States Intelligence Board (USIB), the top intelligence agency charged with supervising and coordinating foreign intelligence.

Sullivan's voice echoes through the documents, exhorting the field to use imagination and daring in the development of new schemes. One encounters types like Sullivan in all bureaucratic structures: the professional who outgrows the established milieu of his agency, chafes at its backwardness, but in the end surrenders to it. But even such wing-flutterings were barred in the Director's domain. The Director was the father-ruler of a family of agents bent to his will by the power of his personality and their fear of jeopardizing extremely well-paid jobs. History had cast Sullivan in the role of Hoover-slayer, but had placed the cudgel of an Oedipus in irresolute, fear-palsied hands. His dreams of defiance were thwarted by fear, not only of career consequences but of the Director's manic fury,* while his hopes of succeeding to the throne, based on the opportunistic patronage of the Nixon administration, faded as soon as the Director showed his muscle. Memos reflect his conviction that the Director's priorities and methods had undermined intelligence as a useful weapon against radicalism. But his transient discontents were salved by intellectual vanity and pride in intelligence actions more imaginative than the common run.

Sullivan objected particularly to the Director's primitive standards of target selection (such as the National Council of Churches), his power-centered maneuvers (such as the expansion of the legat network), his exaggeration of the Menace, and his feud with the CIA. In a sense, Sullivan's discontents distilled a conflict between nativist fundamentalism and the professionalism associated with the CIA. On the surface, the conflict appeared to reflect a long-overdue challenge by an infidel to an outworn religion, and it was so viewed by many liberals. But Sullivan's gods were far more destructive than Hoover's. What Sullivan wanted was carte blanche for a no-holds-barred professionalism, in which break-ins, wiretaps, and mail openings, for example, would be routinely

*The record is full of examples of Sullivan's behind-the-scenes criticism and face-to-face fawning in the style of his abject reversal of position on the influence of communism in the movement for racial integration. Most revealing was Sullivan's panicky retreat from his Huston Plan proposals for lifting restraints on the FBI's intelligence collection techniques. He first deceived Hoover about his role in drafting the document, falsely portraying himself as the embattled defender of the Director and the Bureau against efforts by other members of Huston's panel to expand the FBI's operational scope. Then, when the proposal, which he had largely drafted himself, was circulated, he informed the Director he had not approved it. The harsh voice of the Director cowed Sullivan even from the grave. Thus, he told a newsman in an interview that toward the end Hoover had slipped into madness, but precipitately retreated after a denunciation by the Director's congressional supporters.

On Sullivan's Huston Plan maneuvers, see Church, Book III, pp. 965–966, and "FBI Counterintelligence Plan Against Radicals Outlined," Washington *Post,* March 19, 1974, reprinted in HISC Hearings, 1974, p. 3544. Sullivan's claim that Hoover was insane in his last years was made in an interview with Los Angeles *Times* reporter Jack Nelson. "Aide Says Hoover Was 'Not of Sound Mind,' " New York *Post,* May 15, 1973. The response of Hoover's supporters appeared in CR, May 16, 1973, pp. 15855–15856, vol. 119. A letter of apology, in which Sullivan noted that Hoover's "superior ability, industry, intelligence, and personality set him apart from most men," was published in CR for June 14, 1973, p. 19716, vol. 119.

used to rout the subversive enemy. His unsuccessful attempt to persuade the Director to continue the COINTELPROS when Hoover saw the handwriting of disapproval on the wall measures the difference between this reckless *fantaisiste* and his cautious chief, fearful of a tarnished image. But despite differences in target priorities and style, what bound them together was stronger than what separated them: the conviction enfolded in a passionate self-righteousness that their patriotism justified whatever actions they considered necessary to combat subversion. Sullivan's eagerness to replace the culture-bound crudities of Hoover's intelligence style with a more elegant, imaginative mode ignored the simple reality that techniques employed against a combat adversary or a foreign spy could not be readily adapted for use against powerless, peaceful, and un-threatening domestic dissidents. The substitution of one ambiance for the other added to the Bureau's traditional intelligence operations a sort of unintended grisly humor in the contrast between the elaborate planning of an operation and its puny potential. Like a monumental pop-style bronze of a hot dog or a cigarette butt, a petty end is overwhelmed by a grotesque means.

The new dispensation, for example, contributed the device of a fictitious organization ("notional"), operated in whole or in part by informers solely for the purpose of destruction. A variant version had no real members at all, but existed only as a letterhead such as "The Committee for the Expansion of Socialist Thought in America," a Bureau-sponsored newsletter critical of the Communist Party. The Bureau must have had favorable reports about the project's effectiveness, for it continued for more than two years. Another no-tional which, although approved, was never implemented was an immaculately conceived unit of the DuBois Clubs, a CP youth group, composed entirely of informers and wholly fictitious members to be set up in a Southern area removed from the centers of radical activity. The plan tickled Sullivan's fancy for a variety of reasons, including the fact that it would transfer from the Bureau to the Party the burden of financing the expenses of the informer members of the group required, for example, by out-of-town trips to conventions and schools.

A grimmer sort of organizational disruption was projected in Operation Hoodwink, the code name of a project designed to provoke a feud between the Mafia and the Communist Party, which, in the language of an FBI memoran-dum, "would cause disruption of both groups by having each expend their energies, time and money attacking each other." We can trace attempts to implement this operation over the course of a two-year period (1966–68), begin-ning with the anonymous mailing to Mafia leaders of a spurious leaflet, allegedly from the Communist Party. The contrast between the gruesome implications of the actions and the solemn bureaucratese of the memoranda exchanges between the Director and his field functionaries supplies the kind of unintended humor sometimes found in very bad movies.

In the fall of 1966, after a bomb had damaged Communist Party headquar-ters, the Party's newspaper denounced the alleged "hoodlum" perpetrators and appealed to the FBI to apprehend the bombers. The Bureau's New York office won Washington approval of a proposal to blame the Mafia for the explosion. Three forged anonymous letters, supposedly written by a Communist to local Mafia leaders, denounced the Mafia for the bombing, and concluded: "Long live the revolutionary movement!" The forgeries were duly mailed, but they produced no response. Neither did the Party's appeal for the apprehension of the bombers.

The Director was fussy about granting approval for some proposed actions. For example, he vetoed a suggestion for inserting an item in the column of a friendly newsman stating that "the local commies . . . are now ready to take on local hoodlum elements," on the ground that "it might put the party in a favorable light." But he gave his blessing to a proposal for a forged letter to the Party newspaper, *The Worker,* which was to attack Mafia leaders and to be "written as if coming from a longtime Jewish reader," one "I. Cohen." (How much more Jewish can you get?) Alas, though it was approved by the Director, the letter was never printed. Could it be that *The Worker*'s editor became suspicious of his longtime Jewish reader's bureaucratic style and his repeated reference to "La Cosa Nostra" and "LCN," both of which were FBI usages? The FBI plan for a struggle to the death between subversion and organized crime ended not with the hoped-for bang but with a whimper. But there can be no doubt about the violence and bloodshed that would have followed if such a confrontation actually had been ignited, as in the Bureau-inspired feud between the Black Panthers and Ron Karenga's US, discussed below (see page 219).

A more ingenious form of disruption is the charge of informing, or "putting the snitch jacket," on an individual. The classic, highly successful snitch jacket project was Operation Splinter Factor, activated by the CIA to disrupt eastern European Communist régimes in the post-World War II era by exploiting the paranoid suspicions of Josef Stalin. Although many of the victims were lifelong Communists with unassailable records of commitment, the CIA's frame-up charges that they were American spies were extraordinarily effective. One of the victims, a Hungarian Communist, Lazlo Rajk, was executed in December 1949 on false charges that he was an American secret agent and Titoist. A month later John Lautner, a minor functionary of the American Communist Party, was expelled from the Party as a Rajk accomplice under the control of the Office of Strategic Services (OSS, predecessor of the CIA). Whether this expulsion was the result of a CIA maneuver (as was probably the case) or lock-step Stalinism by the domestic Party is impossible to establish conclusively. But the CIA could hardly have planned it better. Lautner was expelled and, embittered by the Party's rejection of his protestations of innocence, became the leading witness against the Party in a series of Smith Act conspiracy cases.

The snitch jacket formula depends for its effectiveness on the fear of informers within the target group. The spymaster's sense of power over his targets, born of knowledge secretly acquired, is confirmed and strengthened by their fear, frequently groundless in fact, of his spies. These psychic fruits of intelligence are not only rewarding but easy to harvest. All that is needed is a credible stimulation of latent anxiety. Instilling and exploiting fear of informers might, on the face of it, seem unprofessional and foolhardy; why alert the target and thus make infiltration more hazardous? It is simply that, as already noted, the by-product of infiltration outweighs the importance of the product. Many techniques are used to harden an already existing fear of informers. The simplest is some action by a Bureau agent, such as an interview to suggest knowledge secretly acquired from a particular individual (Who else but Y would know that X is on vacation?). But the problem of credibility is formidable. Far more reliable is the planting of evidence. If the victim, method, and evidence are carefully chosen, the false accusation may stick, eliminating the target and producing a train of disruptive consequences. The falsely accused subject may, as in the case of Lautner, be induced to become an active informer out of resentment or revenge and thus retroactively convince the accuser of the truth of the original charge. A common snitch jacket technique is to use a genuine (if that is the word) informer as the accuser; the charge not only diverts attention from the accuser himself (the thief crying, "Stop thief!"), but strengthens his image as a militant member concerned with security. Sometimes, however, cruder techniques are required.

In October 1959 the Senate Internal Security Subcommittee (SISS) held a hearing in Philadelphia ostensibly to adduce testimony on the subject: "Revitalizing of the Communist Party in the Philadelphia Area." The suspiciously nonlegislative theme for the hearing was no accident. An ulterior purpose was confirmed by a preliminary observation of the subcommittee's counsel that the inquiry might depart from its announced purpose, "and may develop other areas of questioning which . . . would be of value [to] the internal security of the country." And matters grew curiouser and curiouser when Chairman Roman Hruska placed in the record a recently published essay by the Director ("Communist Illusion and Democratic Reality") totally removed from the hearing's professed purpose, followed by a particularly fulsome tribute to the Director.*

In fact, the hearings were entirely bogus, and were set up by the Bureau to place a snitch jacket on a member of the Philadelphia group. At the Bureau's suggestion, SISS subpoenaed a number of individuals to appear as witnesses and called all of them to testify, with a single exception—the target of the snitch jacket plan. In the Bureau's script, SISS's failure to call him would create the suspicion among his comrades that he had made a deal with the committee. But, in contrast to the usual case, the intended victim was in fact an informer who had already fallen under suspicion by the group members. Surely the Bureau would not have gone to such lengths to snitch-jacket one of its own informers? Indeed not; the intended victim was an infiltrator planted by a right-wing group, and feared by the Bureau informer in the CP branch as a threat to his own security. The target's failure to testify confirmed prior suspicions and he was expelled, presumably leaving the Bureau informer free to function without competition. In an affair in which ironies clamor for notice, we cannot ignore Senator Hruska's indignant rejection of the charges that the hearing lacked legislative purpose, and his admonition to a harassed witness that he had no right to respond "so as to question the good faith of the committee."

A classic example of use of the snitch jacket technique is the Albertson

---

*"It is the acting chairman's judgment, which I have expressed many, many, many times, that J. Edgar Hoover is one of the better things that has happened to America in this last one-third of a century. The record of his achievements and the achievements of the Federal Bureau of Investigation not alone in this field but other fields is one that has been outstanding and in which law-abiding citizens who have the well-being of this Nation in mind have a good deal of pride and take a good deal of comfort."

affair.[19] William Albertson was fifty-four years old and a top leader of the Communist Party when he was expelled in disgrace as an informer in 1964. In spite of his denials and his continuing legal efforts to clear his name, neither his Party nor the government relented in the devastating judgment of informer that was to follow him and his family even beyond his death. Buried among documents released in August 1975 was a five-page report dated January 6, 1965, containing an item that reads as follows:

> [Name deleted], the most active and efficient functionary of the New York District of the Communist Party USA and leading national officer of the party, through our counterintelligence efforts has been expelled from the party. Factors relating to this expulsion crippled the activities of the New York State communist organization and the turmoil within the party continues to this date. Albertson's exposure as an FBI informant has discouraged many dedicated communists from activities and has discredited the party in the eyes of the Soviets.

In the course of processing the document, an FBI clerk apparently eliminated the name William Albertson at its beginning, but neglected to delete the name when it recurred at the end. In any event, the factual background confirms the identification of Albertson as the "leading officer" of the Communist Party expelled in 1964 as an FBI spy. The evidence that led the Communist Party to expel Albertson consisted of a document—seemingly in his handwriting, and found in a car in which he had been a passenger—that purported to be an informer's report, presumably to an FBI contact, on certain Party decisions. Albertson vigorously protested his innocence and offered to cooperate by supplying a handwriting sample. When experts confirmed the charges, he repeated his denials. Alleging a frame-up, he offered to take a "lie-detector test, a truth serum test, or any other test—psychological or otherwise." All his proposals were rejected; the handwriting analysis by itself was considered conclusive.

The Communist Party proclaimed Albertson's expulsion in clichés that must have delighted the COINTELPRO author of the action:

> With callous and malicious intent, he violated the confidence entrusted in him to perform the role of stool pigeon and informer against those whom he called his comrades, his friends, men and women who are devoted fighters for peace, freedom, and equality. Albertson lived a life of duplicity and treachery—posing as a dedicated defender of the workers' interests while in actuality betraying them. . . . It should come as no shock to communists that the ruling circles in the United States employ the tactic of infiltrating working class and people's organizations to cause dissention and disunity . . . hoping to defeat the people's struggle.

Albertson had been a dedicated Communist since his youth. Both his mother and his wife were Party members. During a 1953 Smith Act trial in Pittsburgh, Albertson was sentenced to jail for sixty days on a contempt charge when he refused to name others present at a meeting. He told the court: "My wife and I have tried to raise our children in the best tradition of the American labor movement. We have given them a hatred for spies, stool pigeons, and scabs. I could not look my children in the face if I violated those sacred traditions."

Albertson was subsequently convicted, along with four co-defendants, on Smith Act charges of conspiracy to teach and advocate the violent overthrow of the government. But the convictions, based on the testimony of seven informer witnesses, were later reversed by the Supreme Court when the government admitted that one important informer witness, Joseph D. Mazzei, was a liar. In 1957, the government dropped the case rather than retry it.

After thirty years in various Party posts, Albertson reached the highest rung in 1959: membership in the Communist ruling body, the National Committee. In May 1962 he was hauled before the Subversive Activities Control Board by Attorney General Robert F. Kennedy; this was the first step in a proceeding under the McCarran Act requiring his registration as a member of the Communist Party.

After Albertson's expulsion in July, and while his McCarran Act case was pending in the Supreme Court, the government moved to drop him from the case on the ground that he was no longer a CPUSA member. But Albertson, pointing to the fact that he had not exhausted his appeal, successfully opposed the government's motion and again denounced as a frame-up the charge that he was an informer. Party leaders remained unconvinced. Not only did his accusers deny the possibility of a forgery; they refused to entertain the hypothesis that the document had been planted by a real FBI informer, the driver of the car. The incriminating letter was addressed "Dear Joe" and signed "Bill," a practice strictly forbidden by the FBI to protect the identity of its informers. Routinely, an informer is assigned either a false name or a code number, but the Bureau had to ignore its own practice to make sure that the snitch jacket was successfully put on Albertson. The alleged report also was undated, so worded that a change in the date of its discovery would not affect its timeliness, and ended with a "request for a raise in expenses," a rather artless attempt to impute a financial motivation to Albertson.* But, as he contended in the course of his long efforts at vindication, there was simply no change in his chronically precarious financial situation.

Albertson's life had been plagued by informers, and he pointed this out to his CPUSA accusers. Attacking the handwriting evidence, he submitted an article from a technical journal, a description of a handwriting computer developed at the Massachusetts Institute of Technology. In response to his inquiry, Professor Murray Eden, the computer's co-designer, wrote that "computer-generated handwriting which had been modeled on the script of a single person would be very difficult to distinguish from the natural handwriting of that person." But all in vain.

The Bureau had chosen its victim with cunning. Along with fears of betrayal, the snitch jacket technique exploits the victim's political vulnerability. To finger a popular leader supported by all factions would boomerang and invite suspicion of a frame-up. But the Bureau knew that Albertson had powerful Party enemies who would seize on the forged report. The spy charge is sometimes used in left polemics as an epithet or metaphor (X is "in effect" or "might just as well be" a spy for the other side). Here was actual "evidence," the discrediting image miraculously transferred into reality. Albertson's defense

---

*Victims, with good reason, typically charge that informers and defectors are motivated primarily by greed. The Bureau knows this and invariably weaves financial considerations into its snitch jacket scripts.

was thus rejected from the start by those with a political stake in his disgrace. Although proof of the frame-up was subsequently brought to the Party's notice, it declined to retract its expulsion or grant requests for Albertson's rehabilitation. As in an expertly played confidence scam, the mark's needs had converted a lie into the truth.

As soon as reports of his expulsion from the CPUSA were published, Albertson's wife and his mother were shunned, and his three children suffered the stigma and ostracism that have been visited on the children of informers throughout history. In this setting the FBI played out the last act of the snitch jacket scenario: the instigation of a pressure campaign designed to "turn" the already embittered, unjustly accused victim through instigated harassments intended to be attributed to retaliation by his former comrades. Mysterious crank calls, abusive and obscene, came at all hours. Stores called about the delivery of merchandise which the family had never ordered; on at least two occasions, vans filled with unordered furniture pulled up to make deliveries at the Albertson home. Increasingly distraught, the Albertsons were forced to move and were faced with renewed hostility and ostracism. The family attempted to save itself from disintegration through therapy. At this point an FBI agent approached Albertson with an offer actually to serve as an informer; the Party had thrown him out and harassed him; why should he persist in his loyalty? The IRS made a similar offer and, after he refused it, pursued him with spurious tax charges. Against the strongest advice, Albertson refused to abandon his quest for vindication. His widow recalls: "He was constantly involved from the day of his expulsion in one appeal after another, in corresponding with the Party and doing everything possible to have his name cleared and to be reinstated, to also do his own investigation to try to find out how he had been framed. The most painful thing that I ever had to experience in my whole life was watching a destroyed man try to save himself." Albertson never recovered from the trauma of the frame-up. In February 1972 he died as the result of an accident, protesting his innocence to the end.

Paralleling the earlier COMINFIL investigative coverage, COINTELPRO-CPUSA, beginning in 1960, targeted a variety of non-Communist organizations. This expansion was justified by an article in the Communist official organ *Political Affairs,* exhorting its readers "to bring such issues as disarmament and peaceful coexistence" to "organizations of the people." Non-Communist organizations were attacked through anonymous press stories on the ground that they harbored Communists, and in a further expansion, individuals were victimized by COINTELPRO actions because they were allegedly under Party influence or committed to goals also supported by Communists, from integration to the abolition of the House Un-American Activities Committee.* By the mid-sixties,

---

*The program was launched by a memorandum of instruction to the field offices in sixteen American cities setting forth the criteria for initiating an action. But, as was so often the case, the memorandum at the same time invited disregard of the criteria: "Since it is rather difficult to draw up all-inclusive criteria for every case, no office should hesitate to submit its recommendation if it has a case it feels falls within the approximate criteria set forth above." The subsequent pressures to produce results led inevitably to increasingly remote approximations of the governing criteria. "There were no 'Stops' only 'Go's' in Washington's case advice on subversive matters," a former agent recalled in an interview. In targeting anti-HUAC groups for aggressive action, a self-protective

COINTELPRO-CPUSA embraced a broad spectrum of actions against non-Communist targets—especially in the civil rights sphere. For example, even prior to the formal adoption of the program the Chicago office, in 1959, learned from an infiltrator that a left caucus was planning to run a slate of candidates for election as delegates of the Chicago branch to a national NAACP convention, and anonymously communicated this information to the branch president. According to Bureau documents, the alerted official defeated this threat by keeping the election site secret and packing the meeting with his newly enfranchised supporters. The Director recommended a commendation to the agent who had initiated the operation.

While this extension of aggressive techniques to non-Communist targets was internally justified by claims of CP resurgence and mounting influence, the Director contemporaneously boasted about the success of the COINTELPROS in disrupting and neutralizing the CP itself. Thus, in a 1965 statement, one in a series of secret briefings of the Appropriations Subcommittee, reporting on the effectiveness of the program, Hoover gloated over what he described as "the most effective blow ever dealt the organized Communist movement."*

SWP—Election Campaigns, Rummage Sales, Summer Camps, and Other Threats to the National Security[20]

Long before October 1961, when the "SWP Disruption Program" was formally launched, indeed since the late forties, the FBI had exploited the historic

---

rationale was advanced: if the abolition drive succeeded, the FBI itself would become vulnerable to attack by the same forces.

*What was this "most effective blow"? The Bureau deleted from the document submitted to the Church Committee the Director's description of this action "as it tends to reveal a highly sensitive technique." In a communication to a member of the Church Committee staff, an intelligence official reaffirmed its effectiveness, stating that it had caused a "radical decrease" in Party membership, but again refused to describe its workings on the ground that it involved "sensitive" foreign intelligence. The Church Committee's failure to press further for a disclosure of this data reflects, in an otherwise quite vigorous investigation, a pervasive lack of concern, for "internal security" reasons, about abuses involving communism and the Communist Party—Church, Bk III, pp. 15, 72.

Presumably, this alleged blow was delivered in the previous year, 1964. But a Bureau report covering Communist Party COINTELPRO actions for the year 1964 refers only to the Albertson matter, a letter-writing campaign dealing with Soviet anti-Semitism, and the frustration of a legacy of a piece of land allegedly worth $50,000. According to students of the Party's history, the "most effective blow" ever dealt the Party resulted from the circulation of Khrushchev's remarks at the 20th Party Congress in 1956, an action for which the Bureau could hardly claim credit. They are without exception mystified by the Director's boasted coup, which may indeed have been invented to impress the subcommittee.

The Bureau's testamentary obstruction in 1964 encouraged it to more valiant efforts, in 1967, to block a larger bequest (over $1 million) in a carefully drawn will probated in New York City. It contacted relatives of the deceased in order to instigate a contest, leaked information about the will to the press to influence the probate court's decision, and prompted federal and state tax authorities to take action to deplete the estate as much as possible. An agent even interviewed the probate judge who, in a cooperative spirit, requested the Bureau to investigate whether the widow would be willing "to take any action designed to keep the Communist Party from getting the money." The widow refused to cooperate and the entire campaign came to naught.

rivalry between the Soviet-oriented Communist Party and the Socialist Workers' Party (SWP), followers of Leon Trotsky. Like the Communist Party, the
SWP, then and now a minuscule group,* was targeted for ideological reasons
and because "it had been openly espousing its line on a local and national basis
through running candidates for public office and strongly directing and/or
supporting such causes as Castro's Cuba and integration problems arising in the
South." Much of this program consists of colossal sculptures of cigarette butts:
elaborate bureaucratic processing of petty harassments. Schemes—proposed,
revised, rejected, revived, modified, approved—are processed by streams of
memos debating, sometimes for months, such matters as whether an anonymous
letter should be mailed to blacks as well as whites, to the national or local
leadership, in the name of a fictitious committee or a disaffected member. Should
informers be utilized to allay suspicion, or is the risk too great? The wording
of an anonymous letter intended to disrupt the already hopeless prospects of an
independent mayoral candidate in San Francisco is anxiously submitted for
Washington's approval ("errors and misspellings are intentional") and solemnly
evaluated: "The letter should be handwritten on a cheap grade of paper and
contain the spelling errors set out in the sample. The letter definitely has disruptive potential." Praise and even bonuses reward puny triumphs, while failures
are salved by consolations and encouragements for future efforts. Thus, when
the "disruptive potential" of the San Francisco letter failed to materialize, a
letter from Washington offered comfort: "You should be encouraged by the fact
that your anonymous letter . . . was received and considered although no action
was taken. It could have been discarded without comment upon receipt."

Responding to Washington's pleas for madder music and stronger wine, the
field sought the help of the arts. Because the Milwaukee SWP leader was a
published poet and his CP counterpart a bookseller, an office versifier composed
a taunting limerick, which was sent anonymously to the bookseller in the hope
that he would attribute it to the poet:

> *There was an old radical named* ——————
> *Who swapped his soapbox for a bed*
> *He lives in the past*
> *Drinks beer to the last*
> *And from militant action has fled.*

The CP chairman rose to the bait and wrote back:

> *Revolting* ——————, *the King of the Trots*
>
> *Don't make a fetish*
> *Of being Reddish*
> *There's someone Redder I'll bet.*
> *At plain revoltin'*
> *None can match* ——————
> *He's quite the revoltin'est yet.*

*The FBI's application for the mail cover in 1973 described in the previous chapter typically
strains to magnify the group's status: "The Socialist Workers' Party is the largest Communist-
Trotskyist organization in the United States, with a membership of approximately 1,100."

Don't bother with wherefores,
Or thus-es or therefores,
Or whereas-es, which-es or whats.
The Ultra-revoltin'
Is no one but ———
The Pontiff, and King of the Trots.

Dizzy with its success in the use of verse, the field office drafted plans to exacerbate the quarrel through satirical cartoons.

The SWP's vulnerability to factional splits made internal disruption an attractive gambit. The Bureau relentlessly fomented internal disagreements and intensified existing ones, in some cases around ideological issues and in others by "polarizing black and white within the SWP," to use the language of one of the documents. The Los Angeles SWP is wracked by an ideological disagreement, the "Sino-Soviet Ideological Dispute," as it is grandiosely referred to by the Bureau. Should the Bureau informers be instructed to encourage the formation of a "splinter group," or should they align themselves with the majority against the malcontents (all five of them) and thus "keep the turmoil at its highest possible level"? Los Angeles endorsed the latter course because of its optimal disruptive potential: the constant internal bickering would cause the withdrawal of new recruits. Then too, it reasoned, the minority group would recruit past ideological dropouts and thus provide a potential source of new informers who would intensify the existing discord. In fact, one informer, already playing a leading role in "fanning the flames of discord and discontent," is running for membership on the executive committee along with another informer; if both are elected, even greater disruption may be anticipated.

An annual Christmas fund-raising bazaar to support an SWP-sponsored school in New York City auctioned articles donated by local merchants. An anonymous letter by a fictitious disillusioned member was dispatched to the New York Better Business Bureau pointing out that, in view of the connection between the school and the SWP, the merchants were being solicited under false pretenses. The bazaar was canceled because it could no longer be run at a profit. But an SWP Los Angeles fund-raising rummage sale was a tougher nut to crack. How to sabotage a sale of used merchandise and clothing donated by friends and well-wishers? Publicity about the SWP would not deter either the proprietor of the shop where the sale was conducted nor the potential purchasers—all friendly to the group. "It appears," the memo notes, "that the only possible way to disrupt the rummage sale is the physical destruction of the available material." No principled objection to such a step was raised; it was simply that the small amount of profit "does not justify drastic measures which would be necessary to physically destroy the rummage material."

The Los Angeles office was also deeply concerned about a vacation school, which had in the past netted the local SWP branch sufficient profit to repay an indebtedness to the national office. Fortunately, a minute inspection by the U.S. Forest Rangers—prompted by the county sheriff—as well as other harassment, created problems resulting in a sharp drop in income. This misfortune, Los Angeles noted with satisfaction, followed the collapse of earlier arrangements for another site, resulting in a forfeiture of a $150 deposit and requiring the preparation of new announcement mailings and area maps of the new inferior site. The entire fiasco cost the Los Angeles SWP branch a loss in anticipated profits and, the memo regretfully adds, there would have been a net loss had not the site owners, the Unitarian Church of Los Angeles (a longtime Bureau target), agreed to renegotiate the lease. For this slightly flawed triumph, the Los Angeles office claims some credit since it was already trying to wreck the deal for the initial site when it fell through. Heartened by these developments, Los Angeles promises that the disruption of the camp will again receive priority consideration when a quest for a new site is undertaken the next year. All this is noted in minute detail (three single-spaced pages) in the Los Angeles report to Washington. The Los Angeles office was right on the ball when the group selected a new site in 1964. Its informers were instructed to spread the word that the facilities were inadequate, and the office tried a variety of pressures to force cancellation of the arrangements for the new site. Its desperation is measured by its attempt to obtain publicity by mailing a Bureau brochure about the school to *Tocsin,* a far-out anti-Communist weekly.* But *Tocsin* failed to come to the rescue, and the school was conducted without interference.

Disruptive proposals were often implemented through other government agencies, a technique used in all the COINTELPROS. Only a few months after the beginning of the SWP operation, the Philadelphia office obtained approval to seek the eviction of the SWP local branch, located in offices rented from the Philadelphia Redevelopment Authority. But the Authority reported that it could not act against the SWP without legally justifiable reasons. As soon as the SWP missed a rent payment, the Authority had a sheriff attach all its furnishings and instituted eviction proceedings. But the SWP quickly made up the back rent, and the Authority backed off, despite further Bureau urgings.

The Newark, New Jersey, SAC, working in cooperation with the State Alcoholic Beverage Control Board, developed a plan for a Labor Day, 1962, raid on an SWP-operated camp in the hope of finding violations of the state liquor laws. The Bureau prepared a detailed drawing of the camp's facilities, including the building housing the bar, and transmitted it to the Control Board agents. Bureau informers within the SWP were warned not to serve as bartenders during the time when the raid was scheduled so as to avoid arrest. At the appointed hour while a dance was being held, the raid scenario unfolded, complete with marked bills, axes wielded by state troopers, and the confiscation of liquor. Two arrested SWP members were held overnight in jail until $1000 cash could be raised for their bail, a source of great satisfaction to the Bureau. Indeed, the apprehension of a vicious criminal could hardly have yielded greater gratification. A chain of difficulties followed, including four indictments (when two of the violators could not be located, the Bureau made their addresses available to the police), property damage, and discouragement of potential members. Even the SWP's efforts to dispose of the camp did not dull the Bureau's ardor. It desperately sought to develop pretexts for another raid,

*The publication was forced out of business in 1965 when, in the course of a libel action, it refused to disclose its sponsors.

consulting with local officials as to possible violations of township health and sanitation regulations, only to discover that most of the local ordinances had never been formally recorded. It debated internally the planting of exposés in local newspapers, hoping to intimidate potential buyers. The legal proceedings against the indicted SWP members were closely monitored, and information about their eventual guilty pleas and $200 fines was sent to local papers but never published. In September 1965, three years after the raid, the camp was finally sold. Related pressure techniques included prodding the IRS for audits of subjects of interest to the Bureau and the New York State Department of Labor for an investigation of possible violations of the Unemployment Insurance Laws, as well as first aid and safety requirements.

The pressures on individuals included anonymous letters to parents (the Bureau's strong suit was a do-you-know-where-your-children-are? appeal), warning of their offspring's political aberrations, and to employers seeking the discharge of target employees, but anonymous letters sometimes created problems of credibility, which in turn required corroborative communications from a second anonymous source. Even more important was the need to forestall the suspicion raised by the nature of the information, that it originated with an informer, as was usually the case. Planted press stories were used for this cover purpose.

A number of SWP members who taught in public schools or state universities were targets of attempts to remove them from their jobs. In these cases two drives are intertwined: the ideological concern that capitalism cannot generate long-term loyalties and is threatened by generational defection; and the more immediate, nativist fear of mind-poisoning and, even worse, the fatal corruption of youthful souls, a consequence of the mere contact—especially by "little children"—with subversives.* Besides, the Bureau's efforts in this field were frequently crowned with success. Consider the case of Morris Starsky, once an assistant professor of philosophy at Arizona State University, under surveillance since 1968 because of his well-publicized leadership role in the campus anti-war movement and his prominence in the local SWP. Both the State Board of Regents and the conservative Arizona legislature were eager to find a removal pretext, and the Bureau watched the situation in the hopes of finding a COINTEL-PRO opening. After a two-year search, an opportunity presented itself when, on April 5, 1970, Professor Starsky became involved in an argument with an SWP member of a campus group over the possession of a box of leaflets. The other member reported the incident to the police, and threatened to swear out a complaint against Professor Starsky for disturbing the peace. But tempers rapidly cooled and later the same day the complaint was withdrawn. The Bureau, however, lost no time preparing an anonymous letter to the faculty disciplinary committee, describing the incident in lurid detail (omitting the amicable conclusion) and accusing Professor Starsky of using the tactics of Himmler and Beria. The faculty committee remained unconvinced, but continued Bureau and other pressures through anonymous letters eventually induced the Board of Regents

---

*The Director himself was a longtime prey—from the twenties to his death—to such fears, fueled by the sentimentality that is the counterfeit of compassion.

to cancel Professor Starsky's contract. When the story of this COINTELPRO became known, the American Association of University Professors took the unusual action of writing a protest to Attorney General Saxbe, charging the Bureau with carrying on a "planned attack on the academic community" through a program "designed to stifle dissent and freedom of expression." In at least three other teachers' cases, the Bureau tried to effect termination, in one of them (a substitute music teacher in Cleveland) solely because of a spouse's SWP activity. Another, Evelyn Sell, conceded by the Bureau to be "an intelligent, excellent teacher who was well qualified in her field," was faced with a contract cancellation as a result of Bureau pressure on the Austin, Texas, school board when the Head Start Program that employed her was removed from the school district's supervision to that of a local administrative unit.

At a meeting in Orange, New Jersey, of an SWP unit to which his wife belonged, an automobile salesman named Walter Elliott was overheard by an informer talking with a local SWP organizer about the amount of time Elliott devoted to his post of Scoutmaster for a local Boy Scout troop. Outraged to learn that someone associated, even by marriage, with the SWP was a participant in the Boy Scout movement, the Bureau began a search for the unit Elliott belonged to. A Bureau memo voices the classic horror at the prospect of such defilement: "Individuals who have subversive backgrounds, especially those as Elliott who remain in the scouting movement for the expressed purpose of influencing young minds, represent a distinct threat to the goal of the scouting movement and should be removed or neutralized."

Unable to locate a newspaper clipping or similar "public source" material to send to the Scouts to discredit Elliott, the Bureau threw caution to the winds and risked a direct phone call to Boy Scout National Headquarters by a self-identified FBI agent. The agent obtained a promise that Elliott would not be re-registered as a Scoutmaster when his current term expired. Some small snags developed in the plan, but the agent persisted with bimonthly proddings until finally he was able to report mission accomplished.

The Bureau's highest priority was to undermine the SWP's role in the anti-war and civil rights struggles of the sixties, primarily through the sabotage of joint action with other groups. It fired an opening gun in the spring of 1966, an anonymous letter intended to discredit the SWP's participation in a broad anti-war coalition, the National Coordinating Committee to End the War in Vietnam. In 1968 another anonymous letter was disseminated throughout the entire anti-war community, this time to drive a wedge between the Young Socialist Alliance (YSA) and other members of a campus anti-war coalition, the Student Mobilization Committee. A draft of a follow-up letter was sent to Washington for approval, fastidiously marked "Obscene" (cover requirements, the New York SAC apologetically explained, "necessitate[d] the use of a certain amount of profanity"). This mailing was approved by Washington, as was another subsequent campaign against the Mobilization Committee to End the War in Viet Nam (MOBE), which included anonymous letters, memoranda, and cartoons, some scurrilous. Media coverage helped solve the problem of credibility and anonymity—at least where the outlet was respectable and not a far right exposé sheet—but in many instances the Bureau's splitting games were too esoteric for general audiences, with the result that even its media friends sometimes let the Bureau down, forcing its reliance on anonymous letters alone.

The college campus was the ideal COINTELPRO theater. The reasons need only be briefly restated: student radicalism is a major Bureau concern; a large corps of student informers provided an abundance of information; "established sources" (deans, administrators) helped out not only in supplying data but as collaborators. Especially agitated because the YSA was recruiting in high schools, the Bureau tried to warn educational groups (the Educational Research Council of America and the American Federation of Teachers) of the subversive threat. An anonymous letter to the UCLA chancellor and Board of Regents from a "perturbed parent"—the final approved text emerged only after six weeks of memo exchanges—expressed horror that the YSA had been recognized as an official campus organization. Other campuses (among them San Francisco State, Wayne State, American University, University of Florida, San Diego State College, University of Texas) attracted aggressive action programs. The D.C. Bureau office proudly launched, for the enlightenment of conservative American University students, the *Rational Observer.* Although the anonymous author's pride in this newsletter is poorly concealed, it was little more than a crude assemblage of cartoons and one-liners. Its "rational" side is exemplified by messages such as this: "If you recognize evil and want it eliminated, call or write President Williams, your rabbi, minister or priest, the Bureau of Narcotics, the FBI or the Metropolitan Police Department."

In October 1970 Texas Governor Preston Smith, incensed by heckling he received during a speech on the University of Houston campus, assigned no less than six staff lawyers to look into ways to eliminate YSA and similar groups from all of the state's campuses. Only the week before the Bureau had consulted with the university's security department in an attempt to devise just such a plan, and sent word to the governor's office offering help. But to the Bureau's great disappointment, the governor did not respond to its overtures for a state-wide campus ban on the YSA and similar groups. Undiscouraged by this failure, the Bureau then explored a new scheme, this one to encourage a suit against YSA for violation of IRS regulations in its use of student funds.

Perhaps the most gung-ho of all the campus-oriented attacks on YSA and its allies took place on the Indiana University campus at Bloomington. In June 1968 the Indiana field office prepared and circulated a detailed, overheated summary of anti-war activities on the university campus that served as a basis for a multi-pronged plan of attack for the next school year. Proposals included furnishing incorrect dates and times for meetings, mailing letters from "A Concerned Alumni"* (a standard Bureau usage) to parents of student activists, and the publication and distribution on a regular basis of a newsletter, *Armageddon News* ("Don't Let the New Left Win the Armageddon at IU"). Overcome by its pride of authorship and its conviction about the potential impact of *Armageddon News,* the Indianapolis SAC requested Bureau permission for a first run of 25,000 copies. But Washington cruelly vetoed the proposal, pointing

---

*This error may have been deliberate—to establish the writer's wholesome illiteracy. Or it may be that in a super-bureaucracy like the FBI, the ignorance of the original user became institutionalized; or that it simply reflected the Director's usage and, for that reason, was unchangeable.

out that such a large run would jeopardize the security of its authorship, and cut it down to 200 copies, to be mailed anonymously to individual fraternity, sorority, and faculty members. As a further security measure, a sentence linking the SDS with the Communist Party was ascribed in a Washington revision to "responsible government officials" rather than, as in the original, to J. Edgar Hoover. The Washington supervisor also had his doubts about the tone of *Armageddon News,* especially a final exhortation: "TAKE A STAND FOR LAW AND ORDER." Bureau headquarters felt that this might not appeal to the broad mass of college students in 1968, and suggested rewriting the newsletter to reflect a more liberal point of view. The SAC was delighted with the final product's reception: one issue was reprinted by a local newspaper, as well as by an American Legion magazine, and a second by a conservative organization on campus that distributed 5000 copies. The field, flushed with triumph, pleaded with Washington for permission to put out a second volume with a press run of 3000, but approval was again limited, this time to 400 copies. The new issues were aimed specifically at YSA and SDS, and were coordinated with a program of disruptive action by Bureau informers within each group. The university administration, by a suspicious coincidence, added its own crackdown, with the result that by the fall of 1969 the campus anti-war movement was virtually stifled.

By February 1970, in fact, the anti-war campus activity had become so quiescent that the Indianapolis office suggested the local COINTELPRO operations be deactivated. A memo from the Director quickly rejected this proposal, pointing out that "every evidence points to the fact that militant Leftists are continuing their efforts to disrupt higher education," and ordering that all agents remain continually alert for opportunities to institute further COINTELPROS. Properly chastised, the field office soon located another target for a COINTELPRO scheme. In November 1970 the university student body president, Keith Parker, traveled to North Vietnam with a group of student leaders. The Bureau saw this as an opportunity to discredit Parker and his student political party, which was allied with the YSA on campus. A leaflet attacking Parker for allegedly using student funds for his trip and for support of other anti-war activities was prepared by the Bureau, and sponsored by a fictitious organization, "Concerned Students at IU." Five hundred copies were distributed to fraternities and other student groups, and other copies mailed anonymously to members of the university board of trustees and to Parker's parents and friends. The university once again delivered the *coup de grâce.* The board of trustees soon thereafter deprived the student government of its financial support, and imposed censorship on programs sponsored by the student government.

Attempts to influence the educational authorities were not always successful. When the Student Mobilization Committee (SMC) scheduled an anti-war rally at the Washington, D.C., campus of Catholic University in 1971, FBI headquarters canvassed its field offices for action suggestions to stop the gathering on the ground that the SMC was dominated by the SWP. Pressure proposals included anonymous telephone calls by agents pretending to be irate Catholics, anonymous letters, and press leaks of a bogus leaflet, "Trotskyists Welcomed at Catholic University." The campaign assumed that the anti-Communist Catholicism of the fifties could readily be mobilized to block the conference. But the New York office pointed out that "various forms of radical philosophies had gained a foothold among many priests and nuns." In fact, New York warned, the radicalized clergy, learning of the FBI's involvement, might embarrass the Bureau by publicly exposing its pressure campaign. San Antonio shot back that "with respect to New York's patronizing comments," Washington "should be aware that there is a great number of Catholics, both religious and laymen who do not subscribe to this radical philosophy." Indeed, if the Bureau had taken "effective counterintelligence actions" when "so-called permissive attitudes" first became evident among youth and religious groups, "the Bureau's investigation of New Left and other such matters would not have been as great as it is today."

Anonymous mailings for wedge-driving purposes were also used against the SWP in the civil rights area, beginning with successful efforts in New York City—notably frustrating proposed cooperation with the Malcolm X movement. More prolonged efforts along these lines targeted the Committee to Aid the Monroe Defendants (CAMD), a group formed following the indictment of a number of individuals charged with offenses committed in connection with civil rights activities in Monroe, North Carolina. In 1962 the Bureau began its efforts to destroy CAMD by sowing disruption among its members and supporters, especially over the handling of funds. When the NAACP offered CAMD support, the Bureau renewed its efforts, including anonymous calls and letters to Roy Wilkins as executive director of the NAACP, pressure on a local of the United Automobile Workers' Union, investigation of all the active members of the committee, and disruptive anonymous mailings to a broad range of activists, editors of newspapers for rival groups, and known leaders of minority factions within the SWP. An opportunity for more drastic action presented itself when the home of a respected leader of the Monroe area civil rights movement was broken into, and several thousand dollars in defense funds taken. The only person in the house at the time was George Weissman, a member of the SWP National Committee and a supporter of the CAMD. Weissman reported to the police that the robbers had forced their way into the house, tied him up, and broken into the wall safe. Although there was no evidence to contradict Weissman's account, the Bureau sent an article about the theft to the group of activists, editors, and minority faction leaders it had previously circularized. Along with the clipping, the Bureau included the following bit of doggerel:

> *Georgie-Porgie, down in Monroe,*
> *Found himself alone with the dough,*
> *Called the cops, and what did he say?*
> *"Bad guys came and took it away."*

The outcome of the mailings was closely monitored by informers in the hope of qualifying for the laurels so eagerly sought by every field office engaged in COINTELPROS.

White Hate Groups—In the Footsteps of 007[21]

The Klan-White Hate Groups program, which ultimately accounted for 255 actions, was authorized on September 2, 1964, and directed at 17 Klan organizations and 9 "hate groups" such as the American Nazi Party. Although subcaptioned "Internal Security," it was designed to prevent violence by wiping out its targets. Federal legal remedies against violations of civil rights by groups such as the Klan were available (state laws were another matter): the Civil Rights acts of 1875, 1957, 1960, and 1964. Moreover, in contrast to the organized crime area, where the agency held the Kennedy Justice Department at bay while it tried to overcome its prior apathy through wide-scale bugging, the Bureau had developed law enforcement intelligence resources. But civil rights prosecutions did not stir the eager cooperative response that marked the agency's role in countersubversive prosecutions (or, for that matter, in the prosecutions of bank robbers, kidnappers, or car thieves). No superordinate "responsibility" was distilled from the constitutional guarantee of equality to overcome bureaucratic inertia. Thus, from the emergence in the fifties of civil rights violations as a federally prosecutive subject matter, the agency successfully persuaded the Department of Justice to permit it to play a limited, passive role.

The reasons for the Bureau's abdication were both personal and institutional. The agency's Southern offices were staffed by nativist types who, if not in accord with the Klan's methods, endorsed its values from anti-communism to race hatred, from super-patriotism to puritanism. Resident agents who had opted to return to their Southern hometowns could chill luncheon audiences with countersubversive horror stories, but would not be caught dead reminding them of the legal and constitutional limits on bigotry and vigilantism. Beyond this, the roots of the modern Klan and the Hoover Bureau's anti-radicalism are entwined in the nativist soil of the twenties. The linkage becomes apparent in the Bureau files of the era, such as those dealing with ACLU members characterized as "radicals," "Socialists," "Russians," "Jews," "parlor Bolsheviks," and "parlor Pinks."

The Bureau's institutional racism is perhaps best seen in its systematic refusal to intervene to protect the victims of federal law violations by local law enforcement officials, or to exercise its conceded powers of arrest and apprehension even when federal offenses were committed in the presence of Bureau agents. Similarly, on the ground that "the FBI is not a protection agency," it refused to take steps to warn potential victims or arrange for their safety when it was alerted to planned violence. Klan informer Gary Thomas Rowe, Jr., gave the Bureau three weeks advance notice of the planned beating in May 1961 in Birmingham of a group of Freedom Riders. Although he informed the Bureau that the Klan had arranged with the Birmingham police for a fifteen-minute period to complete their attack free of interference, the local office not only failed to take preventive action on its own, such as notifying the targets in advance, but did not even alert the Department of Justice. When FBI headquarters learned that violence was planned, it merely sent out an alert to various Bureau offices along the route of the Freedom Riders that the attempt to integrate bus service would be made, that mass meetings and rallies would be held, and that "all offices receiving copies of this airtel should alert their informants, local authorities and furnish the Bureau promptly all developments. . . ."

Nor did the intensification of racial violence and federal law violations after the 1961 Freedom Rides change the Bureau's negative role. Like the legendary Austrian general who hated war because it disturbed the order of his troops, the Hoover Bureau shunned initiative and vigorous evidence collection for prosecutive purposes out of fear of jeopardizing relationships with local (state and urban) law enforcement units, which when not themselves violating the rights of blacks were all too frequently in sympathy with the aggression, and even harbored Klansmen and their supporters. The Bureau's continuing foot-dragging was especially damaging because of the nature of the law enforcement problem. The reactive investigative techniques used in conventional criminal situations, through which evidence of a particular crime and the identity of the criminal is collected, processed, and submitted to the prosecutor, are wholly inadequate to deal with an ongoing course of criminal conduct. Here teamwork, a day-to-day, hour-by-hour collaboration, is required in which the prosecutor gives direction to the investigation. But such on-the-spot submission to "outside" direction, however functionally necessary, violated the ritualized bureaucratic practices through which requests for investigative services were channeled via a multi-layered hierarchy and decisions subsequently rerouted by a reverse process. Thus, quite apart from value preferences, the Bureau's deep-rooted resistance to threats to its power and autonomy played an important role in its sabotage of the civil rights enforcement program. Not that the Director or his subordinates flatly rejected bids for cooperation in direct confrontation with the Attorney General or his representatives. Bureau agents simply returned from promising investigative assignments empty-handed, conducted interviews that frightened victims and cosseted suspects, delayed compliance with the simplest request, treated assignments with obfuscatory literalism or deliberately misconstrued them, sat on their heels ignoring obvious leads, and generally substituted a sullen negativism for the zeal which—the Bureau boasts—distinguishes it from other law enforcement agencies.* Then too, again in contrast to its countersubversive expansiveness, it discovered jurisdictional hazards, repeatedly rejected by legal scholars, in every distasteful investigative levy. These the Director voiced with a special piety, the bogus humility typically invoked to justify declining uncongenial assignments (alone he resisted the blandishments of empire-building and stood guard against the dread emergence of a national police force).

By 1963 the Bureau loomed, in the eyes not merely of the "movement" but

*The special agents were almost entirely white. A Civil Rights Commission staff report shows that at the end of 1962 the Bureau had 10 black special agents among its 6030 special agents, with 3 additional in a category called "Special Agents Limited," assigned to chauffeuring and other menial duties. Five special agents were added in 1963, and by 1964 the total of all agents did not exceed twenty-eight. Even more revealing: as of 1961, of the entire Bureau staff of 13,649, only forty-eight were black, the lowest percentage of any government agency—Carl M. Brauer, *John F. Kennedy and the Second Reconstruction* (Columbia University Press, 1977), pp. 82–83; Navasky, p. 108; Wechsler, "The FBI's Failures in the South," *Progressive* (December 1936).

of lawyers, commentators, and bodies such as the President's Commission on Human Rights, as a hostile symbol of a broken promise. The placatory stratagems of the Kennedy Justice Department had, as Victor Navasky has written, won scattered transient victories over the Bureau, but at the cost of entrenching its powers and alienating the Kennedy administration's civil rights constituency. The agency fought its detractors with traditional weapons: criticism of the Bureau became, more than ever before, a touchstone of subversion; the Communist Influence on Racial Matters (CIRM) program was used as a resource against Bureau critics; dossiers were circulated to discredit civil rights leaders, especially those with administration influence and, perhaps most important, the figure viewed both as the movement's leader and as the sinister source of an anti-Bureau crusade, the uppity Dr. King, was blueprinted for concentrated attack. But a series of fifty murders, beatings, and bombings in the spring of 1964, culminating in the Klan murder in Neshoba County, Mississippi, of three civil rights workers (Goodman, Schwerner, and Chaney), undermined this counteroffensive and left the Bureau highly vulnerable.* After a Justice Department team was dispatched to the scene "to get something going on the Klan," Allen Dulles, CIA chief on a separate assignment by President Johnson, reported back that a greater FBI presence was required. In response to these and other pressures, the Director, in July 1964, opened a Bureau office in Jackson, Mississippi, brought in new leadership, and enlarged the local staff of agents. On July 30, intelligence responsibility for Klan activity was shifted from the General Investigative Division to the Domestic Intelligence Division, which was charged with developing a covert action program. A month later, the Klan-Hate Group project was approved.

This decision starred the Klan as the counterpart in "extremism" of the Communist Party in "subversion." There was one significant difference: the anti-Communist intelligence targets embraced, as we have seen, broad non-Communist intelligence sectors; but the anti-Klan operation, although modeled on the earlier program, was confined to the organization itself. This was true not only for dirty-tricks purposes but also in the conventional passive-surveillance operations. For example, the White Citizens' Councils—in many areas Klan fronts and certainly influenced by the Klan—were not brought under surveillance, let alone subjected to aggressive intelligence.[22]

---

*In a letter sent before the murders, Attorney General Kennedy pressed President Johnson for a stronger intelligence program with a law-enforcement focus. Apparently reluctant to tangle with the Bureau directly, he advised the President

> that consideration should be given by the Federal Bureau of Investigation to a new procedure for identification of the individuals who may be or have been involved in acts of terrorism, and of the possible participation in such acts by law enforcement officials or at least their toleration of terrorist activities. . . . The unique difficulty as it seems to me to be presented by the situation in Mississippi (which is duplicated in parts of Alabama and Louisiana at least) is in gathering information on fundamentally lawless activities which have the sanction of local law enforcement agencies, political officials and a substantial segment of the White population. The techniques followed in the use of specially trained, special assignment agents in the infiltration of Communist groups should be of value. If you approve, it might be desirable to take up with the Bureau the possibility of developing a similar effort to meet this new problem.

Church, Vol. 6, p. 214.

The decision to turn to aggressive tactics was ironic; while the Bureau had regularly complained of jurisdictional excess in its investigative assignments for prosecutive purposes, it was ready to swallow an intelligence offensive completely outside the forms of law. Similarly, while the Bureau had fought off its critics with the reminder that in the civil rights area, as elsewhere, the FBI "functioned strictly as a fact-gathering and fact-reporting agency" and did not "make prosecutive recommendations or otherwise assume the role of accuser, prosecutor, jury or judge," it was now ready to assume all of these roles on its own.

Unlike other programs, this one was imposed on the agency as a result of external pressure, generated by a loss of confidence in its commitment to law enforcement. History had conspired to "embarrass the Bureau," threatening not only its image but its power and autonomy. Yet, as in earlier conflicts with the Department, token submission to higher authority left the agency stronger and more autonomous than before. The advantages of secret investigation and extra-legal punishment were impressive: intelligence was entrenched as an alternative to law enforcement in connection with activities unrelated to internal security even under the most extravagant interpretations of that term; new frontiers were staked out for Sullivan's Domestic Intelligence Division, which were to be systematically expanded in the years that followed. The program enabled the Bureau to increase and monopolize its supply of secrets, thus providing a highly efficient weapon in fending off eager-beaver Justice Department lawyers. Finally, by operating in secret, the agency avoided a damaging public clash with local law enforcement authorities and a consequent damage to a valuable "buddy system."

The effectiveness of the program was viewed as contingent on an acceleration of information collection. Burglaries and bugs were used to obtain information, but the sovereign priority was the immediate beefing up of the corps of Klan informers. Though the Klan was already infiltrated, the Bureau, within the space of a year, added 774 new plants* for a grand total of 2014. In at least half of the Klan units, informers were elected to top leadership positions. While this army of spies fattened the Bureau's files, it did not measurably contribute to peacekeeping. The informers' instructions to discourage violent tactics could not prevail in the councils of the Klan, then deeply committed to violence and bombings; such restraining efforts would only destroy the spy's credibility and perhaps even endanger his life. And compliance with a formally communicated policy of avoidance by informers of personal involvement in violence presented the same risks even more sharply, especially when the agent had, as previously instructed, penetrated activist cells. The COINTELPRO made the conflict even more severe because of its heavy reliance on a flow of information. Thus, when informer Gary Thomas Rowe asked, in an interview with his contacts, how to reconcile the Bureau's caution against violence with its post-COINTELPRO demands, he was told: "You can do anything to get your information . . . we don't want you to get involved in unnecessary violence, but the point is to get the

---

*In a typically self-aggrandizing formulation, the Bureau noted in a memo to the White House that this represented "an average of more than two each day for every day in the past twelve months."

information." It was not merely that the collection of information became an end in itself; the necessity of protecting its swarms of informer sources from disclosure and their active involvement in violent crimes barred the resort to prosecutive remedies. Indeed, the Bureau's reluctance to proceed in the 1963 Birmingham church bombing despite the impressive evidence in its possession, and its refusal for more than four years after a 1971 request to cooperate with a state investigation, suggests the persistence of this protective rationale.*

Informers were instructed to concentrate on "compromise-type data," which was used to exploit rivalries (a notable Klan vulnerability) and otherwise to discredit leaders. A second priority was data, principally stolen membership lists, for use in mass postcard mailing programs exposing the secret affiliations of Klansmen. The cards were embellished with cartoons and brief messages since, as Washington put it, "Klansmen are not intellectuals." In April 1966 nearly 6000 cartoons with captions such as: "KLANSMAN, trying to hide your identity behind your sheet? You received this. Someone KNOWS who you are!" were sent out from twenty-one field offices.

The exposure campaign in turn intensified already festering fears of informers ("the feds"), by 1967 so numerous that the Intelligence Division briefly considered a plan to replace Imperial Wizard Robert Shelton with one of them. The embattled Shelton proposed that all members of his Imperial Board be subjected to sodium pentothal (truth serum) and lie-detector examinations. The Bureau fought back with a planted denunciation of "Gestapo-like tactics." (When the proposal was renewed in 1971, the Bureau responded with a reissuance of the old article.) The informer panic made the snitch jacket a highly fruitful technique. The Louisiana Klan, for example, was severely disrupted by a Bureau plot to frame an Assistant Grand Dragon on informer charges. Another target, the National States' Rights Party (NSRP), an anti-Semitic group, was victimized by a scheme to portray one of its members as an informer, not for the FBI but for the B'nai Brith Anti-Defamation League, a Jewish organization. This was accomplished by preparing a phony "informant report" à la Albertson with inside information and a request for money addressed, seemingly inadvertently, to NSRP headquarters rather than the Bureau. A 1970 memo describes a successful program for discrediting adherents of the American Nazi Party by leaking facts about their Jewish ancestry.† Since the looting of Klan

*With the aid of clues belatedly supplied from FBI files, a state prosecution in the fall of 1977 —fourteen years after the bombing—resulted in a guilty verdict against an ex-Klansman. And a year after that, Rowe was indicted by an Alabama grand jury for the murder of civil rights demonstrator Viola Liuzzo, a crime for which two Klansmen were convicted in a federal court in 1965 on the basis of Rowe's testimony. Accounts of Rowe's undercover career and subsequent indictment are collected in *Hearings of Subcommittee on Administrative Practice and Procedure on FBI Statutory Charter,* Part 2 (1978), pp. 273, 275–80, 283–86. See also Church, Bk. III, pp. 229–34, Vol. 6, pp. 115–19, 123–24, 127–31, 134, 144–45 and 841–91. In July 1979, the Michigan ACLU brought an action for damages against the FBI on behalf of members of the Liuzzo family charging the Bureau with responsibility for the alleged murder by its informer. If Rowe's culpability is established, the court will be squarely confronted with the issue (discussed in chapter 5) whether Rowe was in effect the Bureau's employee, responsible for acts committed in the normal course of his duties.

†The memo claims credit for the expulsion in 1970 of Frank Collin from the American Nazi Party, but does not refer to two earlier cases. One of them involved Daniel Burros, a KKK organizer and former American Nazi Party official, who committed suicide in October 1965 after the *New York*

treasuries was a recurrent abuse, informers were regularly instructed to raise questions at Klan meetings concerning the misuse and misappropriation of funds and to demand an accounting. One such charge by an informer led to an armed confrontation between the bodyguards of an Imperial Wizard and the rank and file of the Hattiesburg, Mississippi, Klavern. There was no shooting, but the state organization was effectively disrupted. In another case, an Assistant Grand Dragon was portrayed in a series of anonymously mailed cartoons as a friend of Fidel Castro. At the instigation of an informer, the Klan conducted an investigation into the Dragon's former associates. Before the smoke cleared, the Dragon had resigned and the Klavern had had its charter revoked by the state organization.

The instigation of tax and other official harassments, both federal and local, pressures on hotel managements and college trustees, press leaks, and other practices already discussed were frequent tactics.* Material obtained from bugs and informers was leaked to "cooperative news media," including Atlanta *Constitution* columnist Ralph McGill, described as a "staunch and proven friend" who would "not betray our confidence," and thus converted into "public source material" for recirculation.

The Klan program was, after all, a brainchild of Sullivan's division, and Sullivan's influence is reflected in a pattern of stylish initiatives such as "The National Committee for Domestic Tranquility"—a fictitious organization, the source of an intermittently published bulletin attempting to exacerbate factional disputes within Klan organizations. The committee, pseudonymously headed by "Harmon Blennerhasset" (the name of one of Aaron Burr's co-conspirators and financial angels), mailed material to Klan members who were thought by the Bureau to be ripe for conversion into informers, or were active participants in some internal dispute that might weaken the organization. Klan leaders were attacked for pleading the Fifth Amendment before a congressional committee ("joining hands with communists who also always hide behind the Fifth Amendment"),† or for acting "in league with the Anti-Christ." Other committee newsletters spread false reports of the collapse of Klan chapters. It was

---

Times published a front-page story that he was of Jewish ancestry. Two days after Daniel Burros committed suicide, a press story appeared that one Robert Burros (no relation to Daniel), the national secretary of the National Renaissance Party (NRP), a pro-Nazi anti-Semitic organization, had concealed the fact that his father was Jewish. He was thereafter promptly expelled from his party post—A. M. Rosenfeld and Arthur Gelb, *The Life and Death of an American Jewish Nazi* (New American Library, 1967); "FBI Bares COINTELPRO Highlights," Washington *Star,* Aug. 16, 1975; Jonathan Miller, "Frank Collin's Roots," *New Republic,* July 1, 1978. The Bureau predicted that the circulation of a report that Collin is half-Jewish would "demolish" him. Instead, after his expulsion, he formed his own group, the National Socialist Party of America, which gradually overshadowed the official Nazi party in the Midwest. As we have seen, during the struggle for hegemony the Chicago FBI office's informers were instructed to promote violence between the two groups.

*Documents released in August 1979 in connection with a Chicago lawsuit established a wide range of harassments against white neo-Nazi groups by the Chicago Bureau office. However, the documents make no mention of two organizations, committed to violence and illegal operations, which were quite active in the Chicago area—the Minutemen and the Legion of Justice. (See chapter 12.)

†Klan leaders were subpoenaed by the House Un-American Activities Committee in 1965 and subsequently cited for contempt for refusing to answer the committee's questions.

succeeded by another fictitious organization, the "National Intelligence Committee" (NIC), which undertook to expel Imperial Wizards and Grand Dragons on invented charges. Both notionals used their communications as a means of directing suspicion at an individual who was either already faced with informer charges or under attack for other reasons.

This entire operation—the notionals and the newsletters, the disruptive games and the kiss-of-death gambits—may be said to reflect a new professionalism. For example, the rhetoric of the newsletters, a mixture of Christian fundamentalism and right-wing populism, is uncannily accurate. The choice of the name "Harmon Blennerhasset" is perhaps a bit overmuch. Its nativist resonance was apparently so appealing that risk of discovery (after all, some Klansman might have recalled the name from his history books) was overcome by intellectual vanity.* But a novelist might well have been envious of the skill and imagination reflected in the letter—set forth below—sent to the wife of a Grand Dragon, typed "on plain paper in amateurish fashion" by the fictitious mate of a Klan member:

My Dear Mrs. [A],

I write this letter to you only after a long period of praying to God. I must cleanse my soul of these thoughts. I certainly do not want to create problems inside a family but I owe a duty to the klans and its principles as well as to my own menfolk who have cast their divine lot with the klans.

Your husband came to _____ about a year ago and my menfolk blindly followed his leadership, believing him to be the saviour of this country. They never believed the stories that he stole money from the klans in _____ or that he is now making over $25,000 a year. They never believed the stories that your house in _____ has a new refrigerator, washer, dryer and yet one year ago, was threadbare. They refuse to believe that your husband now owns three cars and a truck, including that new white car. But I believe all these things and I can forgive them for a man wants to do for his family in the best way he can.

I don't have any of these things and I don't grudge you any of them neither. But your husband has been committing the greatest of the sins of our Lord for many years. He has taken the flesh of another unto himself.

Yes, Mrs. _____ , he has been committing adultery. My menfolk say they don't believe this but I think they do. I feel like crying. I saw her with my own eyes. They call her Ruby. Her last name is something like _____ and she lives in the 700 block of _____ Street in _____. I know this. I saw her strut around at a rally with her lust-filled eyes and smart aleck figure.

I cannot stand for this. I will not let my husband and two brothers stand side by side with your husband and this woman in the glorious robes of the klan. I am typing this because I am going to send copys to Mr. Shelton and some of the klans leaders that I have faith in. I will not stop until your husband is driven from ——— and back into the flesh-pots from wherein he came.

I am a loyal klanswoman and a good churchgoer. I feel this problem affects the future of our great country. I hope I do not cause you harm by this and if you

*To one familiar with the names of real-life Klan leaders, such as "Lycurgus Spinks" or "Alton Pate," Harmon Blennerhasset must have seemed irresistible. However, the historical Blennerhasset, an émigré younger son of a landed Irish family with snobbish aspirations and a wife to match, was hardly a Klan type.

believe in the Good Book as I do, you may soon receive your husband back into the fold. I pray for you and your beautiful little children and only wish I could tell you who I am. I will soon, but I am afraid my own men would be harmed if I do.

A God-fearing klanswoman

This new professionalism is also reflected in an action involving Imperial Wizard Robert Shelton. When Shelton complained to the Bureau resident agent about a bogus letter from the NIC suspending him and firing the North Carolina Grand Dragon, the agent contacted the local postal inspector after explaining to Shelton that the complaint was not within the FBI's jurisdiction. Using its investigation of Shelton's complaint as a cover, Washington headquarters monitored the Post Office investigation and sent a letter to the local Bureau office stating that since Shelton's charges "appear to involve an internal struggle" and "since the evidence of mail fraud was somewhat tenuous in nature," no further investigation was contemplated either by the Post Office or the criminal division of the Department of Justice. Neither agency was informed that the Bureau had drafted and mailed the letter that was the subject of the complaint.

But the Klan program was not all fun and games. A chilling product of the program was the entrapment and ambush of Mississippi Klansmen in a 1970 bombing attempt, resulting in the death of one of the would-be bombers and the wounding of another. The bombing attempt was set up by two Bureau informers who were paid a total of $36,000, of which $30,000 was raised by the Meriden (Mississippi) Jewish community for first entrapping and then springing the trap, under instructions by the Bureau and local police.

While the Klan program did not improve the agency's civil rights posture, it was highly useful in the Director's post-Kennedy reconsolidation of his power and standing. On September 2, 1965, the first anniversary of the launching of the Klan-White Hate Groups project, he transmitted a memo to the White House and the Attorney General describing, in addition to claimed law enforcement successes, the program's achievements. A communication to Attorney General Ramsey Clark on December 1967 refers to "infiltrating the Ku Klux Klan with informants, neutralizing it as a terrorist organization and deterring violence," providing illustrative examples. In addition, "The Resurgent Klan" and "The FBI's Secret War" emerged as themes for the Director's publicity ghosts and congressional drumbeaters. Thus by 1970, when there was hardly any Klan left to disrupt, the Director nevertheless continued to brag of the Bureau's triumphs and, at his insistence, kept alive the disruptive program. And after the Director's death, when all the trees in the forest began to fall, defenders of the entire operation (such as Sullivan) proudly pointed to the Klan program as evidence of a larger concern for democratic values. In the same way, President Nixon cited the Bureau's attack on the Klan (specifically, a burglary of an office) as an example of an acceptable law violation when he felt it necessary to respond to the shocked reaction to his observation in a TV interview that "when the President does it it isn't illegal."[23]

Black Nationalist-Hate Groups—Toward
A Final Solution[24]

With its 360 operations, the Black Nationalist-Hate Groups program was second in size only to the COINTELPRO-CPUSA, and considering its short time span, was the most intensely pursued of all, involving nearly 100 operations a year between 1967 and 1971. Moreover, the numerical total of actions approved under this formal caption is supplemented by others undertaken under New Left and CPUSA code designations, simply listed as "Racial Matters" or conducted entirely outside of a formal bureaucratic framework. In contrast with the Klan program, it was comprehensively directed against an entire movement, including groups that had rejected violence but were labeled as "Hate" because they opposed institutionalized racism. (Nativists like the Director had in the same way in the twenties denounced Communists and labor organizers as immoral because "they preached class hate.") That the label imposed no limitations on the program was admitted by its supervisor, who told Church Committee investigators that it was directed at "a great number of organizations that you might not today characterize as black nationalist but were, in fact, primarily black."

Approved in August 1967, the program had a standard "neutralize-disrupt" objective. In March 1968 it was expanded from twenty-three to forty-one field offices, in a letter from Sullivan that put flesh on its bones. "An effective coalition," the letter warned with chilling hyperbole, "of black nationalist groups might be a first step towards a real 'Mau Mau' in America, the beginning of a true black revolution." Target groups were to be discredited among "responsible" blacks, "responsible" whites, as well as misguided liberals and, through "special measures," among black radicals. Here, as in all the programs, youth was a special concern.

The range of organizational targets under this program ultimately included Black Student Unions (BSUs), Student Non-Violent Coordinating Committee (SNCC), Southern Christian Leadership Conference (SCLC), Deacons for Defense/Revolutionary Action Movement (RAM), Junta of Militant Organizations (JOMO), Republic of New Africa (RNA), Poor People's Campaign, United Slaves (US), Black Economic Development Corporation (BEDC), and Black Panther Party (BPP). The goals included the full range of those already listed, and in particular fomenting internal factionalism and external rivalries, incitement to violence, the instigation of pretext raids and arrests by local city police, the vandalization of publications, and the organization of heckling claques. The techniques include the use of provocateurs, anonymous letters, snitch jackets, cartoons, forgery, burglary, sexual exploitation, impersonation, defamation, blackmail, and extortion.

What was new in the black nationalist program was the stress on punitive action against individuals. This motif is sounded clearly in the priority given to the need to "prevent the *rise of a 'messiah'* who could unify and electrify the militant black nationalist movement. . . ." (italics in the original). For the first time, an aggressive intelligence program listed individual targets by name; agents were explicitly exhorted to "pinpoint potential troublemakers," to make a census of area leaders of the black nationalist movement, and check it against the Bureau's "Rabble Rouser Index" in order to identify targets for aggressive action. This uniquely personalized emphasis eloquently bespeaks a racism that perceived black leaders as corrupt, criminal, oversexed demagogues, who had to be destroyed and replaced by "respectable" figures who alone could be trusted to lead the ignorant blacks. Since approval and reward turned on the readiness of field agents to propose and implement actions injurious to these leaders, already powerful racist trends in the agency were intensified. The need to justify these vigilante exercises in turn led to even greater distortions of the character and intentions of the black targets.

The enlarged scope of the COINTELPROs against high-profile black leaders and their followers is dramatized by a special project directed against the nonviolent Nation of Islam (NOI). A boxing match featuring its most prominent adherent, Muhammad Ali, was sabotaged on the ground that his purse would enrich the NOI. An April 1968 memo from Chicago SAC Marlin Johnson reports that anonymous letters were sent to NOI members protesting the "lavish extravagance" of NOI leader Elijah Muhammad. Another gambit to discredit Muhammad was a forged letter, planted in a variety of periodicals and newspapers, purporting to come from his wife and charging him with extramarital affairs.

In an effort to remove Herbert Muhammad "as a possible successor to his father as head of the militant black nationalist Nation of Islam," Johnson probed his federal income tax returns for possible irregularities. The effort failed to produce evidence of tax evasion. But the Bureau did not flag. On January 7, 1969, the Director wrote Johnson: "When [Elijah Muhammad] dies a power struggle can be expected. . . . We should plan now to change the philosophy of NOI to one of strictly religious and self-improvement orientation, deleting the race hatred and separate nationhood aspects." Johnson agreed on this strategy. "Chicago continues its contacts with its sources whose identities are known to the bureau and feels these sources will be of possible extreme value at the time of the demise of Muhammad."

That same month, in order to "cause factionalism among the leaders and discredit them," the Chicago office fed a Chicago *Tribune* reporter information regarding the Nation of Islam's extensive commercial holdings. The resulting article appeared on page 1 of the *Tribune* on January 26, 1969. One week later, gunmen robbed a top Nation of Islam official of $23,000 in cash. In a memo of March 13, 1969, Johnson concluded that one of the tangible results of the Bureau's use of the *Tribune* reporter was that "articles authored by him may have had the effect of rendering NOI officials vulnerable to robbery efforts. . . ."*

---

*The Chicago office, however, could hardly claim the planted story as a triumph. The Muslims were so pleased that Elijah Muhammad wrote and publicized a letter praising the paper and the reporter. And this same March 13 memo reported that "a Black Muslim functionary attempted to pay [the reporter] $1,000 as a token of NOI appreciation."

This personalized stress is most dramatically reflected in the campaign to destroy Martin Luther King, Jr., an initiative launched almost four years before the COINTELPRO operations against black groups and their leaders. The all-out pursuit of King began in the fall of 1963 when, as we have seen, he became a symbol of the civil rights struggle. But its roots ran deeper: in his earlier effectiveness as a leader and his criticism of the Bureau's civil rights performance. To these must be added the Director's racist fury. The rage against King that howled in the Director was rendered uncontrollable by a violated sense of his own power and importance. A "no-good" black man had dared to criticize the agency and the Director himself, and had even failed to respond to telephone calls by FBI officials in an effort to "set him straight." This wound was periodically salted by tributes and citations that King received and that were beginning to overshadow the Director's— how much more fitting that such high honors should crown the homage of a grateful people to the Director himself, in the twilight of his career. Nothing was so shocking as the proposed award of an honorary degree to King by an institution (Marquette University) that had so cited the deserving Director! Particularly galling was King's 1962 citation as "Man of the Year" by *Time* magazine, a coveted honor that had eluded the Director. "They had to dig deep in the garbage to come up with this one," he wrote. But it was King's Nobel Prize award, announced in November 1964, which blew his fuse altogether, resulting in the "most notorious liar" and "moral degenerate" outbursts in that month.

Hoover's racist hatred was refueled by taped conversations allegedly dealing with King's love life, confirmation of the bigoted stereotype of black hypersexuality and threat to the purity of white womanhood.* Not only did Hoover personally play the tapes and proffer transcripts to congressmen and other dignitaries, but he directed their use by senior staff members in a media program to discredit King. Not that the men around the Director or the SACs in the field needed encouragement—Bureau memos about King bristle with vituperative characterizations. The entire operation was imprinted with the special Bureau hallmark already noted: a moralizing, self-righteous anger. Although attempts to destroy King were entirely illegal in both objective and method, neither Hoover nor his vicars took great pains to conceal the Bureau's role in their

*This familiar obsession of Southern white males (a Klan article of faith) is sometimes ascribed to the guilt deposited by the historic sexual exploitation by Southern whites of black women. In the Director's case, it may also reflect a well-grounded anxiety about his own sexuality and sexual fears of women. After King's assassination in 1968, Hoover sent an emissary to columnist Jack Anderson, with whom he was then on good terms, to inform him that James Earl Ray had been hired in Los Angeles to kill King by an outraged white husband of a woman who had borne King's child. Anderson flew to Los Angeles, personally investigated the matter, and subsequently wrote: "I returned to Washington satisfied that the FBI story was erroneous and half convinced that it was a deliberate hoax"—Jack Anderson with Les Whitten column, Washington *Post*, Dec. 17, 1975. FBI files released in October 1968 further document Hoover's sex-centered bigotry. Hours after the murder in Birmingham of Viola Liuzzo, a white woman from Detroit active in the civil rights movement, Hoover, in what appears to have been an attempt to deprecate the seriousness of the crime, stated in a memo to President Johnson: "A Negro man was with Mrs. Liuzzo and reportedly sitting close to her." In a subsequent memo to his aides, he said that he had informed the President on the telephone that "she was sitting very, very close to the Negro in the car; that it had the appearance of a necking party."

dealings with third parties,* in marked contrast with the furtive style of the formal COINTELPROS, and frequently fed file material to public officials and press without resort to "public source" pretenses. Nor were they deterred by the inconsistency between their derogatory characterizations and the "no-evaluation" canon.

On October 18, 1963, Alan Belmont, Assistant Director, with the Director's approval, began distribution to the White House and a number of executive agencies of a document drafted by Sullivan and intended to discredit King, entitled "Communism and the Negro Movement—A Current Analysis." The personal character of the attack outraged Attorney General Kennedy, who ordered the document withdrawn on October 25, 1963. This disapproval was not altogether unanticipated. In a memo dated October 17, Belmont had written:

> This memorandum may startle the Attorney General, particularly in view of his past association with King, and the fact that we are disseminating this outside the Department. He may resent this. Nevertheless, the memorandum is a *powerful warning against Communist influence in the Negro movement* and we will be carrying out our responsibility by disseminating it to the people indicated in the attached memorandum.

It has been suggested that Robert Kennedy traded the stop order for his approval of an FBI request to tap King's phones.[25] But the decision to circulate the document was made at least a week *after* Kennedy approved the FBI's request for authorization to tap King's phones. Kennedy's disapproval was hardly a deterrent either to Hoover or to Sullivan, finally emerging from the doghouse and eager for the Director's blessings for an aggressive program. Now he would make amends for his past folly in a way that would please the Director most—by neutralizing King, Hoover's (literal) *bête noire.* At the close of the year Sullivan convened a high-level conference, which met for nine hours, reviewing anti-King proposals, and shortly thereafter sent Belmont a memorandum with the fruits of his months-long "thinking about this matter," which proposed the removal of King from his "pedestal" and his replacement by the "right kind of a national Negro leader. . . ."† The exceptional qualifications of his proposed candidate, Sullivan wrote to his superior, Alan Belmont, on January 8, 1964, had become apparent after he had explored the matter "from a philosophical and sociological standpoint. . . ." This nominee, who could potentially "overshadow Dr. King and . . . assume the role of the leadership of the Negro people when King has been completely discredited," was none other than Samuel R. Pierce, Jr.[26] A prominent black lawyer, subsequently elevated to the bench, Pierce had played no special role in the civil rights movement. Nor did Sullivan or anyone else in the FBI consult him about their plans to elevate him to leadership of the entire movement. If Sullivan's proposal was a fantasy, perhaps it was in character; it was not for nothing that he was known in Bureau circles as "Crazy Billy." But what is to be said of a report drafted in November

---

*Journalists were told that if they revealed their source, the Bureau would deny its involvement.

†Sullivan told the Church Committee, "I am very proud of this memorandum, one of the best I ever wrote. I think here I was showing some concern for the country."

1964 by the canny operator Cartha DeLoach, that the NAACP's Roy Wilkins had agreed in a conference that King should be replaced and had hinted at the need for Bureau support in this endeavor? This would seem to be outright distortion by a wheeler-dealer (DeLoach not only wrote a memorandum for internal use but sent a letter to President Johnson as well) of a conference requested by Wilkins* after Hoover's Loyola speech with its "moral degenerate" reference, for the purpose of halting such attacks, which he felt were damaging to the civil rights movement.

On January 4, 1964, the Domestic Intelligence Division began implementation of its anti-King program by installing in King's room at the Willard Hotel, Washington, D.C., the first of a series of microphones for the specific surveillance purpose of developing information about King's private life. Information to implement the campaign was also obtained through surreptitious entries and photographic surveillance. (On one occasion, a specimen of King's handwriting was obtained.) Informers (including one who had concededly embezzled SCLC funds) were also used to penetrate the SCLC and report on King's activities. The fruits of this coverage along with the tape transcript were incorporated in packets for subversion-cum-immorality briefings of legislators and journalists. Agents were assigned to designated journalists and editors to persuade them to change their attitude toward King. Eugene Patterson, a former editor of the Atlanta *Constitution,* recalled that in the spring of 1964 he was requested by an FBI agent to tell his readers that King was immoral. These private interviews were also used to persuade journalists to put hostile and potentially embarrassing questions to King at gatherings and demonstrations; to prevent the publication of articles favorable to King; and to sabotage the circulation of his own writings.

In November 1964 Sullivan put into effect a plan to send to Mrs. Coretta King edited tape material with the intent of breaking up the marriage and silencing King's criticism of the Bureau. Mailed from Tampa, Florida, with elaborate security precautions, it was accompanied by a note stating that "there is only one thing left for you to do" to prevent the threatened release of the tape in thirty-four days (when King was scheduled to receive the formal award of the Nobel Peace Prize). That the letter was an invitation to commit suicide (as King's associates interpreted it) seems reasonably clear from its wording: "There is but one way out for you. You better take it before your filthy, fraudulent self is bared to the nation." Undoubtedly drafted by Sullivan—an original version was found in his files—it could not have been sent without the Director's approval. The decision to mail the tape and the note appears to have been triggered by King's answer on November 19 to the Director's "notorious liar" charge in which, with remarkable prescience, King suggested that the Director had "apparently faltered" under the burdens of office.† The notion of

*Wilkins has on at least two occasions strongly denied DeLoach's version of what took place in the conference. His denial is credible in view of the undisputed purpose for which Wilkins sought the conference, to protest Hoover's smear. DeLoach has not corroborated his memorandum of the conference but instead professed not to recall what happened there.

†On the same day, November 19, the Bureau called in from the Washington field office the most useful of all the King tapes, the recording of Willard Hotel room conversations.

promoting marital discord is also a Hoover giveaway, obsessed as he was with such matters. And the background further points to the Director as the only begetter of the tape-letter plan. In September, despite the Bureau's strenuous efforts to spare the Pope "embarrassment," he met with King. The Director noted on the memo informing him of the meeting: "I am amazed that the Pope gave an audience to such a [excised by FBI]" and, at another point, "astounding." In November, at about the same time as the mailing of the tape, the Director approved a printed, updated version of Sullivan's monograph of the previous year, which had been ordered recalled by Attorney General Kennedy. The new edition was transmitted to the White House with a request for permission (granted by Johnson's Special Assistant Bill Moyers) to disseminate it to executive branch offices. In addition, the tapes were played for LBJ—both to enlighten and to entertain him.[27] UN representatives, diplomats, and foreign office personnel from Great Britain, Denmark, and Sweden (among other countries) were bombarded with releases and briefings, including a new memorandum, "Martin Luther King, Jr. His Personal Conduct," to discourage their participation in ceremonies honoring King. In November 1964, after King expressed the hope of meeting with high British officials while in England, the officials were briefed by a Bureau representative about King's alleged subversion and private life. When King returned, a team headed by Sullivan and DeLoach was dispatched to Atlanta to block the organization of a banquet in his honor.

The attack ranged over a variety of other fronts. The second edition of the monograph was used in an attempt to convince the National Science Foundation (NSF) to eliminate the SCLC from participation in its scholarship award program for black students from Southern schools. Even when discouraged by the IRS, the Bureau persisted in pressuring it for audits of King's tax returns. In desperation, it began a wild goose chase for a rumored foreign bank account described enthusiastically by the Director as "the most important, presently pending" operation of the entire King investigation, only to halt shortly thereafter when it became apparent that the stimulus for the entire investigation was the hearsay surmise of an unidentified friend of a Bureau supervisor. The contemplated Marquette University honorary degree already referred to was dropped after a Bureau briefing. (The Director was so pleased that he sent the agent involved a letter of commendation along with a bonus.) But a similar proposed degree from Springfield College could not be stopped—although De-Loach tried hard—because the offer had already been made, and besides, the board of trustees was dominated by "liberals."

The fact that King shared the Director's religious faith was bad enough; but that he was, in the Director's usage, a "man of the cloth," a respected religious leader, was intolerable. In December 1964 Hoover authorized the disclosure of data relating to King's personal background to the Baptist World Alliance (BWA) to block an invitation to speak to the BWA 1965 Congress in Miami. Similar Bureau efforts to discredit King in the Christian community continued until his death. Nor did the Director's personal involvement flag: in January 1965 he conferred with an Atlanta police official in Washington attending the inauguration who, on returning to Atlanta, relayed to the senior Dr. King a "good deal" of information about his son imparted by the Director.

A concentrated press campaign in 1966 successfully thwarted an attempt by the King group to solicit a contribution from the Teamsters Union. At about the same time, the Domestic Intelligence Division attempted to sabotage a tentative offer of a grant by the Ford Foundation to the SCLC. Hoover approved a plan to send a former FBI agent who was then a vice-president of the Ford Motor Company to McGeorge Bundy, director of the Ford Foundation, to brief him on the "subversive backgrounds of King's principal advisers." The ex-agent agreed to contact Bundy for the purpose of preventing the grant. But, DeLoach reported, Bundy had refused to discuss King, insisting that he would talk only with a source having first-hand knowledge about King. DeLoach recommended that the Bureau drop the effort, pointing out: "I personally feel that Bundy is of the pseudo-intellectual, Ivy League group that has little respect for the FBI." The Director agreed, noting on the DeLoach memorandum: "Yes. We would get nowhere with Bundy."

A King speech in April 1967 opposing the Vietnam War refueled the Bureau's campaign, which had temporarily flagged. Here, finally, was proof of Communist influence. (His remarks were "a direct parallel of the communist position on Vietnam. . . .") A week after this speech, a third edition of Sullivan's monograph was prepared and distributed, and the press campaign intensified. In mid-May the Director sent a memo to all SAC's warning of a contemplated presidential peace slate consisting of King and Dr. Benjamin Spock. The memo alerted the field to the necessity of discrediting such a ticket by linking it to communism through the circulation of bogus election material, such as flyers, buttons, and bumper stickers "with the name of the CPUSA prominently displayed." The Chicago SAC suggested a more cautious response: leaks to a reliable political columnist. Less shielded procedures, "if ever made known or even hinted at, would be the source of the most severe sort of embarrassment for the Bureau. It could be asked with the most telling cogency 'What does the FBI have to do with the selection of Presidential candidates?' The only possible answer could be, 'Nothing.' " The more discreet tactic, the SAC added, promised a fruitful return. "Effectively tabbing as communist or as communist-backed the more hysterical opponents of the President on Vietnam question in the midst of the presidential campaign would be the real boon to Mr. Johnson." Johnson, of course, did not run for reelection in 1968, nor did the peace groups field a presidential ticket.

In October 1967, the Director approved the dissemination of an editorial in order to "publicize King as a traitor to his country and his race and thus reduce his income" from a fund-raising promotion.

The announcement at the end of 1967 of the planned Poor People's March (the Washington Spring Project) spurred a fourth revision of the Sullivan monograph, in the hope that its dissemination would "serve again to remind top-level officials in Government of the wholly disreputable character of King." Discrediting proposals and propaganda discouragements of contributions and support were supplemented by DeLoach briefings of congressional leaders seeking material to discredit the planned March. To exploit the violence that had erupted at the King-led Memphis demonstration of March 28, the Bureau prepared for media circulation an attack charging that the violence proved the planned April demonstration would not be nonviolent as King had pledged; and, on the basis of DeLoach briefings, anti-King legislators, led by Senator Robert C. Byrd, delivered speeches to their congressional colleagues linking the Memphis riot with the upcoming March on Washington. The day after the approval for circulation of the violence article, the Domestic Intelligence Division recommended a second piece, this time chiding the black leader for hypocrisy in urging the boycott of white merchants but himself taking refuge in a white-owned hotel instead of the Hotel Lorraine, owned and patronized exclusively by blacks.*

Even after his death, King remained a Bureau target. On learning in March 1969 that Congress was considering a proposal to declare King's birthday a national holiday, DeLoach recommended a briefing of key congressmen. The Director approved, but noted: "it must be handled *very cautiously.* "

The March 1968 expansion of the Black Nationalist aggressive action program specifically added King to the list of individual targets, leading one to speculate what new harassments the Bureau could possibly have devised under this program had King not been assassinated on April 4. Both King's Northern advisers (Levison and Rustin) and his Southern associates (Young and Abernathy) were formally targeted under counterintelligence programs prior to the assassination. Less than a month after the assassination, the field was instructed to collect information on the "immoral activities" of Young and Abernathy (Atlanta agents were dispatched to obtain a sample of Young's handwriting and Abernathy's bedroom was bugged). The Director approved a DeLoach proposal to leak a press story that King's widow (Coretta King) and Abernathy had deliberately charged an assassination conspiracy in order to profit from a continuing flow of contributions. In May 1970 Director Hoover agreed to supply Vice-President Spiro Agnew—who had professed concern over "inflammatory statements" attributed to Abernathy—with material that could be useful in destroying Abernathy's credibility.

The SCLC-sponsored Poor People's Campaign itself was heavily infiltrated by Bureau spies, and, according to one of its leaders, Reverend Hosea Williams, by provocateurs. The Bureau's COINTELPRO action concentrated on planting press stories and photographs depicting the Washington encampment as dominated by wild, violence-prone youths and its participants as more affluent than claimed. A particularly inept effort charged the American Friends' Service Committee, the Quaker organization, with plotting to take over control of the demonstration from the SCLC.

Another victimized black liberation movement leader was Muhammad Kenyatta, who, under his original name of Donald Jackson, was active in the Jackson, Mississippi, civil rights movement. The recipient of a Ford Foundation grant to create black economic cooperatives in the Deep South, Jackson early on became a Bureau target, and was listed in the Agitator Index. The local Mississippi field office transmitted his name to local and state police with instructions to "carefully scrutinize . . . for any indications that [he] may be

---

*Mark Lane and Dick Gregory's *Code Name 'Zorro'* (Prentice-Hall, 1977) urges that these two articles were part of a Bureau plot to compel King to return to Memphis, where he was targeted for assassination. This thesis is quite far-fetched—See Donner, "Why Isn't the Truth Bad Enough?" *Civil Liberties Review* (Jan.–Feb. 1978).

breaking state or local laws." In short order Jackson was arrested and charged with driving with an expired driver's license in a car with improper tags. For this he was sentenced to pay a $125 fine and serve thirty days in jail. His persistence both as a teacher of teenagers and as a student at Tougaloo College prompted further attack. The Bureau prepared a letter from the fictitious "Tougaloo College Defense Committee" to Jackson, denouncing his "intimidation methods and nihilistic doctrines" and warning him to leave the campus, threatening to contact the local police or to take measures "which would have a more direct effect." Intensive surveillance and the dissemination of information about his background and activities not only forced his departure from Mississippi but the withdrawal of funding and subsequent closing of the Jackson Human Rights Project, a respected civil rights enterprise.

Similar troubles plagued Charles Koen, leader of the St. Louis Black Liberators. When Koen and an associate were invited in the fall of 1968 to give a series of lectures, the Bureau, through an anonymous letter, sabotaged the arrangement and incited the associate's animosity. Thereafter, Koen left St. Louis on a trip; a power struggle within the organization placed his former lieutenant in command. Delighted with this development, because in its view the new leader lacked Koen's intelligence and ability, the St. Louis office decided on a program to prevent Koen's comeback. Rumors that Koen was an informer, already planted by Bureau spies and Koen's unexplained absence, made the snitch jacket a promising ploy. An anonymous letter warned that Koen had been seen entering the Justice Department building in Baltimore, where the local FBI office was located. When Koen did return to St. Louis, he was forced to resign as head of the organization in favor of the Bureau's candidate.

Though separated for some time, Koen continued to provide support for his wife and their two daughters, an arrangement the Bureau nevertheless determined to exploit. An anonymous letter informed Mrs. Koen, who, as the Bureau noted, "appears to be a faithful, loving wife," that her husband had slept with at least two female members of the Black Liberators, and that he had bragged about how he could keep his wife off his back with just a few support payments. The Bureau hoped this letter would create sufficient problems to force Koen to sacrifice his political activity to save his marriage. To ensure optimal disruption, a second copy of the letter was prepared and sent to Koen himself, along with a forged cover letter ostensibly from a minister concerned with the immorality revealed in the communication.

The cumulative impact of personal and organizational problems created by the Bureau led to the collapse of the Black Liberators, and Koen's departure from the St. Louis area for Cairo, Illinois, where he organized an effective boycott of white merchants by the black community protesting discrimination. The Bureau's contribution was another COINTELPRO action aimed at Koen: a series of cartoons ridiculing his modish attire and exaggerating its cost. Koen barely survived this hounding. In the case of Stokely Carmichael (head of SNCC), the results were more dramatic. A pretext call to Carmichael's mother warning of a fictitious Black Panther plot to murder him led to his decision to leave the country and the subsequent dissolution of a projected alliance between the two groups. A variety of dirty tricks were devised to harass comedian-activist Dick Gregory, including a proposal to the Director to incite crime syndicate violence against him in reprisal for his attacks on organized crime.

The Director's characterization in 1968 of the Black Panther Party (BPP) as the greatest threat to the nation's internal security—another pronouncement that mocked the evaluation disclaimer—marked the beginning of all-out warfare. On the face of it, the charge was absurd: by the most generous police estimates, the entire organization nationwide boasted no more than 2000 members and only 500 activists, a substantial number of them self-preening generals without a base in the black community, spouting doomsday rhetoric and proclaiming "demands" they were powerless to enforce. When it became apparent that this abrasive, fear-engendering style brought headlines, the rhetoric escalated. The flourishing of (legally acquired) arms as a symbol of defiant strength and the abrasive challenge to police oppression in the ghetto ("off the pigs"), including a demand that the black community be armed for self-defense, set the stage for a crushing response by local police units all too ready to take the word for the deed. The Bureau orchestrated this hostility in a nationwide anti-Panther campaign, which in turn enlisted police cooperation generally in filling a vital COINTELPRO need—punitive sanctions.

There was more: the Panther leaders flourished Mao's *Little Red Book* and reproduced quotations from it in their speeches and publications. This made the group, in the Bureau's view, a revolutionary conspiracy, "schooled," as the Director hyperbolically put it, "in the Marxist-Leninist ideology and the teaching of Chinese Communist leader Mao Tse-tung." The Panthers were thus classified as both ideological felons and violence-prone "extremists." Doubly armed, the Bureau proceeded after Hoover's 1968 pronouncement to move in on the Panthers, although ironically the BPP had not even been listed as a target when the program was initially launched. But the Bureau rapidly overcame that lag, making the BPP the subject of 233 out of 295 (79 percent) authorized black nationalist COINTELPRO actions.*

The Panther offensive was marked, from the start, by a special recklessness. The record illuminates the intensity of the attack, beginning with a memo of July 30, 1968, to every field office with an active BPP unit, and setting a ten-week deadline for concrete counterintelligence proposals along specified lines. Dis-

---

*In addition, a super-secret support program, "Counterintelligence and Special Operations," concerned with hostile intelligence services both here and abroad, devised anti-Panther actions, presumably because of the BPP's claimed foreign ties. On May 11, 1970, the research section of this unit invited the San Francisco SAC to consider a detailed plan for a "disruptive-disinformation operation targeted against the national office of the Black Panther Party (BPP)" to be implemented with the active help of the local (either San Francisco or Oakland) police force. A source in the local police department, posing as a disgruntled employee, was to mail to a Panther office batches of documents, some genuine, some forged, on the stationery of the police department and the Bureau, in such a manner as to give the recipient the impression that they were stolen. The police documents would falsely record that certain Panthers were informers, that others were inept or irresponsible. Supporting tactics would include: "indicating electronic surveillance where none exists; outlining fictitious plans for police raids or other counteractions; revealing misuse or misappropriation of Panther funds; pointing out instances of political disorientation, etc." This disruption operation would develop the source's credibility by including information that was true. The letter ends on a reassuring note: "Although this proposal is a relatively simple technique, it has been applied with exceptional results in another area of intelligence interest where the target was of far greater sophistication."

satisfied with the pace of the operation, Washington dispatched a second memo on November 25, instructing the field that beginning a week later and every two weeks thereafter, "imaginative and hard-hitting counterintelligence measures aimed at crippling the BPP" were to be submitted. In May and July of the following year (1969) memos addressed to the San Francisco field office (charged with operations directed against the national BPP headquarters in Oakland) and distributed to other field offices rebuked the SAC for slighting "our responsibility" under the program. In pointing out that there was little likelihood of the BPP seeking to overthrow the government, the SAC had ignored the "obvious conclusion" that the group had embraced the "principle of violent overthrow and would go any lengths to further this aim." The second memo changes the tune somewhat: the weakness of the group caused by local harassment had created new opportunities for disruption of the national organization, which must not be neglected.

The techniques and impact of the Bureau's disruptive efforts are well illustrated by the following chronology of a power struggle which by a directive from Washington the Bureau kept alive and exacerbated between the BPP and a rival group, United Slaves (US), headed by Ron Karenga:

Nov. 5, 1968. A Bureau memo describes the tension between the two groups culminating in death threats and suggests already fearful Karenga followers be told of these threats as a means of recruiting them as informers.

Nov. 25. Fourteen field offices are alerted to the feud and instructed to submit "imaginative and hard-hitting counterintelligence measures" exploiting the rivalry.

Feb. 20, 1969. Subsequent to the killing (by US members) on the UCLA campus on Jan. 19, 1969 of two Panthers (Carter and Huggins), the San Diego office requests permission to circulate cartoons ridiculing the BPP as ineffectual and corrupt, and inviting the inference of US origin.*

March 12. The San Diego office notes that BPP has attributed the cartoons to US and on March 17 reports the critical wounding of a BPP member in a retaliatory raid accompanied by a shooting into the home of a US member.

March 27. The San Diego office obtains approval of another mailing of three cartoons in the name of the US, again ridiculing the BPP in order to thwart an attempted reconciliation of the two groups.

April 10. San Diego reports that it has mailed the cartoons—a day after it learned of a second attempted reconciliation. The same report boasts to Washington that a cartoon had succeeded in destroying the fragile truce and stirring up new animosity, resulting in violence.

May 23. A BPP member is shot and killed by a Karenga follower, a fact reported to Washington on June 5, along with a self-congratulatory observation that the confrontation had generally escalated from "mere

*Two US members were later convicted of the murders, but in 1974 escaped from San Quentin, an unprecedented feat. An affidavit by an informer, Darthard Perry, in a Black Panther lawsuit against the government *(BPP* v. *Levi et al.)* charged that the US members responsible for the slaying were known to him as FBI informers, in support of a claim that the murders and the prison break were engineered by the FBI. The government has denied the allegations.

harassment up to and including beatings of various individuals."

June 13. San Diego reports to Washington that US members are not only holding firearm practice but purchasing a large quantity of ammunition, described in detail.

June 17. San Diego, impatient with the laggard reaction of the BPP, receives approval to send a letter under the forged signature of the local BPP to Oakland headquarters in the hope of hastening a confrontation.

Aug. 14. The BPP reports the wounding by a US gunman of two members, and the killing of a third (Sylvester Bell) the next day. This bloodshed is followed on Aug. 30 by the bombing of the US office in San Diego.

Sept. 18. Delighted with this carnage, the San Diego office reports that among the follow-up actions it is contemplating to exploit the situation in the future is a new cartoon which, especially in the wake of the Bell murder, "will assist in the continuance of the rift between BPP and US." As for the past, the office bids for a meed of praise: "it is felt that a substantial amount of credit for the unrest is directly attributable to this program."

Nov. 12. Learning that Karenga fears assassination by the BPP, San Diego receives permission for a letter purporting to come from a supporter inviting retaliatory action against the BPP for a hostile article in its newspaper.

Jan. 29, 1970. Headquarters approves distribution of a third series of cartoon caricatures hostile to the BPP, attributable to the US, in the hope of further intensifying the feuding.

May 15. Washington invites San Francisco and Los Angeles to submit recommendations for exploiting a BPP newspaper article attacking Karenga. The proposals, Washington delicately explains, must bear in mind "two aspects, one against US and Karenga from obvious subject matter; the second against BPP, because inherent in article is admission by BPP that it has done nothing to retaliate against US for killing of Panther members attributed to US and Karenga, and admission that the BPP has been beaten at its own game of violence."

May 26. LA reports back that area BPP members are reluctant to attack US members, but hopes that its informers in both groups will create opportunities, "in order that the two organizations might be brought together and thus grant nature the opportunity to take her course."

The Bureau, it is clear, was criminally complicit in the violence that enveloped the two groups; more specifically, it engaged in a conspiracy to deprive individuals of their constitutionally protected rights and to life itself, a conspiracy of the very sort it is charged with policing. Here, as elsewhere, the law enforcer turns law violator. On occasion, this conflict gives rise to a grisly irony. For example, a proposed letter was submitted by Los Angeles (purportedly from an anonymous source but identifiable as US) to BPP headquarters, warning of the writer's intention to kill leader Huey Newton. Regretfully Washington denies approval, fastidiously noting that such conduct might be a violation of a federal statute, and hence "may subsequently be embarrassing to the Bureau."

The BPP-US operation paralleled the Bureau's attempt to promote a confrontation between the Chicago BPP and a violence-prone street gang, the Black Stone Rangers, headed by a seasoned felon, Jeff Fort. In the stated hope that it would provoke a retaliatory response, the Chicago field office prepared a letter to Fort, warning him that the Panthers had a "hit out for you." The Bureau's purpose, the memo explained, would not be promoted by a similar bogus letter to a Panther leader because "the BPP at present is not believed as violence-prone as the Rangers to whom violent-type activity—shooting and the like—is second nature." As in the BPP-Karenga situation, the letter was followed by a series of violent clashes. Internal factionalization between the followers of Eldridge Cleaver and Huey Newton was inflamed in the same way by false charges and forged letters—again with a fallout of violence.*

The effectiveness of the BPP newspaper, the eloquence of its leaders, the appeal of its children's breakfast program, and the emergence of a sympathetic white constituency, placed a high priority on actions to sabotage their media access and to discredit them through unfavorable publicity. In May 1970, in response to Washington instructions to eight field offices to submit proposals for immediate action to undermine the BPP newspaper, suggestions were advanced for harassments ranging from tax audits to spraying the newspaper's printing plant with a foul-smelling chemical to anonymous letters from enemy groups. Agents successfully pressured a commercial airline to demand a higher rate than that charged other organizations for shipping similar printed matter, and to seek payment retroactively. In the same way, they persuaded the postal service to charge higher postage rates for mailing the Panther newspaper than applied to similar publications. A Bureau-inspired newspaper column by Victor Riesel, proposing that union members refuse to handle the publication, was reproduced for local dissemination. A scheme was concocted to create friction between the Panther publication and the Nation of Islam (NOI) publication *Muhammad Speaks,* which "with careful planning and close supervision" might develop into "an open dispute between the two publications." Distributors of the newspaper were regularly harassed, and speaking engagements were sabotaged, including the arrest of Chicago Panther leader Fred Hampton in a TV studio prior to his scheduled appearance. "Cooperative news media" were supplied with a steady stream of discrediting stories and, more ambitiously, plans were made to use "established and reliable sources in the television and/or radio field" to prepare programs discrediting the BPP.

Anonymous letters, newspaper stories, phone calls, and open pressures were used to force evictions, to destroy marriages, to attack BPP attorneys and the attorney-client relationship, to frighten parents by false charges of immorality into forcing their children to end their Panther associations. An elaborate program to discourage white support included harassments, death threats, snitch jacket attempts, poison pen letters to the trade press attacking Hollywood figures, and employment pressures. The Bureau's greatest fear was that BPP projects such as its breakfast program might modify its violent image and

---

*A member of the Cleaver faction in New York City was shot by Newton followers while selling the BPP paper. In retaliation, the circulation manager of the paper, controlled by the Newton faction, was killed.

overcome its isolation. The already mentioned May 1969 memo rebuked the SAC:

> You state that the Bureau under the CIP [Counter Intelligence Program] should not attack programs of community interest such as the BPP "Breakfast for Children." You state that this is because many prominent "humanitarians," both white and black, are interested in the program as well as churches which are actively support-ing it. You have obviously missed the point. The BPP is not engaged in the "Break-fast for Children" program for humanitarian reasons, including their efforts to create an image of civility, assume community control of Negroes, and to fill adolescent children with their insidious poison.*

An inflammatory children's coloring book depicting police as caricature pigs played an important part in a drive to eliminate the program. This comic book, which has been rejected by the Panther leadership as a distorted expression of the party's views, was afterwards transmitted by an informer to the Bureau. In a COINTELPRO operation the Bureau added captions advocating violence, and printed thousands of copies in the party's name, circulating them widely, espe-cially to merchants and businesses contributing to the breakfast program, who were told that the books were given to participating children. Another aspect of the COINTELPRO called for anonymous protest letters to churches supporting the program. As the result of such a letter from "A Concerned Christian," a Catholic priest in San Diego was transferred ("completely neutralized"), thus forcing the program's termination in that city.

To implement its assault, the Bureau recruited an army of informers, com-parable in number to its Klan coverage. Some BPP units were run by spies who looted Panther funds, secure in the knowledge that draining BPP treasuries could hardly displease their agent-handlers.[28] The flow of information from its spies promoted an unprecedented collaboration between local police units and the FBI. (Running informers was a financial drain and only the generously funded feds could afford a substantial number of them.) Informers supplied the evidence of "probable cause" needed for the most destructive police blow (short of outright gunfire): raids on offices or private premises. Such police raids, usually based on the reported storage of arms or explosives (bought, in many cases, by Bureau spies and provocateurs), became routine against Panther offices in 1969–70. Indeed, beginning in the early summer of 1967, the Philadelphia police intelligence unit under the command of Frank L. Rizzo had conducted a series of raids at Bureau instigation based on tips that explosives were stored in the raided premises (invariably referred to as an "arsenal" or "fortress"). Exorbitant bail kept the arrestees in jail for months or even longer; but in eight cases the charges were ultimately dropped, and in three others reduced to weapons charges resulting in probationary sentences.

Similarly, information obtained from Bureau informers channeled to the Philadelphia unit served as the basis for harassing pretextual arrests of activists,

---

*This is, of course, a variant of an old standby: the disclaimer of violence is a device to conceal, and hence make even more threatening, the subject's basic commitment to violence. Since potential Bureau critics might not be impressed with such explanations, the Director instructed the field to "Insure that no implication is created that we are investigating the [Breakfast Program for School-children] itself or the church where it is held."

to quote a Bureau document, "on every possible charge until they no longer can make bail" and are "incarcerate[d] . . . for as long as possible." In other cities, too, the Bureau briefed the police on Panther activities and reviewed opportunities for harassing arrests. Not that the police needed much urging; a pattern emerges from the records of local police units throughout the country of hundreds of arrests on such charges as conspiracy to commit murder, car theft, robbery, carrying concealed weapons, drug use, riot, felonious assault, resisting arrest, disorderly conduct, arson, possession of explosives, and an assortment of traffic offenses. Whenever possible, prohibitive bail was set, so as to keep the accused locked up until the charges were ultimately dropped or reduced to a face-saving formality. In addition to setting up arrests, the Bureau's contributions ranged from transmission of information to grand juries, to the supplying of "background information" to law enforcement agencies, and (in at least one instance) an anonymous communication to a judge.

But far more than in any of the other counterintelligence programs, fear of informers, not information, was the most destructive Bureau weapon. The fear of FBI and police spies replaced the ethos of mutual trust that is the lifeblood of effective group functioning with suspicion and mistrust. Anonymous spy charges created an organizational climate in which "man is wolf to man," while actual informers, encouraged to become spy hunters in "security" posts, falsely accused the innocent, their credibility protected by fears of betrayal and the unwillingness of doubters to risk charges of working with the police.* This susceptible paranoia-ridden setting provided an ideal camouflage for disturbed power-hungry types—like William O'Neal, the Chicago informer in the Hampton case (discussed below), whose prison doctor had recommended psychiatric treatment and whose behavior patterns included the bull-whipping of a falsely accused informer and involvement in violent crimes and murder threats.

Spy-hunting even without FBI prodding became an outlet for suppressed violent tendencies, as in the case of George W. Sams, Jr. A seriously disturbed individual, with uncontrollably violent impulses, Sams had spent two years in an institution for the mentally retarded. In May 1969, not at the time demonstrably a Bureau agent, he showed up in New Haven, Connecticut, as a Panther security enforcer and, only a few days after his arrival, engineered—in what may have been the ultimate snitch jacket—the torture-murder of Panther Alex Rackley, falsely charged as an informer. Along with other local Panthers, Sams pleaded guilty to an assortment of state court charges and emerged as the principal government witness. Pardoned after serving four years, he was groomed as a witness in the Chicago Hampton trial, placed under a federal witness security program, and given a new identity, but was jailed for parole violation in 1977, a result of a series of arrests including violent assault charges.[29]

The informer-instigated raid scenario was tragically played out in the case of Chicago Panther leader Fred Hampton. Hampton, along with an associate, Mark Clark, was killed on December 4, 1969, in the course of a raid by state attorney's police and detectives sparked by information supplied by FBI in-

*When the BPP launched a purge of suspected spies, the FBI, with the aid of membership lists stolen by its informers, dispatched letters on forged stationery and over forged signatures to scores of others, telling them that they too had been purged.

former William O'Neal, whose bureau control agent, Roy Mitchell, was assigned to the Chicago Panther COINTELPRO unit.[30] O'Neal became the Panthers' "Captain of Security"; a former bodyguard for Hampton, he was himself arrested on a variety of charges ranging from drug possession to the attempted illegal purchase of firearms. A classic informer type, O'Neal earned about $30,000 from 1969 to 1972, exclusive of such expenses as car maintenance and bonding fees. His elevation to the post of security captain (the wolf guarding the sheep) won him the Bureau's gratitude, expressed in the form of a substantial pay increase and special additional emoluments when his regular salary payments ran out. His security role produced predictable ironies, such as a homemade electric chair for use in ferreting out informers. On one occasion a Bureau tap of Panther headquarters that he had helped arrange established his own involvement in a drug sale. In a more traditional vein he played a provocateur's role, urging members to participate in armed robberies and bombings with explosives that he purchased and stored. These initiatives were part of an assignment that included, to quote a Bureau document, "harassing and impelling the criminal activities of the Black Panther Party locally."

A June 4, 1969, raid led by Marlin Johnson, the Chicago SAC, stemmed from an O'Neal tip that the Panthers were harboring Sams, in flight after the New Haven murder. Although the raid failed to turn up the alleged fugitive, it did yield a list of contributors, the entire treasury, and eight arrests on charges that were quickly dropped. (There are persuasive indications that the fugitive hunt was a pretext for COINTELPRO harassment.) Three police confrontations in July and October resulted in gun battles, arrests, and, again, dropped charges, which were followed by a shootout on November 13 resulting in the deaths of two Chicago policemen.

Although Hampton was out of town at the time, he was suspected of responsibility for the two slayings.* Hampton was a key Bureau target for other reasons. A highly effective leader, his charisma enabled him partially to overcome the Bureau's divisive efforts, and was principally responsible for a truce with the Black Stone Rangers as well as an alliance with the SDS, itself the subject of a special COINTELPRO operation. He had instituted a number of successful community welfare, medical, and educational programs, activities that had earned him a Rabble Rouser Index listing. If he survived the decimation of other leaders—Newton, Seale, Cleaver, and others in New York and New Haven either in jail or facing criminal charges—he was slated for national leadership. The evidence that Hampton was deliberately targeted for elimination is persuasive.

On November 19, six days after the police slayings, Mitchell, on the basis of information supplied by O'Neal, sketched out a floor plan of the Panther "crib" on Monroe Street, including the designation of the bed where Hampton slept. O'Neal also gave Mitchell requested information about Hampton's movements and his use of the apartment. Representatives of the state attorney's office, provided with the layout drawing and orally conveyed details (including the

---

*Tom Charles Huston, of Huston Plan fame, told an interviewer for *New Times* that the Bureau had identified Hampton as the culprit—*New Times*, May 31, 1974.

assurance that Hampton frequently slept in the apartment), prepared a plan for a raid based on a claim that two illegal weapons were stored in the apartment. This justification for the raid was curious in view of the fact that before the final raid-planning session was held in early December, a memo by Mitchell to Washington sent on November 21 and summarizing O'Neal's report of the 19th stated that the weapons in the apartment were legally purchased and registered. The raid, conducted at 4:00 A.M. ostensibly to seize this contraband, was accompanied by a fusillade of between eighty-three and ninety-nine shots. One shot was fired in return.

When public shock over the killing forced the convening of a federal grand jury in the winter of 1970, the Chicago SAC, in accordance with a plan previously agreed on with Department of Justice officials, concealed the roles of O'Neal and Mitchell from the grand jury and publicly disclaimed Bureau involvement.* In a subsequent civil law suit filed in 1976 by the families of the victims and the raid survivors, four of whom were seriously injured, the Bureau tried to continue its cover-up, withholding from the court a great mass of documents (more than 90 percent of the total number) until a witness inadvertently revealed their existence. SAC Marlin Johnson's insistence on the witness stand that the Bureau's role in the affair was confined to a routine dissemination of material that might be of local concern ("What they did with the information was none of our concern") was questionable in the light of two unsuccessful Bureau attempts in October and November to persuade the Chicago police to conduct the raid before the state attorney's office agreed to do so, the Bureau's June 4 raid, and earlier pressure on the Chicago police to arrest Hampton on a warrant charging mob action. The attempt to disclaim responsibility was shattered by the discovery of a memo to Washington on the eve of the fatal raid (December 3), which reported that "local law-enforcement [agencies were] . . . currently planning a positive course of action relating" to the information supplied by O'Neal. This was communicated in a "periodic progress letter" captioned "Counterintelligence Program," under the subheading "Operations Being Effected and Tangible Results Obtained." Plainly, the raid was a tactic in a Bureau counterintelligence strategy. Nor did the Bureau satisfactorily explain why Mitchell, the field chieftain of the anti-Panther counterintelligence activities and O'Neal's control, participated in a series of off-the-record pre-raid conferences with a representative of the state attorney's office. SAC Johnson was similarly evasive when confronted with documents reflecting the agency's hostile designs on Hampton. He insisted that the word "hit" in the letter sent to Jeff Fort (see p. 221 above) did not mean a murder contract at all, but "something non-violent in nature" (despite an accompanying memo stating that its

---

*Convened to allay suspicion of a planned execution, the grand jury investigation was a cover-up in the true sense of that much-abused term. Apathetic about the Bureau's involvement, it was equally incurious about the circumstances of the raid: the timing (when the occupants would be sure to be asleep and on the premises rather than earlier in the evening, when it was known they would be occupied elsewhere), the unnecessarily heavy arms, the large raiding force, the massive gunfire despite lack of response, and the rejection of conventional search procedures used effectively against the Panthers on earlier occasions. Hampton slept through the raid, apparently drugged, though he was not a drug user. The grand jury found that he was not drugged, but there is substantial evidence to the contrary.

purpose was to inspire "retaliatory action"), and that "impelling criminal activities" (the function ascribed to O'Neal) meant to "curb or constrain" them.*

In his efforts to dissociate the Bureau from the raid, Johnson had help from the raiding party's chief, Sergeant Daniel Groth, who testified that the "probable cause" evidence in his affidavit for a search warrant submitted to a court on December 3 came not from O'Neal but from another informer whom he refused to name. This claim neatly solved other problems: O'Neal's last pre-raid report, as we have seen, had stated that there were no illegal weapons in the raided premises. In addition, disclosure that he had relied on O'Neal's information, relayed to him by Mitchell, would have invalidated the "probable cause" affidavit on hearsay grounds: a legally valid affidavit would have required execution by Mitchell himself. But the signature of a Bureau functionary would in turn bring to the fore a sticky embarrassment: possession of the weapons referred to in the affidavit was per se a violation of federal law. Why had the Bureau, or the Treasury Department's Alcohol, Firearms and Tobacco Division, with which the Bureau had previously consulted on this very matter, failed to pursue the investigation? Such an inquiry would obviously have exposed the Bureau's counterintelligence role.†

These deceptions, dictated by the need to answer courtroom charges, could not change the fact that immediately after the raid, according to one of the documents that had been withheld, O'Neal's supervisor, Robert Piper, requested Washington for the award of a special bonus in this "successful action" because O'Neal had supplied information that was "the only source of the raid." In January 1970 Washington authorized a special payment of $300 as a reward for O'Neal's "uniquely valuable services."

This reward request was only one of a number of documents revealing the Bureau's instigation of the raid, which had accumulated in its files by the time of the convening of the federal grand jury. The script concealing the role of the Bureau required that such documents be suppressed and hidden from grand jury

---

*Johnson solemnly averred on the witness stand that the COINTELPRO attack on the BPP was based on the fact that it was a "Black Nationalist" group, which he defined as one with offices across the nation, as opposed to a purely local organization that would not be of Bureau concern.

†The plaintiffs contended that Groth's informant was invented both to validate the warrant and to conceal an alleged conspiracy between the FBI and state law enforcement officials. But the court accepted Groth's unsupported claim that identification would endanger the life of his mysterious source. In thus upholding the claim of "informers privilege," the decision conflicts with a ruling of the federal court in the same district (*Alliance* v. *Rochford* and *ACLU* v. *City of Chicago*) ordering city and FBI defendants in two consolidated lawsuits to reveal the identity of 180 Chicago police and over 200 Bureau informants. Judge Griesa in the SWP case above made a similar ruling. A federal appeals court, in May 1979, issued a sweeping decision ordering a new trial and rejecting the trial court's ruling upholding Groth's concealment of the identity of his informant. A central issue in such a trial will be whether O'Neal was in fact the "reliable informant" whose information was the basis for the search warrant. More broadly, the 122-page decision reversed the trial court's ruling dismissing the case against certain defendants and concluding that the plaintiff had established a *prima facie* case of conspiracy against the state and federal officials in whose favor the trial court had ruled. The appellate court decided that the plaintiff had made a *prima facie* case of two conspiracies—the first implicated the defendants in the preparation, planning, and execution of the raid, and the second involved a post-raid conspiracy to cover up the evidence of the first, and further to harass the survivors of the raid. The appellate court also rebuked the FBI and its attorneys for suppressing some 40,000 pages of evidence and expunging additional documentary material in the course of the 18-month trial.

inspection. But this was hardly a problem: the investigation was assigned to a Bureau agent under the close supervision of Marlin Johnson. The prosecutor in charge of the grand jury was none other than Jerris Leonard, the Nixon administration's civil liberties division chief and coordinator of a Justice Department intelligence operation geared to the elimination of the Panthers. ("Nothing but hoodlums," Leonard had insisted.) But there was no assurance that the Bureau's role could be effectively concealed simply by indicting others—the state's attorney and his raiding party. *Any* indictment would result in a trial that might open up sealed doors. There was a further problem: State's Attorney Edward Hanrahan had procured state indictments on attempted murder charges of seven remaining Panthers. A trial on these charges was equally threatening; it was bound not only to reveal the Bureau's role but to raise a host of "taint" issues, such as electronic surveillance, burglaries, and police misconduct—a classic instance of a conflict between intelligence and law enforcement. Leonard, after consulting with Attorney General Mitchell, neatly solved all his problems. Early in April 1970 he informed Hanrahan that the federal grand jury would not issue any indictment at all, but simply a report in exchange for Hanrahan's dismissal of the state court's indictment of the Panthers. What made the offer particularly attractive was the inclusion of an undertaking by Leonard not to press for the identification of Groth's claimed informant, or even for confirmation that he existed at all. (Hanrahan knew that the raid was based on the O'Neal report and said so in a radio interview in February 1975, which was read into the record of the 1976 civil action.)*

A Baltimore variant on this pattern of police collaboration involved a young white lawyer, Arthur Turco, who, along with seventeen local Panthers, ex-Panthers, and supporters, was charged in April 1970 with a variety of offenses arising out of the alleged New Haven-style torture-murder of a suspected spy.[31] The indictments came six months after the discovery of a skeleton buried in a park, which was first described by the local examiner's office as that of a white man, aged twenty-five to thirty, whose death was ascribed to a drug overdose. But when the skeleton returned from the FBI laboratory in Washington, the remains became those of Eugene Leroy Anderson, a black man, age twenty, killed by a shotgun blast. The local prosecutor filed charges after a conference with Baltimore police, the FBI, and Attorney General Mitchell along with Jerris Leonard. Nor did the federal presence end at that point: the prosecutor received trial guidance from Washington, Bureau investigative support, and the benefit of a series of Bureau lectures on "How to Deal with Panther Cases." Turco had represented the Baltimore Panthers in legal matters, but the prosecution rested on the theory that he master-minded Anderson's execution as a spy and that his orders were carried out by three Panthers: Mahoney Kebe, Donald Vaughn, and Arnold Loney. The three men were produced by the FBI as participant witnesses and turned over to the Baltimore police intelligence unit, headed by Major Maurice DuBois, who had been a Bureau agent for twenty years.

All three witnesses turned out to be Bureau informers and received immu-

---

*Although his concession was unambiguously worded and is explained by the fact that at the time there appeared to be no risk of embarrassment—the state indictments had long since been dropped—Hanrahan disavowed it on the witness stand in the civil trial.

nity, free room and board, and a salary—an extravagance in view of their confused testimony. The judge, on his own motion, ordered Kebe, the star witness, removed from the stand and his testimony stricken. A new prosecutor offered deals to the remaining defendants, dropped all charges against them, and substituted drastically reduced charges against the rest. He subsequently admitted that from the beginning the charges lacked evidentiary support, adding that his predecessor had engaged in "improper prosecution practices," but said nothing about the federal pressures that had generated the indictment and the Bureau's informers who had tainted the trial. Perhaps the most arresting aspect of the entire prosecution was the attribution to a young white lawyer of power to direct and control the actions of the Panther defendants, a by-product of a counterintelligence-style attack against lawyers for radical clients initiated by the Nixon administration.*[32]

The role of the informer as a link between the Bureau and local police dominates the ambush-slaying in Seattle of Larry Ward.[33] In January 1970, Bureau informer Alfie Burnett was mysteriously released from the Kings County, Washington, jail where he was awaiting trial on a robbery charge. When Burnett subsequently pleaded guilty, his parole officer, who had originally objected to his release, demanded his arrest because of his failure to appear for sentencing on another criminal charge. The Bureau had the officer overruled for a second time because Burnett, according to the Bureau, was a source of valuable information on ghetto violence. In actual fact, Burnett was sprung to provoke violence, and used his freedom to scour the ghetto offering money for the bombing of buildings. After many false starts and fruitless stakeouts, he found a victim—not the ex-Panther Jimmy Davis he was looking for, but his best friend, Larry Ward, a black veteran who was recruited for the job at the last minute by Burnett's offer of $75. By prior agreement, the police arranged for a stakeout coordinated with a series of alerts from the Bureau agent who was running Burnett. On May 14, the agent relayed to the Seattle police a report from Burnett that a bombing of the Hardcastle Realty Company had been arranged for that night. A second call at about 11:00 P.M. confirmed the report, and a third, received between 2:00 and 2:30 A.M., relayed Burnett's message that the bombing would take place in minutes. According to Burnett, in his last call to the Bureau he "distinctly told them that it was Ward instead of [Davis]," and "that he was unarmed. . . ." Ward was killed almost instantly in a police ambush. Seattle intelligence chief Williams blamed the Bureau: "As far as I can tell, Ward was a relatively decent kid. Somebody set this whole thing up. It wasn't the police department." The Bureau took care of Burnett, a marked man as a result of the shooting, by having him transferred from a state to a federal prison.

The Panther assault claimed twenty-eight dead over an eighteen-month period, some direct victims of aggressive intelligence actions and others traceable to Bureau-assisted feuds. The Bureau unleashed a reign of terror that crushed the organization and neutralized its leadership through death, impris-

---

*Turco's original capital charges were, after a mistrial, reduced to common assault, to which he reluctantly agreed to plead guilty. The decision resulted from permanent damage to his health by imprisonment in the Baltimore city jail (subsequently closed down as a health hazard) without bail for ten months prior to his first trial, police harassment of his wife, and other pressures.

onment, and exile. Its ferocity and cruelty can only be explained by a racism that holds the lives of blacks cheaply.* For the FBI, its black targets were not merely outlaws deprived, as in the case of Communists, of civic identity but bestial and inhuman. The black COINTELPROs plunge us into a fen of horror, a nativist Final Solution, justified as violence prevention and bureaucratically programmed in a stunning gloss on Hannah Arendt's "banality of evil."

New Left—Of Satyrs, Sissies, Strumpets, and Studs[34]

The "New Left" program started in May 1968 and was stepped up by a series of implementing directives following the Columbia campus disturbances in the spring of 1968. Altogether lacking in limiting standards, it quickly emerged as an attack on the entire youth movement and particularly its anti-war segment. Neither lack of ideology nor nonviolence served as a restraint on the Bureau. Thus, a free speech demonstration, admittedly "not . . . inspired by the New Left," was attacked because it "shows an obvious disregard for decency and established morality." Nonviolent anti-war groups were targeted because they "lent aid and comfort" to disruptive allies; faculty members sympathetic to the New Left were similarly attacked and subjected to job pressures for "using [their] good offices" to promote objectionable programs and policies.

The counterculture of the sixties had finally recognized what was the blood-and-marrow of the Bureau's heritage, that culture is politics, the first line of defense of the capitalist economic order. The New Left COINTELPRO was an undisguised assault by the self-appointed defenders of the American way of life against an entire milieu. The tactics were familiar and had worked well enough in the past: disruption of groups and discrediting of individuals through planted propaganda, anonymous mailings, interviews, snitch jackets, "disinformation," notionals, letters to relatives, and the use of right-wing groups as enforcers. But the Bureau had bitten off much more than it could chew. The program's broad and amorphous scope, the diffused and unstructured character of its targets, which made them largely immune to organizational traumas, the popularity of their anti-war goals, the crude quality of the offensive actions, and the bonds of trust among the leaders that limited the effectiveness of snitch jacketing—all these considerations fatally handicapped the program. The anonymous-letters

---

*The callousness of American society generally to the loss of black lives has been the subject of frequent comment. For a summary see Arnold Rogow, *The Dying of the Light* (Putnam, 1975). In the context of this book, it is well illustrated by the letter referred to above seeking a special reward for O'Neal. The letter praises O'Neal for an alleged contribution (the floor plan), which "saved injury and possible death to police officers" while the killing of the two blacks is routinely (and falsely) noted as a consequence of their resistance. This callousness also is notable in actions against other minorities. An FBI memo dealing with Hispanics involved in the Puerto Rican independence movement describes an attempt to provoke a "violent confrontation" between two groups; a second memo records an agent's "pleasure" in the heart attack suffered by a leader in the movement, Juan Mari Bras, because it showed that threatening telephone calls and personal harassment "seem to be having an effect." A description of the released files relating to the Puerto Rican independence movement appears in William Lichtenstein and David Wimhurst, "Red Alert in Puerto Rico," *Nation,* June 30, 1979.

device, the most popular weapon, did not produce impressive results. The fictional irate parents, "A Concerned Alumni," the disaffected group member —the entire cast of characters of the Bureau's intelligence repertory theater— are typically given lines grotesquely unsuited to their roles.

There was, however, one organization that, being more structured than most New Left targets, did prove vulnerable to dirty tricks: Students for a Democratic Society (SDS). The most popular tactic was the use of trained black infiltrators to stigmatize SDS as racist. In December 1968, the Bureau attempted, through invented charges of racism, to force the eviction of the SDS from its headquarters at 1608 West Madison Street, Chicago, in a black neighborhood. When the Chicago office learned from an SDS headquarters wiretap of a planned national council meeting in March 1969 at the University of Texas, it persuaded university authorities to bar the SDS on the grounds that the group's use of the campus would be "an insult to Lyndon Johnson."

In order to disrupt SDS and its June 18, 1969, national convention, SAC Johnson enlisted the cooperation of the Chicago *Tribune* and its leak specialist, Ron Koziol. On June 16, 1969, Koziol met with Johnson, Field Supervisor Hugh Mallet, and Special Agent Robert B. Glendon, who "provided background information" and "sharpened the understanding of Koziol relative to the underlying political dispute between the factions vying for the control of SDS." The resulting story, "Red Unit Seeks SDS Rule," was a front-page banner headline story in the June 17, 1969, *Tribune.* On June 24, Johnson reported that "It is felt that this article forced all groups to harden their stances, thereby alienating a large number of non-members and leaving a number of disillusioned delegates who do not have a strong commitment to any of the factions. This, it is felt, has weakened SDS severely." On June 30, 1969, Johnson concluded that the article "which resulted from the Bureau authorized contact by SAC M.S. Johnson with [deleted] of the Chicago *Tribune* aggravated a tense situation and helped create the confrontation that split SDS."

The pursuit of the SDS embraced its friends and supporters. In order to "develop possible counterintelligence actions to cause Mrs. Montgomery to withdraw her financial support of SDS," the Chicago FBI office, through the use of an informer in the Chicago IRS office, on December 12, 1968, illegally acquired the confidential 1967 income tax return of Lucy Montgomery, a Chicago area benefactor of the SDS and other anti-war and civil rights groups. Chicago FBI Agent Paul L. Timmerberg noted in his December 12, 1968, report to Johnson detailing the contents of Ms. Montgomery's tax returns that "DISCLOSURE OF THE SOURCE OF THIS INFORMATION COULD RESULT IN GREAT EMBARRASSMENT TO THE BUREAU." When an IRS audit found no irregularities in her tax returns, Hoover directed the Chicago office to "detect any weakness which may be utilized" to pressure Ms. Montgomery into ending her SDS contributions.

Individual SDS leaders were likewise subjected to politically motivated tax and draft pressures. As in the case of the Panthers, the FBI collaborated with local police to have SDS activists arrested on bogus charges or served with subpoenas. Such tactics were used intensively to prevent delegates from attending the SDS June 1969 convention in Ann Arbor, Michigan. A drive to curb campus war-connected unrest (especially pressures on college administrators to use local police to control demonstrations) was implemented through anonymous letters to university officials, members of Boards of Regents, state legislators, and the press. A prominent target was Richard E. Flacks, an assistant professor of sociology at the University of Chicago, who had been active in SDS as a student and subsequently joined the New University Conference, a radical faculty group. The Bureau hoped that the university administration's tolerance of Flacks's political activities could be reversed by pressures applied to the board of trustees, which included such people as John D. Rockefeller III. An anonymous letter with appropriate warnings from "A Concerned Alumnus" (correcting the standard FBI usage) was mailed to the board and to the conservative Chicago *Tribune,* then an important ally. A similar letter, deploring the use of Yale University facilities by the Black Panther Party, was sent to the conservative columnist and Yale alumnus William F. Buckley, Jr., with the objective of reversing administration policy by mobilizing alumni opposition.

A more ambitious program was launched against Antioch College, a small institution in Yellow Springs, Ohio, proud of its reputation for involvement in social causes. The president of Antioch, Dr. James Dixon, had already demonstrated his unfitness as an ally of the Bureau by challenging the claim that marijuana use was harmful. Unable to enlist Dr. Dixon's aid, the Bureau decided on a massive program of attack against the entire college. The local field office carefully identified thirty or forty former student leaders, and set out to follow their careers after graduation in the hope of uncovering a consistent record of low achievement, which, according to Bureau plan, could then be publicized through a contact in the Cincinnati *Inquirer.* The aim was nothing less than to "force Antioch to defend itself as an educational institution." But the whole plan collapsed when the investigation showed that the Antioch graduates under investigation did quite well in the outside world.

Another priority dictated by the Director's self-assumed role as head of the entire police establishment in this country was the defense of urban police forces against charges of brutality. When the Chicago police were criticized for their excessive use of force in curbing demonstrations at the 1968 Democratic Convention, the Director irately told his agents that

> Once again, the liberal press and the bleeding hearts and the forces on the left are taking advantage of the situation in Chicago surrounding the Democratic National Convention to attack the police and organized law enforcement agencies. When actual evidence of police brutality is not available, it can be expected that these elements will stretch the truth and even manufacture incidents to indict law enforcement agencies. We should be mindful of this situation and develop all possible evidence to expose this activity and to refute these allegations.

Cooperative news media were to be enlisted in the effort to portray the Chicago police in a more favorable light. Within a week it became obvious to Hoover that the growing weight of evidence was against his version of the events. He reacted with an urgent teletype to selected field offices ordering the collection of any information that might provide some mitigation of the police reaction. Agents were given just one day to find evidence of provocation of the police by demonstrators. Hoover further ordered the collection of evidence of violation of anti-riot laws, which ultimately was used as the basis for the indictment of the Chicago 7.

But it was the immorality of the young radicals that disturbed the Hoover Bureau most. A key assignment, stamped with the Director's rhetorical horror, requested reports for distribution to the news media on the "scurrilous and depraved nature of many of the characters' activities, habits, and living conditions representative of New Left adherents." This directive, sent in May, was followed by an angry communiqué in October 1968 in which Hoover chastised his agents for ignoring the "mounting evidence of moral depravity," and instructed them to be especially alert to demonstrate "the depraved nature and moral looseness" of student radicals. In an almost predictable projection of his authoritarian-father role, he exhorted agents to transmit to the parents of every student found engaging in an "obscene display" a suitable report, along with photographs if possible. (Compare his relaying of dirt about King to his father.) The fruits of such sexual snoopery were also to be distributed to school authorities and the local press.

Whether prompted by eagerness to please the Director or by an institutionalized puritanism, the field was quick to attack what it conceived to be moral looseness among the youth. Pornography, obscenity, "taking the Lord's name in vain," all were faithfully reported. The documents positively leer with accounts of nudity, extramarital sex partnerships, and sexual promiscuity, and shudder with disgust over the subjects' living conditions, personal hygiene, and eating habits. The Newark office breathlessly wires Washington of its acquisition of a copy of *Screw* magazine, described as "containing a type of filth that could only originate in a depraved mind," and reportedly sold on the Rutgers University campus by " 'hippie' types in unkempt clothes, with wild beards, shoulder length hair and other examples of their non-conformity." The abomination was forwarded to Washington as "Enclosure, 1: OBSCENE," and a copy sent along with an anonymous letter from "A Concerned Student" to the chairman of the State Senate's Education Committee.* This comstockery is reflected in a pattern of harassment and raids instigated by the FBI against underground publications by local police units on obscenity and related grounds.

The eroticizing of the New Left renewed a link with radicalism forged by the response to the Russian Revolution. Sexual license ("the nationalization of women," "free love") ranked next to godlessness among the horrors perpetrated by the Bolsheviks, and was domesticated in the social unrest and bohemianism of the twenties. The Director's personal (and well-grounded) sexual fears and anxieties intensified this linkage, not only in the agency's investigative priorities (spies were regularly encouraged to report sexual "hang-ups" and to use sexual relationships to obtain information)† but in puritanical internal codes of dress,

---

*In order to maintain standards of internal purity and decency, even in its internal communications, the field offices were required to use chaste circumlocutions and asterisks. When an anonymous letter or publication was proposed using obscene language, the writer would invariably explain that such usage was required for purposes of deception. In order to spare the sensibilities of typists in the stenographic pool, letters with offensive language were typed outside the agency.

†Research on prostitution triggered the Bureau's counterintelligence pursuit of California professor Vern L. Bullough and contributed to his inclusion in the custodial detention index

private behavior, and language. In this sexually haunted world, white males traditionally stereotyped as "panty-waists," "queers," "fairies," and "faggots," were now depicted as licentious. Washington approved hiring a diseased prostitute to infect California New Left leaders, on the assumption that if they contracted VD their disgrace would alienate potential campus followers.* Indeed, much of the agents' New Left COINTELPRO output is roiled by an undertow of sexual prurience; young leftists, as the agents see it, "dig the grass bit and balling them radical chicks," and, in a verse format, "go for grass and Jewish ass . . . " Radical females, as in the past, are viewed as strumpets (*pace* Emma Goldman and Louise Bryant Reed) seeking in politics an outlet for their insatiable lust, betrayers of the purity of American womanhood.

The San Antonio office distributed a press account of the practice of communal living on the University of Texas campus in Austin, along with an anonymous "irate parent" letter to the chairman of the university's Board of Regents—a friend of Lyndon Johnson—and a Texas state senator, the brother of Governor John Connally. Extramarital cohabitation was seen as merely the first step toward revolutionary activism: "if we can 'nip this in the bud' it could prevent the development of another New left such as that at Columbia University."

A related stereotype, also deeply embedded in nativist culture and, as we have seen, a Hoover obsession, casts the black in the role of stud. This role was assigned to the fictional authors of anonymous letters complaining of black leaders' collaboration with white groups,† dominated by white "faggots" or by horny adventurers lusting after sexually preferable black women. Another stud script singled out effective black leaders and denounced them for their lack of virility. As already suggested in the discussion of the pursuit of Martin Luther King, Jr., movements for black liberation were perceived in Washington as threats to the purity of white womanhood. Hence resistance to such movements was justified not for political reasons alone but as an imperative of sexual morality. Because of their potential impact on both black and white sensibilities, COINTELPRO scenarios involving interracial sex, the black stud and the white

---

(Category IV). See Vern L. Bullough, "How the FBI Spotted Me," *Nation,* July 9, 1977.

*In 1961 prostitutes were recruited to entrap leaders of the Fair Play for Cuba Committee. *Newsweek,* "The FBI's Turn," Feb. 13, 1975; Chicago *Sun-Times,* "Report FBI Bugged Two Houses of Prostitution," Feb. 2, 1975; *Time,* "FBI Dirty Tricks," Dec. 5, 1977. According to FBI records, a wiretapped telephone call from California to the headquarters of a New Left group in Chicago overheard on December 9, 1969, yielded the information that a woman leader of the group had contracted gonorrhea—apparently from one of two male national officers. Eager to exploit this disclosure, Washington advised Chicago to check whether the caller's infection had been reported, as required by law. Perhaps it would be possible to neutralize the entire group by having its leaders arrested for failing to report the infection. And, why not leak the story to a friendly newsman? But these suggestions were vetoed by Chicago out of fear of discovery of the illegal tap. It has been argued, without supporting evidence, that the source of the infection was the prostitute mentioned in the text.

†The disruption of white-black coalitions was a major priority of both the Black Nationalist and the New Left programs of the Bureau. One of the more successful of these actions was described to the author by ex-agent Robert Wall. In order to undermine a 1969 Washington anti-war rally, the Bureau forged a letter in the name of the Black United Front (BUF), demanding that the planners of the rally pay a $20,000 "security bond" to the group. The letter was approved by the Bureau's counterintelligence desk and signed with the forged signature of a leader of the group. The scheme was implemented by a Bureau plant, who also reported back on its effectiveness.

strumpet, were valued and encouraged by Washington. One such script involved a white woman in St. Louis who, an informer reported, was active in both the Women's International League for Peace and Freedom (WILPF) and ACTION, a local biracial civil rights organization. The woman's husband, according to the informer, did not share his wife's political interests, resented the amount of time she spent in civil rights and anti-war work, and suspected that she had been unfaithful. The Bureau decided to send the following anonymous letter in the hope that it would create a marital tempest and thus distract the woman from her political activities:

> Dear Mr. ———,
>
> Look, man, I guess your old lady doesn't get enough at home or she wouldn't be shucking and jiving with our Black Men in ACTION, you dig? Like all she wants to integrate is the bedroom and us Black Sisters ain't gonna take no second best from our men. So lay it on her, man—or get her the hell off Newstead.
>
> A Soul Sister

The Bureau was pleased to report a few months later that the marriage had broken up and that the letter had contributed to the split.

An even more successful version of the strumpet-stud gambit was a campaign directed against the film actress Jean Seberg. To discredit her support of the Black Panthers, discourage further financial contributions, and, more generally, "to cheapen her image with the general public," the Los Angeles SAC in April 1970 requested Washington's permission to circulate a rumor that Ms. Seberg was pregnant with the child of a prominent BPP leader. The source of the rumor was to be a letter to a columnist from a fictitious friend:

> I was just thinking about you and remembered I still owe you a favor. So I was in Paris last week and ran into Jean Seberg who was heavy with baby. I thought she and Romain had gotten together again but she confided the child belonged to [name deleted] of the Black Panthers. The dear girl is getting around. Anyway, I thought you might get a scoop on the others.

Delighted with the proposal ("Seberg should be neutralized. Her current pregnancy . . . while still married affords an opportunity for such effort."), Washington suggested a timing refinement: ". . . to insure the success of your plan, Bureau feels it would be better to wait approximately two additional months until Seberg's pregnancy would be obvious to everyone."

The blind "item"—in the usage of the media gossip souks—was first published in a Los Angeles *Times* column and then widely disseminated, a result for which L.A. claimed credit. When *Newsweek* published it in 1970, Ms. Seberg and her then husband, the French diplomat and author Romain Gary, the actual father, successfully sued for libel. After the actress committed suicide in August 1979, Gary charged that the publicity had led to the stillborn delivery of the child, a psychotic breakdown, and ultimate suicide, the culmination of a series of attempts every year on the anniversary of the stillborn delivery.

The Propaganda Campaign

In attempting to neutralize the protest movements of the Vietnam era, the Bureau relied heavily on its already developed "friendly" press sources and tried to cultivate a more extensive media network to combat the new challenges. In March 1965 FBI offices were requested to compile lists of reliable reporters who could be called on for COINTELPRO work. A memo in response from the Chicago field office listed some twenty-five friendly area sources, including leading newspapers, television, and radio stations; similarly the New Haven, Connecticut, office listed twenty-eight media contacts. But an immorality–drug abuse attack on the New Left was not a resounding media triumph, except in the hinterland where it was redundant. The field agents' planted stories of depravity were too preachy and lurid even for established mainstream urban "cooperative news media," with the result that they were forced to rely increasingly on far right organizations and publications with little or no influence. Red taint charges had a broader market of old standbys, provided they were based on hard information which, given the limited role of communism, was difficult to produce. And even if credible, these did not stir the juices of a post-McCarthy generation of reporters, columnists, and editors. However, some journalists in addition to those moonlighting as paid informers could always be counted on to peddle the Bureau's wares, especially when baited with file information or an assurance of future favors, a trade-off perfected by Cartha DeLoach in the fifties. One such mouthpiece, the editor of the Jackson (Miss.) *Daily News* ("friendly, discreet, reliable and . . . a loyal American"), produced a seven-part series on the New Left based on FBI file material and studded with the Director's pronouncements.[35] (The author had been introduced to Hoover and other FBI worthies by his friend, Senator James Eastland.) The St. Louis *Globe-Democrat* was an equally zealous collaborator to the very end ("especially cooperative with the Bureau . . . its publisher is on the Special Correspondents list"). When its rival, the St. Louis *Post-Dispatch,* in a series of articles on COINTELPROs, documented the fact that the FBI had taken credit for its success in planting stories in the *Globe,* the infuriated *Globe* publisher denounced the charge as a "villainous lie." "We are at a loss to account for the FBI memoranda," he wrote, "unless the explanation is that some overzealous agent sought to advance himself by taking credit for what the *Globe-Democrat* produced in its normal pursuits."

To overcome media apathy, the Director recommended sex and money items as effective lures; it was "immaterial" that the planted story was baseless ("the Bureau feels that the skimming of money is such a sensitive issue that disruption can be accomplished without facts to back it up"). Particularly important media outlets were wooed with tidbits about prominent personalities on the left, such as Jane Fonda, Paul Krassner, Alger Hiss, and David Dellinger.[36] Hoover reviewed the pieces with a sharp eye and did not hesitate to rebuke even the cooperative media for lapses from his fundamentalist political standards.

The entire propaganda attack against the New Left was marked by a klutziness born of ignorance of shifting media concerns, on the one hand, and of the targets on the other. No less than 6000 specially ordered copies of a pamphlet on the New Left, *The Anarcho-Communist Coalition,* published by the right-wing American Security Council, were distributed to individuals and groups who, for the most part, thought it either funny or biased. Jewish intellectuals on the left were mailed copies of a *New York Times* article recording the emergence of anti-Semitism among radicals and of a speech by an obscure Jewish chaplain in support of the war in Vietnam. And one wonders what returns the Bureau expected from its involvement in the production of a booklet critical of the New Left under the sponsorship of the Mississippi American Legion. In support of the project, the Bureau provided the Legion with thirteen articles, including several written by J. Edgar Hoover.

The field agents also made a bid for television and radio support. A Tampa television station was anonymously sent information to aid its preparation of a program on local radical groups. Bureau executives were invited to a showing and gave it their effusive endorsement. At the Bureau's suggestion, copies of the film were made for distribution to church and civic groups. But its greatest conquest was Miami television station WCKT, with which it developed a pattern of collaboration in the production of programs on the National States Rights Party, the Ku Klux Klan, the New Left, and the Nation of Islam (NOI). In describing the collaboration on the NOI film, a thirty-minute production entitled *Fear of the Secret Dark,* the Miami field office gloated that the information had been transmitted to the station "without the Bureau's interest becoming evident," and that "Each and every film segment produced by the station was submitted for our scrutiny to insure that we were satisfied and that nothing was included which could in any way be contrary to our interests." To crown the Bureau's triumph, "This exposé ended with quotations from the Director, with excellent results. . . ."* Another fruitful area of collaboration lay in the station's use of FBI-prepared questions in interviews with radicals. When the Communist Party's presidential candidate was scheduled for an interview, a WCKT representative "offered his cooperation in any way possible, including the handling of any questions which the FBI desired asked." The Miami SAC thereupon requested "authority to furnish an updated and revised list of 44 questions previously furnished by the Bureau calculated to place a communist spokesman on the defensive." As with other co-productions, the grateful station provided the local office with tapes of the program.

The FBI's Boston media allies—such as Gordon Hall, the freelance exposé specialist for radio station WMEX and television station WBZ—were especially cooperative.†[37] The Bureau did not hesitate to use the media to meddle in foreign

---

*This production was presented by WCKT on October 9, 1969, and was the second of two "specials." The first, "Black Nationalists and the New Left," was aired on July 7, 1968. Here too, according to FBI records, "a great deal of work was done by Miami agents." In addition to providing extensive background material, "especially important was the FBI's choice of the individuals to be interviewed, as they did not have the ability to stand up to a professional newsman." The interviewees "seemed to have been chosen either for their inability to articulate or their simpering and stupid appearance," Washington crowed in a memo sent to forty-one field offices praising Miami's work.

†The Bureau regularly ran checks to verify the credentials of media representatives offering cooperation. A reporter would earn bad marks if he had written unfavorably about the war or about the Bureau; on the other hand, a high opinion of the Director was *prima facie* indication of a

policy matters. Bureau agents stationed in American embassies in London and Tokyo were encouraged to plant stories in the local press downgrading the importance of the huge anti-war demonstrations in October 1969. It was suggested that if such articles could not be placed, a suitably deprecatory article should be selected and mailed directly to the North Vietnamese delegation in Paris.[38]

After the formal abandonment of the COINTELPROs in April 1971, the field reverted to the more casual patterns of aggression of earlier years. Thus, in 1975, the Socialist Workers' Party compiled a list of some 229 post-April-'71 incidents of harassment directed against the party and its youth branch, in which agents denounced the group's members to employers, landlords, parents, and associates, characterized the organization as subversive, procured their discharge from jobs, ran informers with destructive assignments, and perpetrated political burglaries and break-ins.[39]

The ease with which punitive, affirmative action can be spun out of the conventional investigative process (even a snitch jacket can be justified as an attempt to protect a Bureau informer in place)[40] leaves little confidence that this mode of intelligence will not flower in a changed climate. Confronted with the need to reverse political and cultural trends that had finally surfaced after years of suppression, the FBI in the sixties significantly altered its style. In discharging its new "responsibility," the agency could no longer rely on a broad mainstream anti-Communist consensus; reduced to a core nativism, the agents became commissars for a besieged Americanist orthodoxy. And in the process the Bureau, repeating a familiar historical pattern, completed a journey from countersubversion to subversion in the most basic definition of the term: it resorted to deception, illegal acts, and suborned violence to destroy its enemies.

---

reporter's reliability. In the case of Boston's WBZ, its then general manager and later vice-president, Lamont Thompson, had been a Bureau agent, and the station's investigative reporter was described as "extremely cooperative, discreet and reliable with this office in the past, not only in regard to counterintelligence activities, but to all other phases of the Bureau's investigative interests." Gordon Hall's credentials were just as lustrous. He had earned his spurs in the fifties as a compiler of dossiers and exposés, and subsequently graduated to the role of talk show host. Hall fell from grace for a brief period and was denied access to inside information when he publicly boasted of his special relationship with the Director.

Media employees also served unknowingly as Bureau sources, as in the case of Clarence McDaniels of Seattle radio station KIXI. McDaniels, the Bureau proudly reported, was twice sent on Wounded Knee assignments without knowing that he was serving the FBI. An internal Bureau dispatch of March 1973 reads in part: "According to UPI, New York, WK [Wounded Knee] Indians will not talk to their correspondent; however they have implicit trust in McDaniels and will talk to him. . . . McDaniels is expected to continue furnishing complete coverage of activities at WK to KIXI by phone and tapes. . . . He is unaware that his stories are not being publicized in full or that the intelligence information and his tapes are being furnished [to] the FBI. KIXI officials request he not be contacted at WK; however, if any specific information is needed by FBI, KIXI is willing to pass on request as normal duty assignment with no reference to FBI. McDaniels will be made available to FBI, Seattle, at [which] time it is hoped all of the Seattle area participants will be identified."

7 Intelligence as a Mode of Governance — The White House

National Security—Meat for Caesar

The Hoover Bureau, we have seen, atavistically transformed its narrow mission as defined in the 1939 Roosevelt directive into the tribal Americanism of the twenties, and in the process the *Volk* ("the American people," "society") was substituted for the presidency as the source of its "responsibility." Nominally under the direction and control of the Attorney General, the President's representative, the Bureau functioned for a generation as though its authority flowed directly from the wellsprings of American nativism. However, the cold war and the worldwide conflict with Soviet communism brought a new emphasis to the role and power of the presidency generally, and a heightened awareness of the executive as *the* source of intelligence power in the political sphere—not merely a label on a chart but a fact of political life. Once intelligence was forced out of the closet of nativist countersubversion and located in the White House, the gaps between its practice and purpose became apparent.

The President's power to authorize political surveillance and related activities against domestic targets is derived from his role under Article II of the Constitution as commander in chief of the armed forces and chief foreign relations representative and spokesman for the nation as a whole. The interest confided to the President's protection, "national security," trenches to the heart of the nation's safety and stability; and only a serious threat such as that posed by the involvement of a foreign country in an attempt to overthrow by violence or replace by conspiracy the country's political structure and institutions can justify the use of this power. In the same way, the President may be called upon to exercise his Article II powers through intelligence initiatives in order to thwart foreign espionage or sabotage on our shores. It was on these grounds that President Roosevelt proceeded in the issuance of the 1939 intelligence directive

and a wiretap authorization in 1940.* But the emergence in the sixties of executive power as the acknowledged source of intelligence did not produce a cognate
limitation on the intelligence function. Far from seeking to discipline or control
the Bureau's targeting overkill and operational abuses, the White House promoted new domestic intelligence agendas for crassly political and partisan purposes. And the new excesses were justified by a grand deception—that they were
required to protect the nation's security from external threats. The "internal
security" formula of the forties and fifties merged into an equally spurious
"national security" justification.

The emergence during the Johnson and Nixon years of the White House
as a prime source of intelligence abuse is ironic. The fifties incubated a cold war
consensus that envisioned a strong executive, a White House that would serve
as the command post of a society mobilized by a liberal élite to meet the external
danger of communism. As "leader of the free world," the United States, inspired
by and unified behind its President, would replace totalitarianism with a *pax
Americana* shaped by a commitment to freedom. This goal required the domestic suppression of the left in the name of freedom. By the mid-fifties, anti-
Communist liberals in droves abandoned the defense of civil liberties, ignored
the FBI's repressive practices, and protested only the "methods" of congressional witch hunters. But the marriage of nativism and liberalism on the altar
of anti-communism—perhaps most clearly seen in the close ties between ACLU
officers and the FBI, described in Chapter 5—was an uneasy one. Those elements of the liberal consensus which were repelled by the crude anti-intellectualism and nationalism of the nativist style as reflected in the operations of the
Bureau and congressional committees became willing auxiliaries of the more
sophisticated Central Intelligence Agency. In contrast to the Bureau, which
viewed liberalism as communism-in-the-soft, the CIA recognized from the outset that liberalism, because of its influence and access to power, was the most
important and effective anti-Communist force in the country. Beginning in the
early fifties, the Agency had little difficulty enlisting the support of scholars,
journalists, youth, labor, church and cultural leaders, writers, missionaries,
scientists, businessmen, political figures, and educators.

As the domestic repression spread, some liberals were embarrassed by the
gap between our professions abroad and our practices at home and by the
domestic growth of the ultra right. But they, too, refused to permit such concerns to distract them from their cold war priorities. Besides, these were temporary difficulties, to be resolved with the election of a strong, all-wise President
who would maintain the consensus without resorting to repression. Sensitive to
the needs of a democratic image, he would curb "populist" anti-Communist
excesses through the sheer prestige of his office and hold the Bureau to more
enlightened practices (not by relaxing vigilance against the left but by requiring

---

*While President Roosevelt knowingly permitted an expansive interpretation of these direc-
tives, he assumed that they were required for defensive counterintelligence purposes alone. In
October 1938, after the conviction of members of a Nazi spy ring, he stated, "We do not need any
secret police in the United States to watch American people, to watch our own people, but we do
need our own people to watch the secret police of certain other nations. . . ."—Joseph P. Lash,
Roosevelt and Churchill (Norton, 1976), p. 139.

the surveillance of the far right as well). The presidency, like the FBI in the forties and fifties, was thus conceived as the keystone of the "right way" to fight communism, an insurance against emergence of a serious domestic challenge on the left *and* a safeguard against a renewal of McCarthyism.

But the protests of the sixties wrecked these fond hopes: far from curbing the Bureau, the White House encouraged its repressive practices and moved from its fifties role of passive approval to active spur until, in the Nixon years, national security intelligence was lifted altogether from its limited protective context to become a Bureau-style "responsibility," that is, a free-floating, moral-sounding pretext for violating law and Constitution. So it was that in President Nixon's speech of May 22, 1973, defending his administration against charges of intelligence abuses, he used the term "national security" twenty-three times and "security" by itself thirteen more times.[1] In a telecast of May 19, 1977, the ex-President, when asked by his British television interviewer whether he had given his approval to an intelligence program that contemplated clearly illegal acts, replied: "Well, when the President does it, that means that it is not illegal." When his interrogator interjected, "By definition," he said, "Exactly. Exactly if the President . . . approves something, approves an action because of a national security, or . . . because of a threat to internal peace and order of significant magnitude, then the President's decision in that instance is one that enables those who carry it out to carry it out without violating a law." When pressed with a suggestion that this rationale would also permit a President to order murder, he replied: "There are degrees, there are nuances which are difficult to explain"; "the dividing line," he went on, was "the President's judgment."*

This grossly exaggerated assertion of executive power made explicit a thesis that has evolved since the Roosevelt era that executive power, unchecked by the Bill of Rights, is all but boundless—especially when exercised in the asserted interest of national security. The exercise of intelligence power in this country has since the forties typically outrun its legitimate purposes in order to handicap and repress political dissent. This decades-long perversion, conducted under the banner of the presidency, was tolerated, encouraged, and unredressed because it reinforced the existing order. And the possibility of protesting these abuses was further reduced because they were perpetrated in secret, and shielded by claims of executive prerogative. Besides, in American public life we almost invariably reduce power conflicts to issues of due process, of individual rights;

---

*In a taped conversation of March 21, 1973, President Nixon and his aides, H. R. Haldeman and John Dean, discussed the problem of how to make a convincing defense of the break-in at the office of Dr. Lewis Fielding, Daniel Ellsberg's psychiatrist. Dean says, "You might put it on a national security ground basis." Haldeman agrees: "It absolutely was." Now the President: "National security. We had to get information for national security grounds. . . . With the bombing thing coming out and everything coming out, the whole thing was national security"—Impeachment Hearings, Transcripts of Eight Recorded Conversations, p. 112.

Four months later in hearings before the Ervin Committee (the "Watergate Hearings"), John D. Ehrlichman, chief domestic adviser to President Nixon and later convicted for his role in the Fielding break-in, testified that he believed the President had the inherent legal authority to order warrantless break-ins in the name of "national security." When asked if that power would include the right to order a murder or other crimes for the same objective, Ehrlichman replied: "I do not know where the line is, Senator." He added that the Fourth Amendment protection against unreasonable search and seizure "has been considerably eroded over the years, has it not?"—Watergate Hearings, Bk 6, pp. 2600–2601.

the one is typically abstract, and the other more accessible because it is specific and "human." Finally, a need for stability, a desperate dependence on institutional order and continuity, makes us reluctant to confront claims of usurpation of power, as though the very recognition of such a possibility would deny meaning to the American experience. But public awareness of the link between executive power and intelligence abuses crystallized in the wake of the Watergate Hearings and the Nixon impeachment proceedings. A more precise measure of the asserted inherent executive power to engage in intelligence activities without legal or constitutional restraint is supplied by the record of electronic eavesdropping of domestic targets undertaken without judicial warrant.

National Security Electronic Eavesdropping

At least since the twenties electronic eavesdropping—the overhearing of conversations by telephone interception or the planting of microphones in a residence or office—has been used as a surveillance weapon in the political arena.[2] In May 1940 President Roosevelt authorized such surveillance subject to the approval of the Attorney General, indicating that it was to be confined to threats posed by political spies and saboteurs. But this limited authorization suffered the same fate as the September 1939 instruction to the FBI already discussed: it was contemporaneously stretched to embrace domestic leftists generally, and its original intended purpose was subsequently obscured by Attorney General Tom Clark, who doctored its language.[3] Beginning in the fifties, "fronts" and alleged supporters of the primary targets were subjected to electronic eavesdropping. Over a thirty-year period thousands of taps and bugs were deployed against individuals and organizations. Perhaps the most revealing measure of the expansion and distortion of the delegation by President Roosevelt of electronic surveillance authority was Attorney General Kennedy's authorization in 1963, in response to repeated requests by the Director, of taps on the home and two office phones of Martin Luther King, Jr.—the core of a network of taps and bugs that ultimately embraced King's advisers, hosts, visitors, and associates, fifteen hotel rooms where he stayed, and, it is claimed, even his pulpit. During the Kennedy years right-wing groups, including the Ku Klux Klan and their leaders, were extensively tapped. In 1964 the *possibility* of Communist infiltration of the Student Non-Violent Coordinating Committee (SNCC) was deemed sufficient to justify a tap. Similarly, the "extremist" justification was used to obtain tap authorizations for a wide range of black targets, including Malcolm X and Elijah Muhammad.

Beginning in the forties, and with minor exceptions, Attorneys General routinely approved FBI requests for authorizations for electronic surveillance under a national security rationale.* In 1954 Attorney General Brownell author-

---

*Attorney General Robert H. Jackson found the Roosevelt order so distasteful that he transmitted all requests to the Director without passing on them—Biddle, *In Brief Authority,* p. 167. In 1950 Attorney General Tom Clark, "in view of his extended absences from the city," gave advance blanket authorization of wiretaps subject to approval on his return—Memorandum of Nov. 10, 1950, in the Director's private "O C" files.

ized "unrestricted use . . . in the national interest" of microphone surveillance even when, as was typically the case, a trespass was involved. This ruling, surely a prize-winning example of executive irresponsibility, was intended to circumvent if not flout a Supreme Court decision condemning as violative of the Fourth Amendment the installation by the police of a microphone in the home of a suspected gambler. Thus ironically until 1965, when Attorney General Katzenbach applied the approval requirement both to taps and bugs, the Bureau enjoyed wholly unsupervised power to install through surreptitious entries the far more intrusive bugs and hence was provided with a ready means of circumventing the authorization requirement for taps.

Despite a directive by President Johnson in 1965 requiring that taps be limited to national security matters as certified by the Attorney General (an attempt to tighten the earlier practice), the Bureau had no difficulty in doing business at the old stand. Indeed, Attorney General Katzenbach reassured Hoover that no new stringency would be invoked to limit the number of national security wiretaps and bugs. Katzenbach not only made no attempt to end the tapping and bugging of Martin Luther King, Jr., but in fact himself approved further microphone surveillances of the black leader. Attorney General Ramsey Clark, however, took a more responsible view and insisted on a rigid definition of "national security." He told a congressional committee that "Every installation approved involved a foreign nation, its embassy, or other office, its personnel or agents or persons allegedly acting directly in the behalf of a foreign nation. . . . I sought to confine the area of approval to international activities directly related to the military security of the United States." On the basis of this standard, he rejected all requests by Hoover for new surveillance authorizations —some on several occasions.* As a result of his stringent policy, Clark succeeded in sharply reducing the number of national security electronic surveillances.

The nationwide network of countersubversive taps continued to expand in the late sixties. Since these installations were secret and for intelligence, not law enforcement, purposes, courts were not called on to rule whether their national security justification was valid. But a point is reached in the intelligence process when, as I have tried to show, the need for sanctions and publicity takes precedence over the secret collection of information, especially when it serves no genuine intelligence purpose. In American intelligence practice, such a prosecutive option has always been considered highly important, and when the Nixon administration took office it became paramount. This goal was, however, blocked by a number of obstacles. After a 1967 Supreme Court decision (the Katz case) condemning warrantless electronic surveillance as an unreasonable search and seizure within the meaning of the Fourth Amendment, Congress passed the Omnibus Crime Control and Safe Streets Act of 1968, authorizing

*The requests Clark rejected included such subjects as Martin Luther King, Jr., Southern Christian Leadership Conference, African-American Heritage Association, Student Non-Violent Coordinating Committee, Stokely Carmichael, H. Rap Brown, Leroy Eldridge Cleaver, Fred Allen Hampton, Black Panther Party, Robert Alfonso Brown, demonstrators at the Democratic National Convention, Students for a Democratic Society, Student Mobilization Committee, Fifth Avenue Peace Parade Committee, Jerry Rubin, National Mobilization Committee to End the War in Viet Nam, and *Liberation* magazine.

federal courts to issue wiretapping warrants at the request of the Attorney General when "there is probable cause for belief that an individual is committing, has committed, or is about to commit" any one of a long list of crimes.

In the Katz case, the Court had specifically reserved for later decision the question "whether safeguards other than prior authorization by a magistrate would satisfy the Fourth Amendment in a situation involving the national security. . . . " and Congress similarly did not resolve the question of whether the President has inherent power to authorize electronic surveillance without obtaining a judicial warrant when the nation's security is threatened. The statute merely stated that nothing in it "shall . . . limit the constitutional power of the President to take such measures as he deems necessary to protect the United States against the overthrow of the Government by force or other unlawful means, or against any other clear and present danger to the structure or existence of the Government." The Court's decision precipitated a problem that had plagued the Department of Justice for a long time: the possibly destructive impact of electronic surveillance on criminal prosecutions.[4] Unless the administration could convince the courts that warrantless wiretapping was not barred by the Fourth Amendment, the road to prosecution of radical and dissenting groups, winding through a thicket of national security surveillances, might be quite risky. This dilemma became even more acute as the result of a Supreme Court decision in March 1969, in the Alderman case, which ruled that in a criminal proceeding the trial court must be notified of any overhearing of the defendant through electronic means. If the court determined that the eavesdropping was illegal, the defendant was entitled to inspect the logs and summaries in question with a view to determining if the illegal overhearings had tainted the evidence in the case. A refusal by the government to disclose the fact of wiretapping or its extent was ground for dismissing the case.

The government was stunned by the decision, and protested that compliance would be highly embarrassing. In a press conference and interviews with reporters, Justice Department spokesmen warned that in a number of cases convictions might have to be overturned and indictments abandoned because the defendants had been overheard over the tapped lines of foreign embassies. The Department of Justice may have been legitimately concerned over the possible airing of surveillance of embassies. But this outcry concealed a deeper fear: the impact of the decision on the prosecution of domestic radicals and dissenters who had themselves been targets of microphone surveillance and wiretaps. If the records of such surveillance were released to the trial court, the entire national security game, with its dubious claims of linkages between domestic targets and foreign principals so substantial as to justify executive intervention, would be exposed. Nor was this idle speculation: the 1967 Supreme Court decision and the Congress in the 1968 statute had indicated that the executive power to authorize warrantless electronic surveillances was limited to the gathering of genuine "foreign intelligence"; that is, information necessary for the conduct of international affairs and the protection of national secrets and installations from foreign spies and saboteurs. Attorney General Mitchell was deeply concerned, and with good reason, that disclosure of countersubversive wiretap records even to a court, let alone to the defendant, would not only jeopardize the prosecution but effectively outlaw the use of electronic surveillance even for intelligence purposes against radicals.

The Justice Department filed a petition for rehearing before the Supreme Court and, in a most extraordinary pressure maneuver, dispatched the Department's information chief to two Supreme Court Justices (Chief Justice Warren Burger and Justice William Brennan, Jr.) with some "highly detailed and highly classified defense information" in support of a plea for reconsideration of the decision. Nor was this all: on the eve of the filing of its petition for rehearing, Attorney General Mitchell appeared before a Senate committee, condemned the Court's decision, and warned that the enforced disclosure of transcripts of countersubversive taps would endanger not only the safety of the nation but the lives of federal agents as well.[5]

After the Supreme Court had rejected the Attorney General's petition, Mitchell made a new bid to break out of the "dismiss or disclose" dilemma in a series of arguments submitted to courts where the tapping issue was under consideration. The "Mitchell Doctrine," as it came to be called, insisted that the President, acting through the Attorney General, has the inherent constitutional power to authorize electronic surveillance without judicial warrant in national security cases and to determine unilaterally whether a given activity threatens the national security. Moreover, Mitchell insisted, this power was exclusive. Application to a court for a warrant would be inappropriate: a court lacked the competence to assess national security dangers and, besides, the risk was too great of leaks of the sensitive matters that would be the subject of warrant applications.

But the foundation of the Mitchell Doctrine was the contention that the President's awesome responsibility for the safety of the nation was all-encompassing; his power to authorize warrantless wiretaps could not be made to turn on the target's foreign ties. If anything, Mitchell insisted, the domestic threat was more exigent than the foreign one. This contention was rejected early in January 1971 by a California court which ruled that the government "cannot approach dissident domestic organizations in the same fashion that it deals with unfriendly powers."[6] The attempt to amalgamate domestic and foreign intelligence was also rejected in a number of other cases, on the ground that warrantless eavesdropping directed against domestic political dissent would reintroduce into our national life the very evil the Fourth Amendment was intended to prevent.

The Attorney General had another string to his bow: the eavesdropping had not been initiated for the purpose of prosecuting the target but was part of an ongoing domestic intelligence investigation. In many cases, the government called the court's attention to the fact that the defendant had been accidentally overheard in the course of intelligence electronic surveillance directed at someone else. In a case in Buffalo, Judge John Curtin noted that this intelligence argument in effect meant that "where a person is only suspected of some kind of, let us assume, subversive activities," he can be the subject of surveillance "for years and years. . . . (I)t appears in intelligence gathering, the government with much less information, with only a touch of suspicion, would be able to conduct long, drawn-out surveillances, merely for the purpose of intelligence gathering, while the warrant procedure would be much more rigidly limited."[7] This position, like the national security contention, seemed to many to be not a reason for withholding the protection of a warrant but rather for insisting on it. In the case of an ordinary criminal investigation to obtain evidence of crime, a defendant could call upon the court to protect himself against electronic surveillance. But where there was no intention to prosecute, the defendant might suffer violation of his rights without ever even learning about it. In addition, in a so-called intelligence investigation, there was no natural terminus of the surveillance, in contrast to a criminal investigation, in which the accumulation of wiretap evidence culminates in a decision either to seek an indictment or to end the investigation. The courts uniformly concluded that such open-ended presidential surveillance would revive the roving commissions and arbitrary searches pursuant to general warrants and writs of assistance that had kindled the struggle for independence from England.

A 1972 decision by the U.S. Supreme Court in the Keith case eliminated altogether the tattered remnants of the Mitchell Doctrine.[8] The Court ruled that intelligence-related wiretapping requires a warrant where "there is no evidence of any involvement, directly or indirectly, of a foreign power." Subsequent lower-court decisions further limited the permissible scope of warrantless taps by insisting on a more rigorous foreign-intelligence standard. In the wake of the Keith case—and in some instances even before the decision was handed down —the administration moved to dismiss indictments in a number of cases rather than disclose wiretap records. In May 1973 the trial judge dismissed the indictment of Daniel Ellsberg, on trial for releasing the Pentagon Papers to the press, on grounds of prosecutorial misconduct which included the failure to inform the court that Ellsberg had been overheard through a telephone tap of the phone of Morton Halperin, a former National Security Council staffer, and the subsequent failure to produce the logs pursuant to the court's direction. This result was richly ironic: the logs had been secreted in a White House safe on the personal orders of the President, specifically to protect the Ellsberg prosecution from legal attack. Eight years later, Halperin's claim for damages against President Nixon for warrantless wiretapping was upheld against a contention that the President was immune to civil damage suits. The Federal Court of Appeals for the District of Columbia, reversing a lower-court ruling, held that "The President is the elected chief executive of our government, not an omniscient leader cloaked in mystical powers."

Leakers and Plumbers

The Halperin tap was one of seventeen taps on government officials and newsmen authorized by the Nixon administration ("the Kissinger taps") and maintained over a twenty-month period beginning in May 1969. These were not traditional countersubversive surveillance but rather leak-plugging efforts.*

---

*Ironically, the Kissinger-taps story became the subject of a musical-chairs-style series of leaks by FBI sources engaged in an internecine struggle for power after the Director's death. In February 1973 an official (thought to be William C. Sullivan) leaked the story of the Kissinger taps—

Such taps, installed at White House initiative, allegedly for defensive "security" purposes to detect leaks of "classified information," had been a hallmark of the Roosevelt administration: President Roosevelt felt no hesitation in ordering the tapping of the home telephones of White House aides whom he suspected of leaking war-related secrets.*

The Kennedy administration initiated such security wiretap requests on two newsmen, Hanson Baldwin of the *New York Times,* along with his secretary, and Lloyd Warner of *Newsweek.* (In addition, it requested electronic surveillance in connection with an investigation of Dominican sugar lobbyists that included the bugging of the hotel room of a congressman.) Another media target (in 1965) was Frank Capell, editor of an anti-Communist newsletter, and his attorney, suspected of leaks of classified information.†

Electronic surveillance of U.S. citizens to trace leaks of classified information became a priority of the Nixon administration, and leaks to newsmen a mania:[9] in addition to four reporters included in the seventeen Kissinger taps, columnist Joseph Kraft was briefly tapped in Washington; while in Europe his Paris hotel room was bugged under the supervision of William C. Sullivan. The Washington tap, however, was an installation not by the FBI but by Nixon's Plumbers. In the Vietnam era the release of secret information by officeholders served as a channel of bureaucratic protest both against government policies and against the secrecy with which they were formulated. The spread of opposition to the war and the increasingly adverse role of the press institutionalized the anonymous press leaks by government insiders, a contemporary *trahison des clercs.* And ready access to copying machines gave the practice a new, documentary dimension.[10] The monitoring and prevention of leaks quickly became an intelligence concern entrusted to a specially created unit, the Plumbers (so-called because of their leak-plugging mission, although in intelligence vernacular "plumber" is a term used to characterize an inept, bungling operative). The

themselves a leak-plugging enterprise—to *Time* magazine. In his confirmation hearings shortly thereafter, Acting Director L. Patrick Gray III denied that he had known about the taps prior to the publication of the *Time* story. Top secret documents indicating that he did know were then leaked to a *New York Times* reporter. After publication of a news story based on these documents, the Watergate special prosecutor began an investigation to verify a third leak, that the source of the leak to the *New York Times* was Mark W. Felt, the second-highest-ranking Bureau official, before his resignation in May 1973 as a move in an internal power struggle. Felt denied these charges, as well as broader allegations that he was "Deep Throat," the prime source of Watergate secrets for the Washington *Post*'s investigative reporters Robert Woodward and Carl Bernstein.

*In at least one case, that of Thomas C. Corcoran, a tap was continued by the Truman White House until May 1948 because of its purely political value.

†The taps, requested by the Director, may well have been a pretext to protect him from embarrassment. In 1963 Hoover had engaged in correspondence with Capell, an ardent admirer. Subsequently, Capell wrote to Hoover about his researches into alleged improprieties by Attorney General Robert F. Kennedy, confident that the Director shared his low opinion of the Kennedys. Capell's labors resulted in the scandalous and *farouche The Strange Death of Marilyn Monroe,* published in 1964 and linking Attorney General Kennedy with the film actress. The next year, shortly before Hoover requested authorization for the taps, Capell published *Treason Is the Reason,* incorporating material from his newsletter dealing with the alleged subversive background of members of the Kennedy administration, including Adam Yarmolinsky, its reputed candidate to succeed the Director, and reproducing an earlier signed letter from Hoover. This was bad enough —the Director was not infrequently embarrassed by his far right devotees—but much of the material in Capell's book of dossiers suggested a Bureau source.

Plumbers were an intelligence unit with a classic three-tiered structure: operations (G. Gordon Liddy and E. Howard Hunt, Jr.), control agents (Egil Krogh and David Young), and White House supervision (John Ehrlichman).

The significance of the Plumbers unit has too often been misunderstood. For the first time in American history a chief executive organized an intelligence capability answerable only to himself and operating outside the legal-constitutional system, not only for the purpose of passive information-gathering but to develop aggressive means of injuring and neutralizing targets. The potential for Caesarism, the utility of such an operation as a spearhead for a pretorian coup, is self-evident. Nothing more clearly substantiates this appraisal than the attack on Daniel Ellsberg.[11] Initiated on White House instructions in a plan to discredit Ellsberg as a foreign agent, Project Ellsberg quickly embraced a variety of aggressive tactics, including:

> The burglary of the office of Dr. Lewis Fielding, Ellsberg's psychiatrist; pressure to block an investigation by the Justice Department of the Fielding burglary and the concealment from the Ellsberg trial court of the facts about the Fielding burglary;
>
> The use of the CIA to supply psychological profiles, disguises, and similar amenities;
>
> The organized attempt to assault Ellsberg on the Capitol steps on May 19, 1972;
>
> A campaign to influence the outcome of the Ellsberg trial, first by the dissemination of derogatory matter about Ellsberg and then by offering Judge Byrne, the trial judge, the directorship of the FBI.

The frenzied search-and-destroy quality that characterized Project Ellsberg also marked the Plumbers' attack on newspaper columnist Jack Anderson and his suspected sources.[12] In the fall of 1970 White House sleuth Jack Caulfield verified the suspicion that Anderson had accurate sources in high places and recommended that the way to plug leaks to Anderson was to identify and fire his source wherever found. But Haldeman insisted on sterner measures—criminal prosecution; however, attempts to bring criminal charges against a suspected Anderson source (an obscure Pentagon clerk) and Anderson's associate, Les Whitten, both fizzled.

White House rage over the publication in July 1971 of information in an Anderson column about the SALT talks was in turn topped by its response to Anderson's publication—in a series of columns beginning on December 13, 1971 —of documentary material from top secret National Security Council (NSC) sources dealing with the India-Pakistani war. The get-Anderson campaign resulted in aggressive attacks designed to destroy his credibility: physical surveillance of his movements, the tapping of the phones of his suspected sources, the illegal seizure of the records of his telephone calls, a year-long tax audit by the Internal Revenue Service, the deployment of CIA agents for round-the-clock surveillance of his house and of the movements of his reporters, and the search of FBI files for blackmail material. The Pentagon, according to ex-Pentagon investigator W. Donald Stewart, authorized at least eleven investigations on its own of Anderson and his sources. David Young, the master Plumber, asked

Stewart to develop bogus evidence that Anderson was a homosexual. When Stewart refused, Young shouted: "Damn it! Damn it! The President is jumping up and down and he wants this and we're always telling him everything can't be done." As the frustration increased, the proposed tactics to get Anderson grew wilder, culminating in a suggestion attributed to Charles Colson that Anderson could be discredited by drugging him so that he would babble incoherently on his live radio program. Hunt and Liddy, the two operational Plumbers, met with a retired CIA physician to discuss the project. After a conference exploring three possible ways of drugging Anderson—including rubbing the steering wheel of his car with a drug that would enter his body through his skin —the plan was abandoned as unworkable.

The Plumbers' investigation of Anderson's source for his Pakistani war story ultimately took a bizarre turn when in 1972 it uncovered evidence that a Navy yeoman, Charles E. Radford, collected top secret "eyes only" information on national security for transmission not to Anderson but to a trio of admirals. The saga of this leak in high places was itself revealed in 1974 as the result of a series of leaks to *New York Times* investigative reporter Seymour M. Hersh.[13] Radford, a court stenographer, was assigned in September 1970 to the White House office of the Joint Chiefs of Staff (JCS), set up to maintain liaison with the National Security Council headed by Dr. Henry A. Kissinger. After the Plumbers worked Radford over for three weeks, he persisted in his denial that he had spied for Anderson, but admitted that he had transmitted, via two admirals to Joint Chief of Staff Admiral Thomas H. Moorer, top secret and highly sensitive information not intended to be viewed by the Pentagon.*

Radford later told a Senate committee (in 1974) that he was specifically instructed to take "anything I could get my hands on," and that his spying activities won high praise. Radford explained that military duty obligated him to obey his superiors despite fleeting doubts of the propriety of what he was

*When Radford testified behind closed Senate doors, he told the senators that his interrogators had cursed him and that Stewart "told me, did I know that I could do a long prison sentence for this . . . and he called Jack Anderson and his kind sons of bitches and bastards and he was very profane. . . . He told me," continued the yeoman, "that did I not know that three of my Army buddies had been killed the day before . . . in Vietnam . . . because of what I had done. . . . He used a lot of other words, just the whole list of gutter language."

"Were they intermingling polygraph tests with these threats and intimidations against you?" he was asked.

"Yes. I was on the machine, and then I went back in the other room and talked to [them], and then I came back on the machine."

"Did they use the rubber hose on you?"

"No," said Radford, "but I would not have been surprised. He was pretty angry. He was almost hysterical. . . ."

"Were you physically threatened in any way?" a senator asked.

"No, he did not lay his hands on me in any way," Radford replied. "He pounded the desk. He made motions like he would leap across the desk at me at any moment. But he did not touch me in any way. He did not physically harm me."

"Then you would be threatened this way and then you would be taken for a polygraph examination?"

"Yes, sir. As I recall, that is how it happened."

"And you were in a highly emotional state?"

"Yes, sir. I was rather upset. . . .," Radford said. "After I broke down that is when they let me go home. That is when it ended after I told them I was passing information from [the White House] to the Pentagon, then they stopped. Then they let me go home."

doing. The admirals denied the whole business and suggested that it was all invented to divert attention from Radford's "treason," the claimed Anderson leak. But their denials made no sense at all in view of their admitted receipt of the pilfered material. As a *New York Times* editorial writer noted, "Such things do not happen except in musical comedies about life in the military. Enlisted men do not take it upon themselves to embark on unauthorized missions against the White House. Nor are they likely to drop in on admirals with secret booty."[14] Radford's home telephone was tapped and on the basis of identification gleaned from the logs, additional taps were placed on the home phones of two of Radford's friends.

The charges against the yeoman were abandoned for insufficient evidence, and Radford himself was exiled to a post in Oregon, where taps were installed first in the home of his stepfather with whom he stayed temporarily and then in his new residence. In addition, coverage was initiated at the training center where Radford worked. The tap on his residence was not terminated until June 20, 1972, one day after the Supreme Court's decision in the Keith case. The President later, in an attempt to justify his cover-up of the Plumbers' activities, referred to the affair as a matter of extraordinary sensitivity involving "information of interest to other nations."

But if the Radford matter was indeed so sensitive, why was no action taken against Admiral Moorer? A tenable explanation is that it would have been embarrassing, if not worse, to charge the nation's supreme military leader with stealing secrets relating to vital civilian concerns at a time when the administration was placing its entire weight behind the Ellsberg prosecution. But Ellsberg and Anderson are linked more tightly. In both cases, the embers of hidden grudges were pumped to flame by an enormous bellows: the secret power to take reprisal and to escape responsibility on national security grounds.

The organization of the Plumbers reflected the Nixon administration's disgust with the Bureau's lack of responsiveness to its intelligence needs. In a sense, this frustration began in the Johnson years with the recruitment by the White House of the Bureau's countersubversive intelligence resources. While the Director was permitted to continue on his own course, for the first time the demands of the President played an important role in determining the Bureau's investigative priorities.

The White House Takeover

President Johnson, well acquainted with the Director and a former neighbor of his, had no compunction about demanding countersubversive intelligence products for use in buttressing his policies.[15] The anti-war movement was especially troublesome, and he impressed the Director personally with a need for ammunition to silence congressional doubts. To this end he commissioned the SDS investigation (complete with electronic eavesdropping) already referred to. A strong priority was information that could be used in the right places to discredit the anti-war movement as subversively inspired without exposing him to the charge that he was reverting to McCarthyist tactics. He pressed the

Director for evaluative material, reports on trends for use in bolstering the Communist influence theme; but none of the reports was made public, since they said little more than that the Communists had participated in anti-war meetings and demonstrations and that they wanted to influence policy. The President, instead, dispatched Bureau functionaries to the Hill to impart to congressional leaders, in off-the-record briefings, exaggerated accounts of Communist involvement in the peace movement.

Like President Roosevelt before him, Johnson commissioned the Bureau to check the files of individuals who, by letter or telegram, opposed his foreign policy. In March 1966 Johnson requested the Bureau to develop dossiers on legislators and prominent citizens who opposed the Vietnam War. These reports, submitted on a bimonthly basis, also included material derived from wiretaps of foreign embassies. LBJ was particularly interested in what Senator J. William Fulbright, chairman of the Foreign Relations Committee, had to say to the Russian ambassador. Johnson also assigned the Bureau to monitor the Fulbright Committee televised hearings on the Vietnam War in order to prepare memoranda comparing Fulbright's statement and positions with "the Communist Party line." A notable Johnson initiative in the abuse of the Bureau's functions was the conversion of the name check—a practice used in the investigation of applicants for government employment—into a perquisite of executive power. He requested such checks and reports on all persons employed in Senator Goldwater's office during the 1964 campaign; on seven newsmen, including David Brinkley and John Chancellor of NBC, Peter Arnett of the Associated Press, and columnist Joseph Kraft; and on Kennedy holdovers suspected of disloyalty. (LBJ wanted no record made of this request. The file also indicates that the Bureau refused a request for a wiretapping device in one case.)

On White House instructions, the Bureau conducted penetrative surveillance and compiled dossiers on critics of the Warren Commission Report, which even contained references and photographs dealing with the subjects' sex lives. Certain that a Republican plot had resulted in discrediting his aide Walter Jenkins, Johnson ordered an investigation of Jenkins's arrest in the fall of 1964 in an incident involving homosexuality. On another front, ghetto unrest, it was again the fear of a Republican plot that led Johnson to commission the Bureau, in the summer of 1964, to report on the causes of urban riots. Similarly, the suspicion of a plot by Robert Kennedy and others involved in the investigation of Bobby Baker, his former senatorial aide, prompted a requested Bureau investigation with the caution that he wanted no record made of the request. Convinced that Kennedy and his associates had organized the investigation to ensure Baker's conviction and his own downfall, Johnson became incensed because the head of the Criminal Division of the Department of Justice had arranged to have a witness "wired" in the Baker investigation. The Bureau, which had declined the wiring job for security reasons, was in turn instructed to probe those who had in fact undertaken to do so. Johnson's political fears also resulted in instructions to wiretap Mrs. Anna Chennault (the "Dragon Lady," a Republican concerned with Asian affairs) and to check the telephone toll-call records of vice-presidential candidate Spiro Agnew to determine whether he had communicated with Mrs. Chennault or the South Vietnamese

Embassy on a specified date. This assignment, too, was the product of a suspicion of a conspiracy—this time to sabotage the current peace negotiations by persuading the South Vietnamese to stall until a Nixon victory, which would give them a favorable bargaining position.

Almost without exception, all of these assignments were channeled through and directed by LBJ's personal Bureau representative, Cartha Dekle ("Deke") DeLoach.* LBJ had a private line installed from the White House to DeLoach's bedroom and showered him with assignments, typically demanding that no record be made of them. If Sullivan was the moody intellectual, DeLoach, a Georgia backwoods product with limited education, was the extroverted wheeler-dealer. After taking over the Crime Records Division in 1959, he developed a highly successful network of relationships with the media; his duties also covered, less openly, liaison with Congress. DeLoach's blend of confidence-sharing, Southern "poor boy" humility, and fundamentalist piety ingratiated him with an important constituency on the Hill. And to help out with the unpersuaded, he made effective use of the Bureau's secret files on legislators and their relatives which, in contrast to the officially acknowledged "public record" Congressional Relations Service (see above, p. 116), included private accusations and gossip.†

DeLoach was also the Bureau's voice in the American Legion; he ascended to the post of national vice-commander and, more important, public relations chairman. While his dealings with the press and Congress called for a low-keyed pragmatic style, he learned how to sound the full ideological register when the occasion called for it. In 1968 the Freedoms Foundation, the super-patriotic steward of the American way of life funded by the far right sector of corporate enterprise, honored DeLoach for one of his speeches defending America "for her refusal to become a welfare state. . . ."

DeLoach's congressional liaison duties had brought him together with Senator Lyndon Johnson, and when the senator became President, DeLoach came to enjoy an intimacy with the chief executive unmatched before or since by any FBI official. He had begun as a protégé of the Director's; now the President had taken him under his wing. But he remained the Director's obedient servant. In 1963 when the Director was involved in one of his endless feuds —this time with Supreme Court Justice Warren's Commission investigating the assassination of John F. Kennedy—he used DeLoach as his emissary to Gerald

*The Bureau also undertook investigative chores against LBJ's enemies on its own initiative. The Director assumed with good reason that LBJ was as unforgiving toward his critics as the Director himself, and without White House instructions ordered investigations of LBJ critics. A notable example is the case of Barbara Garson, author of the satirical play *MacBird*, who was investigated and personally denounced by the Director in a public statement.

†A former Bureau agent recalled in congressional testimony the following colloquy between DeLoach and a member of a group of Bureau agents who had returned to Washington for a refresher course: "Somebody asked him, 'What do we use all this memorandum stuff we put in about things we see—what do you do with it?' DeLoach said, 'You fellows have been in the Bureau for more than 10 years, so I guess I can talk to you off the record.' He said, 'The other night we picked up a situation where this Senator was seen drunk, in a hit-and-run accident, and some good-looking broad was with him.' He said, 'We got the information, reported it in a memorandum,' and DeLoach —and this is an exact quote—he said, 'By noon of the next day the good Senator was aware that we had the information and we never had any trouble with him on appropriations since' "—Pike Hearings, Pt. 3, p. 1068.

R. Ford, his secret ally on the Commission. Ford assured DeLoach "that he would keep [him] thoroughly advised as to the activities of the commission on a confidential basis." When, in recognition of his growing power and influence, he was promoted in 1965 to Assistant Director in charge of all investigative services, DeLoach retained his crime record public relations responsibilities. These enlarged Bureau powers enabled him to execute his White House assignments more efficiently, and at the same time ensured a favorable reception in lobbying on the Director's behalf: DeLoach was, for example, commissioned by the Director to obtain LBJ's approval of pocketing a $75,000 fee from Warner Brothers for the film rights of *Masters of Deceit.* Similarly, it was DeLoach who at the Director's request peddled the King transcripts and Sullivan memos to a receptive LBJ and his aides—Walter Jenkins and Bill Moyers. They apparently agreed with the Director that, to quote a DeLoach memo, "The FBI could perform a good service to the country if this matter could somehow be given to members of the press."[16] (LBJ listened to the tapes with gusto, and Moyers, overruling an earlier prohibition by RFK, approved the distribution throughout the executive department of Sullivan's memo, based in part on hotel room overhearings.)*

DeLoach earned the Director's gratitude by orchestrating his duel with Robert F. Kennedy in 1966 over responsibility for the tapping and bugging of Las Vegas casino operators, a campaign that included drafting a letter of inquiry from a congressman as well as the answer for insertion in the *Congressional Record.* Similarly, DeLoach played a role in a Bureau plan to milk the investigation and capture of the assassin James Earl Ray in June 1968 for its maximum publicity value by bypassing the Attorney General. On the day of Ray's capture, DeLoach arranged for the issuance of a self-congratulatory press release in defiance of departmental regulations requiring clearance by the Attorney General and captured the media headlines at the time of the funeral of Robert F. Kennedy.

Perhaps DeLoach's most extraordinary service to the Bureau was his successful neutralization of a threat of an investigation headed by Senator Edward V. Long of Missouri into Bureau wiretap practices. In 1966 he worked out a deal in which, solely on the basis of assurances that Bureau wiretapping was confined to "the most important and serious crimes either affecting the internal security of the nation or involving heinous threat to human life," the committee agreed to clear the Bureau of all charges of impropriety. In exchange, Long was to

---

*LBJ's callousness, if not actual malice, about the King eavesdropping, despite his professed opposition to the practice, was inspired by the fact that King was identified with the Kennedys. In November 1964 Ben Bradlee, then *Newsweek*'s Washington bureau chief, reported to Acting Attorney General Katzenbach that DeLoach had offered to play the King tapes for one of his reporters. Katzenbach testified before the Church Committee that he was so shocked that together with Burke Marshall, then retiring head of the Civil Rights Division, he flew to LBJ's ranch to protest. But it happened that Bradlee, the source of the charge, was a JFK intimate. DeLoach could hardly have hoped for a more vulnerable accuser. According to DeLoach's memo to the files of Dec. 1, 1964, the President expressed displeasure over Bradlee's condemnation of the Bureau's electronic invasion of King's private life. DeLoach's memo adds that the President wished to alert the Bureau not to trust Bradlee. It continues: "Moyers also stated that the President felt that Bradlee lacked integrity and was certainly no lover of the Johnson Administration or the FBI. I told Moyers that was certainly obvious."

receive a letter signed by the Director anointing the investigation. DeLoach subsequently upped the price and received a requested commitment that the senator "would in no way embarrass the FBI" in the future. But Long and his staff were unhappy; why couldn't the Bureau furnish a witness to testify in public along the lines of the private assurance? DeLoach refused: such a "token witness" would invite more criticism from the Bureau's media enemies than the bare statement. (It should be recalled that the King eavesdropping was, by this time, well known to the press.) DeLoach also vetoed an alternative proposal by the committee's counsel to call a former agent to the witness stand. Having received full payment, the Director on January 20, 1966, pronounced his promised blessing, a letter hailing "the close examination," "exhaustive studies," and "penetrative inquiry marked by complete objectivity and fairness," which persuaded the committee's chairman and staff to clear the Bureau.

DeLoach was still worried about media leaks, but he had insurance against such a double-cross: detailed, tabbed dossiers on the personal lives of the senator and his committee colleagues (which undoubtedly had contributed to silencing the probe in the first place). In the spring of 1967 the committee opened hearings on a wiretap bill. The Bureau rose to the occasion: in May Life magazine published an article by one of the Bureau's "leak men" stating that Long had received $48,000 in referral fees from a lawyer in St. Louis for the Teamsters Union and its president, James R. Hoffa, as a concealed bribe to prevent or reverse Hoffa's conviction on criminal charges. The hearings were effectively discredited and as the storm broke around Long he dusted off the Director's letter of January 20, 1966; surely, he told his colleagues, "Director J. Edgar Hoover is a more competent authority than Life magazine." But the Bureau giveth and the Bureau taketh away. Long's comprehensive wiretap bill was shelved in favor of a more limited measure and shepherded to final passage in 1968 by another subcommittee. By that time, Long's Senate career was over.*

DeLoach's labors on behalf of the Bureau in the Long affair were matched by his services to the Johnson White House. In 1964, in response to a White House request, a team of twenty-seven Bureau agents under DeLoach's direction descended on the Democratic Convention site in Atlantic City, and from August 22 to August 28 meshed the entire convention proceeding in a web of surveillance that included the installation of a tap in Dr. King's hotel room and a bug (presumably by means of a surreptitious entry) in a store-front headquarters of civil rights leaders who had come to Atlantic City in substantial numbers to participate in the convention proceedings and pre-convention negotiations on a civil rights resolution.[17] In addition, information was obtained by the interception of a two-way radio communication between convention staffers, by agents posing as reporters and by briefings of friendly NBC newsmen. A network of

---

*On August 9, 1968, Life published an exposé of the involvement of Congressman Cornelius E. Gallagher with organized crime that could only have been derived from FBI wiretaps. Gallagher was subsequently convicted on tax evasion charges. Was it merely a coincidence that he had chaired a House investigation beginning in 1965 that was a counterpart to the Long investigation? Tongsun Park, the South Korean rice dealer, testified in 1978 that he paid Gallagher a total of $221,000 between 1970 and 1975, the largest payment made to any congressman—"Park Tells Hearing of $850,000 in Gifts," New York Times, April 4, 1978. The Bureau was careful for obvious reasons to avoid involvement in investigations of such congressional law violations.

informers, some brought in (including a number of plants in the Mississippi Freedom Democratic Party) and others recruited *in situ,* channeled reports to a central control room, where summaries of overheard conversations were also processed. The entire intelligence product was in turn telephoned to the White House over a special direct line.

The purpose of the surveillance is no longer in dispute: LBJ was concerned with pre-convention developments within the Democratic Party, particularly with the activities of Robert F. Kennedy, his paranoiacally feared rival; the controversy over the seating of a Mississippi black delegation; and the threat to his domination by civil rights groups, among whom Robert Kennedy had strong support. But DeLoach insisted, both to the Watergate Committee and more fully to the Church panel, that the purpose of the entire operation was to develop intelligence about planned demonstrations and violence and to protect the person of the President. The targets were such highly respected leaders as King, James Farmer (then national director of CORE and later a Nixon administration appointee), Bayard Rustin, and the beloved Mississippi activist, the late Fannie Lou Hamer. While DeLoach denied the claim by the local Atlantic City Bureau chief that the Secret Service—the agency primarily concerned with the protection of the President—had not been kept informed, he was unable to deny the fact that the operation was concealed from Attorney General Robert F. Kennedy. Indeed, though he kept RFK in the dark about the entire operation, understandably enough in view of its purpose, he seriously claimed there was no need for further clearance even for the installation of wiretaps. RFK's authorization of the previous year was, he insisted, carte blanche! (Although conversations of King and various legislators were overheard and reported back to the White House, the record is unclear as to whether RFK—the asserted source of the eavesdropping authority—was himself overheard.) The store-front office bugging was justified by the Bureau on the suggested ground that "an apparent member" of the Communist Party was becoming active in the civil rights group.[18] Despite the claim that violence prevention was the sole purpose of the surveillance, the reports deal far more extensively with pre-convention maneuvers and pressures than with threats of disruption, let alone injury, to the President. And in fact, the convention itself was viewed as a model of pre-programmed smoothness, a tribute, most observers at the time wrote, to the President's advance knowledge of what was unfolding behind the scene. De-Loach insisted on the ritualized defense that had served the Bureau in good stead over the years: the Bureau was not a political agency; it was engaged in a purely investigative activity, which did not even involve surveillance. But his own self-congratulatory contemporaneous report boasts that "we were able to keep the White House fully apprised of all major developments during the convention's course,"[19] and a special investigation by the Bureau itself at the request of the Church Committee referred to the recollection of a special agent involved in the project that DeLoach sought to impress Jenkins and Moyers "with the Bureau's ability to develop information that would be of interest to them." In response to Moyers's congratulations on the success of his mission, DeLoach wrote that he was glad that his "vital tidbits" had been helpful to the White House. Indeed, the entire affair produced bouquets for everyone in sight:

DeLoach's final report proposed letters of recommendation for the twenty-seven squad members and three others. The Director added that DeLoach himself had earned a meritorious award, and the President had Jenkins call Hoover to congratulate him on "one of the finest [jobs] the President had ever seen."

DeLoach denied to the Watergate investigators in 1973 that he had spoken directly to LBJ, but he was contradicted by the Atlantic City SAC, who recalled hearing conversations between DeLoach and LBJ. Before the Church panel, DeLoach hedged his denial with "to the best of my knowledge," but insisted that he did not even have a direct line to the White House. But his final report states: "I kept Jenkins and (Bill) Moyers constantly advised by telephone of minute-by-minute developments," and telephone company records confirm that such a direct line was, in fact, installed.[20] Similarly, he insisted to a senatorial interrogator that he had refused to comply with LBJ's request for name checks on Goldwater staff members, "not because of the fact that we did not have information in the Bureau's files but simply because the Bureau did not desire to be involved in such a request." The record shows that of the fifteen requested name checks, the Bureau returned reports on two of the individuals involved and advised Moyers, the source of the requests, that there was no derogatory information on the others.[21]

DeLoach's services further enhanced his qualifications as the White House candidate for the Director's job. But in the Director's power-centered scripture, one could not serve two masters, even (especially!) if the other was the President himself. Although DeLoach tried to appease the Director by diverting kudos to him, he failed because he had won LBJ's favor. His emergence as official heir-apparent was in itself sufficient to haunt the Director's dreams of unending power. DeLoach's popularity in high places became in the Director's moralizing rhetoric proof of his "disloyalty." Recognizing the indefiniteness of his future —the Director made a point of boasting that he had never felt better—DeLoach in mid-1970 accepted a post as an executive in Pepsico Corporation offered to him by Nixon backer and financial angel Donald Kendall.[22] By accepting the offer, he became for the second time guilty of "disloyalty." But a final service helped heal the breach: he responded to the Director's pleas to intervene with Attorney General Mitchell to reject the Huston Plan (discussed below).

Yet for all the Bureau's submission to White House control, it could not meet the Johnson administration's basic need: a countersubversive intelligence product sufficiently persuasive to discredit the anti-war movement. To begin with, the Bureau lacked the resources to produce an impressive report, a document that would link opposition to the war to subversion. But this was not the major problem; the thesis that such opposition was inspired by domestic communism would be inherently unconvincing and backlash into charges of McCarthyism. The administration was thus directly confronted with the dilemma latent in the liberal blueprint for *pax Americana:* how to use executive power to suppress domestic opposition to foreign policy and at the same time escape the stigma of anti-libertarianism. The most promising means of resolving this dilemma was the time-tested charge of foreign sponsorship and funding, not via the almost visibly decrepit domestic Communist movement but by "foreign powers" with designs on our security. If accepted by mainstream constituencies,[23] this charge could justify a defensive counterintelligence response on national security grounds, making it possible to portray the anti-war movement as a treasonous conspiracy and its surveillance as a form of foreign intelligence-gathering peculiarly within the President's stewardship and immune from the requirements of the Fourth Amendment to the Constitution.

The Futile Quest for Evidence of Foreign Influence

Despite the Bureau's shortcomings, the Johnson administration pressed it hard for evidence of a connection between domestic anti-war protest and foreign sponsors. The Bureau strove to please: its informers and ghetto plants were instructed to give high priority to evidence of foreign influence, travel, and funding. But little or nothing could be produced and, indeed, the Bureau's intelligence brass became convinced privately that none existed. Yet they could hardly be expected to put professionalism over ideology and thus condemn the very ground on which the Bureau's entire anti-subversive edifice had been constructed. Much less could such an alarming conclusion be contributed to President Johnson or the Congress. The administration turned to the CIA for help: CIA Director Richard Helms subsequently recalled that President Johnson was "after us all the time" to produce evidence of foreign involvement in the domestic peace movement; "this was something that came up almost daily and weekly."[24] The desperation of this quest for such evidence—it led in the summer of 1967 to the CIA's full-fledged domestic intelligence mission discussed below—is reflected in the administration's readiness to ignore a statutory ban on CIA domestic security functions, and to risk further embarrassment in the wake of the disclosures about secret CIA funding of domestic groups that had rocked the country. The President ordered a ban on such subsidies and appointed an investigatory commission, which made recommendations at the end of March, subsequently adopted by the White House, prohibiting covert CIA financial support of a comprehensive spectrum of organizations. But this scandal, far from discouraging the administration, seems to have whetted its appetite for access to CIA resources for prohibited domestic intelligence projects.

The White House demand for usable intelligence material intensified with the announcement of a planned demonstration on October 21, 1967, at the Pentagon by peace groups from all over the country. An initial pre-demonstration CIA memorandum provided no useful evidence of foreign involvement, and immediately after the demonstration Justice Department spokesmen told the press that there was no evidence of foreign influence. Nevertheless, a week later President Johnson confided to Republican leaders, in a private White House briefing, that he did have evidence of such influence. Johnson was a master of the whispered confidence, the off-the-record confab. The would-be critic is so flattered by being let in on a portentous secret that he swallows his objections. But this time the master stumbled: when pressed by one of the conferees, LBJ agreed to release the supporting evidence. The next day White House officials refused to make the promised disclosure. Attorney General Clark visited the office of one of the White House conferees, minority leader Gerald R. Ford, and according to Ford, urged him not to press for the release of the evidence.[25] President Johnson once again turned to the CIA to obtain the evidence which he had claimed was already in his possession and which the CIA had been unable to supply him. On November 15, 1967, Helms submitted a report concluding that there was no substantial proof of foreign involvement. (Two succeeding studies, the last sent to the White House on January 5, 1968—"part of our continuing investigation of this general subject matter"—confirmed and expanded these initial findings.)

After the November 15 report, and despite its negative conclusions, administration spokesmen continued to beat the foreign-influence drums.* Thus, in a speech on November 20 in Atlanta, majority leader Carl Albert charged that the Pentagon demonstration had been "basically organized by international Communism." And Dean Rusk made the same charges but refused to release the claimed documentation on the ground that it would refuel the fires of McCarthyism. So the administration dutifully played its assigned role in the liberal consensus script: through invented proof it stigmatized the anti-war protest movement as subversive, and at the same time struck a blow for "freedom"—by withholding the nonexistent proof.

LBJ applied direct pressure on Helms to produce a usable intelligence product. In closed-door testimony before a House committee in March 1975, Helms testified that the demands from Johnson at one point became so great he secretly taped the President's instructions as a guide to what was needed. But the role of Walt Whitman Rostow, National Security Council staff chief and LBJ's national security adviser, cannot be ignored. Rostow not only strongly influenced White House intelligence planning but served as liaison to the intelligence community, including the CIA.† One could hardly find a better exemplar of the liberal élite, whose influence on the Johnson war policies has been well documented. A legatee of the European Socialist-Menshevik tradition,‡ as deep-fibered and culture-bound as Hoover's nativism, Rostow had served an intelligence apprenticeship as a major in the OSS. His brilliant postwar career reached a plateau with a professorship at Massachusetts Institute of Technology, where

---

*U.S. News and World Report published in its Nov. 13, 1967, issue a sensational story with a London dateline based on "Western intelligence sources" that "Russia is plotting, guiding and helping to finance anti-American and anti-war demonstrations throughout the world" in order to force the United States out of Vietnam and blacken its reputation. The circulation of this story at the very time when the White House was desperate for such "evidence" could hardly, in the author's opinion, have been a coincidence.

†A revealing indication of Rostow's role as CIA liaison is reflected in a secret report by Helms dated Sept. 1, 1967, to Rostow and John A. Gardner, Secretary of Health, Education and Welfare. The report dealt with the activities of the National Student Association after the CIA's subsidies to the group were terminated in the wake of the exposé discussed above. Helms wrote to Rostow: "I am not distributing it, except to you and John Gardner, because the agency should not be reporting at all on domestic affairs of this sort. I simply make this exception because I thought you would be personally interested."

‡His father, Victor Rostow, a proud adherent of the Second (Socialist) International, had expressed his political convictions in the naming of two of his three sons—one of them after the poet of democracy, Walt Whitman, and the other after America's Socialist folk hero, Eugene Victor Debs.

he became a leading and "witting" figure in a CIA front (it was subsidized by the CIA and headed by a former CIA official), the Center for International Studies. In 1953 he collaborated in a CIA-funded book, *The Dynamics of Soviet Society,* primarily for the use of the intelligence community. In 1960 he joined President Kennedy's "best and brightest," and after a brief stint in the White House transferred to the State Department. Ironically, his European social-democratic brand of anti-communism aroused deep suspicions among the fundamentalists charged with his security clearance, a resistance overcome finally by White House pressure. In April 1966 Rostow returned to the White House at LBJ's request and quickly entered the Johnson inner circle. "I've never had a man in whom I have more confidence than Walt," the President declared in the fall of 1967.[26] Rostow's hard-line counsels were characteristically laced with libertarianism: the triumph of our arms in Vietnam was the best hope of defeating totalitarianism worldwide.

In September 1968 Helms transmitted to President Johnson, pursuant to an earlier White House request, a report on youth and student movements, with particular stress on foreign Communist influence and sponsorship.[27] The report ("Restless Youth") stated quite plainly that "International Communism has not been able to employ its student/youth to channel dissent in support of its objectives. . . ." and indicated further that European Communist parties were also suffering headaches over the radicalization of youth. Helms conveyed his disappointment over the failure of CIA researchers to meet White House needs. "I fear," he said in his suave prose, "that we may be lacking that precision of information which would make a more positive report possible." Helms had a suggestion for more satisfactory results: why not authorize the Bureau to operate on a less restricted basis in monitoring U.S. radicals and use "more advanced investigative techniques"? In view of the fact that the report contained a section on SDS's activities in the United States, Helms felt constrained to alert the White House to its "peculiar sensitivity."[28]

The Quest Grows More Desperate

Anti-war, ghetto, and campus unrest panicked the incoming Nixon administration into a siege mentality almost from the day it took over. Nixon was haunted by the fate of Johnson, ambushed by what seemed to be the revolt of an entire generation. Those long years of powerlessness, of wandering in the wilderness, was it all to be for naught? Were the country's unruly dissenters to be allowed to frustrate his too-long-delayed entry into the promised land? But how to contain them; how to make credible the claims of an endangered national security? The President requested a top-level briefing on the domestic peace movement's foreign support, influence, and funding. Helms transmitted the "Restless Youth" report in February to Dr. Henry Kissinger, then the foreign intelligence czar, along with an expression of his readiness to brief President Nixon on the subject. He expanded his original "peculiar sensitivity" caveat. "This is an area not within the charter of this Agency, so I need not emphasize how extremely sensitive this makes the paper. Should anyone learn of its existence, it would prove most embarrassing for all concerned." Two months later Nixon assigned John Ehrlichman to assemble the views of the chiefs of the domestic intelligence community's component agencies on the extent to which foreign influence or support contributed to campus demonstrations. Ehrlichman and subsequently the President rejected the ensuing, uniformly negative reports, insisting that more penetrative techniques would produce the missing proof. The frustrations of the Johnson administration in this area had simply resulted in a "Go back and look again" response and in the quest for other institutional assistance, but a demand for broader and more intensive coverage became a refrain of the Nixon era.[29]

In June, Ehrlichman assigned the newly recruited White House staffer Tom Charles Huston to develop a carefully researched report from all intelligence sources on the link between domestic unrest and foreign revolutionary movements. Huston was a logical choice: a lawyer and former national head of the conservative Young Americans for Freedom (YAF), he had served in military intelligence and, at least equally important, he alone of the White House staffers knew something about the politics of the New Left. At a White House briefing he was pointedly told by the President that intelligence concerning "foreign influences and financing of the New Left" had the highest priority.[30] After consulting Sullivan, Huston sent a memorandum to the CIA, FBI, the National Security Agency, and the Defense Intelligence Agency pleading for a helpful response to White House intelligence needs: " 'Support' should be liberally construed to include all activities by foreign communists," not only to "assist" but to "encourage" domestic revolutionary protest movements. The President, Huston added, also wanted to know all about the adequacy of the resources available to monitor foreign-connected protest. The CIA's answer, submitted on June 30, 1969, was bleak: the available evidence showed "only a very limited amount of foreign communist assistance" to domestic protest movements, a conclusion that was repeated in two subsequent updates. The contrast in the Bureau's response, both in tone and conclusion, illuminates an important difference between the two agencies. Unlike the CIA, it shrank from bringing the king bad tidings and tried to accentuate the positive: there was still ground for concern about the Menace, the potential effectiveness of hostile (Communist) foreign intelligence services in snaring U.S. youth and the likelihood that the new movements, already boldly and openly participating in international conferences, would in the future develop into "hard-core revolutionary elements." Once this transformation occurred, "increasingly closer links between these movements and foreign Communists" could be expected.

Hardly headline stuff. The reasons for the Bureau's dusty answer seemed clear enough both to Huston and to the CIA and NSA chiefs. Indeed, it was hinted at in the report itself, which contrasts the "strong reliance" on "live informants" and "physical surveillance" with the "highly selective and limited use of electronic coverage." The Bureau's inability to produce evaluations in support of White House needs thus created pressures for the more expanded use of illegal techniques, which could colorably be justified only by proof of the very foreign linkages sought to be established. Nor, for the reasons already suggested, could the Bureau escape this dilemma by undercutting the White House "foreign influence" thesis altogether. Instead, it strove harder to deliver the goods. In November 1969, citing what he called "recurring allegations," the Director dispatched a field alert concerning the financing of movement groups by individual "angels" or tax-exempt foundations. The financial sources of revolutionary groups were the subject of a special White House request and Bureau report in February of 1970. With the exception of a section dealing with the Communist Party, withheld from publication on security grounds, the Bureau's report concerning the funding of twelve such groups indicated that income was uniformly derived from dues, sales of publication, or donations. Almost all of the groups reported on were chronically in financial straits. A few weeks later the Director once more ordered a field survey of funding, calling attention to the "high level interest in the financial aspects of revolutionary activity."[31]

But there is a heads-I-win-tails-you-lose quality in a charge of secret influence: the failure to find evidence can be used to confirm the effectiveness of the deception and the inadequacy of the investigation. Huston's initial views on the Bureau's shortcomings were strengthened by his association with Sullivan, a classic example of the bureaucratic defector in search of an ally—in this case on behalf of a more vigorous intelligence attack on the new dissenters through bolder Bureau operations, especially taps, bugs, and break-ins, as well as a greater interagency coordination. Huston, who saw himself as a potential domestic intelligence czar but who altogether lacked experience, found in Sullivan's grievances a ready-made agenda for Bureau reform. In the past, both the administration and the Attorney General had tiptoed around the aging lion, but now he was being prodded by whippersnappers (he called Huston a "hippie intellectual") to perform in ways that were risky and status-threatening.

There was another dimension to the problem: other intelligence agencies, long unhappy about the Bureau's obsolete priorities and methods, began to voice complaints. As early as 1967, the National Security Agency (NSA) had tried unsuccessfully to persuade Hoover to expand his collection techniques.[32] As we have seen, in 1968 Helms delicately tried to push the Bureau into the use (or revival) of more effective methods. After the Pentagon demonstration in November 1969, both the CIA and the NSA renewed their demands for more penetrative Bureau coverage. It seems apparent that the pressures on the Bureau from other intelligence components were, at least in part, a way of diverting White House heat for proof of foreign influence: a repetition on an institutional level of a familiar intelligence buck-passing process in which a control officer defends himself to a dissatisfied superior by blaming the field operative.

The Huston Plan

The pressures for change intensified when, early in 1970, the Director broke off entirely a deteriorating relationship with the CIA over its refusal to identify a Bureau agent who had furnished the CIA with information concerning the whereabouts of one of its contacts, Thomas Riha, a university professor. By May the Director, to demonstrate his impartiality, had terminated liaison arrangements with all other intelligence agencies except the White House. It was grotesquely poor timing; in the spring of 1970 the country shook with escalating violence and bombing. March saw the explosion of a bomb assembly operation in a Greenwich Village townhouse, followed in early May by campus demonstrations protesting the Cambodian invasion.

The White House reaction was predictable. In mid-March President Nixon told the Congress that the bombings were the work of "young criminals posturing as romantic revolutionaries." In April one of his advisers told the press: "It wouldn't make a lot of difference if the war and racism ended overnight. We're dealing with the criminal mind, with people who have snapped for some reason." A key official in the administration added: "We are facing the most severe internal security threat this country has seen since the depression." He said that the President had "expressed distress that the intelligence system was not capable of pinpointing the activities of these people," and insisted that there was a desperate need to improve government intelligence. One White House aide proclaimed: "The greatest safeguard for the rights of individuals is to have good information on what (the radical fringes) are doing." He urged that the government substitute, for traditional criminal prosecutions, the collection of information to "prevent the perpetration of an act of violence."[33]

The scene was set for basic alterations in intelligence structure, coverage, and operations under direct White House control. The significance of this decision becomes plain when we recall that centralized political police systems, answerable only to the head of state, have historically emerged in response to the release of powerful movements for change beyond the control of conventional police units.* The demand for structural coherence, brought to a head by the Director's pique, is rooted in the history of the domestic intelligence system. From the very inception of the Bureau's intelligence mission in 1939, intelligence institutional structures were highly diffused; federal, state, and urban intelligence was served by a variety of wholly uncoordinated units. The Bureau dominated the federal intelligence sector because of its vast operational resources, appropriations, and manpower. But even here other agencies developed an autonomous investigative capability and jealously guarded their jurisdictional turf. On the state and urban levels the situation was particularly chaotic; the Bureau, largely because of the egomania of its Director, had not developed fruitful liaison arrangements with urban anti-subversive police units, which increasingly, as the sixties unrolled, were locked in front-line combat with anti-war, campus, and ghetto activists and demonstrators. This balkanized domestic system contrasted with the more integrated foreign intelligence community. But it was this diffused institutional condition and relatively low profile that had permitted the system to survive and flourish beyond the reach of democratic control and libertarian restraint. Coordination and centralized control would, inevitably, expand the range of the targets and sharpen the techniques for dealing with them. Spontaneous pressures for coordination had already, as we have seen, made an impact on the traditional go-it-alone Bureau intelligence posture. The administration's frenzied response to the turbulence of the time

---

*One need only recall Sidmouth's England, Fouché's France, and the European continent after 1848.

placed the large-scale restructuring of intelligence on the agenda for immediate action, despite the obvious pitfalls.

On June 5, 1970, Nixon personally initiated a project to draft recommendations for improved domestic intelligence coverage at the White House. In addition to the President, the Oval Office conferees included H. R. Haldeman, White House chief of staff; John Ehrlichman, then domestic counselor to Nixon; Huston and the chiefs of four intelligence agencies—J. Edgar Hoover; Admiral Noel Gayler, director of the National Security Agency; Lieutenant General Donald V. Bennett, director of the Defense Intelligence Agency (DIA); and Richard Helms, director of the CIA. The President set the tone for the new effort in a talking paper that touched all of the familiar intelligence bases: Thousands of young Americans are agitating the citizenry and exploiting legitimate grievances for their own sinister political ends and in behalf of foreign principals. "They are reaching out for the support—ideological and otherwise —of foreign powers and they are developing their own brand of indigenous revolutionary activism which is as dangerous as anything they could import from Cuba, China or the Soviet Union." The Interagency Committee on Intelligence (Ad Hoc) as it was formally called (referred to here as ICI) was all too aware of what was expected. The threat evaluation section of the committee report played assorted changes on the foreign influence theme, beginning with the observation that the Communists are a "distinct threat to the internal security because of extremely close ties and total commitment to the Soviet Union." Besides, there are many "thousands of people in the United States who are Marxists and agree with the basic objectives of the Communist Party, although they do not identify themselves specifically with the organization." Despite the fact that "there is little likelihood that the Party will instigate civil disorders and use terrorist tactics in the foreseeable future," continued surveillance is imperative. At one fell swoop the absence of a threat of violence is brushed aside and the scope of surveillance broadened to include Marxists of every hue and commitment.

The same foreign influence theme and variations dominate the discussion of New Left groups: "These individuals must be considered to have potential for recruitment and participation in foreign-directed intelligence activities." As for black militants: "BPP (Black Panther Party) relies heavily on foreign Communist ideology to shape its goals. . . . The Marxist oriented philosophy of the BPP presents a favorable environment for support of the Panthers from other Communist countries." Similarly,

> although there is no hard evidence indicating that the black extremist movement is substantially controlled or directed by foreign elements, there is a marked potential for foreign-directed intelligence or subversive activity among black extremist leaders and organizations. These groups are highly susceptible to exploitation by hostile foreign intelligence services. . . . Communist intelligence services are capable of using their personnel, facilities and ancient assets to work in the black extremist field. The Soviet and Cuban services have major capabilities available.[34]

The recommendations of the ICI, the handiwork of Sullivan, included domestic electronic surveillance of "individuals and groups in the United States who pose a major threat to the internal security," and of "foreign nationals ... of interest to the intelligence community"; official support of the interception of communications of citizens of this country using international facilities; covert mail coverage (the opening of sealed materials for delivery); surreptitious entry; an increase in the number of "campus sources"; and an expansion of the Army's domestic counterintelligence mission (although not the domestic use of military intelligence agents).

The Huston recommendations were ultimately rejected because of the Director's opposition. Hoover had thought, or preferred to think, that the President wanted his ripe seigneurial views on the Menace ("a historical overview of the problem of revolutionary violence," as Huston put it). But he was left with the bleak realization that the report reflected on the effectiveness of the Bureau's intelligence services. The ICI proposal to transfer operational coordination, allocation of resources, and evaluation to a new White House unit would block his direct access to the President, a prerogative doggedly developed and defended for over thirty years. These objections could hardly be voiced openly; instead, Hoover fell back on the claim that the risks of exposure were intolerable. It has been argued (by Huston) that the Director had no personal principled objection to tactics such as mail opening, burglary, and wiretapping; yet his fear of a backlash cannot be questioned. Helms and Admiral Gayler were outraged at the Director's failure to respond to the needs of the hour. But Hoover was chained to the past in more ways than one. His critics had not been burnt as he had by the Palmer Raids and the subsequent outcry. Nor had they been required, pursuant to a Supreme Court order in the Black case in 1966, to account for break-in-related microphone surveillances, abandoned by an Attorney General (Ramsey Clark), and confronted by a congressional investigation (the Long Committee) as in the Johnson years.* Another Palmer Raid scandal might bar him from the American Pantheon and even erase his name from the majestic portals of the new Bureau headquarters building. These reservations were quickened by the resentment, endemic to field functions, of the operative or informer who senses that he is being used, exposed to all the risks—almost literally "holding the bag"—while others claim credit.

The ICI's report was organized around a series of options from which Huston extracted the most draconian (and illegal) alternatives as recommendations to the President. These proposals were ratified by the President in mid-July and a week later were incorporated into the document later known as the Huston Plan. For the first time in our history a chief executive had expressly authorized a political police structure with a range of powers in conflict not only with established law but with the provisions of the Fourth Amendment as well. And what seems quite clear is that neither Huston nor the intelligence brass gave any thought even to the fact that they had authorized the commission of crimes —either because the participants thought it irrelevant altogether or inapplicable to targets who, in their view, served foreign interests. Huston himself justified the entire enterprise after the fact as a laudable attempt to avoid a repressive

---

*His ban on "black bag" break-ins in December 1966 reflected the Director's sensitivity to these pressures. And his fear of exposure was ultimately vindicated by the May 1971 dissemination of the Media documents.

rightist blacklash by using the professionalism of intelligence to forestall potential leftist violence. Huston also felt confident—or so he claimed later—that the
use of informers, mail opening, and bugging could enable local authorities to
close in on would-be bombers, a view which, if sincerely held at the time, is
questionable. The Bureau's army of informers had failed to uncover bomb plots
(except those which they had instigated or provoked) and would-be bombers are
hardly likely to confide their intentions to the mail or discuss them over the
telephone. As for the lawlessness of the recommended techniques, the President,
Huston thought, was immune from such legal and constitutional restraints.

The President did not think the Huston Plan was all that extraordinary. In
response to a Church Committee question, he said: "My approval was based
largely on the fact that the procedures were consistent with those employed by
prior administrations and had been found to be effective." As to the plan's
overkill (the President himself noted that the plan contemplated the "use of CIA
informants within the United States"), the President embraced the Loki defense.* There was no way, he explained to the Church Committee, to ascertain
the extent of Communist influence on terrorism and premeditated violence
without comprehensive surveillance directed at legitimate dissent: "unfortunately, the tools available to get at the one while avoiding the other were not
as delicate as the surgeon's scalpel."

On July 23, the approved plan was dispatched to the four intelligence chiefs
as the White House charter. It did not escape the notice of some that this
document was signed not by the President, or even by Haldeman or Ehrlichman,
but by the young and lowly Huston, suggesting in the language of a DIA staffer
that the higher-ups "didn't have the guts" to sign themselves.[35] As Sullivan
recalled, the Director "went through the ceiling," and immediately successfully
appealed to Attorney General Mitchell (already sympathetic since he had not
been consulted) to have the plan revoked. Its termination on July 27 made little
if any difference operationally: the agencies represented on the ICI concealed
from each other that they were already engaging in some of the practices for
which approval was sought—and continued to do so (in some cases on an
expanded basis), despite the withholding of approval.

The intelligence chiefs (with the exception of Hoover) viewed the plan as
a trade: in exchange for the legitimation of their activities by the executive and
access to the Bureau's operational capability, they would deliver the goods—
evidence of foreign influence and funding. To the White House, the goods were
worth almost any price. As for the Director, he lost no time in repairing the
damage to his White House relationship and overcoming the threat to his
precarious tenure. To complete the record, he assured Attorney General Mitchell that he had no objection to the implementation of the plan by other agencies,
a meaningless gesture since only the Bureau had the necessary operational
capability. Moreover, he told Mitchell, "the FBI is prepared to implement the
instructions of the White House at your direction," provided he received specific
authorization for each assignment. But this was calculated naïveté: as the Direc-

*Loki, the Norse god of mischief, condemned by a judgment of his peers to lose his head, foiled
the executioner by insisting that his neck be left untouched.

tor well knew, what the White House wanted was a kamikaze operation at the field level, which would permit a plausible denial in the event of exposure.

But he also took more positive steps. On July 27, 1970, the very day that Hoover transmitted his counterproposal to the Attorney General, the White House requested wiretap summaries of embassy taps, like those previously furnished President Johnson. Two days later the Bureau sent over the logs of three years of conversations—from June 1, 1967, through July 1970—a gesture that won the Director warm thanks. Among other services, the Bureau provided Vice-President Agnew with public record material on Reverend Ralph Abernathy, the head of the Southern Christian Leadership Conference, requested over the telephone, in order, as the Vice-President put it, "to start destroying Abernathy's credibility"; circulated a blind compilation of public record material attacking one of Daniel Ellsberg's lawyers; and probed with great zeal the background of a Harvard professor who had attacked the qualifications of Nixon's Supreme Court nominees. In the early fall of 1970 the Bureau responded more positively to the Huston recommendations. It enormously expanded informer quotas, lowered the requirement for informers from twenty-one years of age to eighteen in accordance with an earlier recommendation of the Huston panel, ordered the field to infiltrate black groups "on a continuing basis," and sanctioned new surveillance techniques. In addition, all SDS members were placed under surveillance, and an enlarged coverage program for youth and student groups agreed on that contemplated the opening of over 10,000 new cases.[36]

But the Director's efforts did not heal the White House breach resulting from the Huston affair. Certainly there was nothing personal separating him from the White House: the President honored Hoover as an ally in his own past triumphs and as an icon of the America for which he considered himself a spokesman. More than this, the Director was the President's kind of man; the bond between them was symbolized by their common antipathy to CIA's Richard Helms. This suave and evasive patrician irritated and frustrated the President, while the semi-literate Hoover was enraged by the "Ph.D. intelligence," as he derisively referred to it, that his Agency practiced, and jealous of his power. But the Director had simply outlived his usefulness; he had become a human fossil who, like many of his species, endlessly relived an invented past. One could listen just so long to Hoover's recitals of bygone conquests of John Dillinger or Ma Barker, or to his endless ramblings about the Menace and how he had wrestled with it. Sentiment could not halt the march of progress: nativism was outmoded both as a social control and as a power-centered operational style.[37] Unable to fire the Director, the Nixonites yearned for his speedy departure and the politically lucrative canonization that was bound to follow.

The CIA—At Home Abroad

Presidential irritation with Helms (both Johnson's and Nixon's) resulted from his Agency's unwelcome conclusions and reports, not from a lack of zeal in the collection of information. Its resources must have seemed well suited to the needs of the hour. If there was a foreign dimension to domestic unrest, the

CIA specializing in foreign intelligence could surely dig out the proof; and it could present it in usable forms since evaluation was its prime intelligence function. Besides, it ran little or no risk of courtroom or congressional exposure, had virtually unlimited funds, ample manpower, and an extensive cloak-and-dagger repertory ("cutouts," "safehouses," "fronts," "proprietaries") to ensure operational secrecy. But there was one obstacle: the National Security Act of 1947, the CIA's charter, had confined it to the collection of intelligence abroad and explicitly barred it from "police, subpoena or law-enforcement powers or internal security functions." It is plain from the legislative history of this enactment that, with the exception of the overt public collection from willing sources of information about foreign matters, Congress intended to ban *all* domestic intelligence-related activities, leaving the Agency free, of course, to maintain a headquarters and to train personnel. This statutory prohibition was not wholly a reflection of libertarian fears; it was also a prime demand of Hoover's congressional supporters. Unable to resist the cold war pressure for a new permanent foreign intelligence agency, despite the Director's opposition, they made certain that the Director's turf would be respected.

The CIA from the beginning viewed this prohibition as a sort of public relations placebo and, on another plane, as an intelligence problem to be solved by deceptive intelligence techniques. Thus, despite the outcry in 1967 over its use of domestic organizations as conduits or proxies for its overseas operations, the CIA deputy director for plans, Richard Bissell, told a closed-door seminar in 1968 that, "if the agency is to be effective, it will have to make use of private institutions on an expanding scale, though those relations which have 'blown' cannot be resurrected. . . . We need to operate under deeper cover, with increased attention to the use of 'cutouts.' . . ."

In this spirit that it was above the law, the CIA involved itself in a variety of ways, sampled in the footnote below, on the domestic scene—not in response to special assignments or requests by hierarchical superiors but on its own, in autonomous implementation of its intelligence functions.* These earlier pro-

---

*The 1967 press disclosures and subsequent congressional investigations and documents released under the Freedom of Information and Privacy Acts (FOIPA) and lawsuits have revealed a long train of CIA involvements in American life, including the following:

Between 1952 and 1966 the National Student Association (NSA) received an estimated $3,-300,000 in funding from the CIA which, during certain years, amounted to as much as 80 percent of NSA's entire budget. This subvention resulted in the cooperation of "witting" NSA officials and representatives who influenced the policies of the organization in directions favored by the Agency. In addition the CIA provided, through a variety of foundation conduits, funds for a considerable number of labor, business, church, university, and cultural groups. A minimal estimate of $12,-442,925 was secretly channeled to these groups by the CIA.

The anti-Communist and highly influential Congress for Cultural Freedom, a private group of intellectuals, writers, and artists, from 1950 to 1966 received over $1 million in secret subsidies from the CIA. Through the AFL-CIO's American Institute for Free Labor Development and other domestic labor organizations operating in the international sphere, the Agency supported anti-Communist labor unions and officers in Europe, Africa, and South America.

From 1949 through 1972 the agency used the United States, in particular its academic institutions, prisons, mental hospitals, medical and research facilities, as a laboratory for testing its "sources and methods." Studies were commissioned at an estimated cost of $25 million on mind-control and brain-washing experiments, using drug-induced behavior modification, electrode implant and sensory deprivation procedures—sometimes without the knowledge of the subjects and frequently without their "informed consent." In one project, LSD subjects were recruited from bars

grams largely (but not entirely) avoided domestic surveillance and related activities, and were justified as ancillary to the Agency's foreign mission. But prodding from the Johnson and Nixon administrations led to the expansion of some domestic initiatives and to ambitious new programs, implemented by intrusive surveillance techniques, that completely nullified the statutory ban.

The first product of this collaboration was Operation CHAOS, which emerged in August 1967 in response to intensified demands from the Johnson White House to uncover foreign influence behind domestic unrest. Authorized by CIA chief Richard Helms, conceived and justified as a defensive counterintelligence project,* it was supervised by counterintelligence chief James J. Angleton and headed by his deputy, Richard Ober, who had already begun a similar operation complete with a computerized array of files developed in connection with an investigation of the *Ramparts* exposé of the CIA's funding of the National Student Association.[38] (Ober has replaced the FBI's Mark Felt as a suspect for the role of Deep Throat, the secret source of the disclosures of Washington *Post* reporters Woodward and Bernstein.)

All domestic intelligence agencies become, for reasons already suggested, willing victims of what might be called the "collage syndrome"—the develop-

---

and lured to plush hotels for sexual behavior studies with prostitutes while under the influence of the hallucinogen. Researchers watched through two-way mirrors. In 1977 the CIA notified eighty academic institutions that, during the fifties and sixties, they had been involved in some way in mind-control research.

In the late sixties and early seventies recruitment and other university-related activities also led to considerable CIA campus involvement with both students and faculty. In addition to monitoring the politics of students in connection with obstruction of recruitment (discussed below) and of faculty members under consideration for grants, overseas "tasking," the CIA maintained confidential relationships with professors and administrators for recruitment purposes, and used covert allies and agents to identify and recommend for employment or other relationships campus-based prospects who were then investigated.

Beginning before 1950 over a period of twenty-five years a large number of American journalists abroad, including correspondents for the *New York Times,* CBS News, *Time* magazine, and many other organizations, served as conduits for planted CIA stories, shared information with the CIA, and in some cases provided operational assistance. A number of journalists, full-time correspondents for general-circulation news organizations, functioned as undercover contacts and were paid on a regular basis, in some instances with the full knowledge of their employers. About twenty-five part-time journalists—freelancers and stringers—were employed by the Agency on a regular salaried basis. In addition, major news organizations such as the *New York Times* allowed CIA employees to pose as clerks or part-time correspondents and provided cover for others at the Agency's request. Propaganda and "disinformation" disseminated abroad through the CIA's worldwide network of news services was unwittingly reprinted as bona fide news by U.S. newspapers. Through a project initiated on April 1, 1967, the Agency directed its "propaganda assets" in the field to take actions to discredit critics of the Warren Commission Report on the Kennedy assassination through book reviews and feature articles, not only attacking their conclusions but suggesting that they were subversively motivated. Material was transmitted that included excerpts from countersubversive files about the authors of books challenging the Report's conclusion.

The Agency subsidized a publishing house to issue books in support of its intelligence mission and established in 1950, through a grant of $300,000 to the Massachusetts Institute of Technology, the Center for International Studies, which turned out books both for public distribution and in a more confidential version for dissemination in intelligence circles. This program, funded by substantial grants, continued until 1966. But it was only a small part of a huge (allegedly still continuing) propaganda effort that has resulted in the production or subsidization of more than 1,250 books, concealing the identity of the sponsor or author or both.

*By placing CHAOS in a counterintelligence structure, Helms tried to ensure not only that it would not be known on the outside but also, since Angleton's operation was highly secretive and compartmented, within the Agency—Colby, p. 318.

ment of a data base beyond the scope of their mission or functional needs. Operation CHAOS was no exception. Between 1967 and 1973 Operation CHAOS had amassed some 10,000 files on individuals and over 100 domestic groups, some of which ran to several volumes. In addition, a computerized index system (HYDRA) permitted prompt retrieval of over 300,000 references, with few exceptions, to American citizens and organizations. The organizational targets included: Students for a Democratic Society (SDS); Women's Strike for Peace (WSP); Young Workers Liberation League (YWLL); Student Non-Violent Coordinating Committee (SNCC); Nation of Islam (NOI); Youth International Party (YIP); the women's liberation movement; the Black Panther Party (BPP); the Cuban Venceremos Brigade; and Clergy and Laymen Concerned about Vietnam.

The files on individuals for the most part reflect intelligence concern with domestic dissenters, many of them well known in public life. Typically but not uniformly, the triggering mechanism for the surveillance and file compilation was foreign-related activity. Former Congresswoman Bella Abzug became a file subject beginning in 1953 as the result of the interception and opening of her mail to the Soviet Union in connection with her work as an attorney. Her subsequent anti-war activity with no special foreign aspect was routinely monitored. In the same way, three other members of Congress active in opposition to the war became file subjects. A file was opened on the black entertainer Eartha Kitt, which recorded personal details of her early life, the fact that at the age of twenty she had performed with a group said to be headed by a "sponsor or endorser of a number of communist front activities," and that she had signed an advertisement in support of Dr. Martin Luther King, Jr.'s, civil rights drive in the South along with a number of persons, some of whom had been "identified in the past with a Communist party." But the CIA justified the accumulation of this information and the file itself on the ground that she had become involved overseas with individuals in whom the CIA was interested. A claimed concern with foreign contacts was frequently not merely strained but manifestly contrived, as in the targeting of Supreme Court Justice William O. Douglas, Representative Claude Pepper of Florida, former Representative Cornelius E. Gallagher of New Jersey, and the late Senator Edward V. Long of Missouri. Douglas became a CIA subject in the mid-sixties after he visited the Dominican Republic; contacts with the same country also served as the reason for the Gallagher surveillance. In the case of Senator Long, an alleged involvement with foreign companies triggered the investigation,* while then-Senator Claude Pepper's relations with Cuban refugees invited the CIA's interest.

Operation CHAOS was fed by other CIA domestic intelligence programs such as the Agency's Domestic Contact Service (DCS). Organized to collect foreign intelligence information on an open basis from Americans through the Agency's field offices, it was used as a conduit for information about the foreign involvement of domestic dissidents and also as a channel for background material without foreign implications. In addition, a quite separate intelligence system, based on a "security" justification, also generated information about do-

---

*The CIA also compiled a dossier on Bernard Fensterwald, who had been Senator Long's aide in charge of his committee's investigation of wiretapping and bugging.

mestic targets. Here there was no assertion of a foreign influence rationale; the predicate was the protection of the CIA's personnel and installations and, beyond this, of "intelligence sources and methods from unauthorized disclosure." The quoted phrase had been included in the CIA's 1947 grant of authority in order to authorize it to take measures necessary to secure intelligence secrets, but was converted into a pretext for evading the internal security functions ban as well as the prohibition against engaging in law enforcement activities. Under this authority, the Agency's Office of Security conducted special "security" investigations on the most tenuous grounds of a wide range of targets, including many not employed by the Agency, which were implemented by such techniques as wiretapping, intensive physical surveillance, mail covers, examination of tax data, unauthorized entry, and mail opening. Security was used as a warrant for wiretapping domestic journalists and for targeting columnist Jack Anderson, an intensive surveillance effort undertaken by CIA operatives on behalf of the Plumbers through Howard Osborn, head of the Office of Security and CIA liaison to the Plumbers.

But the Office of Security's primary concern was with political activists on the left. Beginning in 1950, only three years after the 1947 enactment, the Agency began to develop campus contacts to protect its recruiters from harassment and possible violence. In February 1967, in response to a request by CIA top brass, the Office of Security conducted a survey of left groups that might in the future become sources of opposition to recruitment activity by CIA representatives.

The close of that year saw the birth of Project Resistance, which was charged with the collection of material on student protest activities generally that might result in hazards not only for the CIA but for recruiters of all government agencies. A second phase of the program predictably developed in the fall of 1968 when a Targets Analysis Branch was set up to process the information pouring in from the field as well as from FBI reports. From an initial campus focus, the Targets Analysis Branch quickly expanded to include assessments of protest movements and demonstrations, first in the Washington area, then in other centers, along with a file and index system. In addition to reports on specific targets requested by other components of the Office of Security, the project produced weekly Situation Reports analyzing current events and presenting a calendar of demonstrations and meetings.

Resistance was considered a success. An Agency report dated January 15, 1970, "Operational Support for Recruitment," states:

> The field offices responded extremely well. They used existing contacts at the various colleges, developed new informants and came up with information that could indicate that they attended some of the dissident meetings. They developed files on the universities and colleges, came to know all the campus security people, special units in the local and state police as well as other knowledgeable people not further identified.

The report also indicates that the Agency's field offices developed direct liaison with the FBI at local levels and even ran their own informers.* Resistance

---

*A Church committee study (Book III, p. 723), relying on data submitted to the Rockefeller Commission, concludes that the project developed an estimated 600–700 files and indexed some

remained in being until mid-1973, when its major functions in the Washington area were taken over by the more ambitious Project Merrimac—an early warning operation supposedly designed to alert the Office of Security to threats to CIA facilities by Washington area groups. By the fall of 1967 this initial self-protective impulse could no longer be traced in the project's surveillance activities against such targets as Women's Strike for Peace, the Washington Peace Center, the Congress of Racial Equality, and the Student Non-Violent Coordinating Committee. All four groups were surveilled and infiltrated not because they threatened CIA facilities or engaged in violent tactics but on the ground that they were "indicator" organizations, that is, bellwethers of possible future violence.* By August 1968 this initial grouping had expanded to ten and the coverage became more intensive. Infiltrators were required to supply information about planned demonstrations, as well as finances, sources of support, associations with other groups, and what was said and resolved at meetings.

Another anti-radical operation launched in 1964 did not trouble about even a strained justification for its surveillance. Controlled by the Domestic Operations Division, it concentrated on urban areas marked by vigorous protest movements, especially anti-war activities, and deployed a wide variety of intelligence techniques including wiretapping, photography, informers, and break-ins. One agent recalled that the CIA had supplied him with more than forty psychological profiles of political activists during his service. According to this same source, a four-year veteran of surveillance activity in New York, more than twenty-five agents were assigned to monitor anti-war activity by the fall of 1968 in New York City alone.†

12,000–16,000 names. But subsequent CIA file releases indicate that this estimate is far too low: no less than 50,000 names were indexed of members of the California Peace and Freedom Party alone, and a substantial number of its key leaders were subjects of dossiers.

*Women's Strike for Peace (WSP) was formed in 1961 by a group of American women opposed to the Vietnam War. Because of its peace aims, it was considered a tool of a foreign principal and thus a CHAOS subject under a "counterintelligence" rationale. But it was metamorphosed into a "security" subject, a potential source of violence against CIA personnel and facilities, when Project Merrimac was launched with a security mission. This transformation reflected no change in policy, simply the fact that WSP's Washington-based headquarters made it a convenient Merrimac target. Surveillance of the organization commenced in 1962. Five years later, it was penetrated by a CIA informer who attended meetings, photographed demonstrators, and confiscated the organization's records and lists. Even after the infiltration was terminated at the end of 1968, the surveillance continued until 1971. As the CIA's file swelled with accumulated leaflets, announcements, newsletters, and identifications of members and leaders, no attempt was made to evaluate the surveillance in the light of either the physical security or counterintelligence rationales. In February 1967 it was disclosed that a CIA cover organization, the Intercontinental Research Co., Inc., occupied Washington offices one floor above the WSP headquarters. This proximity was treated by both the WSP and the press as an ironic coincidence. However, subsequent disclosures suggest that the Intercontinental Research Co. may well have undertaken domestic operations against its neighbor in addition to its main assignment in Latin America.

†Watergate burglar E. Howard Hunt, Jr., in congressional testimony and a confirmatory interview, stated that he spent four years in the service of the Domestic Operations Division, beginning shortly after the unit was launched in 1962, and that his duties included a daily pickup of "any and all information" available in 1964 at the presidential campaign headquarters of Senator Barry Goldwater, then running against President Johnson, for delivery to a White House aide who was a former CIA official. In addition, he told of projects involving the subsidizing and manipulation of news and publishing organizations—See "Underground for the CIA in New York: An Ex-Agent

Although the evidence is far from clear, a covert action project of the Domestic Operations Division may well have been responsible for a wave of office burglaries, in 1969 and 1970, of the files and lists of a number of groups such as the United Servicemen's Fund, an organization supporting dissidence in the Armed Forces; the National Welfare Rights Organization; and a variety of anti-war groups, including the Fifth Avenue Peace Parade Committee in New York City.

The CIA's domestic programs were fed by an unusual diversity of surveillance techniques. Like all intelligence enterprises with a dubious provenance, the Agency's domestic efforts were at the outset largely confined to "public sources," transmittals from other agencies, and related materials available without surveillance. But external pressure and internal momentum soon changed things. The intensity of its coverage by the late sixties is reflected in its use of intelligence satellite photographs of demonstrations. According to documents declassified and released in July 1979, the space spying operation was conducted by the top-secret National Reconnaissance Office (NRO), which conducts satellite photography programs for the entire intelligence community. The extraordinarily detailed photographs ("too 'sensitive' for public release") were reviewed by CIA identification units concerned with domestic anti-war protest activities.

The Agency also developed what it prefers generically to call "assets": individuals who monitor open meetings as well as infiltrator members and penetration agents in leadership roles. In some cases, these assets were Agency employees and their relatives; in others, outside firms and fronts were used for infiltration assignments. One group of CHAOS agents recruited for service abroad participated in radical activities in this country for the allegedly limited purpose of establishing and improving their cover before an overseas assignment—a process known in the trade as "reddening" or "sheep-dipping."* In the same way, returning CHAOS agents were debriefed after they reentered the radical community pending reassignment and, in some instances, were expressly brought back from overseas to cover a target of particular interest to the FBI. Another program, "Project 2," was launched in 1969 by a CIA component for the purpose of ultimately infiltrating foreign intelligence targets. Here, too, the informer candidates developed their leftist credentials in the United States by participating in domestic radical activities. In the course of this work they filed detailed reports, were debriefed by their case officers, and provided considerable information. Many of the recruits for this project, as well as the forty candidates recruited and trained for CHAOS service abroad, infiltrated university campuses

---

Tells of Spying on Students," *New York Times,* Dec. 29, 1974; and "Hunt Tells of Early Work for CIA Domestic Unit," *New York Times,* Dec. 31, 1974.

*The Bureau term for such apprentices is Potential Security Informant (PSI); the contrast between these two usages tells us worlds about the differences in the style of the agencies. The contrast in operational techniques is reflected in the use made by both agencies of the Communist Party journal, the *Daily World* (formerly the *Daily Worker*). The FBI's multiple subscriptions were obtained to serve the needs of bureaucrats charged with monitoring the Party. But the CIA's heavy contributions to the paper's support were made to ensure the continued existence of a source "in place." It "mirrored the enemy," and "we didn't want to lose our enemy"—Interview with former CIA intelligence supervisor Tom Braden, Ch. 5 telecast, Sept. 21, 1975, "The Rise and Fall of the CIA."

such as Brown, Boston, California (Berkeley), Columbia, Utah State, Cornell, and New York University. One CHAOS asset submitted detailed reports on domestic left movements, and a Project 2 asset put in a lengthy report describing activities over a three-week period in connection with demonstrations, group meetings, and women's liberation activities. A highly clandestine project was blueprinted in the early seventies to monitor the Black Panther Party, primarily through a corps of specially recruited black surveillants and infiltrators. In addition to monitoring domestic BPP units, black Americans were dispatched to such places as Algeria, Kenya, and Tanzania to ferret out BPP links to foreign governments. The mission was unproductive, hardly surprising in view of the earlier report of the Kerner Commission, a body on which the CIA was represented, that foreign influence played no role in black protest movements.

Eager to expand its sources, the CIA wooed local and state intelligence agencies. The local agencies provided information, but also cover in the form of badges and identification cards as well as other services. In return, the CIA offered courses of instruction, briefings, demonstrations, and seminars for various police departments throughout the United States. It showed its gratitude in other ways, such as providing "safehouses," transportation, gifts, gratuities, electronic equipment, transmitters, audio devices, cameras, and gas masks. In December 1967 the Agency sent two agents to Chicago to evaluate the Chicago Police Department's intelligence-gathering capability and make recommendations for improvements. The return for this service was soon forthcoming: red squad reports on groups planning to demonstrate at the 1968 Democratic Convention, a detailed report on a newly formed radical association, and files on a number of individuals active in the peace movement.

Communications Interception—HTLINGUAL, MINARET, and SHAMROCK

A key source of information for CHAOS was the CIA program HTLINGUAL for monitoring mail to foreign countries, especially but not exclusively to the Soviet Union and other Communist countries.[39] Begun in 1952, it expanded over the following twenty years and involved not only the inspection of envelopes but also the opening of mail which it shared with the FBI and other agencies. In 1972, the last year before the termination of the program, the New York City intercept project examined the outside of some 2,300,000 mail items, photographed 33,000 envelopes, and opened 8,700 letters. Over the 20-year duration of the project, records indicate that a total of 28,519,414 letters were reviewed, over 2 million envelopes photographed, and more than 215,000 letters opened. Those victimized included members of Congress, authors, church leaders, activists, and even a President.[40] Information obtained from the contents of the letters or the surface of the envelopes was used to supplement existing files, to open new ones, and to service an index system that embraced no less than 1,400,000 entries.

Richard Helms conceded HTLINGUAL's illegality, but a Department of

Justice investigative report (released in January 1977) refused to recommend prosecution of the responsible officials (both CIA and FBI) on the principal ground that the program may have been justified as an exercise of the President's national security power, although evidence of presidential authorization or even knowledge is lacking. Counterintelligence chief James Angleton, who headed the program from 1955 until 1973 when the Agency was forced by the Post Office to call a halt, defended the program, insisting that it had produced valuable information, and rejected as "inconceivable" the notion that an intelligence agency like the CIA should be required to conform to law.*

From the late forties continuously for three decades, the National Security Agency (NSA)—the most secretive, lavishly funded, and largest of all the agencies in the intelligence community—monitored international cable communications for intelligence data (Operation SHAMROCK).[41] The targets were not confined to embassies and other foreign intelligence sources but included domestic political subjects without grounds for suspecting espionage. SHAMROCK was implemented by physically scanning the text of cables made available by the three major companies in the field, and by directly monitoring international telephone and cable traffic. The latter operation was initiated in the fall of 1967 when an Army intelligence chief (General William Yarborough) requested the NSA to provide information in support of the Army's civil disturbance responsibilities, pinpointing the role of foreign governments in fomenting domestic discord. Other intelligence agencies in hot pursuit of proof of foreign influence and control submitted similar monitoring requests, watch lists of designated individuals considered dangerous to the domestic order for one reason or another. As Operation MINARET (the signal-monitoring program's code name) expanded, the NSA—far removed from its basic military and diplomatic concerns, without executive authorization, and in deep water because of its violation of statutes prohibiting such interceptions—became increasingly secretive about its participation. Before MINARET was halted in 1973, the NSA had intercepted the messages of 1680 American citizens and groups in compliance with requests by the FBI, CIA, the Secret Service, and other agencies. The accumulated data was incorporated in reports—ultimately about 2000 in all—hand-carried to the requesting agencies and marked: "Background use only." Operation CHAOS received 1100 pages of such material from the NSA. The FBI justified its extended submissions (950 names out of a total of 1200 in the "civil disturbance" category) on the theory that its listees were bent on destroying the government and hence were "natural allies of the foreign enemies of the U.S."

The civil disturbance listees to be watched were the familiar mix of radicals, liberals, celebrities, and ordinary citizens involved in one-time protests, and of organizations ranging from the liberal left to pacifist. Interceptions of private,

*It is quite certain that William Colby, then CIA chief, initially leaked the story of the mail interception program to *New York Times* reporter Seymour M. Hersh in an effort to force the ouster of Angleton, with whom he had been feuding over the recruitment of Soviet defectors as counterspies. Hersh subsequently published a rather unflattering, spookish profile of Angleton in the *New York Times Magazine.* Angleton tried to parry these thrusts through Edward Epstein, an investigative journalist whose book *Legend* reflects Angleton's KGB-spy mania. Angleton has since gone all the way with the charges that Colby may have been duped by KGB moles—See Victor Marchetti, "Twilight of the Spooks," *Inquiry,* July 10, 1978; and Powers, pp. 281–282, 288–289.

personal communications were frequent. The functional responsibilities of the requesters were largely ignored, notably in the case of the Secret Service, which submitted names of individuals and organizations active in anti-war and civil rights movements not considered a direct threat to protectees on the theory that they might participate in demonstrations against United States policy that would endanger the physical well-being of government officials.[42] As far as the record shows, these three programs were no more successful in flushing out evidence of foreign influence than any of the other intelligence pursuits of the Vietnam era triggered by the political desperation of the Johnson and Nixon administrations.

The Bottom Line

In 1973 CIA Director Richard Helms testified in connection with his nomination as ambassador to Iran and denied that the Agency had been involved in domestic intelligence activities.[43] The following colloquy is significant:

> SENATOR CASE: It has been called to my attention that in 1969 or 1970 the White House asked that all intelligence agencies join in the effort to learn as much as they could about the anti-war movement, and during this period U.S. Army intelligence became involved and kept files on U.S. citizens.
>
> Do you know anything about any activity on the part of the CIA in that connection? Was it asked to be involved?
>
> MR. HELMS: I don't recall whether we were asked, but we were not involved because it seemed to me that was a clear violation of what our charter was.
>
> SENATOR CASE: What do you do in a case like that?
>
> MR. HELMS: I would simply go to explain to the President this didn't seem to me to be advisable.*

But Helms himself in the comments already referred to indicated as early as 1967 both that his Agency was involved in anti-war activities and that he knew it was improper. Tom Huston wrote a memorandum in July 1970 to Haldeman, discussing the preparations that ultimately produced the Huston Plan, in which he stated: "I went into this exercise fearful CIA would refuse to cooperate. In fact Dick Helms—Director of Central Intelligence—was most cooperative and helpful, and the only stumbling block was Mr. Hoover." Equally illuminating is a memorandum transmitted by Helms to the White House on the activities of the Women's Strike for Peace, with an attached note to President Johnson's assistant, Marvin Watson, requesting: "Would you please put this in the President's night reading?" When complaints about the program's impropriety came back to him, he insisted that "CHAOS is a legitimate counterintelligence function and cannot be stopped simply because some members of the organization do not like it."

Helms, ultimately forced to retreat from his earlier denials, claimed that his arm had been twisted by President Johnson and later by President Nixon's

---

*Even before this testimony, Helms had insisted in a public address in 1971 that the Agency had not surveilled domestic targets: "We do not target American citizens. The nation must to a degree take it on faith that we who lead the CIA are honorable men, devoted to the nation's service."

underlings. Unquestionably, Helms's arm *was* twisted; but such Johnson administration officials as Secretary of State Dean Rusk and Joseph A. Califano, Jr., have denied knowledge of any presidential authorization to collect domestic intelligence. Walt Rostow stated that he had "no memory" of a formal presidential order directing the White House CIA to engage in domestic surveillance, and added, "I suspect I would have." The cautious quality of this denial is understandable in view of Rostow's role in conveying White House instructions to the Agency and in checking its performance of assignments.

Even if, as Helms contended, the domestic surveillance ball was handed to his Agency by the President, the CIA certainly ran with it. Much of its overkill was inspired by James Jesus Angleton, the agency's counterintelligence chief, a committed believer in the long twilight struggle. Following a distinguished undergraduate career at Yale, Angleton spent two years at Harvard Law School and then, in the footsteps of his father, a businessman with extensive foreign connections who became a lieutenant colonel in the OSS, he too entered the intelligence fellowship. Angleton is one of those rare real-life figures whose career and personality overshadow conventional spy novels and authenticate the more imaginative contributions to the genre. A sensitive, complex, literate man, a gourmet, wine connoisseur, and grower of prize-winning orchids, he has been well described as a "spook's spook, completely obsessed with the tactics of espionage." Angleton's devout Catholicism, passion for poetry—he once edited a poetry journal—and cold war obsessions mark him as a Graham Greene archetype. And to complete this fusion of life and art, Angleton's fanaticism had made him a burden and embarrassment to the CIA, a classic version of Greene's burnt-out case. When forced to retire after the publication in December 1974 of an exposé of domestic CIA operations that blew his cover, he protested that his career had been devoted to protecting the United States from its arch-enemy, the Soviet Union, and that he was the victim of a secret KGB plan to destroy confidence in U.S. intelligence operations.[44]

Less ardent defenders of the program have nevertheless insisted that executive pressure to come up with definitive conclusions concerning the foreign sponsorship of domestic dissent necessarily required overkill. In order to defend negative conclusions from White House attack, the entire field of domestic dissent had to be covered—not merely a particular organization that might seem receptive to foreign influence. In the same way, to dispel anticipated skepticism about a particular target, it was required to "prove a negative," that is, that no influence at all could be found which tainted or compromised the organization's policies and tactics. The bloated character of the operation was further extenuated as a striving for thoroughness and efficiency—a familiar justification for the pathology of overkill. It was admittedly possible through intelligence activities abroad to determine whether nuptials or even an engagement was in the offing between a foreign and domestic partner and thus avoid the entire sphere of domestic activities. But it was more efficient to monitor the domestic partner as well, to record the first awakening of desire.

The CIA domestic operations yielded eight reports to the White House alone, in addition to a great many memoranda on particular subjects and events disseminated both to the White House and other agencies. Far from helping the embattled Presidents who had requested them, these reports proved an embarrassment. But the Agency persisted in the face of what it surely knew to be a fact: namely, that the Vietnam era movements were indigenous. And, like the Johnson administration, the Nixonites refused out of desperation to abandon the hunt. Indeed, even when the game was ending, the Nixon administration continued to play the same losing cards. So it was that when the Watergate investigation, in 1973, turned up evidence of assaults on hostile demonstrators at Nixon rallies, Haldeman, in a White House conversation on February 10, instructed Dean to "Get our people to put out the story on the foreign or Communist money that was used in support of demonstrations against the President in 1972."

What indeed did the White House finally glean from the stream of intelligence activities that it released from 1967 to the early 1970s focusing on the foreign connections of domestic dissident groups? This prime mission of the entire intelligence community over a period of years yielded only the charge of "support," not money or cadres but approval of objectives. President Nixon did the best he could with the available materials in his apologia of May 22, 1973, when, referring to campus violence, he said: "Some of the activities were receiving foreign support." How could the war opponents be condemned because others overseas were attracted to their cause? But such reasoning is anathema to intelligence. "Support" plays a special role in the invention of subversive linkages; it justifies intelligence activity not by reason of the improper conduct of the target but solely because of the approval, in unspecified ways, of a negative reference group (foreigners, subversives, or enemies of the United States).*

"Support" works equally well in reverse. Thus a military intelligence document charges war opponents with subversion because "they are supporting the stated objectives of foreign elements which are detrimental to the United States." This formulation has many proleptic variants: foreign elements are hopeful about, or pleased with the prospect of, or would welcome supporting domestic activity. And even if these anticipations never mature, the targets must be watched because of their potential receptivity to overtures seeking support; even worse, the subjects might at some unspecified later time be approached to spy for a hostile intelligence service like the KGB. The remoteness of the contingency is discounted by the gravity of the risk; why wait until the dissenter is approached to become a foreign spy? Or, even more sinister, the tool of a foreign spy.

The foreign influence thesis became a courtroom issue in the spring of 1977 in connection with the Kearney wiretapping and mail interception indictment (see chapter 5), based on FBI efforts to locate and apprehend the Weather Underground fugitives. A 400-page "top secret" report *(Foreign Influence— Weather Underground Organization)* was prepared by FBI researchers and leaked to the press to establish that no crimes were committed because the fugitives were in fact foreign agents and thus subject to inherent executive power, unrestrained by legal or constitutional requirements. The taps and mail

---

*A homely version of this device draws a negative inference from the fact that a subject is "mentioned favorably" in the Communist Party newspaper, the *Daily Worker* (now the *Daily World*). Bureau files bulge with such clippings.

interceptions, the report argued, were legitimate counterintelligence practices, sanctioned by a reservation in the Keith case, excluding targets with "significant connections" with a foreign power from the requirement of prior judicial approval for wiretaps (and, by necessary inference, break-ins). The report's attempt to provide a defense for Kearney and for Gray, Felt, and Miller (whose activities were under grand jury scrutiny at the time it was leaked) required conformity not only to the Keith case standard. In June 1975, the vague language of *Keith* was sharpened by an appellate court ruling (*Zweiborn* v. *Mitchell*) that mere influence or support of a foreign power did not deprive a domestic group of the protection of warrant requirements in the absence of a showing of an actual agency relationship or collaboration.

The press response to the leaked report was not encouraging: a *New York Times* summary indicated that the militants, before or after they went underground, received limited aid from Cuban intelligence officers in the United States and Canada. The North Vietnamese were similarly reported to have offered advice in the late sixties but nothing more. As for the Communist bloc countries, including China, the report, the *Times* concluded, "appeared to be more significant for the paucity of [their] support than for the extent of it."[45]

When the report was subsequently released, its tendentious character became apparent, particularly its resort to the familiar intelligence formula of assimilating shared ideological assumptions to direction and control. The most damaging of the report's allegations concerning the Weather Underground Organization—charging that money and explosives passed between the Cuban mission and the Weathermen—was based solely on a news story, not supported by documentation or confirmed by the FBI's own intensive investigation. Indeed, the FBI's case files make no reference to a foreign intelligence rationale in either their coding or their content, and leave undisturbed the conclusion apparent from other portions of the report that no financial or other tangible assistance was rendered the Weather Underground Organization by any foreign country—including Cuba and Canada.

Intelligence Evaluation—The Triumph of Countersubversion Over Social Need

It is a hornbook precept that the chief executive of a large complex organization such as the United States government needs advance information to set goals, formulate policy, and make decisions. Such information, we are told, must be analyzed by specialists and transmitted in the form of reports to a higher level of administration for assessment in a broader context as a guide to official action. This process has been put forward as a formal model for political intelligence gathering. Commonly called "pure" or "preventive" intelligence, this domestic peacetime intelligence mode insists on its professionalism, based on principles borrowed from the disciplines of social research on the one hand and conflict-related intelligence gathering on the other. Such professionalism teaches that, as in the nonpolitical sphere, intelligence cannot be entrusted to the inevitably biased collector to whom the material is invariably significant, but must be reviewed and evaluated by a specialist. Similarly, the "line" intelligence product, however correctly formulated, must at some point be transmitted to higher internal levels and to other intelligence agencies for corroboration and cross-checking. Finally, these intermediate appraisals must be sorted out by experts at the policy action level, in command of a broader range of data, for a determination as to whether a government response is appropriate or necessary ("threat assessment").

In the broad social and economic domain, this information-gathering process has lagged far behind the needs of policymakers and planners.* The political intelligence schema here outlined has served as a façade to legitimate countersubversion and to conceal systematic operational abuses.

In the preceding section, we have seen how an attempted exploitation of countersubversion to discredit the peace movement for political purposes institutionalized an illegal domestic CIA surveillance system. Here we explore, on a lower executive level, the way in which the countersubversive Moloch swallowed up an emerging need for information thought to be indispensable for social ends. The seed of this corruption of a governmental process was not, as in the case of the CIA, the peace movement, but ghetto unrest and riots. Familiarly enough, the tale begins on a succession of promising notes.

In 1964, in the wake of nine serious urban ghetto disturbances, President Johnson—for the semi-paranoid reasons already suggested—commissioned an FBI investigative report. The report took pains to reject claims of police brutality as a cause of the rioting (a traditional Bureau posture) while it pinpointed individuals connected in one way or another with proscribed groups. It nevertheless conceded that the riots were caused for the most part by mass frustrations and deprivations. Further, the report concluded, despite a seemingly common pattern of recurring riots within a short time span, that there was no evidence of a subversive conspiracy to incite the disturbances.[46]

But the report had no significant consequences: no steps were taken on the executive level to prevent future riots either through social planning or, on a short-term basis, an intelligence alert system. The civil disorders of 1965–66 found the Department of Justice, in particular, wholly unprepared and the Bureau exclusively committed to countersubversive surveillance. The newly created President's Commission on Law Enforcement and the Administration of Justice urged that local police establish "procedures for the acquisition and channelling of intelligence" to higher government echelons, so as to facilitate a coordinated response to "a true riot situation" in the future. This recommendation cemented the Bureau's liaison with urban police units for the exchange of information about activities with "a potential for violence." In practice, it

---

*   . . . Upon this gifted age, in its dark hour
Rains from the sky a meteoric shower
Of facts . . . they lie unquestioned, uncombined,
Wisdom enough to leach of us our ill
Is daily spun, but there exists no loom
To weave it into fabric.

—Edna St. Vincent Millay, *Collected Sonnets of Edna
St. Vincent Millay* (Washington Square Press, 1959), p. 140.

merely served to bolster the existing countersubversive, agitator-oriented intelligence system, rather than to stimulate a professional police capability for assessing potential violence. Continuing pressure for predictive intelligence about ghetto violence came from the White House as well as a number of Justice Department aides. (As will be shown in the next chapter, reliance on predictive intelligence was, in any event, a risky guide to preventive action.) The first step in this direction was an experimental student project in the summer of 1966 to assemble and coordinate readily available materials on developments in black communities.

Planning for a more formal information-gathering project began in the fall of 1967, in a direct response to ghetto disturbances in Newark, Detroit, and other cities. After unsuccessful Justice Department efforts to use the Bureau as a ghetto-monitoring instrument, the White House turned the job over to the Army, whose civil disturbance intelligence activities are described in the next chapter. Attorney General Clark continued on a more modest level to develop intelligence resources. As Clark has since pointed out in an interview, he and his associates knew what they needed: a barometer to help the Civil Rights Division answer such questions as what urban ghetto will blow next, what can we do to alleviate or prevent it? But they were operating in and succumbed to an intelligence milieu that personalized unrest, attributing it to conspiracies of identifiable subversives.*

A report by Assistant Attorney General John Doar, dealing with the new intelligence effort, reflected this ambiguity, recommending the collection of data to facilitate logistic and conciliation initiatives but at the same time focusing on dissident individuals and groups classified Bureau-style by countersubversive categories and indexed. A Clark memorandum urges the collection of: "The most comprehensive intelligence possible regarding organized or other purposeful stimulation of domestic dissension, disorders and riots."[47] While Clark pressed the need for an early warning system, he also referred to the need for information about "individuals and groups who may play a role in either instigating or spreading disorders or in preventing them." Clark's Interdepartmental Information Unit (IDIU) might have escaped the clutches of countersubversion had it been administered by departmental personnel with genuine civil rights concerns. But the unit relied primarily on countersubversive Bureau reports, which were processed by personnel with a background in the Department's Internal Security Division. It was not long before IDIU was rigidly gripped in the countersubversive matrix, proud of the growth of its files and its access to countersubversive sources of information. Yet dossiers were no answer to the need for information about causes and conditions. Nor was the incongruity between supply and demand improved by weightier and more numerous dossiers, or by acquiring a computer to process them.

This scapegoating thesis about the causes of the unrest of the late sixties became entrenched in law enforcement circles in part through the efforts of the prestigious Director. In his 1967 testimony before the National Advisory Com-

---

*As in the case of his 1964 assignment, President Johnson instructed the FBI to investigate the Detroit 1967 riot with specific instructions to ascertain whether it was instigated by a subversive conspiracy. Despite prolonged pressure, the agency failed to find evidence of a conspiracy.

mission on Civil Disorders (the Kerner Commission), and in 1968, before the National Commission on the Causes and Prevention of Violence (the Eisenhower Commission), Director Hoover charged that civil disturbances and violence of all kinds were the fruits of scheming subversives, especially Communists. The Kerner Commission Report rejected his countersubversive dogmas and urged broader social intelligence programs to provide a barometer of potential civil disturbances. But the report, actually the most carefully researched and documented assault on countersubversion in our time, invited the distortion of its basic message by loosely formulated recommendations for "intelligence units," served by "undercover police personnel and informants." It was promptly converted by intelligence apologists into support for the very thesis it had rejected.

The Nixon administration eagerly embraced this intelligence thesis. It renamed the IDIU the Interdivisional Intelligence (instead of Information) Unit, enlarged its staff and its file-processing capability, used its resources to start an "extremist" file collection for the IRS, and disseminated its file holdings to other intelligence units, including the CIA and a special Panther intelligence-oriented task force. Even the Community Relations Service (CRS), created by Clark to mediate racial tensions, was converted into an intelligence source. (Clark's aides had refused to use the CRS in this way lest it compromise its relationships with ghetto dwellers.)

As with the Johnson administration, the march of countersubversion could not be broken by the counsel of thoughtful men. The 1969 Report of the Eisenhower Commission, which had been authorized in 1968 in the wake of the King and Kennedy assassinations, continued the Kerner Commission's attack on the individuation of the causes of civil disturbance and violence.[48] Similarly, the President's Commission on Campus Unrest (the Scranton Commission) issued a report in September 1970, which emphasized two of the conclusions drawn in both earlier reports: that the campus disturbances were rooted "in unresolved conflicts in our national life," and that the rights of protesters had been needlessly sacrificed in the pursuit of order. The Nixon administration ignored the Eisenhower Report and repudiated the Scranton document altogether. In fact, it expanded the IDIU's mission to cover campus dissidence.

As it became increasingly ideologized, the IDIU adopted the intelligence dogma that political affiliation is in itself a ground for predicting violence, a view reflected in an IDIU report excerpted for the press by John Dean on November 6, 1969, stating that violent confrontations would be staged during an anti-war demonstration scheduled for November 15 of that year. No violence occurred. In November 1970 the IDIU came under the leadership of Robert Mardian, newly appointed head of the Department's Internal Security Division. Shortly after Mardian took over, the unit's chief James T. Devine conceded that the data collection was "of practically no value" in achieving its intended purpose as a barometer of possible civil disorder, but insisted on its usefulness for federal law enforcement purposes, a questionable justification in view of the fact that disorders and violence at demonstrations involve questions of local law enforcement. Devine unpersuasively claimed that the information was needed to determine whether anyone had crossed the state line to incite a riot, conduct made a federal offense by a 1968 statute. For the remainder of its bureaucratic life, the IDIU played variations on countersubversive themes, while it expanded its computerized files—over 14,000 separate entries by April 1971—to include everyone connected with civil rights protests from prominent public figures to lowly demonstrators.[49]

The degeneration of the quest for accurate line intelligence is paralleled on higher levels which, in the intelligence blueprint, are assigned an evaluative or "threat assessment" role. The super-agency proposed by the Huston planners was to be entrusted with this responsibility. The threat assessment concept is especially attractive to intelligence planners because it provides a functional justification for a top-level bureaucratic intelligence czar. The lure of systemic centralization and hierarchy—a vertical expression on the federal level of the pressure for horizontal institutional coordination already referred to—had, even before the adoption of the Huston Plan, resulted in the creation in May 1969 of a top-level agency, the Intelligence Evaluation Committee (IEC), with a mandate to evaluate and assess threats of civil disturbances. The IEC was organized after consultation with CIA Director Helms and functioned in secret with the IDIU as cover. It was headed by Assistant to the FBI Director Cartha DeLoach, and included representatives of five other Justice Department units, the Secret Service, and military intelligence.[50] Liaison with the CIA was also maintained in order to give the committee the benefit of the Agency's evaluative expertise and sophistication. Because of the "political implications," CIA Director Helms declined Mitchell's invitation to assign a CIA employee on a regular basis. The IEC became moribund and was succeeded by the Civil Disturbance Group (CDG). After Director Hoover persuaded Mitchell to veto the Huston Plan in 1970, Mitchell proceeded to revise the IEC and again sought the advice of the CIA—not only that of Helms but of CIA officials in charge of domestic surveillance. After consultation with these officials, John Dean, then a Justice Department personal assistant to the Attorney General, proposed the creation of an interagency unit with operational* as well as evaluative capability. The defunct IEC was reactivated with a new, broader representation, including (in addition to the Justice Department participants) the CIA, the Department of Defense, the National Security Agency, and the Secret Service. It began functioning in December 1970 with Assistant Attorney General Robert C. Mardian as chairman and John Dean as White House representative. It is quite clear that the IEC's ultimate purpose was to revive and implement the Huston Plan. Dean and Mardian hoped that Hoover's earlier objections could be overcome if the new unit went through the motions of evaluating the available intelligence and *only then* recommending more penetrative coverage.[51] As early as January 1971 the IEC addressed a memorandum† to Mitchell, Ehrlichman, and Haldeman urging that the adoption of the ICI's June 1970 recommendation was imperative. Similarly, pressure to implement at least some of the recommendations of the Huston Plan was renewed at a conference in March 1971, with Helms, Gayler

---

*A memorandum from Dean to Attorney General Mitchell concerning the proposed unit advocates "the creation of a [sic] interagency intelligence unit for both operational and evaluation purposes. . . ." But there is no evidence that the IEC became operational.

†Written on Department of Justice stationery, but unsigned and attributed to Robert Mardian.

(of the NSA), Hoover, and the Attorney General.[52] The Director refused—for at least a third time.

In contrast to the 1969 version, the revamped IEC did not enjoy Bureau support. Hoover limited the Bureau's official participation and grudgingly assigned to the staff two Bureau analysts who made what were considered worthless contributions. The Director was playing dog in the manger. The Bureau wasn't supposed to engage in evaluation at all; why object to a project designed to complement its own collection efforts? But the Director preferred to have it both ways: he disavowed the evaluation responsibility when self-interest counseled, but presented himself as king of the evaluation hill in his personal dealings with Congress and the White House. And, by the end of 1970, he must have become quite fed up with the widespread deprecation of the Bureau's skills in this area.*

But fear of a congressional backlash and the lack of even an executive authorization for departmental countersubversive intelligence activities beyond the Bureau's fief forced the IEC into an increasingly furtive, hole-in-corner style and the ultimate abandonment of a planned formal structure to be headed by a Washington state judge sponsored by Ehrlichman. IEC's liquidation in 1973 because of its vulnerability to congressional attack was not considered a great loss to the intelligence community. During its two and a half years of life its staff turned out some thirty papers considered of uniformly poor quality by intelligence experts and fifty-five intelligence calendars, a stock intelligence compilation of coming radical events.

It can hardly be doubted that all of these evaluation efforts totally failed to achieve their purpose: to provide decision makers with early warnings of potential disturbance, initially in the ghetto and later on the campus and at other demonstration sites. These successive failures were caused not by the Director's hostility, as has been claimed, but by the unwillingness or inability of the intelligence bureaucracy to break the hold of the countersubversive mystique. At a time when society heaved with unrest on a scale almost unprecedented in our history, these domestic intelligence professionals blindly accepted the fiction of their trade that the road to prevention and containment was the monitoring of targets unshakably assumed to be the effective causes of unrest. An objective, nonideological view of the matter would have required the recognition that the riots, demonstrations, and bombings would not end without some meaningful recognition of their causes. Even the repressive nineteenth-century spymasters perceived this simple truth. Nor could the underlying reality be altered by greater Bureau cooperation or implementation of the illegal Huston proposals. How could more information about individuals, already endlessly surveilled and dossiered, make possible effective, preemptive intervention in civil disturbances? And, for that matter, how could after-the-fact "incident" reports, written in the Bureau's stationhouse style and perspective, tell even the most gifted analyst what future course to advise in order to forestall a recurrence? This obsession with countersubversion distorted and

*Hoover said as much in testimony before the House Appropriations Subcommittee in the spring of 1971. See Chapter 4.

homogenized virtually all the intelligence efforts of the sixties, whatever their formal purposes, from the collection of taxes by the IRS to the protection of the safety of public officials by the Secret Service. And it is perhaps most sharply demonstrated by the massive domestic military intelligence programs directed against civilian dissent, to which we must now turn.

8 Military Surveillance of Civilian Politics — Countersubversion in Uniform

The Institutional Setting

By the late sixties the intelligence units of the armed forces had become, next to the FBI, the most important single component in the domestic intelligence community. As in the case of the CIA, the latter-day bloating of military surveillance of political expression and activity in this country must be seen, in part as yet another flowering of the liberal quest for benign, presidentially sponsored forms of repression, and in part simply as a "natural" response.

In every modern state, the military has played an important role in the development of institutions to monitor civilian politics. Even when these surveillance functions pass from military into civilian hands, the influence of military attitudes, assumptions, and practices continues to be felt. But here we are concerned not with the residual influence of the Army on civilian intelligence practices, but rather with a huge intelligence system operated by the Army itself without civilian authorization or control.

The system as a whole is marked by a quality of excess reflected most notably in its gargantuan coverage. Individuals from every area of dissent, leaders and followers, were surveilled and dossiered; literally every organization of a liberal or radical hue was similarly covered. This same passion for excess is reflected in the Army's intelligence resources. An intelligence unit may have impressive operational capability, but only limited authority and resources for planning; manpower to collect information, but meager technical equipment to process it; reasonably efficient overt surveillance facilities, but no clandestine capability; its own information input, but no access to other systems (liaison intelligence) or opportunities for operational collaboration with other units; extensive files, but no resources to evaluate their content. These limitations and imbalances—the combined product of history, legal restraints, inadequate funding, jurisdictional barriers, institutional rivalries, and plain caution—handicap the functioning of most of our intelligence institutions, serving, incidentally, as

287

a practical if temporary curb on abuses. (Indeed, this arrested state of institutional development—an important spur, as we have seen, for the Huston Plan —reflects a pervasive ambiguity on all governmental levels about intelligence, an impasse between our democratic constitutional commitment and subversion-mongering.) But few, if any, shortcomings marred Army intelligence structures. Unlimited funds, ample field manpower, specialized command personnel, planning and training resources, and the most sophisticated communications and data-processing capability ensured a unique versatility.

What makes this over-involvement even more striking is its contravention of constitutional and legal prohibitions. All American intelligence programs are, in varying degrees, maimed by the Achilles' heel of illegitimacy. This challenge confronts us with a special sharpness in dealing with the Army's surveillance of civilian politics, because its power generally to intervene in civilian affairs is severely limited. The Constitution and specific statutes, and the republican principle they implement, subject the Army to civilian direction and control, and confine military intervention in domestic affairs. Article I, Section 8, of the Constitution entrusts to the Congress the power to authorize domestic use of the military but solely to repel invasion, suppress insurrection, and execute the laws. The President is authorized to use troops only if necessary to protect the states against invasion and against domestic violence, and in the latter case only on prior application of state authorities. Congressional enactments further precondition the use of troops by the President to repel an invasion on the issuance of a proclamation ordering the dispersal of the invading forces and, in the absence of such a proclamation, ban the use of any part of the Army or the Air Force, as a Posse Comitatus or otherwise, to execute the laws.[1]

The austere provisions I have cited, with their insistence on formal measures in response to a clear emergency, preclude the implication of a free-floating power to conduct military surveillance of legitimate political civilian movements.[2] As will be shown, the only authority to collect information about civilians and their politics that may be implied from this civil disturbance mission is tightly confined to tactical and reconnaissance data, not political and ideological intelligence of the sort that has obsessed the Army. In the same way, a concentration on political dissent led to routine disregard of the prohibitions of the Posse Comitatus Act through extensive cooperation with civilian law enforcement agencies. A rejection of the forms of law is similarly reflected in the use of the Army Security Agency (ASA) to monitor private radio transmissions. The ASA is a link in a signals intelligence system headed by the National Security Agency (NSA) and, like its parent, is entrusted with a foreign intelligence mission: the interception of international communications. In the footsteps of its parent, it was improperly put to domestic countersubversive use. Originally, the ASA got its feet wet domestically as a support unit for troops called out in connection with the civil disturbances of the early sixties, but it then moved to situations where it was not even contemplated that troops would be deployed, such as the October 1967 Pentagon March, the disturbances following the King assassination in April 1968, the Washington Poor People's Campaign, and the 1968 national political conventions. It is undisputable that this activity violated the prohibitions of Section 605 of the Communications Act against interception and divulgence of the content of private radio transmissions. Uncertain of the legality of this surveillance, the Army sought approval of the Federal Communications Commission (FCC), which ruled that it was violative of the statute. Nonetheless, the ASA with command approval persisted in this illegal practice until 1970, when public exposure forced a retreat.

Nor was this expansionism braked by interagency arrangements such as the "Delimitations Agreement," first signed in 1940 and periodically renewed and amended thereafter, which assigned to the FBI the exclusive authority to conduct all domestic internal security investigations not involving active or retired members of the armed forces or defense industry personnel.[3] This same refusal to accept containment is reflected in the readiness of a general and an admiral from the Defense Intelligence Agency (DIA) and the NSA, respectively, to serve on the ICI. (So strongly did they feel about Hoover's objections that they initially refused to go along with the ICI report, but were dissuaded by Huston's assurances that their disagreements would be personally communicated to the President.) The report itself, while rejecting a proposed use of military undercover agents in civilian groups as violating the Delimitations Agreement, nevertheless recommended that the Army's service-connected security mission "should be expanded to include the active collection of intelligence concerning student-related dissident activities," and "the use of trusted military personnel as FBI assets in the collection of intelligence regarding student-related military activities." When the Intelligence Evaluation Committee (IEC) was formed in December 1970, the Defense Department continued its earlier involvement in interagency coordination of civilian intelligence activity.

It seems plain that the bias common to all intelligence agencies is not enough to explain the intensity of the Army's involvement in the surveillance of civilian politics. We must look to influences that are identified with military life and institutions generally. A bulwark of nationalism and its supporting economic structures, the Army is a natural breeding ground of political conservatism. Its isolation from the mainstream of public life and confinement to an autonomous garrison world intensifies this conservatism and generates chauvinist stereotypes and élitist fantasies, especially at the command level. Generals Patton and MacArthur may not be typical, but they do symbolize political and cultural values embedded in military life. Then, too, the functional imperative of obedience makes the military almost instinctively hostile to dissent. And its stake in the threat posed by communism abroad—the guarantor of its bloated budgets—makes it receptive to the exaggerated mythic version of domestic communism. An ideological and cultural reluctance to make distinctions among opponents of the status quo is reinforced by a combat perspective that relentlessly divides civilian attitudes into exclusive categories—friend or foe—an application to people-watching of the Army dictum: "If it moves, shoot or salute." The zealots who find intelligence work congenial are irresistibly attracted to this milieu. The process is intensified by career drives. In the military, the name of the game is advancement, and the ambitious officer will in the (metaphorical) comment of the GI, "kill to get his star." The key to promotion is a good record—and a good record is almost invariably measured by quantifiable achievements: how many surveillance targets, reports, informers, photographs, file entries. Another spur is the competition of rival intelligence structures, fueled by lower- and middle-ranking officers also striving to get ahead, to outshine their counterparts in other commands. The wheel of excess is spun faster yet by the Army's passion for redundancy of function, duplication of bureaucratic structures, and gadgetry. (The fact that an activity lends itself to both elaborate bureaucratization and technology would seem to make it almost self-justifying in the military mind.) One can hardly conceive a setting more favorable to the growth of a countersubversive intelligence commitment and more hostile to restraints on involvement in civilian life and political dissent.

The Shaping of the Domestic Military Mission

The Army's civilian involvement in the sixties was forged in World War I, when it played an outstanding part in the repression of wartime dissidence. Both openly as policeman and covertly, it monitored political dissent, a role institutionalized in 1917 with the establishment of a domestic Corps of Intelligence Police and a Washington-based staff component, the Military Intelligence Division (MID).[4] The surveillance of civilians was structured around twin objectives, which since then have defined the basic areas of military intelligence: the prevention of troop disaffection ("security") and the protection of the nation from a *Dolchstoss,* an attack on its domestic resources and morale that might jeopardize victory in the field. The MID, first under the direction of Colonel Ralph H. Van Deman, and then under General Marlborough Churchill, became involved in a wide spectrum of activities, ranging from "slacker" raids through strikebreaking. Van Deman zealously promoted collaboration of his intelligence operatives, not only with federal, state, and local government agencies but with private vigilante networks such as the American Protective League (APL).[5] In this way, intelligence solved the problem of operating deficiencies, intensified by the requirement that soldiers wear uniforms on duty, and at the same time consolidated a vital constituency by welding together the older tradition of anti-radical nativism with war-borne nationalism. "Disloyalty" thus emerged as a blunderbuss characterization, borrowed from popular usage, of political dissent. In time, "disloyalty" became subversion, and the ideological bonds linking the Army to a civilian constituency were strengthened by a worldwide social and political unrest, viewed as a precursor to a Bolshevik-style revolution for which military intelligence specialists developed contingency plans.

Like every war in our history, World War I served to legitimate the role of surveillance and related practices as instruments of control over domestic civilian dissent. Battlefield strides in the art of intelligence stirred the popular imagination in a new way. Spying was not only exciting, an extension of the war to one's own backyard, but patriotic. While the close of hostilities ended the Army's troop disaffection concerns, it did not curb its broader countersubversive involvement. In the postwar years it remained active in spreading the countersubversive gospel and developing legislative support through countersubversive investigative hearings.[6]* In pursuit of this countersubversive mission the Army developed a committed civilian constituency, more accurately a political subculture dedicated to monitoring radicalism and—an emerging priority— peace movements. A more immediate focus was the postwar labor unrest, which provided military intelligence with a pretext: the preparation for a possible call-out in the event of a strike. Overnight its long-term objectives of holding off a revolution merged with its more prosaic strikebreaking role.

Although restrictions on the Army's intelligence operations against civilians were an irritant, they did not limit its access to countersubversive information. It rapidly developed a network of liaison arrangements with local law enforcement units.† In addition, both active duty and retired G-2 officers developed personal ties with industry, law enforcement, and National Guard units,

*The effort to exploit the prestige of military intelligence to legitimate red-hunting is seen in the career of Archibald E. Stevenson, a young New York lawyer who became a leader in the anti-radical crusade of the twenties and who headed the successful drive to create the New York State Lusk Committee. In 1919 he presented sensational testimony before the Senate Overman Committee, then engaged in an anti-radical probe, the first of its kind. Stevenson's qualifications as a witness were burnished by his claim that he had served on secret assignments from Army intelligence during the war, although it was later established that, in fact, he had never been an Army officer or an employee of the Military Intelligence Division. In the 1930 Fish Committee Hearings a number of witnesses with backgrounds in Army intelligence presented testimony on the growth of the Menace.

†This document tells its own story:

CONFIDENTIAL COPY
HEADQUARTERS
Vancouver Barracks, Washington
Office of the Intelligence Officer

October 16, 1922.

Dear Sir:

The Intelligence Service of the Army has for its primary purpose the surveillance of all organizations or elements hostile or potentially hostile to the Government of this country, or who seek to overthrow the Government by violence.

Among organizations falling under the above head are radical groups, as the I. W. W., World War Veterans, Union of Russian Workers, Communist Party, Communist Labor Party, One Big Union, Workers International Industrial Union, Anarchists and Bolsheviki, and such semi-radical organizations as the Socialists, Non-Partisan League, Big Four Brotherhoods, and American Federation of Labor.

Not only are we interested in these organizations because they have as their object the overthrow of the Government, but also because they attempt to undermine and subvert the loyalty of our soldiers.

With the few scattered military posts in this part of the country, it is obviously impossible to cover all points as thoroughly as they should be, hence it is necessary in many cases to trust to the cooperation of law-enforcement officers whose duties and whose knowledge of a particular locality gives them a thorough insight into such matters.

It is requested that you inform this office as to any of the aforementioned or other radical organizations coming to your attention under such headings as (a) location or headquarters, (b) names of leaders, (c) strength of organization, (d) activities of the organization, (e) strikes and methods of carrying on same, and (f) attitude of members. We will be glad to receive copies of pamphlets, handbills, or other radical propaganda spread in your vicinity.

If from time to time you will keep me posted as to conditions in your vicinity, such cooperation on the part of yourself and your subordinates as the press of your duties permits will be greatly appreciated.

Sincerely,
W. D. Long,
1st Lieutenant, 7th U. S. Infantry,
Intelligence Officer.

patriotic and veterans organizations, and encouraged surveillance and the development of file collections. The Army's concern with radicalism and with strikers was further spurred by postwar cutback drives in appropriations and manpower. It openly courted employers, pointing out that such cuts would leave the country a prey to revolution by subversive strikers. By the end of the twenties military intelligence was entrenched as a counterrevolutionary bulwark and indispensable defense against the Menace.

Depression unrest both intensified and broadened intelligence collection by the G-2s. The extent of its involvement was revealed by its activities in connection with the veterans' bonus march of 1932. The entire domestic structure was tasked with special intelligence preparations because of the veteran status of the bonus marchers. Corps commanders were requested in secret code messages to identify subversives among the marchers and their leaders from their files. Intelligence officers in the field did not hesitate to denounce the marchers as dangerous subversives. As the date of the march approached, G-2 agents solicited information from the Army's civilian support groups, reserve officers, American Legion officials, and volunteer patriots.[7]

World War II renewed the domestic intelligence role of G-2. Despite the Delimitations Agreement, G-2 and a new intelligence structure, the Counter-Intelligence Corps (CIC), became involved in internal security surveillance, targeting radicals, peace activists, labor officials, and suspected fifth columnists. According to a former agent, Willis R. Adams, his G-2 unit attached to the Chicago area Sixth Surface Command, in 1943, engaged in extensive tapping and bugging both on its own and in cooperation with other units. A Chicago hotel room occupied by Mrs. Franklin D. Roosevelt was bugged, among others occupied by prominent individuals passing through Chicago during the war.[8] Nor was there a postwar respite: the cold war and the Korean involvement kept the pot boiling.[9]

During the McCarthy era, Army intelligence personnel secretly collaborated with the Wisconsin senator in defiance of civilian leadership of the Army. The Army-McCarthy Hearings centering on Fort Monmouth strongly suggested that McCarthy's involvement in personnel security at the fort had been instigated by lower-ranking intelligence officers in struggle with their superiors. McCarthy cross-examined the civilian secretary of the Army on the basis of a letter summarizing a confidential FBI report sent to Major General A. R. Bolling, Assistant Chief of Staff, G-2. McCarthy refused to say how he had acquired this document.[10]

In a replay of the twenties, Army elements (especially intelligence) allied themselves with the ultra right as part of a larger effort to entrench military power by exploiting fears of subversion. The warning of President Eisenhower to stand "guard against the acquisition of unwarranted influence" by a conjunction of an immense military establishment and a nationwide arms industry became a reality in the light of a series of disclosures of the involvement of the Pentagon top brass in "educating" civilians on military defense about communism and the cold war. In a series of Army-sponsored seminars, conferences, speeches, and rallies, audiences all over the country from schoolchildren to bankers were pounded with the same message: We are losing to the Communists; civilians have a choice between appeasement or surrender and all-out struggle for survival. These sessions were enthusiastically supported by ultra-rightists, whose political views on domestic as well as foreign affairs were endorsed by most speakers.[11] The authority for this military propaganda crusade was an obscure 1958 directive of the Joint Chiefs of Staff attributed to Admiral W. Radford,[12] authorizing the services to indoctrinate civilians on cold war issues, especially the Communist threat.

The G-2s played a discreet but important role in this drive. Each Army corps to which they were attached issued weekly intelligence summaries on domestic subversion, advised the commanding officer about the political coloration of Army critics—especially the critics of the anti-subversive "educational" campaign—helped plan the seminars and forums, and checked on proposed speakers to ensure what is known in the jargon as "quality control." This movement was strengthened by seminars sponsored by the Industrial College of the Armed Forces and conducted by teams of officers in local communities. The National War College also initiated courses at Fort McNair to train officers for civilian indoctrination. With the blessings of the Joint Chiefs, these programs hit the ground running: in a very short time the trainees of the Fort McNair indoctrination course were successfully peddling their wares all over the country, aided by a proliferating stream of collaborating organizations: the Institute for American Strategy, the Foreign Policy Research Institute, chambers of commerce, right-wing groups such as Harding College at Searcy, Arkansas, the Fourth Dimensional Warfare Seminar, National Security Seminar, and Strategy for Survival (eleven such conferences were sponsored by this last group alone).

Although the Army was forced to retreat from its more vulnerable involvements of the fifties in civilian politics and to curb its rabid, countersubversive hawks, its domestic intelligence mission was left undisturbed. The single most important figure in shaping this civilian mission and consolidating its base was the redoubtable Colonel Van Deman. As World War I intelligence chief, he recognized the importance of civilian operational support, speedily expanded G-2's wartime anti-labor initiatives, and, using a plant security justification, resisted postwar attempts to curtail intelligence. His legacy was as simple as it was enduring: that the role of the Army in civilian affairs, modest though it seemed, could be used to justify military intelligence as a resource to curb movements for change. When Van Deman retired to San Diego in 1929, he launched an anti-radical information-gathering and clearing-house operation with the combined support of military intelligence, employer, and patriotic groups. After his death in 1952 his extensive file collection—fed by materials from his own operatives as well as MI, FBI, and local law enforcement reports—was transferred to an Army unit and later in 1970 to the Senate Internal Security Subcommittee.[13]

Military Intelligence Structures

The civil rights disturbances and demonstrations of the early sixties prompted a limited number of troop commitments and modest Army intelligence activity of a preparatory nature in anticipation of possible troop deployments to selected trouble spots. But as the disorders spread and criticism of the Vietnam War intensified, the earlier restraints were abandoned. By the end of the decade a huge intelligence structure had emerged, which planned, programmed, processed, interpreted, stored, and disseminated civilian-focused intelligence. Its intelligence function, mission, and product are generically described as CONUS INTEL or simply CONUS, an acronym for Continental United States Intelligence. During the period of its greatest activity this apparatus functioned through a hydra-headed bureaucracy, consisting of the U.S. Intelligence Command (USAINTC), the Continental Army Command (CONARC), the Counter-Intelligence Analysis Branch[14] (CIAB) attached to the office of Chief of Staff of Intelligence (OACSI), and the Directorate of Civil Disturbance and Planning (DCDPO), renamed in 1970 the Directorate of Military Support (DOMS).

USAINTC, organized in 1965 and headquartered at Fort Holabird, Maryland, served as the principal instrument of CONUS intelligence. By the late sixties it boasted a nationwide network of some 1500 agents, stationed in over 300 posts scattered throughout the country and organized into seven Military Intelligence Groups (MIG), substructured into regional field and resident offices. The MIGs were responsible for Special Investigations (personnel investigations) and CONUS intelligence, functions that overlapped operationally as the decade progressed. The surveillance of both civilian and military dissidents engaged in anti-war activities involving military personnel was entrusted to a special USAINTC program, Resistance in the Army (RITA). Surveillance operations were primarily the responsibility of the field and resident offices, while the group and regional offices were largely involved in command, review, and administrative functions, and also served as custodians of the more important files.

Following the Newark riots in July 1967, USAINTC established a new post, "CONUS Intelligence Section, Operations IV" (OPS IV), charged with coordinating, processing, and storing the information that flooded the command's Fort Holabird headquarters. A former intelligence officer, "Roger" (a pseudonym), described this in an interview:

> Well, the Operations Center has about fifteen to twenty telephones, which hook the intelligence command up on a direct line basis to every MI group, plus the MI Detachment in Puerto Rico, plus the Army operations center in the Pentagon which is the War Room. They have a direct line to the National Security Administration in case the Army communications system gets messed up, in case of a nuclear attack or a major riot. The room is about twenty by twenty feet, with six or seven desks in the middle, surrounded on the walls by all these telephones, and just outside of the operations center are about six teletype machines plus the AP and UPI, all come into the operations center complex there. These teletype machines receive the spot reports that the MI groups send in. This is all typed out on the tape at the MI group headquarters in Chicago. That tape is run through the machine and it comes out perfect in Baltimore in four copies.[15]

Not very far from Fort Holabird at Fort Monroe, in Hampton, Virginia, is the headquarters of the United States Continental Army Command (CONARC), the umbrella command coordinating most of the Army's stateside forces and responsible for deploying troops in civil disturbance situations. CONARC had, until 1965 when USAINTC was launched, been assigned responsibility for all military intelligence functions in the continental United States, including civilian-oriented surveillance. And the intelligence mission which I have described was evolved through its Military Intelligence Division (MID, or G-2 as it was more commonly called). But, after 1965, it was left with the responsibility for more modest intelligence-related functions, such as personnel, document, and base security. In short order, G-2 perfected a refinement of Parkinson's Law: a military bureaucracy increasingly strives to demonstrate the folly of assigning some of its functions to a rival by persisting in their exercise more zealously than before. Through a familiar dodge, the counterintelligence sections of the MIDs entered the civilian surveillance sweepstakes and even competed in their off-post monitoring with their USAINTC counterparts, a rivalry that frequently became quite intense since the MIDs stateside security functions were not of a demanding nature. The CIAB prepared analyses and forecasts for the use of both intelligence networks. The mission of this unit is worldwide; in 1964, a North American desk was created and subsequently subdivided into "left-wing," "right-wing," and "racial" desks. According to the Ervin Committee, by the fall of 1968 the CIAB personnel assigned to monitor domestic disturbance and dissent outnumbered those covering "matters of counter-intelligence interest emanating from any other area of the world, including Southeast Asia."[16]

The DCDPO, a 180-man command center, was created in 1968 in the wake of the riots in April of that year following the assassination of Martin Luther King, Jr. After a temporary stay in makeshift offices, in 1969 it was housed in a specially constructed Pentagon basement war room (at a cost of $2,700,000).[17] A real-life version of the interior of a Stanley Kramer spaceship, this room was equipped with teletype networks linking CONUS installations all over the country, a special hook-up to emergency centers, situation maps, closed-circuit television, hotlines, an illuminated switchboard, and a computerized data center. The intelligence collected by field echelons was transmitted through "spot reports" in standardized formats. A more detailed "Agent's Report" form permitted the enclosure of documents and photographs. The stress on speed also encouraged the use of telephone reports from the observer or participant to local headquarters, where they were reduced to written form by duty agents and then transmitted by teletype up the chain of command, finally reaching OPS IV. At headquarters the mass of incoming reports was sifted, filed, prepared for computer storage, converted into daily and weekly summaries, and teletyped to a worldwide network of users.[18]

An outstanding aspect of both the USAINTC and the CONARC systems was their extraordinarily comprehensive and sophisticated communication grids— teletypes, hotlines, tie-ins with law enforcement telephones and radio transmissions, and electronic links to virtually all collection posts in the country. According to the Ervin Committee Report, "In some cities, these lines extended to every precinct station and were manned at both ends by Army agents."[19] The sophisticated communication equipment—videotape equipment (mobile and stationary), citizen band broadcast interceptors, miniaturized transmitters with hidden throat mikes—reflected the Army's doomsday assumption that only a lightning-fast response would hold off the holocaust. The spate of raw information from the field ultimately emptied into elaborate file systems at Forts Hola-bird and Monroe. The core Fort Holabird USAINTC collection was stored at the fort's repository, the United States Army Investigative Records Repository (USAIRR), comprising about 8 million dossiers, developed by USAINTC. This central collection was augmented by a number of satellite compilations dealing with civilian political activity, comprising two computer systems, two noncom-puterized collections, and a library of documents, photographs, and videotapes. Of the two noncomputerized files, one was the so-called subversives file, which had been in long-term use as a search file in security clearance investigations and for background material on civilians and organizations suspected of sabotage, espionage, and related offenses. Based on inputs from all sources, this collection included dossiers on elected officials (congressmen and governors) and organiza-tions such as the Friends, the NAACP, and indeed all political groups over the entire left-liberal spectrum, each with a specially assigned dossier number.[20] A measure of the size of the collection: it contains no less than 124 linear feet of raw intelligence on the U.S. Communist Party, all of which duplicates the Bureau's internal security files on the same subject. "Incident" files—descrip-tions and summaries of demonstrations, meetings, disturbances, and the like—made up the second noncomputerized collection. From this latter hoard, intelli-gence personnel at Holabird extracted and summarized the most important of the 1200 monthly field reports upon which the collection was based for computer storage. This computerized system organized and made instantly retrievable minute details about the time, place, setting, and participants identified with virtually every public protest activity in the United States. The biographical data stored by the computer could be independently retrieved in the form of lists of individuals along with details of their personal lives. In addition, these dossiers were cross-indexed in code to the master subversive file already described.[21] Purporting to deal with "hard core militants and civil disturbance individuals, CONUS wide . . .", the file collections indiscriminately run the gamut from priests to comedians, from supporters of Senator Eugene McCarthy to Weathermen and large numbers of public officials. Included as a "personality of interest" is a brigadier general because he was listed as a subscriber to *The Bond* (an "underground" anti-military sheet).[22]

The computerized file alone stored information about some 770 organiza-tions of every political shading and interest—some, indeed, unconnected with public affairs altogether— identified by categories of "target interest" and listing every organization's officers (chairman, secretary, treasurer, steering committee members).[23] These holdings were supplemented by file collections—some of them quite extensive—in the more than 300 USAINTC regional, field, and resi-dent offices scattered over the country.

No less overpowering are the G-2 collections housed at Fort Monroe. Its core collection, dating back to the twenties, was supplemented by a computer-ized system that stored data in three categories: incidents, personalities, and organizations, together comprising the Counter-Intelligence Record Informa-tion System (CRIS). With unimportant exceptions, CRIS duplicated the USAINTC information system: almost a third of the material that it stored originated with USAINTC, and only 10 percent with its own sources. As in the case of USAINTC, CRIS reports are marked by a grotesque sense of overkill.[24] Not only do they frequently mention public officials, but in some cases designate them by a code number, a practice reserved for radical students, militants, and civil rights leaders, and indicating a decision to make data concerning these individuals machine-retrievable. One of the more beguiling features of the CRIS reports is the trend breakdown: the difference in the number of reports on a particular subject from the previous week is computed and labeled "Trend."

CRIS also published a six-volume "personalities" edition, summarizing the political associations and activities of some 5500 subjects, extracted from computerized data.[25] The standard sections of the printout format contained, in addition to the usual vital statistics, an entry for "PLINK," computer shorthand for "personality link," expressed by a numerical identifier which unfortunately is unexplained. There are also cross-indexing identifiers and a list of seventeen informational categories, including "race," "income," "character," and "effectiveness." Picketers, peace protesters, vigillers, writers of letters to the editor are filed cheek by jowl with proven or suspected spies. The "narrative" sections of the printouts tell their own story:

> MEMBER OF FIRST UNITARIAN CHURCH TREASURER OF THE [city] CIVIL RIGHTS COUNCIL-1964 SIGNED LETTER TO PRESIDENT OHIO STATE UNIV APR 64 REQUESTING HERBERT APTHEKER TO SPEAK ON CAMPUS ACTIVE IN ANTI-VIETNAM PROTESTS SPONSOR OF SANE PRESIDENT OF THE [city] COMMITTEE TO DEFEND THE BILL OF RIGHTS.

> ON THE EVENING OF [month] 65, A MEETING OF THE INFORMATION SUBCOMMITTEE OF THE COLUMBIA UNIVERSITY INDEPENDENT COMMITTEE TO END THE WAR IN VIETNAM WAS HELD IN A RESIDENCE HALL LOUNGE AT COLUMBIA UNIVERSITY IN NEW YORK CITY.

> EMMA LAZURUS [sic] FEDERATION OF JEWISH WOMENS CLUBS AMONG LARGER DONORS CONTRIBUTING $500 DURING A FUND RAISING DINNER HELD BY THE EMERGENCY CIVIL LIBERTIES COMMITTEE ECLC DEC 15 1962 AT THE AMERICANA HOTEL NYC IN CELEBRATION OF THE 171ST ANNIVERSARY OF THE BILL OF RIGHTS.

One tells us:

> [x] HAS WRITTEN A NUMBER OF LETTERS TO US GOVERNMENT OFFICIALS CIVIL DEFENSE OFFICIALS AND TO NEWSPAPERS. THE LETTERS ARE GENERALLY VERY CRITICAL OF FEDERAL AND LOCAL GOVERNMENTS BECAUSE OF WHAT SHE CONSIDERS THE FUTILITY OF A CIVIL DEFENSE PROGRAM AND REFUSAL OF COUNTRIES TO DISARM.

On the basis of the last-quoted "narrative" given in its entirety, X's "effectiveness," one of the categories included in the computer program, was designated as "above average," although her "character" was described as "moderate or passive."

Occasionally, we encounter a particularly lurid "narrative" suggesting the contribution of an informer:

> SUBJ HAS A CRIMINAL RECORD AND A REPUTATION AS A SWINDLER HE REPORTEDLY HAD BEEN IN CONTACT WITH CHINESE COMMUNIST OFFICIAL WHO HAD OFFERED APPROX ONE MILLION DOLLARS TO PERSON TO BLOW UP STATUE OF

LIBERTY IN NY WITH ANOTHER MILLION DOLLARS UPON COMPLETION OF THE JOB
SUBJ IN 59 REPORTED THREAT AGAINST PRESIDENT EISENHOWER.

The "data source" for this item is the FBI, as was indeed the case for 80 percent of the entries in the "Personalities Edition." In some cases the sources are designated only by code, suggesting a covert infiltration or interception. Others are anonymous and also suggest snooping on a low level. ("Subject wrote to Soviet Embassy for information for school paper in exchange correspondence with a teacher in the Soviet Union.")

The CONARC personalities compilation is both quantitatively greater and more detailed than the corresponding USAINTC collection. In addition, all of the CONARC Army commands maintained their own organizational and "personality" file collections, some of it duplicating the Fort Monroe collection or the USAINTC MIG compilations in the same geographic area.

But we are not yet through with the Army's file collections. The CIAB maintained a microfilm archive known as the "Counterintelligence Reference File System," which was used to service its research and analysis functions. The index to the archive was computerized to provide rapid access to the contents of some 117,500 documents, broken down into entries of 189,000 activities and events, 113,250 organizational and 152,000 personality references covering both domestic and foreign matters. Master-coded by a series of descriptive categories, the index was designed to make instantly available, simply by the pressing of a button, a microfilm reel and frame for viewing or reproduction. But, frequently, the contents of the documents did not lend themselves to such ready categorization, with the result that the CIAB analysts were forced to assign code numbers in a somewhat arbitrary fashion. In addition, errors in coding were common: by writing 5 instead of 4 in a six-digit number, an analyst could falsely brand a subject a Communist. As a result, according to former CIAB analyst Ralph Stein, many individuals listed as Communists "were students who merely participated in a meeting or rally sponsored by an organization under surveillance."[26]

The United States Strike Command (USSTRICOM), a two-service command (Army and Air Force) headquartered at the MacDill Air Force Base in Florida, also maintained computerized files on civilian political activities, purportedly to facilitate rapid troop deployment in the event of riot. (USSTRICOM was established in 1961 to supply combat-ready troops in emergencies.) An elaborate data storage system was established by USSTRICOM's intelligence director in the late sixties, without civilian authorization of any kind and in complete disregard of the abundance of intelligence materials available from other sources. This computerized collection included a "Counterintelligence Personality File" and a "Counterintelligence Publications File," indistinguishable both in scope and irrelevance from the other compilations already discussed. Presumably to increase its efficiency it was, into the bargain, linked to each of the continental armies by a teletype network similar to the nationwide grid among the USAINTC components.

Finally, the DCDPO operation already referred to, in the Pentagon war room, was served by a computerized data-processing center with a focus on civilian political activities. It too boasted hotlines, elaborate electronic nationwide connections, and a special communications emergency network.[27] Its computer was apparently programmed for storing and retrieving information about specific incidents or events which, from the evidence of one printout, were so routine or minuscule as to leave one particularly baffled about their value as a harbinger of riots. One report in the printout announces an "ANTI-WAR DEMO" at West Point, where Vassar "GIRL STUDENTS WILL OFFER SEX TO CADETS WHO SIGN AN ANTI-WAR PETITION."[28]

Evaluation—The Intelligence Product

The Army published and disseminated a veritable Krakatoa of intelligence material. In addition to USAINTC's daily, weekly, and monthly teletyped summaries, each CONUS Army unit, and indeed some National Guard units, published monthly intelligence summaries (MISs) in booklet form, matched by similar publications of the Navy ("Trends"), and the Air Force ("Counterintelligence Briefs"). And the range of distribution was enormous, extending far beyond the population of possible users. If a high school class in Evanston, Illinois, demonstrated against the war, agents in Europe, Panama, and Hawaii could read about it almost as soon as it was reported to Fort Holabird. Appropriately paired with the MIS is the SOI, the Summary of Information, a genre that flowered from the requests from Army officers—both within the intelligence structure and outside it—for easily read and digested summaries of information about particular targets. Lower-level intelligence personnel were so burdened by such requests that USAINTC organized a special "Summaries and Analyses Branch" to process them. The SOIs quickly became such a popular item that USAINTC ordered them to be printed in its own printing plant in large editions, which were disseminated not only to requesters but, unsolicited, to over 100 intelligence units.

The available evidence about verbal briefings and evaluations by CIAB staff, largely untrained to interpret and analyze such data,[29] establishes that the interpretive function was dominated by the Army's countersubversive mission rather than a genuine concern for the tactical problems involved in dealing with civil disturbances. Apart from a CIAB-compiled city packet containing maps, liaison information, description of approach routes and possible disturbance sites, the intelligence products are obsessively concerned with subversion and the scapegoating of agitators.

CIAB's most important single intelligence reference work—formally known as "Individuals Active in Civil Disturbance," but more commonly called the "mug book," the "USAINTC Identification List," or the "Black List"— resembles the Bureau's "Agitator Index" and "Security Index." The 5 (out of a total of 6) volumes examined by the Ervin Committee profile some 1000 individuals, with 3 entries on a page, each one consisting of photographs and 7 descriptive listings: name, DPOB (date and place of birth), address, occupation, description, arrests, and organizations. The entire compilation is typical of the genre: encyclopedically over-inclusive (the ADA, the National Committee to Abolish the House Committee on Un-American Activities, the War

Resisters League, and many similar organizations are listed), inaccurate, paranoid, and irrelevant. Another CIAB intelligence product was the Compendium, a two-volume set in looseleaf format to permit periodic updating. Classified "Secret," the set was formally entitled *Civil Disturbances and Dissidence,* Volume I focusing on "Cities and Organizations of Interest," Volume II on (again!) "Personalities of Interest." Supplementing this material was a collection of summaries of "Significant Organizational Activity" and a discussion of "Organizations of Interest," dealing with the activities, structure, goals, and methods of over 100 organizations, widely diversified in size and influence. As elsewhere, the benchmark for "intelligence interest" was subversion or subversive influences, nowhere defined. This work was intended as a user's desk book to reduce the number of information requests addressed to CIAB and, like the mug book, was very widely distributed.[30]

From what has already been said about similar works, the reader should have no trouble conceiving the tone of Volume II, with its 345 biographical sketches of "Personalities of Interest." The compilers found "interest" in such matters as the results of medical examinations by physicians and psychiatrists, income, credit, sexual aberrations, family life, and stale background material, some of it dating back to the twenties. Badly skewed selection criteria resulted in the slighting of many prominent "personalities" in favor of obscure or unknown ones.

Collection Plans—Tooling Up for Armageddon

The basic documents that purport to guide domestic intelligence collection are especially important because they emanated from Army command circles and may be regarded, if not as orders, certainly as official statements of collection policy and priority. The first of these internal guides to intelligence collection appears in a section of a Field Manual, dating from the mid-sixties, dealing with "Intelligence Planning" in support of the Army's civil disturbance control mission. The Manual's general emphasis is on the Army's role as a public order force in riot situations, in which the most pressing need is for such information as area maps.[31] The chief sources of such information (the term "intelligence" is used sparingly) are other government agencies and the media. An Appendix dealing with crowd control reflects the Army's weakness for trendy social science theorizing. Crowd behavior, we are told, is not spontaneous but can be forecast through the advance compilation of relevant data. This intelligence will enable the commander to solve his central problem: How to isolate and remove the "3 to 5 percent hard core" from the mass who are in themselves harmless.

In the confident think-tank style that became familiar in the late fifties— the white laboratory jacket is almost visible through the prose—the Appendix assures us that "Always present in the agitation technique is a 'shadow' effect of blending with the other participants to give the 'appearance' of spontaneity, lack of direction, etc." When groups do not yield to traditional dispersal techniques, such resistance is an indication "that an internal control apparatus is present." The nucleus of the crowd's resistance consists of a "number of agitators of the local militant group organization." These agitators, in turn, recruit criminals, arm them with weapons (iron bars, wooden clubs, and placards), and also hire recruits who are unemployed hangers-on but are useful "because they provide a nucleus *responsive to orders* which sincere citizen protestors might *not* be." (Italics in original.) The agitators are organized for maximum destructiveness through an external command, an internal command, an assemblage of bodyguards, couriers, a shock force, sign-carriers, and "cheerleaders," the last being "specially briefed agitators [who] are carefully rehearsed on the slogans they are to chant and the order in which the cries are to be raised." These cheerleaders differ from their high school counterparts "only in that, in a mob situation, the fans will *join the game and riot when all of the . . . 'plays' have been properly executed.*" (Italics in original.)

The assumption of the Appendix that civilian unrest is the work of agitators is clearly apparent in the Army's intelligence preparations for call-outs in the early sixties. Thus, in Texas and Oklahoma, two states not known for their high potential for insurrection, surveillance of individuals and organizations began as early as 1964, apparently because the unit commanders involved discerned threats to the Republic in such activities as membership in the Unitarian-Universalist Fellowship and the Brotherhood of Railway Clerks. It seems quite plain that the more pointed tactical concerns of the Field Manual did not set military intelligence on fire with enthusiasm. In the wake of the Watts riot in 1965, USAINTC instructed its field units around the nation to begin collecting information that might be useful in civil disturbance contingencies. But the 1967 urban riots found the Army unprepared. The commanding officer of the troops sent to Detroit, Lieutenant General John Throckmorton, found himself deploying his airborne forces with only an Esso road map as a guide. Similarly, despite the fact that MIGs kept close watch on the preparations for the March on the Pentagon in the fall of 1967 and, in fact, conducted what Assistant Secretary of Defense Robert Froehlke called a "major covert operation," the Army's response was marked by confusion and bewilderment.

The Detroit fiasco resulted in the commissioning of Cyrus Vance, a former Deputy Secretary of Defense, as the personal representative of President Johnson, to report on how the Army had handled the Detroit call-out and to make recommendations for improving its future performance. Vance urged:

> in order to overcome the initial unfamiliarity of the federal troops with the area of operations it would be desirable if the several Continental Armies were tasked with reconnoitering the major cities of the United States in which it appears possible that riots may occur. Folders could then be prepared for those cities listing bivouac areas and possible headquarters locations and providing police data and other information needed to make an intelligent assessment of the optimum employment of Federal troops when committed.

To this straightforward recommendation, he added:

> The assembly and analysis of data with respect to activity patterns is needed. I believe it would be useful to assemble and analyze such data for Detroit, Newark, Milwaukee, Watts, et cetera. There may be "indicator" incidents; there may be a natural sequence in the order in which the several types of incidents occur.

Vance's logistic intelligence recommendations were largely ignored in favor of the suggestions in the last-quoted paragraph. Although all that Vance proposed was the exploration of possible local patterns of disturbance development, the stress on prediction, on forecast, on strategy rather than tactics became the dominant priority of military intelligence in the late sixties. This obsession with prediction is extraordinary when we remind ourselves again that the function of domestic Army intelligence is simply to guide troop commanders on riot assignments. The Army's intelligence leaders seem to have ignored the fact that the Army cannot on its own intervene in a civil disturbance situation. It is the responsibility not of the Army but of state governors and federal Attorneys General to advise the President when troops are needed. Such judgments are based on information, typically collected on-site by urban and state law enforcement personnel or, in the case of the Attorney General, by employees of the Department of Justice. By the time an urban disturbance reaches the point of troop call-out, its causes and progress have been reported by the news media, law enforcement agencies, the National Guard, and Department of Justice personnel.

The passion for prediction that unifies all of the Army's intelligence collection plans is explained by its assimilation of the sixties' unrest to its historic countersubversive mission. Countersubversive intelligence is future-oriented: seemingly innocent, nonpolitical activities must be surveilled and their participants dossiered to determine the existence of underlying revolutionary patterns and designs. The seed had to be watched because it was sure to ripen into poisonous fruit. In fact, the ripening was already in progress: riots and demonstrations were no more than "urban guerrilla warfare" or, in a formulation that became trendy in the sixties, part of the "political weapons system of the international Communist movement."[32] So it was that at the height of the Detroit riots, Major General William Yarborough ("the Big Y"), then Assistant Chief of Staff for intelligence, told his men at CIAB: "Get out your counterinsurgency manuals, we have an insurgency on our hands."*

It was not only that the prediction role was ideologically congenial to the intelligence mind; it was so much more professional and important than working out nitty-gritty arrangements that would lighten the burdens of a bewildered troop commander. Then, too, in the sixties, social scientists were talking quite hopefully of the utility of "key social indicators" and "trends" as an aid to government planning and policy making for the future.[33] Indeed, Vance's report had referred to "indicator incidents," and the Army had made use of such predictive intelligence for combat purposes in Vietnam. Finally—a seeming paradox—predictive intelligence was enormously appealing to the Army's action-oriented brass. The executive, the man of action, values intelligence precisely because it can unlock the future, give him an advantage over the competition, and tell him what to do at the appropriate time. While, on the one hand, he insists on the "facts," scorning the ambiguous or the tentative, on the other, he demands evaluation of future developments, especially when short-term predictions have already been verified by events. But the forecast of social

*It was Yarborough who initiated NSA's signals monitoring Operation MINARET.

developments, the extrapolation and projection of significant trends in a complex sequence of events, is at best a risky progression through a minefield of contingencies. It is not only that the analyst is forced into re $\cdot$ rvations and bet-hedging; the forecast itself is typically too "soft" to warrant action in reliance on it. Yet the tough-minded executive, "sick for certainty," is tempted to dismiss such dusty answers as speculative and abstract. His practical needs and anti-intellectualism ("That guy couldn't find his way out of a telephone booth") thus combine to encourage the production of forecast intelligence.

Betting on a sure thing is a confidence scam to which the military is especially vulnerable. For an intelligence officer eager to stay on top of his mission, the lure of prediction as a recipe for future action will almost surely prevail over such obstacles as utility and accuracy. It was inevitable that "the Big Y" would turn a deaf ear to the conclusions of the CIAB analysts that urban violence ("the thresholds of violence," to use a think-tank term adopted by Army intelligence) cannot be predicted. All that was needed was more of everything: more information drawn from an enlarged, nationwide network of sources, reported back with greater speed, processed by the most advanced equipment, and disseminated in greater volume—remedies that made an even greater farce of the whole predictive scenario.[34]

After an Army task force had formulated a civil disturbance plan in December 1967, Army intelligence designed a "Collection Plan" as a master blueprint for the collection of intelligence in preparation for a troop call-out. The plan strikes all the familiar conspiratorial chords, especially "the sinister perspective that subversive influence and organized control are distinct future possibilities in the United States civil disturbance problems." It warns of the dangers of foreign linkages with domestic disturbances, and points out that leaders of anti-war groups who have traveled to foreign countries "may be eithe $\cdot$ heavily influenced or outright dominated by their foreign contacts." Thus taixted, they "may, in turn, influence their followers, the majority of whom have no sympathy for the Communist cause, but are unaware of their leaders' affiliations." If, to use the document's formulation, the "Friendly Forces" (USAINTC and the stateside armies) are to triumph over the "Dissident Elements" (the civil rights, anti-Vietnam, and anti-draft movements), field intelligence must develop certain "Essential Elements of Information (EEI)," which will illuminate "the cause of civil disturbance," as well as "the patterns, techniques and capabilities of subversive elements in cover and deception efforts in civil disturbance situations." An important priority is the identification of "instigators and group participants."

After the King assassination riots, the Army on May 2, 1968, adopted an even more expansive plan known as the Department of the Army Civil Disturbance Information Collection Plan (ACDP) (U). As in the case of its predecessor, the document assures us that the Army is convinced that the anti-war and racial movements are, in the overwhelming majority of the cases, supported by "sincere Americans." But there is the traditional serpent in this paradise: "a small and virulent group who are out to tear America apart." They are now familiar figures to us, the "people who deliberately exploit the unrest and seek to generate violence and terror for selfish purposes." In order to frustrate their ends—

lawbreaking, chaos, violence, and revolution—field commanders are ordered to collect information about political activities in all cities where there is a "potential for civil disturbance," pursuant to an intricately calibrated system of priorities. The formation of "covert subversive organizations," as well as attempts by such organizations to penetrate and control civil rights or militant organizations, and "indications of participation or instigation by subversives," are assigned the highest priority, with identification of "friends or sympathizers" of participants—including newspapers, radio, television stations, and prominent leaders—not far behind.

In April 1969 USAINTC published its own collection plan, fully as broad as the ACDP and with the same heavy concentration on theories of conspiracy, a hard core of subversive agitators, and well-organized and effective enemy structures. (Both plans assume that the target subversive groups are a mirror image of the Army in their power, hierarchy, control, and effectiveness.) The USAINTC plan is divided into eleven collection categories, each with a separate computer code number, and then subdivided into EEIs, most of them duplicates of the ACDPs. Here, as in the case of the ACDP, liaison with local and federal law enforcement agencies is considered a major source of information; but direct photographic coverage of target individuals such as leaders or members of a "dissident/militant group" is specifically requested—"In all cases full identifying data concerning personalities, elements or activities depicted in the photograph will appear on the reverse side of the photo." As before, the development of covert intelligence collection sources is prohibited unless specifically authorized by the USAINTC commanding general. Finally, the plan concludes with a partial list of organizations "with dossier numbers of intelligence interest." The collection personnel are instructed that reports on the listed organizations should be prepared with the exact title of the group and the dossier number. The list begins with the African-American Student Movement, and includes the American Friends Service Committee, American Nazi Party, Americans for Democratic Action, Black Panther Party, Congress of Racial Equality, Chicago Area Draft Resisters, Fifth Avenue Peace Parade Committee, National Association for the Advancement of Colored People, SANE, Progressive Labor Party, The Resistance, Southern Christian Leadership Conference, Students for a Democratic Society, War Resisters League, and the Young Socialist Alliance, each of them with a designated dossier number.

These plans with their clotted rhetoric and pseudo-precision could hardly have been more misguided. Far from providing a source of tactical assistance, they rendered spying on civilians legitimate without even attempting to set limits or define terms. The confusion of purpose, absence of restraining guidelines, and ideological bias are all painfully apparent from the field operations that they were supposed to guide.

Operational Patterns

All intelligence operations in the political sphere outrun their asserted purposes. Nowhere is this more true than in the case of military intelligence.

The formal justifications—preparation for emergency troop call-outs and the monitoring of threats to the military function itself—serve as little more than pretexts. The scope and intensity of the field operations of the Army's intelligence personnel established all too clearly that, as in the case of the Bureau's surveillance system, they were at root forms of aggression against legitimate political expression. The limitations on the use of the military in civilian life discussed above barred open, direct actions to suppress protest activities, but still left available intelligence as a weapon, a means of projecting a hostile military presence into dissenting political activity. To be sure, discretion would seem to have been required—some attempt to maintain a low profile, to tread carefully in the political arena, to observe targeting restraints, and to respect the constitutional protections of the individual targets. But caution fell prey to the ideological hostility released by the eruptions of the sixties. If the collection plans summarized in the previous section were intended as a curb, it is not apparent from the field operations.

The assassination of Dr. Martin Luther King, Jr., led in April 1968 to a nationwide military intelligence mobilization, which monitored the King funeral, the urban riots in the wake of the assassination, the Poor People's March, and the subsequent Resurrection City encampment in Washington. Atlanta agents were assigned to monitor the funeral procession in unmarked cars and instructed to report back every fifteen minutes by "hotline" to Fort Holabird with instructions from their commanding officer, Major General William Blakefield, to "beat the AP" in their reporting, and to surveil everyone who attended the funeral, including such dignitaries as the Vice-President of the United States.[35] When the March began a month later at King's gravesite, agents in unmarked cars recorded the license plates of those who visited the grave. Coretta Scott King, the slain leader's wife, predicted to those who were about to start on the trek to Washington that her slain husband's "dream" ("I have a dream") would come true. When an agent reported her words back to his field office, he was told to go "find out what dream she is referring to."[36] The March itself, as well as the encampment, were heavily infiltrated by Army agents who spied on infiltrators planted by civilian units. The demonstration was also closely monitored by law enforcement agencies; there was no prospect of a breakdown of local peacekeeping efforts that might justify military involvement. The Army's informers were, as they subsequently recounted it, alternately bewildered and amused at the kinds of information they were instructed to report.*

Both the 1968 national political conventions were placed under military intelligence surveillance.[37] The August Miami Convention was monitored by ASA electronic technicians as well as by military agents based at Fort McNair, Georgia, in plain clothes.[38] The security coordinator for the Miami Beach Police

---

*At one point they were told to observe whether the mule teams leading the caravan were being abused. Said one agent, "It was a very strong requirement of the Army to know the exact number of mules and the exact number of horses at all times." A black officer assigned to infiltrate the Resurrection City campsite "was requested to get information on the sanitation facilities, the depth of the mud when it rained . . . and information of that nature"—*Ervin Hearings* (1971), pp. 253, 1469, 1471.

Department explained: "The Army intelligence as well as Navy intelligence had rather complete files on people who might be trouble-prone, and they also had contact with Washington and other parts of the country where they could get immediate information on any of these individuals, should that be necessary. The Army circulated in the area with concealed walkie talkies which enabled them to maintain communication with agents who had penetrated the target groups. They had other sophisticated devices as well and many of them were put to use." About sixty agents attached to at least four separate intelligence units monitored the Democratic Convention in Chicago. Operatives infiltrated the protesting groups and also invaded the convention floor without the knowledge of party functionaries. Reports transmitted from the surveillance units back to OPS IV at Fort Holabird were in turn relayed to the newly launched Directorate of Civil Disturbance Planning and Operations (DCDPO), which was also receiving hourly reports from three employees of the CIAB—not supposed to be an operational unit at all. The Army's intelligence coverage of public events peaked with the presidential inauguration in January 1969, which was covered by no less than 107 agents from MIG units all over the country. About eighty of them were assigned to undercover work throughout the District of Columbia and nearby suburbs. Informers were planted in groups considered potential sources of disruption.[39]

The field personnel—especially in the more remote areas—were structured into an identifiable intelligence community, which not only exchanged information occasionally but met together on a regular basis. For example, in Region II of the IIIth Military Intelligence Group (Greensboro and Winston-Salem, North Carolina), regular area intelligence meetings were held. These were attended by members of the FBI, the North Carolina State Bureau of Investigation, local police from nearby police departments and remoter municipalities as well, and sometimes university security officers from Lake Forest University. We encounter frequent examples of joint patrols, seemingly for law enforcement purposes (a clear violation of the Posse Comitatus Act), and even joint undercover operations.[40] The operatives exchanged information about their targets with law enforcement and campus security personnel, and even kept "contact files" on other members of the intelligence community. The field operations were built around a countersubversive axis. A Winston-Salem agent recalled: "We were trained to be paranoid. On the day we graduated from training, the Commanding Officer told us that the Communists already had dossiers and pictures of each one of us."[41]

As already indicated in Chapter 5, the number one target in the military surveillance repertory was the university campus. Every intelligence unit in the country monitored college-level institutions in its area, and in some instances even high schools. The extensive coverage reflected the role of the campus in the anti-war movement, as well as draft resistance; it was extraordinarily intensive because of the ease with which young operatives could pose as students and the readiness of most college administrators to cooperate with field offices. In at least one instance an agent penetrated a New York University course in black studies, recorded the contents of lectures and discussions, and identified the students. But other areas were not slighted. In the Winston-Salem unit, for example, agents had standing orders to follow "any suspicious black man, learn his identity and find out what he was up to."[42] And the scope was matched by the thoroughness of the surveillance. In testimony before the Ervin Committee, Texas State Representative Curtis M. Graves said that he had learned that the data collected about the targets in the Houston area included "how many teeth they had extracted, how many times they complained about back injury, surgery records. . . ."[43]

In addition to monitoring local branches of national groups—such as the Black Panthers, the SDS, the Friends, the Women's Strike for Peace—the regional and field offices spied on local ad hoc groups, meetings, and demonstrations. Agents monitored or infiltrated such targets as:

an anti-war meeting in a Washington, D.C., Episcopal church

demonstrations by a welfare mothers' organization in Milwaukee, Wisconsin

a procession of black Olympic stars

a conference of dissenting priests in the Washington, D.C., diocese protesting Archbishop Boyle's position on birth control

a Halloween party for elementary schoolchildren in Washington, D.C., suspected of harboring a local dissident

a demonstration of welfare recipients in New York City

a meeting of a sanitation workers' union in Atlanta, Georgia

a Fayetteville, North Carolina, church group

a Southern Christian Leadership Conference

Upward Bound—an OEO project

an anti-war vigil in the chapel of Colorado State University

the members of the congregation of the Unitarian Church in Houston, Texas, and of another in Monterey, California

a Godfrey Cambridge concert held in Washington, D.C.[44]

The chartered bus trip to an anti-war demonstration became a military intelligence specialty. Intelligence agents worked with the bus companies to obtain all available information about the sponsor and passengers, and mingled with the passengers en route to a protest site. The November 1969 March on the Pentagon was the most heavily infiltrated of these pilgrimages. MIG agents who traveled from New York with the demonstrators encountered so many other operatives in Washington that they were unable to report back as instructed because the phones were tied up by their colleagues from other areas under similar instructions.[45] An earlier Washington demonstration was similarly saturated by surveillants: "Agents took pains to dress and look like hippies, and when the pictures they took were developed, it turned out that New York agents snapped New Jersey agents. . . ." Obstructive tactics were sometimes used to delay departure or—by substituting an agent for the regular driver—arrival; agents were also permitted to replace drivers in order to monitor the passengers.

The MIG regions were stocked with high-grade surveillance gear: communications equipment, tape recorders, cameras with a variety of lenses, binoculars, lock-picking kits, lie detectors, and interview rooms with two-way mirrors.[46] The larger units in urban centers boasted special command head-quarters, emergency rooms, communications equipment and hotlines housed in an "operations center" mirroring on a smaller scale the OPS IV and Penta-gon facilities. Despite the Army's paper constraints on covert methods, the records shows that they were routinely used. Agents were issued "Leroy Kits," which enabled them to forge such identification as drivers' licenses and registration certificates. The most common kind of deception was of the shal-low variety, such as posing as a peace protester with a hidden transmitter or a camera. Agents frequently used a media cover, equipped with bogus creden-tials as reporters or photographers.[47] As we have seen, the campus was often targeted by such imposters, as well as by infiltrators from Army units and civilians under military direction. An agent of the 116th MIG who infiltrated a Washington, D.C., Yippie commune in 1969 was authorized to use mari-juana and liquor as a cover.[48] This same unit ran two informers who worked for two months undercover in the New Mobilization Committee, an anti-war group, and a third in a GI organizing program held at a Washington area school. The range of infiltration is indicated by the following statement by an operative:

> To gather . . . information, the 116th routinely assigned some twenty of its men as full-time undercover agents to infiltrate political groups and observe politically active persons. . . . Some of these groups have grown beards and long hair to pass as students on local college campuses. In addition, other members posed as mem-bers of the working press to obtain pictures of those involved in political activities; concealed tape recorders were also commonly used to record speeches and conver-sations at political events.

Though not with the scope and intensity of the COINTELPROs, the Army did conduct aggressive intelligence. The Fort Holabird CONUS intelligence sys-tem included an "offensive operations function." Enough evidence of "dirty tricks" has emerged to justify the conclusion that they were part of a deliberate program.*

Despite intensive national intelligence coverage by the seven MIGs, much of this activity was duplicated by the counterintelligence sections of the military intelligence detachments (MIDs) attached to the G-2 divisions and corps com-mands, and to a lesser extent by Navy and Air Force intelligence units. The CONUS operations of one of these G-2 units, the 5th Military Intelligence De-tachment of the 5th Infantry Division, Fort Carson, Colorado, are described in useful detail by two former agents: Laurence Lane, who served eighteen months in the G-2 office at Fort Carson, and Oliver A. Pierce, who, after completing training at Fort Holabird, was assigned in May 1969 to the same Fort Carson unit. Their testimony before the Ervin Committee recorded the cutthroat rivalry between the 5th MID and Region IV of the 113th MIG headquartered at Fort Collins in Denver.[49] The Fort Carson intelligence operation was extraordinarily zealous: intensive penetration and photography of a wide spectrum of targets,

---

*The report of the Ervin Committee indicates that various MI groups conducted offensive operations against targets such as anti-war and student groups. Further information about these operations was withheld through the Pentagon's refusal to declassify the relevant records.

the compilation of detailed dossiers, liaison intelligence pouring in from every law enforcement agency from the FBI to the sheriff's office and university police units, the issuance of weekly (sometimes triweekly) summaries and special reports. One would hardly guess that the 5th MID's mission was supposedly confined to base-related security functions.*

The rivalry was so intense that for a time liaison exchange was ended between the two units, and G-2 authorized the off-post semi-permanent assignment of two of its operatives in order to outdo the competition. This Keystone Kops competition was fanned by the zeal of G-2 commanders who, Lane explained, were not only quite grim about the importance of the intelligence that was being gathered but highly mistrustful of their MIG opposite numbers.[50] In mid-September 1969 a demonstration in Colorado Springs outside the Fort Carson gate provided G-2 units with their finest hour. Thirty MID agents mingled with the crowd monitoring the speakers; a task force was "assigned to follow the other intelligence personnel, so we knew where the 113th individuals would be throughout the whole demonstration." Not that such cross-surveillance was a novelty; a G-2 agent recalled: "I have read reports from the 113th with my name on them."[51]

By the fall of 1969, Region IV of the 113th MIG had gained the upper hand in the struggle over the CONUS turf. But G-2 consoled itself by intensifying its surveillance efforts in less controversial areas. For example, according to Lane, after a new coffeehouse drew the attention of the 5th MID: "I was in the area and stopped out of curiosity. There sat six counter-intelligence agents, the owner and myself in this dingily lighted dive making small talk but attempting not to let on that you knew who the guy next to you was and what he was doing there."[52]

Running Amok in Chicago

The 113th MIG whose activities in the Denver area we have just glimpsed was probably the most zealous MIG and certainly the one with the most intelligence personnel. Headquartered at Fort Sheridan, Illinois, with five regional headquarters, thirteen field, and forty-four resident offices, the 113th is a microcosm of a highly developed intelligence system. The intelligence operations of Region 1, which embraces the entire state of Illinois (except for East St.

*Surveillance of GI involvement in protest movements abroad came to light in 1973 and was made the subject of an ACLU lawsuit. The complaint, filed on behalf of a group of surveillance victims in West Germany, specified in largely uncontradicted and, indeed, extensively documented allegations and supporting affidavits, a startling assortment of undercover practices, including wiretapping, infiltration, photography, interception and opening of first-class mail and, most notably, of eavesdropping on communications between lawyers and their GI clients (invading the lawyer-client privilege), discipline for political reasons, and harassment. The charged offenses also include a cover-up and obstruction of justice. When, for example, embarrassing wiretap logs were made public, the Army quickly ordered the destruction of incriminating corroborative evidence. The Army also maintained file collections on the targets of its "CS" (countersubversive) campaign—lawyers, ministers, journalists, and others involved in responsible work in various political groups and campaigns, all well within the protected freedoms—*Military Surveillance* (1974), pp. 92–94, 360–397.

Louis) and is headquartered in Evanston, a Chicago suburb, were documented in a lawsuit filed in December 1970 *(ACLU* v. *Westmoreland).*

Region 1's civilian-oriented intelligence work was the responsibility of two units run by civilians: Richard Norusis and Thomas Filkins. Norusis—we will meet him again—is an exemplar of the extremist "obsessed" tradition in domestic intelligence. As one of his operatives recalled, he "was an extremely reactionary individual who seemed to take upon himself the task of protecting the U.S. society from everything to the left of center on the political spectrum. He possessed an unbounded amount of energy and, owing to the complete lack of command control of CONUS activities, he was free to direct his energies to whatever activities he deemed fit."[53] In short, here as elsewhere in the intelligence structure, the absence of effective guidelines gave free play to the political bigotry of the collection personnel.

Filkins, like Norusis, was an ICCP (Intelligence Career Civilian Personnel), who after his retirement from military intelligence duties overseas had taken a variety of intelligence courses at Fort Holabird. He testified at the Westmoreland trial that his surveillance blueprint had been the collection plans and that the guideline for the selection of targets was "those individuals and organizations whose activities were likely to result in domestic violence calling for the use of troops." Using this as a standard, Filkins's unit placed under surveillance and compiled files on some 800 subjects, including "virtually every organization"; those with no record of violence or policies in that direction were nevertheless surveilled by a strained standard of predictive or associational guilt. A file was kept on the Southern Conference Leadership Fund, although it had admittedly not been involved in violence, but "associates and affiliates of SCLC had engaged in violence. This was part of the Army's legal monitoring of all large group activities."[54] The Chicago ACLU was included among the region's targets because the Information Collection Plan (ICP) mandated surveillance of any organization or individual offering a legal defense or even making a public statement "in support of individuals who had participated or allegedly participated in civil disturbances. . . ." Filkins explained how the guidelines of the collection plan generated a huge body of files:

> Under the intelligence collection plan, the basic reason for this maintenance of files and monitoring of newspapers, etc. would have been where organizations or individuals were engaged in violence, violent activities, but also under the intelligence collection plan was a responsibility to also maintain at least moderate coverage of the organizations which are intertwined either officially or unofficially with these groups. So here we can see, if I may cite an example where this could have been true, we were obliged to keep files, for example, on the Youth Against War and Fascism, which has engaged in quite a bit of violence and related activities in the Chicago area. And if, for example, a perfectly legitimate and peaceful organization like the American Friends Service Committee, a Quaker action group . . . if they had a demonstration or co-sponsorship of an activity, the intelligence collection plan would have allowed them a maintenance of at least a nominal file on the American Friends Service Committee.[55]

Individual dossiers, described by Filkins as a "large voluminous file that contained all details on a person's life, background, and history," were opened on every subject who "we had reason to believe was in a leadership position in a group that was or could reasonably be expected to be involved in civil disturbance." The subjects included Senator Adlai Stevenson III; Representative Abner Mikvna; Jay Miller, then executive director of the Illinois division of the American Civil Liberties Union; black activist Jesse Jackson; two Chicago black aldermen, A. A. ("Sammy") Rayner and William Cousins; Gordon Sherman, a member and former officer of Chicago Business Executive Move for Vietnam Peace; and Henry de Zutter and Morton Kondracke, Chicago newspapermen. In addition, files were maintained on professors, clergymen, businessmen, and others whose only link to the Army's civil disturbance mission was either opposition to the Vietnam War or support for integration movements.[56] One law professor, Jon R. Waltz of the Northwestern University Law School, was monitored because he served as a legal consultant to the defense counsel in the Westmoreland case.[57]

Like other intelligence operatives called upon to justify their activities, Filkins offered an ingenious explanation of his unit's practices, itself a canon of intelligence professionalism. For example, he insisted that the "primary purpose" of the surveillance of the Reverend Jesse Jackson was "to be aware of Mr. Jackson's activities and to be up to date, because of the significance of his position . . . in the black community in Chicago and . . . in the United States. We felt . . . that Mr. Jackson, along with other civic leaders, would be the ideal person to contact should violence occur in the city of Chicago. He would be the one man to be relied upon to try to put a damper on any violence."[58] But if such were the purpose, a notation of Jackson's address and phone number would be sufficient, instead of, as was actually the case, a file complete with newspaper clippings and intelligence reports from other law enforcement agencies. That Filkins's explanation for the Jackson file was a cover is further demonstrated by the testimony of Ralph Stein, a CIAB analyst who testified that Jackson's file

> contained a great deal of specific information of conversations that he had with members of the Southern Christian Leadership Conference . . . and this information, at the time it was received by our office, was not available to any member of the press or public. . . . The wording of the report made it obvious that it could only have been obtained by someone who was in the confidence of Mr. Jackson or other members of the SCLC, as their very remarks indicated, that they wanted the information kept extremely private and limited.[59]

One must also treat as a cover-up the explanation that a "characterization file" on the ACLU in Chicago was intended to protect that organization against an improper evaluation by inexperienced investigators.[60] Nor can one willingly suspend disbelief in the testimony that the Chicago conspiracy trial became a subject of Army intelligence interest only "because this was to be a precedent setting trial on the use of federal troops in civil disorder."[61]

The files were fed by a number of sources: intelligence generated by the undercover agents; a stream of flyers, circulars, announcements; spot and agent reports and photographs; liaison material from all of the area law enforcement and intelligence agencies, federal, state, and urban; and finally clippings, mounted and annotated by the agent with cross references to other file material dealing with the individual, group, or event. Part of this flow was duplicated for local use before it was transmitted to group headquarters, where it would either be retained or sent on to Fort Holabird.[62] While files and dossiers flowed through the Region 1 offices to group offices and ultimately Fort Holabird, a reverse flow of material, summaries, dossiers, evaluations, and studies poured into the group, regional, and field offices. Requests for information regularly came to the desks of personnel at the regional, field, and resident office level. Local cadres were constantly reminded that the developments they were surveilling and reporting could be properly understood only in a broader focus: the six-states 113th MIG area and the entire nation. This reminder served to enhance the importance of local information that seemed on its face trivial or innocuous—its true meaning could only be deciphered in the context of other seemingly unrelated developments. Only the experts at Fort Holabird could penetrate what might be a deception and fit all the pieces of the puzzle together.

The operations of Region 1 were extraordinarily diversified and quite sophisticated. We begin with the technical equipment:

> The equipment employed included approximately nine vehicles equipped with $1200.00 to $1400.00 two-way radios, about four $1000.00 portable radios, and several cameras for snapping pictures of disturbance leaders. The radio communications network was tied together by a large radio transmitter located atop the Prudential Building in downtown Chicago and rumored to have cost between $900,000.00 and one million dollars. . . . (R)adio vehicles together with agents on foot carrying portable units, spread out over the city flashing back reports of any gathering observed, in excess of three persons, which appeared suspicious.[63]

Richard Stahl, a former operative with thirty months' intelligence service in Region 1, testified that, "on numerous occasions (he) was involved in surveillance, the use of tape recorders at rallies, camera equipment to take pictures and gather information. . . ."[64] Another agent was ordered to wear his hair long and dress hippy-style as he roamed the city, covering and photographing demonstrations, a duty for which he had received special training and equipment, including a camera with lenses permitting photographs at very long distances. "Precisely I was told to take pictures of anyone no matter who they were or why they were there."[65] At Region 1 level, a "mug book" was kept with which agents were required to become familiar, in order to avoid duplication and to concentrate their cameras on "personalities" not already known. The mug books covered the entire political spectrum from pacifists to Minutemen.

Region 1 had an especially close working relationship with the Chicago police anti-subversive unit and its members. At demonstrations the agents wore lapel pins to identify them to other policemen and surveillance operatives; but that was hardly necessary in the case of the Chicago police, with whom they shared photographic and observation chores. The military intelligence agents found the Chicago police arrest records, with their elaborate detail and photographs, particularly useful. They demonstrated their gratitude: "One agent from our office prevented a member of the press from taking a picture of the Chicago police arresting by force a demonstrator, by bumping into the photographer and making him lose his balance every time he attempted to take the picture."[66] The Region I forces also collaborated with a local group with terrorist leanings, the Legion of Justice (see Chapter 12): Former members of the terrorist group alleged that the local intelligence office had provided financial help in activities against left-wing Chicago groups, as well as material such as tear gas, grenades, and bugging devices. While many of these allegations were not supported by corroborative evidence, it is incontestable that the local agents were in contact with the Legion's leader and exchanged information, including material plundered by the Legion in a raid on an office of a radical organization.

Evidence of aggressive intelligence includes arranging for the delivery of unordered fried chicken to the home of a Chicago professor where an anti-war meeting was in progress; posing as a bus driver, collecting bus tickets of departing demonstrators and directing them to a nonexistent bus—a "disinformation" tactic widely practiced in Washington area demonstrations; heckling speakers in order to cause disruptions; and removing notices of rallies and demonstrations from school bulletin boards. The 113th also played an active role in the 1968 national surveillance programs already mentioned, including the identification of members of the Chicago contingent of the Poor People's March; vehicular surveillance of leaders and coverage of the National Democratic Convention.* Under a variety of covers, personnel attached to the 113th infiltrated a number of organizations and rallies organized to protest the Democratic National Convention, including a Lincoln Park rally addressed by Panther leader Bobby Seale, a sunrise meeting conducted by poet Allen Ginsberg ("other than singing and meditation, the meeting was uneventful"), and a Grant Park meeting addressed by pacifist Staughton Lynd, then a professor at Roosevelt University.[67]

The 113th earned national distinction with its two-man team equipped with a complete videotape system housed in a vehicle with the cover name "Mid West Video News." The team's finest hour was an interview, claimed to be exclusive, with Yippie leader Abby Hoffman. The video team was included in the 113th contingent subsequently assigned to support the 116th MIG (Military District of Washington) in monitoring the inaugural in January 1969.

All of the 113th agents reporting for duty were expressly told, whatever their formal assignment,

---

*According to a semi-official account of the surveillance (Ervin Hearings [1971], pp. 1481–1482):

a. Around-the-clock coverage was provided by two shifts. Operations center was located in the existing Evanston, Illinois, unit. Direct communications were established to Fort Holabird, Maryland; Fifth US Army; and Fourth US Army. Direct lines were connected between the FBI and Chicago police to the Evanston office.

b. Concept of coverage consisted of two-man agent teams at focal points, particularly at those selected and manned by Chicago police.

c. Departure of normal coverage by liaison consisted of:
   (1) Roving teams, on foot, equipped with handi-talkie radios, to report on incidents.
   (2) Vehicle roving teams, also radio equipped, dispatched as required. One such team also had still photo cameras.
   (3) Stationary observers at sites manned by Chicago police. Two such places were the Hilton Hotel and a tower near the convention hall.
   (4) One team equipped with a TV camera for recording video tape.

to be alert when visiting local colleges and Universities in connection with personnel security investigations for notices of any marches, rallies, meetings or demonstrations. We were soon instructed to collect any and all newspapers, flyers, pamphlets, or notices relevant to any student political activity and turn them over to the CONUS Intel section. Agents were ordered to visit especially the larger schools, such as the University of Chicago, Northwestern University, Loyola University, and the University of Illinois at Chicago Circle regularly for this purpose. In addition, agents assigned to the CONUS section at Region 1 headquarters . . . about five . . . and the CONUS section at CFO (about two) also visited the same campuses for the purpose of keeping track of student political activity.[68]

The blanket college coverage included the planting of an informer at Loyola University. The plant, a captain in military intelligence, was enrolled as a student and collaborated with other students in the preparation of an anti-war essay. He supplemented his more deceptive tactics with physical surveillance: from his apartment in a building overlooking the campus, he spied on demonstrations with a 30-power telescope pointed down out of his window.

Nor did Region 1 neglect the high schools. Investigative reporter Dave Anderson early in 1971 published a detailed account of such surveillance against student opponents of the Vietnam War. The principal of one high school recalls readily that Norusis had unsuccessfully approached him for information on several occasions, boasting that he had already acquired information about one student from other official sources. A group of guidance counselors did not deny that they had transmitted such information and professed to be unaware of the purpose for which the material was being collected.[69] In a letter dated June 1, 1971, from the Department of the Army addressed to the Skokie Human Relations Commission, the Army justified the collection of the high school data as "simply an effort to obtain information which was thought to be of use in planning and preparing for possible disturbances."* The zealousness of Region 1's intelligence activities was extraordinary but by no means unique. Finally, the nationwide accumulation of excesses made inevitable exposure and the demand for an accounting.

The Ultimate Reckoning—Exposé and Cover-up

The cult of secrecy, the protective cloak of national security, the classification system, the pledge of the individual agent not to disclose what he has learned in the course of his duties ("the debriefing oath")—all provide a protective shelter for intelligence abuses.[70] In the case of military intelligence, the doors and windows were opened wider than those of other intelligence systems as the result of a scouring probe conducted over a four-year period by the Ervin Committee. The effectiveness of the probe is a tribute to efficient staff work and, especially, to the efforts of ex-intelligence Captain Christopher Pyle, who became a consultant to the committee, its principal witness, and the midwife of

---

*The Skokie incident reflects in part a form of surveillance that recurred in communities which were physically close to MIG installations and offices—here, Evanston. The children of intelligence personnel attending local high schools inevitably imparted to their parents news of school activities, especially anti-war demonstrations, which invited investigation.

the second thoughts, criticisms, and recantations of about 125 military intelligence agents, a considerable number of whom testified or gave statements to the committee.

It all started with the publication of Captain Pyle's landmark article in the January 1970 *Washington Monthly:* "CONUS Intelligence: The Army Watches Civilian Politics." Pyle, a lawyer and a Columbia University Ph.D. candidate equipped with a mass of authoritative information about the Army's domestic surveillance practice in the late sixties and a broad knowledge of intelligence theory, rejected the self-serving justifications of the Army intelligence establishment. In exploring the "greening" of intelligence, we begin with the fact that a considerable number of officers in the Vietnam era in the military intelligence structure were not career officers but, like Captain Pyle, individuals with a civilian background and a prospect of return to civilian life. Then, too, the agents themselves were for the most part draftees. With its haphazard assignment procedures—matching the job to the candidate's background (mostly educational)—its short-term service requirements, its ultimate reliance on on-the-job training, the draft lacked the resources to ensure commitment and solidarity of intelligence personnel. Moreover, in contrast to the cadres of the peacetime intelligence services, Vietnam era domestic intelligence attracted many who were ideologically indifferent or hostile to war-connected values and assumptions, choosing it only to avoid combat involvement—a motivation hardly calculated to stir enthusiasm for, say, monitoring anti-war demonstrations. Related inducements like the opportunity to live off base and to wear civilian clothes were likewise dubious assurances of commitment.[71] As in the case of the Vietnam soldiery generally, the hunters frequently identified more sympathetically with their quarry than with their superiors. All of the accumulated discontents of Army officers and agents detailed below were honed by school-room strictures that in this country—in contrast to the role of the military in other lands—the Army is rigorously excluded from civilian life.

The availability of cadres of young men had initially seemed to offer unique opportunities; ironically, it was these same younger agents who later became most bitter and cynical. Many of them were outraged by the institutional bigotry which, for example, viewed student demonstrators as revolutionaries and long hair as subversive. Both at Holabird and in the field, the most resented types were intelligence civilian career personnel (ICCP's), many of whom had retired from military intelligence and while receiving pensions were rehired as intelligence experts. Since the collection plans imposed no restraints, the zealots among them ran wild.

A substantial number of agents surfaced out of a concern for the threat posed by the program to the right of dissent. Such grievances as a disregard of professional norms, poor training, duplication, waste, and inadequate supervision brought many others out of the closet.[72] Others again found repelling the arbitrary exercise of authority, the drive for promotion, and the self-imposed isolation of senior intelligence personnel from the mainstream of democratic life and values.[73]

There were, of course, agents who were untouched by such doubts but nevertheless became disillusioned. Swept up in trench-coated James Bond-type expectations, they were prepared to enjoy the stalking of subversive targets and their access to surveillance gadgetry. Intelligence offered a risk-free road to glory.[74] But the conflict between fantasy and reality was unbridgeable. A light-hearted few—possibly conditioned by exposure to television and film spy comedies—thought the entire program very funny. The Fort Holabird training seemed, in the words of one ex-agent, "hilarious," especially the field exercise in which the junior officers stalked "rabbits" (usually enlisted men posing as spies). After solving the problem by flushing the "rabbits," hunters and hunted would hide from their superiors in a bar for "the remaining two hours of the problem."[75] Field operations came through as Act II of the farce begun in training: a huge force of snoopers, equipped to the nines with surveillance gear, pursuing an elusive hydra-headed enemy without quite knowing what made him the enemy, how to recognize him, or indeed why the pursuit was launched in the first place. The Act III evaluation process brought more laughs.[76] An interviewed agent assigned to preparing summaries at Fort Holabird recalls with a chuckle: "No spot report was ever taken, ripped off the teletype machine, read, [considered] irrelevant and thrown away." Similarly, the irrationality of the security precautions and the classification system became stock sources of jokes and comic anecdotes.* If the intelligence mystique was legitimated by mass culture, its flip treatment by the media in the sixties contributed to a perception of its comic aspects. In both interviews and written accounts, the agents' experiences suggested to them familiar pop-cult treatments: a parody spy thriller (featuring Peter Sellers or Alec Guinness); a musical comedy set in a provincial MIG resident office, *Our Man in Casper, Wyoming;* a Graustarkian operetta— rival teams of spies discover that they have been spying on one another; a science fiction fantasy—data banks, computerized filing systems, microfilmed dossiers, and indices ranged in a to-the-death struggle for survival; a horror spoof— Hawkshaw Frankenstein Runs Amok.[77]

The Army, of course, took a much grimmer view. The disillusionments and defections were themselves made the subject of an intelligence operation. A research team was commissioned to draft a report establishing the existence of a Communist conspiracy that made the preservation of the entire system imper-

*Here are two Fort Holabird stories:

"My job was to read the Communist newspaper. . . . I would arrive in the morning and grab the paper and then take it out of the office with me to read over my coffee. But the sheet was classified 'Secret' so I wasn't supposed to take it out of the office. Why it was classified beats me, but there it was. Anyone could buy it on the newsstand, but once it got into Fort Holabird it was regarded as a classified document."

"Every night all our working papers and notes were deposited in a special safe in each agent's office. The security of the safes and the material in them was the responsibility of an old-timer, a sergeant who had seen thirty years of service and was about to retire. One morning when I came to the office all of the materials which were supposed to be guarded by the sergeant were piled neatly on my desk and topped by a pamphlet dealing with the Jehovah's Witnesses. It wasn't only my safe, but the contents of every safe received the same treatment. There was a crisis in the office; a twenty-four-hour special emergency was declared and an investigation launched. Was this some kind of stunt by the enemy? How had security broken down? It turned out that the sergeant facing retirement had found God and was so fervent in his conversion that he thought he would make a try at converting the rest of us. So ended the great security crisis."

ative. On another front, a "cover your ass" conference was convened to devise an intelligence-type "plausible denial" of Captain Pyle's charges. In yet another rapid flanking movement, Fort Holabird generals physically removed many of the embarrassing files and entries detailed in the Pyle article; telephone calls also went out from OPS IV instructing the field agents to hide, but not destroy, incriminating files.[78]

In mid-January 1971 Army intelligence organized an investigative task force in which the former poachers were recruited to serve as gamekeepers. When the Defense Department civilian leadership began to probe, the high intelligence brass denied the existence of computers and computer records altogether. The mere possibility of a cutback in computer-processing capability terrified Fort Holabird's career officers.* When orders finally came down to destroy or curb Fort Holabird's file collection, they were obeyed—but not before the files had been duplicated. The custodial personnel were made to feel that ingenuity in circumventing file destruction orders would ultimately be rewarded by promotion. One clerk quoted in the Ervin testimony recalled: "The tendency was to keep the information while obeying the order. . . . The order didn't say destroy the information, just destroy the Compendium." This gloss made it possible to transfer both volumes of the Compendium to microfilm before destroying it physically.

The field resources were viewed by the intelligence command as its trump card and it was at the field level that the worst sabotage took place. When attempts were made to implement new, more restrained policies through a council composed of high civilian defense officials, field compliance inspection visits were frequently evaded by crafty ploys reminiscent of Gogol's Inspector General.[79] Intelligence field commanders assured their cadres that the regional files would remain intact and that surveillance operations would continue unchanged. Other forms of field deception consisted of restructuring the intelligence collection process so that when CONUS intelligence sections were liquidated as ordered, the same work was transferred to the section engaged in personnel security investigations. A blunter procedure was simply to juggle files: personality files were merged into organizational files; anti-war surveillance files were relabeled RITA files, even though the subject groups had nothing to do with proselytizing military personnel. In the same way, file collections were secretly transferred to nonfederal units or stored in the homes of agents and officers.

The skirmishes of the Army's intelligence headquarters and field personnel to nullify and circumvent attempts by the civilian leadership to curb intelligence

---

*In the words of a former agent: "The lieutenant colonels and the full colonels at Fort Holabird pride themselves on their ability to retrieve information really quickly. If Colonel or General So-and-So out in Oregon wants to know about so-and-so real quick, then they can get this file out real quick and read it to him over the phone and the general is just snowed. This is the mentality, to try to snow the next rank up so that the next time it's your turn to be promoted they'll look at you favorably. So when you get down to the middle- and lower-ranking officers, that's where they begin to think, 'Well, good heavens, you know, if we destroy this, we might not be able to answer requests and then that's going to put me in a bad light. So we'll remove it and it will look like it was never there, or as if it were destroyed, but we'll just put it in another place, so we'll still be able to retrieve it.' "

abuses, the token palliatives of the leadership itself, the persistent attempt to appease critics without surrendering ground unnecessarily, the promulgation of vaguely worded guidelines—all finally ended in December 1970. A directive was issued setting down guidelines that were entirely new in the sense that, instead of dealing with isolated abuses in piecemeal fashion, they structurally confined the Army's civilian intelligence program within appropriate legal and functional limits. This was achieved simply by liquidating CONUS intelligence and confining its targets to conduct that threatens a legitimate palpable Army interest. The work of liquidation and reform was later (on March 1, 1974) completed by a Defense Department directive covering all of the services. While retaining the potential for abuse,* the new provisions unquestionably pointed military intelligence in a new direction. For the first time, responsibility for the conduct of domestic surveillance was lodged by a positive directive in the civilian Secretary of Defense. To complete the dismantling process, on June 1, 1971, the Army issued an implementing directive, which among other things dissolved the role of CIAD. Under the new dispensation, it was left all dressed up in an analytic capability with nowhere to go. CIAD was authorized to receive from civilian agencies "early warning intelligence" about civil disturbance situations that might, in the future, overtax local law enforcement resources, to be supplemented by public media data. But the agency was specifically forbidden to use the latter source either to collect "background information about the beliefs of civilians or the nature of civilian organizations" or to develop files about such individuals or organizations.

Fixing the Blame

Although there are ambiguities in the record, it is fair to conclude that CONUS INTEL was the creation of Army intelligence and that it simply continued *toutes proportions gardées* in the upheavals of the sixties the tactics with which it had historically confronted domestic unrest.[80] The role of Johnson administration officials in this development parallels the domestic CIA build-up. That there was pressure from the White House and the Attorney General's office for an accelerated flow of information dealing with the urban riots and their causes is incontestable: the hope persisted that somehow the Army with its superior resources would come up with the desperately sought prize—a means of predicting riots. But the Johnson administration cannot escape responsibility for encouraging the Army to enter barred areas, for failing to ensure civilian control of any kind, and finally, for a refusal to recognize that, however well intentioned, its quest for forecast intelligence would be ideologized and implemented by illegal methods.[81] To be sure, the civilian leadership of the Defense Department, the White House, and the Attorney General's office were left in the dark about the military intelligence colossus. But it is fair to conclude that they preferred

---

*Possibly the most serious defect in the new directive is that the Defense Secretary was given carte blanche to authorize the most questionable form of surveillance (undercover penetration) without the specific findings required in more routine monitoring that "there is a distinct threat of a civil disturbance exceeding the law enforcement capabilities of state and local authorities."

it that way. When the Nixon administration took over, "intelligence" wholly replaced "information" (recall the IDIU's transformation) as the key objective. In 1969, Justice and Defense agreed on an Interdepartmental Action Plan (IAP) to share responsibility for civil disturbance intelligence. The plan—a phase in the groping of the Nixon administration for an integrated intelligence structure and hierarchy—assigned the IDIU an evaluative role and rather cloudily left the Army with a collection responsibility. The civilian Defense Department leadership did argue for turning collection over to the Bureau in accordance with the Delimitations Agreement. But by this time it was too late. The Bureau preferred safer passage, and the entrenched intelligence brass viewed such a move as a death sentence. Most important, the Nixon civilian high command, whose knowledge of the scope and style of the collection effort is incontestable, felt that it was vital to its offensive, commenced in the spring of 1969, against domestic dissent. And by that time the Army was also irreversibly committed: in April 1969 USAINTC promulgated its collection plan, even more comprehensive than its predecessors. As an Army intelligence functionary tersely summarized the situation in the spring of 1969: "We created addicts for this stuff all over the Government."[82]

But the armed services were perhaps more addicted to "this stuff" than any other government agency. And nothing shows this more than their involvement in developing the Huston Plan in the summer of 1970 and their subsequent participation in the IEC, at the very time when responsible military and civilian leaders were—by directive, assurances in legal proceedings, and public statements—insisting that civilian intelligence collection had ended. It is doubtful whether addiction to "this stuff" can be cured, short of the severe criminal sanctions that Congress has rejected. The Army as a whole is congenitally vulnerable to shifting winds, and stateside civilian intelligence would seem to exercise a far more precarious hold than other peacetime Army functions. Yet it has maintained unbroken continuity for over half a century. Its survival formula is simple enough: when democratic values are in the ascendant, the intelligence system retires to the shadows to hibernate, so to speak, until social unrest changes the weather—an extension on an institutional scale of a flexibility required in day-to-day intelligence operations. But intelligence professionals regard such a retreat as merely tactical, a temporary setback that confirms the strength of the subversive enemy. The need to avoid destructive confrontations with powerful civilian critics also explains the evasions, the resort to tokenism, and the pseudo-contrition of the "sorry about that" variety all regularly invoked when the demands for an accounting grow strong.

Continuity is assured in a variety of ways, not the least of which is an old-boy network of former agents. As we have seen, after World War I many displaced intelligence officers and agents found similar work either with the government or with private groups. When, after World War II, intelligence became a negotiable skill, former Army practitioners of the art either found private intelligence-related employment or were encouraged to hole up in other intelligence agencies. A similar process is already at work to provide shelter for displaced post-Vietnam intelligence personnel.

These agents form the core of the nativist countersubversive constituency, providing it with literature and file information. Such materials are in steady demand in the countersubversive marketplaces of the nation. It is this sense that countersubversive files will have future value and indeed ultimately serve as a showdown resource that explains the tenacity and evasiveness of the Army's response to civilian cleansing efforts. And it would be folly to take comfort from official directives ordering the destruction of civilian file collections. Given current reproduction technology, the duplication of these collections is a certainty. If history is a guide, copies of the Army collections have been secretly retained by intelligence agents and added to other file holdings on federal, state, and local levels. In addition, again judging from the past, the Army files have surely been acquired by private agencies to augment collections originally built through the same process of clandestine acquisition. Nor, in considering the Army's survival prospects in the domestic civilian intelligence arena, can we ignore its technological "capability" (including computerized data encoding to thwart access by outsiders), its financial resources and spaces on intelligence manning charts for long-established military specialties (MOS).[83] After all, "intelligence" in a battle context is a normal military function, served by specialists and the most advanced equipment. Why, for example, should the sensors developed in Vietnam be mothballed when they could be used to monitor domestic civilian politics?[84] It should be recalled that the Army's cognitive passions also embrace—clumsily, to be sure—the social sciences: information theory, behavior analysis, social indicators. What other domestic intelligence agency, from the FBI to the lowly red squads, is so richly qualified for the task of ferreting out dissent? In the light of both recent and more remote history, how can self-regulation alone create the assurance of protection against future abuse?

9 Internal Revenue Service — Tax Collector as Nation-Savior

Subverting the Revenue-raising Function

In the entire federal bureaucracy, no agency offers such an attractive lure to the intelligence enterprise as the Internal Revenue Service (IRS). A Goliath with 700 offices spread over the nation and some 2800 special agents, it collects and files information about the private affairs of some 80 million individuals who file tax returns every year. As former IRS Commissioner Donald C. Alexander has stated, "We have more information about more people than any other agency in this country."[1] Form 1040, the standard taxpayer's return form, discloses the taxpayer's name, address, social security number, marital status, number and names of children and other dependents, as well as the taxpayer's entire gross income. Schedule A discloses data about the groups or causes the taxpayer has supported, his union membership, and whether he is under medical care.

In addition to the information contained in the taxpayer's return, audits and investigations yield mountains of additional information on demand without the requirement of a subpoena. If the taxpayer is uncooperative, subpoenas are readily procurable to compel disclosure. Beyond the information from the taxpayer himself, the IRS is in command of an extraordinary arsenal of investigative techniques to ferret out hidden sources of income: the undercover capability of the IRS outweighs that of all of the other federal civilian agencies combined. In addition, electronic surveillance, decoys, mail covers, and related practices have, at least until very recently, been part of the everyday intelligence operations of the IRS.[2]

The huge IRS intelligence bureaucracy is linked functionally to other segments of the intelligence community. But the ties are stronger than shared operational techniques and occupational solidarity; intelligence forms a distinct employment market, and veterans of one agency frequently turn up in another retaining useful ties to their former employment. These links form the sinews of a brotherhood, a "buddy system," as it is sometimes called, which promotes the clandestine exchange of information among the units of the intelligence community. The IRS Intelligence Division, for example, has served as a conduit to relay to other branches of the agency special requests from other intelligence agencies, including the proper handling of the tax returns of paid informers.

As I have tried to show, the basic thrust of intelligence is the development of sanctions against proscribed targets. Because the function of the IRS is not confined to passive data collection, it is a vital asset of the entire intelligence community. Few punishments are as efficient for aggressive intelligence purposes as the pocketbook sanctions commanded by the Service. A claimed tax delinquency or other offense by an individual taxpayer hits where it hurts; only slightly less damaging is an audit or investigation by IRS agents. Moreover, the seemingly random character of the conventional tax return verification effectively shelters the IRS from charges of political motivation, even when they are true.

However, such repressive dividends are obtained at great cost. The foundation stone of our tax collection system is enlightened self-enforcement. But the willingness of a taxpayer to reveal sources of income voluntarily depends on his or her trust in the government's assurance that such disclosures will be treated confidentially. The intelligence involvements of the IRS have seriously disturbed this trust-confidentiality dialectic.* Selective enforcement is possibly even more destructive of sound tax collection norms than is breach of confidentiality. It not only destroys confidence in the impartiality of the collection process but invades the protected freedoms by engendering the fear that unpopular politics may result in adverse tax consequences. And these risks are incurred without compensating revenue benefits: radicals, dissenters, and "extremists" are usually impecunious and constitute a rather unpromising source of tax revenue. For the same reason, there is very little tax potential in cause groups: the bulk of such associations are of a transient, ad hoc character, with modest treasuries and limited access to contributors.

The Tax Exemption Ambush

It is as true today as when Tocqueville first remarked on it that "in no country in the world has the principle of association been . . . more unsparingly applied to a multitude of different objects than in America." Our commitment to the encouragement of private associations is reflected in tax statutes granting

*Congressional investigations have established generally that the confidentiality of tax returns has become a joke. A wide range of agencies and commissions enjoy access to tax returns, for both statistical and investigative purposes. Particularly noteworthy is the use of tax returns for criminal investigative purposes by federal strike forces. Such disclosures in a prosecutive context raise serious constitutional issues, for example, invasion of the taxpayer's Fifth Amendment privilege not to incriminate himself and the Fourth Amendment's guarantee against unreasonable searches and seizures. This protection comes into play when the government invades an area of privacy upon which the individual justifiably relies. Certainly the taxpayer files his return in the expectation that it will be used only for tax administration purposes. The use of tax documents filed by unincorporated associations to identify and harass contributors and supporters has also been challenged as violative of the First Amendment protection of free assembly and expression.

exemption from taxation to nonprofit associations engaged in a variety of activities considered important to civil and religious life. At the same time, contributions to certain charitable, educational, and religious organizations are tax-deductible, providing inter alia the organization that itself is exempt from taxation does not devote a "substantial part" of its activities to "carrying on propaganda, or otherwise attempting to influence legislation." But tax-favored organizations are typically priority intelligence targets, both for the information they may yield as entities and as a means of monitoring and identifying individuals, supporters, and contributors. The tax data generated by the exemption process—applications, returns, investigative reports—thus becomes a valuable source to an intelligence operative seeking to identify a group's officers, to verify its claimed objectives and check on its funding, including the names of contributors and the amount of their contributions. Even more attractive than the information yield is the punitive potential: the granting or retention of an exemption can become vital to the group's existence. In the same way, the group's policies and programs may be importantly influenced by the threat, actual or feared, of an exemption being withdrawn. The vague terms of the exemption statute—when does a group move from the sunshine of "education" into the shadow of "propaganda"? how much is a "substantial part"?—make the entire exemption process vulnerable to changes in the political wind, even in the absence of external stimuli.*

Beginning in the late forties, the IRS revoked without a hearing the exemptions of all organizations on the Attorney General's list of subversive groups, including the Joint Anti-Fascist Refugee Committee, the School of Jewish Studies, the Hollywood Writers' Guild, the Ohio School of Social Science, and others. In the Internal Security Act of 1950 Congress provided for the denial of exemptions to Communist front and Communist action organizations registered as such under that statute. Without waiting for a ruling against any organization, let alone compliance through registration, the IRS interpreted the law as a mandate to withhold exemptions from groups which, in its own view, were subversive. Its rationale was simple: "It is our belief that an organization which is truly subversive cannot be considered as exclusively educational."[3] In 1955 it revoked the tax exemption of the Institute of Pacific Relations and an affiliate group then under attack by the Senate Internal Security Subcommittee (SISS). The grounds for the revocation—widely disputed at the time—were that the Institute "had pursued its objectives through other than educational means" and had "to a substantial extent engaged in the dissemination of controversial and partisan propaganda," and that it had "attempted to influence, directly and indirectly, the policies and/or actions of governments and government officials."[4]

---

*The elasticity of the statute is well illustrated by the revocation in January 1963 of the tax exemption of the Fellowship of Reconciliation (FOR). The FOR, an interfaith group opposed to war and weapons of mass destruction, had enjoyed an exempt status since 1926. FOR teaches that the effective force for overcoming evil and transforming society is "love, such as that seen predominantly in Jesus." The IRS concluded that FOR's aims "can only be obtained by legislation," and for that reason revoked its tax exemption. The ruling provoked an outcry from religious leaders who contended that it would in effect silence their teachings not only on the subject of war but on "any radical issue where some governmental or legislative action may be implied." The protests bore fruit: the revocation was rescinded.

Tax-exempt groups are a special prey of Congress, particularly of its anti-subversive committees. At least from the mid-fifties on, the congressional countersubversive bloc exerted pressure on the IRS to crack down on tax-exempt groups on the left.* Tax-exempt foundations with a liberal slant also came under congressional attack in a 1954 probe chaired by Representative Carroll Reese. The investigation was authorized "especially to determine whether tax-exempt foundations and organizations are using their resources for un-American and subversive activities. . . ." and employed FBI personnel and files in the development of hearings. These legislative pressures were peculiarly effective because the Service makes a special effort to court the goodwill and confidence of the Congress, the source of its appropriations. In many cases, congressional attacks were rooted in constituency complaints by political opponents of the challenged groups outraged that subversion was flourishing under a tax shelter and—a nativist *idée fixe*—that it was wallowing in concealed income supplied by subversive principals. These complaints, relayed by the anti-subversive committees and powerful individual legislators, were so effective that the IRS was more quickly moved to act by the fact that an organization had become "controversial" or "notorious" (that is, a subject of complaint from high quarters) than by the fact that it had violated its exemption privileges.[5] So, for example, when in 1956 the IRS investigated the exemption for the Fund for the Republic—a prominent private foundation linked to liberal causes—an IRS official complained, in the words of the Fund's counsel, about its "bad public relations, saying we have not 'sold' the Fund, that we are losing friends, etc. and that some of our officers and directors . . . are controversial or provocative."[6]

While congressional pressure did not always succeed in stripping a target group or foundation of its tax privileges, it invariably produced substantial harassment. In the late sixties, too, the congressional committees persisted in their pressure to curb the support of target groups. Thus, during the Nixon years, SISS collaborated with the IRS in an attempt to dry up the funding by church groups of an underground press service and both congressional anti-subversive committees worked to promote tax difficulties for the Black Panther Party and its leaders.[7]

Paths to the Present

It is no small irony that the one agency of government for which autonomy and independence are functionally indispensable is uniquely vulnerable to external pressures. Over the years the agency has acquired the qualities of Play-Doh or Silly-Putty, permitting itself to be molded to the needs of special intelligence interests. The agency has become a client of political intelligence, ready to do its bidding whatever the cost. When social tensions run high, it anticipates the

---

*The assault by the Southern congressional bloc on the integration movement following the Brown case in 1954 included tax pressures such as the demand, pressed by Southern legislators, for the revocation of the tax exemption privileges of the NAACP. For an account of NAACP's subsequent tax problems, see Jason Berry, "Tax Conflict: A Disaster for Rights Group," Washington *Star,* Dec. 18, 1977.

demands of its patrons and joins the game on its own. Beginning in the late forties and continuing into the fifties, it responded with investigations and audits to "squeal" letters by anonymous informants, sometimes inspired by IRS field agents, charging tax delinquencies against unpopular individuals and groups. IRS informers who supplied information about suspected delinquents for a percentage bounty of the total amount collected were encouraged by counter-subversive field agents to branch out into the political sphere and report the hidden income of radicals. Informers who had acquired tax-related information in the course of their FBI service were similarly encouraged to enter the field. Defectors and lapsed members of leftist groups were frequently approached, under threat of tax pressure, for information about the income of former associates. These informal back-channel practices flourished in a risk-free climate since they generated no "paper."

FBI agents also played a role in this process: they supplied IRS district offices with tax-related information gleaned from informers. (X was claiming deductions for nonexistent dependents; Y had hidden income; Z had filed no return.) The Bureau headquarters maintained liaison with higher echelons of the IRS intelligence division in Washington, through which it obtained requested tax data of suspected subversive targets. The names of listees in the Security Index were, for example, routinely submitted to the intelligence division for tax data in exchange for a promise of confidentiality. Here is a sample extracted from a letter by Director Hoover to the field with enclosed tax information:

> Transmitted herewith are one copy each of an Internal Revenue Service (IRS) report dated 5-27-58 and IRS report dated 6-20-58 pertaining to captioned subject.
>
> In the event the information in these reports is utilized by you, you must take all precautions to protect the IRS as the source of such information. It is also imperative that you not disclose to the local office of the IRS that you are in possession of copies of these reports.

(The caution in the last sentence of the quoted transmittal was not a routine security precaution. The IRS had decentralized its organizational structure in order to ensure control at the field level of IRS resources and to resist pressures from above—historically a source of great abuse—for purposes unrelated to tax collection and compliance with the tax laws.)

The IRS also generously supplied the Bureau with lists of contributors, drawn from a group's tax returns or application for exemptions, or verified whether individual taxpayers had claimed deductions for contributions to suspect causes or organizations. Institutional collaboration between the Bureau and the IRS was cemented with the organization in 1954 of the Internal Security Division (ISD) as a Department of Justice unit. The ISD not only transmitted Bureau requests for tax data but on its own instigated audits and investigations of political subjects. Since taxpayers were rarely able to prove that their difficulties with the IRS were connected with their politics—and in any event lacked the funds for a legal challenge—claims of IRS abuses in the fifties rarely reached the courts. But two court cases offer a glimpse into the agency's ideological zeal. In March 1956 the IRS, alleging nonpayment of taxes, seized and padlocked the offices of the Communist Party in New York, Philadelphia, San Francisco, Los

Angeles, and Chicago, as well as the New York office of the Communist official publication, the *Daily Worker.* The premises were released a week later, but the litigation continued for years. In 1964 a Court of Appeals decision reversed a tax court ruling, which had held that the Party's attempt to obtain review of the tax assessment was rendered invalid by the novel, not to say bewildering, circumstance that it had never been affirmatively shown that the attorney who signed the petition for review of the tax assessment had in fact been authorized to act for his client. The Court of Appeals rebuked the tax court for this hanky-panky.* In 1967 the Court of Appeals again rebuffed and reversed the tax court, this time rejecting the tax court's conclusion that the CPUSA had failed to raise its central contention that, like other political parties, it was not amenable to federal income taxes. "This," the court said, is "wholly at odds with the record."[8]

Another testament to IRS crudities in the fifties is the Lenske case.[9] Beginning in 1955, two special IRS agents investigated every aspect of the life and work of Reuben T. Lenske, a lawyer active in the National Lawyers Guild. Hundreds of witnesses were interviewed, and an investigative report was issued in 1958 recommending criminal action. The report stated that the FBI and the police "have reason to believe Mr. Lenske is a Communist," and that Lenske and another lawyer had called a meeting for the purpose of forming a local chapter of the Lawyers Guild. It also referred to a letter to a newspaper in which Lenske expressed the thought that this country's actions in various parts of the world had been in violation of international law. A jeopardy assessment was levied, tying up all of Lenske's assets for years. A guilty verdict in a criminal prosecution was reversed by the Court of Appeals. The presiding judge wrote in a special concurring opinion:

> I regard what I have recited above as a scandal of the first magnitude in the administration of the tax laws of the United States. It discloses nothing less than a witch-hunt, a crusade by the key agent of the United States in this prosecution to rid our society of unorthodox thinkers and actors by using federal income tax laws and federal courts to put them in the penitentiary.[10]

The Bureau's access to tax returns and investigative reports made the IRS an especially attractive resource against the targets of the sixties. Thus, the Bureau's Klan COINTELPRO offensive included the levy of tax information both to establish a suspect's Klan membership and to determine whether he had reported income from the Klan. Although there is no proof that the information was published as planned, the evidence shows that the IRS released the requested tax data both about the Klansman and the Klan organization. In the same year (1964) the IRS, on the Bureau's bare request, turned over "all available information"—tax returns, investigative files, and reports—dealing with Dr. Martin Luther King, Jr., and the SCLC. IRS employees cooperated further by

---

*"The obstacles placed in the way of this particular litigant seem to us as unusual in character as they are unfounded in either the Tax Court's normal procedures or the law generally applicable in the field. . . . We think that on this record, [petitioner] cannot be thrown out of court, for the reasons and under the circumstances obtaining, without verging too closely towards the wholly unacceptable proposition that the rules of the game vary with the players"—*Communist Party* v. *Commissioner of Internal Revenue,* 332 F. 2d 325, 329 (App. D.C., 1964).

supplying requested information about future IRS compliance action on King and his movement. Since the SCLC was not tax-exempt in the sense that contributions were tax-deductible, the Atlanta Bureau suggested a COINTEL-PRO-style action involving the use of forged SCLC stationery designed to frighten donors and discourage future contributions. For undisclosed reasons, Washington rejected the suggested project.

The enlarged corps of informers recruited to infiltrate the protest movements of the sixties were briefed to obtain information about the income of their targets, which was transmitted routinely by their contacts to IRS offices for possible tax action. With the adoption of the COINTELPROS, requests for Washington approval of such transmittals became common and were routinely granted. As various IRS districts were showered with such information, audits against both individuals and their organizations increased. In a second phase, the Bureau instead of relying on information gleaned from informers turned more boldly to the IRS for access to tax returns. The "intensive" investigative mission in 1968 directed against Key Activists, and later (in 1970) against Key Black Extremists, increased Bureau reliance on IRS tax data. The Bureau requested and was routinely granted access to the tax files of a considerable number of activists—107 in both categories. This focused IRS attention on the activists and invited investigations—most extensively where no return could be found. A stock procedure was the use of information turned over by the IRS to instigate an audit as part of a COINTELPRO gambit. In one case involving an activist on the Chicago University faculty, the Chicago SAC won Washington approval for a proposal to call questionable deductions to the attention of the local IRS office in the hope of instigating an audit, which would be so timed as to divert the subject's attention from his planned involvement in protest activities in connection with the Democratic National Convention.

The record indicates that the IRS unquestioningly granted Bureau requests for tax data, both prior to 1968 when it was channeled through its intelligence division, and thereafter when a reform was instituted—the earlier practice was condemned as "illegal"—requiring approval of the chief of the IRS Compliance Branch. But the change was purely cosmetic. The ISD acting on behalf of the Bureau sent requests in form letters stating that the returns were "necessary in connection with an official matter before this office involving . . . internal security. . . ." But there was no further requirement for particularizing the proposed use of the material. Thus, even if so inclined, the IRS had no means of determining whether the released documents had been used for an improper purpose. Far from curbing the prior practice of indiscriminately releasing tax data, the new request procedure merely institutionalized it. Moreover, the ISD itself sought and obtained, without objection from the IRS, large quantities of tax-related data, and in 1968 went even further. In that year it launched a special "national security case program," which involved not only the examination of tax data but requests for investigations and audits. By the spring of 1969 under this new program the ISD had transmitted national security requests involving seventy-two individuals and organizations and, in response to ISD requests, the IRS conducted delinquency investigations on some twelve individuals affiliated with target organizations.[11]

The CIA was also accorded cooperation both before and after the 1968 procedure. The CIA was not compelled to resort to an ISD channel: it made its requests and received reports from specially designated liaison personnel within the Agency. These employees took care of the tax problems of CIA proprietaries, supplied requested returns of CIA personnel, and furnished information needed for operational purposes such as establishing the cover of an operative. All of this was supplied on request without a record—an embarrassment of the conventional request procedure. When the CIA was engaged in an attempt to suppress a book by Victor Marchetti critical of the Agency, it obtained Marchetti's tax returns for 1970 and reported that its "confidential informant" at the IRS "would be ready to conduct, at our request, a routine audit of [Marchetti's] income tax for the past 3 years." The CIA found the IRS equally cooperative four years earlier, in 1967, when it sought help in counteracting the disclosures in *Ramparts* magazine about its relationships to the NSA (see Chapter 5). The IRS advised the CIA of the status of the NSA's application for tax exemption, and also furnished across the table the tax returns of the publisher of *Ramparts* magazine without complying with established request procedures. "If such a request is made," a CIA executive delicately explained, "the Commissioner will not be in a position to deny our interest if questioned later by a member of Congress or other competent authority."[12]

Moving into Deeper Waters

The involvement of the IRS in political intelligence pursuits described in the preceding sections was for the most part reactive, sporadic, and directed at particular targets rather than a class or category of taxpayers. When demands for special compliance efforts subsided—that is, when the tax-paying entity ceased to be "controversial" or "notorious"—the normal pattern of impartiality revived. And, while the purely passive sharing of information was continuous, it constituted no significant departure from a broad, government-wide practice of tax return disclosure. In the fifties, the agency did make forays on its own against anti-establishment targets. But, as far as the record shows, they reflected only a limited official commitment to the use of its powers for countersubversive purposes. The IRS was primarily an institutional client, not a principal, until the late sixties when as a result of converging pressures from Congress and the White House it was more completely politicized. But this development was foreshadowed by a project initiated in the Kennedy years.

Echoing the pseudo-libertarian demands of his liberal constituency for even-handedness, President Kennedy in the fall of 1961 denounced the ultra right. In the wake of his attack, which included a suggestion for a tax crackdown and follow-up prodding by Attorney General Robert F. Kennedy and an aide, the IRS obtained from the Commissioner's adviser, Mitchell Rogovin,* a list of right-wing groups for the purpose of making an initial probe. The "Ideological

---

*Besides serving as liaison to the administration, Rogovin was the CIA's man at IRS and subsequently became its counsel in the Church Committee investigations—Taylor Branch, "Playing Both Sides Against the Middle," *Esquire* (September 1976).

Organizations Project,"[13] as it was ultimately called, presented two familiar difficulties: first, how, in the troubled language of one memo, "to avoid giving the impression that the service is giving special attention to returns filed by taxpayers or organizations with a particular political ideology."[14] The Service dealt with this problem by procuring from Rogovin a balancing list of left-wing organizations for audit. But such cosmetic flourishes merely exacerbated a second problem: the puny revenue potential in the audit of all tax-exempt groups of whatever ideology. It was not merely that there was not much tax gold at the end of the rainbow, but that the expense and manpower required to extract it were formidable. To validate a claim, for example, that an organization was exempt as an "educational" group, required under the regulations a detailed analysis of publications, speeches, conference reports. Did the entity's communications to the public permit the formation of an independent opinion or was it "propaganda"? At what point could it be said that otherwise tax-favored activities were intended to influence legislation and hence not a proper basis for the deduction of contributions? In a memorandum to the President dealing with the Ideological Organizations Project, the IRS laid bare these problems and concluded that "for every man-year spent on such examinations, there is a potential loss of approximately $175,000 otherwise produced from income tax audits."

Despite these negative conclusions and a discouraging progress report, which recorded that a total of sixteen audits had resulted in two recommendations of exemption revocation, the IRS announced plans in the summer of 1963 for an expanded audit program of "10,000 examinations of exempt organizations of all types." But the problems presented by the plan forced the IRS to abandon it in favor of an acceleration of its existing project. In 1964–65 a task force specially organized to analyze data collected in field audits recommended revocations in fifteen cases (fourteen of them right-wing), but only four were approved. Before the project ran out of gas in 1967, a total of fifty organizations in all were audited. But the significance of the project cannot be measured by its narrow impact: the formalized use of tax compliance measures for nonrevenue purposes exposed a particular class of taxpayers to uniquely aggressive enforcement procedures and demonstrated the eager responsiveness of the IRS to White House political manipulation.

The White House also played a role—albeit a minor one—in the congressional politicization of the IRS. Over the years, it had routinely issued executive orders granting the anti-subversive committees access to tax returns, although these panels had no legitimate interest in tax matters and had repeatedly used tax data for harassment—particularly in the exemption area. In 1967 and 1968 executive orders of this kind were successively issued to Arkansas Senator John J. McClellan's Senate Subcommittee on Investigations, which had been commissioned by the Senate in August 1967 to probe the violence, unrest, vandalism, and disorders then shaking the nation. The shape of the McClellan operation was unmistakable: instead of an exploration of the causes of the unrest, it promptly took the traditional countersubversive scapegoating course made familiar by the standing House and Senate committees (HISC and SISS). But McClellan was bent on developing a new, more punitive thrust. What was the point of merely providing a forum for discrediting protest movements long inured to such tactics? In the process of sharpening his panel's bite, McClellan developed behind-the-scenes operational liaisons with state and local police forces to harass left targets. This new, punitive agenda included a highly effective campaign to end scholarship grants and government assistance to students linked to campus disturbances.[15] Inevitably, the tax compliance structure beckoned. In addition to the traditional lure of exemption revocation, McClellan was eager to co-opt IRS investigative resources for his committee's ambitious program. In the spring of 1970 the McClellan investigators requested the Alcohol Tax and Firearms (ATF) Division of the IRS to develop information identifying suspected users of explosives. The ATF (then part of the IRS but later, on July 1, 1972, transferred to the Treasury Department) scoured the records of urban library systems to identify individuals who had either borrowed or consulted books listed under the catalogue heading of explosives or relating to guerrilla warfare (in one case they flushed the names of two teenagers working on a term paper). One concentration point of this program was the library system of metropolitan Atlanta, Georgia, an important center of Southern militancy and the headquarters of a number of organizations the McClellan unit was actively investigating.

In a number of cities, as in Atlanta, the federal agents met with resistance from librarians and threatened them with subpoenas. One city librarian initially refused the request of ATF agents, but was finally forced to comply by the City Attorney's office. Both the National Education Association and the American Library Association passed resolutions denouncing the investigation and urged member librarians to report any further attempts to obtain access to library lists and to defend intellectual freedom against the IRS. On July 29, 1970, the Secretary of the Treasury, David M. Kennedy, announced a change of policy: agents would no longer be permitted to make a general search of libraries to find out who read certain books, but would be allowed to investigate what books a particular suspect had checked out.[16]

McClellan had begun to plow the exemption field even earlier. At the beginning of 1969 the new administration granted his request for a renewal of return-access privileges, which he used to develop material on organizations such as the SDS, the Black Panthers, the Student Non-Violent Coordinating Committee (SNCC), and the Republic of New Africa (RNA).[17] In response to his request for access by his staff to tax files on twenty-two organizations and conferences with IRS personnel, the Service dashed off a memorandum to the field instructing its district directors to give the committee and its staff full cooperation and, in addition, to prepare a detailed report about each organization in the district.[18] The memorandum noted that, in addition to the McClellan Committee, "Other Congressional Committees also showed an interest in these organizations and National Office officials may be called upon to testify or produce information concerning them. Some are not much more than a name; others have applications for exemption pending; a few have apparently not filed required tax returns. Most are newsworthy and many are controversial."[19]

A request from Capitol Hill or the White House to the IRS for information about a taxpayer may, for form's sake, appear to seek enlightenment, but frequently it masks a barely suppressed prod to get moving against the subject of the inquiry. So it was with McClellan. He soon made known his disapproval of the Service's seemingly relaxed attitude toward the organizations he was investigating. The senator was further put out because the Department of Justice had twice refused to enforce compliance with an IRS summons requiring SNCC to produce its books and records.[20] It became clear that the IRS was not being asked merely to supply material already in its files, but as in the case of the ATF, to divert its investigative resources to the Senate probe, a non-tax-related enterprise, and beyond this to use tax sanctions to check activism. The pressure bore fruit: the IRS collected so much material on the twenty-two organizations that it took the committee's investigative staff six man-days to review and transcribe it. In fact, the IRS Compliance Division was itself so impressed with its investigative haul that it considered taking tax action against some of the groups involved as soon as the committee gave the word. In the meantime, arrangements were made to turn over to an IRS agent the materials collected by McClellan's staff that might be useful in tax actions.[21]

But the coziness of the relationship with the field and the assurances of Washington's cooperation still left the senator impatient with the sluggish pace of the action. Something had to be done to bring the entire agency into line. On June 25, 1969, he convened an executive session of his panel to hear an explanation of the reason why the IRS investigation of SNCC was going so slowly. Broadening his complaint, he scolded the Service for its abandonment of its responsibilities to ensure that militant organizations ("probably dedicated to overthrowing the Government, to violence") were not required to be taxed as he was.[22] The IRS's chief witness, Deputy Assistant Commissioner (Compliance) Leon Green, agreed. Green felt as much shamed by his inability to answer questions about the tax status of this "notorious" group as by the substance of the charges. Something had to be done to provide the Service with the right answers to questions from important quarters about the tax status of "notorious" organizations.

This exercise in congressional arm-twisting was matched by White House pressure. Shortly after the Nixon administration came to power, in the spring of 1969 the "Committee of Six," a group of conservative White House staffers including Tom Charles Huston and Patrick Buchanan, developed a program to replace what it considered to be a liberal intellectual establishment—headed by tax-exempt groups such as the Brookings Institution, the Ford Foundation, Potomac Associates, and the Stern Fund—with a new grouping of conservative organizations. To achieve this change, the committee proposed to "turn the spigot off" to end the flow of contracts, grants, and other benefits to the liberal groups and to reexamine their tax exemptions.[23]

After President Nixon approved the recommendation for action on the tax front at a White House meeting, Huston and Dr. Arthur Burns, then the President's closest adviser on domestic matters and later the Olympian chairman of the Federal Reserve Board, met on June 16, 1969, with Commissioner of Internal Revenue Randolph Thrower, and conveyed to the commissioner, according to Thrower's records of the session, the President's personal concern over the fact that "tax-exempt funds may be supporting activist groups engaged in stimulating riots both in Congress and within our inner cities."[24] Huston added that the exemption policy discriminated against right-wing groups, and urged a reexamination of exemptions previously granted certain groups. Thrower rejected Burns's charge that the IRS was biased in favor of liberal groups, pointing out that prolonged and aggressive investigation of exempt groups was inconsistent with the traditional allocation of resources to areas of maximum revenue potential. (In a congressional hearing on June 25, 1975, before a House Ways and Means Oversight Subcommittee, Burns stated that he did not recall the meeting with Thrower at all.)[25]

But Thrower had misgivings about this rebuff and instructed Roger V. Barth, his assistant and a White House protégé (he had been a member of the Nixon 1968 campaign staff),* to convey to Huston the IRS interest in further information about specific organizations that were suspected of abusing their exemptions. On June 20 Huston, in reply, sent a confidential memorandum to Barth recommending a "close look" at a tax-exempt foundation and three other tax-exempt groups. Huston closed his memorandum with a masterful blend of threat and pressure:

> I advised the President that Mr. Thrower is aware of his personal interest in this subject. The President has indicated that he is anxious to see some positive action against those organizations which are violating existing regulations, and I will assure him that I will keep him advised of the efforts that are presently under way. . . . I would appreciate it if you would keep me advised of what steps are being taken by the Service in this regard.[26]

Barth responded as to a blast of trumpets and promptly made known to Donald O. Bacon, IRS Assistant Commissioner (Compliance), the White House demand for action. On July 1, Huston again reminded Barth to get moving on the exempt organization front and on the same day Bacon's staff completed a promised memorandum on the subject for transmission through Barth to the White House.[27] In the face of the combined pressure from McClellan and the White House, the response of the IRS, historically a pushover even for more modest efforts, was predictable. After a series of organizational meetings, the Service in August 1970 launched for the first time in its history a unit with a political intelligence focus. The significance of this development can hardly be overstated: while in the past the IRS had permitted its resources to be used sporadically against unpopular groups and individuals, these practices were now for the first time institutionalized. Congressional investigators have, understandably enough, never fully attempted to assess the extent of the role of one of their own committees in the birth of the Special Service Staff (SSS). But the nature of the White House involvement is quite clear: the Nixonites wanted tax action against their targets but did not go so far as to specify its institutional form.[28] In this respect, the Nixon administration's role in the emergence of the SSS is not dissimilar from that of the Johnson administration's involvement in the

---

*Barth served both as Assistant to the Commissioner and deputy chief counsel of IRS. His qualifications for these important posts included his service as an advance man for Julie and Tricia Nixon in the 1968 campaign and references from David and Julie Eisenhower which, Commissioner Thrower later stated, "spoke well for him."

launching of the CIA's domestic programs. In both cases, it was the result that was stressed, not the operational form. But it would be misleading to assume that, in either case, the agency's involvement was reluctant. Just as the CIA's enthusiasm was little dampened by the knowledge of statutory prohibition, so the IRS executives who formed the unit knew that it lacked justification but were nevertheless determined to proceed. "From a strictly revenue standpoint, we may have little reason for establishing this Committee or for expending the time and effort which may be necessary but we must do it."[29]

SSS—Mission, Operations, Files

The IRS is a bureaucrat's dream (or nightmare) in the sense that it turns out spates of information about all of its activities—their purposes and norms. But it was quite uncommunicative in informing the public or tax professionals about the Special Service Staff (SSS). The internal documents tell us that the unit's mission was to neutralize "an insidious threat to the internal security of this country."[30] In another place we are told that its mandate was to "coordinate activities in all Compliance Divisions involving ideological, militant, subversive, radical, and similar type organizations; to collect basic intelligence data; and to ensure that the requirements of the Internal Revenue Code concerning such organizations had been complied with."[31] Another (unconsciously) revealing formulation is that the SSS was "directed to the notoriety of the individual or organization and the probability of publicity that might result from their activities and the likelihood that this notoriety would lead to inquiries regarding their tax status."[32]

These were all private, internal formulations. The agency could hardly afford to reduce to writing for public scrutiny what was quite evident from its internal records: that the unit was a hit squad, functioning in the tax field against proscribed organizations (whether tax-exempt or not), their officers, supporters, and members, as well as individual activists. Its chief, Paul Wright, though an intelligence neophyte, quickly learned the rules of the game. As in other intelligence sectors, the absence of mission guideposts or defined operational standards left him free to employ whatever means were at his disposal to save an imperiled nation. How could one suffer the restraints of the tax collection function in, as he put it, "the overall battle against persons bent on destruction of this government"?[33] Such grandiosity not only justified disregarding mundane functional considerations but offered bureaucratic power dividends: it enabled the unit and its head to identify with the nation-saving legions of the intelligence community, to inflate the importance of the unit in the IRS bureaucratic structure, and to boast of its White House connections.

Since the operation was of questionable legitimacy, secrecy was imperative. The minutes of the unit's very first meeting state: "We do not want the news media alerted to what we are attempting to do or how we are operating, because disclosure of such information might embarrass the Administration or adversely affect the Service operations in this area or those of other Federal agencies or Congressional committees."[34] The unit's successive name changes also reflected the fear of adverse publicity. The original name, "Activist Organizations Group," was changed to "Special Service Group" in May 1970 because it "left the connotation of recognizable identification for possible criticism and embarrassment to the Service if knowledge of the action being taken became known to the mass media." But even this name made IRS functionaries nervous, leading to a final change—Special Service Staff.[35] Here, as elsewhere, the secrecy invoked to hide misconduct did double duty as a bit of intelligence puffery enhancing the importance of the operation. Top secret clearance was a staff requirement. The unit operated in a soundproof basement with a "need to know" restriction on access to its documents even within its own staff. Security was considered crucial, not only as a protection against the targets themselves but against younger IRS employees suspected of subversive sympathies who might expose the operation through leaks (it would hardly do for the pursuer to become as "notorious" as the pursued). The cloak-and-dagger style even extended to the use of maildrops and pseudonyms through which the unit dealt with casual informants and received publications. The atmosphere of glamor and high risk was strengthened by the accumulation of files and the hugger mugger of processing and classifying file material. How could one keep SSS down on the (tax) farm after it had seen the Paree of intelligence?

The power sense instilled by the intelligence milieu invariably creates illusions of invulnerability. The agency comes to believe that it is immune to exposure, providing security precautions are taken which in themselves enhance the importance and legitimacy of intelligence programs. But, in mid-January 1972, a former FBI agent, Robert N. Wall, blew the whistle. He described visits to the SSS to check out the tax status of certain New Left activists he was investigating: "The room had no name on the door and it had several locks. Inside were two guys who seemed surprised that I had shown up. On a long table in the middle of the room were piles of Manila folders. It turned out that they were investigating the taxes of these people and my man's folder was on the table." (The IRS investigators told him they were preparing investigations "on anti-war people and draft card burners and black militants.")[36]

The exposé forced the SSS in from the cold, yet it continued to function in a new sixth-floor office of the IRS building, which offered the consolation of a walk-in vault for its files. But conformity to the norms of disclosure required new deceptions. In the Internal Revenue Manual published on April 14, 1972, a new section appeared dealing with the Special Service Staff. However, the entry throws no light on what the unit did apart from the fact that its targets were individuals and groups that "may ignore or willfully violate tax or firearm statutes."[37] In November 1972 at a biennial conference in Charlottesville, Virginia, of all the Service's top officials, a briefing paper (classified "Confidential") was presented on "Special Service Staff: Its Origin, Mission, and Potential."[38] This document, intended to stimulate field personnel to work more closely with the SSS both in supplying and using intelligence, states that information developed during the hearings of the McClellan Committee established the fact that "various controversial organizations presented problems to the Internal Revenue Service." But these groups were not run-of-the-mill, garden-variety tax law violators. The SSS was pitted against a well-laid plot "by highly organized and well financed groups bent on destroying our form of government." Indeed, "there is evidence that transfers of large amounts of money to and from the USA are being used to establish and organize groups with the view of overthrowing this government."[39] This febrile intelligence rhetoric contrasts comically with the entry dealing with the SSS in the April 1973 Supplement to the Internal Revenue Manual, where it was again drably described, but now as the "focal point for information about organizations and individuals involved in tax strike, tax resister, tax protester activities"—a genuine tax concern but hardly an accurate account of the SSS mission.[40] The Manual's new formulation was merely a fresh cover. It was blown four months later through a leak to *Time* magazine. The day after the story appeared, August 7, 1973, Commissioner Donald C. Alexander ordered the unit's abolition on the ground that the project had exceeded the power of the IRS because "political or social views, 'extremist' or otherwise, are irrelevant to taxation."[41]

Starting with the modest capital of 22 files developed with the aid of the McClellan Committee, the SSS in four years built a collection of files on 8585 individuals and 2873 organizations.[42] Files are the mainstay of every intelligence venture, and nowhere is this more apparent than in the emergence and growth of the SSS. The information provided by the collection was of relatively minor importance; but the array of bulging cabinets was visible proof that IRS political intelligence had come of age, ready to do on its own what formerly it had been told to do by outsiders. Processing material for inclusion in the files, clipping newspapers, duplicating items for multiple entries, arranging the folders, devising indices, cross-reference systems, and other retrieval devices provided bureaucratic busy-work. In turn, the need to protect both process and product from disclosure invested the entire enterprise with an ambiance of high risk and transcendent importance. The means (the accumulation and storage of information) did not merely obscure the end (revenue collection) but largely replaced it.

The SSS acquired its assets not through its own collection efforts, which were rather modest, nor, like the military, by drawing on an accumulated stockpile of information. It overcame such handicaps simply by qualifying for membership in the intelligence community. Shortly after the launching of the SSS, Paul Wright advised the FBI that IRS had organized the unit "as a result of considerable pressure from Congress and the White House."[43] His superior, Assistant Commissioner for Compliance Donald O. Bacon, followed up with a formal request to be placed on the Bureau's report dissemination list.[44] The Bureau hailed the program as long overdue: "if properly implemented, [it] should deal a blow to dissident elements."[45] Bureau disseminations poured into the SSS secret headquarters, as one bureaucrat put it, "like a spigot under Niagara Falls," and included dossiers and reports on lists of organizations (2300 in all) classified by political coloration (Old Left, New Left, etc.). When SSS developed its own intelligence priorities, it made special requests for reports on subjects such as underground newspapers, an area on which it concentrated heavily (148 files). Bureau documents received between October 27, 1969, and November 30, 1973 (three months after the dissolution of SSS), ultimately came to the grand total of 11,818 reports on individuals and organizations and formed the bulk of its files. Even when on their face the FBI documents were totally useless, the SSS felt that it had no authority to destroy them.[46]

Another Justice Department source for SSS files was the "Civil Disturbance List" maintained by the Inter Divisional Intelligence Unit (IDIU). The IDIU's disseminations consisted of computer printouts, which included radical and leftist suspects, and also civic leaders considered potentially useful in the control of civil disturbances. They, too, became grist for the SSS files. In the spring of 1971 the IDIU was merged with the Internal Security Division (Analysis and Evaluation Section) of the Department of Justice, which was already exchanging information with the IRS and collaborating with it on the "national security" case program.[47] The congressional committees were also important sources. The McClellan panel not only supplied continuous file data but also guided the SSS explorers of the nether world of subversion to other congressional sources. It was the McClellan staff that arranged for the fledging unit's access to the House Internal Security Committee's vast holdings. In the beginning, the SSS obtained HISC data in response to inquiries about specific organizations; by the end of 1970 it was granted direct access to the entire collection.[48]

The Army's military intelligence units were most generous and made available the four volumes of its Counterintelligence Analysis Division compilations. The Naval Investigative Service (NIS), the Air Force, the State Department, and *Information Digest* (a private publication discussed below) also supplied file material. In addition, the SSS obtained intelligence information via liaison with state and local law enforcement officials, as well as such ad hoc sources as the Subcommittee on Foundations of the House Select Small Business Committee. The SSS received a biweekly intelligence survey of Washington area subversion compiled by an ATF informer, and subscribed to about thirty publications from the *New York Times* to the Communist *Daily World* and *The Mole,* an underground publication, as well as handbooks of special listings of radical and extremist organizations acquired sub rosa and paid for by money orders subsequently reimbursed out of an "Imprest Fund" used by the IRS to buy information.[49] But its most important source was the Social Security Administration, which provided identifying data as well as the valuable history of wage payments made to a subject over a three-year period.

No less than 41 percent of the file subjects were minority groups and activists in race relations movements; 29 percent were drawn from the anti-war and New Left movements. Organizational targets included: the National Council of Churches, the Americans for Democratic Action, the Fund for the Republic, the American Library Association, Common Cause, the Carnegie and Ford Foundations, as well as the Black Panthers, the Ku Klux Klan, the United Jewish Appeal, the American Jewish Committee, the U.S. Commission on Civil Rights, the American Civil Liberties Union (ACLU), and the Friends of the FBI.[50]

The ACLU's SSS file is about 7 inches thick and consists of 395 pages. It apparently is a duplicate of an FBI file beginning with some 18 pages of printouts from computerized sources, followed by about 150 entries dating back to the forties and covering not only the ACLU but individuals whose "subversive inclinations" are established by membership in or support of the ACLU. Like all dossiers of this kind, the entries are heavily slanted; for example, whenever an event or action is recorded both in mainstream sources and in the Communist press, the compiler prefers the Communist version, however uninformative it might otherwise be. In addition, the file draws on a number of right-wing publications *(Human Events;* Manchester, New Hampshire, *Union-Leader; Christian Crusade)* critical of the ACLU. It reproduces copies of ACLU letters to congressmen, brochures, invitations to join, and copies of official publications. The tax relevance of the dossier is baffling.

Individual files were equally ecumenical, covering a wide range of occupations: educators, college presidents, symphony conductors, entertainers, comedians, priests, ministers, rabbis, conservative newspaper columnists, editors and publishers, women's liberation figures, labor union organizers and officers, solicitors and contributors to defense funds, and tax attorneys. The collection also included candidates for public office, both successful and unsuccessful, several U.S. senators from both major political parties, five members of the House and in two instances their spouses, a Democratic mayor and a city councilman, and twenty-five individuals on the White House "enemies list."

Out of its total corpus of files, the SSS referred to the field for collection or audit only a few hundred cases. Of the 136 individual taxpayers whose cases were referred, almost half were members of black militant organizations such as Panthers, CORE, and SNCC. Another fifty-seven were political leftists and civil rights activists. The organizational list of referrals was dominated (eighty-nine) by anti-war and black militant groups. In addition, the field referrals included fifteen underground newspapers, as well as civic, welfare, and educational groups, and seven right-wing organizations. The small number of referrals can certainly not be attributed to a lack of effort. The SSS made a search of the tax and Social Security records of some 3658 individuals and 332 organizations; in addition, it conducted a tax record search of 437 organizations in the IRS exempt organization master file. The transmittals to the field were accompanied by scary exhortations and typically included intelligence data entirely devoid of tax relevance—details sometimes drawn from FBI reports on the taxpayer's politics, covering matters such as speeches, attendance at meetings and demonstrations, political affiliations with radical groups, presumably designed to hasten responsive field action. The organizational referrals were similarly accompanied by dossiers of officers, supporters, and contributors, together with a description of the organization's politics and purpose. Special case-handling procedures were devised. The field was instructed in how to conduct the investigation and to make progress reports of the sort used only in extraordinary cases. Similarly, when an investigation established that an individual taxpayer was not required by law to file a return, he or she was required to file a statement to that effect.[51]

But for all these special enforcement efforts, the SSS could not overcome the reality, already mentioned, that its targets were not promising sources of revenue. When weighed against the costs of funding the SSS efforts, the IRS suffered a net financial loss. A final inventory in 1973 showed that 78 percent of the SSS files had no revenue potential at all. A total net assessment of $580,000 was made against individuals and $82,000 against organizations; but of the individual total, four disputed cases accounted for the sum of $501,000. All in all, less than $100,000 in revenue was actually collected.[52] Moreover, confidence in the IRS's impartiality was seriously impaired. The political motivations of field audits became apparent to many of the subjects and resulted in a spate of litigation. The National Council of Churches' books were audited from late 1969 through June 1972. The IRS agents sought to obtain lists of NCC contributors; when these were denied them, they said, "Never mind, we have them already." The NCC audit of almost three years' duration was particularly curious in view of the fact that a 1969 statute strictly forbids the examination of the books of account of a church or an association of churches to determine whether it is engaged in unrelated trade or business unless the Secretary of the Treasury or his delegate believes that the organization is engaged in such trade or business and so notifies the organization in advance of the examination. No such notification was given to the National Council of Churches.

In February 1970, a month after the publication of the exposé (described in Chapter 8) by Captain Christopher Pyle of the Army's surveillance of civilians, the Army's CIAD (Counter Intelligence Analysis Division) conferred with SSS functionaries and requested an audit—not because it had reason to think that Pyle's tax returns were irregular but to determine whether Pyle's disclosures had been secretly financed by a subversive principal. The New York-based 108th Military Intelligence Group also requested an audit for the same alleged intelligence purposes. Pyle was audited at the end of 1970, but the result was hardly helpful: he received a refund of $150 for an overpayment. In August 1973 the head of an anti-war group, Walter D. Teague III, was advised by the Manhattan District Director of IRS that he had been assessed a tax liability for the years 1961 and 1962 on the ground that he had filed no tax returns for those years. In fact, as he subsequently showed, he had filed returns and paid whatever taxes were due. By a letter dated November 21, 1973, Teague was advised, regarding the years 1961 and 1962, that no "further action need be taken because there is no deficiency or overassessment." In January 1974 Teague received another letter asking him to come to the IRS office to provide information regarding the years 1962 through 1972. Teague's lawyer requested a postponement and the IRS dropped the entire matter. In the course of litigation initiated by Teague, the IRS admitted that its audit had been triggered by the SSS, which in turn obtained information about Teague from the Internal Security Division of the Department of Justice.

Equally serious, if not more so, was the impact of the program on the confidentiality of tax records, already in shambles as a result of the earlier IRS cooperation with FBI and ISD intelligence activities. Once admitted to the intelligence community, the SSS was in no position to deny its sister members requested information. The Pyle case is only one instance of the intimate cooperation with other intelligence units. Not only the Bureau and military intelligence but the NIS, Secret Service, CIA, and other units were supplied with tax information.[53] Regulations limiting access were either waived on national security grounds or circumvented by memoranda summarizing the contents of documents. In the case of the Bureau, the SSS served as a channel for its requests for tax-related sanctions against its targets. In one case, the Director himself alerted the SSS to a need for tax investigation of a black leader and requested a follow-up report from the unit. In another, the FBI used the SSS to obtain for it a list of contributors to the leftist Students for a Democratic Society (SDS) for transmittal to the White House.

The SSS finally brought the tax collection process to the agenda of domestic political intelligence. Its emergence as an intelligence unit dramatizes the shaping power of countersubversion in molding intelligence to a fixed pattern, no matter how irrelevant to the function it is supposed to serve. In the case of the SSS, the gap between revenue collection and its targeting standards is so huge as to be comical. Although the entire program was manned by ideological Keystone Kops, groping and gullible, they took themselves seriously and impressed others with the vital importance of their mission. Citing efficiency and prompt retrieval needs, an IRS internal study recommended in March 1973 that the files should be computerized. The proposal was aborted by Commissioner Alexander's death sentence on the SSS in August of that year.

Intelligence Gathering and Retrieval Service (IGRS)

The SSS was a tactical intelligence operation, concerned with short-term compliance objectives, and duplicating existing compliance structures. The agency entered the political process through another channel as well, the Intelligence Gathering and Retrieval Service (IGRS). Planned in 1969 and sporadically activated in test areas, the IGRS became fully operational as a nationwide intelligence instrument in 1973. The IRS Intelligence Division had since the thirties monitored organized crime through a variety of surveillance techniques against specific targets suspected of law violations, and had performed this role as a component of prosecutorial strike forces. But as in other areas, such as civil disturbance, the forecast intelligence bug began biting. Why wait until it was too late? Why not pinpoint the areas of anticipated noncompliance using the gadgetry of computers, codes, and interlocks to develop a list of *potential* tax law violators? But neither the lure of prediction nor the trappings of computerization could change the fact that what emerged was an institutionalized fishing expedition, a system for collecting and filing data about a huge range of targets, much of it not tax-related.

By mid-January 1975 about one-half million names of individuals and entities, either potential tax violators or subjects of current investigations, were stored in the computerized indices maintained in the forty-five IRS district offices, and interlocked in a network covering the entire nation, linked by master codes that served as a guide both to the collection and storage of information. The system was served in the larger districts by teams of IGRS investigative agents and elsewhere by clerks, who clipped newspaper and other media for relevant material.[54]

The same distorted concern with dissident politics noted in other contexts was built into the IGRS system. The recommendations of the task force for the

IGRS project were supposedly focused on "organized crime, racketeering and corruption"—activities marked by highly sophisticated techniques for concealing huge profits from the tax collector. But the task force took note of the fact that "some of these same techniques are also being adopted by various major subversive and radical elements to further breakdown [sic] the basic fibers of our society," and proceeded to assimilate "subversive activities" to the kinds of illegal enterprises that generate hidden taxable income. This heady perspective was reinforced, the task force observed, by the Intelligence Division's law enforcement mission, which required it to soar above the grubby collection of taxes and to do battle with "corruption which can destroy our society."[55] How could one save the society from corruption and at the same time permit its destruction by subversion?

An IGRS unit in each district was charged with accumulating and processing data broadly dealing with targets suspected of "illegal activities," along with "background information" of a more general character drawn from informers, surveillance reports, law enforcement agencies, the news media, and other IRS investigative files. The investigative cadres for these new units were to be specially selected for their superior ability "to recognize significant intelligence data and their enthusiasm for intelligence gathering and informant contact work." This field intelligence was to be evaluated and transmitted to clerks charged with indexing, filing, and retrieval. Included in a series of alphabetical and numerical codes was a three-digit "Illegal Activities" code. The number 186 was assigned to "Subversive Activities," preceded by Forgery (184) and Hijacking (185), and followed by Abortion (187) and Extortion (188).[56]

Somebody in the IRS must have recognized either that "Subversive Activities" cannot be equated with "Illegal Activities" like forgery, hijacking, and extortion, or that, in any event, it was not a fruitful source of hidden revenue. When the IGRS plan was recast in final form, the old "Subversive Activities" became "Sabotage," but preceded and followed by the same offenses as in the earlier version. Fair enough: sabotage can be an "illegal activity" like forgery and extortion, but it is a no more likely source of concealed profits than subversive activities. Despite the change in the name, the intended countersubversive focus is apparent.[57] For example, a memorandum summarizing a conference of four Western taxing districts, held in November 1970 to iron out certain difficulties in the operation of the IGRS, noted that "each district has a different set of values due to the particular interest of their respected districts. . . . San Francisco is primarily interested in Subversive and Activist Groups and pornographers. . . ."*[58] The IGRS political thrust is confirmed by a selective printout of 102 names of IGRS file subjects leaked to the public in the late spring of 1975, presumably by an IRS employee.† The printout is crowded with political figures —a few conservatives but mostly liberals of assorted hues, anti-war activists,

---

*The San Francisco viewpoint may well have reflected the fact that the district was a center of leftist activity. The Black Panther Party, which had been subjected to a prolonged audit beginning in 1970, is located in Oakland in the San Francisco district, as is the Berkeley campus of the University of California.

†An accompanying memo is subscribed: "An American Who believes in the United States Constitution."

ghetto leaders, and the like, including such personages as Los Angeles Mayor Thomas Bradley, Congressman Augustus Hawkins, and ex-Attorney General Ramsey Clark. Listed groups include the American Civil Liberties Union, the Baptist Foundation of America, the Black Panther Party, the Bay Area Revolutionary Union, the Gay Liberation Front, the Communist Party, the Lower East Side Mobilization Committee, the Medical Committee for Human Rights, and the Church of Scientology.

One IGRS investigative component, Operation Leprechaun, drew national attention through a series of sensational press stories in 1974–75. A Miami, Florida, project, Leprechaun was conceived as a strike force to ferret out suspected tax frauds by prominent Miamians, including federal and state judges and city officials. Operation Leprechaun made heavy use of informers.[59] A GAO investigative report concluded that the spy operation had spent some $87,800 between 1972 and 1974 on a network of thirty-four informers, some of whom were recruited by the paid spies. Both the informers and their sub-agents were compensated either in cash or, according to other sources, by a benign disposition of their tax problems. In some cases the informers had run afoul of narcotics laws, but a few had agreed to spy for ideological reasons, to demonstrate their patriotism (a large number of the spies were Cuban refugees). Two informers from the Cuban community broke into the office of a candidate for Congress, Evelio Estrella, and stole numerous documents. The GAO investigation, as well as an earlier one by the IRS itself, reported that no criminal prosecution resulted from the strike force program, and very little tax revenue ($49,000) was obtained —a predictable result in view of the fact that targets were selected only on the basis of vague suspicion. In January 1975 the entire IGRS program was suspended, and in June its intelligence collection component was dropped altogether. The computerized indexing system was retained, but subjected to strict guidelines and controls, limiting the operation to tax-related objectives.

IRS Informer Apparatus

The potential for political exploitation of IRS procedures devised for revenue purposes seems inherent in the role of IRS in the governmental structure. And the vulnerability of the agency to manipulation for political purposes is magnified by its unique undercover capability. The IRS Intelligence Division runs an elaborate undercover surveillance system manned by its special agents, trained in schools that teach standard courses such as cover protection, the management of infiltrators, and the use of recording equipment. Until reforms were instituted in 1973, these schools also provided gamier instruction in "stress seminars" dealing with problems faced by undercover agents such as liquor and women.[60] A second network consists of nonemployees paid out of the "Investigative Imprest Fund," which finances intelligence projects by secret payments estimated at $2 million annually for informers, cover arrangements, witness protection, and the outfitting of undercover vehicles. Beginning in the early sixties, IRS informers and wiretap know-how were frequently borrowed by Department of Justice strike forces in investigations of organized crime, narcotics, prostitution, gambling, political corruption, and other crimes that yield large returns but are difficult to police. As a result, the IRS informer system is to some extent unchanneled, and is responsible, to the extent that it is at all, to nontax centers. Both as captive IRS units and as strike force components, the IRS informer corps has been widely criticized for involvement in illegal activities and financial corruption.

In the case of Operation Leprechaun, a key informer, Elsa Gutierrez, turned on the IRS. In a series of interviews she claimed that she had been instructed to spy on the private lives of some thirty prominent local figures, including their "sex and drinking habits." A GAO report disputed this alleged priority but did conclude that Leprechaun's informers functioned virtually without any direction, and that some of them often handled cash payments to, and supervised the activities of, others.*[61] As for Ms. Gutierrez, a grand jury reported in December 1977 that while she had been recruited to monitor the private lives of certain strike force targets, there was no evidence that the rights of any taxpayer had been violated in the process. The statements to the press that she and her family had been threatened by her agent-control in a variety of ways if she revealed the Leprechaun scandal were bluntly characterized by the report as false.

The use of the IRS intelligence resources in a criminal investigation by a strike force is illustrated by the bribery trial in 1972 of the controversial and colorful New Orleans District Attorney Jim Garrison, along with two former New Orleans police officers and local pinball machine operators. The case was developed by an IRS informer, Pershing Gervais, who had been a member of the New Orleans Police Department, a criminal investigator, the owner of a number of barrooms, and ultimately the chief investigator in Garrison's office. He took the Garrison job, he explained, in order to "give myself a rebirth . . . to clean up whatever damage I have done to my character in my earlier years."[62] Gervais, by a familiar coincidence, also had tax problems with the IRS, which developed in the wake of an investigation of police corruption when the agency discovered that he had hidden (and illegal) sources of income.[63]

While Gervais acted as a bagman for the bribery scheme charged to the defendants, he was equipped by the IRS with a body microphone and transmitter, which he carried in his armpit or in a coat pocket. In some cases he recorded telephone conversations with the defendants. While he collected, counted, and disbursed the alleged bribes, his IRS case officer recorded the transaction in a nearby station (usually the trunk of a car or a motel room). Many of the taped transcripts—Gervais had recorded some 52 conversations in all—were incorporated in a 113-page affidavit submitted to a federal court by the intelligence chief of the IRS New Orleans District. The transcripts of his telephone conversations establish Gervais as a veritable wizard of the electronic informer's art. An instinctive actor (he had played the part of a corrupt Louisiana sheriff in a film, *Damned Citizen*), Gervais was a master of the secretive circumlocutions—metaphors, aliases, nicknames, code names, and the like—

---

*John T. Harrison, the agent in charge, in a memo to his superior wrote: "There are several informants which [sic] I have never met . . . to help offset limited time and manpower, I used informants to instruct and even pay other informants. . . . Admittedly, this is not orthodox and is a risky procedure."

that are the *lingua franca* of those in fear of eavesdropping. Intended to disarm, they usually confirm suspicion by projecting a consciousness of guilt without wholly concealing the nature of the underlying transaction. (It requires no profound insight to reach the conclusion that recurrent messages such as "The patient needs medicine," or, "Doctor is getting restless," are reminders that a promised payment is due or overdue.) In dealing with his victims face to face, Gervais used another form of semantic bait to gain confidence: he showered them with dirty language. He explained afterwards that obscenity was a useful investigative tool. "When you get guys talking that way they loosen up and tell you what you want to hear. Besides, when they're talking that way they never have any inkling they are being taped."[64] The conversations—whether recorded on the telephone or face to face—resound with witty sardonic overtones, the performance of a man thoroughly in command, knowing that his victims do not suspect the conversations are being recorded. At the end of his last conversation with Garrison, when he had left the house, Gervais delivered to his microphone a version of the cry of assassin John Wilkes Booth: "So perish all enemies of this country."

After Gervais agreed to surface as a witness—the moment of truth, so to speak, in an informer's life—he entered into a protective agreement, authorized under the Organized Crime Act of 1970, with United States Attorney John Wall, head of a strike force with nine federal components (two from the IRS). Gervais insisted that the agreement be reduced to writing when he became furious at the government's alleged failure to adhere to the terms of an earlier understanding.*

Because Gervais wanted to leave the country, both for safety's sake and for the still elusive rebirth and redemption, the Justice Department placed him in

---

*The agreement read:

Mr. Pershing Gervais, care of Mr. Floyd D. Moore, Chief Intelligence Division, Internal Revenue Service, New Orleans District, New Orleans, Louisiana.

Dear Mr. Gervais: This is to confirm the agreement between you and the Department of Justice which you will recall discussing on the night of September 8, 1971, and early morning hours of September 9, 1971, together with me and Floyd D. Moore, Chief of Intelligence Division for the New Orleans District of the Internal Revenue Service.

You agreed that during the period September 1, 1971, to August 30, 1972, you will accept employment commensurate with your ability at the salary offered and the Department of Justice agreed to supplement such income up to $22,000 per year.

You further agreed to accept employment commensurate with your ability from September 1, 1972, to August 30, 1973, wherever such employment is located at a salary of $22,000 per annum and the Department of Justice agreed to secure employment for you at that salary for at least one year, and to pay the cost of moving for you and your family by regular commercial movers at the location of such employment.

It was further determined on September 8, 1971, that subsistence is paid on condition that you do not re-enter the United States without prior approval of the Criminal Division, and that all future payments will be cancelled and the Department of Justice will be relieved of any responsibility if this condition regarding re-entry is breached.

In addition to the foregoing, the Department of Justice agrees, at any date you choose subsequent to August 30, 1973, to pay the cost of transportation and moving of household goods for you and your family by regular commercial movers from wherever you are then located, to New Orleans, Louisiana.

Sincerely, John Wall, Attorney in charge.

—*United States* v. *Jim Garrison et al.*, Criminal Action No. 7–542. Testimony on Sept. 20, 1973, pp. 124–126.

a job in the British Columbia plant of General Motors. He was provided with a new identity, and all members of his family, including his children, were given forged birth certificates. But when he discovered that his job was a sinecure, a poorly disguised bribe, he became embittered and felt that he had been used. Prior to taking the stand, Gervais condemned the government's case as a frame-up in an interview with a reporter, Rosemary James, climaxed by the following colloquy:

> "Now when you say that you went to work for the government, what sort of work did you do?" Mrs. James asked.
> "Well, it was, you see, it's, uh, entrapping people."
> "What people?"
> "The pinball operators."
> "And who else?"
> "And Jim Garrison."
> "Are you saying you participated in a deliberate frameup of Jim Garrison and a whole bunch of pinball executives at the direction of the federal government?"
> "Without a doubt, I'm saying that unequivocally [sic]."[65]

Gervais subsequently returned to the fold and insisted in the course of his testimony that his earlier recantations (there were several) were "absolutely false."[66] But it was too late; his prior statements had fatally discredited him. The jury acquitted the defendants, refusing to believe either Gervais or the tapes. The criminal case acquittals made it impossible to try the defendants on the tax charges set forth in an accompanying indictment.

The major rationale for informer coverage of protest groups is the commitment to tax resistance, either to protest the constitutionality of revenue laws generally or the use of tax money for purposes considered objectionable. But the coverage tends to envelop groups because they are considered potential champions of tax resistance. A documented practice involves the attendance of IRS intelligence agents at open meetings posing as husband and wife. A pretended interest and a more active role lead to an invitation to a position of trust that enables the infiltrator to obtain membership lists, minutes, and financial data. An IRS intelligence memo in the Church Committee files describes this process, which is standard operating procedure in political infiltration:

> After several months of getting acquainted with the movement, we decided we would attempt to infiltrate one of our agents into the inner circle of the (protest group). Despite foreboding warnings from other districts that infiltration was extremely difficult, by November 1973 one of our agents had gained the trust, confidence and money of the (protest group) by being selected as Treasurer. This coup also gained us the entire mailing list of the (organization).

The Church Committee staff report describes a case in which an IRS infiltrator was made privy to the legal defense plans of the defendants in a pending tax case and obtained a draft copy of a brief prepared for submission in a tax protester's trial. His contact turned the brief over to the federal prosecutor in charge of the case.

When, in 1975, Commissioner Donald Alexander proposed reforms and reductions in the IRS intelligence system, he was attacked with heavy artillery.

A Nixon appointee and a former tax lawyer for well-to-do clients, he was charged with deliberately destroying the IRS's intelligence capability in order to serve his Republican corporate constituency. In fact, Alexander himself was investigated for alleged complicity in a shady transaction in behalf of a former client.[67] But the charges that Alexander's reforms were motivated by a desire to protect fat-cats and tax evaders appear to have been themselves the product of an intelligence gambit. Alexander was particularly resented for his attempts to curb the informer system. This is understandable enough; corruption is an occupational disease of informer operations, breeding invented disbursements, padded expenses, and assorted opportunities for graft. When an attempt was made to implement Alexander's reforms, the agents resisted, on moral grounds, requests that their informers be identified. Thus, the auditors become audit-proof because the very practices that generate corruption effectively serve to prevent its exposure.[68]

Alcohol, Tobacco and Firearms (ATF)— The Extremist Beat

The ATF Division is charged with tax compliance functions that require the monitoring of illegal traffic in firearms and explosives. Both when it was an IRS branch and later as a Treasury agency, it developed an extensive political intelligence capability, most of it in response to Nixon administration stimuli. It served as a temporary haven for Nixon White House apparatchiks Liddy and Caulfield, and the White House in 1970 unsuccessfully tried twice to force them on IRS Commissioner Randolph Thrower to lead a crackdown on radicals through the ATF. The increasing resort by fringe groups to violent tactics in the sixties resulted in a shift of ATF focus from particular individuals suspected of law violation to organizations and movements, their leaders and activists. In the process the agency developed a huge surveillance overkill, which embraced many targets not committed to violent tactics on both the far left and the far right. These were cast into the intelligence net by an assumption that, despite the absence of present proof, they were potential sources of traffic in contraband. The agency's expertise and familiarity with the world of extremist politics attracted the McClellan Committee, as we have seen. When in the summer of 1969 the SSS began to develop from scratch an intelligence capability, it drew on the resources of the ATF. The White House also looked to the ATF for help in developing intelligence structures. Eddie Hughes, the national ATF coordinator for militant organizations, was summoned to Washington from his headquarters in Atlanta in June 1969 to brief IRS staff members and help prepare a report for transmission to the White House.[69]

The ATF's expansion beginning in the sixties reflects the conventional intelligence stimuli—overtargeting, unfocused investigations, and claimed concern with future misconduct—as well as its heavy reliance on informers. The agency buys information either through a fixed developed source or from anyone who offers it. Not infrequently, an informer becomes "hooked" on firearms charges and sells information of dubious reliability in exchange for prosecutive laxity. A dealer in contraband who sells information to the ATF told me in an interview a few years ago: "If I'm really broke, I can always sell a piece of information to the ATF. The dope [information] I offer them is true—but sometimes exaggerated. I figure they already have a lead on the person. My agent sometimes asks about a case he's working on; he wants some information, in fact, he gets very palsy. They have got a stake in me; if I'm busted, I can count on them for help."

Freelance informers also are accorded a welcome reception by ATF. In 1971, Larry Shears, then an unemployed laborer and a former spy for the Kern County (California) sheriff's office, entered into an agreement with the ATF for a $10,000 fee in return for information about a plot to assassinate Cesar Chavez. The fee, approved in Washington, included payment for services as an informer and later as witness as well as the cost of relocation after surfacing. The reward was never paid because the alleged plotters were arrested on unrelated charges. Shears received only $500 in payment according to a voucher "for information and evidence necessary to identify those persons who are providing . . . the funds to arrange the arson and murder of Cesar Chavez."[70]

The most important function of the ATF informer is, however, the sale not of information but of hard evidence, usable in a courtroom. ATF informers may set up, as well as participate in, a "buy." But whether the informer or only his agent becomes involved, the use of such evidence is frequently protested on grounds of entrapment and provocation. The uncrowned king of ATF informers is surely Roy E. Frankhouser, former Pennsylvania Grand Dragon of the United Klans of America, organizer of the National States Rights Party, a Minuteman activist, and a member of more than thirty other right-wing groups. Frankhouser reveled in spookery and claimed that he was in fact a double agent, using his role as ATF informer to obtain access to intelligence in the agency's files about his right-wing associates. He even boasted that he had tapped telephone conversations between an ATF control and a Minuteman informant who was also a double agent, and that he had obtained recordings through his own intelligence network of conversations of Attorney General John Mitchell and his successor Richard Kleindienst. Frankhouser tried to penetrate the left with a cover story that he belonged to a "populist" segment of the rightist movement that shared the libertarianism of the radicals. But he kept mum about his ATF connections. After the publication of the Media FBI files in *WIN* magazine, a liberal publication, Frankhouser invited the editors to his Reading, Pennsylvania, headquarters, where he held forth on how he had master-minded counterintelligence tricks to foil the ATF's infiltration of the far right. In September 1975 Frankhouser pleaded guilty to his involvement in the disposal of 139 pounds of dynamite, 245 blasting caps, and 10,000 feet of detonating cord stolen from a local mining company in May and July of 1973. The court rejected Frankhouser's sole defense that he was an agent of the government at the time.

The ATF, like all intelligence agencies, rejects responsibility for its informers on the ground that their lapses are unavoidable occupational hazards. But what can one say in justification of the recruitment of the would-be assassin of ex-President Gerald Ford, Sara Jane Moore? On the day before the attempted assassination, Moore, accompanied by an ATF special agent, visited a dealer in firearms for the purpose of setting up a gun buy. Although Moore was a castoff (she had informed for the FBI from June of 1974 until June of the following year, when her services were terminated), the ATF took her on for a gun-traffic clean-up jointly conducted with the San Francisco Police Department. By the summer of 1975, not only was her identity established but it had become obvious that her reliability was, to say the least, quite dubious. Her disturbed mental state, which ultimately triggered the assassination attempt, was quite apparent from her wild talk. As a Bay Area radical put it, "Everybody but the feds knew she was flakey. Even the feds may have known but they didn't seem to mind."

A similarly unstable but less melodramatic type is Eustacio ("Frank") Martinez, who for two-and-a-half years served as informer and provocateur for the ATF.[71] A former mental patient in a Texas veterans hospital, Martinez was recruited in August 1969 after his conviction for possession of a sawed-off shotgun he said he had acquired in a gangfight. Offered a choice between serving as an ATF spy or a jail term, he signed on. Apart from the fear of jail, Martinez wanted desperately to be "an American first, Chicano second." Between September 1969 and October 1970 Martinez carried out three major assignments: the infiltration of the Mexican-American Youth Organization (MAYO) and the Brown Beret Organization in Houston and Kingsville, Texas; the development of intelligence data on these groups, their leaders, and supporters; and the provocative instigation of violence both to preserve his cover as a "militant Chicano leader" and to set up these targets for arrest. Martinez himself took part in numerous acts of disruption and violence. When he became "hot" in October 1970, he was transferred to Los Angeles to infiltrate the national office of the Brown Berets and the National Moratorium Committee. Under the code name "Adam 26," he also informed for the Los Angeles Police Department (LAPD).

In the quickly assumed role of militant leader, Martinez acquired access to letters, files, and names, which he turned over to the ATF and the police. Soon after arriving in southern California, he led a violent disruption of a speech by Senator John Tunney. Martinez literally went out of control: he attempted to knock in the top of a car driven by one of Tunney's aides, kicked Tunney, and beat his assistant. Martinez later recalled: "Several days later I reported my role in the incident to one of my superiors, Tito Garcia. Garcia's response was that I was to provoke incidents, but I should not go to the extreme of 'kicking a politician in the ass.' I also reported my role in this incident to Agent Fernando Ramos and Supervisor Jim Riggs at a later occasion." Martinez was not play-acting. One organizer in the Mexican-American community stated that "Frank was a time-bomb. They [ATF and LAPD] knew this, and counted on it. In a tense situation where Frank would be pitted against some important authority figure, he'd explode."

As Martinez's reputation grew, his controls instructed him, as he put it, to "start hassles among the people to divide them, create incidents and do crazy things to gain a reputation as a Chicano militant." In November 1970 Martinez paraded in front of the Chicano Moratorium office with a 410 caliber shotgun, with the goal of provoking a police raid. The raid took place later that day, and resulted in numerous injuries, arrests, and convictions. After a Moratorium rally on January 31, 1971, Martinez asserts that he helped provoke a riot by "shouting and throwing things at the East Los Angeles Sheriff Station and talking about doing in police and throwing a reporter in the river." A short time later many Chicanos were hurling rocks, and soon sheriff's deputies arrived with loaded shotguns, not tear gas. The Moratorium swiftly folded. When Martinez's compatriots began to suspect him, he became anxious and tried to withdraw completely. Unresolved complaints of underpayment hastened his return to Texas in April 1971.

In the summer of that year Martinez was brought back to California to help destroy an organization, La Casa de Carnalissimo, suspected by the ATF and the LAPD of serving as a cover for the Chicano Liberation Front, the group credited with a series of bombings in East Los Angeles. His ATF and LAPD sponsors furnished him with membership lists and photographs of leading militants and urged him to engage in bombings as a member of La Casa; the needed explosives would be supplied. When Martinez returned negative reports about planned violence and disassociated the Casa from the Chicano Liberation Front, he was told that his information "was a bunch of bullshit" and that "we are going to close that organization down by any means necessary." His disenchantment mounted when he was asked to plant a drug addict and pusher in La Casa. Soon afterward Martinez resigned and publicly recanted. He said: "I came forward for the simple reason that I was beginning to realize that our people were being railroaded." Other sources say that Martinez balked at any future assignment when the ATF reneged on an earlier promise of immunity from a prosecution arising out of an arrest on August 29, 1971, for inciting a riot and interfering with an officer in East Los Angeles. His ATF control, apparently fearful of Martinez's turn-about, had urged him to plead guilty with the intention of forcing his return to Texas. Martinez's search for identity as an American ended in a devastating isolation. In an interview in 1972 he said: "I cannot join any organization, because, for fear I might be found out—who I was in the past —it has damaged me psychologically. I cannot go to any group gatherings, rallies or anything, because no one will trust me."

The Nixon Administration's IRS Takeover Attempts

The Nixon administration viewed the IRS as a Roman general might have viewed the legions he was preparing to turn loose on a province ripe for conquest. "What we cannot do in a courtroom via criminal prosecution," Huston explained, "the IRS could do by administrative action. Moreover, valuable intelligence-type information could be turned up by IRS as a result of their field audits."[72] The administration's demands on the IRS were unique for another reason: it was not merely that the White House wanted to use the agency to attack a particular class of taxpayers—such as leftist and liberal tax-exempt organizations; it also pinpointed the targets with the highest priority. Its exorbitant demands on the IRS were doomed to failure. The IRS response was too slow, cautious, and, in some instances, quite uncooperative. When, in the fall of 1970, the administration received a progress report from IRS Commissioner Randolph Thrower on the SSS, a bitterly disappointed Tom Huston transmitted it to Haldeman with the observation that it "is long on words and short on action." Top White House political strategist Patrick Buchanan wrote that what was needed was a shake-up in the IRS bureaucracy, and "an especially friendly fellow, with a friendly staff in the Tax Exempt office."[73]

After Huston had followed up with a reminder of the President's continuing interest, the IRS moved on an important front: Commissioner Thrower announced that, "pending further study," the Service would discontinue granting tax-exempt status to public interest law firms. A natural outgrowth of the consumer movement of the sixties, the public interest firms were emerging as watchdogs of neglected areas of national concern.[74] The firms' principal benefactors were the tax-exempt foundations, led by the Ford Foundation, an administration *bête noire*. The IRS warned Ford and all other donors to the public interest law firm movement not to make long-term commitments to the firms pending completion of the study, on pain of losing their own exemptions. The move seemed mystifying: the firms were nonprofit entities and engaged neither in lobbying for legislation nor propaganda. In the wake of a storm of protest against the freeze by congressional leaders, including House Minority Leader Gerald Ford and two members of the Nixon administration (Russell Train and Virginia Knauer, environmental and consumer affairs functionaries, respectively), the IRS reversed itself.[75]

But there was one casualty of the administration's pressure. In September 1970, at about the same time that Huston complained about Thrower to Haldeman, a public interest firm, the Center on Corporate Responsibility, a Ralph Nader group, requested tax exemption which IRS ultimately denied after a two-and-a-half-year delay. In a suit filed in 1973, the Center alleged an unlawful denial of tax-exempt status and discriminatory treatment for political and ideological reasons without basis in the statute and the IRS regulations. A United States District Court on December 11, 1973, ruled that the tax exemption had improperly been denied under circumstances raising an unmistakable inference of political intervention. The court took note of the long delay and the fact that the Interpretive Division of the IRS Chief Counsel's office had unanimously approved the application. The opinion denying exemption had been written under Barth's direction, and a note in the file by the Interpretive Division's Assistant Director read: "Perhaps White House pressure."[76]

The White House also plundered established procedures developed in the past to give the chief executive access to IRS data in order to develop legislative programs and (the "sensitive case" procedure) to prevent abuses in cases involving political figures. Because the tax files sought by the administration were to be used for illegitimate purposes, these procedures, which required formal requests, were bypassed in favor of private channels developed through the administration's IRS contacts. Thus, the White House intervened to defuse and sabotage an IRS investigation of Charles ("Bebe") Rebozo's tax returns, while at the same time Ehrlichman ordered a speed-up of a pre-election audit of

Lawrence O'Brien, Democratic Party chairman, so that it could be used in the presidential campaign.[77]

Even when the IRS was requested to transmit tax data through the established procedures, it was used for partisan purposes.[78] For example, in March 1970 special counsel to the President Clark Mollenhoff obtained through proper channels the tax returns and other related investigative data of Gerald Wallace, the brother of George Wallace, then feared as a threat to the President's reelection. When instructed by Haldeman to obtain the confidential data from the IRS, Mollenhoff was told that it was for the exclusive use of the President. Three weeks later the material appeared in a Jack Anderson column ("IRS Probes Wallace, Lurleen Reigns." "Confidential field reports made available to this column . . . "). Commissioner Thrower stated in an affidavit to the House Impeachment Committee that an investigation convinced him the material had not been leaked by the IRS or the Treasury, and that when he met thereafter with Haldeman and Ehrlichman, he felt compelled to tell them that such unauthorized disclosures constituted criminal conduct.*[79]

The processing of White House tax requests assumed such importance in the Nixon administration's agenda that it was assigned as a fixed responsibility to John Dean and his staff. Dean succeeded in obtaining access to the tax returns of administration critics and supporters for purely political purposes, as well as to the files of tax-exempt groups. In some cases, he transmitted requests directly to administration friends in the IRS, and in others White House hawkshaw John Caulfield served as the conduit. Charles Colson was particularly assiduous in levying information through Dean's office regarding the tax exemption status of opposition groups, including the National Council of Senior Citizens ("this outfit is giving us trouble"), Common Cause, and the Vietnam Veterans Against the War.[80] Information was one thing; but when Dean tried to arrange for audits and investigations, he didn't get very far and complained that the Commissioner had not been "responsive" or "sensitive." Specifically, he reported:

> We have been unable to crack down on the multitude of tax exempt foundations that feed left wing political causes.
> We have been unable to obtain information in the possession of IRS regarding our political enemies.
> We have been unsuccessful in placing RN supporters in the IRS bureaucracy.[81]

In the summer of 1971 the administration, panicked by congressional defeats the previous year, began preparing for the 1972 presidential election. The underlying strategy was to win not by organizing a constituency around positive issues but by making the Democrats lose through dividing their supporters and exploiting mass fears and prejudice. This strategy would avoid the necessity of defending the administration's policies and would transfer the election contest from the market place of issues to the darkened theater of intelligence. It was imperative to devise sanctions to, as Dean put it, "screw our political enemies."[82]

*In March 1971 an Anderson column reported that the Wallace tax files had been made available to the White House but, far from revealing the earlier leak, Anderson asserted: "There is no evidence that the White House has used tax information for political purposes." Here was source protection with a vengeance.

Beginning in June 1971, lists of the administration's political opponents were compiled and circulated by members of Colson's staff.*[83]

Tax harassment was seen as a choice weapon. On September 11, 1972, Dean at Ehrlichman's request asked IRS Commissioner John Walters to investigate McGovern's campaign staffers and contributors: some 490 in all. Walters advised Dean that compliance with the request would be disastrous for the IRS, but agreed to reconsider the matter with Treasury Secretary George Schultz, who subsequently advised him to do nothing.[84] In a White House conference four days later, Haldeman reported that Dean was "moving ruthlessly on the investigation of McGovern people," and was "working the thing through the IRS." But Dean, who subsequently joined the conversation, renewed his complaint about Commissioner Walters's lack of cooperation. The President, especially embittered over the failure of Treasury Secretary Schultz to push the IRS more aggressively, vowed that after the elections there would be changes made.[85] By March 1973 Dean was feeling better about IRS cooperation. When asked by the President whether he needed IRS material in responding to the Watergate developments, Dean replied: "We have a couple of sources over there that I can go to. I don't have to fool around with [Commissioner] Johnnie Walters or anybody, we can get right in and get what we need."[86]

Dean's boasts as well as his complaints about his IRS sources are a Watergate trademark. The Nixon administration's overriding commitment to intelligence inevitably made access to intelligence sources a surefire means of advancement among those who vied for the President's favor. They all—Dean, Ehrlichman, Haldeman, Magruder, and Colson—had, or claimed they had, intelligence pipelines. These boasts of inside information frequently came to nothing. But there was little risk in promising without delivery. Failure could always be ascribed to the scheming Democrats, who had intervened once again to prevent the administration from using power in the same way as its predecessors, or to the need for "harder input." So, for example, Dean blamed his frustration on an alleged anti-Nixon cabal in control of the IRS bureaucracy and not on the fact that his requests were improper.[87]

Operatives like Caulfield and Liddy readily sensed that the market would absorb intelligence of any kind, no matter how paranoid. For example, prior to the appearance in October 1971 of a critical *Newsday* series on Rebozo, Caulfield told Dean that he had learned of its preparation from "New York sources" and that Ed Guthman (a former Robert Kennedy associate and managing editor of the Los Angeles *Times,* which owned *Newsday*) was "close to the matter" because he was, as Caulfield put it, "in New York at the time of the planning stages of the inquiry." In another memorandum, he pointed out that *Newsday* writer Bill Moyers, a former Johnson aide, was a trustee of the Kennedy Foundation.[88] Was it not crystal-clear that the *Newsday* series was secretly financed in violation of the law by the tax-exempt Kennedy Foundation? Caul-

*Both Colson and Haldeman told the Watergate Committee that the lists were intended to avoid the embarrassment of inviting administration opponents to White House social affairs. But this claimed purpose is hardly consistent with the comments on the list, such as, in the case of Morton Halperin, "a scandal would be most helpful here," and in that following the name of advertising executive Maxwell Dane, "they should hit hard starting with Dane."

field had his own assets. One of them was Assistant IRS Commissioner Vernon ("Mike") Acree. In Caulfield's proposal for Project Sandwedge—a private, commercially organized intelligence plan to aid the President's reelection campaign—Acree was designated to head a mission to provide "IRS information input." Acree had demonstrated his loyalty by supplying tax data at Caulfield's request; it was Acree who, according to Caulfield, suggested that an audit be instigated against an administration opponent through an anonymous "squeal" letter. In May 1972 Acree was promoted for his services to the job of Commissioner of Customs.[89]

After the exposure of his role as the White House IRS contact, Acree insisted that, during the twenty years of his IRS service under eight Commissioners and as Assistant to six of them, "sensitive case reports all bubbled up at the top to the White House simply as a matter of national interest. They wanted it for guest lists and other things."[90] But he could find no precedent for his practice of turning over to Caulfield tax returns without the authorization or knowledge of the Commissioner.*[91]

In the end, the pursuit of a sanction, a means of doing injury outside the forms of law, had only a limited success. The IRS is too lumbering an apparatus to strike with the necessary deterrent speed, and its arsenal of tax harassments too unsuited to left targets. Besides, even with the prodding of the zealous head of the SSS, its coverage was confined to the more visible targets and left untouched anonymous armies of protesters, including large numbers not even subject to tax return filing requirements. These deficiencies were overcome by kangaroo grand juries.

---

*Acree's job had nothing to do with tax returns or compliance; he was head of the IRS Inspection Service, an élite corps charged, ironically enough, with keeping the agency honest. Acree's unit itself fell under suspicion of corruption in connection with a Florida project, Operation Sunshine, launched in 1971 to ferret out evidence of bribery.—*Report on Operation Sunshine,* March 26, 1975 and related statements by IRS Assistant Chief Counsel Leon G. Wigrizer (July 8, 1975) and Harry C. Woodington (July 31, 1975) in *Oversight Hearings into the Operations of the IRS* (Part 1), pp. 649–719, 807–895. "Chief IRS Probe Figure Is a Rizzo-Styled Tough Cop"; "Panel Sifts More IRS Spy Evidence," Philadelphia *Sunday Bulletin,* Aug. 31, 1975.

10 Kangaroo Grand Juries

Subpoenas to the Rescue

The spring 1970 panic, described in Chapter 7, over the opposition to White House policies placed repression close to the top of its list of priorities. And the need was seen as desperate: legitimate dissent had been preempted by madmen leading a generational revolt that threatened the American experience in a new way, a vengeful oedipal uprising not only against the Vietnam involvement but against the heritage it symbolized. Even a moderate conservative like speech writer Raymond Price joined in the general surfing on the apocalypse. The campus rebellion was, in his view, "the most profound challenge of the century to the continued stability of the democratic system itself." Desperation mounted as conspiracy prosecutions, a hardy vehicle of political oppression in the fifties, foundered in a series of trials that took place across the country from Oakland to New Haven. For young Turks like Huston and his White House patrons, the answer was clear: traditional criminal law remedies were useless to stem the swelling tide and had to be replaced by "intelligence," in other words, a clandestine offensive outside the forms of law.[1] What secrecy could not conceal could always be justified as a sensible precaution or a defense against threatened violence and foreign manipulation. After the defeat of the Huston Plan in June, the Bureau remained the only available resource for this guerrilla warfare. But again the redoubtable Director loomed as an intractable obstacle. His priorities and methods deepened the bitterness of the White House intelligence types eager to strike hard in new ways at the young rebels. The emergence of a new style of political dissent crystallized what they had privately sensed for a long time —that the Bureau's Mr. Clean nativist version of intelligence, born in the twenties, developed in the forties, influenced by image-building and power goals, and shaped by the *modus operandi* of its principal target, the Communist Party, had finally exhausted itself. Its White House critics and their supporters in the intelligence community pressed, cautiously to be sure, for a change to more

353

daring and imaginative tactics, risk-taking, and deception, all with a punitive rather than a propaganda thrust. Not that the Bureau didn't try hard on both the intelligence and the law enforcement fronts. No less than half of the entries on its "ten most wanted" list of dangerous criminals (now augmented to sixteen) were radicals. In addition, Sullivan had persuaded the Director to extend the boundaries of the COINTELPROs beyond the Old Left. But the Director had kept the program under tight Bureau control, fearful of the consequences of exposure. As a result this entire offensive, with the exception of the attack on black militants, produced only a limited impact on the protest forces and was effective primarily against easily infiltrated targets with a traditional public style—quite different from the amorphous, neo-bohemian new movements.

The Bureau was incapable of developing an intelligence response to the New Left: its concentration on communism as the Menace left little room for developing an awareness of the new movements. Indeed, subversion was such a foul contaminant that it was dangerous to come too close to it, to verify from experience the stereotypes of countersubversion that had shaped Bureau intelligence for half a century. Thus the Bureau entered the Vietnam era far removed from political reality but with a self-deceiving confidence in its effectiveness, based on its intensive informer coverage of the Old Left. Indeed, Old Left informers were easy to recruit and plant. Marxist politics functions in a straight, earnest world, in which acceptance of programs and policies and faithful performance of Party assignments are enough to establish the spy's credibility. But infiltration of the countercultural New Left was far more daunting, involving changes in style of life, dress, hygiene, sex habits, speech, and hair. And beyond this, the targets were far more sensitive to those clues to consciousness ("vibes") that authenticate true political commitment. It was not only that qualified infiltrators were hard to find; the agents responsible for recruiting them did not know where to begin to look, and the movement was still too young to produce defectors who could be induced to return as informers.

Without such input, the frustrated Bureau agents could not deal even with the threshold problem of identification. Before one could open a file on these troublemakers living in remote tribal communities, far from their homes and families, cut off from the mainstream of American society, one had to identify them. Who were they? This was an immense challenge. The world of the New Left seemed isolated and autonomous, and the traditional guideposts of organizational hierarchy—officers, leaders, and members—had vanished, itself a casualty of the new rebellion. The target was an entire milieu, light-years removed from the Bureau's traditional intelligence beat.[2] Its protest sector at least functioned above ground and in the open; but finding the trail of security-conscious bombers and fugitives was infinitely more baffling. The Bureau's hunt, begun in the early seventies, for underground Weatherpeople fugitives (some nineteen in all) was totally unsuccessful despite the resort to illegal wiretapping and mail opening. By the end of 1977 sixteen of the fugitives were still at large; three had voluntarily turned themselves in. This failure is not unrelated to the fact that there is only one known successful Bureau penetration of the terrorist group: informer Larry Grathwohl, who infiltrated a Weather Underground circle in December 1969 and was exposed in April 1970.

It was this setting of wild exaggeration of the threat, combined with a loss of confidence in the available means of containing it, that led to the emergence of a new repressive offensive, the federal grand jury.[3] The congressional anti-subversive committees might have filled the bill. But their legitimacy was discredited and their principal weapon, the public exposure device, no longer effective. The new leftists in any event could not be linked to the Menace and, most important, they were in many cases supported by a broad middle-class anti-war consensus. A new attack would have to be secret, clothed with a more plausible justification than the committees' claimed legislative purpose, and aimed inwardly at the group and its members.

The White House entrusted the grand jury offensive to the Internal Security Division (ISD) of the Department of Justice. This unit, which had languished during the post-McCarthy years, was now enlarged from a complement of six to one of sixty as part of a master plan to deploy all available resources against the new dissenters. At the same time (as will be recalled) the Inter Departmental Intelligence Unit (IDIU) was converted from a riot-alert function to a fully ideologized political intelligence unit, with inputs from the entire intelligence community, and made part of the ISD. A single branch of the Department of Justice was thus entrusted with countersubversive law enforcement and intelligence responsibilities unrelated to law enforcement. This transformation was the work of Robert Charles Mardian, an abrasive right-wing Californian brought in to head the ISD in November 1970. A former HEW general counsel, a member of the hard-line White House junta on civil rights, and a protégé of Richard Kleindienst (the senior Justice Department official who subsequently became Attorney General), he qualifies for admission to the circle of fanatics for whom the pursuit of radicals gratifies combined personal needs and career ambitions. Mardian was a red hunter of the old school, a mind of the fifties with a provincial outlook unpalatable to the more philosophical Tom Huston, who once turned up his nose at his offer of a job. "Mardian," he observed, "didn't know the difference between a kid with a beard and a kid with a bomb."[4] An important White House channel of information about radical doings, Mardian chaired the Intelligence Evaluation Committee (IEC) with its broad representation of all elements of the intelligence community. He supervised the prosecution of Daniel Ellsberg, and reported on its progress to the White House, and on President Nixon's instructions transmitted logs of wiretap conversations in which Ellsberg had been overheard to the White House, to protect the government's case from legal attack. Mardian had acquired the logs from FBI Intelligence Division chief William Sullivan, with whom he developed a personal relationship. This connection gave Mardian direct access to the Bureau's intelligence resources and enabled Sullivan, restive and ambitious, to function in a more spacious intelligence theater without fear of the Director's reprisal. (Not that Hoover had viewed the ISD-Intelligence Division marriage with equanimity. But there was little he could do about it beyond undercutting and disparaging Mardian in White House circles.)

The ISD's principal function under the new dispensation remained what it had been before Mardian took over: the prosecution of offenses involving internal security. Mardian selected as the field marshal of this drive a Kansas City lawyer, Guy Goodwin. With Goodwin in charge of a new unit, the Special Litigation Section,[5] the ISD converted the federal grand jury proceeding from its traditional and recognized function, deciding whether the prosecutor has presented sufficient evidence to justify an accusation of law violation, into a cover for a variety of intelligence-related pursuits divorced from legal ends. The effectiveness of the grand jury proceeding as an intelligence instrument is directly traceable to the subpoena power, the power to compel testimony and the production of documents on pain of contempt. A dominant aim of such compelled testimony was to force a witness to name associates and friends in an ever-widening inquisition, a revival under a law enforcement cover of a practice made familiar by congressional anti-subversive committees under a legislative cover.[6]

Patterns of other intelligence-related abuses for which the grand jury proceedings served as a cover emerged from a series of over 100 grand jury proceedings in 84 cities of 36 states, in which between 1000 and 2000 witnesses were subpoenaed.[7] This nationwide network, which flourished almost continuously between 1970 and 1973, produced a serious impact on many of its targets, which included New Left radicals, anti-war intellectuals, the Catholic left, black militants, anti-draft movements, the women's movement, journalists, lawyers, and the Puerto Rican independence movement. Out of an estimated 400 indictments* returned by the ISD grand juries, the conviction and plea rate was less than 15 percent, compared to 65.2 percent in ordinary criminal cases, an eloquent commentary on the insubstantial character of the indictments.

The framework for the entire program was the conspiracy concept. Concentrating on inchoate offenses enabled the ISD to cast its net as widely as possible without appearing to abandon a law enforcement objective, to use informers wherever available to provide an armature of remembered discussion, even if never implemented, on which to build an investigation. In turn, investigative overkill was assured by an assumption inherent in modern intelligence, that entire areas of protest (women's liberation, the Catholic left, anti-war protest) were linked in a highly reticulated network with a common end. And this shared-end hypothesis was used to justify subpoenaing targets committed to the use of lawful means of achieving it.

As early as 1973 Senator Edward M. Kennedy denounced the ISD grand jury system as "unprecedented" and "a throw-back to the worst excesses of the legislative investigative committees of the 1950s."[8] A highly respected legal authority, Moore's *Federal Practice,* similarly noted that "the federal grand jury has become the battle ground" in a war by the Nixon administration "against the press, the intellectual community and the peace movement generally. . . ."[9] And a judge of the Ninth Circuit Court of Appeals, taking note of the flood of cases "arising out of grand jury proceedings concerned with the possible punishment of political dissidents," remarked: "it would be a cruel twist of history to allow the institution of the grand jury that was designed at least partially to protect political dissent to become an instrument of political suppression."[10]

---

*A generous estimate: it includes both original and superseding indictments, and lists separately multiple indictments arising out of the same alleged offense.

These criticisms and concerns focused only on the broad aspects of the politicized grand jury system. They could not exhaust the full range of abuses blueprinted by ISD grand jury strategists—the legion of Bureau agents armed with subpoenas who fanned out for harassing interviews with bewildered and frightened subjects, followed up by subpoena-enforced appearances, the need to hire a lawyer, the pressure to betray and inform on others however innocent the association, the threat of jail, the public trial for contempt, and the jail sentences where grounds for refusal were rejected. It is not too much to say that during its heyday, the period from 1970 to 1974, the grand jury became a police state instrument.

The Prosecutor Reigns Supreme

More than any other single circumstance, the extraordinary power of the prosecutor made possible the ISD perversion of the grand jury system. Few figures in our criminal justice system are in command of such arbitrary and unrestrained power. The formal usage "grand jury subpoena" should not lead the reader to believe that in fact the grand jury, independently of the prosecutor, uses its process (really the process of the court of which it is an appendage) to compel the witness to appear and testify. Federal prosecutors command the subpoena power in the name of the grand jury. There are no limits to the number of individuals a federal prosecutor may choose to subpoena. For example, in 1971 a Los Angeles grand jury investigating the West Coast anti-draft, anti-war movement subpoenaed more than 100 witnesses, ranging from doctors, lawyers, and draft counselors to the parents of draftees. An irresponsible prosecutor can spray subpoenas wildly over the entire country in pursuit of objectives wholly removed from the grand jury's basic concerns. He may do so on short notice, out of pique, to show his power, to harass the witness, and in the knowledge that it will serve no legitimate purpose. Moreover, the prosecutor can ask whatever questions he chooses and in whatever form suits his fancy since he is unrestrained by the evidentiary requirements of an adversary trial.

The secrecy of the grand jury proceeding cloaks abuses. Although secrecy historically served to protect the independence of the grand jury by insulating it from the pressures of the Crown, there can be little doubt that in the Nixon years grand jury secrecy became an instrument of the very evil it was intended to prevent. This is not to say that a case cannot be made for preserving the secrecy of grand jury proceedings, but rather to insist that prosecutorial over-reaching is promoted by the knowledge that the proceedings are sealed. To be sure, a witness may seek redress from the judge who is responsible for the conduct of the grand jury proceedings. But, traditionally, the judge tends to protect the prosecutor. Judges have pronounced themselves satisfied with the relevance of oppressive questioning on the basis of affidavits submitted *in camera* which the witness is denied an opportunity to challenge. That the witness has in fact little or no protection against an oppressive prosecutor under the existing grand jury system is hardly a novel or controversial contention. The witness cannot even bring his counsel into the grand jury room; he has no right to learn the subject of the investigation, whether a question is material, or indeed whether he himself is a target of the inquiry. The secrecy of the proceedings and the possibility of a jail sentence for contempt so intimidate the witness that he may be led into answering questions that pry into his personal life and political associations, and that, into the bargain, are frequently immaterial and vague. Life in a relatively open society makes him especially vulnerable to a secret appearance before a body considering criminal charges. Alone and faced by either hostile or apathetic grand juries, the witness is frequently undone by his experience. When he seeks protective guidance from his lawyer (outside the grand jury chambers), he learns that the judicial broadening of due process that has occurred in the past two decades has largely ignored grand jury matters, precisely because it was assumed that the grand jury functioned as a guardian of the rights of witnesses and potential defendants. In theory, the power of the prosecutor is subject to a functional limitation on the role of the grand jury itself —a familiar trade-off in our constitutional system—which is expressed in the literature and court cases in a variety of ways: the grand jury is an arm of the court, charged only with judicial and not executive functions; its mandate is primarily to evaluate and appraise evidence developed independently by the prosecutor in order to decide whether an indictment should be returned; its functions are "accusatorial and not inquisitorial"; it cannot engage in a "fishing expedition" seeking information in a haphazard, unfocused way, nor can it be converted into a "prosecutive tool."

But these formulations have been largely ritualized and can no longer be viewed as restraints on overzealous prosecutors. Nor is there surviving vitality in the more positive protective role of the grand jury as expressed by the Supreme Court in this language:

> Historically, this body [the grand jury] has been regarded as a primary security to the innocent against hasty, malicious and oppressive persecution; it serves the invaluable function in our society of standing between the accuser and the accused, whether the latter be an individual, minority group, or other, to determine whether a charge is founded upon reason or was dictated by an intimidating power or by malice and personal ill will.[11]

While this protective responsibility of the grand jury was so valued by the founding fathers that it is enshrined in the Bill of Rights, the reality now is that grand juries have virtually abandoned their historic mission and become unquestioning servants of the prosecution. This surrender has, ironically enough, been most abject in proceedings related to political dissent, precisely the area in which the grand jury emerged most conspicuously as a shield for the innocent against malicious and oppressive prosecution.*

---

*Two historic refusals to indict for state crimes involve Lord Shaftesbury (treason) and, in the American colonial period, Peter Zenger (criminal libel). The return of an *Ignoramus* in Lord Shaftesbury's case in 1681 was said to be the occasion for the writing and publication of Lord Somers's great tract, *The Security of Englishmen's Lives: Or the Trust, Power, and Duty of Grand Juries of England*. The preface to a second edition in 1771 tells us:

> This little book explains the whole duty of Grand Juries, the high importance of them to every individual in the kingdom, as the life and safety of all depends upon them. It also shews their independency of judges; explains the duty and power of judges, and not only of judges but of

It is hardly a matter for dispute that today, as a federal judge has observed, "the grand jury is the total captive of the prosecutor who, if he is candid, will concede that he can indict anybody, at any time, for almost anything, before any grand jury."[12] In the political realm this highly personalized power is peculiarly subject to abuse. As Attorney General Robert H. Jackson warned in his 1940 speech to federal prosecutors (already referred to), when "law enforcement becomes personal . . . the real crime becomes that of being unpopular with the predominant or governing group, being attached to the wrong political views, or being personally obnoxious to or in the way of the prosecutor himself."

While this personalized political use of the grand jury reached its apogee in the Nixon years, it has striking antecedents in the modern period: two grand juries conducted in the early fifties by Assistant U.S. Attorney (later aide to Senator McCarthy) Roy M. Cohn. In both cases, Cohn used the grand jury for non-law enforcement purposes—to issue a report attacking politically unpopular individuals and groups. In 1952 a Cohn grand jury investigated an alleged conspiracy by trade union officials to file false non-Communist affidavits with the National Labor Relations Board. Cohn drafted a grand jury report attacking the trade unionists for pleading the Fifth Amendment before the grand jury and recommending that the National Labor Relations Board deny the union the protections of the National Labor Relations Act. The grand jury foreman and an unidentified "assistant U.S. Attorney" named the officials through press leaks in order to discredit them and increase the pressure on the National Labor Relations Board.[13] District Judge Edward Weinfeld in a landmark decision quashed the report on the ground that the grand jury's power is confined to the issuance of indictments and cannot be used to attack or denounce particular individuals or groups through reports or presentments.[14] In another celebrated case, Cohn used the grand jury to subpoena United Nations staff members over whom it had questionable jurisdiction and interrogated them not with a view to indicting them but simply to determine whether they were Communists. But the matter was not confined to the grand jury room; after each witness was questioned, he was brought next door and reinterrogated by the Senate Internal Security Subcommittee (SISS). Here again the grand jury issued a report; but, to protect Cohn from charges of impropriety, it mentioned no names. The omission was repaired this time not through a leak but through publication of the SISS interrogation.[15]

While Cohn's manipulation of the grand jury process conflicted with higher echelons,* Guy Goodwin's—during the period 1970–73 when he ran the ISD operation—was official policy. Like Cohn, Goodwin appears to be a counter-subversive zealot obsessed with stalking and harassing his targets by any means possible.[16] A veritable Javert in his pursuit of radicals, his animosity undercut

---

kings, and is a full account of that most essential part of the English constitution, upon which all our other liberties depend.

*The issuance of the proposed report was opposed, according to Cohn, by lawyers in the State and Justice Departments. The main objection, Cohn has written, was that the issuance of the document would be politically embarrassing to the Truman administration. Cohn prevailed after soliciting the support of the Director.—Roy M. Cohn, "Could He Walk on Water?" *Esquire* (November 1972).

and compromised the prosecutive function that served as his cover. Low-keyed, impeccably dressed, his gray hair coiffed and styled, he affected a withering stagy hauteur in dealing with uncooperative witnesses. Among his colleagues he commanded admiration for his fingertip knowledge of the left scene, which he used to put down the already resentful local U.S. attorneys[17] and paraded before the grand jurors in gossipy display.

Goodwin used his grand jury operations as an outlet for a compulsive voyeurism. When a group of Catholic anti-war activists raided the Selective Service offices in Camden, New Jersey, they were confronted as they were making their escape in the early morning hours by the suave prosecutor, who flicked on the lights and, greeting them familiarly, handed out to each startled activist a copy of "your indictment." One of the defendants recalled in an interview: "At about 4:00 A.M. Goodwin, elegantly dressed and grinning, greeted each of us. He called me by my nickname 'Cookie' and asked if my brother still played the drums." "Psyching" the target in this way with knowledge acquired through surveillance is a familiar enough intelligence gambit: it is intended to frighten and at the same time to assert power over the target, telling him in effect, "We are watching you and know all about you."

But only a powerful subjective hostility, a compulsion to confront and attack, can explain why a federal special prosecutor, an officer of the court, felt it necessary personally to serve a defendant in a dramatic early morning confrontation with an indictment that could have been routinely served through appropriate means and in due time. This same subjective need is reflected in Goodwin's practice of working directly on an operational level with informers rather than, as is normally the case, confining himself to evaluating the facts developed by investigators and, if necessary, suggesting further areas of inquiry. Goodwin was apparently untroubled by the fact that such involvement might prove embarrassing and even compromising. For example, he did not hesitate to tell a *New York Times* reporter in July 1970 that he had no knowledge that one of the defendants in a Detroit conspiracy indictment, Larry Grathwohl, was in fact a Bureau informer although he had worked closely with him in preparing the case. Three years later Goodwin made a similar denial but with more serious consequences in the Gainesville, Florida, conspiracy case against members of the Vietnam Veterans Against the War (VVAW). In order to frustrate the group's planned demonstration at the Miami political convention in 1972, Goodwin had issued grand jury subpoenas on a wholesale scale. To protect the cover of informers who would otherwise (by reason of office or activity) rate a subpoena, Goodwin subpoenaed Bureau spies as well. When in 1973 the indictment came to trial, defense lawyers had no way of separating out suspected spies and were forced to seek relief from the judge to protect themselves and their clients from exposure to a concealed government agent. Goodwin represented to the court under oath that none of the persons listed by defense counsel, including one Emerson L. Poe, were agents or informers. Poe was in fact a Bureau informer and a close friend and confidant of the defendants' leader, Scott Camil. Goodwin's denial gave him access through Poe to the defendants' legal preparations and plans until the moment mid-trial when he appeared as a prosecution witness. (Poe subsequently admitted that he had met with Goodwin at both his office and his motel room in Gainesville.) "Of course Goodwin was aware that I was working with the FBI." After the defendants were acquitted, they brought a civil suit for damages on the ground that their right to counsel had been infringed during the grand jury proceedings and part of the trial. The complaint also requested that Goodwin be tried for perjury by a special prosecutor. In September 1977 a federal appellate court rejected Goodwin's defense that as a prosecutor he enjoyed absolute immunity from damage actions and ruled that he was not entitled to absolute prosecutorial immunity because he was engaged in investigative activity rather than the quasi-judicial function to which such immunity is attached.[18]

The civil suit and threatened perjury prosecution were not the last of Goodwin's problems. In November 1977, while still employed as a prosecutor in the Department of Justice general crime section, he became the subject of an investigation by the House Judiciary Committee for unprofessional behavior. His principal accuser was Rodney Sager, former head of the Richmond, Virginia, U.S. Attorney's office and a respected U.S. attorney. Sager gave a number of examples of Goodwin's unprofessional behavior. One of them involved a 1975 grand jury investigation in Richmond of alleged FBI misconduct. Goodwin's protective bias and incompetence—Goodwin is a strong FBI supporter and a profound admirer of the late Director*—so disturbed Sager that he moved for his removal from the case. In reprisal, Goodwin called Sager himself to the witness stand for a grilling that lasted fifteen hours. When Sager's subsequent complaint was dismissed by the Justice Department, he resigned in disgust.[19]

Goodwin launched the ISD radical hunt with two new weapons. In the past, grand juries had been tied to the prosecutive personnel attached to the office of a U.S. attorney in a particular judicial district. Roy Cohn, for example, was able to exploit his grand jury power only in the Southern District of New York, where he served on the staff of the federal prosecutor for that district. The Organized Crime Control Act of 1970, however, authorized the Department of Justice in Washington to exercise centralized control over grand jury proceedings whenever it was deemed necessary, and to replace the local U.S. attorneys with special prosecutors, empowered to proceed through specially convened grand juries for an eighteen-month term, with an extension option for a second eighteen-month period. This statutory dispensation, enacted to provide a more effective means of coping with interstate crime, institutionalized a national offensive directed against intelligence targets on the theory that a coordinated conspiracy of highly mobile plotters threatened the security of the entire nation. The solution to what had happened in, say, New York might be found by convening a grand jury in Seattle; an informer's tale about a bombing plot in Detroit could be fleshed out by interrogating witnesses in Vermont or the District of Columbia. In addition, the lengthy term for which a grand jury could be authorized and the renewal option provided a powerful sanction for recalcitrance, since uncooperative witnesses could be jailed for civil contempt during the period in which a grand jury was sitting and then suffer a continuation of their incarceration in the event that the grand jury was extended.

*A framed commendatory letter from Hoover is prominently displayed in his office.

Civil contempt was made more threatening than in the past by a provision in the 1970 statute dealing with immunity. The pressures on dissent in the McCarthy era had resulted in the enactment in 1954 of a provision authorizing the grant of immunity from prosecution to witnesses before grand juries and congressional committees, thus undermining the right to resist compulsory disclosure on Fifth Amendment–self-incrimination grounds. This provision authorized *transactional* immunity, protecting the witness against prosecution for any conduct broadly covered by the subject of his or her testimony—except perjury. The 1970 statute, however, provided for *use* immunity, which barred prosecution only for the conduct directly related to the witness's testimony or its fruits. A resourceful prosecutor like Goodwin was able in this way to force use-immunized witnesses to testify against each other. Moreover, even without immunity, witnesses lacking counsel could be trapped into disclosure by inadvertently waiving the privilege against self-incrimination or, on the ground that the privilege is personal and hence unavailable, could be forced to identify and betray others under threat of a contempt sentence. Finally, unlike the case in the fifties, the pursuit was sheltered by a surface legitimacy: bombings *had* occurred; explosives *had* been bought and sold; destructive crimes had been discussed and planned. But it was precisely the failure of conventional police and investigative procedures in dealing with such that led to the conversion of the grand jury into an investigative tool for the use of frustrated Bureau agents. In this way a legitimate end, the weighing of evidence for accusatorial purposes, both masked and was replaced by indefensible means.

The ISD Pattern

The ISD grand jury program was foreshadowed by a grand jury proceeding in November 1969. The previous year a group called the International Committee to Defend Eldridge Cleaver placed an advertisement in the *New York Times* in support of the Panther leader. A federal grand jury in Philadelphia subpoenaed the names of the group's sponsors and contributors, assertedly in aid of a probe of "mail fraud." But it seems clear that this was a law enforcement cover for an operation of the Justice Department's Panther task force, looking for evidence linking the black militant group to foreign sources of support. This attempted use of the subpoena power was quickly abandoned in the face of a legal challenge that it was an attempt to extend to another forum the compulsory identification procedures of congressional anti-subversive committees.[20] But the ISD attack was directed not, as in the case of the congressional committees, only against formal membership groups but more broadly against unstructured movements defined only by common issues, lifestyles, and religious views (the Catholic left). It was assumed in selecting subpoena targets that those who were least committed would most readily cooperate. Thus the remoteness of the witness from the ostensible concerns of the grand jury served not as a protection but as a reason for harassment.*

*The use immunity provision was intended to provide prosecutors with a means of extracting useful evidence from witnesses with some knowledge of but limited involvement in organized crime.

After several preliminary grand jury sessions in Detroit and Vermont, the ISD grand jury offensive found its style in the fall of 1970 with the investigation of the alleged purchase in Tucson, Arizona, of dynamite by a young man who drove a car registered to a woman in Los Angeles. Several months of surveillance of her home revealed little more than that a group of five young people were living communally and engaging in various open community activities. After the issuance of an indictment against the alleged dynamite purchaser, one John Fuerst, Goodwin proceeded to develop a broad picture of West Coast radical activities through the subpoenaed witness—the owner of the car and her four friends. None of the five was indicted. But the fact that they were interrogated after the indictment had been handed down, as well as the range of questioning, showed that Goodwin had other fish to fry. A pattern that was to become typical of the ISD investigative grand juries is illustrated by questions such as these:[21]

Tell the grand jury, please, where you were employed during the year 1970, by whom you were employed during the year 1970, how long you have been so employed and what the amount of remuneration for your employment has been during the year 1970.

Tell the grand jury every place you went after you returned to your apartment from Cuba, every city you visited, with whom and by what means of transportation you traveled and who you visited at all of the places you went during the times of your travels after you left your apartment in Ann Arbor, Michigan, in May of 1970.

I want you to describe for the grand jury every occasion during the year 1970, when you have been in contact with, attended meetings which were conducted by, or attended by, or been any place when any individual spoke whom you knew to be associated with or affiliated with Students for a Democratic Society, the Weathermen, the Communist Party or any other organization advocating revolutionary overthrow of the United States, describing for the grand jury when these incidents occurred, where they occurred, who was present and what was said by all persons there and what you did at the time that you were in these meetings, groups, associations or conversations.

These questions, it should be repeated, were asked of mere witnesses, people supposedly not themselves under investigation.

The five Tucson witnesses made an initial decision not to cooperate with the grand jury and refused to answer all questions put to them. They were given full (transactional) immunity by the district court, again refused to testify and, beginning in early November 1970, went to jail as each was cited for contempt. They received the conventional civil contempt sentence: until they agreed to testify or until the life of the grand jury (up to eighteen months) expired, which in this case was the following March. Each of the witnesses decided to pay the

However, it failed altogether to achieve its purpose. For a lowly Mafia soldier, a jail sentence for refusing to talk is a badge of honor, a cheap price for an opportunity to demonstrate loyalty to higher-ups. But it was ideally suited for political harassment both because it did not specify the offenses for which the immunity might be granted and because the "movement" witness, however ignorant of the criminal involvements of others, was himself a primary target not of law enforcement but surveillance and harassment.

price of his or her disobedience and remained in jail for the entire period. The grand jury expired on March 23, 1971, but no one informed the jailed witnesses or their lawyers. On March 25, when the witnesses were finally released from jail, each was greeted at the cell door with another subpoena to appear before a new grand jury on April 7. Karen Duncan, one of the five witnesses, in an interview later described the impact of Goodwin's tactic:

> It then appeared that there were no legal restrictions to the kinds of questions a grand jury could ask, or the number of grand juries one could be called before and thus the time one could be jailed for contempt. It looked like we could be continually jailed on repeated 18 months sentences forever. It looked as though the only way we could ever get out of jail was by testifying.

And so, after a surveillance and jail ordeal seven months long, the witnesses —whose refusal had all along been more an act of political opposition than one of personal defense—capitulated. Two of them testified under immunity. After a few questions about the dynamite purchase in which they were not involved, Goodwin again plied them with questions calling for a startling variety of biographical details: friendships, affiliations, communications, meetings, travels, finances, beliefs, habits, and so on.

The Tucson sessions and a series of proceedings that followed made it quite clear that the ISD grand jury network exploited the grand jury format to develop information for the ISD's intelligence unit, the IDIU. Indeed, this strategy, so apparent from the questioning, was virtually admitted. In 1973 the ISD was asked by the editor of the *Columbia Law Review* whether information developed through the ISD grand juries was fed into the IDIU system. Its chief, William Olson, replied with a carefully worded formulation which tells its own story that "no inquiries are conducted *for the purpose* of supplying intelligence information *to any other office of government*"[22] (italics added). It need only be added that once the material entered the IDIU files, it was disseminated to virtually every component of the intelligence community, including the CIA. Bureau agents also acquired information first hand, either from concealed access to grand jury questioning or, more usually, from their collaboration with prosecutors.

Another strand in the pattern was the diversion of a legitimate grand jury inquiry into whether or not the evidence warranted an indictment into a quest for evidence. Grand jury investigative inquiry is typically designed to clarify and supplement a body of evidence, which is itself the product of a completed investigation. Its investigative powers are limited, ancillary to its accusatorial role, and come into play when the scent is warm and the chase is keen. This transformation from accusation to investigation is seen most clearly in the use by field agents of the grand jury process. Frustrated by their failures in pursuing conventional police methods to identify suspects, the agents used grand jury subpoenas to force cooperation from individuals, not actually suspected of criminal conduct but typically selected for interrogation by reason of their visibility or prior identification. Cooperation with Bureau agents was quickly perceived in the radical community as a prelude to informing, a betrayal of the trust that is indispensable to group life. When agents responded to recalcitrance with threats of subpoenas, a continued rebuff became a symbol of commitment. In a second stage, agents sought interviews armed with subpoenas already filled out by the prosecutor and requiring only to be filled in by the agent with the names of uncooperative subjects. Sometimes, when these holdouts appeared in response to subpoenas, the ISD prosecutor would defer questioning until cued by a Bureau agent. On one occasion a witness was subpoenaed for appearance before a grand jury that did not even exist. The impropriety of this phased transformation is apparent: a quasi-judicial deliberative function is swallowed up by one that is executive in character. In a court case in New York, decided in May 1975, a federal district court judge quashed an ISD subpoena served on a lawyer and pointed out that,

> while the grand jury has broad powers to inquire into suspected criminal conduct, these powers are abused when exercised as an adjunct or tool of an FBI investigation. . . . Congress has not chosen to vest the FBI with subpoena powers and it would circumvent the legislative judgment for the FBI to be allowed to instead simply make use of the grand jury process in order to do indirectly what it may not do directly. Just as the grand jury is not meant to be the "private tool of the prosecutor" . . . it should not be allowed to become an arm of the FBI.[23]

The Capitol Bombing—The Grand Jury Goes Fishing

On March 1, 1971, a washroom in the Capitol Building in Washington was bombed. Thereafter, a series of anti-war demonstrations was announced for May 1. The pressure on the government to gain some ground on the radicals was considerable. On the evening of April 27, four carloads of FBI men worked their way through two of the houses in northwest Washington where demonstration organizers were staying, and arrested nineteen-year-old Leslie Bacon. Although she was wanted only as a material witness, she was held on $100,000 bail on the government's unsupported allegation that she was likely to flee if released. Subsequently, a federal Court of Appeals ruled that the arrest was improper on the ground that the mere allegation was insufficient to support the arrest warrant without further evidence.[24] On April 29 Bacon was flown to Seattle, amid proliferating reports leaked to the press that she was a suspected "courier" between radical groups that had been involved in the Capitol bombing and a link between the bombers and the organizers of the upcoming demonstrations. But why Seattle, so far removed from the scene of the bombing? An FBI official later explained: "We didn't know a damned thing. Leslie Bacon was the only thing we had and that was just a fishing expedition. She was called before a grand jury in Seattle because we were more likely to get an indictment out there."[25]

Leslie Bacon testified in Seattle for three days, beginning April 30, with no grant of immunity. As she answered and reanswered Goodwin's questions, which almost parodied his own style, it became clear to her lawyers that she was being used as an intelligence source for purposes not legitimately related to law enforcement. Since Goodwin had by then touched on nearly every facet of her life for the previous six months, it was more than likely that Bacon had already waived whatever rights to remain silent she might have had. This in fact turned out to be the case. After answering more than 250 questions, Bacon began "taking the Fifth." The district court noted her waiver and denied her right to remain silent, but she persisted in her refusal. Goodwin, who had been visibly encouraged by his progress, was now outraged that Bacon, on the advice of a new lawyer, continued her silence despite her waiver. He quickly struck back. When she rejected a grant of limited (use) immunity and persisted in her silence, he had her jailed for contempt. She was subsequently freed on the ground that the government had failed adequately to deny her claim that her interrogation was tainted by electronic surveillance.[26]

The intensity with which the government pressed the Bacon case is explained by her extensive travels and participation in a number of the radical conferences that had been held around the country during the previous year. When arrested, she was working on the May Day demonstration in Washington and had developed ties with the inner circles of the May Day organization. Her grand jury grilling, and the deceptions used by Goodwin as cover, symbolized the systematic transformation by the ISD of grand juries into fishing expeditions, pure and simple. She was asked, for example:

> Where were you in September through January, 1970–71, and who were you living with?

Bacon responded with references to Greenwich Village, the East Village, Boston, Buffalo, Washington, D.C., and California. Goodwin then plucked out the precise details that interested him. About California, a purely social visit, he asked in part:

> What did you do or where did you go in Santa Barbara?
> Who were the people you saw, visited with, or stayed with in Santa Barbara?
> Do you remember the names of the people you travelled to Santa Barbara with?
> What were the conversations in the car during the 56-hour drive?

These questions were followed by an even more detailed probe of Bacon's movements in and around the May Day organization. Goodwin traced every step of every day, asking how she traveled from one place to the next, who was present at all times, what was said by each person, right down to questions about who slept with whom in what specific rooms.

In addition to expanding ISD background information, Goodwin gained from Bacon what he had failed to get in Tucson—a basis for serving further subpoenas on the people she mentioned for appearance before grand juries in other cities. He first issued subpoenas to three May Day organizers for a June 8 appearance before a D.C. grand jury. All three refused to testify. Two of them, both women, were granted transactional immunity, refused again, and were jailed. The third, one of the authors of the field manual for May Day, was dismissed without being offered immunity, presumably because he was considered a possible defendant. But the two women successfully appealed their contempt sentences on the ground that the government, once a plausible claim was made, had to disclose any illegal electronic interceptions of their conversations.

This decision by the Court of Appeals, in the wake of a similar ruling arising out of a Harrisburg grand jury proceeding (discussed below), was a serious blow since it jeopardized the government's strategy of using grand jury interrogations as a means of laundering evidence tainted by warrantless electronic surveillance.

Goodwin next moved to New York, where Bacon had been transiently involved in a bank-bombing plot but had pulled out so quickly that a New York State grand jury had refused to indict her. Goodwin now made overtures to the Manhattan District Attorney's office to reopen the case against her. When he was rebuffed (Goodwin's relations with New York State and federal law enforcement officials were not of the best), he subpoenaed twelve witnesses, allegedly to investigate Bacon's role in the New York bank plot. The interrogations, however, broadly scoured the New Left anti-war scene. The twelve all refused to testify and instead launched a legal attack on the grand jury. The grand jury nevertheless resurrected the charge dropped by the state grand jury and on June 23 indicted Bacon for conspiracy. A week later the twelve subpoenas were withdrawn, and subsequently dropped permanently along with the Bacon indictment, which had been issued in the first place only to give color of legitimacy to the twelve subpoenas.

In late June Goodwin subpoenaed seven people Bacon had connected with May Day activities to appear before a grand jury in Detroit. After one person testified, the remaining six refused, raising the wiretap issue. Goodwin again balked at the wiretap challenge and excused each of the witnesses. In August Goodwin came back to these six with new appearance dates set for the fall. When the first of them appeared in mid-September and again refused to testify, the government moved for a court order compelling him to answer questions. The government requested the court to hold *in camera* sessions in order to avoid public disclosure of the specific questions it proposed to ask. When this request was rejected, Goodwin again abandoned the chase.

All of the ISD grand juries—Seattle, the District of Columbia, New York, Detroit—were used to develop information about individuals and groups in parts of the country removed from the area from which the grand jurors were drawn and who were neither under indictment nor actively suspected of crimes. Many individuals who were the subjects of inquiry were themselves then subpoenaed to appear in a subsequent grand jury, and in turn asked the same questions about others. For example, after Goodwin learned her name from the initial Seattle proceeding, in May 1972 he subpoenaed Sylvia Brown, a Barnard undergraduate, from her home in New York City, for an appearance before a reconvened Seattle grand jury, and asked her some twenty-four questions along these lines:

> I am going to read you a list of names and I want you to tell the grand jury every occasion during the years 1971 and 1972 when you have had any contact with the individuals whose names I give you, describing for the grand jury when the contact was, where it was and what was said and done on each occasion.[27]

He then read off a list of twenty-two names. When the witness refused to answer the questions, she was jailed for contempt. The overriding purpose of all of the grand juries was to develop political intelligence. The justification or pretext for this dragnet procedure was an asserted—but never established—link between legal demonstrations and underground terrorism and bombings. As for the Capitol bombing itself, no indictment was ever returned against Leslie Bacon or anyone else.

Detroit—Accuse First, Investigate Later

Goodwin was forced from time to time to produce charges; after all, he could not indefinitely interrogate uncooperative witnesses without assuring both grand jurors and judges that the chase had a beast in view. But such premature deliveries produced sickly offspring, requiring postnatal nourishment. Thus a cluster of grand juries was used for the improper purpose of developing evidence from friends, relatives, associates, and supporters of the radical SDS Weatherman faction in support of an indictment already handed down. A related purpose—equally improper—was the attempt to use the grand jury subpoena as a "discovery" device, that is, an instrument for learning what the defense strategy would be in a subsequent trial. On July 3, 1970, the first of seven Weatherman grand juries sitting in Detroit returned a sweeping indictment charging thirteen individuals with conspiracy to bomb military and police installations in Cleveland, Detroit, Milwaukee, and Los Angeles. Fifteen unindicted co-conspirators were also named, but the ISD was whistling in the dark: the entire case rested on the testimony of informer Larry Grathwohl who, for cover purposes, was himself named as a defendant. Grathwohl had only limited knowledge of the "overt acts" allegedly undertaken to implement the conspiracy. More evidence was needed and since it was obtainable only through a post-indictment investigation beyond the legitimate scope of the grand jury process, its purpose would have to be concealed.

The Tucson grand jury already had pointed the way: much of the questioning there involved the Detroit charges. In November 1972 another ISD grand jury was convened in Cleveland, which was also used as a cover for an extensive interrogation about the activities charged in the Detroit indictment as "overt acts." In December a Detroit panel handed up a new indictment against fifteen Weatherpeople, superseding the original 1970 indictment with similar charges now fleshed out with evidence gathered in intervening grand jury proceedings in other areas. The superseding indictment in Detroit did not put an end to the hunt for supporting evidence. Early in January 1973 the Cleveland grand jury subpoenaed two witnesses, one of whom had already testified in November. In this round of questioning she was presented with a rerun of the earlier questions, despite the fact that it was the same grand jury. The second Cleveland witness refused to answer a number of similar questions on the ground that they were based on illegal wiretaps. In response, the government dropped her subpoena rather than disclose its sources. On January 10, two days later, indictments were handed down in Cleveland against three of the Detroit defendants. These indictments were based on the testimony of an FBI agent; the two witnesses had been called solely for the purpose of developing information to aid in the prosecution of the new Detroit indictment.

The Cleveland indictments were simply moves in a cover-up game. To provide a justification and to mask its true purpose, the prosecution "indicted" three individuals who were underground and thus not likely to be brought to trial. Moreover, the indictments listed acts identical to those charged by the Detroit grand jury, and were returned only two days after the Detroit defendants sought to intervene in the Cleveland proceedings on the ground that the Cleveland grand jury was being improperly used to develop evidence for use at the Detroit trial.

Another grand jury proceeding activated to develop testimony for use in the Detroit trial began in Madison, Wisconsin, in February 1973, when two women, each named as an unindicted co-conspirator in the Detroit indictment, were subpoenaed. In a familiar development, one of the witnesses was asked about activities described as "overt acts" in the Detroit indictment. When she refused to testify, the government applied for a grant of immunity and an order compelling her to testify. At the immunity hearing the judge, after inquiring into the purpose and scope of the grand jury's investigation, refused to grant immunity or to order testimony on the ground that the Internal Security Division attorney was abusing the grand jury process.

Still another front in the grand jury offensive against the SDS radicals was opened in the fall of 1972 in San Francisco with a volley of eleven subpoenas for a group of individuals, most of them strangers to one another, scattered all over the United States and Puerto Rico. From the questions asked in San Francisco by Goodwin and his assistant, it became clear that this investigation sought information about links between fugitives and techniques for the protection and support of persons in the underground. Subjects covered included maildrops, food stamp acquisitions, transportation, housing arrangements, and travelers checks. Some questions were asked about the bombing of a San Francisco police substation in February 1970. Even at the time, however, police and the local press did not attribute the bombing to the Weathermen, but viewed it as an isolated event with no organizational link. An intensive investigation for more than two years had yielded no suspects. The questioning about the bombing was a gratuitous attempt to link witnesses with terrorism, with the expectation that the questions would be made public when read at the subsequent immunity and contempt hearings.

Other questions involved a San Francisco residence, referred to in the Detroit indictment as having been rented by one of the defendants for the illegal purpose of storing explosives. Again, a deliberate abuse of the grand jury process. But when a number of Detroit defendants sought to intervene, the government insisted that the development of evidence was not the "sole or dominant purpose" of the investigation. One witness, John Davis, brother of Chicago conspiracy defendant Rennie Davis, challenged his subpoena on wiretapping grounds. The government admitted that it had wiretapped Davis, but denied that the information it had garnered was used to prepare either the subpoena or the questions. A hearing was then held to determine possible taint—whether the questions asked of Davis were based on wiretaps—and the government submitted approximately 250 pages of questions. The logs indicated that Davis had been "overheard" on numerous occasions in 1969, when he used telephones in the national offices of SDS. Davis and another witness, who had been subpoenaed in October but never questioned, commenced a civil suit to enjoin the grand jury from questioning witnesses until the National Commission on Individual Rights became operative. The Commission was created by the 1970 Organized Crime Control Act, the same act that created "use" immunity. It never met because President Nixon failed to appoint the seven members as required. Minutes before the witnesses were to appear in court as plaintiffs, the government scrapped the subpoenas and contended that the civil suit was therefore moot.

In all, seventeen witnesses were called in the San Francisco probe, beginning in September 1972. Of these only four actually testified, and one other was jailed for thirty days for refusing to testify, although his conviction was later reversed on appeal. Another witness was also held in contempt, but was ultimately not required to testify because the government refused to comply with a court order that he receive a transcript of his testimony. The subpoenas of the other witnesses were dismissed. After all the smoke had cleared, only one person—a fugitive Detroit defendant—was indicted as a result of the grand jury's work. Despite the government's disavowals, the main purpose of the San Francisco proceeding appears to have been, once more, to dig up evidence for Detroit. None of the four witnesses who testified knew anything at all about the indicted defendant; his indictment was the result of information already in the government's possession.

"With a Little Help from My Friends"

The pressures that transformed the grand jury into an investigative instrument resulted in the development of operational ties between the ISD-FBI and urban anti-subversive units ("red squads"), which the Bureau had traditionally upstaged. Under this new working relationship the Bureau obtained access, for use in grand jury proceedings, to informer and wiretap intelligence, accumulated locally, thus reducing the risk of taint charges. The deployment of federal-urban intelligence teams was standard operating procedure whenever a particular organization (SDS, Panthers, SNCC, the Venceremos Brigade) became a priority target—a decision made either by the Department of Justice or by the White House itself, as in the case of the Vietnam Veterans Against the War.

One such collaborative program, which seems to have been federally conceived and locally executed, was directed at lawyers who represented grand jury witnesses and post-indictment defendants.

The Arthur Turco–Baltimore Panther case discussed in Chapter 6 offers a glimpse of a joint federal-local pattern in the targeting of a lawyer that is equally pronounced in the New Haven (Seale-Huggins) Panther case, where for a two-year period (1969–71) the local red squad engaged in electronic surveillance of local Panthers as well as four of their lawyers. In return for the intelligence product, the New Haven FBI supplied its urban counterpart with installation expertise, tapes, and the rent for an office where an eavesdropping program was conducted. The diversion of operational responsibility provided a cover against the claims of warrantless wiretapping and violation of attorney-client confidentiality,* either of which might fatally taint a prosecution. The record indicates that of all the targets of this joint program, the Chicago 7 conspiracy case defense was the most intensively surveilled. Prior to the commencement of the trial, Captain Charles Kinney, head of the Newark, New Jersey, Police Department intelligence unit (we will meet him again), transmitted surveillance reports (almost certainly based on electronic monitoring) on the lawyers' planning sessions in March and April 1969 to the Chicago red squad. In turn, the Chicago unit briefed a federal prosecutor assigned to the case on the contents of the reports. During the trial the lawyers were plagued by a variety of federal-urban surveillance activities.† After the trial and convictions, a transcript of a bugged lawyers' meeting, held in March 1970 at the Newark office of attorney Leonard Weinglass to discuss plans for an appeal, was transmitted to the Director by coded teletype, the "take" of the same microphone installation that had yielded the pretrial reported overhearings of the previous year.

From 1970 until 1973 more than fifteen cases are reported in court documents of burglaries in cities with active red squads on the premises of lawyers for radical groups and individuals, and in a few instances of those of their clients. According to an affidavit filed by Weatherman lawyer Gerald Lefcourt, his office was burglarized twice, first in the fall of 1970 and again in the winter of that year. On April 12, 1970, a fire, classified "suspicious," occurred at his Manhattan office. Lefcourt said that the contents of one of his files on Weather Underground fugitive Mark Rudd had been scattered about the office. Two burglary attempts were made at Lefcourt's New York City home between the spring of 1970 and the spring of 1971. Nothing was taken in the second break-in, so police were not notified. Of the first, Lefcourt says, a television set was found in the building lobby and taken to a police precinct, where he went to claim it.

At the San Francisco office of attorney Michael Kennedy, burglars rifled files and scattered them about. The San Francisco police confirmed the break-in but professed frustration of their detection efforts. During another burglary of his office, Kennedy's briefcase was rifled. On August 19, 1971, the People's Law Office in Chicago was burglarized. Police verified the fact that a burglary had been committed but were again unable to apprehend the culprits. In a burglary at the Los Angeles law offices of Henry di Suvero on June 8, 1972, files were rifled. In addition, the offices or homes of other attorneys for subpoenaed clients or defendants in conspiracy cases, including Charles Garry, Melvin Greenberg, Jeffrey Haas, Carol Scott, Lee Holly, Carl Maxey, and Michael Lerner (counsel *pro se* in the Seattle 9 case), were entered under circumstances marked by a common pattern: the rifling or theft of files, by perpetrators who uniformly eluded the police and took nothing else of value.

---

*This same concern is reflected in an official FBI caution to agents or clerks on electronic surveillance assignment to suspend their operations during conversations of monitored subjects with their lawyers. But even when alerted in time that such conversations were in the offing or in progress, the eavesdroppers not infrequently continued their activities.

†As will be shown in Chapter 12, a private countersubversive group, the Legion of Justice, also served as a break-in, file-stealing resource.

An example of attempted mail interception is supplied by the affidavit of a Chicago postman:

> I have been assigned to the Lincoln Park Station of the Chicago Post Office since 1968 as a mail deliverer.
> Part of my duties were deliver mail to 2242 N. Bissell Street.
> I was aware that members of the Peoples Law Office staff including Jeffrey H. Haas, Courtney Esposito, Liza Lawrence and G. Flint Taylor, Jr. were living at and receiving mail at that address.
> On several occasions I was approached by men in plain clothes outside 2242 N. Bissell Street who showed me badges which were sometimes of the Chicago Police and sometimes of the Federal Bureau of Investigation.
> These plain clothed officers asked questions of me about inhabitants of said house, took pictures of said house and watched said house.
> On several occasions I was approached and offered a job by some of these plain clothed police which I declined to accept.[28]

Another clue to the *modus operandi* of the ISD network is supplied by two incidents, both involving attempts to develop evidence for the Detroit case. On April 24, 1970, the Chicago apartment of Martha Real, the cousin of Detroit defendant Mark Real, was searched illegally by the Weatherman expert of Chicago's red squad, Maurice (Maurie) Dailey. During this search many items were seized, including Martha Real's personal address book, two sealed addressed letters, and alleged contraband consisting of several firearms. After the material was suppressed by the court as illegally seized, the record of her arrest was also expunged, pursuant to the court's order. The illegally seized items were then turned over to federal authorities, and on July 9, 1970, Martha Real was subpoenaed by the Detroit grand jury. When Miss Real first appeared before the grand jury, she invoked her Fifth Amendment privilege in response to all questions. Thereafter, Goodwin obtained an order granting her immunity from prosecution and requiring her to testify. Goodwin then questioned Miss Real about the contents of the sealed and addressed letters illegally seized in Chicago, about other physical evidence illegally seized there, and about what was said in a tapped telephone conversation with a defendant in the Detroit case. The recitation of an overt act in that indictment was almost certainly based upon material obtained from the illegal search and wiretap. In addition, by inducing Judge Keith to grant immunity, the prosecution made him an unwitting accomplice to the laundering of the illegally obtained evidence by compelled grand jury interrogation derived from this tainted source.

Robert Swartwout, an unindicted Detroit co-conspirator also mentioned in connection with an overt act, was in the early part of 1970 detained and beaten in Chicago by a Chicago policeman and his partner. He was then told he was under arrest because he was wanted on a charge in Virginia and was taken, without process of any court, to the Chicago airport where a ticket was purchased for him with money taken from his person. When the plane landed at the National Airport in Virginia, Swartwout expected to be met by police, but no one appeared and he was never thereafter arrested or charged in Virginia on any warrant. But information gleaned from him as a result of the Chicago beating turned up in the Detroit prosecutor's file.

The ISD network generated a confrontation with the grand jury issue across the country. What had begun in Tucson with an isolated defense committee became a national radical campaign against the grand jury. The underground press published a series of reports and analyses of the government's new strategy. Grand juries in Madison, Cleveland, Los Angeles, Vermont, Detroit, Kansas City, and elsewhere that had gone relatively unnoticed were now seen with a keener retrospective eye. Defense committees sprang up in cities where federal grand juries were in session, spurred by the fear of a revival in another form of the moribund congressional anti-subversive committees as instruments of harassment. This response was broadened as evidence of the political motivation for the distortion of the grand jury process emerged.

The Political Imperative—VVAW, Camden and Fort Worth

The White House itself was extraordinarily concerned about the strength and effectiveness of the Vietnam Veterans Against the War (VVAW). Organized opposition by veterans to policies in Vietnam could, unless curbed, divide and weaken a vital Nixon constituency. President Nixon personally requested that Dean relay to him hourly intelligence reports on the activities of the VVAW. In addition, the VVAW played a role in the Watergate cover-up; the bugging of the Democratic National Committee was justified by the asserted need to protect the Republican Convention from violent demonstrations, specifically by the VVAW. James McCord, security chief for the Committee to Re-Elect the President (CREEP), in his testimony before the Senate Watergate Committee cited ISD reports of planned VVAW violence prior to the Watergate break-in of May 27, 1972. In fact, however, the Internal Security Division convened a grand jury to probe the VVAW only after the Watergate burglars had been caught and the need for a cover explanation became urgent.

The political motivation for convening the VVAW grand jury was further confirmed by its timing. The VVAW and many other anti-war groups had been planning a series of demonstrations at both Miami conventions. On July 6, three days before the Democratic Convention opened, Guy Goodwin sent out the first batch of twenty-three subpoenas. All of those subpoenaed were members of VVAW and almost all were leaders—regional, state, or chapter coordinators. They were subpoenaed from all over the South on July 6, 7, and 8 to appear in Tallahassee the following Monday, July 10. When the grand jury did meet, it was accorded an unusual amount of publicity. On July 11, while the Democratic Convention was in progress and three days before any indictment was handed down, an anonymous "spokesman" for the Department of Justice gave an interview about the case. He described the "pretty bizarre and destructive weapons" that VVAW members had allegedly purchased, leading to headlines like "Bomb Plot Against GOP Probed" (Atlanta *Constitution,* July 10).

After the initial unsuccessful defense motions to enjoin the proceedings on First Amendment grounds, most of those subpoenaed were called before the grand jury, asked preliminary questions (name, address), and eventually excused, after being held under subpoena 500 miles from Miami for the entire week of the Democratic Convention. Several were called back for further questioning, and refused to answer after being granted immunity. Four were summarily cited for contempt on Thursday, July 13. That evening the grand jury voted to indict six VVAW members for conspiracy to disrupt the Republican Convention, scheduled for late August.*

Five days later the Court of Appeals invalidated the contempt citations and remanded the case to the district court for a proper hearing, with notice, formal reporting of the proceedings, and argument—all of which had been disregarded earlier. The hearing was held, and by August 7 the four vets were back in jail for civil contempt, having been denied bail by the district court. They remained imprisoned for a month, until bail was set by Supreme Court Justice Douglas, who said: "I am deeply troubled by the charge that enough evidence had been found to sustain an indictment, making colorable the use of the grand jury for other purposes. . . ."—the "other purposes" apparently including the prevention of VVAW protest demonstrations at the Republican Convention, an objective which the grand jury proceedings successfully accomplished.† The six indicted individuals were arraigned in Tallahassee on August 24, the last day of the Republican Convention. On October 18, 1972, although none of those subpoenaed had been recalled before the grand jury, a superseding indictment was issued. The subpoenas of those who had been imprisoned for contempt were eventually dropped, after the Court of Appeals again reversed the citations for contempt, this time because of inadequate government denial of wiretaps of their attorneys.[29] (In the course of the trial itself, defense attorneys alleged that they had been bugged.)

Anger and desperation in high quarters also influenced a Camden, New Jersey, grand jury probe in the summer of 1971 of Catholic draft board raiders. According to Robert Hardy, the Bureau's informer, on White House orders arrests and indictments were deliberately postponed until the completion of the raids. After the indictments were returned against twenty-eight defendants, a prolonged grand jury investigation was launched to obtain intelligence about other "actions" of the Catholic Resistance and to develop leads for the still unsolved theft of documents from the Bureau's Media, Pennsylvania, office in the spring of 1971.

On September 24, 1971, Goodwin's first grand jury witnesses, Pat and Bruce Grumbles, appeared but refused to answer any questions, citing a variety of

---

*The indictments were used for political purposes. A piece of GOP campaign literature listed among the "52 Reasons Why McGovern Must Be Defeated": "During the McGovern convention in Miami, plotters were conspiring to blow up the Republican convention. They were arrested and taken to Tallahassee where six have been indicted; but these dynamiters and gun shooters and plotters were glorified with the consent of Mr. McGovern in the convention." The "glorification" was a resolution passed by the convention on Thursday, July 13, condemning "this blatantly political abuse of the grand jury to intimidate and discredit a group whose opposition to the war has been particularly moving and effective," and describing the grand jury as "an attempt by the Nixon Administration to deny the veterans their most fundamental constitutional rights to express their dissent and opposition to the war in Southeast Asia."

†G. Gordon Liddy had originally proposed kidnapping possible demonstrators at the Republican Convention, then scheduled for San Diego, and holding them in Mexico for a week.

constitutional claims. Thereafter, in mid-November, they were granted immunity and later jailed on civil contempt charges for refusing to testify. The Grumbles had spent more than six months in prison when they sought release in the district court, on the ground that the grand jury had been inactive since their confinement. The government hastily subpoenaed five new witnesses for June 27, 1972, and asserted that the investigation was continuing. Attempts to quash these subpoenas, based on objections to the government's use of the grand jury to acquire evidence for the already pending indictments, failed. However, despite the government's assertions, these five were never recalled before the grand jury.

On February 26, after fourteen months in prison, the Grumbles made a second bid for release. The trial of the Camden 28 had begun a few weeks before, but the term of the grand jury was not due to expire until the end of March. It was clear that the Internal Security Division intended to keep the Grumbles in jail until the end of the term, despite the fact that the grand jury investigation had long since ended. The petition for release argued that continued incarceration would simply be punitive. The district court agreed, ruling that punishment for civil contempt could be curtailed when a continued jailing becomes punitive rather than an inducement to testify. Pat and Bruce Grumbles had served fourteen months, the longest contempt jail term served by any witness before an ISD grand jury.[30] (The previous record was held by the five witnesses in Tucson in 1971, who were confined for seven months.)

A grand jury proceeding in another political key involved a group of twelve Irish-Americans who on June 21, 1972, were summoned from New York to appear before a grand jury in Fort Worth, Texas. The subject of the investigation was to be the purchase and transportation of Japanese-made arms to the Irish Republican Army by the American-based Irish Northern Aid Society. The abuse in the choice of venue was dramatized by the fact that a grand jury was convened in the southern district of New York in November of that year to investigate alleged illegal gun-running, the same subject supposedly under investigation in Fort Worth. Seven of the grand jury subpoenas were either dismissed or suspended indefinitely before the witnesses were called. Four of these were "high officials" in the Irish Northern Aid Society, the organization allegedly under investigation; the remaining five witnesses had no official connection with the society. The questions put to them related solely to persons and places in the New York City area, Texas being roped in with catch-all queries of the sort that began: "Have you ever known any person in New York, Texas, or elsewhere . . . ?" Given the politically sensitive nature of the investigation, the fact that 1972 was a presidential election year, and that the New York grand jury was not convened until after the election, it seems reasonable to conclude that Fort Worth was selected as a grand jury site because it was not an Irish community and thus would generate little or no local protest.[31]

The five witnesses were interrogated to obtain information in support of a gun-running indictment that had already been handed down. They all refused to answer these and other questions under immunity and were kept in the county jail for over a year. Another grand jury, also dealing with an aspect of the arms shipment investigation, was convened in San Francisco in the fall of

1972. There too a witness, Robert K. Meisel, was jailed on contempt charges in January, with a short period of freedom on bail, granted by Justice Douglas but later denied by the full court. Even though the grand jury was inactive, having heard only one witness after Meisel's incarceration, he remained in jail until the expiration of its eighteen-month term in March 1974. Meisel justifiably charged that the life of the jury was artificially prolonged solely to punish him. The Fort Worth proceeding contributed measurably to the growing movement for grand jury reform: Senator Edward M. Kennedy, a spokesman for the Irish community, denounced the Fort Worth foray in a congressional hearing concerning proposals for grand jury reform.

The Political Imperative—Ellsberg, Russo, and Company

In mid-June 1971, shortly after the *New York Times* began publishing material from the Pentagon Papers, a Los Angeles grand jury, originally convened in March, began inquiry into relevant law violations, and on June 28 a hastily drafted indictment of Daniel Ellsberg was handed down. It can hardly be doubted that the government rushed the indictment as a form of pressure on the Supreme Court, which had heard argument on June 26 in a government lawsuit against the *New York Times;* if unauthorized reproduction and circulation of the documents constituted a crime, then—it could be more plausibly argued—their publication could be enjoined.[32]

The indictment charged that in September and October 1969, Dr. Ellsberg violated two separate provisions of the criminal code: Chapter 31, Section 641, which proscribes selling or converting to one's own use a "record . . . or anything of value of the United States," and Chapter 37, Section 793 (e), which bans the unauthorized possession and willful retention of documents "relating to the national defense." If the value of the property converted exceeds $100, conviction on the first offense can result in a ten-year jail term and a fine of $10,000.

Ellsberg's indictment was not the end, as one might assume, but the beginning of a highly ramified hunt by two grand juries: one in Los Angeles and the other in Boston. The government was assertedly trying to find out (presumably for the purpose of additional or superseding indictments) if Ellsberg or anyone else had violated an espionage provision that punishes anyone who "communicates, delivers, transmits or causes to be communicated, delivered or transmitted, or attempts to communicate, deliver, transmit, defense related documents or information to a person not entitled to receive it. . . ." But this justification for the post-indictment grand jury proceedings was a spurious one, improvised to develop information for the Plumbers' Project Ellsberg, a plan to discredit Ellsberg by projecting in the media and through congressional committees a "negative image," in support of a claim that Ellsberg was involved together with other intellectuals in a foreign-inspired conspiracy to discredit the President's "peace with honor" initiative.[33]

The White House knew from the very beginning that the "foreign spy" thesis was without foundation. Ten days after the publication of the Pentagon Papers, on June 23, 1971, Secretary of Defense Laird told the President and Ehrlichman that 98 percent of the documents could have been declassified. Nevertheless, the administration circulated false reports that a copy of the Pentagon Papers—not the one published in the *Times,* but a secret, more complete version, loaded with defense secrets—had been delivered to the Russian Embassy on June 17, 1971. But if any government agency would know about deliveries to the Russian Embassy it would be the FBI, which deploys an incredible arsenal of surveillance weapons against the embassy. And where would the embassy's receipt of such material serve a vital function? Obviously there is one place where such evidence would be invaluable: at the Pentagon Papers trial before the U.S. District Court on June 18, 1971, and the argument on appeal on June 22. At both of these proceedings the government had a chance to offer support for its key contention that publication of the papers had threatened our national security, especially through the channel of foreign relations. The government could have made such proof in open court or, if it was necessary to protect sensitive national security matters, *in camera.* When this contention was made public in 1973, an inquiry was addressed to U.S. Attorney Whitney North Seymour, Jr., seeking verification. In a letter dated May 5, 1973, he replied:

> I have since looked into the matter and am relieved to be able to report that apparently neither this office nor the court was deceived as to the information available to the government at the time of the Pentagon Papers proceeding here. I have not been permitted to see the actual reports, which are classified, but I have been advised by an official in Washington that the FBI had no information concerning the possibility of the Soviet Embassy having possession of the papers at the time we presented our arguments to the District and Circuit Courts. I should add that I have not been able to learn the actual extent or scope of the papers that may have come into the embassy's possession.

In the fall of 1971 the great spy plot unraveled completely. On November 1, Egil Krogh and David Young, the master Plumbers, wrote a confidential memorandum to their supervisor, John Ehrlichman, casting doubt on the success of the propaganda campaign to paint Ellsberg as a spy, because:

(a) Ellsberg gave classified information to the *Press,* not to a foreign power;
(b) Just a few months after Ellsberg went public, DoD [Department of Defense] published virtually the same material;
(c) There has been no apparent damage as a result of Ellsberg's disclosures.[34]

The legal case was equally unpromising. A superseding fifteen-count indictment handed down by the Los Angeles grand jury on December 29, 1971, added ten new charges to the original June indictment but failed to charge espionage.[35] When asked why, the government prosecutor, David Nissen, replied that an intensive investigation had failed to turn up evidence to support such a charge.[36]

The pressure to expand the Ellsberg case for political reasons reproduced the kinds of distortions in the grand jury function already noted, especially the attempt to develop post-indictment evidence. On June 23, Anthony Russo, a thirty-four-year-old engineer and political scientist, a friend and former colleague of Ellsberg at the RAND Corporation, appeared before a grand jury in Los Angeles pursuant to subpoena, and declined to answer a series of questions about Ellsberg's activities on Fifth Amendment grounds. Offered full immunity, he nevertheless persisted in his refusal and was held in contempt on July 2. Between the time of the refusal and the contempt session, Ellsberg was indicted. Since all the questions put to Russo involved Ellsberg, counsel for Russo argued that the grand jury had no right to inquire further of his client concerning a matter that the grand jury had resolved by indicting Ellsberg. Brushing aside the defense contention that grand jury process cannot be used as a means of pretrial discovery of evidence, but must be confined to the accusatory procedure of indicting on probable cause, the court held Russo in civil contempt, to be confined until he "was disposed to answer the questions." Russo's appeal was rejected by a three-judge appellate panel on August 17. In response to the contention that the grand jury process was being abused, Robert Keuch, chief of the Appellate Section of the Internal Security Division, replied that "there is a possibility of other defendants and a possibility of other activities." If Russo answered the questions, "other areas of investigation might possibly be opened."[37]

Russo was remanded to jail on August 16, the day that Ellsberg appeared for arraignment, and stated that he would rather accept a prison sentence than collaborate in the "attempt to prosecute Daniel Ellsberg by testifying in secret before a grand jury." He offered to tell his story openly, "free of the compulsion of grand jury subpoenas and contempt citations and not as a tool of the prosecution."[38] Russo remained in jail for forty-seven days. When his attorney moved to terminate his imprisonment on the ground that his confinement had been ordered "for the life of the grand jury" and that the grand jury's term had expired, the court accepted the prosecutor's argument that the extension of the term of the grand jury—even though ordered subsequent to the contempt sentence—automatically extended the potential length of the punishment. It also accepted prosecutor Nissen's statement that the indictment of Ellsberg constituted only a small portion of "a very broad investigation." The continuing probe, he insisted, was "not at all" aimed at assembling evidence to support the Ellsberg indictment, but rather sought to identify "who else is involved and who may have committed perjury before the grand jury." Russo finally agreed to testify, subject only to the condition that he receive a transcript of his testimony. The condition was accepted by the court on October 1 over the prosecution's vigorous protests.[39] On returning to the grand jury room on October 18, Russo was bluntly informed by prosecutor Nissen that the court's order requiring that he be furnished a transcript was "unlawful." When the government persisted in its refusal to comply with the order, the court on November 17 ordered Russo's release.[40] The next month he was added as a co-defendant to the superseding indictment.

In the summer and fall of 1971 prosecutor Nissen subpoenaed a number of friends, colleagues, and relatives of Russo, Daniel Ellsberg, and Patricia Ellsberg, including her brother and sister (both of whom were dismissed after refusing to answer questions). The Los Angeles grand jury also heard Robert, Ellsberg's fifteen-year-old son, who was subpoenaed at 7:30 in the morning for an appearance two hours later. He was summoned although his mother, Daniel Ellsberg's ex-wife, had been induced to testify on the representation that her appearance might obviate the need to call her son.[41] A small army of Ellsberg's neighbors, tradesmen, and anti-war acquaintances and colleagues were also interrogated by the FBI.

In September the government subpoenaed parcels stored by Ellsberg at a Beverly Hills warehouse in 1970. This subpoena was initially quashed by trial Judge Matthew Byrne, on the ground that its execution would violate Ellsberg's rights under the Fourth (unreasonable search and seizure) and Fifth (self-incrimination) amendments. A search warrant was thereafter signed by a federal magistrate on a secret showing of "probable cause," and twenty-eight containers of Ellsberg's stored effects were carted off by the FBI. Here again, the government's disavowal and its reliance on a claimed continuing investigation were credited, despite the persistent refusal of the prosecutor to specify his further aims. It ultimately became clear that the post-indictment proceedings were a classic fishing expedition in the hope of turning up evidence to bolster the indictment, and at the same time to discredit opponents of the war, especially intellectuals, as traitors.

The Boston grand jury, convened six to ten weeks before Ellsberg was scheduled to be tried in Los Angeles, subpoenaed more than twenty witnesses, including a group of Southeast Asia scholars, journalists, and other professionals, all of them strong opponents of the war and most of them connected with a university or research institute. Among those subpoenaed were: Richard A. Falk, a Princeton professor of international law; Noam Chomsky, M.I.T. linguistics authority and an influential writer on the war; and Ralph Stavins of the Institute for Policy Studies—all three of whom successfully attacked their subpoenas on wiretapping grounds. Also subpoenaed were two congressional figures: Bernard Rodberg, an aide to Alaska Senator Mike Gravel, and K. Dun Gifford, a former top assistant to Senator Edward M. Kennedy. In addition, subpoenas demanded the books and records of the Unitarian Church and its publishing arm, the Beacon Press, which had published the Pentagon Papers under the sponsorship of Senator Mike Gravel.[42] The grand jury even subpoenaed a seminar paper Ellsberg had delivered before the Council on Foreign Relations in November 1970, seven months before the publication of the Pentagon Papers.[43]

The Boston investigation, first by Bureau agents and then by the grand jury, confirms the view that law enforcement was a cover for a hidden intelligence agenda. One person interviewed by Bureau agents, Everett E. Hagen, director of the Center for International Studies at M.I.T., where Ellsberg had an office, reports that the questions dealt mainly with personal qualities: "I had the feeling that they would have liked me to say, 'Dan Ellsberg's kind of an odd person; he stands on his head in his office every afternoon.' "[44] FBI agents also interrogated Samuel Popkin, then a Harvard faculty member. The interview commenced on a curious note. As Popkin recalled, one agent began by making this observation: "We would like to ask you questions about Dan Ellsberg. We want to understand him and we need your help." The leitmotif of the interview was expressed through terms such as "emotions," "stability," and "psychiatric." "I had the impression the agents were trying to elicit negative comments about Ellsberg. . . . All sorts of questions were also asked me that didn't sit right, like 'Does Ellsberg seem to be a nervous person?' 'Is Ellsberg emotional?' 'Is Ellsberg erratic?'—questions that at the time I thought were there to impugn the person, to try to paint him as a neurotic, or a crazy person, or a person with a grudge or a vendetta."

But the prosecutor was also interested in probing more deeply into what Professor Popkin, a conservative scholar specializing in Vietnam village life and an occasional White House consultant, knew about the secret Pentagon war study before its release by his friend, Ellsberg. In response to a subpoena, Popkin appeared before the grand jury on August 19, 1971. "My first contact with the manipulative side of the grand jury came when I asked the prosecutor, 'May I please be told the subject of the matter under inquiry?' The prosecutor reared up at me and gave a long lecture saying, 'The judge's just told you that you may not ask this question, to appear here immediately and testify. Please don't keep these people waiting. Why are you trying to hold up the process of justice?' " This appearance began an ordeal that stretched on through the rest of 1971. Finally, on March 29, 1972, he was held in contempt for his refusal to answer questions before the grand jury two days earlier.

In his testimony, Popkin denied all knowledge of who might have possessed the Pentagon Papers before their release or how they were distributed to the press. He answered a number of questions but refused answers that would have required naming people who had given him information on a confidential basis in connection with his research. He also refused to give his opinions about who might have had access to the documents. Popkin's contempt citation prompted the Harvard faculty to adopt a resolution urging restraint in grand jury inquiries and insisting that the government show a strong need before putting such questions. It warned that "an unlimited right of grand juries to ask any question and to expose a witness to citations for contempt could easily threaten scholarly research." Twenty-four other scholars filed affidavits on Professor Popkin's behalf. In addition, no less than eighty supporting affidavits of scholars were attached to a motion submitted on behalf of a number of subpoenaed academics, which argued that the Boston probe was intended to take anti-war intellectuals to the woodshed, to cut them off from their confidential sources, and to compromise their relationships with public figures who had used their data to document opposition to the Vietnam War. Among the supporting affidavits are those of John Kenneth Galbraith, Harrison Salisbury, Stanley Hoffman, Edwin O. Reischauer, John K. Fairbank, Samuel H. Beer, Karl Deutsch, and other internationally known scholars.[45]

In May 1972 the first Circuit Court of Appeals in Boston upheld Popkin's right to refuse replies to four questions asking for his opinions of who might have had copies of the papers. One judge went so far as to label some of the questions "repugnant." But the court ruled that Popkin had to disclose the names of other scholars with whom he had discussed the Pentagon Papers, and from whom he might have learned the names of participants in the study.[46] This left Popkin near the end of his rope. On November 10 the Supreme Court, by an 8 to 1 decision (Douglas dissenting), refused to delay the execution of his contempt judgment. On November 16, Popkin filed stipulations offering to answer the questions, but only if he would not be forced to compromise his confidential sources. This offer was rejected by the Court of Appeals, and on November 21, 1972, Samuel Popkin became the first American scholar jailed for protecting sources of information.

One week later the government suddenly decided to dismiss the grand jury, which had been scheduled to run another six weeks, and Popkin was released. The decision came after Harvard president Derek Bok had joined the case as a lawyer to argue in Popkin's favor, and after Daniel Steiner, general counsel to the university, had met in Washington with A. William Olson, then head of the Internal Security Division, to urge that some way be found to release Popkin as soon as possible. Throughout Popkin's ordeal, the prosecution continually asserted that the grand jury was investigating in good faith the commission of federal crimes, and that the questions at issue were necessary to that investigation. Judges routinely accepted that claim. Not until the Watergate Committee Hearings and the impeachment proceedings did it become clear that both grand jury proceedings were leaked to the Plumbers, for use in Project Ellsberg.

The Political Imperative—Harrisburg

Early in January 1971, in the wake of Director Hoover's prejudicial and widely criticized charges of a kidnap-bombing plot (described in Chapter 4), a grand jury was hastily convened, and in what must have been record time on January 12 returned a wide-ranging indictment echoing Hoover's testimony. The convening of the grand jury was protested within the Justice Department, but the alternative was not merely discrediting Hoover but jeopardizing the special relationship between Mardian's ISD and Sullivan's Division 5, which had already stirred the chief's displeasure. An indictment backing Hoover up was the price for its continuance. But where was the proof to be found? Subsequent to the indictment, Goodwin subpoenaed an array of witnesses identified with the Catholic anti-war movement. Unable to find sufficient evidentiary support for the kidnap-bombing plot charged in the indictment, the grand jury returned a superseding indictment on April 30, 1971, which charged a sprawling amorphous plot to cripple the selective service system and subordinated the Hoover kidnap-bombing conspiracy. The Director (as we have seen) expressed his gratitude in a letter to Goodwin commending him for "outstanding service to the country."

But the superseding indictment presented fresh problems. The anti-draft actions that formed the gravamen of the new conspiracy charge had already been investigated or prosecuted by federal or state authorities. For example, a new defendant, John Theodore Glick, was charged with a conspiracy to destroy draft files despite the fact that he was at the time in jail for having (along with seven others) actually destroyed the same files. What was equally curious was that the government for more than a year had known the identities of all the individuals who destroyed the draft files in the places referred to in the indictment, because as a matter of principle they had all taken public responsibility for their acts, and indeed it was alleged to be "part of said conspiracy" that "certain of the defendants and co-conspirators" would "surface" and avow their acts.

Apart from the need to protect Hoover, the retained but now subordinated kidnap-bombing charge served as a pretext for attaching to the superseding indictment alleged correspondence between Sister Elizabeth McAlister and Philip Berrigan, which had discussed kidnapping "someone like Kissinger."* Such pretrial publication of letters between alleged confederates is without legal precedent,† and their release—a gross violation of the right to a fair and impartial trial and an abuse of the grand jury process—was a measure of the government's strenuous efforts to neutralize the adverse reaction to Hoover's congressional performance.

The Harrisburg indictment named twelve individuals as co-conspirators but only eight were made defendants.‡ The practice of naming "unindicted co-conspirators" was a tactic in the ISD total attack program. In the Chicago conspiracy case *U.S.* v. *Dellinger,* twenty individuals were named as alleged co-conspirators, of whom eight were made defendants and twelve were unindicted. In a conspiracy case in a Washington federal district court involving anti-war activists, *U.S.* v. *Marshall,* sixteen individuals were named as alleged co-conspirators, of whom eight were made defendants and eight were unindicted. In the Pentagon Papers (Ellsberg case), four were named as alleged co-conspirators, of whom two were made defendants and two unindicted. In the Detroit Weatherman case, thirty-nine were named as alleged co-conspirators, of whom fifteen were made defendants and twenty-four were unindicted. And in a Weatherman indictment filed in April 1972, forty were named as alleged co-conspirators, of whom twelve were made defendants and twenty-eight were not indicted.

A variety of objectives was served by the "unindicted co-conspirator" practice. It stigmatized the identified individuals without affording them an opportunity to defend themselves; created pressures to inform and thus to escape the stigma; and conveyed to courts, jurors, and the public an impression of more extensive and sinister doings than those set forth in the indictments. For exam-

---

*These letters, along with others of a more personal and private character, had previously come into the possession of the press apparently as a result of a deliberate leak by the FBI.

†The government cited scattered precedents that involve the sending of threatening letters directly to the person threatened. Even if the correspondence could be considered a threat to Kissinger, no threatening communication was sent to him. A second case involving the Catholic left arose out of a civil contempt ruling by Judge Anthony Travia when Sister Carol Vericker refused to testify even after being granted immunity. The Court of Appeals vacated the judgment of contempt, holding that the government had failed to demonstrate that it was investigating a crime for which immunity might be conferred.—*In re Carol Vericker,* 446 F. 2d 244 (C.A. 2, 1971); "Nun Held in Contempt in U.S. Court in Brooklyn," *New York Times,* July 1, 1971.

‡In April 1972 the trial jury deadlocked (10–2 for acquittal) on the main conspiracy charges and convicted two of the defendants, Father Philip Berrigan and Sister Elizabeth McAlister, of smuggling contraband letters into the federal prison where Father Berrigan was incarcerated. In July 1972 after the death of the Director in May, the government dropped all of the remaining charges against the defendants. In June 1973 the smuggling convictions were reversed on all but one count, on the ground that the letter exchange that had inspired these charges was conducted through a prison informer with the knowledge of the prison authorities and hence was not in violation of the law.

ple, one of the unindicted co-conspirators in the Ellsberg case was the mysterious Vu Van Thai, a former South Vietnamese ambassador to the United States who was barely mentioned in the trial and usually in a context suggesting movie-style intrigue (the prosecutor consistently referred to him as "the Oriental gentleman"). A more serious abuse was the practice of listing informers as unindicted co-conspirators as a cover for gaining access to legal defense plans.

In the VVAW case two individuals who, though named as co-conspirators, were not themselves indicted brought an action to expunge references to them in the indictment. A third, who was content to be named as unindicted co-conspirator without seeking legal redress, was an informer, Charles Becker, who subsequently testified at the trial.* The two unindicted plaintiffs were vindicated by the Court of Appeals, which ruled that a federal grand jury is not empowered to accuse a person of crime in an indictment that does not make him a defendant. Noting that the grand jury's action was inspired by the prosecutor, the court concluded that:

> There is at least a strong suspicion that the stigmatization of appellants was part of an overall governmental tactic directed against disfavored persons and groups. Visiting opprobrium on persons by officially charging them with crimes while denying them a forum to vindicate their names, undertaken as extra judicial punishment or to chill their expressions and associations, is not a governmental interest that we can accept or consider.[47]

Like the Harrisburg case, the VVAW indictment resulted in a government setback: the trial jury voted acquittal in a little under three hours. This was the eighth in a series of government rebuffs in conspiracy cases against dissidents. Here, as elsewhere, the pressures on the grand jury process resulted, on the one hand, in indictments that outran the available evidence and, on the other, in a wrenching distortion of the accusatorial function for purposes unrelated to law enforcement.

The Mixture as Before

The grand jury's potential for oppression came home, ironically enough, to the administration sponsors of the ISD program when they themselves began to feel the heat of Watergate. A March 22, 1973, White House colloquy:

HALDEMAN: (Inaudible) Well, there is danger in a grand jury.
DEAN: Well, there are no rules.
PRESIDENT: Well, grand juries are not very fair sometimes—
DEAN: That's right.
MITCHELL: (Inaudible)

Not only were Watergate grand jury proceedings leaked to the White House, but it was widely charged that the prosecutor had protectively contained its inquiries—until a special prosecutor was appointed.

*The naming of Becker was manifestly a cover for continued infiltration; the listing of the other two—whatever its additional purpose—served in turn to protect Becker's cover since listing him alone might invite suspicion.

The use of the grand jury for intelligence-related purposes in the ISD pattern persisted in the post-Watergate era. Two illustrative grand jury proceedings involved the women's liberation and the Puerto Rican independence movements. In these and other cases not discussed here we note the intensification of trends that were apparent in the earlier period: the extent to which the grand jury process has replaced the criminal investigation process; the consequent overshadowing of the local U.S. attorney by Bureau investigators, and the overkill that lumps a primary target (bombers) under criminal investigation with members of a nonviolent group because they share the same ultimate goals.

The Bureau's frustration over its long-time failure to apprehend two fugitives, Susan Saxe and Katherine Powers, under indictment since the late sixties on charges stemming from a Boston bank robbery, triggered a broadside attack on the lesbian and feminist communities in Lexington, Kentucky, and New Haven and Hartford, Connecticut.[48] An FBI agent involved in the Lexington investigation brought six young people who had refused to respond to his inquiries before a Lexington federal grand jury. After being "immunized," they were convicted on civil contempt charges. On leaving the courtroom, their attorney read a statement which they had jointly drafted:

> We believe that we have just cause for our refusal to answer questions propounded to us by the Grand Jury. We state to the Court that none of us know the present whereabouts of the persons who are known to us as Lena Paley or May Kelley [the names which the fugitives had used during their stay in the Lexington area]. We further state to the Court that we had no knowledge or reason to believe that Lena Paley or May Kelley were persons other than the persons they claimed to be, or that they were fugitives from justice.

After five months in jail, during which the contempt sentence was appealed, five of the protesters gave in and testified when the judge ruled on the basis of a sealed affidavit from the U.S. attorney (which they were not permitted even to look at) that the investigation was legitimate. The holdout, Jill Raymond, was forced to spend fourteen months in jail.

A New Haven grand jury was similarly used in connection with the Bureau's efforts to ferret out clues to the fugitives' whereabouts. Again, mass interrogations, threats of subpoenas, and fear of contempt sentences forced reluctant feminists to respond to interrogations by the agents. But two feminists, Ellen Grusse and Terri Turgeon, resisted and spent over seven months in jail. (One of the fugitives, Susan Saxe, was captured on March 27, 1976, when she was recognized while walking in Philadelphia.) The Bureau's shotgun investigative style had, according to many, a destructive impact on the feminist movement. Critics also are convinced that the overreaction reflects the Bureau's readiness to attribute to targets with unorthodox or controversial views broad conspiratorial support.

This tendency is plainly reflected in another grand jury investigation of a series of bombings by a terrorist cell that calls itself the Puerto Rican Armed Forces of National Liberation (Fuerzas Armadas de Liberación Nacional, FALN). Though FALN has "claimed" each of the bombings—a terrorist tactic intended both to achieve the primary end of publicity for its cause and to protect others from unjust accusations—the Bureau has harassed other, nonviolent "independentistas." Grand jury subpoenas have, for example, forced appearances by members of the Puerto Rican Socialist Party (PSP) who reject terrorism, because, the Bureau insists, both groups have called for Puerto Rican independence.[49] The ever-widening hunt for the FALN bombers led in the summer of 1977 to a subpoena of the records of the Hispanic Commission of the Episcopal Church because one of its former employees was suspected of belonging to FALN. The subpoena called for all records, documents, reports, notes, lists, memoranda, statements, books, and all other papers for a seven-year period dealing with the Commission, its membership, finances, employees, meetings, conferences, and the identification of all attendants. The two subpoenaed church employees were released on January 23, 1978, after serving more than ten months in jail for refusal—on the ground of "moral and religious commitments" —to answer questions before the grand jury. In his decision ordering the release (they could have been kept in jail until May), Federal Judge Robert L. Carter noted that while their continued refusal was not justified on the First Amendment grounds they relied on, "no legitimate purpose" would be served by keeping them in custody until the May expiration of the grand jury term.* But a number of others active in the independence movement and not shown to have been involved with the FALN were jailed for long periods of time for refusing to cooperate with grand juries in New York and Chicago.

The grand jury remains as it was during the ISD period an intelligence option and, especially in the political sphere, an investigative tool used by police agents when appropriate detection procedures have failed. These abuses have, in the post-Watergate era, catalyzed a broader movement for the reform of the grand jury system. A wide range of organizations from the National Council of Churches to the American Bar Association have urged a variety of reform proposals that enjoy sympathetic congressional sponsorship.[50] These cover due process rights before grand juries, including the right to advance notice of hearing, the availability of an attorney at the hearing, notification to witnesses of their rights, a ban on use of the grand jury process to gather evidence in support of a pending indictment, the abolition of forced immunity, the freeing of grand juries from prosecutorial controls by authorizing the retention of independent counsel, and a prohibition on the jailing of a witness twice for refusal to answer the same questions.

---

*The court pointed out that there was no ground for disputing their claim that they were "legitimately engaged in the work of their church" or any indication that they were involved in criminal activities, belonged to the FALN, or condoned or espoused its terrorist vices—"2 Women Freed After 10-Month Silence in Bomb Case," *New York Times,* Jan. 25, 1978.

11 Intelligence as a Mode of Governance — The Role of Congress

The Pseudo-Legislative Response

From the twenties on, both state and federal legislative committees have engaged in a wide variety of countersubversive intelligence practices. The prototype for the state legislative units was New York's Lusk Committee, which was launched in 1919. State committees and commissions—most of them legislative offshoots—flourished between the wars, a period when federal involvement in anti-subversion was at a low point. The McCarthy era revitalized the state units, most notably in Massachusetts, Ohio, Washington, California, and New Hampshire. The integration movement produced a second wave of countersubversive responses in many of the Southern states, including Mississippi, Georgia, Alabama, Louisiana, and Florida.

Between 1918 and 1956 Senate investigations of communism were conducted by no less than eighteen standing committees and one select committee, and in the House by sixteen standing committees, seven special committees, and five select committees. While most of the probes were limited in duration and scope, others were of a more comprehensive variety. The progenitor of the federal committees was the 1919 Senate Overman Committee, which began a probe into wartime German propaganda by domestic brewing interests but shifted mid-course to the more congenial subject of "Bolshevik Propaganda." In 1930, the House ordered an investigation into "Communist Propaganda in the United States" by a special committee, under the chairmanship of Representative Hamilton Fish (the "Fish Committee"). A network of surveillance agencies, public and private, had accumulated a storehouse of documents and dossiers on radicals and their organizations and were eager to demonstrate that the turmoil in the country was attributable not to hard times but to a Bolshevik conspiracy, financed by Moscow gold. Resistance to the proposed investigation, fed by the memories of the twenties' red scare, was overcome by a sensational series of documents produced by the New York City police commissioner, and subse-

386

quently shown to be forgeries, purporting to link Communist propaganda in this country with the Soviet Amtorg Trading Corporation.

The Fish Committee heard testimony from an assortment of patriotic and civic groups, private organizations engaged in anti-radical surveillance, labor espionage agencies, employer associations, and military and naval intelligence units. The hearings consolidated and strengthened an emerging countersubversive constituency. The 1930 panel was succeeded, first by the McCormack-Dickstein Committee in 1934, and then in 1938 by the Special Committee on Un-American Propaganda Activities (the "Dies Committee"), with a cautious one-year mandate to investigate "un-American propaganda" and "un-American propaganda activities." The committee's temporary status became a fiction: its mandate was renewed each year until 1943, when its tenure was extended for a term of two years. In 1945 the House gave its blessing to a permanent version of the Dies Committee, the House Committee on Un-American Activities (HUAC), and entrusted it not only with the conventional power of standing committees to consider and propose legislation but with the broader power to conduct investigations implemented by subpoenas. This unit, renamed the House Internal Security Committee (HISC) in 1969, was finally terminated in January 1975 by a post-Watergate Democratic Congress. Two years later the Senate abolished the Senate Internal Security Subcommittee (SISS), the counterpart to HISC, launched in 1951 as an offspring of the Senate Judiciary Committee. Both HISC and SISS were absorbed by the judiciary committees of the House and Senate respectively. A substantial number of former staff members of both committees have found congressional refuge elsewhere and, like other displaced toilers in the countersubversive vineyards, wait for a change in the political climate to permit the resumption of their activities.*

The anticipation that Congress will at some future time resume countersubversive investigations is hardly quixotic. The congressional countersubversive investigation has become an institutionalized weapon in the struggle over the direction of public policy. Resistance to movements for change recurrently flowers in the form of countersubversive investigation when conservatives dominate the Congress. Just as conventional legislative committees tend to ally themselves with the interests they regulate, so the pseudo-legislative mode is allied with clearly defined lobbies and pressure groups—business interests, veterans organizations, fundamentalist churches, anti-Communist ideologues, civilian and military foreign policy hawks, defense contractors, and nativist ultras. Indeed, since the pseudo-legislative committees are far removed from the main business of the Congress, they tend to be tied even more closely to the private groups whose values they share and to intelligence units engaged in related activities.

The countersubversive investigations by congressional committees are es-

*HISC staffers have been dispersed, but a substantial part of the SISS staff transferred *toute ensemble* to the Senate Judiciary Subcommittee on Criminal Laws and Procedures and was permitted by its sympathetic chairman, the late Senator John L. McClellan, to continue to conduct hearings on subversion-related subjects. On McClellan's death, the equally sympathetic chairman of the parent Judiciary Committee, Mississippi Senator James O. Eastland, continued the former practice. But these survival expedients were abandoned when Senator Edward M. Kennedy succeeded the aging Eastland, who retired in 1978.

sentially intelligence operations. However, unlike other intelligence activities, they are typically public and open—designedly so. The pseudo-legislative process consists of three structural components, the first and most important of which is the identification of subjects as subversive through a variety of techniques, beginning with the compulsory requirements of testimonial self-disclosure ("Are you now or have you ever been . . . ?") and of informing on others. This tactic maximizes the punitive impact of the hearing and places the recalcitrant witnesses under the drastic threat of a contempt sentence. A complementary purpose is to expand the boundaries of subversion in order to discredit as many groups and causes as possible by linking them to stigmatized witnesses. The third ingredient in the pseudo-legislative mix is the use of the committees' almost unlimited resources for printing and circulation of material to create the climate of fear and dependence that is the elixir of all intelligence systems. The propaganda also serves to arm the committees' constituency with useful materials in harassing stigmatized witnesses on the one hand and influencing the political process on the other. I have called this process "pseudo-legislative" because it serves no legislative purpose; on the contrary, the punitive exposure of individuals—the keystone of the process—is a form of legislative punishment without trial, condemned by the constitutional ban on bills of attainder.*[1] The two remaining stages, First Amendment objections aside, involve activities without a plausible relevance to the lawmaking function with which congressional committees are primarily concerned.

As we have seen, the intelligence activities of official bodies—the FBI, the military, the CIA, and grand juries, to list some outstanding examples—are typically sheltered by the cover of a legitimate role, such as law enforcement, security protection, riot control, or spy-catching. The systematic use of such covers is itself a wearisomely familiar intelligence practice by which deception becomes a handmaiden of usurped authority. Nowhere, however, over the entire spectrum of American institutional intelligence has a legitimizing pretext worked so effectively. The sham of legislative purpose went unchallenged for reasons of institutional comity, and, more important, out of fear of the political consequences.

The insistence that the committees were pursuing bona fide legislative goals led the courts to seek refuge in the separation-of-powers principle, dodging challenges to a claimed legislative purpose, the validity of the committees' mandates, and the relevance of the investigation to these mandates, and preferring instead to resolve contempt cases on narrow, frequently strained grounds. Given the implicit assurance of a free hand and a favorable climate, the pseudo-legislative investigation became almost irresistible for the ambitious politician seeking fame overnight. Senator Joseph R. McCarthy leaps to mind, but one may also recall the rise to high office of former HUAC member

---

*The exercise of legislative power to harass, stigmatize, and punish identifiable individuals and organizations, the congressional counterpart (and forerunner) of the COINTELPROs, cannot be distinguished from the classic bills of attainder associated with the seventeenth-century English Parliament. Such legislative punishments have recurred in periods of intolerance and hysteria in response to subversion-related charges, supplanting conventional law enforcement either because the conduct condemned was not a legal offense, there was no proof of guilt, legal process was deemed too slow, or the punishment inadequate.

Richard Nixon. And the opportunities are especially alluring for a committee chairman: the congressional committee system imposes few formal restraints on its chairmen beyond an observance of protocol in dealing with other members of the majority, the minority, and the House or Senate as a whole. As long as the tribal customs are observed, the committee chairman can write his own ticket and know he is protected by the institutional majesty of the legislative process. Senator McCarthy fell because he refused to play the game by the rules. The Senate intervened, not to repudiate the pseudo-legislative mode but to protect it from permanent damage. But, beginning in the early 1960s, the entire operating formula—the hearings held all over the country for an invented legislative purpose, the "friendly" witness (frequently a surfaced informer) placing in the record a list of names of alleged Communists, followed by the clutch of "unfriendly" witnesses consisting of those named by the "friendly" witness, the applause from its patriotic constituency and the press headlines—all this fell apart. A changing climate produced a crop of outraged demonstrators, a new breed of articulate and *really* unfriendly witnesses, and a hostile press.[2]

The Wrong Way—And the Right Way

In 1969 the House panel came under the leadership of Representative Richard Ichord of Missouri, who in 1968 had introduced a measure to abolish HUAC and to create a new committee with a new mandate. It was no longer to serve as a watchdog of "un-American propaganda," that sloganistic survival of the 1920s. The key term now was "internal security," the cold war phrase that had served as the jurisdictional foundation of the committee's Senate counterpart. The rechristened House Internal Security Committee (HISC) was supposed to monitor organizations and their affiliates that sought to establish, or to assist in establishing, a "totalitarian dictatorship" in the United States or to overthrow the government, not only by force but by "any unlawful means." In addition, it was to police the activities of groups that used unlawful means "to obstruct or oppose the lawful authority of the Government of the United States in the execution of any law or policy affecting the internal security of the United States. . . ."

The new charter, approved by the House in February 1969, was hardly an improvement on the old. It remained vague; at one end of its grant of authority it collided with the First Amendment, and at the other, it simply authorized investigation into conduct that was patently criminal and covered by existing legislation. HISC promptly became an outlet for the anti-Communist line of the geopolitical pundits of the 1950s (Stefan Possony, William Kintner, Gerhart Niemeyer), and the cold war policies ("struggle for survival," "the unending conflict," "the front is everywhere") of such institutions as the National War College, the Hoover Institution, and the Foreign Policy Research Institute. In the 1960s the American Security Council (ASC, discussed in the next chapter) became the chief torchbearer of this movement. Ichord is the ASC's representative in the corridors of governmental anti-communism, a contributor to ASC radio broadcasts, a prominent participant in Operation Alert, an ASC lobby, and an editor of the ASC newsletter, *Washington Report*. Two former ASC staff members joined the HISC staff in 1971 and were discovered buying index cards at reduced government rates for ASC use.[3] ASC had, of course, always supported HUAC; but the emergence of one of its own as HISC chairman gave special impetus to its efforts. When in 1974 reform proposals threatened HISC's future, ASC launched a campaign of full-page newspaper advertisements and coordinated the counterattack through the "Safe America Committee." But ASC's most important contribution was ideological: it helped reformulate the committee's mission and priorities. This transformation produced a piquant irony: the pseudo-legislative mode was invented in the 1930s for the claimed purpose of exposing "un-American propaganda" by the agents of hidden principals. But HISC's relationship with ASC involved precisely such dissemination of the propaganda of unacknowledged sponsors.

The role of the committee as a front for unseen principals was strengthened in 1970, when HISC partitioned itself into a Democratic majority and a Republican minority under the leadership of John Ashbrook. The newly formed minority rapidly made itself spokesman for the organized far right. Before 1970, the committee had not found such a division necessary: its Democrats (typically Southerners) and Republicans shared the same views. But the adoption of the two-party format was admirably designed to enhance HISC's budgetary appeal, broaden its sources of congressional support and, most important, provide a forum for John Ashbrook, an energetic ultra rightist. Moreover, the minority gave Ichord's far-out views an even more forthright airing than he could afford to express as chairman, thus enhancing his image as a moderate.

Ichord's survival strategy was to blunt potential opposition to HISC by a claimed commitment to due process and the First Amendment, pursuing the "right way" to fight communism in contrast to HUAC. As a first step on the path to righteousness, HISC scrapped the compulsory self-identification and informing component of its exposure structure and replaced it by third-party and documentary identification, thus reducing the occasions for judicial scrutiny arising out of court review of contempt punishments. This abandonment of the classic instrumentality of self-exposure was also not without irony. When the Special Committee was created, Chairman Martin Dies acknowledged that any attempt to prevent or punish "un-American activities" by legislation "might jeopardize fundamental rights far more important than the objectives we seek." Instead of introducing legislation, he promised to confine himself to "exposure" —independent of a legislative end. Thus identification, preferably by the witness himself, became the "right way." HISC not only dispensed with the unfriendly witness scenario but adorned the process of third-party identification with due process trimmings. No longer, as in the bad old days, were witnesses to be charged with subversion without solid proof. Under the new dispensation, a witness is solemnly asked (an actual question): "Tell us of your own knowledge whether Gus Hall [National Secretary of the Communist Party] is a member of the Communist Party." And in another proudly proclaimed departure from the disgraceful past, the rules accorded Gus Hall (or any other individual charged without proper proof) an opportunity to reply and to correct the record. In the same spirit, Ichord campaigned to defeat a proposed repeal of the "concentration camp" provisions of the Internal Security Act of 1950. What was objectionable, Ichord protested, was not the detention camp provisions but rather the failure to mandate hearings before such drastic restraints on freedom were imposed. A professed concern for freedom similarly inspired Ichord's attack on proposals to sequester and seal HISC's file and dossier collection as "anti-intellectual," "book-burning," and a "violation of the First Amendment."[4]

But Ichord's pious embrace of the "right way" did nothing to modify his fanatic commitment to the countersubversive tradition or to change in any basic respect the pseudo-legislative system. Shortly after Congress approved the revised mandate and the reorganized committee, Ichord launched an investigation into "the financing of revolutionary groups," a subject that has ever obsessed the intelligence mind. Questionnaires requested some 179 colleges and universities to supply the names, sponsorship, and honoraria of "all guest speakers on the campus from September, 1968 to May, 1970." The committee thereafter, on Ichord's initiative, published a list of speakers whom it charged with being members or "supporters" of fourteen specified subversive organizations, including John C. Bennett of the Union Theological Seminary, Muhammad Ali, the boxer, John Ciardi, poet, and a number of others whose listing was based only on their membership in groups that opposed the committee.

On October 28, 1970, District Court Judge Gerhard A. Gesell barred publication or distribution of the list on the grounds that it was a blacklist, intended "to inhibit speech on college campuses," and that "it is without any proper legislative purpose and infringes on the rights of the individuals named therein." He concluded that it would be "illegal to publish the list at public expense." Nevertheless, the committee defiantly distributed the list under the protection of a House resolution asserting the immunity of the House from judicial interference with its legislative function. The committee's printed report listed the organizations considered subversive (based on such sources as Director Hoover's congressional testimony and its own hearings and reports), and also the names of those colleges that had refused to cooperate by returning the questionnaire.[5]

Although this defiance was justified by the need to protect the integrity of the legislative function, Chairman Ichord never bothered to explain to his colleagues what legislative purpose could be legitimately served by printing and circulating the list. This abuse of legislative power contributed to strengthening opposition to the committee in the House. An even more important stimulus was the committee's expansive jurisdictional claims. HISC inherited the identity crisis that had plagued its predecessors: what was its legislative function? As a standing committee, HUAC had, over a twenty-three-year period, produced six measures that became law—most of them transiently until they were ruled unconstitutional. The basic reason for this dismal record is that the committee's limited and ambiguous jurisdiction could not generate a body of legislation. Neither "un-American propaganda" nor "internal security" is a subject matter which, standing alone, raises recurrent problems justifying a separate legislative entity. And once the problem of subversion (whatever that may mean) is linked to some concrete threat or concern, a conflict arises with the congressional committee assigned to this particular subject. The clash is inevitable because under the committee system delegations of power are generally inclusive—a subject matter in all of its aspects. Nor was the position improved when, instead of considering bills for statutory enactment, the committee engaged in at-large investigations; it could hardly investigate in areas where it had no authority to consider legislation.

All of the major HISC hearings from the very beginning thus involved subjects to which other committees had a more convincing jurisdictional claim. For example, in 1969 it held hearings on obstruction of the armed forces and on industrial, vessel, and port security—two subjects plainly within the purview of the Armed Services Committee. In 1970, 1971, and 1972 it considered various proposals, mostly originated by its own members, regarding the renovation of the federal employee loyalty program—a subject more appropriately within the jurisdiction of the Post Office and Civil Service Committee. The 1971 hearings on "Attempts to Subvert the United States Armed Services" again involved problems more appropriately handled by the Armed Services Committee. Similarly, its 1972 hearings on proposed restraints on travel to hostile areas and on the subversive causes of prison unrest invaded the jurisdiction of other committees. In the case of the committee's prison probe, three other panels had already launched inquiries. In particular, an exhaustive series of hearings was held in 1971 and 1972 by a House subcommittee of the Judiciary Committee under the chairmanship of Robert W. Kastenmeier, who protested HISC's intrusion.

Ichord brushed aside objections to HISC's jurisdictional trespass—voiced most strenuously by HISC's gadfly member and most eloquent critic Robert F. Drinan, also a member of the Kastenmeier panel—by announcing a new theory: the vertical subject matter divisions of the committee system are not absolute. Jurisdiction is also horizontally layered, so that each committee may deal with its specialty, extracted from a larger setting already within the competence of another committee. Under this new rationale, the Judiciary Committee could probe prison unrest but the specialized aid of HISC was needed to evaluate the extent to which subversive influences (rather than genuine grievances) were responsible for that unrest. In short, Ichord saw HISC's role as a sort of anti-subversive House detective, with, in his words, an "investigative function which is intended to serve all Committees of the House."

HISC's jurisdictional difficulties reinforced the perception that the legislative process was a crude cover for a countersubversive intelligence operation. And the underlying abuse of power for exposure-propaganda purposes is corroborated by the pseudo-legislative investigative style. Every bona fide legislative investigation must necessarily be selective; not even the most conscientious legislative probe can examine *every* manifestation or example under inquiry. Thus, for example, an investigating committee looking into migrant labor would try to elicit representative views from the growers, contractors, and laborers, then reach a conclusion and make recommendations. It would hardly think it useful to call every single migrant laborer, grower, and contractor to gain an understanding of the problem. By contrast, there was something curiously exhaustive about pseudo-legislative hearings. Both HISC and SISS were eager to identify every last member of an organization under inquiry. This is, of course, a practice associated with law enforcement and intelligence gathering rather than with legislative investigation. A prosecutor must proceed against every law violation; an intelligence officer prides himself on the comprehensiveness of his coverage and files. Similarly, the migratory labor probers would not, unless some unforeseen new problem arose, promptly reinvestigate after issuing a report. But both committees dove into the same subject matter again and again. The printed output of only these two principal countersubversive committees, HUAC/HISC and SISS, is in excess of 165,000 pages.[6] In no other area have congressional investigations generated a remotely comparable volume of printed materials and contributed so little to the lawmaking process.

The Pseudo-Legislative Agendas of the Sixties

The protest movements of the sixties confronted the pseudo-legislative congressional bloc with the same challenge as the White House; indeed, even more urgently. In view of the decline of domestic communism both in membership and in influence, how could the public be persuaded through hearings and propaganda that the growing unrest was the product of Communist manipulation? The political realities led to a split in the intelligence world. The fundamentalists insisted that communism was indeed the primary source of the new disturbances and that the basic task of intelligence remained what it had been since the twenties, to link the new movements to the Menace. They brushed aside the arguments—based on informers' reports, wiretap logs, and internal documents—that the new dissent was basically nonideological, promoting instead their own time-worn ideological formulations, which had succeeded so well in the past in suppressing cognitive embarrassments. A concession to political reality might deal a death blow to the Menace and undermine the entire countersubversive system of containing domestic dissent and influencing foreign policy. The countersubversive establishment itself was under siege: anti-communism had fathered the pseudo-legislative mode, shaped its operational techniques and file collections, provided the career opportunities for red hunters, both committee members and staffers. Nor was the threat confined to the pseudo-legislative mode: the entire system of interlocking official and private countersubversive structures required reinforcement. But the obstacles were formidable; it was no longer possible as in the past to begin with an identifiable Communist core and work outward to other movements. And it was unrewarding to plow the same shrinking Communist field over and over again. The FBI had already pointed the way to the only feasible solution: monitoring and measuring degrees of Communist influence, "the extent of subversion," in the target organizations. To reinvigorate the Menace itself, both SISS and HISC pounced on minuscule Marxist sects, factional mutants, Maoists, Trotskyists, and third world grouplets, as newly discovered threats to the national security. These investigative exercises, invariably crowned by tendentious "staff studies," were used both to provide ideological resources for tainting the broad protest movements of the day and to fuel opposition to the Nixon administration's Soviet and Chinese détente initiatives.

The pseudo-legislative attempt to ideologize the unrest of the sixties is perhaps best illustrated by hearings on the causes of and cures for urban riots and disruptions. The most significant treatment of this theme was developed in a twenty-five-part, three-year investigation by the Permanent Subcommittee on Investigation of the Senate Committee on Government Operations, headed by the late Arkansas Senator John L. McClellan (the "McClellan Committee"). In August 1967 McClellan, a hard-line opponent of civil rights legislation and court decisions, obtained authorization to conduct a congressional inquiry into the cause and cure of urban rioting. As we have seen, Southern legislators, in the wake of the 1954 decision by the Supreme Court, systematically used the Communist scapegoating technique to resist integration. Indeed, the febrile Southern model of the "red peril" is the prototype for the pseudo-legislative version. McClellan's probe was designed to strengthen this attack. Even before he received congressional approval, McClellan announced that the investigation would stress "law enforcement rather than the social causes underlying the disorders." He was certain that racial unrest was the work of subversive agitators and that peace could be restored by strict law enforcement measures. Republican Senator John Sherman Cooper had vainly tried to amend the resolution to direct the panel to search specifically for "economic and social factors involved," but this was rejected by a committee vote on the ground, as voiced by some members, that concern with social causes would amount to "condoning lawlessness."[7] The strongest supporter for the McClellan line was Senator Robert Byrd of West Virginia (later majority leader) who, shortly before the investigation was launched, had made a Senate speech demanding that riots be brought under control by "brutal force," even if it meant the shooting of adult looters on sight.

Before the hearings were half over, McClellan proclaimed that "a climate or condition has been created by agitators—perhaps by an attitude of some Negroes, though certainly not a majority of them—a condition which is ready to be sparked by any incident which could be seized upon and built into a riot. . . . Of the four cities covered by our hearings to date, we definitely have established that militant agitators were present and had been holding hearings in three of them. . . . I would say that they were fanning the prejudice, deliberately inciting to riot, and were ready to, and did, seize upon an incident." He then added that he was dissatisfied with the way the government had dealt with these agitators and demanded "more vigor in prosecutions." The senator was "confident that subversive influences are present, though not in every instance. . . . I think the Communists are at work through every channel that is available to them to sow the seeds of discord and to exploit any dissent that they can find among our people. There isn't any question in my mind about that. I think you will find that Communists are right now planning to get into this 'poor peoples' march' on Washington that is scheduled to begin soon."[8]

The conservative members of the committee, and especially Senators McClellan and Karl Mundt, warned about a "master plan," an intricately coordinated subversive conspiracy, national in scope. Endlessly repetitive identifications of suspected conspirators were received into evidence. The walls of the hearing room were paneled with "power structure charts" of the SDS and Black Panthers, together with pictures of activists in both organizations. In addition to staff testimony, the record was filled with the testimony of police officers and undercover agents (some sixty-three in all). Names and photos were selectively leaked to reporters for local and regional coverage. Urban police witnesses readily furnished expected assurances that the Menace was alive and flourishing. Sergeant Joseph P. Grubisic, operating head of the Chicago Intelligence Unit, after supplying the committee with "200 or 300 names," assured the legislators that "the Communist threat . . . does exist . . . and poses a major threat to the peace and security of our Nation."[9]

The effort to develop sanctions against members of the alleged conspiracy included the pressures on the IRS discussed above and an attempt to cut off scholarships and other forms of federal aid to campus troublemakers. About a dozen major American universities were subpoenaed to provide the names of every student involved in campus disruptions.[10] To placate liberal Democrats on the committee, McClellan regularly made obeisances to due process, evenhandedness, and the First Amendment, but matters got out of hand shortly after the hearings commenced. In September 1967 a committee investigator made arrangements with a Kentucky prosecutor to obtain papers and documents, seized in a raid on the home of Alan and Margaret McSurely, organizers for the Southern Conference Educational Fund (SCEF), who were leaders in the civil rights and poverty movements in Pike County, Kentucky. Shortly thereafter, a federal court invalidated the Kentucky sedition statute used to justify the raid and ordered the seized documents sequestrated "until final disposition of this case by appeal or otherwise" (no appeal was ever filed). Despite this order, the McClellan investigator took the papers to Washington. After the McSurelys obtained a court order restoring the papers to their custody, they were served with a committee subpoena for their production at a committee hearing on the ground that they might be useful in the committee's probe of riots that had occurred in Nashville, Tennessee, in April 1967.* In a subsequent contempt case, the committee conceded that its investigator's initial inspection of the documents alone prompted the subpoena. An appellate court concluded that, in the light of this concession, the subpoena itself was invalid, the fruit of an illegal

---

*There is no evidence either in the committee's investigative files or in the record of the trial involving these disorders that in any way suggests the McSurelys or SCEF had anything to do with the riots. The theory, apparently improvised by the committee to give the color of legitimacy to its subpoenas, was that since Stokely Carmichael, a leader of the Student Non-Violent Coordinating Committee, had spoken at Vanderbilt University before the Nashville riots and, a few days previously, had addressed a staff meeting of SCEF, somehow the committee was entitled to the papers. But a more plausible explanation of the committee's maneuvers was a planned collaboration with the prosecutor in ridding Pike County of the McSurelys. (The McSurelys finally did leave Kentucky in December 1968 when their house was bombed in the middle of the night.) The abuse of legislative power by McClellan's probe is further shown by the seizure and retention of personal correspondence between Margaret McSurely and newspaper columnist Drew Pearson. McClellan directed that a love letter from Pearson be placed under lock and key and shown only to himself and two staff members but not to his colleagues. Pearson had strongly attacked McClellan in a number of columns, including one on Aug. 10, 1967, the day before the illegal raid and seizure.

search by a committee agent of the McSurelys' property, originally obtained by state officials through an unconstitutional search and seizure.*[11]

The McClellan investigation overlapped a multi-volumed HUAC hearing on the same subject intended to demonstrate that riots were part of the Communist "international weapons system." Captain Charles Kinney, Newark's intelligence chief, was a star witness. When asked by committee member William Tuck about social conditions in Newark, he assured the congressman that conditions were fine, that Newark was "the first city in the United States to become part of this federally funded program," and that there had been no previous riots; that "economic conditions in Newark are probably better than in most cities in the United States"; and that "employment opportunities are ample." Tuck thereupon concluded: "then all this razzle-dazzle we have read in this report about economic conditions and racial injustice just did not exist prior to this time."[12]

The document referred to by Congressman Tuck was a report of a New Jersey commission, which had made an investigation of the riot and concluded that its primary causes were economic and political. But that was not the way Captain Kinney saw it. He insisted that:

> In Newark, certain individuals conspired, and are conspiring, to replace the leadership of the Newark Police Department.
> Still other individuals conspired, and are conspiring, as part of the movement to replace this system of government under which we live in the United States of America, using any means to do so, including the use of force and violence.
> To these conspirators, the insurrection that occurred in 1967 was a means to an end which they welcomed and exploited to serve their plot.[13]

This was a variant on Captain Kinney's earlier television charge that the 1967 Newark riots were instigated by a subversive organization, the Newark Community Union Project (NCUP). Kinney claimed that NCUP director Tom Hayden "traveled with both black and white people from Newark to Bratislava, Czechoslovakia, for a meeting behind the iron curtain where they received instructions. That we know. Some of this information is coming right from Peiping, as a matter of fact, and it's coming here from China by way of Canada. . . ."

In another advance on the urban riot front, HUAC in May 1968 published a tract, *Guerrilla Warfare Advocates in the United States,* as told to the committee (for a fee of $1000) by its author, Phillip A. Luce, a former member of the Marxist Progressive Labor party (PL) and editor of its official organ. Luce defected from this neo-Maoist group to become a right-wing propagandist who "cooperated with government agencies." Luce's sixty-one-page printed report, an expansion of an earlier effort, *Communist Plan for Guerrilla Warfare in the*

---

*The McClellan Committee's collaboration with the Kentucky officials was a rerun of an uncannily similar attack on SCEF in 1963, when the Louisiana Joint Committee on Un-American Activities and the New Orleans police teamed up with SISS in a series of raids seizing documents and records. Here, too, the authorizing statute was invalidated; the captured records were removed from the state in defiance of a court order, reproduced by SISS in Washington, and then returned to Louisiana officials who also copied them before returning them to SCEF in belated compliance with the court order—*Dombrowski* v. *Eastland,* 387 U.S. 82 (1967).

U.S., published by the American Security Council, outspooked the field, averring that domestic Communists had received "guerrilla warfare instructions in Spain during the civil war of 1936–1939" and had more recently attended "guerrilla warfare training schools behind the Iron Curtain." Unfortunately, no evidence of such training or of actual Communist involvement in guerrilla warfare could be supplied. The Communist students had also been trained in concealment and, in addition, were shielded by "court decisions which have nullified effective U.S. controls of the international movement of American Communist agents." The report's bizarre conclusion is that, although lack of mass support would logically lead even Communists to reject guerrilla warfare as a tactic, still "logic and rationality are not necessarily ingredients in the plans of some Communists in the United States. They are obviously capable of making mistakes, and it would be just as grievous a tactical error to overestimate their intellectual capabilities as to underestimate their fanatical revolutionary zeal."

In addition to tracing "subversive influences" on the protest movements of the time, HISC and SISS worked ceaselessly to identify each participant. While the former effort was, as I have already suggested, frustrating, the latter was a thumping success. As a fruit of its collaboration with urban intelligence units (discussed in the next section), the committees acquired detailed police blotter-style IDs, biographies, and spates of photographs. For example, in the five HUAC/HISC investigations conducted between 1968 and 1972,* a total of 378 identifying photographs appear in the appendices, sandwiched between a fantastic variety of "documents"—a twenties-style haul of literature, plus private letters, maps, Xeroxed checks, informers' reports, surveillance logs, transcripts of interviews, membership lists, press releases, publication lists, invitations to conferences, minutes of meetings and lists of participants, delegates to conferences, newsletters, rent receipts, flyers, file transcripts, constitutions of target organizations, articles of incorporation, university rules and regulations, organizational registration and application forms, posters, student newspaper articles, bank signature cards, agendas for demonstrations, petitions to Congress, newspaper articles, and financial data of all kinds.

Both committees concerned themselves with a familiar intelligence theme, the funding of subversive groups, and subpoenaed their bank records in an effort to intimidate contributors. SISS was particularly aggressive. It launched its multi-volumed hearing on "Extent of Subversion in the New Left" (1970) with sensational testimony by Sergeant Robert J. Thoms of the Los Angeles Police Department Intelligence Division. In his fifty-odd-page presentation, dense with names, charts, and lists, Thoms charged that the subversive groups had been subsidized to the tune of $5 million by the government, over $1 million by the Ford Foundation, and over $200,000 by the Episcopal, Methodist, and Unitar-

---

*"Subversive Involvement in the Disruption of the Democratic Party National Convention" (1968)
"Students for a Democratic Society," Parts LA-7B (1969)
"Subversive Involvement in the Origin, Leadership and Activities of the new Mobilization Committee to End the War in Vietnam," Parts I–III (1970)
"National Peace Action Coalition (NPAC) and People's Coalition for Peace and Justice (PCPJ)," Parts I–IV (1971)
"Subversive Influences Affecting the Military Forces of the U.S.," Parts I–II (1972).

ian churches. And these estimates, he assured the subcommittee, were understated since they were limited to the witness's necessarily incomplete sources. To be sure, not all of the organizational beneficiaries were subversive; some were umbrella organizations, which deliberately brought innocuous civic groups within their representation as a calculated cover "to give [them] an air of respectability."

Shortly after Thoms testified, SISS began its own funding investigation with a subpoena for the bank records of Liberation News Service (LNS), an agency organized in 1967 to provide coverage, largely for underground and college newspapers, of events and issues neglected by the straight press. LNS resisted the subpoena in court—after notification by its bank—but was finally compelled to surrender. When SISS discovered from the LNS bank records that the group had received a modest grant ($5000) from the Episcopal Church, it promptly leaked this piece of news both to favored columnists and to a church publication hostile to such benefactions. The resultant pressure forced the discontinuance of the grant.[14] (A similar subpoena for the bank records of the United Servicemen's Fund, an anti-war group active in the GI peace movement, was successfully resisted in the courts for over four years until the Supreme Court ruled in favor of SISS.)

The Thoms testimony was followed by the publication in the same series of the Illinois Crime Commission's "Report on the SDS Riots, October 9–11, 1969." Before the report was released locally, a number of Chicagoans brought an action seeking to restrain publication on the ground, among others, that the report violated the constitutional rights of free expression, especially of those mentioned who had no connection at all with the riots. For example, the report printed diaries, letters, address books naming individuals not even remotely involved in the affair, dossiers of the owners of cars used by the demonstrators to come to Chicago, and background reports on individuals who supplied bail for the demonstrators. A federal court denied the relief sought but not without reluctance. Two months after the Commission had assured the court that the report, despite its manifest intelligence orientation, was intended for state legislative enlightenment alone, on June 10, 1970, its executive director and chief investigator appeared before SISS and submitted for SISS publication the 400-page document, along with copies of materials seized in the course of the investigation, a maneuver to ensure a wide (and free) distribution throughout the intelligence community.

The desperation of the quest for a more efficient countersubversive stimulus is reflected in the embrace of terrorism—political kidnapping, airplane hijacking, bombing—as a Communist tactic. But again, obstacles loomed: neither in the mid-seventies when the committees seized on it nor thereafter (see Epilogue) did terrorism emerge as an important political phenomenon in the United States, let alone as fuel for rekindling anti-communism.

The committees were undaunted by such details. In 1973 HISC published "Political Kidnappings—1968–1973," pinpointing this tactic as a new worldwide Marxist Communist weapon. Presumably to justify HISC's jurisdiction over a subject beyond its mandate, which is limited to domestic matters and so clearly within the competence of the Foreign Relations Committee (all the data in the report were furnished by the State Department), the report cites a dispute among members of a faction of the domestic Socialist Workers' Party (SWP) about support for terrorist and insurrectionary tactics in South America, and concludes that, although SWP's leaders were opposed to kidnapping and related tactics, the party's position might change with changed circumstances.

Persistently thwarted by political realities, Ichord reacted with fervor to the kidnapping six months later of Patricia Hearst by the Symbionese Liberation Army (SLA). Here, he insisted, was an honest-to-goodness political kidnapping —of the very sort predicted in the earlier document! From the viewpoint of Ichord and his ASC support group, the kidnapping could hardly have come at a more opportune time: HISC was threatened with extinction through a proposed House committee reorganization plan. The emergence of the SLA and the kidnapping in the setting of a worldwide spread of terrorism presented a possible reprieve. Despite the universal denunciation of the Hearst kidnapping by virtually all radical groups, including the Marxist left, the committee set about to expand the old Menace to embrace the new evil of terrorism. Its position was well summarized by the American Security Council's Washington "Report of the Air," which invited all Americans to "agree with Ichord's warning that terrorist tactics" already posed "a severe threat to our security." And here is how it all fits together:

> The committee is particularly interested in developing the extent to which terrorist groups give direct or peripheral support to the world Communist objectives through their espousal of Marxist-Leninist-Maoist revolutionary concepts. Despite the clear and present danger of terrorism and despite the need for Congressional action, critics of the House Committee on Internal Security have begun a new drive to abolish the committee.

The Hearst kidnapping had overnight, the ASC insisted, proved that "it can happen here" and restored the Menace to its pristine *Schrecklichkeit.*

Eager to exploit its new opportunities, the committee, by mid-February 1974, had compiled all of its news clippings on the SLA and hastily issued them as a "study." Even before this document was printed, the committee transmitted the file to FBI Director Kelley for his use in solving the crime.[15] It breathlessly announced that the SLA "study" was merely a prelude to a more comprehensive investigation of worldwide political terrorism. The new hearings were launched with Ichord's announcement that "Work in the internal security field . . . is probably more important today in view of the increase of terrorist organizations activities than at any time in our history. . . ."[16] The hearings and "study" were rushed into print in time for the House deliberations in September on HISC's future. On September 30, Chairman Ichord delivered a long speech (eleven pages in the *Congressional Record*) in support of his amendment to retain the committee without change. The speech looted language and logic, politics and history, to find nourishment for the Menace in domestic terrorism. But Ichord won only a short reprieve before the ax fell in January 1975.[17] During this same period SISS also commenced its campaign against the newly discovered threat of domestic terrorism, again designed to fend off threatened dissolution.

The reliance by both committees on developments abroad to justify their existence was not confined to terrorism. The internal decline of communism and foreign policy initiatives in the direction of détente and co-existence combined to force a new focus on the foreign scene. This global concern was projected by SISS Chairman James Eastland in an introduction to the first of "a series of documentations" entitled "Communist Subversion and American Security (1972)":

> No meaningful study can be made of Communist activities in the USA in isolation from the worldwide pattern of Communist activism. Communist activity is internationally orchestrated, so that what the Communists do in this country is intended to dovetail with and support what they are doing in other countries—and vice versa.

The committees became a standard forum for defectors, escapees, and émigrés from Communist countries. From 1970 to 1973 HISC held eleven hearings to air the revelations of sixteen such witnesses, supplemented by its corps of foreign policy hardliners. The threat of improved relations with the Soviet Union and China spurred a special response. In June 1972, for example, HISC circulated a report on two tiny Maoist groups (one of them promptly went out of business) warning that they "constitute a political threat to the internal security of the United States," and pointing to the fact that the organizer of one of them "now resides in Newark, N.J., coincidentally permitting ready access to the Red Chinese delegation to the United Nations." Only the naïve could fail to conclude, the report adds, that these indigenous Maoists would not receive financial backing from "such excellent friends." In contrast to the committee's customary timetable, the report was printed before the publication of the testimony upon which it was based and at a time when the Nixon administration's planned opening to China was made public.*

From the beginning of the Castro takeover, SISS staked out the Caribbean generally and Cuba in particular as its turf and even took on a Latin American chief investigator to give it an inside track. In 1971 it published the twenty-fifth installment of a probe begun in 1959, *Communist Threat to the United States Through the Caribbean.* In addition, in 1962 it issued a "study" of "pro-Castro influence on the American press" (112 pp.) and in the same year some 630 pages of hearings (in 9 parts) on the Fair Play for Cuba Committee, followed the next year by 400 pages of documents on the theme of Latin American subversion. Barely catching its breath, it plunged onward in 1964 with a study of subversion of the Latin American educational system, followed by testimony in 1965 from four defectors (three from Cuba). In 1967 it again presented a study on the Cuban peril. In 1969 it began an intensive continuing investigation of the SDS-sponsored Venceremos Brigade. On March 16, 1970, SISS Chairman Eastland offered his Senate colleagues tidbits from the investigation in a speech entitled,

*SISS had already demonstrated its concern about possible improved relations with China. In February 1970 it published an 1800-page collection of documents, most of them already printed and circulated, which had been seized 25 years earlier in an FBI raid on the offices of *Amerasia,* a magazine with pro-Chinese Communist leanings, whose editors were charged with discrediting the Nationalist régime in China by using reports allegedly turned over to them by diplomat John Stewart Service. In 1971 it weighed in with *Human Cost of Communism in China.* The exhumed Amerasia papers as well as the subsequent publication were intended both as warnings against a conciliatory policy toward Communist China and as a plea for support of the Chinese Nationalists.

"The Venceremos Brigade—Agrarians or Anarchists," to which he attached a list of 216 individuals who had returned from Cuba. In a repeat performance on November 8, 1972, he listed a total of almost 2000 names broken down by state of residence, comprising all four brigade contingents after the first.[18]

Beginning on October 16, 1972, HISC held hearings on "Theory and Practice of Communism 1972 (Venceremos Brigade)" at which it received the testimony of two Cuban defectors and an infiltrator, Dwight Douglas Crews, employed as a deputy sheriff by the Jefferson parish, Louisiana, sheriff's office. The hearing record includes Crews's 110-page diary, 30 pages of sightseer style photographs, and Senator Eastland's two Senate speeches together with his lists of names. At the end of Crews's performance the subcommittee chairman presented the witness with an American flag flown from the Capitol (as certified by the Capitol architect) and a letter of commendation. This gesture reminds us that the pseudo-legislative investigation is strongly influenced by constituency values and political benefit. For this reason, Southern legislators have specialized in race-related targets. The gratified chairman in this case was Miami Congressman Claude Pepper; the hearing was held in Miami, where over 350,000 anti-Castro Cubans are concentrated, and the time was the eve of the 1972 congressional elections.[19] Pepper also presided over HISC hearings in 1971 on communism in Latin America, in 1973 on a pro-Castro cultural exposition (EXPOCUBA),* and in 1974 on the overthrow of the Allende régime in Chile.†

These and other pseudo-investigative explorations of the foreign scene, far from achieving their intended purposes, crystallized a growing awareness in Congress that the investigations were increasingly poaching on areas entrusted to other congressional committees in order to project right-wing policies and viewpoints frequently in conflict with the legislative consensus. In the process of trying to make itself relevant, countersubversion had grown too big for its britches.

---

*Before the exposition opened, it was bombed; an organized opposition forced its early closing by threats of more bombings, physical attacks, and missile-throwing at the attendants and at the police. The head of the group that had organized the anti-Castro protest denounced the "provocation" of New York City Mayor John Lindsay in refusing to bar the exposition and the conduct of the police in protecting it. A HISC "study" (a collection of dossiers) was placed in the record to demonstrate the exposition's subversive sponsorship. But no investigation was made, staff study conducted, or a single question asked about the violence and bombing—"Blast Damages Union Quarters," *New York Times,* July 25, 1973; "Cuba Exposition Set for Tonight," *New York Times,* July 26, 1973; "3 Men Arrested As Violence Flares Outside Expo-Cuba," *New York Times,* July 27, 1973.

†This hearing developed the thesis that the overthrow of the Allende régime in Chile was really a countercoup by a reluctant, freedom-loving military junta, summoned by an oppressed civilian population to free it from the brutal yoke of socialism. When the hearings were distributed to all members of Congress by the Chilean Embassy to bolster its claims of legitimacy, California Congressman Robert L. Leggett observed:

"I am curious as to why the Internal Security Committee, whose mandate is to inquire into internal matters, has taken the time and effort to compile a 225-page hearing record on Chile's internal problems. Dictatorships are not uncommon in this world—we should know, we support some of the best that money can buy—but none of them have been deemed worthy of the energy and efforts of the Internal Security Committee. It appears that what we have here is a case of selective security: it does not matter how repressive, how undemocratic, or how dictatorial a government, it is OK with HISC—as long as it is not Communist"—*Congressional Record,* July 24, 1974, p. 24830, Vol. 120.

The New Operational Styles

The sixties' expansion of target areas was matched by more aggressive techniques in collecting information. The pseudo-legislative investigative process had long shared the assumptions and evaluative norms of other domestic intelligence institutions. In a new development, it perfected its latent affinity for data collection techniques. Staff members—most of them recruited from other intelligence units such as the FBI, military intelligence, or local police units— engaged in physical surveillance, photographed targets such as peace demonstrators and convention delegates, and recruited informers. In addition, both committees used their powers to gain access to bank records, leases, the names of applicants for post office boxes, tax returns, and passport files. HISC's Republican minority pursued even more aggressive undercover procedures, including the use of informers recruited by right-wing groups such as the Young Americans for Freedom (YAF). In 1972 the minority's chief investigator, Herbert Romerstein, and Richard Norusis, his aide,* were caught bugging a room in the Midland Hotel in Chicago where an alleged Communist group was scheduled to hold a conference. This eavesdropping attempt violated both federal and Illinois law. The surveillance team remained during the convention to complete their mission, which, according to Romerstein, was a probe of the "Theory and Practice of Communism."[20]

To these new in-house modes of data collection, the pseudo-legislative investigators added the resources and assets of the urban police. For the greater part of the decade, local and state anti-subversive police units, either already in existence or newly activated, had extensively monitored the new movements. Just as the depression unrest had fattened local intelligence files until the Fish and Dies committees provided an outlet, so the accumulating take of local intelligence units required a committee channel for exhibition and dissemination. Proud of their cloak-and-dagger achievements, the local sleuths lacked either the legal justification or the funds to make public the fruits of their labors. Their needs for a forum and publisher were complemented by the tactical propaganda and identification requirements of the pseudo-legislative mission. The committees swiftly recognized that the contributions of the local units were also indispensable to the achievement of their strategic objective: demonstrating that seemingly disparate local disruptions were the forerunners of a centrally directed revolutionary plot. In a hearing in 1970, SISS chief counsel Jay R. Sourwine described the subcommittee's goal in these words:

> We seek information with respect to the persons who head these subversive organizations and are active in them and who participate in them, the persons who support

*Romerstein's intelligence career is described below. Norusis was, as we have seen in Chapter 8, a gung-ho veteran of military intelligence in the Chicago area. He was hired by Romerstein because of his extensive contacts with federal, state, and local intelligence units, as well as with security officers and informers in Illinois colleges—"Ex-Army Spy Is GOP Sleuth Here," Chicago *Daily News,* Jan. 31, 1972.

them; about the interconnections, the channels of authority, and the sources of funds.

We are asking police departments from all across the country to sift their records and bring these facts here for the committee . . . by gathering all of the available information from leading police departments throughout the country, the committee hopes to be able eventually to present a picture. We are charting the organizations in each area, the persons in each area who are connected . . . and we hope when we finish we will have a picture which will show just what this country is up against.[21]

Initially, the hearings were based on the oral testimony of local police officers and supplemented by their submission of documents and photographs. But by the early seventies these testimonial exercises had produced a train of criticism of both the police target selections and methods, including at least three damage suits. To protect these now cautious sources, the committees made heavy use of the "staff study" format, based on interviews with police officers and their documents. The absorption of local police intelligence resources and styles explains the committees' obsession with the minute details of identification and the reproduction of photographs. The pseudo-legislative investigators plunged into an operating intelligence milieu in which trivia were invested with portentous significance. For example, HISC solemnly reproduced a photograph of the very watch used by an East German defector, undoubtedly the first subversive timepiece. The concreteness and specificity of information, however innocuous, about individuals were somehow seen to confirm their assumed dangerousness. In open alliance with their police sources, the committees laced their hearings with praise of the embattled intelligence establishment. In 1973–74 HISC issued a "study" and conducted lengthy hearings in support of the FBI's claim to internal security investigative authority.* Insisting that their political surveillance efforts had been misunderstood and unfairly criticized, HISC presented bouquets to the urban red squads.[22] SISS added its voice; in addition to a series of protective hearings, it maintained "almost daily liaison" with intelligence agencies throughout the country.[23]

Playing the Intelligence Game—Debriefing Informers

The pseudo-legislative process has always cherished informer witnesses. Their public disclosures stir cloak-and-dagger images of dangers surmounted and plotters outfoxed by courageous patriots. And what could be more credible than the revelations of the personal experiences of the witness himself? Over the years, the Bureau has made its surfaced informers available to the committees (because of the Senate Judiciary Committee's close ties with the Bureau through its chairman, Senator James Eastland, SISS was the prime beneficiary of the Bureau's favor). The absorption of informer debriefing into the pseudo-legisla-

---

*HISC's claimed authority to conduct the hearings was as dubious as its case for the FBI. It insisted that its charter conferred oversight authority to conduct the hearings, despite the fact that FBI oversight was an assigned responsibility of a subcommittee of the House Judiciary Committee.

tive process strengthened the committees' ties to the Bureau and provided a forum for informers already blown or seeking an official send-off for a planned book or lecture career.

The abandonment by HISC of the compulsory disclosure tactic—SISS had dropped it by the end of the fifties—and the scarcity of defectors from the depleted ranks of the Communists and the still inchoate New Left increased committee pressures for informers to deal with the special problems of the sixties. To supplement the limited Bureau supply, the search for informers broadened to the urban and state levels. Committee staff members scoured the intelligence community for prospects and, once arrangements were completed, conferred with them in debriefing sessions preparatory to appearances on the witness stand. But the committees went even further: they developed their own informer networks.

Among the informers who swarmed through the Labor Day 1967 National Conference for a New Politics was an SISS operative who broke into the conference office in Chicago's Palmer House. The informer rifled the organization's files and stole correspondence and documents mailed from the Mississippi Freedom Democratic Party (MFDP), whose offices were also entered. On September 22, 1967, Eastland made a speech on the floor of Congress describing the seized papers and entering a number of them in the *Congressional Record.* He reminded his colleagues:

> Since the early part of 1961, I have discussed publicly, from time to time, what I referred to in May of 1961, in a Senate speech, as the activities of provocateurs who have descended upon the Southern states in the name of so-called civil rights, but whose sole purpose was the stirring up of discord, strife, and violence. I have warned repeatedly that if such tactics were permitted to go forward in the South, they would be spread to other parts of the country when it suited the purposes of the Communist Party. Now we have seen these predictions borne out.[24]

Eastland denounced MFDP involvement in Mississippi politics as subversive, using as "documentation" a stolen card index, and charged that federally funded Mississippi anti-poverty groups were affiliated with "a national organization apparently infiltrated by the Communist movement." His proof consisted of a letter from a member of a Communist organization requesting an invitation to the conference. This "evidence" of subversion led him to the conclusion:

> We are approaching a crisis in this country, where it will be determined whether law and order is to triumph over revolution and anarchy, whether the black power is to be substituted either in the country as a whole or in any of our states for normal and peaceful processes; and whether the Communist Party, U.S.A., is to be permitted to grasp the reins of political power through the machinations of the National Conference for New Politics and other cooperating organizations.

When pressed to identify the agent who had obtained the documents for him, the senator kept his silence. His office insisted, "He doesn't have to divulge the names of his informants."

In the fall of 1971, HISC Congressman Roger H. Zion admitted to an investigator for National Educational Television that HISC had developed a spy network. One surfaced operative, Gerald Connolly, was recruited by Herbert

Romerstein in June 1970. Connolly—then a student at the John Jay College of Criminal Justice, a police training school in New York City—became an undercover agent for HISC through the efforts of Ruth I. Matthews, who introduced him to Romerstein. The broker in this transaction was a doyenne of right-wing circles and the widow of J. B. Matthews, a leading figure in the modern countersubversive tradition (discussed in the next chapter).

In early January 1969 Donald Meinshausen, a Young Americans for Freedom (YAF) activist at a New Jersey community college, made arrangements through the national leadership of YAF to meet spymaster Romerstein, who recruited him for undercover work on behalf of the committee, sealed by an assurance of generous expense payments in advance. In an interview with the author, Meinshausen explained that he received a short course in the rudiments of spying from Romerstein, who had acquainted himself with the art in order to act as the "case officer" for a number of HISC informers. Meinshausen was instructed "to try to find connections between SDS and the CP." The young agent repeatedly insisted that there wasn't too much connection between the SDS and the Communist Party, that the radical student group was primarily anarchist in character and rejected the dogmas of the traditional Old Left. But he was nevertheless told to persevere. Under Romerstein's directions, Meinshausen made a series of SDS penetrations, reporting back to Romerstein on a number of occasions and at various places in the New York area. Romerstein assured his young protégé that when his oral reports were entered in the HISC files, they would be so written that, as Meinshausen put it to me, "a person could not tell from looking at the conversation who was the informant and who wasn't."

Of all Meinshausen's numerous HISC-financed spying jaunts, the most important was his trip to the June 1969 SDS Chicago convention. After each convention session Meinshausen reported to Romerstein, who set up headquarters at a hotel suite where he received reports from a sizable group of HISC plants at the convention. In addition, Romerstein himself, together with local red squad agents, monitored the convention from a post on the outside and took photographs.

Romerstein told Meinshausen that no less than six committee staff members were running informers in leftist groups, but he was not allowed to meet them. However, "I was allowed to look at other persons' reports and I remember seeing about twenty or thirty just about the Chicago convention alone." Romerstein explained that the purpose of this duplication was to obtain verification of the reports by other informers. Romerstein would show him a report and ask: "Do you recognize any of the names here?" ("I freaked out," he recalled, "when I read my own name.")

At the end of July 1969 Meinshausen was called to Washington for an executive session with a committee staff member prior to his scheduled public appearance immediately thereafter as a witness. He was asked to identify certain documents that had been circulated at the convention, as well as film that was shown at the convention, and was led through a question and answer script. The process was highly selective: "Well, we went through everything I gave them and they said, 'Well, this is no good but we can use this' . . . like, you know, they would want statements on revolution, things like how a guy wants to learn instructions on how to make Molotov cocktails . . . it was all very heavily slanted. The guy who I was sort of coaching with was a former FBI agent."

The night before the hearing, Meinshausen drafted a statement condemning the committee. When he appeared the next day, the staffers learned of his change of mind and maneuvered him off the witness stand with a show of strong-arm tactics. Meinshausen then circulated his recanting statement, denouncing the committee to the press. The response was predictable. One committee spokesman darkly hinted that the statement had been drafted by some subversive Svengali and that HISC would have to reevaluate all of Meinshausen's earlier reports to determine the extent of this plot to defame the committee.

Meinshausen was recruited via the New Jersey state police, for whom he also performed undercover services. But the most promising informer source remained the Bureau, whose spies surfaced from time to time as witnesses in the Subversive Activities Control Board (SACB) proceedings. After appearing as a witness before the SACB, Gerald Wayne Kirk, an FBI informer, testified for two days before HISC in August 1959, in a hearing that was part of an extensive investigation of the SDS. The thrust of his testimony was that the Communists had exerted a subversive influence over the SDS—precisely what the committee wanted to hear, since its own hearings had indicated that the SDS had largely scorned the Communist Party as archaic and unresponsive to the needs of youth. In addition, in reply to detailed committee questions, he supplied the names of former associates in the Communist movement in the Chicago area. In March of the following year Kirk made a second appearance, this time for three days before SISS. His assurances in the course of his testimony of the continuing power of the Menace in New Left circles was considered so valuable as to warrant a press release by Senator James Eastland himself.*

The bulk of Kirk's testimony consists of a rerun of his earlier identification performance. The classic pseudo-legislative identification procedure calling only for names sharply contrasted with the new intelligence demands for ID-style descriptions. After initially furnishing a long list of names and descriptions of former associates, upon request to search his memory further, the witness supplied a supplementary list of names. He was then interrogated in this fashion as each name was mentioned:

MR. NORPEL: And what is the address for her?
MR. KIRK: [address given] in Chicago. It is the same as the first name I mentioned . . . [name given].

*The press release offered the Kirk testimony in refutation of "The commonly held belief that the Communist Party, USA has little influence in the New Left movement . . ." and an accompanying insertion reproduced a speech by Charles D. Brennan, Assistant Director of the Bureau in charge of the Domestic Intelligence Division, which also offers a comfort: "The old Left, the New Left, the pacifist element and the Black Nationalist groups [are] beginning to arise and going together. . . . The Communist elements [are] increasingly beginning to move in to play a more influential role in the leadership of the New Left [which has] unmistakably put itself into a revolutionary, Communist posture."—*Congressional Record,* Dec. 17, 1970, p. E 10461.

MR. NORPEL: How do you recall this particular woman?

MR. KIRK: I believe I met her in connection with some SDS people at the University of Chicago in one of those regular little sessions we usually had to talk over things.

MR. NORPEL: Would you describe her for us?

MR. KIRK: I hope it is the same person. I believe she was, oh, a bit medium to heavy-set, about five-four or five-five, black hair.

MR. NORPEL: Is she white?

MR. KIRK: White, yes.

MR. NORPEL: Female?

MR. KIRK: Female.

MR. NORPEL: What color of eyes, do you recall?

MR. KIRK: Dark brown or black, I believe, that is it.

MR. NORPEL: Did you only see this person once?

MR. KIRK: Yes, I remember the name though.

MR. NORPEL: How did the name come to your attention at that meeting?

MR. KIRK: She was introduced to me; I am sure there was a girl in Hyde Park. The one in question was connected politically with some SDS people. So I am going on that basis that it may very well be the same person.

When the witness could not recall any identifying characteristics, he was exhorted to try to do so after he left the stand and his memory was refreshed, so that the printed record would reflect the full identification.[25] With these descriptive identifications (which, apparently unknown to the witness, included at least one other Bureau infiltrator) completed, the witness was requested to identify a series of subjects from photographs.

Kirk was invited to give his views on a number of subjects. He disposed of the women's liberation movement by pointing out that it was "almost a carbon copy" of movements abroad that were Communist offshoots. Dr. Benjamin Spock, the anti-war activist and baby care authority, fared no better. Kirk recalled that "He used the terms peace and the terms revolution [sic] in a way that only a very sophisticated Marxist would use them. . . ." He might have deceived others in the audience, but Kirk went on: "To a person like me . . . he seemed to be speaking the kind of a code that Marxists use. . . ."[26] Shortly after he testified, Kirk joined a lecture team of surfaced informers sponsored by the John Birch Society.

The Life and Death of SISS

Like HISC, SISS tried to neutralize opposition by broadening the scope of its investigations. For example, in 1974 it published a massive study (over 400 pages) charging that marijuana traffic constituted an unprecedented threat to American security, an attempt by radical groups to sap our moral strength and power to resist subversion. (This theme of strength overcome by cunning conspirators is a stock feature of countersubversive nativism; SISS first explored the drug subversion scene in a series of hearings the year before and returned to it with publications in 1975.) But the hunt for fresh investigative subjects to replace its frayed hearings on communism intensified the problem of jurisdiction. Despite strenuous efforts to increase their legislative output, the committees' record dramatized the fact that the endless investigations lacked legislative purpose. In 1972 committee member Robert F. Drinan acidly noted that HISC had spent in excess of $11.5 million without producing any legislation and that its staff of fifty, including many among the highest-paid in Congress, exceeded all but six other standing committees. SISS, Senator Mark Hatfield observed in 1975, had spent more than $3 million over a six-year period, conducted only eight days of public hearings on legislative measures, and produced virtually no legislation.

The extravagance of supporting large unproductive staffs was in part explained by the fact that the committees offered haven and sustenance for a corps of intelligence types, an old boy network of anti-Communist bureaucrats. The key personnel of both committees typically consisted of former Bureau agents (frequently retirees); the lower echelons were staffed by recruits from police units, service organizations (Veterans of Foreign Wars and the American Legion), ultra-rightist supporters, and, in the early years, Communist defectors. The countersubversive personnel traffic is illustrated by the career of Louis Russell, who left the Bureau to become chief HUAC investigator and, in his retirement, was employed by James McCord, who was in charge of intelligence work for the Committee to Re-Elect the President (CREEP) (although Russell was never involved in any Watergate-related activities). The committee's man in the State Department was Otto F. Otepka, another countersubversive giant. Otepka, a security investigator, was originally dismissed from his State Department post in 1963 for passing classified documents to SISS without authorization. After prolonged departmental hearings, he was, in 1967, reprimanded and demoted by Secretary of State Dean Rusk. In the meantime he became a *cause célèbre* in right-wing circles, in large part because of SISS drumbeating in more than 3000 pages of hearings that stretched from 1963 to 1965. In January 1969 the Senate approved his appointment by President Nixon to the Subversive Activities Control Board (SACB) at a salary of $36,000, more than double that of his last State Department job.[27] After the SACB folded, Otepka became a lecturer on the far right countersubversive circuit. SISS also developed close ties with the Passport Division's Frances Knight, and when her policies and authority were challenged, she too sought protection from SISS.[28]

Busy senators could hardly be expected to run SISS and keep track of its many operations. The heart of the SISS machine was a staffer, Jay R. Sourwine. A former Reno, Nevada, newspaperman and protégé of Judiciary Committee Chairman Senator Patrick McCarran (who founded SISS), Sourwine became famous in the fifties as the Capitol's outstanding red hunter; his power earned him in some quarters the title the "97th Senator."* Sourwine's abrasive interro-

---

*His HUAC counterpart was for a time Richard Arens. Like Sourwine, Arens discharged his responsibilities in an intensely personalized style, most evident in his treatment of lawyers for uncooperative witnesses. But in 1961, Arens was banished (his sponsors took care of him with a judgeship) when it became known that he was a paid consultant for the Draper Foundation, organized to demonstrate the biological inferiority of blacks. HUAC Chairman Francis Walter and SISS Chairman James Eastland also served on Draper Foundation committees.

gations terrified witnesses, but his trademark was his scorn for legal niceties. His credits (if that is the word for it) include collaboration with Roy Cohn in the UN employees case discussed in the previous chapter; a long-running investigation of the Institute of Pacific Relations spearheaded by an illegal raid; an attack on newspaper reporters in the New York City area; the sponsorship and dissemination of a document (he hailed it as a "work of some scholarship") denouncing the Supreme Court as "an instrument of Communist global conquest"; and the master-minding of the face-saving attempt to rescue the credibility of SISS testimony from a recanting informer, Harvey M. Matusow, who repudiated his earlier performance on the witness stand as a collection of lies. At the close of his long career, Sourwine reportedly made use of his extensive contacts with FBI and CIA sources to gain access to materials he published as the work of his own staff. In a farewell statement, he warned that the Communists were conspiring to dominate the world and that subversion still stalked the nation's Capitol and threatened its security.[29]

Despite its dim record, SISS never generated the kind of opposition encountered by HISC. The explanation for its seemingly charmed life begins with its early adoption of a relatively discreet, nonconfrontationist style, which reduced court challenges by hostile witnesses. As a subcommittee of a powerful committee of the Senate, it enjoyed multi-layered protection and, in any event, few senators were prepared to make an issue of its abuses. To defuse potential criticism, the panel's chairmen tactfully acceded to discreet pleas of their colleagues on behalf of prominent constituents. Beyond this, SISS benefited from the principle of comparative legitimacy: Senator McCarthy's committee gave it a "right way" cachet even among Senate liberals.[30] But after HISC (another wrong way foil) was abolished, the hard rain began falling on SISS. It responded to a proposal to reorganize it out of existence by distributing on Capitol Hill a special confidential edition of committee testimony, "Hostage Defense Measures," to provide legislators with guidance in the event they were kidnapped by terrorists. Apart from the remoteness of this contingency, the document merely repeated advice the State Department had for some time made available to possible kidnap victims. It was extracted from lengthy hearings in 1975–76, chaired by South Carolina Senator Strom Thurmond, which aired charges that the domestic intelligence system was under attack by a subversive conspiracy to render the entire national helpless to cope with disorders such as terrorism. A star witness was again the defector Phillip A. Luce, who, as in his HISC performance eight years earlier, insisted that terrorism is an ideological component of Marxist communism and that the Communist abstention from violence was merely a tactic to be abandoned when the time was ripe. The witnesses included police functionaries from cities (Chicago, Los Angeles) where the classic countersubversive style dominates the police response to disorders; Georgia Congressman Larry McDonald, whose activities are explored in the next chapter; and Francis J. McNamara, still another old guard zealot. A veteran of World War II military intelligence, a former national director of the VFW anti-Communist program, editor of *Counterattack* (a blacklisting service of the fifties), HUAC staff aide in 1958 and staff director from 1961 until 1969, McNamara ended his career in the countersubversive bureaucracy as executive secretary of the Subversive Activities Control Board from 1970 to 1973.

SISS commissioned a special report on terrorism from Herbert Romerstein, one-time member of a Communist youth group who had spent all of his adult life in the anti-Communist trenches, including a long stint as a HUAC staffer, followed by service as chief investigator and spymaster for the HISC Republican minority. When HISC fell, he became for a time a consultant to the Friends of the FBI, a Chicago-based group headed by Efrem Zimbalist, Jr., star of the television series "The FBI," then returned to his former haunts on the Hill as an aide to Congressman Larry McDonald, and ultimately joined the minority staff of the newly organized House Select Committee on Intelligence as aide to committee member John Ashbrook, his former sponsor at HISC.[31]

But the terrorist theme and variations brought SISS no closer to reprieve. A more promising opportunity was presented by planned leftist activities in connection with the Bicentennial celebrations in Philadelphia and Washington. In May 1976 SISS issued a lurid report seeking to exploit outraged patriotism, "The Attempt to Steal the Bicentennial," charging two groups, the People's Bicentennial Commission (PBC) and the July 4 Coalition, with subversive designs on the celebrations. It returned to the attack with a series of hearings in which Dr. William R. Kintner, both an HISC and SISS favorite witness, charged in a lengthy statement that the July 4 Coalition was "commanded" by a Weatherman "support group"* and the terrorist Puerto Rican Armed Forces of National Liberation (FALN). SISS rushed a release to the press detailing his wholly inaccurate testimony and that of Philadelphia red squad chief, Inspector George Fencl, which more cautiously warned of a "potential" for violence. A third witness, a Washington, D.C., police officer, referred to reports of planned disruptions and attributed an admitted lack of "hard intelligence" to the restraints imposed on the police intelligence function. On June 28 a group of senators pleaded on the Senate floor for the preservation of SISS, while on the House side, Congressman McDonald inserted in the *Congressional Record* the first of a three-part series of intelligence reports on the radical plot to disrupt the Bicentennial.[32] In the meantime, a White House informal task force was authorized "to co-ordinate counter-terrorist activities." The July 4 Coalition—a loose confederation of 200 organizations, including church groups—was targeted in a special FBI investigation, and Philadelphia Mayor Frank A. Rizzo requested 15,000 troops to monitor a second planned demonstration by radicals in Philadelphia. The Bureau inquiry failed to turn up evidence of planned violence and the troop request was rejected. The SISS alarm—its first and last venture into predictive intelligence—proved false: all the counter-rallies (two in Philadelphia and one in Washington) were peaceful and orderly.[33]

In March 1977 SISS was finally forced to close up shop. Its functions were continued on an ad hoc basis by a subcommittee headed by Senator James O. Eastland. As a last hurrah before Eastland's retirement, the subcommittee

---

*Today this term, with its sinister, intelligence-related overtones, serves much the same purpose in justifying surveillance as did "front" in the forties and fifties.

issued a lengthy report in December 1978 on *The Erosion of Law Enforcement Intelligence and Its Impact on Public Security,* intended as a resource for embattled domestic intelligence units.

Pseudo-Legislative Indices and Files

The investigative activities described in this chapter proclaim quite clearly that the countersubversive committees functioned as intelligence agencies under a legislative cover. This conclusion is independently established by the committees' indexing and filing practices.[34] Every document published by the committees—hearings, studies, annual reports—is indexed, but in a peculiar way: the only information supplied is a list of names (first of individuals mentioned, then of organizations and publications). No guide at all is offered to substantive content; the index tells us nothing about the topics dealt with (trade unionism, violence, prison unrest, government employment, urban riots), events, dates, places mentioned, or the like—the range one finds in a conventional index. However, if the reader is kept completely in the dark about "what, when, and where," he is dazzled by the glaring searchlight on "who."

In addition, no matter how extensive and multi-volumed a hearing, every volume is published serially and separately "indexed." The object is to make the publication available as quickly and in as useful a format as possible. Congress obviously has no legislative need for a listing of all the names mentioned in a committee hearing even at some future time, let alone at the time of publication of each hearing volume. But why should the consumers of the committees' wares in the private sector have to wait until an entire investigation is concluded when they could be using an index of each hearing as it is published?

Yet this does not complete the description of the pseudo-index apparatus. It would be most inconvenient if a search for a subject's political background required an examination of individual indices appended to a long series of volumes of hearings, studies, and reports. The committees expedited the search by means of a "cumulative index." The first of these documents was "Cumulative Index of the Committee on Un-American Activities, 1938–1954." This compilation, which includes the Dies Committee years, was itself a consolidation of five earlier indices. It was followed by seven biennial supplements, all in turn replaced by a 1000-page consolidated supplement, covering the years from 1955 to 1968. Like its component indices, the 1938–54 volumes and its 1955–68 supplement are lists of names (more than 100,000) of individuals and organizations. A second update covering the HISC years was in preparation when the ax fell.

In 1971 SISS published a super-index, a "Combined Cumulative Index to Publications and Reports, 1951–1971," a two-volume, 1685-page giant. Like its HISC counterpart, it is a torrent of names, the quick and the dead: Chiang Kai-shek alone generates two-and-a-half closely printed pages of references. According to SISS, its 21-year index contains a total of 62,705 different page references and consolidates 3 previous cumulative indices. The compilation of this super-index was, SISS tells us, "a tedious job but the advantage of being able to find all entries under one letter is obvious."* A 1976 supplement covering 1972 to 1975 was issued shortly before SISS went out of business.

The pseudo-legislative committees never bothered to illuminate the relevance of the indices, why Congress had a need to identify the politics of particular individuals who testified or were mentioned at a hearing more than a generation ago. All the indices are prefaced by a caveat that no reference is to be drawn from a mere index entry without a reference check. This concern is explained by the fact that the indices ecumenically list *every* name mentioned in the hearing or report. Such impartiality—lumping John Doe and Richard Doe with Dwight Eisenhower and Christopher Marlowe—hardly serves to make the index less useful to the patrioteers, blacklisters, security services, and other components of the countersubversive constituency. As a supplement to its massive indices, the HISC published "Guide to Subversive Organizations and Publications," which continued to circulate in the sixties despite the fact that most of the groups and publications listed had become defunct.

HISC also maintained a separate internal index to serve its huge file collection, comprising over 750,000 reference cards, the responsibility of the HISC File and Reference Service (its official title), which collected and processed bales of material—flyers, letterheads, conference calls, mailing lists, legal briefs—on a range of intelligence targets. In addition to this assertedly "public source" collection, a separate investigative file system was also maintained, which included dossiers on congressmen. These were eliminated when the committee fell under attack.†

Summaries of the files were on request prepared and transmitted to members of the House and Senate ("as a courtesy"). In addition, such dossiers and reports were made available directly to "private individuals" who had "a sincere and genuine need for information of a type such as is available here." Disseminations were, like the indices, prefaced by a "right way" disclaimer to the effect that the committee made no evaluation but merely offered as a convenience the "recorded public material" about the subject. The information set forth was not to be construed as an indication that the subject was subversive, "unless specifically stated." In addition, HISC Chairman Ichord assured Congress that the staff, when compiling a subject's "record of subversive activities," also took note of his "opposition to communism or some other forms of subversion . . . or any known statement which may serve to clarify his record."

Like HISC, SISS also developed a file and dossier collection and a dissemination capability. When the file collection of Major General Ralph Van Deman, which the Army had acquired after Van Deman's death in 1952, became an

---

Annual Report (FY, 1973), p. 30. It should be further noted that the usefulness of a quick reference source to identify subversives did not escape other legislators identified with policies of countersubversion. In 1956 Senator John L. McClellan's Senate Committee on Government Operations published a "Summary-Index" of all "Congressional Investigations of Communism and Subversive Activities" not confined to HUAC and SISS; its index to individuals alone runs to seventy columns of names.

†Republican committee member Roger Zion, in the interview already referred to, complained: "We have members of Congress on whom we had rather extensive files and the files have disappeared." He thought this a reprehensible lapse in "the government's responsibility in keeping them [officeholders or candidates] under surveillance and watching [their] activities." Zion charged the Democrats with thus endangering national security.

embarrassment as a result of a congressional investigation, the Army turned to SISS. By prearrangement SISS Chairman Eastland in 1972 formally requested the records. "They were examined," Eastland reported, "and found pertinent and germaine [sic] to the subcommittee's purpose."[35] This, despite the fact that the files antedated the launching of SISS in 1951. Copies of dossiers from committee file collections—now sequestered—have turned up in the files of police intelligence units, presumably the fruits of past liaison arrangements. And the network of private groups and lobbies—those with "sincere need"—were, long before the doors were closed, granted access to the committees' file resources to continue in the private sector the politics of deferred reckoning.

As in the case of the FBI, the compilation and dissemination of dossiers played an important role in the final assault on the committees, especially HISC. Perhaps even more effective ammunition was the dismal cost-legislative benefit ratio that marks the operations of both committees. These issues—the invasion of privacy and the waste of tax dollars—enabled legislators to minimize the political risks of clashing with anti-Communist constituencies. This is not to say that both houses did not harbor members fed up with the basic abuses of the pseudo-legislative process: red baiting, personalized investigations, and repressive propaganda. But most of them were of the closet variety, finally induced to emerge by a changing climate, a post-Watergate reaction to the use of extra-legal sanctions against individuals, and the realization that pseudo-legislative investigation is a bulwark of the status quo. While overshadowed by the more dramatic operations of the FBI, the pseudo-legislative process functioning continuously over four decades has more effectively handicapped movements for change in this country than any other component of the American intelligence apparatus. Its effectiveness and duration are tributes to the hold of countersubversion on American life.

12 Countersubversive Intelligence in the Private Sector

Nativist Roots

A pattern of support and collaboration between government and private intelligence forces dominates the history of radical-hunting in this country. The values and priorities of American nativism have decisively influenced both official and private intelligence activities. As a vital ideological resource of American capitalism, nativism has kept the countersubversive tradition burning by continuing and enlarging its own private intelligence activities. At a time when established governmental systems for monitoring subversion have been cut back, these private countersubversive operations acquire special importance; they must continue the data collection and storage practices formerly shared with government agencies, intensify their propaganda efforts, and—a new mission—promote renewed official involvement in surveillance and related activities directed against dissent.

Beginning in 1918, private intelligence forces emerged to combat radicalism, labor unionism, and opposition to the war. Government agents on all levels worked with corporate officials, labor spies, super-patriots, amateur detectives, and assorted vigilantes in infiltration, provocation, raids, and the dissemination of propaganda. The leading groups became Bureau insiders, proclaiming the achievements of Chief Burns in saving the country from bloody revolution. The National Civic Federation even helped Burns raise money to finance a state prosecution of Communists. In return, the patrioteers and their allies were given access to radical literature seized in raids by official police agencies. For example, the documents seized in a 1922 raid of a Communist Party convention, at Bridgman, Michigan, were exclusively made available by Bureau Chief Burns to R. M. Whitney, of the American Defense Society, and together with other material from confidential Department of Justice files formed the basis for his pioneering compilation, *The Reds in America.* Patrioteering, vigilante-style contingents enjoyed official recognition from both the Department of Justice and the Army. The American Protective League (APL) and similar groups viewed themselves as a "counter-espionage corps" with a mission to ferret out the nation's domestic enemies. The officially promoted vigilantism of the World War I era spawned stereotypes of subversion that permanently gripped the American imagination; the drab reality of a frustrated and repressed radicalism was replaced with images of planned ferocity. These images, in turn, legitimated surveillance and self-help by private citizens as indispensable defensive measures.*

But resistance to radicalism was not confined to amateur sleuths and vigilantes inspired by ideology and patriotism. Private detective agencies formed the core of the extra-legal assault. The transplanting to the United States of revolutionary ideologies and the need to contain the growing labor force presented problems to American capitalism that were beyond the scope and jurisdiction of the local police. In contrast to the European police system, under which political investigation and law enforcement were consolidated into centralized national institutions closely linked to the exercise of power, American police arrangements have been characteristically local and restrained by peacekeeping functions. To fill the need for a professional-style response to movements for change that were not in violation of law, private detective agencies, independent bodies of investigators for hire, emerged equipped with techniques of surveillance, impersonation, deception, infiltration, and dossier keeping, borrowed from their official European counterparts.

This peculiarly American phenomenon ("Pinkertonism") was nurtured from the 1870s on by the fear of the social and political unrest that accompanied economic dislocation and depression. Its principal stimulus was the drive by American industry to combat labor organization. Labor espionage, its principal tool, was initially justified as a protection of private property, but it soon acquired a more compelling sanction as a safeguard against radicalism and revolutionary violence. The need to link labor unions and their organizers with revolution brought the private detectives into the political intelligence field. Large corporations, industrial and trade associations, developed their own surveillance and blacklist capabilities. In many cases detectives recruited for surveillance and espionage by particular industries ("Coal and Iron police," "Railroad police," and similar units) were commissioned and clothed with official authority. Following the lead of the amateur volunteers, the private agencies

---

*An illuminating account of the information flow between the public and private sectors is supplied in Senate testimony by a military intelligence officer dealing with preparation for the 1919 steel strike:

> Information comes to us from various sources, all sorts of information, and we try to file, index it and give it to the proper authorities. Information of that sort came to us from Gary . . . away back in March or April at which time the so-called Reds were planning a nationwide strike in order to free political prisoners.
>
> When we arrived in Gary, we found that the sheriff had sworn in a great many deputies and that he was running a little intelligence office of his own; and the Loyal Americans' League, composed of citizens who were either deputy sheriffs or special policemen—I believe to a man —also had a little intelligence service of its own. So did the American Legion. They were all of them lined up on this Red proposition and had a mass of information—"Report of Committee on Education and Labor, U.S. Senate Investigation of Strike in Steel Industry," 66th Cong., 1st Sess. (1919), p. 911.

developed what Louis F. Post called "cooperative arrangements with local police officials."[1] This partnership was particularly pronounced in the labor field, where an intermingling of personnel was not uncommon. For example, William Hynes, head of the Los Angeles "Red Squad," took a leave of absence in 1934 to work as a guard and strikebreaker for private employers. Private detectives paid the police for information, and "cooperated" with them by performing illegal services in exchange for immunity from prosecution. Undercover agents sometimes reported both to their private clients and to the police. And the expanding detective agencies regularly recruited cadres from police ranks and indeed used job offers as a bribe to obtain access to confidential information.

The involvement of career personnel with some claim to professionalism in political surveillance did not reduce the hysterical quality of the radical hunt. The private agencies deliberately took an overheated view of the Menace because it was good for business. The operatives for hire sold their services by grossly exaggerating the machinations of the "labor agitators" and the "radical element," or by deliberately provoking violence. (See Chapter 3.) The agencies performed another function: they offered career opportunities to military personnel who, after every war, seek private employment in intelligence specialties acquired in military conflict.

The File Mystique

Private political interests form both the clients and the constituency of the official intelligence community. The connection is not merely ideological; it is functional in the sense that the collection of material and the development of files dealing with subversive individuals and groups is the basic *modus operandi* of rightist countersubversive organizations—what they routinely do and instruct members to do. Indeed, the history of private intelligence institutions in this country may be charted by tracing the accumulation and transfer of file collections. Maintaining a file on a particular subject serves two purposes: (1) the collection and consolidation of material in order to maximize the subversive character of the subject, whether an individual or an organization; and (2) identification for aggressive purposes, the compilation of an "enemies list" for adverse present action, and as targets in the eschatological politics of deferred reckoning. The filing imperatively reflects the deeply rooted conviction that the enemy is a conspiracy of real people, cunning deceivers who must first be identified, then cornered, and ultimately destroyed. The mere act of opening a countersubversive file on a subject is an exercise of power, an outlet for hostile emotion and intention. File work also has an objective, political dimension. It fortifies resistance to change by linking it to governmental overthrow and social disruption. In this respect, it distills the essentially negative quality of American conservatism, which typically seeks to generate political energy by attacking measures that threaten the status quo without submitting its own premises to the test of the democratic process.

American conservatism—especially its more rigid versions—cannot, in short, make an affirmative politics out of its professed political and economic values. To escape this dilemma, it concentrates on social and moral issues, and invites approval as a defense against threats to values more precious than materialistic self-interest. The exploitation of fear is the leitmotif of this political strategy; and the great fear—the one that enfolds all of the other threats to the nation, society, family, and the self, and is hence most effective in influencing political behavior—is subversion. But this politics of fear cannot be supported by rhetoric alone: it must be fueled by a supply of identifiable people, the source of the threat. This need explains the prominence of procedures for identifying and labeling individuals through intelligence procedures such as the pseudo-legislative process. Indeed, because American countersubversion has developed such a boundless demand for file subjects and dossiers, information of this kind has become, so to speak, "commodified," a marketable product that can be sold, despite its seemingly perishable character. And its value depends not only on its quantity but its quality, that is, the extent to which it is based on surveillance and related sources not accessible to the public.

Blacklisting for anti-labor purposes was the chief inspiration for the file mania. The most extensive file collection of the twenties and thirties was assembled by Chicagoan Harry A. Jung's American Vigilant Intelligence Foundation. Jung commenced his operations as a labor spymaster for a trade association, National Clay Products Industries. In the thirties he expanded the files, developed through a network of informers, into a well-paying confidential service, which he sold to banks, industry, and the frightened rich. He also used his files as "documentation" for his anti-Semitic Fascist-style publication, *The Vigilante.* In the fifties he found a new supply of patrons to subsidize the enlargement of his files, which he ultimately sold to the American Security Council.[2]

The publication of file material in the competition to influence political policy began with the R. M. Whitney American Defense Society publication already referred to. It was updated by Elizabeth Dilling's *Red Network.* First published in 1934, it became an overnight success. Its 350 closely printed pages list 460 "Communist, Anarchist, Socialist, I.W.W. or Radical-Pacifist-controlled organizations," plus the names of 1300 individuals who "knowingly or unknowingly have contributed in some measure to one or more phases of the Red movement in the United States." The effectiveness of exploiting the Menace in fighting the New Deal led to the subsequent publication of Dilling's *Roosevelt's Red Record,* an equally detailed compendium of dossiers. Both publications were based primarily on letterheads of organizations and the reports of the New York State Lusk Committee and the Fish Committee.

During the cold war years the collection and filing of information about the political affiliations and personal lives of liberals and radicals became standard operating procedure not only in the traditional far right but in conservative circles generally. In 1948 the United States Chamber of Commerce published an elaborate "Program for Community Anti-Communist Action," which included instructions for the development and maintenance of a file collection of individual dossiers for use in eradicating Communist influence. Military intelligence also contributed to the development of a civilian network of file collections. After former military intelligence chief Major General Ralph H. Van Deman retired in 1929, he established his data collection and processing facility in San Diego with the support of the Army, which paid for two civilian assistants, his filing cabinets, and working materials.

When the general died in 1952, he had earned a reputation as one of the giants of anti-communism, a super-hawk, tireless in his warnings against subversive conspirators. And his files were legendary. He ran an undercover network that reportedly penetrated not only the Communist Party but a whole spectrum of liberal targets, including religious, civil rights, and labor organizations. The files include a huge photographic collection of subjects and also of the general's own agents. Van Deman's public utterances and lectures to anti-Communist seminars revealed him as a phobic nativist red hunter, equipped with all the prejudices of the breed: racism, anti-unionism, anti-liberalism, anti-intellectualism, and anti-Semitism. The collection contains files on prominent politicians, actors, writers, educators, from Pearl Buck to Linus Pauling. Included in the gallery of subversives is former Chairman Emanuel Celler of the House Judiciary Committee, whose dossier characterizes him as a "Jew playing the Reds." In transferring the collection to SISS, the Army understandably concluded: "There may be some embarrassment to the Army because of the information contained on labor and civil rights movements. The question of the Army's relationship to Van Deman could also be embarrassing."[3] There was another source of embarrassment. Only a portion of Van Deman's archives had been transferred to the Army in 1952. There remained in San Diego a forest of files and documents in the custody of the "San Diego Research Library," organized by three former Van Deman associates, two National Guard officers, and a local businessman. The library, supported in part by the state of California as a National Guard project and in part by a group of employers, and housed in the San Diego National Guard Armory, was used to screen individuals for public employment as well as private industry. It regularly exchanged material with federal and state intelligence agencies (including the McCarthy Committee) and accumulated confidential data from volunteer informers as well as clippings from the press and left-wing publications.[4]

In December of 1961 the intelligence functions of the National Guard were deactivated. And in February 1962 the files were seized from the San Diego Armory on the orders of Major General Roderic Hill, state adjutant general, on the ground that they had been used by "unauthorized persons for political purposes."* The confiscation of the files triggered a lawsuit by the library's president, a retired National Guard general, who demanded the return of the files and $320,000 damages. The case became a rallying cry for the right wing: the plaintiffs insisted that the files were the private property of the research library, that they were housed in the Armory by permission of the proper authorities, and that in exchange for the use of the space, the library had

---

*The seizure was sparked by a complaint of San Diego State Senator Hugo Fisher that in the 1958 election campaign a Republican opponent had tried to smear him with the aid of material from the library indicating that Fisher had been seen in the company of a "known Communist," had been an ACLU member, and had once debated the issue of whether the FBI was abusing the rights of citizens. Fisher won the election, but he and others in the Democratic administration feared that the files would again be used as smear material by right-wing Republicans in the upcoming 1962 elections.

provided clearance information to public officials, including the proposed appointees of three governors, Warren, Knight, and Brown. The library's lawyers also argued that its director, Colonel Frank Forward, ran the library in his private capacity, not as commander of counterintelligence of the National Guard Reserve, and that the library's upkeep between 1952 and 1962 had been partially funded by private contributions. The state's version was that the files were public property, that they had been compiled by various National Guard units, housed by the state under the supervision of a National Guard functionary (Forward), and that the state had paid for the file cabinets, index cards, boxes, folders, stationery, and telephone bills. When the smoke cleared away, it became apparent that an intelligence facility (more than 200,000 files) initially supported by the Army and later jointly by the state and private employers as a screening and blacklisting aid, flourished in the favorable political climate of southern California for over thirty years.*[5]

File collections and dossiers became an indispensable weapon of fundamentalist churches in dealing with their liberal adversaries. Thus a special issue of *THINK,* a student organ of Christian Patriots, Inc., devoted to "Filing Suggestions for Conservatives," reminded its readers that, "Among re-awakened Americans, one of the most neglected needs is an adequate filing system. . . ."[6] A more substantial group, Circuit Riders, Inc., specialized in the publication for reference use of the records of liberals and leftists—notably clergymen. Its publications include the following dossier collections:

2109 Methodist Ministers

1411 Protestant Episcopal Rectors

660 Baptist Clergymen

614 Presbyterian U.S.A. Clergymen

42 percent of the Unitarian Clergymen

6000 Educators (Vol. I)

658 Clergymen and Laymen connected with the National Council of Churches

In order to meet the competition, to provide research material for his followers as well as "documentation" for sermons and polemics, Billie James Hargis in the early sixties purchased for his Christian Crusade the anti-Communist files (30,000 subjects) and library of Allen A. Zoll, an anti-Semitic demagogue prominent in the thirties.

The cold war and the McCarthy eras saw a growing use of file resources for punitive purposes against nonindustrial personnel. A pioneer in the field was the American Business Consultants (ABC). Organized by three former FBI agents in May of 1947, it offered clearance services to the East Coast entertainment industry. Its modest goal was to stimulate voluntary sanctions against

---

*While the San Diego battle raged, a separate brouhaha was stirred by charges that Major Robert Backus of the California National Guard Reserve had attempted to organize an informer network to penetrate industry and foil saboteurs. The major admitted the charge but insisted that he was acting without official authorization—Los Angeles *Times,* March 10, 1962.

subversives and fifth columnists because government action had proved ineffective. To develop a favorable climate for its operation, it published a newsletter, *Counterattack,* and to stimulate sanctions against prominent targets, a manual, *Red Channels: Report of Communist Influence in Radio and Television,* which became a desk reference source for industry executives, advertising agencies, and their clients.[7] ABC's "consultant" functions were inherited by Vince Hartnett, a freelance who from 1952 until 1956 worked, according to his own description, as "a professional consultant on the Communist front records of persons working in the entertainment industry."[8]

The Documented Exposé

Counterattack was the forerunner of a new countersubversive genre that flourished in the fifties and throughout the sixties, the "exposé" of individual targets. The exposé is a form of action in the soft, an interim incitement to a deserved injury pending an ultimate eschatological accounting. Its primary purpose is to discredit the target and to injure him or her personally—frequently the address and sometimes the telephone number of the target is supplied—by generating community and employment sanctions. From established file collections and new intelligence sources, a stream of newsletters and broadsides (*Combat, Heads-Up, Tocsin, Facts for Action, Herald of Freedom,* to name a few of the prominent ones) emerged to carry the exposé message to a right-wing constituency.

While the exposé draws on a variety of sources, including letterheads, advertisements, briefs, its bedrock is the oeuvre of the anti-subversive committees. Beginning with the Lusk Committee Hearings and Report of 1920 ("Revolutionary Radicalism"), nativism has drawn sustenance from the pseudo-legislative mode. HISC and SISS improved on past practices by specifically gearing target selection, hearings, and index formats to the needs of the exposé market. The pseudo-legislative process consciously became nativism's friend at court, ready to provide the bullets needed to attack its enemies. The exposé thus emerged as a means of implementing the hostility of government intelligence agencies, leashed by official constraints; and in performing this service, nativism was transformed from an outsider into an insider.

Use of committee publications enables the nativist to claim that his intelligence product is not based on prejudice or rumor but is a "documented exposé," based on an official publication. The cachet of documentation, which serves to justify an attack on an "identified" (a talismanic usage) subversive, is then borrowed to authenticate the structure of inferences used to expand the attack.* Indeed, the mountains of government publications on subversive themes enables countersubversion to preen itself on its scholarship. For example, Stoner's *None*

---

*For example, Frank Capell's *Herald of Freedom* once published an exposé of George Ball, a State Department Under-Secretary under President Johnson, which "proved" his subversiveness by a chain of evidence which included the fact that his former law partner was at one time a member of the board of directors of a publication, the wife of whose editor was once a law partner of an "identified Communist."

Dare Call It Treason (a 7-million-copy best seller) boasts 819 footnotes, most of them based on government publications.*

The exposé in its modern form is the legacy of Joseph B. Matthews. Matthews blazed the exposure trail by his ingenuity in weaving seemingly disconnected and innocent political activities into a "case" of subversion.[9] A former radical and clergyman, Matthews made his debut as a witness before the Dies Committee in August 1938. It was in the course of this testimony that he charged that "Shirley Temple . . . unwittingly served the purposes of the Communist Party."†[10]

Shortly after his appearance, Matthews became the committee's chief investigator and served until 1945. In this role he was primarily responsible for the famous Appendix IX, a 2000-page, 7-volume collection of material prepared in the closing days of 1944 by a subcommittee of the Dies Committee for the claimed purpose of preserving the committee's files against their anticipated destruction with the expiration of its mandate the next year. With its prodigious listings of subversive organizations and individuals, Appendix IX laid the foundation—in both its political assumptions (the equating of dissent and subversion) and its methodology (guilt by association)—for the "documented exposé." Its descriptions of hundreds of organizations and index of some 22,000 names, together with exhibits drawn from the committee's files, made Appendix IX a prime intelligence resource, the *vade mecum* of political sleuths, anti-subversive experts, and blacklisters. Originally published in an edition of 7000 copies, the hastily compiled set proved to be too rich for the committee's blood and it was suppressed. But some copies had already been sold and others distributed to government agencies. In a short time, the Appendix became the most important single asset of the dossier trade, a "documentary" treasure.

It was reissued in 1963 by California Contemporary Classics of Los Angeles and is widely advertised in the right-wing press. When Matthews (known as "J.B." in right-wing circles) left the Dies Committee in 1945, he enriched and refined the art by building, on the foundation of Appendix IX, a unique collection of files that he used as a basis for lectures and as a reference source for the dossier trade. He became the Pope of anti-subversion.

When Robert Welch founded the John Birch Society in 1958, he warned that it would not be easy to ferret out the cunning subversives. "One of the hardest things for the decent American to realize is that a secret Communist looks and

---

*Richard Hofstadter, in *The Paranoid Style in American Politics* (Knopf, 1965), comments that rightist literature "is nothing if not 'scholarly' in technique. McCarthy's 96-page pamphlet, *McCarthyism,* contains no less than 313 footnote references, and Mr. Welch's fantastic assault on Eisenhower, *The Politician,* is weighed down by a hundred pages of bibliography and notes. The entire right-wing movement of our time is a parade of experts, study groups, monographs, footnotes and bibliographies" (p. 26). Similar right-wing works dense with "documentation" are Phyllis Schlafly, *A Choice Not an Echo* (Pere Marquette Press, 1964), and J. Evetts Haley, *A Texan Looks at Lyndon* (Palo Duro Press, 1964).

†Matthews stood on the shoulders of an earlier witness, Walter S. Steele, editor of the *National Republic* and chairman of the American Coalition of Patriotic Societies. This grand master of dossiers boasted prodigious files fed by a variety of sources: "red squads, detective agencies; defectors and informers." In his two days of testimony he listed no less than 640 subversive organizations, including the ACLU, the CIO, all pacifist organizations, a number of Catholic groups, and even the Boy Scouts and Campfire Girls—*Dies Committee Hearings,* pp. 278, 428, 455, 706.

acts like anybody else. One needs not only experience," the founder explained, but a "feel for the way a Communist works." Welch was certain of his own "feel" because his conclusions consistently echoed Matthews's. "And of course I also have the benefit of J.B.'s files, almost incredible memory and judgment built out of long experience."

The nation was offered a sample of Matthews's *modus operandi* in an article he wrote for the *American Mercury* magazine in 1953 on "The Reds and Our Churches," which asserted that 7000 Protestant churches had served what he called the "Kremlin conspiracy." The article charged that "The largest single group supporting the Communist apparatus in the United States is composed of Protestant clergymen." Protests from clergymen, in which President Eisenhower joined, forced Matthews's resignation as executive director of Senator McCarthy's investigative subcommittee after only eighteen days of service. Matthews died in July 1966; his wife carried on his work as co-editor of the right-wing newsletter *Combat,* published by William F. Buckley's *National Review.*

The Big Two

The twin pillars of the private countersubversive establishment are the Church League of America (CLA) and the American Security Council (ASC), the former an outgrowth of the jihad of fundamentalism against the National Council of Churches and the Christian modernist movement, and the latter of the response to labor unionism, welfare state liberalism, and peace movements.[11] Headed by Edgar C. Bundy, a former Air Force intelligence officer and ordained Baptist minister, the CLA boasts that its countersubversive file collection, with 7 million index cards, is "the most reliable, comprehensive and complete, second only to those of the FBI."[12] This collection, based on the original contribution of the files assembled by ultra-rightist George Washington Robnett, became the core of a major intelligence enterprise as it expanded over the years. The growth is attributable in part to the efforts and prestige of Matthews, who served as CLA's research director and consultant in his last years. After his death, the CLA acquired his file collection, as well as compilations from exposé operations such as *Tocsin* and ABC, which were forced by libel suits to abandon ship.[13]

In 1968, Bundy realized his dream: the J. B. Matthews Memorial Library was completed to house the CLA's 100 tons of computerized files and huge library. In his never-ending appeals for contributions and subsidies, Bundy's pitch stresses the CLA's working relationship with law enforcement and intelligence agencies; the value of its resources to the entire countersubversive network; and the extraordinary comprehensiveness of its file holdings ("every name of every person, organization, movement, publication or subject of significance has been put on a reference card. . . ."). Through a subsidiary, the *National Laymen's Digest,* the CLA offers its regularly issued "documented exposés" to contributors and subscribers, and for an additional fee "name checks" (the limit is four) based on "documented information." All contributions, CLA assures its prospects, are tax-deductible as charitable contributions.[14]

To "American businessmen faced with a grave problem" of troublemakers and radicals in the work force, CLA offers a special service: name checks of suspected employees and applicants for employment.[15] But no matter how large the file collection or how well documented, there remains the challenge of the subject who is not already dossiered. To deal with this problem, which in the sixties confronted all of the major countersubversive file repositories, the CLA developed an investigative capability. In addition to retaining detective agencies, it organized its own network of undercover agents, who infiltrate, make tape recordings, take photographs, and steal mailing lists. The better to serve the needs of its clientele and especially to tap the most generous source of funding, large corporations, it allied itself in 1969 with a newly formed investigative unit, National Goals, Inc., an enterprise of John Rees, a countersubversive activist whose shadowy career is explored in a later section.

The employer countersubversive market is dominated by the ASC. Organized in Chicago in 1955 by ex-FBI agents as the Mid-West Library, it was sponsored and funded by corporations and conceived as a reference source from which employer members could obtain information about the politics of employees or applicants for employment, as well as reports on "questionable" organizations.[16] Today it has over 3200 members, led by the industrial giants who pay dues based on the size of their work force. Its file archives, in excess of 6,400,000 entries, are based on Harry Jung's American Vigilant Intelligence Foundation collection, augmented by the acquisition and consolidation of six other file systems, and kept up to date by informer reports, government documents, leftist publications,[17] and clippings from a huge array of newspapers and magazines.

Its reference library, filing, and clearance functions place ASC in a familiar category of employer-financed data collection operations organized by ex-FBI or military intelligence personnel in the fifties, such as the Western Research Foundation, the American Library of Information, and the San Diego Research Library. But ASC has from the beginning also projected the super-patriotic strain in the nativist subculture, best exemplified by the American Legion and its Americanism Commission. ASC's "library" style and tone yielded to martial, patriotic concerns. Today, the ASC is the voice of the military industrial complex, with a board membership glittering with top brass from all the services, and supported by the leading defense contractors. It engages in political lobbying and drumbeating to boost military appropriations, runs a cold war propaganda arm, and sponsors a number of institutes as well as the "Freedom Studies Center," a bastion of hard-core hawks, "the private West Point of psychopolitical warfare."[18]

Of all the components of the private intelligence community, the ASC has the closest ties with established power centers, especially Congress, and is a tireless lobbyist for the pseudo-legislative mode. It master-minded Ichord's terrorism strategy to save HISC and provided it with investigative leads. But the promotion of countersubversion is a tactical measure to create a favorable climate for increased military appropriations and a more aggressive foreign policy. As the richest and most politicized component of the private intelligence community, ASC maintains close liaison with its hawkish sectors and works with lobbies of displaced intelligence operatives. For example, James Angleton, whose fanaticism forced his retirement from the CIA in 1978, turned up as the director of the "Intelligence and Security Fund," an ASC offshoot devoted to the rehabilitation and defense of intelligence and its personnel. Such linkages are not new; in the early fifties Lee Pennington left his job in the Bureau, where he served as liaison with the American Legion, to direct its Americanism Commission, and then joined other ex-agents in organizing the ASC. The Watergate investigation revealed that Pennington, then a CIA operative, was dispatched to the home of Watergate burglar James McCord to ensure that incriminating Watergate evidence would be destroyed. Pennington was at the time a top ASC official, head of its Washington office.

The Private Eyes

Private detective agencies have historically made significant contributions to the development of the countersubversive intelligence system. Discredited by the 1936–37 LaFollette Committee probe of espionage, they were restored to importance by the defense-employee screening programs of the cold war era. According to a Rand Corporation estimate, as early as 1967 there were already 4280 private agencies in the field. During the past decade the industry has grown at a rate in excess of 10 percent a year. Today, with estimated income of $5 to $10 billion a year, the "industrial security industry," as it is called, is a commercial phenomenon. Its services are concentrated on physical plant protection and crime prevention, and over an estimated 90 percent of its personnel are engaged in such work.[19] But the countersubversive investigations have been discreetly reduced to avoid government scrutiny, or referred to smaller freelance operations, typically manned by former government (federal, state, or urban) intelligence personnel.[20] The opportunities for earning a good living in the industrial countersubversive field are attractive. In contrast to the past, when an accumulation or purchase of files was indispensable for entry into the intelligence market, in the late sixties intelligence personnel could acquire the necessary capital through the buddy system: by enlisting the cooperation of former colleagues in reproducing needed documents or trading information with members of the intelligence community. These assets also opened the door to in-house security departments of corporations, which have beefed up their surveillance and screening procedures as a protection against radical infiltration of the work force. The institutionalization of political surveillance was stimulated by bomb scares in the late sixties. Corporate employers throughout the country organized special security programs for their plants and offices. Industrial defense programs and seminars for screening out radicals and potential saboteurs were developed by the National Association of Manufacturers (NAM) in consultation with the FBI and the Army. The American Society for Industrial Security, a professional organization composed mainly of corporate security executives, provided security guidance for its members and a stream of countersubversive propaganda.[21]

Of the three private detective agencies (Pinkerton, Burns, and Wackenhut), the most ideological is Wackenhut. Headquartered in Coral Gables, Florida, and organized in 1954 by George Wackenhut and three other ex-FBI agents, it is the third largest industrial security agency in the country.[22] By the mid-sixties, twenty-one of its forty-eight executives were former Bureau agents or supervisors, including two former high-ranking officers in the Bureau's domestic intelligence division. Until the late sixties and early seventies, when countersubversive intelligence came under attack, Wackenhut led the countersubversive private detective industry. A 1965 prospectus claimed a 2.5 million name file, with 10,000 additions weekly. "The Company believes it is the only organization which can offer its clients a central file of this magnitude and full investigative services to supplement and verify information in the files."[23] Thereafter, the firm acquired the file collection of Karl Barslaag, a former naval intelligence operative, editor of the American Legion's countersubversive publication *Firing Line,* and a HUAC and McCarthy Committee staffer. The firm then boasted that it owned "one of the largest independent collections" of countersubversive files and literature in the United States, with command over "more dossiers than any other organization in the country outside of the FBI."[24]

The agency's professional concerns reflect the political values of its director, George Wackenhut. A rightist of the old blood, he selected as his directors an assortment of ultras prominent in the John Birch Society, the ASC, and other right-wing groups. The agency's monthly house organ, the *Wackenhut Security Review,* systematically decried the subversive inspiration in virtually all the protest movements of the sixties, from civil rights to peace. This vigilance earned the publication the accolade of right-wing organizations, including (in 1962) the George Washington Honor Medal and the Freedom Foundation Award at Valley Forge, Pennsylvania; and (in 1965 and 1966) the Vigilant Patriots Award from the All-American Conference to Combat Communism.

Wackenhut's priorities shifted with changes in the post-Watergate climate, the passage of legislation designed to protect privacy, and the shift in client concern from ideology to physical security. The agency turned over its countersubversive file collection to the CLA—gratis. Now, it claims, it declines active countersubversive investigative work and levies on the CLA's collection to meet client requests for dossiers and background information.

All in the Family—The Intelligence Community's Private Deputies

The World War I era alliance between the intelligence community and the private sector was strengthened by the cold war and later by the challenge of the movements of the sixties. "Intelligence"—with its glamorous rhetoric and "good guy" images—served to invest the collaboration ("liaison") with an aura of legitimacy and professionalism. This trend was solidified by the interchange of countersubversive cadres and the informer traffic between the Bureau and right-wing groups that served both as a source of recruits and a haven for surfaced informers. From its early days, the FBI cultivated the private sector for political and propaganda support. Bureau intelligence was channeled not only to the media but to such groups as the American Legion (the FBI's most important ally), the National Council of Catholic Bishops, and the Chamber of Commerce. In at least one case (see Chapter 5) the FBI provided information to the Ku Klux Klan that enabled it to prepare and carry out a brutal assault on Freedom Riders in the Birmingham, Alabama, bus terminal in May 1961. According to official documents, the FBI transmitted information in advance about the itinerary of the civil rights group to the Birmingham Police Department, with the knowledge that it was infiltrated by the Klan; further, on the day of the Freedom Riders' arrival, it supplied a Department intelligence officer with the schedule of their planned activities for the day. This information was furnished despite an earlier memorandum stating that the Bureau was aware that the officer in question "has been furnishing information concerning political violence given him by the Birmingham FBI office" to the Klan.*

The COINTELPROs frequently scripted aggressive roles for the FBI's traditional allies, such as the Legion and the Catholic War Veterans, as well as media clients. In addition to using the mainstream media used for this purpose, the Bureau also recruited for its dirty tricks operations the fanatic and racist exposé sheets of the far right.

A more functional public-private linkage is often found on the urban and state levels. Indeed, intelligence units have themselves organized a private intelligence network, the Law Enforcement Intelligence Unit (LEIU). Formed in 1956 and headquartered in California, the LEIU was conceived primarily as a countersubversive national structure, a vehicle for the exchange of dossier-type information about radicals and radicalism. The formation of the group reflected an attempt by urban intelligence units and the strong personalities who led them to declare a measure of independence from the Bureau, which then dominated the field, and to restore urban operations to their former prominence. Although LEIU comprises 225 representatives of major cities in the United States and Canada connected with law enforcement agencies supported by public funds, it nevertheless insists that it is a purely private confederation of individuals, without any official status or connection. While member agencies undertake to respond to requests for investigation of a mobile subject, LEIU's main focus is on information exchange. Until the early seventies LEIU's ideological focus was unconcealed: information about dissidents was regularly exchanged at regional meetings, which also hosted speakers on subversion and foundation funding of radical groups. But this emphasis was suppressed in the group's application for funding to convert a portion of its manual file collection to the federal computerized Interstate Organized Crime Index (IOCI). Using a law enforcement cover, LEIU units have continued to accumulate files on political dissenters and radicals, successfully evading courtroom attempts to verify its disclaimers by transferring records to the LEIU national and regional centers.† The LEIU has also

---

*The documents also show that the Bureau knew from the reports of its informer, Gary Thomas Rowe, that the Birmingham police had agreed to keep clear of the bus station for fifteen minutes to give the Klan time for their attack.

†Finally, in the fall of 1978, a court-ordered release of Chicago red squad records revealed a continuing course of surveillance and dossier compilation directed against anti-war, black and

served another needed function in countersubversive intelligence: the recycling of blown informers and undercover operatives. According to Douglas Durham, prior to his recruitment as a Bureau informer against the American Indian Movement (AIM), as a result of an LEIU arrangement he was detailed by the Des Moines police to work undercover for police departments in Lincoln, Nebraska, and Cedar Rapids, Iowa, on assignments that included the surveillance of leftists.

In a number of cities, cooperation between urban intelligence units and local right-wing groups flourished in the sixties. A notable example is Chicago, where linkages were forged that reproduced the themes and relationships portrayed in Costa-Gavras's *Z,* the motion picture about pre-Fascist Greece. The star of the Chicago real-life script is a group known as the Legion of Justice, the instrument of a prominent Chicago divorce and corporation lawyer, the late S. Thomas Sutton. Formerly a liberal and a charter member of the United World Federalists, Sutton, in 1966, helped organize homeowner groups in opposition to the open housing demands of Martin Luther King, Jr., and his supporters. His Legion of Justice, based on a white suburban Chicago ethnic constituency, came to public notice when, in February 1968, a team of student members physically assaulted participants in a University of Chicago sit-in. In a bolder foray, the Legion, then based in suburban Berwyn (Sutton's home) and Cicero, opened an attack on a local YMCA coffeehouse for serving hippies. Pressure mounted until May 1969, when one of Sutton's cronies, "Cicero Sam" Oleinick, shot some arrows from his crossbow into the crowded coffeehouse. Affixed to the arrows were leaflets from both the Minutemen and the Legion of Justice. (The insignia for both groups are quite similar: for the former, a rifle sight, and for the latter, a guillotine superimposed on a rifle sight with the motto: "Treason Must Be Punished.")

The Legion then began to organize and concentrate its operations in Chicago, either in its own name or behind fronts. In a little over a year it claimed five or six units in Chicago, each with forty to sixty members, four in the suburbs of equal size, as well as affiliates in Ohio, Indiana, and Wisconsin.

Court records, a grand jury report, interviews with victims, and the disclosures of defectors establish that in 1969 and 1970 the Legion in collusion with the Chicago police intelligence unit (the red squad) engaged in a series of terrorist-style raids against leftist groups.[26] In some cases the targets, especially of break-ins to obtain files, were suggested by Chicago police who met with Legion members at a motorcycle shop. ("In a way it was funny. The burglaries would be reported to the Chicago police. Then a few days later, we'd be giving the police copies of records we had taken in the burglaries.") The Legion also maintained "liaison" with the police in De Kalb and other northern Illinois cities. The Army's Evanston-based 113th Military Intelligence Group (see Chap-

American Indian activists. The released dossier-style cards focused on political and organizational involvements as well as criminal activities and were submitted for dissemination to the LEIU network by member units in a number of cities. At least one state police unit (South Dakota) also contributed such file material for nationwide dissemination. This and other aspects of LEIU's involvement in countersubversion are examined in detail in Linda Valentino's "The LEIU: Part of the Political Intelligence Network," *First Principles,* January 1979.

ter 8) supplied the Legion with tear gas, mace, and electronic surveillance equipment, in addition to money. Both the red squad and the 113th shared the fruit of its file raids. But a point was reached when the intelligence chief, Lieutenant Joseph Grubisic, announced the proposed absorption of the Legion into his operation because it was unseemly for the Legion to bypass his unit and transmit files directly to Army intelligence.

The Legion's Chicago operation apparently began in July 1969 with the burglary of the office of Newsreel, a film collective. Three Chicago police cars were parked outside the group's offices when the break-in took place. No arrests were made, although one of the victims chased the escaping burglars while the police looked on. The loot—films and documents—was turned over to Army intelligence. This was followed by an incident in February 1970 when, again in the presence of the police, Legion members assaulted a participant in a Young Workers' Liberation League meeting in a Chicago hotel and then threatened the victim with arrest. In March a peace rally was disrupted and the invaders burned the hand of Norman Roth, one of the organizers. When regular squad cars were called to the scene, the red squad officers helped the Legion members flee and later arrested Roth.

An elaborate campaign of Legion/police harassment targeted the Young Socialist Alliance (YSA), a youth arm of the Socialist Workers' Party (SWP). On November 1, 1969, the YSA bookstore-office was raided by a group of eight Legionnaires. After macing one YSA member and clubbing another, the raiders made off with books, files, records, tapes, and a cash box. At a press conference shortly thereafter Sutton proudly displayed the stolen material "liberated," as he put it, by the Legion. Richard Hill, Chicago organizer for the SWP, identified the stolen material and demanded that the police who were present arrest Sutton and two Legionnaires whom he identified as members of the raiding party. Asked if the raid was illegal, Sutton proclaimed: "We find that there is no law to protect a traitor." The police evidently agreed with Sutton. They conducted an amiable first-name conversation with him and refused to arrest him. Two days after the conference Hill swore out a warrant against Sutton for "unauthorized possession of property," a charge later dismissed on the ground that the prosecution had failed to show that Sutton had intended to keep the property, although the resolve was made quite clear from the videotape of the conference, which the prosecution refused to subpoena. (The "liberated" material was burned in a public ceremony on November 15 by Legion members as a counter-demonstration to an anti-war rally.)

On the same day as the press conference, November 13, a Legion supporter, Greg Schultz, attempted to gain entry to the YSA-SWP office, but was barred when he was recognized. Although he left without incident, he claimed that he had been forcibly excluded, and two leftists who had barred his entry were arrested on November 30 on charges of "illegal restraint" as well as assault and battery. On December 6, 1969, two days after the Fred Hampton Black Panther raid, a detail of thirty police, some with guns drawn, entered the YSA-SWP headquarters after several "anonymous" tips that a shootout was in progress. When the police learned that the tips were bogus, they nevertheless proceeded with a detailed search of the office. In the meantime, phone messages were received at YSA-SWP offices all over the country from a caller posing as Hill, that the Chicago "office has been tommy-gunned. People are lying on the floor bleeding and unconscious and pleading for help." These false calls were clearly part of a collusive arrangement between the police and the Legion, the source of the calls, to provoke the called occupants to take protective measures by obtaining weapons and thus justifying an affray in the style of the Panther attack two days earlier.

A few days later, on December 9, Hill—who had already received a number of telephoned death threats—found the following note posted to his door:

> Richard Hill has been found guilty of treason. Treason must be punished and believe us treason will be punished!
> We missed you in your office. We missed you in De Kalb. We missed you at home. Where the hell are you, Rich!

The police deliberately deleted all possible fingerprints after it was explained that the note had been handled so as to preserve the prints. The campaign against the group intensified with another raid in December by men wearing ski masks and armed with mace, bats, and tire irons on a student apartment at the Northern Illinois University campus at De Kalb. The occupants of the apartment, which was also a bookshop, were maced and beaten, one of them so severely that he was hospitalized. The Legion's responsibility was undisputed.* But the De Kalb police ignored the Legion and, instead, quizzed the victims about their politics, blamed the raid on black militants, confiscated books and literature, and tried to get the students evicted.

The Legion repeatedly harassed the Guild Bookstore, where leftist books are sold. On one occasion four men entered, maced one of the owners, overturned book and magazine racks, and dropped a hand grenade that turned out to be a dud. This was followed by a threat of further violence. Complaints about the original raid and follow-up warning drew the usual blanks from the police. In March 1969 a Legion hit man and eight of his friends visited the shop for a third time. When they refused to leave, Richard Wunsch, who was in charge of the shop, picked up a shotgun and repeated his demand. They left, but returned within minutes accompanied by a dozen policemen. Instead of arresting the Legion members, the police arrested and booked Wunsch for aggravated assault, possession of an "unregistered" gun, and refusal to produce the registration card for the "unregistered" gun. The gun was registered but Wunsch almost went out of his mind trying to get the police to accept the registration. When another collective member again presented the registration document, the desk sergeant rejected it because Wunsch had already been booked.

Another Legion concentration was the defense in the case of the Chicago 7, the anti-war activists, tried in 1969 and 1970 for conspiring to incite a riot at the 1968 Democratic Convention. In pursuit of defense plans, the Legion stole records from the defense office, planted a bug in the office of the American Friends Service Committee (Quakers), which, for security purposes, was sometimes used for defense planning, and another in a Catholic church in Cicero

---

*A few months later, a young Legionnaire bragged at a Pro America forum, "We went to De Kalb and closed down a liberal bookstore by beating all hippies and niggers in there."

suspected by military intelligence officers as a secret repository of legal defense files. (In the course of this break-in an armed robbery was committed in which about $1000 in cash and four watches were stolen.) Red squad members checked out in advance whether the church had a burglar alarm system and reported their findings to the Legion's break-in team.

Both the Army and the red squad played a role in Legion gas-bomb attacks that disrupted the performances of Russian ballet and Chinese acrobatic troupes in 1970 and 1971. Army intelligence agents furnished the grenades to the Chicago unit which, in turn, it passed to the Legion through an intermediary, a right-wing businessman. The Legion's style became increasingly bold as its ties with the police and military units strengthened. An effort by a Chicago civic group, the Independent Voters of Illinois (IVI), to induce a state law enforcement official to investigate was leaked by police officers to Sutton, who constantly bragged to his victims and critics of his friends in high places.

The linkages between the intelligence community and the private sector are best illustrated by the John Birch Society (JBS). The brightest jewel in the right-wing intelligence diadem was, in the late sixties and early seventies, one David Emerson Gumaer, who claimed to be, and was billed in the John Birch Society lecture publicity as, an "undercover operative for the Intelligence Division of a major metropolitan police department" who had "successfully infiltrated the SDS, the DuBois Clubs and the National Conference for a New Politics" and "rose to key positions inside the New Left."* Gumaer presented his readers and lecture audiences with claimed disclosures drawn "from intelligence files," and labeled an "intelligence report" the fruits of his consultation with "intelligence sources" presumably eager to share their secrets with him because of his own background. One such report is "California, Pilot Project for Red Revolution," which appeared in the July 1969 issue of *Review of the News*, a Birch-sponsored newsletter. The chilling thesis of this article is that a revolution was then in progress, "which aims for complete victory" in 1972. The tone is super-spookish: at "a recent intelligence meeting . . . this reporter was told that intelligence personnel in the Bay Area have affirmed detailed evidence of Communist subsidies to radical groups"; "in a highly confidential Intelligence Summary issued last August fifteenth by the Office of Military Intelligence for the State of California"; "during an interview with several intelligence officials at the Alameda County Courthouse, I discovered . . ."; "discussing Communists' activity in the Oakland area with police intelligence officers, your reporter was shown a document . . ." and so on. Like Rees, Gumaer turned up on the staff of a congressional Bircher, Representative John Schmitz.

A major JBS intelligence exposé in recent years develops the thesis that the attempted assassination of Governor George Wallace on May 15, 1972, was the result of a Communist plot, deliberately covered up by the federal government.

---

*Advertisement in the Santa Ana *Register,* Nov. 6, 1970; *American Opinion* (September 1969), p. 57. The "major metropolitan police department" is the Chicago Police Department, which initially denied that Gumaer was ever employed by it in any capacity. However, subsequent admissions, confirmed by documents, establish that Gumaer, using the alias David LeMarc, spied for the Chicago red squad from October 1965 until September 1967. The "key positions" claim is a bit of puffery.

The conspiracy charge was the brainchild of JBS investigative reporter Alan Stang, and Timothy R. Heinan, a former undercover agent for the Milwaukee Police Department. Heinan insisted that while he was working undercover in the Marquette University branch of the SDS in the fall of 1969, he saw would-be assassin Arthur Bremer at a number of SDS meetings. But the SDS members vigorously denied ever seeing Bremer at a meeting or even knowing about Bremer. A number of the SDS members recalled that Heinan had attended a few meetings in the fall of 1969 but was expelled at a meeting in November 1969, after admitting that he was a spy. (Heinan's credibility is further impaired by the fact that the university records establish that, contrary to his claim, Heinan never graduated.)

Stang asserted, in both an article and a press conference, that his pursuit of Heinan's leads had confirmed the fact that Bremer was the instrument of a Communist assassination conspiracy.[27] His account abounds with references to a "mystery man" in the service of the Communists (and later found dead of a heroin overdose), midnight meetings with an identified FBI undercover agent in hippy dress, a three-year-old copy of a Communist newspaper found in a bar, "documentation" that documents nothing, and wild surmise. It glistens with emanations of buried secrets finally unearthed by "fearless investigation." The reader is told that "Your correspondent has . . . gone into the underground for the facts with a special . . . investigation team. Intelligence collection is strange work. Things arrive in the mail with no return address, and there is no way of knowing who sent them. The telephone rings and someone whispers information, but you don't know who is he—and you don't ask."

The JBS embrace of intelligence spookery complements its conspiracy obsession. Nativist groups like the Birchers are no longer remitted to fantasy, invention, and forgery to establish the conspiracy. The rhetoric and assumptions of intelligence ratify the conspiracy premise, and at the same time legitimize operational techniques to combat the phantom plotters. And this conspiracy-intelligence dialectic is not confined to the established far-right spectrum. The National Caucus of Labor Committees (NCLC), for example, labeled for a time a left revolutionary group, has planted its banners on the farthest shores of spookery.

An offshoot of the splintered student left of the sixties, the NCLC emerged in the seventies as a faction dominated and controlled by Lyndon H. LaRouche, Jr., who has also used the name "Lyn Marcus"—a derivation from Lenin and Marx. A member of the Socialist Workers' Party from 1948 until 1966, he began in the late sixties building his own movement to make a reality of a resolve born in the thirties that "no revolutionary movement was going to be brought into being in the USA unless I brought it into being." Although initially self-proclaimed as a Marxist-Communist cadre group, the NCLC overnight became a cultist instrument of LaRouche's enormous power drive. His authority and control over his alienated middle-class youthful followers flow from an authoritarian style of leadership combined with a bizarre Freudianism that equates resistance to such leadership with sexual impotence ("a mother complex"), and the use of brainwashing sessions ostensibly for the purpose of protecting his anxiety-ridden, psychologically dependent cadres from the machinations of their political adversaries. In 1973, the NCLC entered the political process through the U.S. Labor Party (USLP), now its major enterprise and institutional alter ego.

The NCLC derives its program and style from its enemies: a vast byzantine conspiracy dominated by the Rockefeller family. Ironically, large segments of the right—not merely its crazies—also place Rockefeller power at the center of an international subversive conspiracy. But hostility of this kind is largely explained by the hatred of the political zealot for the betrayer-heretic, frequently more intense than for the enemy-infidel. For LaRouche, however, the Rockefellers—Nelson and his banker brother David—were *the* enemy, rulers of a hidden police state plotting a "world holocaust" through a network of agents planted in an assortment of institutions and social movements. Convinced of his destined greatness, he proclaimed his wedding day in 1978 an international workers' holiday. A veteran of World War II military intelligence, LaRouche has made a fetish of "intelligence" as an NCLC priority in foiling the never-ending machinations of the conspiracy to frustrate his deserved ascent to power.* As with the Minutemen, the SAO, the Posse Comitatus, and similar groups, intelligence is not a casual or optional activity but is a trademark of the NCLC, as well as of its offshoots and fronts such as the USLP, the International Caucus of Labor Committees, the Labor Organizers' Defense Fund, and the Revolutionary Youth Movement. A special intelligence staff functions to monitor and deceive the enemy, complemented by an élite security unit to foil attempts to undermine the solidarity of the membership. Its New York office bespeaks, in the words of a *Wall Street Journal* reporter, "the tight security and the serious mood [of] some sensitive government intelligence post." Its numerous publications include two with an intelligence focus, *Counterintelligence* and *Executive Intelligence Review,* a weekly journal.

To prepare for aggressive actions, NCLC organizers are routinely instructed to submit intelligence reports on rivals and opponents. Deception, the use of false names, the formation of bogus groups with the acronymic tags of already existing organizations, phone calls from impersonators, post office boxes disguised as offices, infiltration, counterfeiting, the reporting on non-events, and the deliberate bloating of its numerical following—these are all integral to the NCLC mode, as is the projection phenomenon, common to many groups that play intelligence games, by which critics and opponents are almost instinctively denounced as spies.

A prime weapon in the NCLC's intelligence arsenal has been direct violent action against its adversaries on the left. For this purpose, it has maintained a squad of thirty to forty members, as well as a school in an upstate New York farmhouse that conducts classes in the martial arts, weapons systems, explosives handling, and demolition tactics. To clear the way for LaRouche's ascent to the revolutionary summit by wiping out more successful rivals, the NCLC in 1973 organized Operation Mop Up, which mounted some sixty armed attacks in a number of cities on activities of the Communist Party, its youth affiliate, and

---

*FBI documents speak of LaRouche in this way: "He reports that key aides were programmed for his assassination. His concept of his own destiny is grandiose. The fate of the world is riding on his shoulders."

the Socialist Workers' Party. Organized gangs of NCLC'ers with clubs, pipes, and numchucks (a karate weapon consisting of two chain-linked cudgels) inflicted scores of injuries on their hapless victims, some of whom required hospitalization. Planned disruptions of meetings, physical threats, and ruthless takeover raids became stock practices.

Collaboration by NCLC with official intelligence structures began in 1974, when field workers were instructed to brief local police on the activities of political enemies. Since then the NCLC has admittedly acted as an informer for both urban and state intelligence units. In 1976, after renouncing its former professed leftism in favor of an authoritarian conservatism, it developed a special intelligence mission to monitor and analyze "terrorist" groups. (In LaRouche's lexicon, "terrorist" is simply an epithet used to characterize virtually the entire left-liberal spectrum, a means of mobilizing official intelligence resources against USLP rivals and enemies.) It was the NCLC's intelligence briefing of Philadelphia Mayor Frank Rizzo, predicting a terrorist disruption of the Bicentennial celebration, that led to his request for federal troops. Despite the inaccuracy of its briefing, the NCLC, in a subsequent ten-page "Open letter to Philadelphia Police," nevertheless claimed credit for the peaceful character of the demonstrations because "after the Labor Party informed Mayor Rizzo [of the alleged planned violence], the Mayor acted to defuse the situation by focusing national attention on that danger."

The extent of NCLC's collaboration with police structures is suggested by its role as an intelligence arm of the New Hampshire state police in the April 30, 1977, demonstration by the Clamshell Alliance against a proposed nuclear power plant at Seabrook, New Hampshire. On April 1, 1977, NCLC's New England representative telephoned the New Hampshire governor's office to warn of the subversive danger of the ecology movement generally and of the planned Seabrook demonstration in particular. To buttress its proposal for further action to check the nuclear power opposition, the NCLC suggested to the governor's press office:

> We do have a full brief of the environmentalist movement and where every group is funded from, and we have another brief which we drew up for the Bicentennial Movement, which we could send you both of them [sic] and you could cross-grid them and we could discuss exactly how to have a Congressional investigation—that is the idea.[28]

Subsequent disclosures from the New Hampshire state police files revealed a number of communications and meetings between Lieutenant Donald Buxton and NCLC activists, as well as NCLC briefing documents, including a copy of *Information Digest** dealing with Clamshell Alliance. Buxton's intelligence report states that "these well-informed gentlemen" viewed the demonstration as "nothing but a cover for terrorist activity."

NCLC has also collaborated with federal agencies. Initial denunciation of Bureau surveillance (as a tactic of the Rockefeller conspiracy) has given way in the NCLC's counterterrorist phase to a new amity. Released Bureau files show that the NCLC has instigated national security investigations of its political

*See p. 446.

targets and fed material into the agency's files designed to discredit them and assure continuing surveillance. In addition to written and telephone briefings on terrorism, usually followed by mailed presentations from its ever-expanding library of published and manuscript documents on intelligence themes, representatives from its executive hierarchy have visited Bureau offices for briefing conferences. In June 1976 one such meeting was held for the purpose of "furnishing information concerning Rockefeller and the Institute for Policy Studies plan of nuclear attack on Philadelphia during the People's Bicentennial celebration on July 4, 1976."

The bid for police and intelligence cooperation was subsequently broadened. In 1976 the NCLC dispatched a three-page letter to ten federal and state agencies, warning of a terrorist conspiracy to harass the group and to assassinate LaRouche, its candidate for President. Its 1976 publication, *Carter and the Party of International Terrorism,* charges that a terrorist apparatus on the left and an array of government agencies, foundations, and research institutes in league with the Carter administration and the Rockefellers are plotting a world nuclear holocaust. The NCLC's policies and propaganda have won a measure of rightist favor and endorsement, since, as one conservative journal explained, "It is not supported by Rockefeller money, as are all similar groups." NCLC's personalized leadership style and ruthless power drive carry us into realms of cultist messianism in which the gratification of personal needs for submission to authority, for packaged dogmas, and for group reinforcement dissolves all unwelcome realities. The convert, aflame with the passion to preserve his new-found salvation at all costs, turns on challengers and critics with the savagery made familiar by holy wars.*

In the fall of 1977, in the wake of the U.S. Labor Party's intensive involvement in the previous year's elections, the Justice Department announced the termination of the Bureau's seven-year investigation of the NCLC and its Labor Party clone. But the group's journey from violence to respectability has not altered its intelligence-style targeting of dissidents through infiltration, deception, and disruption in order to ease the path to power. In the late seventies, it developed propaganda and intelligence programs directed against Jewish and

---

*L. Ron Hubbard's Church of Scientology, a religious therapy group that has frequently clashed with government agencies, is also high on aggressive intelligence, especially the security/counterintelligence version. Among the items seized by the FBI in two raids in 1977 were dossiers on the church's critics, lock-picking and bugging equipment, a blackjack, and a vial labeled "vampire's blood." An indictment filed by a Washington, D.C., grand jury in August 1978 charges eleven Scientologists with a conspiracy to infiltrate government offices, the planting of two underground agents in government jobs, bugging an IRS conference room, and pilfering files from the IRS and the Department of Justice. In January 1979, the prosecution charged the defendants with ordering the investigation of at least 14 members of the judiciary to insure that a friendly judge would be selected for the trial. In October, eight defendants were convicted of a conspiracy to steal government documents dealing with the Church and a ninth of stealing government records. Like the NCLC/USLP, the Scientologists have responded to critics and defectors with fierce hostility. Court-released files reveal an extraordinary program of deception, infiltration, dirty tricks, disinformation projects, and related tactics designed to silence or harass its enemies—not only government agencies but individual targets as well. The files show, for example, that a member was placed in a job as a stenographer with a New York firm in order to obtain access to secret grand jury minutes in a case involving the Church. "We have had some success (limited) in the past with getting this type of data," states a 1977 memo. A subsequent entry indicates that the mission was successful.

anti-apartheid groups in this country, in courting racist domestic constituencies and, investigators charge, as bait for Arab and South African financial backing. Its continuing intelligence priorities are reflected in cadre training programs in counterintelligence, conducted at "The Farm" in Powder Springs, Georgia, by Mitchell Wer Bell III, a legendary private intelligence operative. Wer Bell is also LaRouche's personal security consultant, hired to protect him against the never-ending assassination conspiracies which he claims threaten him on all sides. The group's intelligence-gathering activities support the production through a variety of methods of a stream of profiles and evaluative reports, uniformly gleaming with LaRouche's ideological obsessions and used for both propaganda and a service to paying clients. According to one investigative reporter, Dennis King, its files "may well be the largest single collection of intelligence data in the United States." In promoting his 1980 presidential campaign, LaRouche has allied himself with the countersubversive drive to restore the CIA's intelligence powers. On February 27, 1979, he publicly appealed for support for a private intelligence agency to perform the functions "that ought to be the proper domain of the CIA." What he proposed, LaRouche explained, "is a de facto augmentation of the resources of the U.S. Labor Party, thereby combining the core contribution to be made by the USLP with the resources otherwise befitting a U.S. government intelligence service into an independent agency . . . endowed by corporate and other private sources. . . ."

California-style Spookery—Ducote and Company

Countersubversion dominates California politics in a special way. Its ruling élites—corporations, agribusinesses, banks, and the press—have since the twenties effectively exploited the fear of communism in curbing challenges to their power. The countersubversive constituency in the state is substantial and passionate, and it has influenced mainstream politics in a unique way: one need only recall Richard M. Nixon and his heir, Ronald Reagan. As countersubversion has entered the political process, its intelligence techniques have turned from passive data collection to more aggressive initiatives. And this California style —break-ins, deceptions, dirty tricks, and the like—is evident in the pattern of aggressive intelligence activities that culminated in the Watergate break-in.

History has supplied us with a dramatic rendering of this politicization of crime in the saga of Jerome Ducote. A deputy sheriff in Santa Clara County for ten years, a one-time member of the State Republican Central Committee, a leader of the Young Republicans, and county chairman of the John Birch Society, Ducote in 1976 admitted having committed seventeen burglaries of the files of various organizations and pleaded guilty to reduced charges contained in a twenty-one-count indictment.[29] Ducote's control—to use the intelligence term—for most of his operations was R. Kenneth Wilhelm, secretary of the Santa Clara Farm Bureau. A super-conspiratorial type and a certified Communist loather, Wilhelm is the very model of the intelligence middleman who woos political and corporate powerholders with the intelligence product, or the promise of it, obtained from the risk-taking soldiers in the trenches, many of them initially motivated by ideological considerations alone. After Ducote had been introduced to Wilhelm in 1964, he was retained at an $800 monthly salary, supplied by Stephen D'Arrigo, a wealthy grower, to develop countersubversive intelligence.

His first assignment was to put together a file demonstrating that Grace MacDonald, a local supporter of the Cesar Chavez United Farm Workers (UFW) movement, had a Communist past. When Ducote turned over the fruits of his labors to his grower sponsors, their monthly publication refused to print out of fear of a libel suit. The editor proposed that the material be laundered by insertion in the *Congressional Record* by Republican area Congressman Charles Gubser. To avoid embarrassment, Gubser in turn arranged for a colleague, John Bircher James Hutt, to insert the material in the *Record*. [30] Another investigative assignment not involving a burglary brought Ducote to the trash depository of the Communist newspaper *People's World,* which he stalked for a number of nights waiting to snatch a subscription list that, he had been tipped off, was about to be discarded. Ducote recalled that when the list was finally dumped into the trash, a struggle ensued: three other men, each apparently unknown to the others, representing the FBI, military intelligence, and the San Francisco police respectively, made a dive for the same booty. The policeman prevailed by threatening to arrest the others, but generously agreed to reproduce copies for them. Ducote also recalled how in 1968 a top Reagan associate, one-time Lieutenant General John Harmer, raised money to send him east in the disguise of a priest to infiltrate a meeting of liberal Catholics and obtain material for use in developing support among southern California's conservative Catholics.

Wilhelm relayed the papers in the MacDonald investigation to the Western Research Library, a now familiar countersubversive resource maintained, in this case, by corporate clients such as the Pacific Gas and Electric (PG&E), the Southern Pacific Railroad, and Standard Oil of California. PG&E was particularly grateful for the MacDonald disclosures because she had been lobbying the state legislature for public power, and it presented Ducote with supplies to facilitate the dissemination of the MacDonald material. The Western Research Library itself was then headed by the late Harper Knowles* and directed by Laurence Cott, an ex-FBI agent who subsequently left to edit, along with Ruth Matthews, the exposé sheet *Combat.* As a result of a meeting between Cott and Wilhelm in the fall of 1966, Ducote was commissioned to obtain the mailing list of the San Jose Peace Center and was assured by D'Arrigo of a $1000 fee. Ducote broke into the Peace Center and stole the lists with the collaboration of one

---

*A pioneer of the file and dossier trade, Knowles began his career in World War I military intelligence. Afterwards he became head of the "Radical Research Committee" of the California Department of the American Legion. In the late thirties he testified copiously before the Dies Committee and placed in the record extracts from his file collection, which even then was extraordinarily detailed. In collaboration with Nat Piper, a former FBI agent, Knowles set up Western Research Foundation. In the early sixties Western Research expanded its focus from labor militants and migrant farm workers to security checks for the expanding West Coast utility industry—Bill Wallace, "The Intelligence Laundry," *Nation,* May 6, 1978.

Henry Scherling, like Ducote a devout Catholic, a dedicated member of the John Birch group, and Santa Clara County chairman of the Young Republicans. Wilhelm, to whom the San Jose files and lists had been turned over, transmitted them to the Western Research Library for storage and dissemination to other intelligence agencies in the area, including the FBI.

In the Peace Center break-in and a number of others Ducote operated according to a set spooky formula: he was instructed to make contact with a stranger by matching half of a torn dollar bill with the other half mailed to him by Western Research. When the contact was completed, he was given a detailed map of the premises by the stranger. The fruits of the burglaries were circulated in right-wing channels—to members of the California legislature, U.S. congressmen, investigators for state and federal committees, ASC functionaries, California grandees of the far right (such as Patrick J. Frawley, Schick razor tycoon, and oilman Henry J. Salvatori), and prominent members of the Reagan inner circle. The San Jose caper brought a measure of fame and an offer from a wealthy rightist of $1400 for a Berkeley break-in. Ducote's blooming prospects led to the recruitment of a third hand, the current chairman of the Santa Clara County Young Republicans. In early 1967, in response to D'Arrigo's suggestion, the three burgled Ms. MacDonald's home and removed eight boxes of files, which were turned over to Cott at Western Research.

In the spring of 1967 D'Arrigo and Wilhelm arranged for a meeting with an unidentified security agent (almost certainly a CIA agent), as a result of which the Ducote team broke into the office of *Ramparts* magazine—then under CIA scrutiny because of its revelations concerning the Agency's domestic involvements—and made off with a huge haul of material. D'Arrigo arranged for Ducote to take this to Washington, where it was shown to Congressman Gubser and the CIA. D'Arrigo also arranged for a meeting with HISC's general counsel and chief investigator. After viewing the MacDonald, Peace Center, and *Ramparts* material, Ducote recalled: "They asked that if we get anything like this in the future," to provide copies. When Ducote returned home, a second CIA man again reviewed the documents, making certain that his examination would leave no incriminating trace since, as he pointed out, they were stolen.

Shortly after his return to California, Ducote was contacted through Wilhelm and summoned to a meeting of ranchers in Fresno, where an appeal was made by D'Arrigo for financial support for the burglaries. At the suggestion of Jack Pandol, a powerful figure in the state's grape industry and a Reagan appointee to the state Board of Agriculture, Ducote broke into the Cesar Chavez Delano headquarters and removed files for dissemination. A few days later, according to Ducote's confession, his grower sponsors (Pandol and D'Arrigo) requested a second Delano entry, this time in the Filipino hiring hall where, he was informed, Chavez's main files were kept. Supplied by Pandol with a key and $1400 in cash, the Ducote team delivered the goods, which turned out to be enormously useful in the growers' fight against the UFW; the haul included boxes of names and addresses of dues-paying UFW members, lists of supporters and contributors, strategic plans for organization and negotiations. But a perfect job was marred by a getaway snag: the license plates of Henry Scherling's departing car were noted and he was apprehended.

Through the intercession of the growers, charges were dropped. Ducote did some softening up on his own; in a secret meeting he explained to a sympathetic Delano police chief that, as he knew, "Chavez . . . was bringing a great many radicals into the area, people from the Free Peace Movement in Berkeley, known identified Communists, etc. . . ." Ducote also intimated that he was working for the FBI.

Using the torn-dollar-bill-and-diagram procedure, Ducote and Scherling next, at Wilhelm's instruction, broke into the offices of two San Jose lawyers, John Thorne and William Stanton, and stole files dealing, in the case of the former, with the National Lawyers Guild. Stanton, an assemblyman in the California state legislature, was a primary target because he had undertaken an investigation of Western Research (whether in his public or private capacity is unclear) on behalf of a number of individuals who had been denied employment on the basis of information supplied by Western Research to corporate clients. (When the heat continued to rise around Western Research, it transferred its file collection and merged with an Oakland counterpart, Research West, Inc., also run in clandestine fashion by ex-Bureau intelligence types and financed by employers).*

Saul Alinsky, the professional organizer of community movements, became a priority target because, while living in Carmel, California, he had served as a consultant for the Chavez organizing campaign. Shortly after the theft of documents and keys from his Carmel home, D'Arrigo arranged for Ducote to case the Chicago office of Alinsky's Industrial Areas Foundation. It was subsequently burgled with the help of a professional supplied by his sponsors, a practice employed in another case as well. The Alinsky dual break-ins were followed by a number of others, including the Palo Alto and San Jose peace centers, the Student Non-Violent Coordinating Committee (SNCC), the United Committee Against the War, the People's World, Catholic Social Justice, and the East Side Farm Workers' Organization.

The pursuit of the Chavez-Alinsky connection led to a trip east to enlist help from conservative leaders of the Presbyterian Church, including J. Howard Pew, board chairman of the Sun Oil Company, who donated $1000 to the cause. With the Chavez campaign as a lure and the stolen documents as exhibits, Ducote also undertook fund-raising efforts on his own that ultimately resulted in a number of counts in the indictment referred to above. These accused him of grand theft in connection with an alleged scheme in 1973–74 to obtain funds from San Jose businessmen by falsely representing to them that he needed front money, to be returned subsequently by the growers, to pay for the subsistence of Mexican nationals who would link Chavez to communism. Ducote's earlier fund-raising efforts on behalf of his principals included a foray into the counter-subversive vineyards of southern California where among his benefactors were a Du Pont heir and publisher, George Hearst, Jr. Ducote's southern California sponsor was Norman Moore, a former Los Angeles Police Department sergeant,

---

*Research West has been described by its president, Patricia Athowe, as "experts on the ideological left." According to Federal Power Commission records, from 1971 to 1976 PG&E paid Research West nearly $90,000 for "investigative services," which neither firm would describe in further detail—Script, NBC News, "Utility Security," Dec. 25, 1977.

who was head of the Fire and Police Research Association ("Fi-Po"), another in the chain of California file exposé operations.*

As Ducote tin-cupped his way through the inner circles of ultras, he shrewdly came to recognize that what loosened the pursestrings of potential contributors was only in part ideology; they all seemed to respond with a special *frisson* to the sharing of secrets penetrated by cloak-and-dagger methods. As Ducote's statement puts it, in addition to ideological satisfaction, "the excitement gets a hold of you too. There's a certain excitement to it, there's a thing of having knowledge of organizations from the inside, being able to use that information." Ducote shrewdly concluded that not only were his clients vicariously turned on by spy work but their needs were practical; "that is [it] wasn't so much the patriotism or a cause but . . . a matter of dollar and cents with them." The awareness that his take was a negotiable commodity led ultimately to a commercialization of the operation and, in the final stages, a confidence scam.

In addition to the regular Wilhelm-Western Research dissemination channels, Ducote's take was shared with Senator Burns's pseudo-legislative California Un-American Activities Committee, which used the Chavez material in an official report in order to discredit Chavez's organizing drive. The secretary of the Burns Committee, Rena Vale, a veteran of the California school of countersubversion, was called to index the stolen documents and to identify Communists.† Another dissemination channel was the American Security Council (ASC). After the Alinsky break-in, Ducote conferred in Chicago with James Galvin, chief executive of Motorola Corporation and actively involved in ASC affairs. Galvin was particularly interested in learning about Alinsky's proposed plans to campaign for proxy votes against corporate involvement in weapons technology, a field in which Motorola functions as a prime contractor.

While his supposed sponsors and confederates (such as Wilhelm and D'Arrigo) have denied the extent of involvement or knowledge attributed to them by Ducote, the evidence is incontrovertible that Ducote committed the burglaries to which he confessed and that he did not act on his own. Nor have disavowals of direction, participation, or knowledge been supported by more than characterizations of Ducote as a "constitutional liar" and "con man." Ducote freely admitted the burglaries in the course of an investigation, in the belief that no charges could be filed against him because the Statute of Limitations on the burglaries had run out. But after his arrest on charges of receiving stolen property and loan fraud, he bitterly complained that he had been made a "fall guy for higher-ups."

Even less credible than the disavowals of his alleged confederates and sponsors is the Bureau's claim that it knew nothing of Ducote's burglaries prior

---

*Organized as an extracurricular enterprise to combat "dope, obscenity and subversion," Fi-Po allied itself with the right-wing countersubversive California subculture and used its newsletter to publicize file material discrediting liberals. When it was forced to disband in 1975 as a result of a political scandal, its file collection was transmitted to a right-wing church group, the United Community Churches of America.

†Vale made her debut as a Dies Committee witness in 1940. A Communist defector, she earned headlines with charges that California Communists had infiltrated a great number of organizations and controlled the Young Democrats.

to his arrest in December 1975. The Bureau's cautious insistence that it never "knowingly" dealt with Ducote is overshadowed by a pattern of involvement beginning in 1967, when the Bureau acquired a microfilm of a stolen membership list, and continued until January 1975, when a confession by Ducote's confederate, Henry Scherling, including a statement that Ducote had previously turned over the stolen documents to the FBI, was transmitted to the Bureau by the agent who recorded it. Perhaps even more compelling is the sworn courtroom testimony of UFW attorney Jerry Cohen, that the FBI had known of Ducote's activities at least since 1974. Early in that year Ducote had approached Cohen, offering to return the stolen records to the union for $25,000; Cohen met with Ducote and after refusing the demand notified the Bureau. A second meeting with Ducote was arranged, which was monitored by Bureau agents, Cohen testified. No action was taken by the Bureau after the second meeting. Cohen's testimony, never contradicted or rebutted, lends strong support to the assertion of a former Bureau agent that the agents in the San Francisco office were instructed to leave Ducote and his operation undisturbed. Circumstantial evidence buttresses the charge of Bureau involvement. The burglaries began after the Bureau itself had banned such "black bag jobs," which occurred during the period when aggressive actions (COINTELPROS) were official policy; the mysterious, unidentified torn-dollar-bill matcher with his detailed diagrams and drawings is precisely the part played by Bureau informers who are routinely instructed to report the location and content of files and the layout of offices where they are housed. Ducote himself stated that he was under the impression these strangers had Bureau ties.

California-style Spookery—Howard Godfrey and the Secret Army Organization (SAO)

As the above account indicates, the services performed by the more committed countersubversive cadres to property interests are not confined to propaganda and exposure. They also act as an operational spearhead both for investigative and counterintelligence purposes. This role involves risks but, as in the case of Ducote, it is played out in a protective institutional context. The risk-takers know that they enjoy a measure of community support and approval even among those who do not wholly share their zeal, that the threat of legal sanctions is reduced by the sympathetic attitudes of the law enforcement establishment, and that "national security" can transform felonies into heroism. Moreover, the FBI field office interprets its duties in the light of the standards and values of the community from which its operative personnel are largely drawn. Finally, the perception of risk is reduced by an alliance with corporate angels in whose behalf the risks are undertaken and who can be called on for protection or financial help when the going gets rough.

The sheltering power of a highly conservative institutional environment also explains the extraordinary lawlessness of the San Diego Minutemen, an "extremist" group, and its offshoot, the Secret Army Organization (SAO), which flourished in the San Diego area (and in a number of states in addition to California) in the late sixties and early seventies.[31] An ultra-conservative nesting ground, San Diego is the home of an influential John Birch Society, a stratum of right-wing retired and active duty naval and military officers, a conservative Republican movement, matching religious institutions, a cluster of vigilante sects (Alpha 66, Phantom Cells, and the National States Rights White People's Party), and the right-wing Copley press.

Over the five-year period 1967–72, the Minutemen-SAO ran rampant in the San Diego area; it engaged in intensive physical surveillance, infiltration, burglaries and file thefts, photography, and terrorist violence against leftist targets. Its tactics included an assortment of "pranks" and dirty tricks such as effigy burning, strewing of carpet tacks (to maim barefoot hippies), interference with telephone communications, and the sabotage of meetings through disinformation practices. But the group's trademark was violence and terror: vandalism, fire-bombings, tire slashings, shootings (bullets and lug nuts), assassination threats, dumping piles of tear-gas crystals, and the posting of stickers with cross-hair rifle sights. This entire campaign was not spontaneous but a planned implementation of a programmatic commitment to violence.*

Among the Minutemen-SAO terrorist targets were the local anti-war movement; the Convention Coalition, a project organized to demonstrate at the Republican Convention then scheduled for San Diego; the Movement for a Democratic Military (a GI organizing project, focused on nearby Camp Pendleton, the base of 200,000 active duty GIs); and porno bookstores. High-priority targets were the left San Diego *Street Journal* and a successor paper, as well as local Marxist faculty members, notably Peter Bohmer, an economics instructor at San Diego State, his associates and supporters. The San Diego *Street Journal* enraged the entire San Diego conservative establishment by its anti-Vietnam reportage, its attacks on James Copley (owner of both major San Diego newspapers) and banker C. Arnholt Smith, a prominent Nixon backer and Republican fund-raiser.[32] Beginning in November 1969, a Minuteman team opened warfare on the *Street Journal.* It fired bullets into the *Journal*'s offices, smashed its windows, stole 2300 copies of a current issue and dumped them into San Diego Bay; terrorized the paper's distributors; broke into its offices, vandalized equipment, and stole records, including its subscription list; destroyed its street-vending machines and slashed tires of staff members. The attack on Bohmer began in the spring of 1971 with the dumping of tear-gas crystals in a car parked outside his residence. In May 1971 he received two telephoned death threats from SAO callers. The harassment intensified after a student demonstration at an administration disciplinary proceeding against Bohmer. But open warfare commenced when, in the summer of 1971, the Republican Party announced plans (subsequently altered) to hold its August 1972 convention in San Diego. In the wake of the announcement, Bohmer and his

---

*A Minutemen instruction sheet reminds its members that "research alone doesn't hurt the enemy. All research should be followed up with a complete investigation of the enemy to determine the strength and weaknesses of their organizations and leaders. A combination of surveillance and infiltration lays the groundwork for harassment, sabotage, subversion and other steps possibly needed to destroy the effectiveness of the enemy. In summary: investigate, infiltrate and devastate."

followers in the radical community organized a Convention Coalition which, it was announced, would hold mass protest demonstrations. Law enforcement officers concluded that as many as 250,000 demonstrators would converge on San Diego.

The vigilantes responded with a plan for massive infusion of LSD or poison in the punch served at anti-war meetings, kidnapping, fire-bombing vehicles, and the planting of explosives in homes and offices. In November a target car was fire-bombed, followed by warnings of greater destruction and the posting of threatening stickers bearing the SAO rifle-sight cross-hair symbol on Bohmer's office, residence, and car, as well as those of his roommates and associates. On January 6, 1972, a call to the Bohmer household warned: "This time we left a sticker, next time we may leave a grenade. This is the SAO." A subsequent call was more explicit: "Say Good Bye to your friends down the street." That night, two shots from a 9mm pistol were fired into the Bohmer residence, wounding Paula Tharp, a *Street Journal* staffer, and causing permanent damage to her elbow. On January 7, a woman inaccurately named in an SAO *Bulletin* as Bohmer's girlfriend received a phone call: "You're next."

The Tharp shooting, despite the attention it attracted, did not end the terrorism, which continued throughout 1972. To implement a grand strategy of eliminating the Coalition altogether, the SAO rented garages in the San Diego area and stockpiled them with weapons, explosives, and food. These and other SAO operations were finally exposed in the course of investigating the bombing of the Guild Theater, a local porno moviehouse. The bomb, which was placed on January 19, 1972, virtually demolished the theater, destroyed its screen, and bulleted two-by-four's and other debris through the audience. The caper stirred the perennially apathetic San Diego Police Department into action, a tribute to the fact that two prominent law enforcement officers were in the audience to determine whether the film being shown *(I Am Curious Yellow)* should be banned. The investigation led to the arrest and subsequent conviction of one William Francis Yakopec. The entire web of SAO activities and involvements soon began to unravel. Yakopec was a member of an SAO action cell in El Cajon, a San Diego suburb. The cell was led and organized by Howard Berry Godfrey, a San Diego fireman who taught Yakopec how to use incendiary devices and supplied the explosives for the Guild job. Godfrey's control and influence over Yakopec were not solely organizational; he was a friend, a next-door neighbor, who had converted Yakopec to Mormonism and was his church-designated "family adviser." The Guild job was only one of a number of planned bombings of porno moviehouses discussed by the two men.

Godfrey played another role that Yakopec did not know about: he was a highly valued FBI informer. After Godfrey's arrest in 1967 on criminal explosive charges, he was put in touch with the FBI by a local Mormon stake president who was subsequently elevated by President Nixon to the federal bench and mentioned as a candidate for a Supreme Court post. In a not unfamiliar trade-off, the charges against Godfrey were dropped and Godfrey signed on as a Bureau informer in the paramilitary Minutemen, one of a cluster of such sects that flourished in the hospitable San Diego climate. What distinguishes groups of this stripe is their commitment to violence, a predilection for firearms and explosives and "intelligence," glamorized by James Bond-type cloak-and-dagger rhetoric.*

While Godfrey subsequently claimed that he was instructed to reduce his own involvement to the minimum required to preserve his cover and indeed to prevent violence, the evidence is overwhelming that he was quite at home in SAO circles, initiated and led its most aggressive activities (including most of those outlined above and many others), and that the Bureau was fully informed about his involvements and protected him from their consequences. Whatever may be the case today, the Bureau's San Diego office during the years when Godfrey served it was a hotbed of far-out countersubversion. Like Godfrey, a number of the Bureau agents, including two of his controls, were Mormons convinced that a Communist conspiracy was about to destroy the nation and debauch its purity.

Under the tutelage of his control agents, Godfrey rose to a prominent position in the Minutemen and, after the group folded, in its successor the SAO. In an extraordinary infiltration coup, Godfrey became assistant chief SAO state commander, San Diego County coordinator, and most importantly, "intelligence" consultant of the organization statewide, its principal source for pamphlets on such subjects as explosives, booby traps, and guerrilla warfare. As the director of the El Cajon activist cell, missioned to devastate the local left by any means possible, he began rather modestly with Ducote-style burglary and file thefts from homes and offices of left targets. The haul was used to build the SAO collection of "intelligence files" and then turned over to the Bureau. Godfrey explained that the SAO file collection was a sort of "hit list" to identify targets in the event of a Communist takeover. On one occasion, parents of students on a stolen list of Student Mobilization Committee members were called and, as Godfrey recalled, "those who stuck up for their kids were put in the file too." In response to a Bureau assignment, Godfrey stole the briefcase containing a membership list from Donald Freed, chairman of the "Friends of the Black Panthers," when Freed came to speak on the San Diego State Campus. According to the Bureau, this stolen list was "the biggest single bit of intelligence ever stumbled across." After processing the information for two days, the Bureau turned the material over to the SAO for its files. For this effort Godfrey received a bonus, one of two he was awarded during his five years of informer service.†

The SAO's targets were hardly distinguishable from the Bureau's and when, beginning in 1968, the New Left COINTELPRO was launched, Godfrey's operation became in effect the Bureau's counterintelligence program. This is not a matter of conjecture. Godfrey's $250 monthly earnings were supplemented by bonuses and a generous expense account, from which he contributed to SAO's operating costs such as office rent and the dissemination of literature. While there may be exaggeration in the charge of his embittered superior, Jerry Lynn Davis, that "the SAO was a federally funded poverty program of the right," the fact that the Bureau knowingly helped subsidize the SAO is beyond question.

---

*The substantial San Diego John Birch Society movement was too moderate for these bloodthirsty types, who scorned it as "the eat and retreat crowd."

†The second was a reward for material obtained from the files of the Peace and Freedom Party.

Nor can it be disputed that, following a familiar pattern,* the Bureau used Godfrey and his resources to supplement its own formally passive surveillance.

Godfrey's informational haul about his leftist targets traveled through three separate channels: the SAO file collection, with its estimated 20,000 entries; the Bureau; and the San Diego Police Department's redoubtable red squad, the Investigative Support Unit (ISU).† The ISU deployed its own informers, in some cases jointly with the FBI, against the SAO's targets (including the *Street Journal*), and collaborated with the Bureau in the creation of that sense of invulnerability that encouraged Godfrey's vigilantism. The ISU also lent a helping hand to the El Cajon unit's covert action work. When, in December 1969, Godfrey's action team all but wrecked the *Street Journal*'s offices, an ISU infiltrator, John Paul Murray ("Jay King"), was the last person to leave the premises before the burglary. Forced to look for new offices as a result of SAO death threats against the owner of its premises, the *Street Journal* entered into a lease agreement with one Bill Joe Reeves, the manager of the new premises. An ISU officer, Sergeant Jack Pearson, demanded that Reeves cancel the agreement "as a personal favor," and when Reeves refused, Pearson transferred the pressure to the building's owner. In reprisal for his refusal to cooperate, Reeves was arrested on a murder charge, held for an hour while his premises were searched, and released. The *Journal*'s leasing arrangements were then canceled. The police openly cooperated in the suppression campaign by arresting *Journal* vendors on trumped-up charges. Godfrey reported to his Bureau contacts about the SAO's activities (fire-bombing, shooting, tire slashing, and the like) and the *Journal* itself complained to the police. No arrests were made, or even a serious investigation undertaken.

Nor did the Bureau stay Godfrey's destructive course. In court testimony and in an interview in January 1976, he admitted the SAO's responsibility for a broad assortment of illegal acts in which he personally had participated. Although, as he put it, "many of the acts were spontaneous" and reported after the fact, others were planned in advance. Despite these forewarnings, the Bureau did not intervene. At the Yakopec trial, Godfrey admitted that the Bureau had reimbursed him for the explosives used in the Guild Theater bombing, knew he had them, and knew he gave them to Yakopec prior to the bombing—for which Yakopec was found guilty. Asked by Yakopec's counsel why the FBI failed to act against the SAO, Godfrey's control, Agent Steve Christensen, replied: "We didn't want to disclose Mr. Godfrey as an undercover informant."

At the trial of George Mitchell Hoover for the Tharp shooting the star witness was again Godfrey, who testified that Hoover was riding in his car and had used a weapon that had been in Godfrey's possession. Godfrey not only witnessed the shooting but reclaimed the gun from Hoover and told him to think up an alibi. For six months after the shooting, Christensen concealed the fact that he had received the weapon from Godfrey; when asked to explain why, he

---

*In some respects, Godfrey's role resembles that of Denver informer Timothy Redfearn, an activist member of the American Nazi movement, who committed burglaries both to serve his cause and to provide information for the Bureau.

†This appears to have been a cosmetic cover name; the unit was also called the Internal Security Unit.

testified that disclosure would have revealed Godfrey's identity.* It was not merely the need to protect Godfrey that accounted for the Bureau's deliberate sabotage of the law enforcement process; after his retirement to Utah, Christensen stated that the Bureau had in mind Godfrey's value in monitoring the convention protest: "They wouldn't let him out. He desperately wanted to get out of that situation. . . . They were going to use Godfrey during the convention, he was a valuable man." These concerns explain why the Bohmer-Tharp shooting remained unsolved for at least eighteen months. Leftists were no better than they should be, but the Guild movie bombings endangered the lives of two law enforcement officials. That was going too far. Following the theater bombing, seven members of the SAO were swiftly arrested for a number of prior "unsolved" crimes.

Godfrey and his SAO team of criminals gave the San Diego area intelligence establishment and its ultra-conservative constituency an operational capability that brazenly flouted the demands of the criminal law, public order, physical safety, and personal property—let alone First Amendment freedoms. For example, there was no one to respond to complaints when Godfrey's team disrupted the local Peace and Freedom Party's activities by breaking windows and terrorizing its supporters. The campus police on the La Jolla campus of the University of California cooperated in a caper by Godfrey and others to hang left-wing philosopher Professor Herbert Marcuse in effigy. Given the encouragement of the local conservative community and the indifference of the law enforcement establishment, Godfrey felt free to take on the Peace and Freedom Party. On one occasion he engineered a delay in a mailing of an upcoming speaking engagement until the speaker had left town and, for good measure, placed Minutemen stickers in each envelope.

While the invulnerability of the Godfrey operation was dissolved by the June bombing, it began to crack when, in May 1972, the Republican Party announced that the convention would be held in Miami—not San Diego. Godfrey's team was therefore no longer necessary as a guerrilla force against the planned demonstrations, for which Godfrey and his associates had prepared a series of proposed actions, including the kidnapping of prominent radicals, that bear resemblance to the so-called Liddy Plan. According to the disputed claims of two former SAO militants, Jerry Busch and Phil Robinson, Donald Segretti, the director of "dirty tricks" in the field for the Committee to Re-elect the President, posing as "Don Simms," in the summer of 1972 met with Godfrey and other SAO'ers at the Gunsmoke Ranch in El Cajon, regularly used by the SAO as a target range. Busch reported that after the Gunsmoke Ranch conversations (which took place prior to Segretti-Simms's official appointment), Godfrey emerged with bizarre proposals to take care of what he called "those red punks." Both Segretti and Godfrey denied that such meetings took place.† What

---

*There was a further difficulty: The gun was stolen. When the owner of the weapon appealed to ISU Sergeant Pearson to investigate the theft, he strongly urged that she abandon the inquiry. Shortly after the gun was discovered, Agent Christensen left the Bureau and took up residence in Utah. He and his wife agree that "the FBI is taking good care of us," and acknowledge that the decision to conceal the gun was not made on his own but that the Bureau knew of it.

†Godfrey's extraordinary candor in revealing a long train of gruesome involvements and activities enhances the credibility of his denials about the Segretti connection.

has been confirmed is that Segretti canvassed the San Diego area for infiltration and covert action resources to neutralize the proposed demonstration by the Convention Coalition.

Godfrey was protected by the Bureau to the end; he was not permitted to surface as a witness until the Bureau had obtained a promise from the local authorities to find him a new job in another area. For five years he had been allowed free rein to act out his ideological hostility and indulge his mania for intelligence hugger mugger. As he put it, he had had "fun."

Closing the Information Gap

The emergence in the sixties and early seventies of new areas of dissent and previously unidentified dissenters sharpened the market demand for exposé material. How to establish the subversive character of such post-Vietnam domestic movements as environmental control, prison reform, and opposition to nuclear energy? The pressure for countersubversive ammunition was further intensified by foreign policy developments—over China, Cuba, Rhodesia, South Korea, and South Africa—and armaments struggles—the SALT talks, the IBM missile crisis, proposed arms reductions, and nuclear arms limitation.

Only in diehard fanatic circles could the Communist Party continue to serve as the exclusive negative reference group. The accumulated acres of files, totemistic tributes to the Menace, had to be updated without sacrificing the continuity of the countersubversive tradition. The times demanded a J. B. Matthews; indeed, a troop of them, to renew the energies of nativism in the waters of a new "communism" not identified with the Communist Party alone but equally capable of activating a modern countersubversive constituency.

The task of revising old norms interlocked with that of identification. The reindoctrinated constituency had to be led through the many mansions of a modernized Menace, then introduced to their occupants. One important response to the new challenge of evaluation and identification is the *Information Digest,* a biweekly newsletter published by a couple, John and S. Louise Rees (their real names; they have, as will be seen, also used pseudonyms).[33]

The circulation of *Information Digest* is limited to a small select group of about forty police agencies, corporate security offices, private detective agencies, and some media outlets (*Reader's Digest;* a TV network). A core group of subscribers disseminates the material but under instruction to disguise its content so as to protect the identity of its sources.[34] In addition, the ID, as I will call it throughout, maintains a file collection and reference index for use of subscribers. Documents obtained through Freedom of Information Act proceedings further reveal that a considerable number of federal intelligence units and operations have made use of the ID: the FBI, CIA, IRS, National Security Agency, ATF, SISS, HISC, the Custom Service, and the Drug Enforcement Agency. An investigation in 1976 by a New York State legislative committee of the files of the New York state police revealed that the state police used ID as a source for its political file collection of over 1 million names. The New York State Police Department unsuccessfully resisted disclosure of the ID material to the investigators, claiming the newsletter as a "confidential informant," hence privileged against disclosure.* The Michigan state police have also regularly received copies of ID with Congressman Larry McDonald's office as the return address. The ID's relationship with the Maryland state police was so close that Rees was able to obtain their help in renting a post office box in Baltimore, Maryland, where the ID is produced. Also authorized to receive mail addressed to the box was John Norpel, Jr., former research director of SISS, which had used Rees as a witness in a number of hearings.† The ID's coverage includes some right-wing and paramilitary groupings (the Ku Klux Klan, Minutemen, Aryan Brotherhood, the National States Rights Party, American Nazi Party, Posse Comitatus), but its major concentration is leftist and liberal organizations and individuals. ID reflects a new intelligence style, which blends traditional countersubversion and a more sophisticated treatment of contemporary movements, preserving the continuity between the old and new by treating gaps and discordances as themselves the result of deliberate deception by an overarching conspiracy.

The ID is full of reminders that it is a product of a collection network which includes infiltrators. One issue tells its readers that a reproduced list of radical entertainers has been stolen. While this is a familiar form of Ducote-style puff spookery—letting the reader in on secrets acquired at great peril—it is abundantly clear that the ID blooms with the fruits of infiltration.[35] Indeed, both Rees and his wife are seasoned veterans of operational countersubversion. The British-born Rees first made his appearance on the countersubversive stage in 1968 when he launched "National Goals, Inc.," to provide an investigative source for various branches of government and (left unsaid) to generate material for the CLA's exposé publications. Rees himself edited the CLA's *National Laymen's Digest* in 1968–69 and used his position to plug National Goals' first project, *Information Digest.*

In the late sixties the Reeses developed cover credentials in the New York area "youth culture" while secretly reporting its activities in *Information Digest.* In May 1971 they entered the District of Columbia radical community under the names of John Seeley and Sheila O'Connor. In addition to writing and editorial work for ID, Louise Rees, under a pen name or anonymously, published articles in such right-wing journals as *Human Events, National Review,* and the John Birch Society publication *Review of the News.* On arriving in the D.C. area, Rees signed on as an informer for the D.C. police and together with his wife launched the police-supported "Red House Book Store," which was used to collect literature of the left and information on the fertile D.C. counterculture. A bid for more useful material was contained in a letter sent by Rees to certain foreign

---

*The basis of the claim was simply a stamp on each page of the ID: "The information contained herein is of a classified nature intended solely for the use of the New York State Police and any other Agency authorized by them."

†Norpel told investigators that "Rees' information was invaluable to the intelligence community. . . . I don't think he got his information from federal agencies. It was my impression that the federal intelligence community was more dependent on him than he was on them." Investigators seeking further enlightenment about the Rees-Norpel connection were referred to Otto Otepka, a former Norpel associate in the State Department's old guard security section, which had been a special SISS fief.

embassies, requesting advice "as to the means you consider most appropriate for increasing the contacts between your country and the tendencies we represent."[36] When the request brought no response, the Reeses moved into deeper waters: they abandoned Red House in favor of a bogus think tank, Coordinating Center for Education in Repression and the Law (CCERL). Under the cover of fighting the evils on the agendas of leftist intellectuals, it was designed to monitor and penetrate such targets as the Institute for Policy Studies, the Center for National Security Studies, and the American Civil Liberties Union.[37] While both Red House and CCERL failed in their larger purposes, they did spawn small ironies: Robert Merritt, Bureau informer, was instructed to monitor the bookstore by his contact, apparently unaware that it was a police operation,[38] while the CCERL was listed with approval by a left-oriented publication as one of a number of "community organizations presently engaged in work around the police. . . ."

The CCERL was headquartered in the Reeses' home, a commune which they made a gathering place for local left groups and a *pied à terre* for out-of-towners, all of whose activities were duly recorded in ID. A locked room was subsequently discovered to have housed arms and wiretapping equipment, which however was not used for bugging the premises, although the D.C. police had in fact authorized Rees to install the equipment. Another location rented by the police intelligence unit and used by Rees as an office was bugged.

Rees ended his D.C. police connection in 1973, but both before and after that time he developed liaison relationships with right-wing and police sources for the clandestine dissemination of intelligence (his readers are repeatedly reminded that they can obtain additional information through previously established contacts) and data collection. A police informer for a number of Eastern urban intelligence units assisted Rees in producing the ID. In dealing with local police, Rees used a familiar scam: he would hawk information to one department (typically a lurid tale of a violent plot) and in the course of this transaction, pick up information that he would in turn peddle to a unit in another city. In the same way, he enlarged his network of sources for ID by inviting follow-up inquiries from police units, which in turn supplied him with file material. Within a short time Rees's confidence scams, first developed in his infiltration apprenticeship, established his ID as unofficial broker for the exchange of countersubversive information among Eastern police departments. By citing his connections with other police departments, he induced D.C. police to pull him off the street.

Rees became a sort of Renaissance man of countersubversive intelligence, covering a wide spectrum of functions including an investigative stint for Wackenhut,* deceptions and impersonations so professional as to deceive both his sponsors and victims.†

In the early seventies he posed as a lawyer under the name John O'Connor,

---

*Although the Wackenhut agency's records confirm that an individual with Rees's name, address, and Social Security number was hired on two separate occasions, Wackenhut's personnel department (after hearings held on Wackenhut's investigative practices by the Privacy Protection Study Commission) denied that he had in fact been employed by the agency.

†The Chicago Police Department refused to buy one of his lurid items. Instead, it opened a file on him, characterizing him as a " 'confidence man type' who possesses all of the unreliable characteristics associated with such a person."

and subsequently as a cleric, Reverend John Seeley. Under clerical cover, complete with collar, he infiltrated the Georgia Power Project, a dissident group, on behalf of the security department of the Georgia Power Company organized in 1973 to identify subversives, that is, in the language of a former Georgia Power Security Department investigator, those who "for any reason would be against . . . rate increases or would have some type of critical opposition to the operation of the power company."[39] Rees's gleanings became the subject of an ID report inserted in the *Congressional Record* by Georgia Congressman Larry McDonald. In 1978 McDonald provided Rees with a special assignment: to supply research assistance to a group of Iranians encouraged to seek an injunction against student demonstrators protesting the visit to Washington of the Shah.

McDonald also provided a sanctuary for the other member of this odd couple, S. Louise Rees, who is fully as versatile as her husband. Like him, she spiced her editorial research and writing activities with operational deception. Using the name Sheila O'Connor, she first developed a cover as a participant in a prison project conducted by the Institute for Policy Studies. Next, she successfully infiltrated the D.C. chapter of the National Lawyers Guild (NLG), where for a year and a half she made herself indispensable through her efficiency and hard work and at the same time did her best to sabotage its activities. A registration list of attendants at the Guild convention in February 1973, including "Sheila O'Connor," was reproduced in ID and disseminated four days after the convention ended. The list was also incorporated in a more extended exposé of the NLG published by the CLA in 1976, "Lawyers for Treason." Unaware of Ms. O'Connor's ID connection—or for that matter that ID even existed—the local Guild officials defended her against the suspicions of a few (O'Connor herself denounced an accuser as "sexist"). In August 1973, two months after she had been elected to the Guild's national executive board in recognition of her contributions, she disappeared. In January of the next year, reverting to her Louise Rees identity, she was taken on as an HISC research aide, and when HISC folded in 1975, she turned up on McDonald's staff along with Herbert Romerstein. Ms. Rees works at her Baltimore home, where she uses the name "Seeley." Her husband, when not responding to pretrial examination demands in three civil suits brought by his victims, promotes a news service for the countersubversive market, collecting information from concealed sources under the cover of a freelance journalist and correspondent for the John Birch Society's *Review of the News.* He now denies that either he or his wife ever engaged in espionage or infiltration. "We were reporting. And we didn't use aliases. We used pen names." The FBI, however, could not permit itself such conceits. In responding to questions in a lawsuit, it stated: "Louise Rees served as an FBI informant from August 1973 to February 1976 and reported on domestic security matters. . . . Mr. Rees furnished information to the FBI on a voluntary basis from at least 1971 until 1974." But it is time we took closer notice of the Georgia congressman and his operation in support of the private intelligence sector.

The Revival of the Documented Exposé

The post-Watergate revolt that produced the 94th Congress and closed down HISC's marathon countersubversive investigation also brought to Congress Laurence G. (now "Larry") McDonald, a physician and the youngest member of the national council of the John Birch Society. McDonald promptly converted the *Congressional Record* into an organ for disseminating countersubversive propaganda and dossiers, focusing on the new radicals and dissenters. From the time when he began service in 1975 until the end of 1977, McDonald placed in the "Extension of Remarks" section of the *Congressional Record* over 1000 insertions, including some 220 detailed dossiers, exposé-style identifications of individuals and organizations characterized as subversive. Whenever available, the insertion provides the addresses and even the telephone numbers of the subjects.

Sympathetic members of Congress have always used their legislative prerogative to serve nativist causes by publishing material in the *Record* in the form of floor speeches or, in the case of House members, with more limited access to the floor, as an "Extension of Remarks" to be printed in the Appendix to the *Record*. This procedure was frequently used to supplement countersubversive committee hearings and reports, either on the legislator's initiative or as a favor to a constituent or a colleague. Perhaps the most notable of all of these insertions was the publication in the *Record* of HUAC dossiers on the "Communist front records" of ten directors of the National Association for the Advancement of Colored People (NAACP).[40] Such insertions were used to attack policy and legislative proposals by discrediting their supporters as subversive, as in the case of the civil rights debate of the fifties and early sixties; to execute an assigned role in a larger countersubversive intelligence campaign; and to recycle and authenticate with an official cachet ("documentation") for broader dissemination exposé material based on questionable sources.

But by the mid-seventies these offerings were reduced to a trickle, a consequence of the change in climate and a faltering in the momentum of countersubversion. The rise in the demand (for reasons already explored) was matched by a curtailment of the supply. What was needed was some central governmental source, which could process and disseminate printed material at the taxpayer's expense. Equally urgent was the need for a laundering function to consolidate and legitimize the reports of a network of "informants" and informers in place in leftist groups (like Sheila O'Connor), red squad operatives, and infiltrators from the ranks of the political right.

In addition to himself enjoying a haven from libel that he has resolutely refused to abandon when challenged, McDonald's methods help to reduce the libel fear generally of the exposé constituency. As we have seen, Ducote used a congressman to allay a journalist's concern about libel, and indeed, libel suits became an occupational hazard of the exposé trade in the sixties.[41] While the fact that a subsequently distributed statement or characterization originated physically in the *Congressional Record* is no defense to a libel charge,[42] it does embolden the timorous.

To advance his mission of reviving the exposé system, McDonald added John Rees and Herbert Romerstein to his staff. Since the processing of information into exposés is labor-intensive, McDonald has been forced to allocate the better part of his expense allotment to staff salaries, at a cost of more than $200,000 a year. As the champion of countersubversive intelligence and, according to experts, the most prodigious "extender of remarks" in history, McDonald has taken Rees and his *Information Digest* under his protective wing, reproducing many of its major reports. His other dossier-style *Record* insertions are fed by detailed material, which bears the stamp of reportage by informers and surveillers.

The congressman's range of exposé targets is enormous: National Lawyers Guild, Institute for Policy Studies, American Indian Movement, Medical Committee for Human Rights, the Martin Luther King, Jr., Memorial project, the World Peace Council, Breira (a group organized to support a just Israeli Mideast peace settlement), the American Civil Liberties Union, and scores of other groups and *ad hoc* committees and conferences. Individuals targeted include disarmament specialist Paul Warnke, former Kennedy aide Theodore Sorensen, Sam Lovejoy (an opponent of nuclear power), Helmut Sonnenfeldt (a Kissinger State Department protégé), and the author. In addition to the traditional countersubversive concerns, McDonald gives special emphasis to movements seeking to curb political intelligence excesses, and sounds a ceaseless alarm about the Menace of terrorism.

McDonald himself, while inveighing against the violent proclivities of his targets, was discovered (after a six-month investigation by the Atlanta *Constitution*) to have collected a hidden cache of as many as 200 high-powered weapons transferred to him at his request by dying patients, many of them cancer victims under Laetrile treatment, the John Birch cancer drug of choice. In Congress he has been a prime mover in a variety of conservative projects, ranging from a drive to remove then-UN Ambassador Andrew Young, to a successful campaign blocking the confirmation of White House nominee Sorensen for the post of CIA chief, to reviving HISC. McDonald serves as "Secretary of Defense" in a "Citizens Cabinet" sponsored by the Conservative Caucus, one of a constellation of right-wing political action organizations that have come to life in the mid-seventies. While pursuing separate agendas, they are unified by the nativist conviction that subversion threatens both government and society.

Intelligence operations and harassment by private groups have been on the rise in the 70's.[43] With the intensification of intergroup political, racial, and social conflicts, the future resort to self-help and vigilantism on an increasing scale is hardly open to doubt. Moreover, the likelihood is high that surveillance and covert action will escalate into violence. As Alan Wolfe has written, "A population which [in sports, the media, and everyday speech] is increasingly addicted to violence is preparing itself subconsciously for using the real thing."[44]

Epilogue

The abuses and usurpations of domestic intelligence institutions have, from 1972 to 1975, been subjected to unprecedented scrutiny and exposure by congressional investigators. These disclosures have been supplemented by an outpouring of documents released under the Freedom of Information and Privacy Acts (FOIPA), which in turn have generated lawsuits and further revelations through pretrial discovery procedures. "Whistle-blowers" and investigative reporting have contributed additional harvests of information. The reasons for the attack on intelligence are varied. Certainly, the self-questioning in the wake of the Vietnam War and Watergate contributed to the consciousness that we have betrayed the principles by which we have agreed to live as a people. And the threshold exposure of the excesses of intelligence institutions, both domestic and foreign, in scope of targeting as well as in the use of illegal techniques, undermined the resistance to further investigation. The critical mood also owed much to the felt need to open FBI doors and windows after the death of the Director in May 1972, as well as to the emergence of a widely felt sensitivity to the issues of privacy, candor in government, and White House autocracy, and to the decline in the affective power of anti-communism. The fruits of these pressures are perceptible: HISC was abolished and SISS forced to retreat. Its caseload in the domestic security field cut back as of October 1977 to 130 individuals and 17 organizations, the FBI promised to sin no more. The CIA, the IRS, and the Army joined in the *peccavi* chorus. Intelligence oversight panels were set up in both houses.

Yet the prospect is far from remote of a revival of domestic political intelligence activities in response to the same social and political pressures that have in the past dominated American public life. Intelligence as a means of containing movements for change, as a system of control, is simply too powerful a weapon in a highly conservative economic and social order lightly to be abandoned. The continuing worldwide erosion of capitalist economic and social structures has clothed the defense of the status quo with a new urgency in a political order governed by constitutional norms restraining official state action. Intelligence is an almost inevitable weapon of choice: secrecy permits it to function without accountability or control by the constitutional standards that prohibit interference with political expression.

We begin with the fact that the political conservatism which is the matrix of intelligence structures has not merely persisted but grown in the recent period. This intelligence constituency cannot function without an enemy, a hostile "they," a "Communist" scapegoat. By the late sixties the fear that anti-communism might be played out as a political strategy had set in motion a drive to reinvigorate the myth of subversion with the emotions that are stirred by social and cultural change. The Nixon administration sought to channel the energy of anti-communism into a *Kulturkampf* against an enemy who combined in one sinister stereotype all of the then prevalent varieties of protest and dissent. The objective was to associate political nonconformity—especially opposition to the Vietnam War—with forms of behavior that touched the most exposed social nerves, and thus to encourage a grass-roots conservative consensus while at the same time strengthening and expanding countersubversive intelligence agencies.

The contemporary "New Right" reflects a continuing and more vigorous exploitation of this process interrupted by Watergate. To counter class-oriented interest politics, strengthened during periods of economic stringency such as the present, the managers of conservative movements concentrate even more heavily than in the past on social issues: busing, crime, abortion, affirmative action, gay rights, the Equal Rights Amendment, capital punishment, gun control, and free access to Laetrile.[1] The effectiveness of these and related appeals is echoed, for example, in the increasing attacks on abortion clinics—arson, vandalism, and even physical assaults—a vigilante-style movement against obscenity, and the frenzied quality of the campaign against the Equal Rights Amendment. To an increasing extent the backlashes generated by specific issues are merging into an overarching, consolidated constituency based on a new sense of shared values, a "movement identity" not unlike that which marked sections of the left in the sixties. In this context, the lure of "subversification" of the opposition as a means of unifying and expanding the right is irresistible: fear of communism has, after an initial decline, increased from 69 percent of the population in 1974 to 74 percent in 1976. The preconditions for a socially rooted, "way of life" politics, in which scapegoated subversives and intelligence stalkers play key roles, are plainly present.

The co-star in the script for the revival of domestic countersubversion is the influential grouping of foreign policy and military defense hawks, which ranges from the American Security Council to the Coalition for a Democratic Majority (CDM), composed of moderate Democrats (Senators Henry M. Jackson and Daniel P. Moynihan are honorary co-chairmen), to an offshoot, the Committee on the Present Danger, and other cold war forces. The potential for an alliance even more durable than in the fifties between nativism and this élitist sector has been strengthened by the emergence of a sense of the decline of America's role as a world power. It was reflected in the scope of condemnation of the cancellation of the B-1 bomber, reduction of troops in South Korea, and the Panama Canal Treaty. The subsequent debate on SALT II, and the fevered response to developments in Cuba, Iran, and Afghanistan, have created a climate in which countersubversion flowers. If the past is a guide, moderates and liberals who share these views will readily accept a politics of countersubversion as a cheap price to pay for consensus on hard-line foreign policy and military armament issues. Revived intelligence programs would surely win favor, especially if they offered "right way" solutions.

The argument which has historically proved most efficient in legitimizing intelligence as a system—as well as the most penetrative operational techniques —is foreign influence and, in particular, the fear of foreign spies. On this espionage ground American Communism has continued to be targeted as a threat to the national security under a "counterintelligence" rubric.

A series of widely publicized charges of KGB espionage in the United States floated in the mid-seventies to curb drives for cutbacks in intelligence. Legislators allied with the intelligence establishment warned that the KGB, exploiting our relaxed defenses, had flooded the country with huge numbers of agents of a far more sophisticated character than formerly.[2] At the same time, efforts to discredit the investigations of intelligence practices in the House and Senate were climaxed by charges on the floor of Congress of KGB infiltration of congressional staffs.[3] Some fifty congressmen requested a Church Committee investigation. Although the FBI reported after an investigation that it had no evidence of such infiltration, the campaign persisted.* In April 1976 then-Vice-President Nelson A. Rockefeller charged in an off-the-record session in Georgia that two Communist agents had infiltrated Senator Henry M. Jackson's staff.[4] He subsequently apologized and admitted that he lacked supporting evidence. A *Reader's Digest* article in January 1978 by John Barron, author of a work on the KGB secretly nurtured by the CIA, alleged that an unprecedented flood of Soviet spies has overwhelmed the available counterintelligence resources.

These charges—they echo similar ones by the FBI—undoubtedly reflect a greater accessibility to American life and institutions by Soviet nationals in the wake of détente. They deliberately lump all such nationals (diplomats, trade representatives, computer technologists, and the like) into an ideological "professional spy," in the "disciplined," "highly trained" category, and ignore at least comparable U.S. activities in Communist countries, as well as the fact that much of the alleged spying is open and legal. Related efforts have focused on the practice by domestically based Soviet intelligence of intercepting and recording telephone conversations within the United States. This right-wing crusade to restore countersubversive intelligence and to silence its critics is dominated by the image of a Soviet "mole," deeply entrenched in a key CIA post, from which he orchestrates a master KGB plan to neutralize U.S. intelligence structures.[5]

---

*Intelligence requirements may have made the Bureau's disclaimer over-broad. In March 1976 Kenneth R. Tolliver, a former aide to Senator James O. Eastland, admitted that he had supplied information to Soviet agents for about seven years—not, however, as a true spy but as a double agent under FBI control. "Ex-Senate Aide Says He Was Double Agent," *New York Times,* March 12, 1976.

The theme of a foreign espionage threat is not confined to the propaganda of rightists and their intelligence establishment allies. Early in 1978 President Carter issued an executive order imposing limitations on intelligence agencies but authorizing electronic surveillance of a subject, even though a citizen of the United States, if the government has reason to believe that he or she may be "an agent of a foreign power." Under this order an intelligence agency could wiretap an American citizen by convincing the Attorney General in secret representations that the subject is such an agent. This, in effect, reaffirms the Nixon administration claim to an inherent executive power to bypass the search and seizure warrant requirements of the Fourth Amendment. This assertion of power was not made in the abstract. Shortly thereafter, the Department of Justice brought an espionage indictment against Ronald L. Humphrey, U.S. Information Agency officer, and David Truong, a young Vietnamese expatriate, for allegedly passing secret documents to Hanoi.[6] The alleged conspirators were indicted on the basis of information gathered by warrantless electronic surveillance, as well as by surreptitious entry and search, authorized by the Justice Department with President Carter's personal approval. In the pretrial proceedings the court accepted the government's contention that "the very nature of foreign intelligence gathering" made the warrant requirement inappropriate. However, it directed the suppression of the fruits of seven months of electronic surveillance on the ground that once a prosecutive decision had been reached, a warrant was required. The dubious importance of the documents in question (most of them low-level diplomatic cables carrying a "Secret" classification in only a few cases) and the virtually unprecedented step of demanding the ouster of the Vietnamese diplomat to whom the documents were allegedly relayed, confirm charges that the case was deliberately shaped, in the language of one State Department official, "as a test of presidential power and nothing else . . . they seemed to want confrontation."*

While the foreign espionage fear may be exploited for broadly repressive ends, as in the past, the dynamic of such an expansion requires a more efficient and credible stimulus. The primary contemporary candidate for expanded intelligence operations is terrorism, a phenomenon that has profoundly shocked popular consciousness in all countries in the West, even those that are not so far theaters of terrorism. Its intent as a tactic is to generate fear, and it has unquestionably succeeded.† Like the word "subversive," "terrorist" has ac-

---

*The Carter administration subsequently retreated. It sponsored a bill, passed by Congress in September 1978, requiring, with narrow exceptions, a prior judicial warrant for all foreign intelligence electronic surveillance in the United States, subject to more rigid standards when directed against United States citizens and resident aliens than in the case of foreign nationals but still not as exacting as the standard ("probable cause that a crime is being committed") imposed in the conventional criminal sphere.

†According to a Dec. 5, 1977, Harris survey:

90% of Americans view terrorism as a serious problem;

76% view the cause that has stimulated the growth of terrorism as "countries of the world have been too soft in dealing with terrorists";

by 55 to 29%, Americans would support a "special world police force which would operate in any country to investigate, arrest and put to death terrorists"; and

by 55 to 31%, Americans favor the death penalty for terrorists.

quired vague and sinister overtones, which recommend it for use in creating a climate favorable to the renewal of countersubversion. This semantic murkiness is matched by the fact that tactics associated with terrorism (hostage taking, bombing, skyjacking) are used in nonpolitical crimes, and that terror itself may be an intended element of such crimes, as in the case of kidnapping, robbery, extortion, and rape. Thus bank robbery, the seizure of an airplane by a criminal fugitive, or the bombing of a gangster's car sow images that reinforce the consciousness and heighten the fears of political terrorism.

Exploitation of terrorism as a major tactic in a psychological warfare campaign to restore intelligence recalls the saturation technique of the *pieds noirs* in their 1962 attempt to force a reversal of de Gaulle's decision to pull out of Algeria. The terrorism scripts hastily improvised in a last-ditch blitz to rescue the two anti-subversive committees initiated an agitprop genre that has been elaborated in a mounting campaign to restore not only the committees but the entire intelligence system.[7] A major theme in this propaganda assault is the warning that we have been left defenseless against European-style terrorism by a left-led dismantling of our intelligence structures. Scenarios of helplessness to prevent a seizure of the Capitol by a handful of *enragés* are floated in congressional testimony. Aldo Moro's murder is attributed to Communist insistence on curbing Italy's political surveillance capability.

Hardliners have cast the KGB as the secret master-mind of terrorist bombing by the FALN—the nationalist, anti-colonial group that has been responsible for terrorist bombings in this country to promote its objective of Puerto Rican independence. FALN, it is charged, is a secret arm of Cuban intelligence (CINCO, as it is acronymically called by those seeking to establish their qualifications as experts), an alleged KGB puppet. But these claimed linkages are pure invention. Similarly, the SDS-sponsored Venceremos Brigade, which made trips to Cuba in the late sixties, is, again without proof, described as a cover for a domestic bombing-sabotage mission operation trained by Cuban intelligence. In these circles, too, Cuban intelligence (not to speak of the KGB) master-minded the assassination of John F. Kennedy and the Panama Canal Treaty. The terrorist theme has monopolized numerous hearings of the Senate Judiciary Subcommittee that inherited the SISS operation. In his campaign to revive HISC, Congressman Larry McDonald floods the *Congressional Record* with terrorism-related items, charges that terrorist sympathizers are in the forefront of the attack on intelligence, and, in a bid for support of the Jewish community, claims that PLO backers are financing domestic terrorists.* Nor has ex-HISC Chairman Richard Ichord deserted the ramparts. In a foreword to a 1978 tract proclaiming the Communist "globalization of terrorism" *(International Terrorism—The Communist Connection),* he deplored the "wholesale dismantling of police and governmental intelligence units," and stressed the need for new structures to prevent the spread of domestic terrorism. With full-throated out-

---

*By early summer 1978 he had already obtained 177 out of a needed 218 co-sponsors to force submission of his HISC revival resolution to a House vote. According to staffer Louise Rees, "Every time the FALN throws a bomb or the PLO hijacks a plane we get two or three more co-sponsors" —Quoted in Rosen, "Lugosi-like HUAC Rises from the Grave in New Committee Body," *New Times,* July 24, 1978.

cry over foreign-inspired terrorism, leaders of the congressional countersubversive bloc are mobilizing to revitalize the dormant Internal Security Act and to defeat long-overdue revision of the immigration exclusions of the 1954 McCarran-Walter Act. An immediate tactical goal of such forces is the restoration of file secrecy, threatened not only by legislation (such as the FOIPA) but by court proceedings as well. Congressional right wingers have enlisted the support of a network of law enforcement units in a campaign to depict both terrorism and nonpolitical crimes as consequences of profligate record access. A right-wing document ("Terrorism in America: The Developing Internal Security Crisis") disseminated in August 1978 as a briefing paper in Congress and the law enforcement community warns that response to a mounting terrorist threat is being effectively crippled by legislative and judicial provision for file access. Shortly after the publication of this brochure, Chicago Police Superintendent James E. O'Grady in testimony before the House Select Committee on Intelligence harshly attacked a lawsuit against the Chicago red squad to halt police spying and harassment of peaceful lawful activity. Without proof, O'Grady charged that the plaintiffs' judicially ordered access to Chicago informer files had rendered the Chicago Police Department "virtually helpless to protect the city from terrorist activities," and "completely frustrated any legitimate intelligence activity." This argument entirely ignored the fact that the access was confined to files unrelated to law enforcement, dealing with targets engaged in activities protected by the First Amendment.

A commodity in enormous demand, terrorism is in pitifully short supply. Political terrorism in its modern form—politically motivated exemplary violence, indifference to human life, symbolic targets, the intended creation of overwhelming fear—is not a serious problem in the United States. As the 1976 report by the Task Force on Disorder and Terrorism of the National Advisory Commission on Criminal Justice Standards and Goals pointed out, not only has terrorism been exclusively domestic and unconnected with terrorist activities in other countries, but "it has been neither sustained nor effective." The report concludes that "conditions in the United States do not seem to indicate a massive expansion of terroristic activity or radical change in its nature or its extension into formal guerrilla warfare." Similarly, surveys of bombing incidents published by the Justice Department show a continuing downward trend. A listing in the 1978 report of known causes of bombings in 1977 attributed 4 to "subversion"—out of a total of 1318 reported incidents—a continuation of a downward trend and reflecting the lowest number of bombings since 1972, when the FBI first began collecting data for publication in an annual "Bomb Summary."* The terrorist scare lobby resolutely ignores or distorts this data, typically by claiming that all reported bombing incidents, whatever the investigatively established cause, are the work of terrorists or that those for which causes are unknown (697 in 1977) are actually terrorist-inspired. We are assured such an attribution is warranted by the left's political inactivity in recent years: the radicals' public agitation and demonstrations have been replaced by bombings

---

*The FBI attributed a further decline in 1978 (52 as against 100 "terrorist-related" bombings recorded for the previous year), to the "deterrent nature" of its counter-terrorist program—*Congressional Record*, October 16, 1979, p. H9219.

and explosions. An equally desperate chorus of hardliners has claimed that both the gruesome Jonestown, Guyana, mass suicide-massacre and the subsequent assassinations of San Francisco Mayor George Moscone and Supervisor Harvey Milk were committed by "terrorists" free to work their will now that "we have dismantled the official agencies that used to monitor and guard us from such excesses."[8]

The campaign to exploit terrorism as a means of refueling domestic counter-subversion is confronted by another obstacle. According to the Task Force's chronology, from 1965 to 1976, of incidents involving political violence, a substantial number are attributable to right-wing and racist sources and thus are useless as documentation for a countersubversive offensive. Many groups linked to violence at both ends of the spectrum were transient products of the sixties and are now defunct. The difficulties are compounded by the fact that groups on the left which are violence-oriented have a cultist nonideological thrust that resists, even by the most strained exegesis, the "Communist" label. Finally, of the small number of U.S.-based terrorist operations in support of overseas movements, the most prominent are rightist, notably the Cuban exile group which, under the direction of DINA (Chilean Secret Service) agents, carried out the assassination of Orlando Letelier, former Chilean diplomat.*

Intelligence propagandists nevertheless insist that the domestic version of terrorism is a manifestation of a worldwide phenomenon rooted in shared ideology. The Baader-Meinhof cells, the Italian Red Brigades, and the PLO are all—so the argument runs—constituents of a common conspiracy against "the West," which also embraces domestic groups such as New World Liberation Front (NWLF), Red Brigade, and Weather Underground, all California-based. Improved channels of communication and financial support (from the Soviet Union) will in the future, it is alleged, establish the now hidden connections between the domestic bombers and their transnational counterparts. Even if the threat is still inchoate, special intelligence initiatives are required to monitor and prevent its emergence; considering the gravity of the danger, it would be foolhardy to wait until it is too late. Ideology satisfies a second, equally important, need: it preserves the expansive rationale of imputation developed by domestic intelligence over the past four decades. A nonterrorist organization can be tagged for surveillance as a terrorist front, or a support group, defender, source of cadres, suspected protector of fugitives, or simply—because of its failure to denounce terrorism with sufficient vigor—an apologist.

To maximize its leverage, the specter of terrorism must be tied to revolutionary violence, to "Communism" (for, it will be recalled, the violence stereotype is the life blood of the Menace myth). It is precisely the image of bomb throwers that is identified in the nativist consciousness with revolutionary communism. Although historically an anarchist political tactic, bomb throwing has been popularly associated with all revolutionary movements. The 1919 bomb scares cradled the stereotype of the bearded Bolshevik, armed with a smoking bomb. To be sure, the minuscule corps of left-wing bombers concentrate on

---

*Afterwards Letelier was depicted, in a right-wing "disinformation" campaign complete with invented documents, as a KGB agent. Taylor Branch, "The Letelier Investigation," *New York Times Magazine,* July 16, 1978.

property and seek to avoid injury to persons, and thus fall short of the "reckless disregard of human life" formula of the twenties. But that is a mere detail, as is the fact that domestic terrorist groups have limited aims (prison reform, ecology, health care, reduction of utility rates) and that, historically, political violence in this country has not been insurrectionary in intent, although bombings are frequently announced in the febrile rhetoric of revolution.* The terrorist group in this country with the most extensive bombing record is the FALN, which is notorious for its unique indifference to personal injury and possible death randomly inflicted by bombs planted in public places.

The alarm concerning terrorism is not confined to the anti-radical grass-roots sector—it resounds throughout the law enforcement community. In the wake of the emergence of kidnapping as an occupational hazard of American businessmen abroad, detective and consultant agencies have developed new counterterrorist specialties, which include intelligence programs, surveillance-detection training, hostage survival guidance,† and the organization of crisis management teams. One of the smaller agencies in the field, Rayne International, grosses $1 million a year and offers its clients a monthly newsletter, *Counterforce,* which deals with all aspects of counterterrorism. A competitor, Risks International, headed by a retired Air Force intelligence officer, sells intelligence data to the business community on terrorist-related activities in every major city in the world. According to Richard Kobetsky, director of behavioral research for the International Association of Chiefs of Police, counterterrorism is "one of the fastest growing businesses in the country . . . a cash-in opportunity." Large corporations have organized their own security seminars and training programs to deal with terrorism. A document used in a course on "asset protection," prepared by the International Association under contract with IBM's Security Department, stresses the need to develop a comprehensive counterintelligence program, including dossiers on potential bombers, kidnappers, and extortionists. It adds that since IBM has "successfully resisted unionization, likely specific radical efforts will center on attempts to organize and manipulate IBM workers."‡

Terrorism has also become a priority concern in government circles. A number of established and ad hoc bureaucracies, headed by a twenty-six-agency Working Group on Terrorism under the direction of a smaller Executive Coordinating Committee of the National Security Council, have emerged to deal on policy and operational levels with existing and potential terrorism. It is assumed, for example, that airplane hijacking and hostage taking similar to those involving West German and Japanese airliners at Mogadishu in Somalia and Dacca in Bangladesh will take place in this country in the near future. Preparations for this and other contingencies cover three areas: intelligence identification;

---

*As Richard H. Hofstadter has noted: "An arresting fact about American violence, and one of the keys to an understanding of its history, is that very little of it has been insurrectionary. Most of our violence has taken the form of action by one group of citizens against another group, rather than by citizens against the State"—Hofstadter and Wallace, eds., *American Violence: Documentary History* (Vintage, 1971), p. 10.

†SISS's contribution to this specialty has already been noted in Chapter II.

‡The corporation repudiated the document after it was published as not reflective of management policies—"IBM Repudiates Terrorism Lesson," *New York Times,* Nov. 23, 1976.

negotiations and crisis management; and commando liberation, an area in which the Defense Department has already organized a special assault capability. Combating terrorism through a program that features the development of intelligence resources is also a top FBI priority, along with organized crime, white-collar crime, and public corruption. The Bureau has restructured its domestic intelligence operations in a new Domestic Security-Terrorism Section of the Criminal Investigative Division. In congressional testimony and a press conference of March 1978, FBI Director William H. Webster stated that the "Bureau's domestic intelligence unit was under instructions to identify groups and movements with a potential for terrorism so as to be prepared for its emergence as a major factor in this country."

Federal intelligence preparations and activity have been especially intense in the nuclear field.[9] The fear of "high-technology" terrorism has resulted in the creation of intelligence units by both the Nuclear Regulatory Commission* (the Intelligence Assessment Team) and the Department of Energy. The NRC-IAT has developed an interface with all other radical-watching elements of the domestic intelligence community. However, the present focus of these intelligence efforts by both the Energy Department and the NRC is not suspected terrorism but monitoring of anti-nuclear movements and activities by environmentalists and others concerned about nuclear proliferation. The IAT communicates such intelligence to utilities involved in nuclear projects, which have themselves through security departments become increasingly committed to surveillance programs, not for the purpose of defense against terrorism but to spy on and neutralize their opponents. A major goal of the intelligence community—both public and private—is putting terrorist trousers (ironically enough) on nonviolent anti-nuclear protest movements.[10] A clue to this priority is the marketability of such intelligence as reflected in the NCLC's tactics (described above) in bidding for intelligence aid in attacking its rivals. Indeed, this group regularly denounces all forms of protest against nuclear power as "terrorism."

In addition to private detective resources, utilities such as Georgia Power work closely with local police units which, as in the past when the federal presence was reduced, continue to conduct traditional anti-radical intelligence operations. These units have not escaped the criticisms and pressures that have forced a retreat in federal intelligence activities; but to an extent not possible on the federal level, they have invoked law enforcement, peacekeeping, and counterterrorism as covers for a continuation of their traditional radical watching.

It seems plain that, as in the past, these urban intelligence units, using deceptive covers, will dominate political intelligence, at least until a full restoration of a federal presence. It is in the cities and states that the tradition of countersubversion, renewed by social anxieties and the competition for power, is still strong. Surely it is a portent that in the 1978 race for governor of the

---

*The NRC commissioned three reports (in 1974, 1975, and 1977) that uniformly recommend the development of an intelligence capability to cope with the terrorist threat to nuclear materials and facilities. Apart from the recommended monitoring techniques (electronic surveillance, informer infiltration), the danger inherent in such proposals is that no reliable guideposts are offered for the selection of targets. As the history of domestic intelligence so clearly demonstrates, the process of vetting—the preliminary investigation to determine the target's goals and style—soon becomes an end in itself.

nativist heartland, California, the two leading contenders for the Republican nomination were Los Angeles police chief Edward Davis, a general in the war on political and cultural dissent, and Attorney General Evelle J. Younger (the winner), a one-time FBI agent involved in the 1941 Bridges wiretapping. (A third candidate was State Senator John Briggs, a crusader against "gays, grass and godlessness.") Despite promises of reform and the shredding of files, a Los Angeles Police Department team in March 1978 invaded the city council chamber and made still and videotaped photographs for intelligence files of witnesses against a proposed nuclear power plant. A claim that the picture-taking was for purposes of police training was later admitted to be false.

The themes of decentralization and concealment of the political intelligence function are exemplified by another California unit, the Organized Crime and Criminal Intelligence Branch (OCCIB), a component of the state's Department of Justice under the direction and control of Attorney General Younger.[11] Founded in 1970, ostensibly for "controlling and suppressing organized crime," it has devoted much of its resources to data collection on the backgrounds of leftists such as Joan Baez and Jerry Rubin. When the heat rose, its former targets ("revolutionaries," "subversives," and "militants") were metamorphosed into "terrorists." In 1975 it broadly characterized prison reform groups as "effective conduits of terrorist-type activities." OCCIB agents and affiliates infiltrated the Chavez United Farm Workers movement and the Abalone Alliance, a nonviolent anti-nuclear group. The official in charge of the latter operation served as a lecturer on an OCCIB course on terrorism, "particularly . . . groups operating under the cover of a legitimate front . . . or legal activity." As for its claimed organized crime mission, the California Legislative Analyst's office has repeatedly noted, in its annual evaluations, OCCIB's continuing focus on activities by "militant groups and motorcycle gangs far removed from 'organized crime' activity for which the unit was established."

OCCIB runs a school, financed by the Law Enforcement Assistance Administration (LEAA), which teaches police from thirty states and a number of foreign countries the use of surveillance techniques in dealing with a variety of crimes, including urban terrorism.[12] Western Regional Organized Crime Training Institute (WROCTI) has flourished in part because of the glamor of its intelligence curriculum (electronic surveillance, the penetration of fronts, informer recruitment) touted in Orwellian jargon: a course in "informant development and maintenance" instructs police students in the refinements of such "human resource and management tools" as "dossiers, contact reports, biographical data and resource banks." LEAA has justified its substantial subsidy as a needed boost to the creation of a "national police intelligence force" with professional standards. WROCTI's disclaimers of concern with noncriminal intelligence are not persuasive; WROCTI-trained forces in various areas have been involved in surveillance of dissidents, such as anti-nuclear groups. (One of the instructors in the "informant development" course is the now familiar Larry Grathwohl, whose résumé boasts that he is the only successful Weather Underground infiltrator.) And WROCTI administrators, while protesting their commitment to law enforcement intelligence exclusively, admit that "there really isn't any way to control this. . . . Guys get power and just abuse it."

Nothing more dramatically demonstrates the grip of subversion both as a pretext for protecting the status quo and as a folkish taboo than the congressional reluctance to confront the basic question of the FBI's authority to conduct internal security investigations. The extensive investigations and reports on federal domestic intelligence in the seventies focused primarily on its excesses, the propriety of its standards for initiating an investigation, its scope and techniques. These matters have been the subject of guidelines such as those prescribed by Attorney General Levi in 1976. But it is universally admitted that the FBI today, as in the beginning, lacks authority to engage in domestic intelligence activities. Three years since the last of the probes ended, Congress still refuses to face the issue whether to grant or withhold political intelligence authority, inherently vague and necessarily secretively exercised, beyond established, clearly understood law enforcement jurisdiction. Should the FBI have the power to select targets (groups and individuals) on ideological grounds, accumulate background information on their noncriminal activities, conduct year-long non-stop investigations of key targets, surveil individuals solely because of their association with such targets, and use techniques that violate basic freedoms?

The Bureau and its Justice Department spokesmen have insisted that not the probability of violence (the criminal standard) but the mere possibility of future violence and bombing, however remote, requires legislative approval of domestic intelligence activities. This bid for an internal security mandate is accompanied by assurances of monitoring to prevent the abuses of the past by linking security investigation more closely to criminal law objectives. The need for a special, more extensive authorization is justified primarily on the ground of prevention: advance information will enable the agency to intervene and forestall planned violence. But a GAO report, made public in November 1977, concludes that the Bureau's efforts had yielded "few visible results . . . only a few cases produced advance information of planned violent activities useful in solving related criminal investigations."* One is left with the GAO's observa-

---

*An earlier (1976, see above) GAO audit of 19,000 FBI open investigative case files concluded that actions of some kind were anticipated in a bare 17 cases, with only 6 involving potential violence. The FBI was unable to supply evidence either to the GAO or when challenged by the Church Committee that it had in fact prevented violence in a single case. Despite massive surveillance of the SDS, the establishment of a New Left desk in 1970, and informer saturation of college campuses, the Bureau neither anticipated nor prevented organization within the SDS of the Weatherman force with its explicit commitment to symbolic bombings. Similarly, surveillance of the entire Black Muslim movement failed to prevent the murders in Washington, D.C., of members of the Hanafi Muslim sect and the subsequent (March 1977) siege by survivors in reprisal for the unsolved murders. Natural barriers (race, style, political tribalism), coupled with the security precautions that are second nature to groups at risk, make violence-prone targets virtually inaccessible through standard penetration techniques such as infiltration and electronic eavesdropping. Thus, frustrated, the intelligence operation focuses instead on secondary nonviolent targets, in the hope of penetrating to the plotters of violence.

This goal of lateral movement along an ever-more-militant continuum typically produces a swollen data base dealing with legitimate activity, but rarely reaches the tiny terrorist-style cells, which because of ideological differences, are frequently intensely hostile to the nonviolent groups, surveilled *faute de mieux*. A related difficulty arises from the fact that terrorist operations groups are frequently dominated by a single commanding figure difficult to identify, let alone to track down and neutralize. Nor does the monitoring of isolated individuals provide a predictive data base: would-be assassins Arthur Bremer and Sara Jane Moore, as well as President Kennedy's assassin, Lee Harvey Oswald, were all under FBI surveillance not long before they made their moves.

tion that it was possible that the FBI's "continuous coverage" in itself might have prevented the implementation of plans for violence by extremist groups— a view unreservedly endorsed by the FBI itself, and long pressed by intelligence lobbies. But, by the end of the seventies, a broad consensus supported the view that the predictable abuse of intelligence power in chilling and repressing legitimate dissent far outruns its protective benefits, whether measured in positive or negative terms.

This view is reflected in the administration-sponsored "FBI Charter Act of 1979," introduced on July 31, 1979, by Senator Edward M. Kennedy. The bill is a retreat from a more expansive earlier claim by the Department of Justice for FBI domestic intelligence powers. Most notable is a requirement that the Bureau confine itself to investigations of criminal conduct only. An investigation may not be initiated unless the facts and circumstances "reasonably indicate" the prospect of a criminal violation. The legislation has been attacked by the countersubversive lobby as a threat to internal security. Libertarian groups have objected to its failure to delineate adequately the threshold standards required to prevent investigative intrusion into areas protected by the First Amendment, and to the lack of higher authorization and review procedures in this area. The bill's vague definition of "terrorism" and a cognate prevention investigative authority have brought warnings of potential abuse as a curb on legitimate domestic dissent. Also questioned is the measure's treatment of the use of informers, including: failure to establish warrant requirements, an open-ended authorization to provide cover for infiltrators; the grant of authority to deploy physicians, lawyers, clergymen, and journalists as informers; the guarantee of informer confidentiality whenever the privilege is asserted by the Attorney General; and, in certain cases, permission for Bureau informers and agents to engage in law violations (federal, state, and local) with impunity. In addition, critics point to the charter's failure to prohibit COINTELPRO activities; its excessive reliance on internal guidelines rather than explicit statutory regulations; the absence of civil remedies; the creation of new exemptions for FBI records under the FOIA; and the failure to provide for effective congressional review.

The outcome of the charter debate is uncertain; the danger is a "right way" trade-off which grants substantive approval to intelligence-type activities in exchange for procedural limitations. The possibility of such a result—the low-profile institutionalization of domestic security as a police responsibility—surely cannot be excluded, given the political stake of conservatism in the social myth of subversion, a society programmed for fear, and a nation wracked by long-suppressed tensions and poised on the cusp of upheaval. Moreover, the history of the modern state reinforces the prospect of planned provocation of violence to justify repression in the United States and to increase dependence on the "defensive" and "preventive" security role of a political police force.

Appendix I

A Note on the Language of Intelligence

The absorption into popular culture, in the wake of World War II, of high-risk, cloak-and-dagger style intelligence, identified with foreign and military conflict, glamorized both the calling and its vocabulary. Usages previously considered inapplicable to a libertarian political order became emblems of legitimacy and professionalism. The word "mission" is a prize example. To the notion of special assignment or trust it adds overtones of religion, diplomacy, and military hazard, thus professionalizing and ennobling at the same time. Director Hoover once indignantly rebuked a university official who complained of FBI campus spies for presuming to interfere with the Bureau's "mission." In this category must also be added "sensitive" and "compromise," as in "to compromise a sensitive operation." This phrase is best taken to mean that the conduct in question is of doubtful legality and that its disclosure would be highly embarrassing.

Operational terms have, over the years, been coated with the gloss of professionalism. This semantic facelifting substitutes "informant," "confidential source," or "asset" for "informer" (he is not hired, but "recruited" or "persuaded" to "cooperate with the FBI"), "surreptitious entry" for break-in, "technical" or "electronic surveillance" for wiretapping and bugging,* "microphone surveillance" for bugging, "highly confidential coverage" for wiretapping, bugging, or an illegal entry, "to secure a residence" for breaking in without a warrant, and "covert action" for a variety of forms of disruption, sabotage, and dirty tricks.† ("Covert" is noteworthy for an additional reason: it is used by

---

*In a trial in September 1975, Nelson Bunker Hunt, a son of the billionaire H. L. Hunt, testified that he would not have authorized wiretapping of his employees if he had known it was illegal. He explained: "Wiretap has a bad connotation since Watergate. This was before Watergate—electronic surveillance was the term we used here"—"Bunker Hunt Says He Was Unaware Taps Were Illegal," *New York Times,* Sept. 26, 1975.

†Such practices were called "negative campaigning" by CREEP spies.

intelligence people to describe an operation which, while functioning openly, is disguised to conceal its source. "Clandestine" describes an operation that is hidden but not necessarily disguised.)

Much intelligence rhetoric has successfully entered the language. "Cover" and "cover story" are now household words. When a cover is "blown," an informer may be "burnt," depriving the "agent," "handler," "control," or (a softer term) "contact" of further intelligence from his "reliable source." (Such exposure is particularly damaging in the case of a "deep cover," "penetration" agent or—a classic spookism—"mole.") Not all applicants for admission to popular discourse have an easy time of it. Director Hoover tried hard to substitute "informant" for "informer," which he condemned as a subversive usage ("sabotage by semantics") despite the fact that his verbal preference describes only a casual source of information and not the continuing, usually paid relationship characteristic of Bureau practice. Equally thorny has been the intelligence struggle to banish "dossier." Former Acting FBI Director L. Patrick Gray III and James Adams, head of the Bureau's Domestic Intelligence Division, bridle when they hear the word; they prefer "file." Former FBI second-in-command Cartha DeLoach is allergic to "surveillance"; he insists on "investigation."

Another source of intelligence usage is trade craft, the jargon developed internally by intelligence people to protect themselves, their operations, and their informers from the enemy who, by an intelligence fiction, is assumed to be everyone and everywhere. A now familiar example is the reference to a burglary as a "black bag job" or a "break." This furtive intelligence style is well described by John le Carré in *The Looking Glass War:*

> Lansen. It was odd to hear a name spoken out like that. In the outfit they simply never did it. They favored circumlocution, cover names, anything but the original: Archie boy, our flying friend, our friend up North, the chappie who takes the snapshots; they would even use the tortuous collection of figures and letters by which he was known on paper; but never in any circumstance the name.

Internal euphemism and circumlocution are found in other intelligence contexts. It is sometimes required, for purposes of "plausible denial," to enable a superior to disavow responsibility or advance knowledge in the event the operation miscarries. A related type of circumlocution is sometimes required to shield the operator himself and his superior from confronting a distasteful reality, as in the case of a proposed assassination. ("To terminate with extreme prejudice" is a particularly ornate example of such word play.) The Church Committee notes in this connection:

> Euphemism may actually have been preferred not because of "plausible denial" . . . but because the persons involved could not bring themselves to state in plain language what they intended to do. In some instances, moreover, subordinates may have assumed, rightly or wrongly, that the listening superiors did not want the issue squarely placed before them. "Assassinate," "murder" and "kill" are words many people do not want to speak or hear.

The Watergate scandals generally illuminate both the destruction of meaning and the role of language as a mirror of that destruction. Outstanding intelligence examples emerged in the trial of John D. Ehrlichman or his involvement in the break-in of the office of Dr. Lewis Fielding, Daniel Ellsberg's psychiatrist. The evidence indicated that Ehrlichman did not expressly authorize a break-in but a "covert operation" to examine Dr. Fielding's files. And in his testimony he referred to the break-in as "the California matter" or the "operation." He denied—not only at the trial but to FBI investigators and the grand jury also—that he had authorized a break-in or, for that matter, any illegal activity. The jury refused to believe him in the light of evidence which showed that he had removed two incriminating memoranda from the Plumbers' file, because, in Ehrlichman's language, "they were a little too sensitive. . . ."

Perhaps the master euphemism of intelligence is "intelligence community," a benign successor to "intelligence establishment." With its connotations of warmth and good fellowship it quite effectively masks the realities of operational hostility and the frequently savage competition among the "community's" constituent units.

Appendix II

Hoover Communicates

No government official has ever communicated to a national audience in such volume as J. Edgar Hoover. Nor has any single contributor, however lustrous, published in an array of periodicals remotely comparable in number and diversity. Hoover also stands alone in the number of his articles, speeches, and interviews that have been reprinted both by the government and private groups, as well as his output of officially sponsored pamphlets. Although the necessarily incomplete listings that follow begin with 1940, when he first emerged on the stage as a nation-savior, his use of the media and the speaker's platform for self-promotion was already well developed. The September 1939 assignment enabled him to subordinate crime and law enforcement to the more congenial themes of Americanism: patriotism, citizenship, freedom, democracy, morality, sabotage, subversion, political violence, Godlessness, communism, the Communist threat, Communist fronts, Communist influence (in movements for change of every sort, peace groups, unions, civil rights activities, student and youth protests), Communist duplicity, Communist propaganda, and the endless perils of straying from the American way of life. Before examining the appended listings, we need to be reminded that they reflect still another unique distinction: never has authorship been claimed for so many publications that were in fact written by others.

Radio and television programs as well as motion pictures are included here; the use of these media was an integral part of the Hoover image-building propaganda effort. The FBI did not merely encourage such productions but provided material, script reviews, and production consultation to receptive media collaborators, and even personnel to play agents' roles. Finally, it must be borne in mind that the field agents served as a distribution network for the Bureau's public relations output and, in addition, were required to cultivate the local media on their own to promote a favorable image of the agency. SAC's regularly gave interviews (television, radio, and press) and delivered addresses on special occasions and, more routinely, at luncheon meetings.

Articles: 1940–1972, by J. Edgar Hoover

1940

"Crime's Law School," *American Mag.,* February.

"Photography in Crime Detection," *Scientific Amer.,* February.

"Presentation of the Marcellus Hartley Public Welfare Medal: With Response," *Science,* May.

"Third Degree," *American Mag.,* May.

"Test of Citizenship: Our Job Is to Keep to the Path of Americanism," *Vital Speeches,* May 1.

*"Is There a Spy Menace?" *N.Y. Herald Tribune,* THIS WEEK, July 21. CR A4498, vol. 86.

"Enemies Within Our Gates," *American Mag.,* August.

*"Americanism in Peril," *Signs of the Times,* Sept. 4. CR A5461, vol. 86.

"Camps of Crime," *American Mag.,* November.

"Criminals Are Home Grown," *Rotarian,* April.

"The Man I Want My Son To Be," *Parents Mag.,* February.

"Stamping Out the Spies," *American Mag.,* January.

1941

"The Big Scare," *American Mag.,* August.

"War Begins at Home," *American Mag.,* September.

1942

"Policing a Nation at War," *Popular Science,* February.

"Nation's Call to Duty," *Vital Speeches,* July 1.

"Beware of Frauds in Uniform," *Colliers,* Dec. 26.

1943

"Man Without Fingerprints," *Colliers,* Jan. 30.

"Hitler's Spies Are Experts," *Colliers,* April.

"Traitors Must Die," *Colliers,* July 16 (F. L. Collins).

"Battle on the Home Front," *Vital Speeches,* Sept. 15.

"Spy Trap," *Popular Mechanics,* December.

"New Tricks of the Nazi Spies," *American Mag.,* October.

"The FBI Is On Guard," *Kiwanis Mag.,* February.

"Slickers in Slacks," *Colliers,* Oct. 16.

"Wild Children," *American Mag.,* July.

1944

"How the Nazi Spy Invasion Was Smashed," *American Mag.,* September.

"Hitler's Spying Sirens," *American Mag.,* December.

"Enemies at Large," *American Mag.,* April.

"Jokers Worse than Saboteurs," *Science Digest,* February.

"Mothers Are Our Only Hope," *Woman's Home Companion,* January. (F. L. Collins).

"First Pan American Congress on Criminology," *Bulletin of Pan American Union,* November.

"Third Front Against Juvenile Crime," *New York Times Mag.,* Feb. 27.

1945

"Post War Crime Unless—," *Rotarian,* April.

"FBI Laboratory in Wartime," *Science Monthly,* January.

1946

"Crime Wave We Now Face," *N.Y. Times Mag.,* April 21.

"Rising Crime Wave," *American Mag.,* March.

"Blaster," *Reader's Digest,* September.

"Enemies Masterpiece of Espionage," *Reader's Digest,* July.

"Fortune in the Grave," *Reader's Digest,* July.

"Our Achilles' Heel," *Vital Speeches,* Oct. 15.

"Reconversion of Law Enforcement," *Vital Speeches,* Feb. 7.

"Spy Who Double Crossed Hitler," *American Mag.,* May.

"Spy Who Double Crossed Hitler," *Reader's Digest,* June.

"Communists Among Us," *Washington News Digest,* December.

1947

*"Red Fascism in the United States Today," *American Mag.,* February. CR A536, vol. 93.

*Reprinted in the *Congressional Record.*

*P "How to Fight Communism," *Newsweek,*
June 9. CR A2811, vol. 93.

"How Safe Is Your Daughter?" *American
Mag.,* July.

"Trigger Finger Clues," *Reader's Digest,*
June.

1948

"Communism in the United States,"
Confidential—From Washington, June.

"Deceit Is a Red Virtue," condensed from
Red Book in the *Catholic Digest,*
September.

"Dangerous Freedom," *American Mag.,*
January.

1949

"God or Chaos," *Redbook,* February.

1950

"50,000 Communists," *U.S. News & World
Report,* May 12.

*"How Communists Operate," *U.S. News &
World Report,* Aug. 11. CR A5725, vol.
96.

"Law Enforcement Views Education for
Leisure," *Education,* October.

*"Hoover Answers Ten Questions on the
FBI," *N.Y. Times Mag.,* April 16. CR
A3331, vol. 96.

"Unmasking the Communist Masquerader,"
The Educational Forum, May.

P"Foe to Freedom," *Elks Mag.,* October.

"Underground Tactics of the Communists,"
Coronet, December.

"Uphold Our Laws," *Scholastic,* Nov. 8.

"When Reporting Subversive Activities,"
American City, October.

1951

"Responsibility of Public in Guarding
Security," *Assoc. Press,* February.

"Communist Threat in the United States,"
U.S. News & World Report, March 30.

*"A Good Christian Is a Good Citizen,"
Lookout, Aug. 12. CR A5269, vol. 97.

"Communism—Enemy of American Labor,"
American Federalist, September.

"Crime of the Century," *Reader's Digest,*
May.

1952

"Make the Communists Show Their Own
Colors!" International News Service
Release, April 18.

*"The Insidious Communist Game: FBI
Chief Cites Reds' Trickery," *N.Y.
Journal-American,* April 12. CR A2488,
vol. 98.

*"Could Your Child Become a Red?"
Parade, May 11, CR A3085, vol. 98.

"Red Spy Masters in America," *Reader's
Digest,* August.

"You Versus Crime," *Rotarian,* November.

"My Most Memorable Christmas," *Coronet,*
December.

1953

"The Communists Want You," *Woman's
Day,* January.

*"Communism and the College Student,"
Campus, Boston, Mass., March. CR
A4750, vol. 99.

*"Your Child Could Become a Communist,"
Washington *Times-Herald,* June 21. CR
A3694, vol. 99.

"Red Infiltration of Labor Unions," *AF of L
Labor Guide,* fall preview issue.

*P "How the FBI Tracks Reds and Spies,"
Pathfinder, Nov. 5. CR A293, vol. 99.

"Hoover Speaks Out on Spies After Years of
Chasing Them," *U.S. News & World
Report,* Nov. 27.

"U.S. Communists Today," *American
Mercury,* May.

"What J. Edgar Hoover Did about White,"
U.S. News & World Report, Nov. 27.

"What J. Edgar Hoover Did about White,"
Time, Nov. 30.

1954

"U.S. Communists Hide Deeper," *U.S. News
& World Report,* Feb. 19.

*"Red Infiltration of Labor Unions," *AF of
L Labor Guide,* February. CR A1565,
vol. 100.

"J. Edgar Hoover Cites Red Threat,"
Brooklyn Tablet, Feb. 27.

*"Where Do We Stand Today with
Communism in the U.S.?" *American
Legion Mag.,* March 1. CR 2297, vol.
100.

"B-R-E-A-K-I-N-G the Communist Spell,"
American Mercury, March.

"U.S. Communists Today: Excerpt from
Testimony Before H. App. Com.,"
American Mercury, May.

*"Hoover Address to 63d Continental
Congress of the DAR," *American
Legion Mag.,* July. CR A4943,
vol. 100.

*"What Makes Men Strong?" *N.Y. Herald
Tribune,* THIS WEEK, July 21. CR
A5299, vol. 100.

*"B-R-E-A-K-I-N-G the Communist Spell,"

P Reprinted in pamphlet form.

N.Y. Herald Tribune, THIS WEEK,
Nov. 1. CR A6062, vol. 100.
P "The Communists Are After Our Minds,"
American Mag., October.
P "Basis of Sound Law Enforcement,"
*Annals of the American Academy of
Political and Social Science,* January.
"Communism and Schools," *U.S. News &
World Report,* Nov. 26.
1955
*"22,663 Red Spies," Shreveport *Times,*
April 15. CR A2605, vol. 101.
"What Makes an FBI Agent?" *Coronet,*
June.
"They Make Your Hometown Safer,"
American Mag., August.
"Communism Is a False Religion," *Fact
Forum News,* December.
"How Safe Is Your Youngster?" *American
Mag.,* March.
"Man's First Need," *American Mercury,*
March.
"Our Common Task," *Vital Speeches,* Nov.
1.
"Why Crime Is Dropping," *U.S. News &
World Report,* Sept. 30.
"Why U.S. Uses Ex-Reds as Informants,"
U.S. News & World Report, Oct. 14.
1956
*"Twenty Thousand Dangerous Few," *The
Pilot,* Boston, Mass., Feb. 20. CR
A1550, vol. 102.
"How U.S. Reds Use Pseudo Liberals as a
Front," *U.S. News & World Report,*
April 13.
P "Communist 'New Look'—Study in
Duplicity," *Elks Mag.,* August.
"Challenge of Crime Control," *Vital
Speeches,* July 1.
*P "Twin Enemies of Freedom," *Vital
Speeches,* Dec. 1. CR 6148, vol. 103.
"Worthwhile Guidance in the Making of
Good Citizens," *National
Parent-Teacher,* November.
"FBI Chief Warns; Reds Still Recruit Ready
Help in the U.S.," *U.S. News & World
Report,* March 8.
1957
*"KO Red Menace—It's Everybody's Job,"
guest editorial in *The Times &
Democrat,* July 3. CR 11187, vol. 103.
*"American Ideal," *Vital Speeches,* March
15. CR A1337, vol. 103.

"American Ideal," *U.S. News & World
Report,* March 8.
"American Ideal," *American Mercury,*
October.
*P "The Twin Enemies of Freedom," *FBI
Law Enforcement Bulletin,* January.
CR 6148, vol. 103.
"Free World Slow to Recognize Communist
Approach," *U.S. News & World Report,*
March 8.
*"What America Means to Me," *N.Y.
Herald Tribune,* THIS WEEK, June
30. CR A5216, vol. 103.
* "*Hold Yourself Accountable,* " guest
editorial in *The Times & Democrat,*
July 4. CR A5749, vol. 103.
P "How to Beat Communism," *The Lion,*
October.
"Legion Alert as Guest Speakers Decry
Public Apathy," *American Legion
Mag.,* November.
P "God and Country or Communism?"
American Legion Mag., November.
"Perpetuation of Our American Heritage,"
Vital Speeches, Oct. 1.
1958
"Should I Force My Child?" *American
Mercury,* February.
"Deadly Menace of Pseudo Liberals,"
American Mercury, January.
*"Masters of Deceit" (at least ten items on
this text by Hoover are cited in the
CR, vol. 104).
*"Communism: A False Religion," *Human
Events,* April 23. CR A3702, vol. 104.
*"The Hoover Report," Los Angeles
Examiner, April 23. CR A3819, vol.
104.
*"The Challenge of the Future," *Christianity
Today,* May 26. CR A5124, vol. 104.
"Juvenile Delinquency and Juvenile Crime,"
ThisWeekMag., Oct.26,Nov.2,Nov.9.
"How to Keep Your Car," *Good
Housekeeping,* March.
1959
"Communist Illusion and Democratic
Reality," *Foreign National Strategy
Seminar,* July.**
"I Challenge Your Right to Drive," *National
Business Woman,* February.
*"Youth, Communist Target," *Our Sunday
Visitor,* National Catholic Action
Weekly, Jan. 18. CR A357, vol. 105.

**Like a great many other articles by the Director, this was reprinted at Bureau expense, and
widely disseminated and reprinted.

*"Hoover Sees Greater U.S. Peril," Washington *Post,* Jan. 17. CR A551, vol. 106.

"Citizenship," *Vital Speeches,* Aug. 15.

1960

*"Communist Party, U.S.A.," *Ave Maria,* April 30.

"What Faith in God Has Meant to Me," *These Times,* September.

P "One Nation's Response to Communism," adapted from an article by Hoover and translated into Spanish to be distributed by the U.S. Information Agency in Latin America.

P "The Communist Menace: Red Goals and Christian Ideals," *Christianity Today,* Oct. 10, Oct. 24, Nov. 7.

"Soviet Rule on Christian Renewal," *Christianity Today,* Nov. 7.

"Student Riots in San Francisco," *U.S. News & World Report,* July 25.

1961

"These Fighters Against Youth Crime Need Your Help," *Reader's Digest,* April.

*"Operation Alert—Campaign Against Communism," Washington *Daily News,* September 15; CR 20194, Vol. 107.

*"Efficient Mr. Hoover," Sept. 19. CR 67408.

*"Reds Try to Convert Pulpit to Own Use," *Christianity Today,* Jan. 10. CR A164, vol. 107.

*"Christianity: An Anti-Red Armor," *Christianity Today,* Jan. 9. CR A118, vol. 107.

*"J. Edgar Hoover Warns Communism Poses Never-Ending Threat," Los Angeles *Examiner,* January 30, CR A703, vol. 107.

*"Top G-Man Warns Against Hysteria," editorial quoting Hoover, *Bakersfield Californian,* April 11. CR A2558, vol. 107.

*"Communism: Menace to Freedom," *Our Sunday Visitor,* National Catholic Action Weekly, April 30. CR A2860, vol. 107.

P "A View of Reality," *General Federation of Clubwomen Mag.,* May–June.

*"Finds U.S. Reds Growing Bolder: FBI Head Sees Spy Set-Up," editorial quoting Hoover, Chicago *Tribune,* May 20. CR A3983, vol. 107.

"Wholly Loyal," *Crusader,* June.

*"Lenin or God," *Christianity Today,* June 12, CR A165, vol. 107.

P "What Does the Future Hold?" *Christianity Today,* June 19.

*" 'Let Joiners Beware' Is Advice from FBI Chief," *Gladwin County Record,* July. CR A5059, vol. 107.

"The Deadly Contest," *Columbia Mag.,* August.

*"J. Edgar Hoover Warns of Blind Attacks on Reds," Los Angeles *Examiner,* Sept. 22. CR A7905, vol. 107.

"Case of the Faceless Spy," *Reader's Digest,* January.

*"America—Freedom's Champion," *Vital Speeches,* Jan. 15. CR A256, A430, vol. 107.

1962

*"The Power of God: Our Ultimate Weapon," *Future,* Jr. Chamber of Commerce, January. CR A811, vol. 108.

"Time of Testing," *Christian Action,* January.

"Let's Fight Communism Sanely," *Christian Herald,* January.

*"Communism and the Knowledge to Combat It," *Retired Officer,* Jan.–Feb. CR A848, vol. 108.

"Deadly Duel," *The Airmen,* February.

*"Shall It Be Law or Tyranny?" *American Bar Assoc. Journal,* February. CR A1496, A1814, A3592, vol. 108.

*P "The Courage of Free Men," *FBI Law Enforcement Bulletin,* April. CR A2034, 3188, vol. 108.

"Communism—Slavery of Mind and Spirit," *N.Y. State Education,* April.

"Who's to Blame for the Rising Wave of Crime," *U.S. News & World Report,* Jan. 1.

P "Young People Can Help Defeat Communism," *Junior Review,* April 16.

*P "Why Reds Make Friends with Businessmen," *Nation's Business,* May.

*"Communist Agents May Try to Get Your Secrets or Sway Your Opinion," *Nation's Business,* May. CR A3902, vol. 108.

"My Answer to Communism and Crime," *The Collegiate Challenge,* May–June.

*"Communist Youth Campaign," *Follow up Reporter,* August. CR A6288, vol. 108.

"Storming the Skies: Christianity Encounters Communism," *Christianity Today,* Dec. 21.

*"An American's Challenge," *Vital Speeches,* Dec. 1. CR A7516, A7546, 23335, 22069, vol. 108.

"Negro in the FBI," *Ebony,* September.

"Two-Edged Sword," *National Education Association Journal,* February.

1963

"When a Child Is Missing," *Parents' Mag.,* March.

*"What I Would Tell a Son," *Christian Science Monitor,* Sept. 21. CR 17480.

*"The Indispensable Supports," *Our Sunday Visitor,* National Catholic Action Weekly, March. CR A1613, vol. 109.

"The Communist War Against Human Dignity," *Christian Herald,* July.

"Hoover's Warning: Be Alert to Fanatics," *U.S. News & World Report,* Dec. 16.

"Vital Role in Building a Stronger America," *PTA Mag.,* February.

"The Inside Story of Organized Crime and How You Can Smash It," *Parade,* Sept. 15.

1964

"The U.S. Businessman Faces the Soviet Spy," *Harvard Business Review,* January–February.

*"Wholesale Defilement and Universal Downgrading of Our Treasured Institutions," *FBI Law Enforcement Bulletin,* June. CR A3058, vol. 110.

*"FBI Chief Sees No Change in Reds," Orangeburg (S.C.) *Times & Democrat,* guest editorial, July 11. CR 16345, vol. 110.

*"Challenge—Not Compromise," *New Age,* September. CR A4724, vol. 110.

"Faith of Our Fathers," *Christianity Today,* Sept. 11.

"FBI and Civil Rights," *U.S. News & World Report,* Nov. 30.

"Enforcing the Law," *U.S. News & World Report,* Dec. 21.

"J. Edgar Hoover Speaks Out on Reds in the Negro Movement," excerpts of testimony before the H. App. Com., *U.S. News & World Report,* May 4.

"If God Be for Us, Who Can Be Against Us," *FBI Law Enforcement Bulletin,* Nov.

"What J. Edgar Hoover Says about Pressure Groups," *U.S. News & World Report,* Dec. 7.

"FBI Chief Speaks Up: Summary of News Conference," *Senior Scholastic,* Dec. 2.

1965

"Communist Gains among Youth," *U.S. News & World Report,* Nov. 1.

*"Faith of Freedom," *Vital Speeches,* Nov. 15. CR A5907, A6081, 27622, vol. III.

"From J. Edgar Hoover: A Report on Campus Reds," *U.S. News & World Report,* May 31.

"Warning from J. Edgar Hoover," *U.S. News & World Report,* Sept. 13.

P "America's Ideals—Its Mark of Greatness," *Union Central Advocate,* 1965 Yearbook of Union Central Insurance Co.

"Continuing Threat of Soviet-Bloc Espionage," *Law Enforcement Bulletin,* April 15.

"Police Brutality: How Much Truth; How Much Fiction?" *U.S. News & World Report,* Sept. 27.

"We Mollycoddle Criminals," *U.S. News & World Report,* Aug. 9.

"When Criminals Are Set Free Too Soon," *U.S. News & World Report,* May 17.

1966

"FBI's War on Organized Crime," *U.S. News & World Report,* April 18.

"How to Fight Pornography," *Columbia Mag.,* March.

1967

"An Analysis of the New Left—A Gospel of Nihilism," *Christianity Today,* Aug. 18.

"Now: Instant Crime Control in Your Town," *Popular Science,* January.

*"What ABC's Are Our Children Learning?" *VFW Mag.,* February. CR H840 Jan. 31.

"The U.S. Businessman Faces the Soviet Spy," *Harvard Business Review,* January.

1968

"Sex Books and Rape: FBI Chief Sees Close Links," reprint *U.S. News & World Report,* March 11.

*"Violence in American Society—A Problem of Critical Concern," *George Washington Law Review,* Jan. CR Vol. 114, pp. 8248–8253.

"Story of Crime in U.S.," statement, Sept. 18, portrait, *U.S. News & World Report,* Oct. 7, same with title "Violence," *Vital Speeches,* Nov. 1.

"War Against Crime Is Your War," *Reader's Digest,* November.

"Violence—A Knife Pointed at Heart of U.S.," *N.Y. Sunday News,* March 24.

"Careers in Crime," St. Louis *Globe Democrat,* August 27, 1968.

1969
"Interval Between," *Christianity Today,* Dec.
19.
1970
*"SDS and the High Schools," *PTA Mag.,*
January—February. CR E1479.
"The Role of Money in Soviet Espionage
Operations," *Industrial Security,* June.
"The Red University," *VFW Mag.,*
September.
"Open Letter to College Students," for UPI,
Sept. 21.

1971
"Mao's Red Shadows in America," *VFW
Mag.,* June.
"Mao's Red Shadows," *New York Times,*
Aug. 17.
*"Hoover Warns of Red Chinese Subversion
in U.S." June 8. CR E5573.
1972
"Focus for Tomorrow," *School and Society,*
February.
"Portraits in Courage," *Today's Health,*
March.

Additional Pamphlets: 1940–1972 by J. Edgar Hoover

(all except * published by the Government
Printing Office)

1947 "Menace of Communism"
1950 "Statement of J. Edgar Hoover,
Director of Federal Bureau of
Investigations"
1957 "An Analysis of the Sixteenth Annual
Convention of the Communist
Party of the U.S."
1958 "Communist Infiltration and Activities
in the South"
1959 "Communist Illusion and Democratic
Reality"
1960 "Statement on Soviet-Bloc Intelligence
Activities"
"Statement Concerning Seventeenth

National Convention, Communist
Party, U.S.A., New York City,
Dec. 10–12, 1959"
"Communist Target—Youth,
Communist Infiltration and
Agitation Tactics"
1961 "A Statement on the Communist Party
Line"
"A Statement on Internal Security"
1962 "The Current Communist Threat"
1965 "What Young People Should Know
about Communism"
1966 "Statement Concerning the Eighteenth
National Convention, Communist
Party, U.S.A., June 22–26, 1966"
1970*"J. Edgar Hoover Testifies," the Radio
Dept. of the Assemblies of God

Speeches: 1940–1972 by J. Edgar Hoover

1940
P"Fifth Columns of Destruction,"
graduating class of Nat. Police Acad.,
Washington D.C., Oct. 5 (released by
the FBI).
*"The Test of Citizenship," 49th Continental
Congress of the DAR, Washington,
D.C., April 18. CR A2229, A2281, vol.
86.
*"America's Duty to the Future," N.Y.
Federation of Women's Clubs, NYC,
May 3. CR A2694, A2800, vol. 86.

*"An Adventure in Public Service,"
graduating class of Drake University,
Des Moines, Iowa (on radio), June 3.
CR A3584, vol. 86.
*"Protect America," Fed.-State Conf. on
Law Enforcement Problems of National
Defense, Dept. of Justice, Washington,
D.C., Aug. 5. CR A4849, vol. 86.
*"Present Task of Law Enforcement," 47th
Annual Conv. of Internat. Assoc. of
Chiefs of Police, Milwaukee, Wis., Sept.
9. CR A5691, vol. 86.

P Reprinted in pamphlet form. Many of Hoover's speeches were reproduced either verbatim
or in summary format or both by the FBI's Crime Records unit and were subsequently reprinted
—not infrequently with new titles—in obscure journals, house organs, news letters, and newspapers.
In some cases it was not the Bureau's release but a *Congressional Record* or pamphlet reprint which
sparked a second round of reprints. In addition, his testimony before Congressional committees and
his periodic "Statements" on public issues were also regularly reproduced in the *Congressional
Record* and disseminated through reprints.
*Reprinted in the *Congressional Record*.

*"The Test of Americanism," 22nd Annual Nat. Conv., American Legion, Boston, Mass., Sept. 23. CR A5895, vol. 86.

1941

P "There Is No ISM but Patriotism," graduating exercises of University of the South, Sewanee, Tenn., June 9 (released by the FBI).

*"Youth and Democracy," radio address to Youth of America, Feb. 24. CR A821, vol. 87.

*"On Fifth Columns," graduating class of the Nat. Police Acad., Wash. D.C., April 3. CR A1598, vol. 87.

P "There are those that hold that the Gov't of U.S. can be overthrown," graduating class of the Nat. Police Acad., Oct. 11 (released by the FBI).

*"Those who would undermine America are quick to accuse the FBI of any disgraceful tactic," graduating class of the Nat. Police Acad., March 29. CR A1598, vol. 87.

"The Challenge of Youth," Boys Town, Nebraska. June 1.

1942

*"Our Nation's Strength," radio address over WEAF, March 22. CR A1183, vol. 88 (sponsored by the Knights of Columbus).

*"Our Future," commencement exercises of Notre Dame University, May 10. CR A1715, vol. 88.

*"A Nation's Call to Duty," St. Johns University Law School, June 11. CR A2245, vol. 88.

*"The Present Task of Law Enforcement: Maintain Internal Security," Annual Conv. of the Internat. Assoc. of Chiefs of Police, NYC, Sept. 21. CR A3362, vol. 88.

*"Operations of the FBI in Wartime," radio address over WSOO in Sault Ste. Marie, Mich., Oct. 18. CR A3735, vol. 88.

*". . . Protect the homefront, not only from surges of lawlessness, but from any national foe that penetrates our gates," graduating class of FBI Nat. Police Acad., Washington, D.C. Nov. 2. CR A3859, vol. 88.

*"An American's Privilege," Annual Banquet of the Holland Soc. of N.Y., NYC, Nov. 9. CR A4057, vol. 88.

1943

*"Your Call to Duty," graduating class of Rutgers University, N.J., May 23. CR A2590, vol. 89.

"Battle on the Home Front," Annual Conv. of the Internat. Assoc. of Chiefs of Police, Detroit, Mich., Aug. 9.

1944

*"The Internal Defense of America," 53rd Continental Congress of the DAR, NYC, April 17. CR A1884, vol. 90.

1945

*"Vigilance urged against the insidious work of the Communists operating behind a thousand guises within the ranks of labor," Internat. Assoc. of Chiefs of Police, Miami, Fla., Dec. 10. CR A5410, vol. 91.

"Reconversion of Law Enforcement," 52nd Annual Conv. of the Internat. Assoc. of Police Chiefs, Miami, Fla., Dec. 10.

1946

*"Communist Propaganda," commencement of the Holy Cross College, Worcester, Mass., June 29. CR A4117, vol. 92.

*"Our Achilles' Heel," Annual Conv. of the American Legion, San Francisco, Calif., Sept. 30. CR A27, vol. 93.

*"A Foe of All ISMS Except Americanism," Intro. of Francis Cardinal Spellman, graduation of FBI Nat. Police Acad., Washington, D.C. June 28. CR A3806, vol. 92.

1947

*"Methods by Which FBI Is Protecting the Internal Security of the Nation," Com. on Un-American Activities, H.R., March 26. CR A1330, vol. 93.

1950

*"Fifty-five Thousand Communists," Grand Lodge of Masons, NYC, May 2. CR A4358, A3495, vol. 96.

"Boys Clubs of America," Washington, D.C. May 18.

"Statement to Jewish War Veterans," Washington, D.C. July 26.

1954

*"FBI and Communism," 63rd Continental Congress of the DAR, Washington, D.C. April 22. CR A3350, A2982, vol. 100.

1955

"Our Common Task," 62nd Annual Meeting of the Internat. Assoc. of Chiefs of Police, Philadelphia, Pa., Oct. 3.

1956

"The Challenge of Crime Control," Nat.

Parole Conf., Washington, D.C., April
10.

"The Twin Enemies of Freedom," 28th
Annual Conv. of Catholic Women,
Chicago, Nov. 9.

1957

"The American Ideal," Freedoms
Foundation Annual Awards, Valley
Forge, Penn., Feb. 22.

"The Perpetuation of Our American
Heritage," Nat. Conv. of American
Legion, Atlantic City, N.J., Sept. 19.

1958

"Law Day Proclamation," Washington,
D.C., April 30.

1959

"What the World Needs Is Love—
Brotherhood Love," acceptance of Nat.
Interfaith Award from Wash. Interfaith
Com., June 9.

*"Citizenship: A Call to Duty," Biennial
Conv. of Junior Order, United
American Mechanics, Charleston, W.
Va., June 16. CR A5180, vol. 105.

1960

*"America—Freedom's Champion," Nat.
Conv. of American Legion, Miami,
Fla., Oct. 18. CR A256, A430, vol. 107.

"Faith or Fear," Quinn Chapel, African
Methodist Episcopal Church, Chicago,
April 18.

1961

*"The Faith to Be Free," Mutual of Omaha
Criss Award, Washington, D.C., Dec.
7. CR A23, A94, 1412, A2062, vol. 108.

1962

*P "The Courage of Free Men," George
Washington Award of Freedom
Foundation, Valley Forge, Penn., Feb.
22. CR A2034, 3188, vol. 108.

NBC *Monitor* program, July 15.

*"An American's Challenge," Nat. Conv. of
American Legion, Las Vegas, Oct. 9.
A7516, A7546, 23335, 22069, vol. 108.

*P "The Current Communist Threat," radio
address, NBC, July 15. CR 10475, vol.
112; CR 6413, 7482, A5817, vol. 108.

1963

*"Communist Backing of Civil Rights,"
remarks to House, March 3. CR
A4979, vol. 109.

*". . . Target of Red Masters is to destroy
America's freedom," receiving medal of
merit from Jewish War Veterans,

Washington, D.C., Nov. 9. CR A547,
vol. 109.

*"Keys to Freedom," Nat. Catholic Youth
Organization, N.Y.C., Nov. 16. CR
A7179, A7205, A7292, A7344, vol. 109.

*"Faith in Freedom," Brotherhood of
Washington, D.C., Hebrew
Congregation, Dec. 4. CR A7475,
A7434, 23545, 23681, vol. 109.

1964

*"Time for Decision," Loyola University,
Chicago, Ill., Nov. 24. CR A511, vol.
III.

*"Our Heritage of Greatness," Penn. Soc.
and the Soc. of Penn. Women, NYC,
Dec. 12, CR A13, vol. III.

1965

*"Espionage and Counterintelligence," before
H. App. Subcom., March 4, CR A6227,
vol. III.

*"The Faith of Free Men," Supreme Council
33rd Degree, Scottish Rite of Free
Freemasonry—Southern Jurisdiction,
Washington, D.C., Oct. 19. CR A5907,
A6081, 27622, vol. III.

1967

"Faith, Freedom and Law," Mich. State Bar,
Rochester, Michigan, June 8.

1968

"A Time of Tribute," National Police
Academy, Law Enforcement Bulletin,
June.

"Violence—The Communist Party," Nat.
Commission on the Causes and
Prevention of Violence, Washington,
D.C., Sept. 18.

1969

"SDS: A Growing Danger," U.S. Chamber
of Commerce, Washington, D.C., April
27.

1971

*"On Weathermen," testimony of Hoover
before H. App. Com., March 17. CR
25893, vol. 117.

*"It is time to stop coddling the hoodlums
and the hippies," 25th Anniv. Dinner,
Wash. Chapter, Society of Former
Special Agents of the FBI, Inc.,
Washington, D.C., Oct. 22. CR 38560,
vol. 117.

1972

*"J. Edgar Hoover—Totally Credible,"
WBBM, Channel 2 (CBS), Chicago,
May 2. CR E5141, vol. 118.

Interviews: 1940–1972 with J. Edgar Hoover

1947
"Loyalty Checks," Bert Andrews/*N. Y. Herald Tribune,* Nov. 16.

1948
* "Communism and Subversive Activities," radio, Feb. 16. CR A872, vol. 94.

1950
*"Hoover Answers Ten Questions on the FBI," *N. Y. Times Mag.,* April 16. CR A3331.

*"FBI Director Hoover Tells How Communists Work in U.S." *U.S. News & World Report,* Aug. 11. CR A6237, vol. 96. *Elks Mag.,* September.

1951
"Communist Threat in U.S.," *U.S. News & World Report,* March 30.

1953
*"How the FBI Tracks Reds and Spies," *Pathfinder,* Nov. 5. CR A293, vol. 99.

1954
*"Our Country Is in More Imminent Danger from Internal Causes Than from the Cold War," Meet the Press, NBC, Aug. 5. CR A7052, vol. 105.

1955
*"Hoover Warns of Red Boring—Says Hard Core Members Still Alive," Baltimore *Sunday American,* Jan. 2. CR A1625, vol. 101.

1962
NBC *Monitor* program, Sept. 2.

1965
Hoover interview, Napa (Calif.) *Register,* May 27.

Hoover interview, *Christian Science Monitor,* July 3.

1966
"Hoover Views Crime-Communism-Columbus as a Key Espionage Target," Columbus (Ohio) *Dispatch,* Feb. 20.

1967
"Hoover on Crimes, Criminals and Precautionary Measures," *Banking Magazine,* June.

1968
"The Increase in Violence," National Commission on the Causes and Prevention of Violence, September.

"Statement on Crime Wave," column by David Lawrence, Washington October.

"Reversing the Crime Trend," *U.S. News & World Report,* Aug. 26.

*"Hoover Hits Civil Dis-obedience," Birmingham (Ala.) *News,* June 23. CR 19000, vol. 114.

1970
"Bull Market in Stocks and Bond Thefts," *Nation's Business,* March.

1971
Hoover interview, Assemblies of God Booklet.

1972
Last Hoover interview, Springfield (Mo.) *News & Leader,* May 12.

*"J. Edgar Hoover Speaks Out," *Nation's Business,* January. CR 371, 675, vol. 118.

Films: FBI

1945	*The House on 92nd Street*	1951	*I Was a Communist for the FBI*
1946	*Notorious*	1952	*Big Jim McClain*
1948	*Walk a Crooked Mile*		*Walk East on Beacon*
	Street with No Name	1959	*The FBI Story*

Radio

Nov. 1944–Nov. 1958   ___ *FBI in Peace and War*
April 1945–Dec. 1952   ___ *This Is Your FBI*
1962–1965   NBC *Monitor* (5 minute segment): "Know Your FBI" and "National Alert"

Sept. 1962–Feb. 20, 1975

     ABC   *FBI Washington*

*Reprinted in the *Congressional Record.*

Television

Sept. 1965–Sept. 1974	ABC	*The FBI*
Dec. 1957–Aug. 1959	CBS	*I Led Three Lives**
	CBS	*FBI Story,*

"The FBI vs. Alvin Karpis," Nov. 8, 1974
"Attack on Terror," Feb. 20, 21, 1975

*With this lone exception, all of the films and television and radio programs listed were produced with varying degrees of Bureau involvement. It hardly need be added that all of them, without exception, glorified the Bureau and the Director. The FBI also assisted in supplying material for, promoting, and distributing books penned by its supporters such as Don Whitehead, Andrew Tully, Frederick L. Collins, Harry and Bonaro Overstreet, and Herbert Philbrick (author of *I Led Three Lives,* the book on which the television series was based). Journalists whose political credentials passed muster were also fed image-burnishing materials. At the same time, as already noted in Chapter 4, the Bureau went to great lengths to attack and suppress unfavorable books.

Appendix III

Internal Security Themes—
Comparable Treatment by the FBI
and Attorney General

A. *Importance of Internal Security Jurisdiction*

". . . . internal security field involves a discharge of primary responsibilities for guarding the Nation against threats from within its own borders," FBI Ann. Rep., 1950, Introduction i. To the same effect, see:

FBI Annual Report		Attorney General's Annual Report	
1941	1,3	1940	151
1942	3	1941	177
1950	10, Intro.i.	1946	10
1955	13	1948	10
1956	17	1949	2,5
1957	15	1950	12,13,21,22
1958	21	1951	2
1959	Intro. 1	1952	6,7
1960	1	1953	19
		1955	195

B. *Sept. 6, 1939 Presidential Directive*

"By Presidential Directive dated September 6, 1939, the FBI was designated the civilian intelligence agency having primary responsibility for protecting the Nation's internal security," FBI Ann. Rep., 1959, 21.

FBI Annual Report		Attorney General's Annual Report	
1940	2	1940	152
1941	3	1941	178
1942	3	1942	6
1950	10	1944	6
1951	4	1950	22
1953	10	1951	7
1955	13	1953	24

1956	17		1955	191
1959	21		1956	209
1962	25		1959	338
1964	21		1960	345
1965	23		1961	345
1966	23		1962	322
1969	21		1964	373
1970	21		1965	357
1971	21		1966	89
1972	21		1967	388
			1971	118
			1972	157

C. *Constantly Growing Red Menace*

"The Communist Party, seeking respectable outlets for its activities and propaganda, has established front groups which voice the Party's programs, and it has attempted to infiltrate unsuspecting legitimate organizations," FBI Ann. Rep., 1953, 12.

FBI Annual Report		*Attorney General's Annual Report*	
1950	Intro. 2	1949	2
1951	4,6,7	1950	23,24
1953	11,12	1951	7,9
1954	13,15	1952	13
1955	14	1953	26
1956	18,19	1954	18,19
1957	16	1955	177,190,192
1958	22,23	1956	211
1959	Intro., ii.	1957	187,198,200,202
1962	28,31,32	1958	319,335,336
1963	21,23,25	1959	322,323,339,340
1964	21	1960	328,346
1965	23,26	1961	329,347
1966	23,24	1962	311,232,236
1969	21,22,23	1963	361,364,365
1970	22,23,27	1964	373,375
1971	24,25,26,27	1965	346,357,358,360
1972	21–28	1966	377,390,391
		1967	374,388,390
		1970	146,147,148
		1971	118,119,120
		1972	157,158,159,160

D. *Heroism of and Debt to Agents*

"Information furnished by these dedicated men and women has proved invaluable to the protection of America's internal security," FBI Ann. Rep., 1955, 16.

FBI Annual Report		*Attorney General's Annual Report*	
1954	13	1942	7
1955	15,16	1955	177,193,194
1956	19,20	1956	212
1957	17,18	1957	186

1958 21,23	1958 336,338
1964 24	1964 358
1969 1	
1970 1	

E.   Attacks by Subversive Critics

"A campaign of vituperation has been directed against informants by communists and their sympathizers who desire to deprive law enforcement of the use of this time-tested and valuable technique. This campaign poses a dire threat to the security of the United States," FBI Ann. Rep., 1956, 20.

FBI Annual Report		Attorney General's Annual Report	
1950	Intro. 2	1950	23
1956	20	1955	190
1958	25,26	1956	212
1959	21	1958	319
		1960	328
		1963	361

F.   Inhuman Workload

"The speed-up in the preparedness and the increasing recognition of the need to render full protection against espionage, sabotage, and related activities in view of tumultuous world conditions, taxed the facilities and personnel of the FBI to the utmost," FBI Ann. Rep., 1941, 3.

FBI Annual Report		Attorney General's Annual Report	
1940	2	1940	151
1941	3	1941	177,178
1962	25	1955	177
1963	Intro. i	1957	185,198
1969	1	1958	318,336
1970	Intro. i	1959	322
1971	1	1960	328
		1961	345
		1963	345
		1964	358

G.   Achievements not Measurable by Law Enforcement Yardsticks

". . . since this work of domestic intelligence is primarily preventive in nature, its successes cannot be measured in terms of arrests and convictions," Att. Gen. Ann. Rep., 1953, 24.

FBI Annual Report		Attorney General's Annual Report	
1940	5	1941	178
1941	3,4	1944	6
1942	3	1946	14
1950	10	1953	24
1951	4,5	1955	191
1953	10,11	1956	196
1954	13	1957	199
1957	15	1960	345
1958	21	1961	345
1959	21	1964	373

1964   21
1966   23

1966   389
1967   388

H.   *Never-ending Struggle Between Communists and Bureau*
"This clandestine activity [of the Communist Party] has required increased vigilance of the FBI," FBI Ann. Rep., 1953, 12. To the same effect, see:

FBI Annual Report		*Attorney General's Annual Report*	
1950	2,10	1949	2
1951	4,6,7	1950	23,24
1953	11,12	1951	7,9
1954	15	1952	13,14
1955	14	1953	26
1956	19,21	1954	18,19
1957	16,19	1955	177,190
1958	25	1956	211,212
1959	Intro. ii	1957	185,198,202
1962	28,31,32	1958	318,336
1963	22,23,25	1959	322
1964	21	1960	328
1965	23	1961	329
1966	41	1962	311,232
1969	21,24	1963	361
1970	21,22,27	1964	373
1971	25	1965	346,358
1972	21	1967	374
		1970	146
		1971	118
		1972	157

Appendix IV

Arrest and Search Warrants Prepared for Use in Connection with the Custodial Detention Program

Master Warrant of Arrest

WARRANT

To the Director of the Federal Bureau of Investigation:

In pursuance of authority delegated to the Attorney General of the United States by Proclamation of the President of the United States, dated ——————, 19——, I hereby authorize and direct you and your duly authorized agents to arrest or to cause the arrest of the persons whose names are set forth on the attached list and whom I deem dangerous to the public peace and safety of the United States.

These persons are to be detained and confined until further order.

I further authorize and direct you and your duly authorized agents, upon or subsequent to the arrest of any person set forth on the attached list and without regard to the place where such arrest may be made, to search any and all premises owned, occupied or controlled by such person, as well as any and all premises where such person is, or during the preceding twelve months period has been, employed or engaged in any regular activity, wherein it is believed that there may be found contraband, prohibited articles, or other materials in violations of the Proclamation of the President of the United States, dated ——————, 19——, and as set forth in the Regulations issued pursuant thereto, and to seize and hold any such articles which you may find and make return thereof to the Attorney General.

I further authorize and direct that this warrant may be executed at any hour of the day or night.

By order of the President:

————————————————
Attorney General

Dated:

Master Search Warrant

WARRANT

TO THE DIRECTOR OF THE FEDERAL BUREAU OF INVESTIGATION:

In pursuance of authority delegated to the Attorney General of the United States, by Proclamation of the President of the United States, dated _____, 19____, I hereby authorize and direct you and your duly authorized agents to make immediate search of certain premises located and described on the attached list wherein it is believed that there may be found contraband, prohibited articles, or other materials in violation of the Proclamation of the President of the United States, dated _____, 19____, and as set forth in the Regulations issued pursuant therto, namely, firearms, weapons or implements of war or component parts thereof, ammunition, bombs, explosives or material used in the manufacture of explosives, short-wave radio receiving sets, transmitting sets, signal devices, codes or ciphers, cameras, means for promoting biological warfare, radioactive materials, atomic devices, or component parts thereof, propaganda material of the enemy or insurgents, propaganda material which fosters, encourages or promotes the policies, programs or objectives of the enemy or insurgents, printing presses, mimeograph machines, or other reproducing media on which such propaganda aforementioned has been or is being prepared, records, including membership and financial records of organizations or groups that have been declared subversive or may hereafter be declared subversive by the Attorney General, cash funds either in currency or coin, promissory notes or checks, securities of any nature, papers, documents, writings, code books, signal books, sketches, photographs, photograph negatives, blue prints, plans, maps, models, instruments, appliances, graphic representations, papers, documents, or books on which there may be invisible writing relating to or concerning any military, naval, or air, post, camp, station or installation or equipment or of any arms, ammunition, implements of war, devices or things used or intended to be used in the combat equipment of the land, naval or air forces of the United States, or of any military, naval, or air, post, camp, station or installation, and any and all files, dossiers, records, documents or papers of any kind which relate in any way to the identity, activities or operations of any person who is or may be engaged in espionage or sabotage against the interests of the United States.

I further authorize and direct you to seize and hold any such articles which you may find and make return thereof to the Attorney General.

I further authorize and direct that this warrant may be executed at any hour of the day or night.

By order of the President:

_____
Attorney General

Dated:

Notes

Books listed in the Bibliography are referred to here by author's name only; the full citations appear in the Bibliography. Abbreviations for legislative hearings and related sources are set forth in the notes when first referred to; again, full citations are given in the Bibliography.

2. The Emergence of the American Political Intelligence System

[1] Thomas E. May, *Constitutional History of England* (Armstrong, 1899 [3rd ed.]), Vol. 2, p. 112.

[2] Tooke was prosecuted (*Rex v. Tooke,* 24 How St. Tr.) 1 (1794) for his expressions of sympathy for "our beloved American fellow-subjects" who died at Lexington and Concord. Wilkes was even more popular—see Chafee, *Free Speech,* pp. 242–247. On his prosecution by Crown spies, see May, Vol. 2, p. 276.

[3] Annals of Congress, June 21, 1798. Livingston was not engaging in hyperbole. Only four years earlier the testimony of Anne Fischer, a domestic servant, had been used in an effort to convict John Horne Tooke (*Rex v. Tooke,* 20 How St. Tr., p. 651).

[4] On the use of informers and police spies to curb political opposition in England in the 1790s, see Philip A. Brown, *The French Revolution in English History* (Lockwood, 1918), pp. 88–95, 132–175; William T. Laprade, *England and the French Revolution* (Johns Hopkins University Press, 1909), pp. 129–130,

135–136; and Arthur Sutherland, "British Trials for Disloyal Association During the French Revolution," Vol. 34, *Cornell Law Quarterly* (1949), p. 303. On the use of spies to break English reform movements in the early nineteenth century, see J. L. and Barbara Hammond, *The Town Laborer* (Longmans Green, 1925 [new ed.]), pp. 243, 258–262, and E. P. Thompson, *The Making of the English Working Class* (Pantheon, 1964), pp. 485–494. For a summary of European developments, see Chapman, pp. 20–49.

[5] Wayne Broehl, *The Molly Maguires* (Harvard University Press, 1964), pp. 131–238; Arthur H. Lewis, *Lament for the Molly Maguires* (Harcourt Brace and World, 1964), pp. 75–169.

[6] Robert A. Pinkerton, "Detective Surveillance of Anarchists," *North American Review,* Vol. 173 (November 1901), p. 615.

[7] See Gellhorn, ed., *passim.*

[8] *Attorney General's Annual Report* (1918) (cited hereafter as *A.G. Ann. Rep.*), p.

105. For a full account of the APL and of the "slacker raids," see Jensen, pp. 189–213.

9. See, for example, John Tipple, *Crisis of the American Dream* (Pegasus, 1968), p. 37.

10. *N.Y. World,* June 19, 1919; Coben, p. 212.

11. *N.Y. World,* June 27, 1919.

12. *A.G. Ann. Rep.* (1919) p. 13.

13. Senate Investigation of Activities of the Department of Justice, *Report of A. Mitchell Palmer,* Nov. 14, 1919 (cited hereafter as Palmer), p. 30.

14. Hoover's title was Special Assistant to the Attorney General; he began working for Garvan some time before he was officially named to his new post.

15. Hoover was called "Speedy" in high school and one of his sponsors described him in 1924 as "an 'electric wire' with the trigger response"— Alpheus T. Mason, *Harlan Fiske Stone: Pillar of the Law* (Viking Press, 1956), p. 150.

16. Hoover's principal aide in his initial study of radical teachings was George R. Ruch. A close friend, Ruch left the Department in 1923 to head a labor espionage operation for the H. C. Frick Coal Co.

17. Hearings before Committee on Rules on *Charges Against Department of Justice, By Louis E. Post and Others* (1920) (cited hereafter as *Rules Hearings*), p. 166; Palmer, p. 10.

18. *A.G. Ann. Rep.* (1920), pp. 172–173.

19. *Ibid.,* pp. 178–179.

20. *Ibid.,* p. 180.

21. *Congressional Record,* May 10, 1920 (cited hereafter as CR), p. 6835.

22. *Rules Hearings,* pp. 68–69.

23. Walsh, pp. 347, 660–661; *Rules Hearings,* p. 174; Murray, pp. 196–208; Preston, p. 216; Coben, p. 221; and Higham, p. 230.

24. Hoover told the press that this was but the first in a planned series of deportation arks—Lowenthal, p. 238.

25. Preston, pp. 226, 228–229.

26. *Rules Hearings,* pp. 68–69; Walsh, p. 354; Lowenthal, pp. 156–172.

27. *Report Upon the Illegal Practices of the Department of Justice* (National Popular Government League, 1920) (cited hereafter as *Lawyers' Report*), pp. 39–40; Walsh, p. 14.

28. *Rules Hearings,* p. 53.

29. Walsh, pp. 10, 12, 19, 21.

30. Preston, p. 211.

31. *Ibid.,* p. 219.

32. *Ibid.,* pp. 218–225; Jensen, p. 282.

33. Post, pp. 78–79.

34. *Lawyers' Report,* pp. 6–8, 64–65; Levin, pp. 52–55; *Rules Hearings,* pp. 00–00.

35. Mary Heaton Vorse, *A Footnote to Folly* (Farran and Rinehart, 1935), pp. 305–306.

36. Paul Murphy, "Source and Nature of Intolerance in the 1920's," *Journal of American History* (January 1964), pp. 17, 66.

37. In addition, young Hoover wrote briefs in support of the deportation of anarchists Emma Goldman, Alexander Berkman, and L. C. A. K. Martens, a representative of the Soviet Russian Foreign Affairs Commissariat— Whitehead, pp. 48–49.

38. Palmer, pp. 321, 141, 375; *Rules Hearings,* pp. 115, 141, 321, 375, 448.

39. Palmer, p. 142.

40. *Ibid.,* p. 150.

41. *Rules Hearings,* p. 154.

42. Whitehead, p. 350.

43. Francis Russell, *The Shadow of Blooming Grove* (McGraw-Hill, 1968), p. 516.

44. Andrew Sinclair, *The Available Man* (Macmillan, 1955), p. 252. Burns, a master of self-promotion, luridly celebrated his sleuthing triumphs in the McNamara case in his book *The Masked War,* published in 1913 and reprinted (by Arno Press) in 1969.

45. It could hardly be argued that the GID's budgetary limitations were flexible enough to extend to the "detection and prosecution" of *state* crimes.

46. *A.G. Ann. Rep.* (1921), p. 131; see also *A.G. Ann. Rep.* (1920), p. 176.

47. Spolansky, pp. 23–30; Theodore Draper, *Roots of American Communism* (Viking Press, 1957), pp. 366–372. Morrow's work for the GID began in 1919. He was considered an employee, with the code name K-97. Initially he received a daily stipend of $41, and later when his services became more valuable, $45— Draper, *op. cit.,* p. 366.

48. *App. Hearings* (1925), pp. 92–93.

49. Hapgood, ed., p. 100. See also Levin, pp. 191–192.

50. Coben, p. 188.

51. *App. Hgs.* (1924), pp. 91–92; *A.G. Ann. Rep.* (1920), p. 176.

[52] *A.G. Ann. Rep.* (1920), p. 178.

[53] *Rules Hearings,* pp. 189–190, 614–619; Palmer, pp. 161–187. Hoover's Communist Party brief states (*Rules Hearings,* p. 155): "Thus we see the cause of much of the racial trouble in the United States at the present time . . . the Communist Party is pledged to stir up and agitate racial prejudices throughout the entire country."

[54] Walsh, pp. 274–275; Palmer, p. 186; Coben, p. 235; Murray, p. 252; Higham, p. 233; and Vorse, p. 301.

[55] Murray, p. 193. See also Walsh, p. 73; Coben, pp. 244–245.

[56] Based on a memorandum in the archives of the American Civil Liberties Union.

[57] *App. Hgs.* (1922), p. 131.

[58] *Ibid.,* p. 145.

[59] *App. Hgs.* (1924), pp. 92–93.

[60] Max Lowenthal, *The Federal Bureau of Investigation,* pp. 274–275.

[61] *Ibid.,* p. 276.

[62] "Charges Inciting Red Outrages," NYT, Feb. 13, 1923; "Death Threat Here Laid to Burns Man in Spy's Testimony," NYT, Feb. 14, 1923.

[63] Cummings and McFarland, pp. 382–383.

[64] Samuel Hopkins Adams, *The Incredible Era* (Houghton Mifflin, 1939), pp. 233, 319, 326–327, 330, 399.

[65] Quoted in Cummings and McFarland, pp. 430–431.

[66] The Baldwin memo on the interview in the archives of the American Civil Liberties Union, at Princeton University, is especially noteworthy on the subject of the termination of the Bureau's intelligence responsibilities: "The department dealing with radical activities has been entirely abolished. There is not a single man in the department especially assigned to that work. There are no more radical experts. The examination of radical magazines and the collection of data on radicals and radical organizations has been wholly discontinued by specific orders of the Attorney General. The Bureau is functioning only as an agency to investigate cases in which there is a probable violation of the federal law. Investigations of radicals are made for the Department of Labor on request, but none are undertaken on the initiative of the Bureau."

[67] The propaganda mystique made intelligence agencies tireless collectors of radical literature (even to the extent of republishing out-of-print documents).

[68] Levin, p. 101.

[69] Lusk Committee Report, *Revolutionary Radicalism: Its History, Purpose and Tactics* (Albany, N.Y., 1920), Part 1, pp. 501–502.

[70] *Special Committee to Investigate Communist Activities in the U.S., Hearings* (1930), Part 2, Vol. 1, p. 36.

3. The Bureau's Spurious Intelligence Authority

[1] In the discussion of the FBI's intelligence authority I have relied extensively on the 1975–76 Hearings, staff studies, and findings of the Senate Select Committee to Study Governmental Operations with Respect to Intelligence Activities, headed by Senator Frank Church. Book III of the Committee's *Final Report* (hereinafter referred to as Church, Book III). The testimony and documents appended to Vol. 6 of the Hearings (hereinafter, Church, Vol. 6) were especially useful.

[2] Church, Book III, p. 393; Church, Vol. 6, pp. 558–559; Whitehead, p. 162.

[3] See Church, Vol. 6, pp. 542, 554.

[4] Hoover recognized as early as 1925 that the Bureau's investigative jurisdiction hinged on violations of federal penal statutes—Church, Vol. 6, p. 553.

[5] Church, Book III, p. 394.

[6] Church, Vol. 6, pp. 561–562; Church, Book III, p. 395.

[7] Church, Book III, p. 394. Presumably because of the questionable authority for the mission, Hoover directed that this investigation "should be handled in a most discreet and confidential manner"—Church, Book III, p. 396.

[8] Church, Vol. 6, p. 562. As the General Accounting Office (GAO) concluded in an investigative Report (1976) (at p. 190): "From the earliest times [Hoover] acted as if the Bureau had received broad authority to investigate subversive activities in general whether by groups or individuals, not just the Communist and Fascist movements . . .

controlled or directed by foreign governments."

[9] Church, Book III, pp. 396–397.

[10] Church, Book III, p. 398; Church, Vol. 6 p. 566.

[11] Church, Book III, pp. 398–399; Church, Vol. 6, p. 567.

[12] Church, Book III, p. 402.

[13] Church, Vol. 6, pp. 570–572; Church, Book III, pp. 404–405, and Book II, pp. 26–27.

[14] "All Local Officers Called to Spy Hunt," NYT, Sept. 7, 1939; "Declare United States Ready to Run Down Spies," NYT, Oct. 1, 1939; S. Woodford Howard, *Mr. Justice Murphy* (Princeton University Press, 1968), pp. 212–213. In quoting Hoover's speech, the *New York Times* account attributes "lecherous enemies" to the Director; he may have said "treacherous." Murphy's hopes to avoid a witch hunt were not realized. FBI field offices were flooded with crackpot complaints and paranoid tips. "Vigilante groups including volunteer firemen and female rifle clubs sprang up overnight. Before long, requests for investigation of aliens suspected of espionage activities were coming into the Department of Justice at the rate of 3,000 a day"—Biddle, *In Brief Authority*, p. 109.

[15] *Emergency Supplemental Appropriations Bill, Hearings*, Nov. 30, 1939, pp. 303–307. In February 1941 Hoover gave the committee similar assurances—*First Deficiency Appropriations Bill, Hearings*, Feb. 19, 1941, pp. 188–189.

[16] *Justice Department Appropriation Bill, Hearings*, Jan. 5, 1940, pp. 151ff.

[17] *Supplemental National Defense Appropriations, Hearings*, June 6, 1940, pp. 180–181.

[18] CR, Vol. 84, p. 10370.

[19] Chafee, *Free Speech*, p. 443. Reviewing the debate, Professor Chafee wrote (at p. 444): "I never realized how Nazis feel toward Jews until I read what Congressmen say about radical aliens."

[20] HUAC, *Hearings*, Vol. 5, June 5, 1939, p. 3694. For an account of the Roosevelt administration's conflicts with Dies and his committee, see Ogden, pp. 101–103, 166–167; Richard Polenberg, "Franklin Roosevelt and Civil Liberties: The Case of the Dies Committee," *The Historian*,

Vol. 30 (February 1968), pp. 165–178.

[21] The March letter appears in CR, May 7, 1940, Vol. 86 at pp. 5642–5643. Subsequent to the April speech, Jackson published an article in which he noted that there are "no definite standards to determine what constitutes a 'subversive activity' such as we have for murder or larceny"—R. H. Jackson, "The Federal Prosecutor," *Journal of the American Judicature Society*, June 1940, at p. 18. The remarks of Jackson and Hoover at the August conference appear in *Proceedings of the Federal-State Conference on Law Enforcement Problems*, Aug. 5–6, 1940.

[22] 28 Code of Federal Regulations, Section 0.85(d).

[23] From Official Files, FDR Papers, Hyde Park, N.Y.

[24] Church, Book III, pp. 459–461.

[25] Church, Book III, pp. 461–463; Church, Book II, pp. 45–46. The National Security Council (NSC) had, by virtue of the National Security Act of 1947, inherited the coordination functions of the Inter-departmental Intelligence Conference (IIC), which had been organized by the FBI and the military services to implement the White House directive of June 26, 1939, by eliminating jurisdictional conflicts. The IIC produced a series of Delimitation Agreements (1940, 1942, 1949), which set up jurisdictional boundaries. In 1962 President Kennedy transferred the IIC from the NSC to the Attorney General's office—Church, Vol. 6, pp. 572–574; Church, Book III, p. 464. The history of the IIC and the successive Delimitations Agreements reflects an assumption by the FBI of a generous scope of intelligence authority, but in no way supports an interpretation of the Sept. 6 document as a "subversive activities" investigative assignment from the White House.

[26] Church, Book III, p. 463.

[27] *Ibid.*, p. 464; HISC, *Hearings, Domestic Intelligence Operations for Internal Security Purposes*, Part 1 (1974), pp. 3337–3338. It was hardly necessary to issue a statement on the subject of the FBI's investigative authority in connection with the atomic energy matters. The Atomic Energy Act of

1946 had already explicitly charged the agency with this function. The only explanation for the issuance of the document was to revalidate the White House precedents (especially the Truman directive) and at the same time to promote the FBI both as an instrument to "spike vigilante activity" and the "right way" foil to a rampaging Senator Joseph McCarthy. See Athan G. Theoharis, "The FBI's Stretching of Presidential Directives," *Political Science Quarterly* (Winter 1976–77), pp. 649, 669–670.

[28] *GAO Report* (1976), p. 197.

[29] Senate Internal Security Subcommittee, "Interlocking Subversion in Government," *Hearings,* Part 16 (1953), p. 1143. Columnist Drew Pearson wrote in his diaries that Hoover's testimony contributed to Brownell's strategy of reviving the White case to improve Republican electoral prospects—*Diaries, 1949–1959* (Holt, Rinehart and Winston, 1974), p. 284. Hoover's testimony, involving matters eight years old and rejected by a grand jury as grounds for indictment, invited political risks of the very kind that he had shrewdly shunned in the past. But vengefulness overcame caution: this appearance, reckless as it was, was a way of getting back at the peppery Truman for refusing to contribute to his apotheosis.

[30] *Confirmation Hearings,* Senate Judiciary Committee (1973), pp. 7, 15.

[31] The earlier (May 25) speech, "Challenges We Face Together," was reproduced in an FBI release; the October speech, "A Standard of Excellence," appears in CR, March 1, 1973, p. S3787.

[32] *Confirmation Hearings,* p. 640.

[33] Richard Cotter, a retired chief of the Research Section of the Bureau's Intelligence Division, has written a valuable account of the background of the adoption of the 1973 *Manual Guidelines*—"Notes Toward a Definition of National Security," *Washington Monthly* (December 1975), pp. 9–11.

[34] For Wannall's testimony, see HISC, *Hearings* (cited above, note 27), pp. 3568–3569, 3606–3607. Wannall relied on the August 1936 assignment as a

source of the agency's countersubversive intelligence authority —*Ibid.,* pp. 3571–3572. Maroney's testimony appears at 3362–3363; see also pp. 3385–3388, 3392–3393.

[35] *Ibid.,* pp. 3620–3621.

[36] *GAO Report* (1976), pp. 138–140. A follow-up report based on 319 case samples issued on Nov. 9, 1977, reached the same conclusion—*GAO Report* (1977), p. 41.

[37] "Kelley Puts His Mark on the FBI," NYT, March 3, 1974.

[38] Church, Vol. 6, pp. 540–544; *Joint Hearings on Warrantless Wiretapping and Electronic Surveillance* (1974), pp. 31–32.

[39] Department of Justice Release, Nov. 4, 1973, summarized in NYT above, note 37.

[40] Quoted in "Supercop Takes Over at the FBI," Washington *Star-News,* March 15, 1974. Kelley's views on the preventive role of internal security surveillance are set forth in speeches before the Federal Bar Association (Washington, D.C. Sept. 6, 1974), the Veterans of Foreign Wars (Washington, D.C., March 10, 1975), and a joint meeting of the National Conference of Bar Presidents and the American Judicature Society (Montreal, Canada; Aug. 9, 1975).

[41] *GAO Report* (1976), pp. 140–144; *GAO Report* (1977), pp. 45–46.

[42] *Ervin Hearings* (1971) Part I, pp. 598, 602–603, 863–864. I refer in this way to the *Hearings on Federal Data Banks, Computers and the Bill of Rights,* of the Subcommittee of the Senate Committee on the Judiciary, chaired by Senator Sam J. Erving, Jr.

[43] *GAO Report* (1976). An FBI memorandum of Feb. 5, 1976 (at p. 212) disputed "the GAO's finding that the Bureau was not granted investigative authority based upon a Presidential delegation in 1936 or by means of subsequent Presidential Directives. We believe a careful analysis of all pertinent documentary evidence bearing on the question of limitations on the 1936 delegation would convincingly reveal that the authority was granted the FBI at the instruction of the President and that this authority extended to subversive activities in

general." The Wannall memorandum is summarized in Church, Book III, p.

4. The Lengthened Shadow of a Man

1 *Memorial Tributes,* pp. XVII, XXIV, XXVI. The referenced volume was published as a Senate document in 1974 pursuant to a resolution introduced by Mississippi Senator James Eastland and passed by both houses of Congress. This handsomely bound 329-page book contains, in addition to the eulogies cited in the text, a record of the funeral services and a compilation of newspaper articles and editorials in tribute to Director Hoover that alone runs to over 150 closely printed pages. See also "Hoover and His FBI: An Era Ends," *Newsweek,* May 15, 1972; "J. Edgar Hoover Dies, 77, Will Lie in State in Capital," NYT, May 3, 1972.

2 These and other tributes are all detailed in a two-and-a-half-page document distributed to the public by the Bureau. A more elaborate version appears in *Memorial Tributes,* pp. XI–XIV.

3 Gallup Poll, release of Dec. 25, 1953: "Poll Finds FBI Losing Support," NYT, Aug. 9, 1970; *Newsweek,* May 10, 1971; *Editorial Research Reports,* June 25, 1971, pp. 1–2.

4 Fritz Redl, quoted in Ernest Becker, *Denial of Death* (Free Press, 1973), p. 135.

5 Schott, p. 162.

6 James Phelan, "Hoover of the FBI," *Saturday Evening Post,* Sept. 25, 1965, pp. 23–24.

7 See, for example, Orlando Patterson, *Ethnic Chauvinism* (Stein and Day, 1977), p. 45.

8 Paul Radin, *The World of Primitive Man* (Schuman, 1953), p. 85.

9 Ollestad, p. 239.

10 Provided by the sponsor's advertising agency with the writers' names deleted.

11 *Life,* Letters to the Editor, April 30, 1971. The quoted letter is one of a series protesting a *Life* article by Tom Wicker, "G-Man Under Fire," April 9, 1971, and a cover caption, "Emperor of the FBI."

12 Patrick J. Murphy, *Commissioner* (Simon and Schuster, 1977), p. 86; Watters and Gillers, eds., pp. 140–167; de Toledano, pp. 261–263.

558 and Church, Book II, pp. 134–135.

44 Cotter, *op. cit.,* pp. 11–12.

13 Smith, pp. 19–21, 366.

14 Television interview of H. R. Haldeman by CBS reporter Mike Wallace, March 23, 1975; Evans and Novak column, "The FBI Abroad," *N.Y. Post,* Jan. 21, 1972.

15 "Nixon Okd FBI Overseas Role," Washington *Sunday Star and Daily News,* June 10, 1973.

16 "FBI Said to Have Cut Direct Liaison with CIA," NYT, Oct. 10, 1971. This disclosure was the result of a leak by William C. Sullivan, FBI domestic intelligence chief, who was fired the week before.

17 Quoted in Stevenson, p. 244; see also pp. 24, 163, 185, 249 for one of many accounts of the difficulties posed by Hoover's publicity hunger to an effective wartime counterespionage program. The FBI's most successful use of a double agent both for counterespionage and prosecutive purposes involved William Sebold, a naturalized American of German birth, secretly trained by the Germans in a full range of espionage techniques. But Sebold was not turned; he voluntarily submitted himself to the FBI's direction and control—Stevenson, pp. 409–410; Ungar, pp. 104–105; Hyde, p. 219.

18 Tricycle's encounters with Hoover are described in Popov, pp. 135–141, 155, 164, 166–169, 175; and corroborated in important parts by Cave Brown, pp. 461, 471; Stevenson, pp. 257–260; Masterman, pp. 79–81, 95–96, 138, 196–198; and Hyde, pp. 219–221.

19 See Corson, pp. 84–87.

20 See, for example, Gordon Lonsdale, *SPY: 20 Years in Secret Service* (M. Spearman, 1965), p. 66, and James B. Donovan, *Strangers on a Bridge* (Atheneum, 1964), pp. 108, 302–304.

21 "F.B.I. Reported to Have Halted Efforts to Detect Foreign Undercover Agents," NYT, Feb. 27, 1976. For a reply by the Bureau, see "F.B.I. Says It Still Hunts Foreign Spies," NYT, Feb. 28, 1976. For an account describing how Hoover's leak to the press for publicity purposes blew a potentially important

spy surveillance and embarrassed the
State Department at the same time, see
"F.B.I. Believes a High Soviet
Intelligence Official Is Visiting the
United States Under an Alias and Is
Trailing Him," NYT, April 19, 1967,
and "On the Way to Ohrbach's," NYT,
April 23, 1967. The previous year
Hoover decided to break a spy case
involving a Soviet attaché, Valentin A.
Revin, and a double agent, John
Huminik, in order to improve his
image, which had suffered as a result of
wiretapping disclosures and an ensuing
controversy with Robert F. Kennedy.
The decision forced the abandonment
of a previously agreed-on plan to try to
"turn" Revin. The State Department,
to head off a trial and the retaliatory
consequences, ordered Revin deported.
But the Russians promptly ousted an
American diplomat in reprisal. Hoover
had to content himself with press leaks
for his needed publicity. In addition,
the blown spy was made available to
Senator Karl Mundt to testify against
the Soviet Consular Convention
discussed below—John Huminik,
Double Agent (NAL, 1967), pp. 171–172,
and Drew Pearson column ("The FBI's
Cover Story"), Sept. 24, 1966.

22 *Anecdotes de l'Empire et de la Restauration*
(Brussels, 1839), pp. 223–224. The use
of invented or assisted conspiracies by a
political police chief to prove his
indispensability is described in P. J.
Squire, *The Third Department—The
Political Police in the Russia of Nicholas
I* (Cambridge University Press, 1968),
p. 152; Hubert Cole, *Fouché*, (McCall,
1971), pp. 139, 178, 179; and Ronald
Hingley, *The Russian Secret Police*
(Simon and Schuster, 1970), p. 104.

23 The Copley, Hearst, and Gannett
newspaper chains were preferred press
outlets. Favorite newspapers were the
Chicago *Tribune,* the Washington *Star,*
and the San Francisco *Examiner.* Press
insiders included Walter Trohan,
George Sokolsky, Frederick Woltman,
Ralph de Toledano, Howard
Rushmore, Victor Riesel, Walter
Winchell, Jeremiah O'Leary, and
Willard Edwards, and a score of
lesser-known right-wing journalists. On
the use of reporters both as outlets and

informers in covert action programs,
see Chapter 6. The FBI's practice of
supplying file material to
anti-Communist journalists is described
in James Boyd, "From Far Right to
Far Left—and Farther with Karl
Hess," *N.Y. Times Magazine,* Dec. 6,
1970, and in an interview by the author
with Hess in October 1971. See also
Kruger, "Hoover's FBI: The Media and
the Myth," *feed/back* (Spring 1978).
Accounts of the use of one journalist
(Sam Jaffe) as a spy appear in *MORE*
(March 1977), "The Reporter Who
Came in from the Cold," and of
another (Jacque Srouji) in the following
NYT stories: "Paper in Nashville
Dismisses Writer Linked to the FBI,"
May 8, 1976; "Writer Threatened over
Link to FBI, Is Reported Missing,"
May 9, 1976; "Ex-Reporter Denies that
She Gave F.B.I. Information about
Nashville Paper or Its Staff," May 19,
1976; "F.B.I. Bars Data on Ties to a
Nashville Journalist," May 21, 1976;
"Not Entirely Pure," column by
Anthony Lewis, Aug. 25, 1976. See also
"A Special Relationship," *Time,* May
24, 1976. The FBI's media manipulation
is briefly described in Church, Book II,
pp. 15–16.

24 "More Companies Find Management
Talent Among Ex-FBI Agents," *Wall
Street Journal,* Oct. 16, 1962.

25 Jack Anderson columns, May 11 and 12,
1971.

26 Ungar, p. 273.

27 *America,* March 8, 1969.

28 Official and Confidential ("O C")
Document Summaries, No. 160; Robert
Sherwood, *Roosevelt and Hopkins*
(Harper, 1948), p. 250. According to H.
Montgomery Hyde (p. 206), Hoover
promptly told Drew Pearson, a prime
beneficiary of the leaks, about his
leak-plugging assignment.

29 Robert J. Donovan, *Conflict and Crisis,
The Presidency of Harry S. Truman,
1945–1948* (Norton, 1977), pp. 183–184,
217; Church, Book II, p. 37; Demaris,
pp. 104–115.

30 Eisenhower, *Mandate for Change* (NAL,
1963), p. 127.

31 Hoover's private ("O C") files did not
contain memoranda only about the
Exner-Mafia-White House connection.

Hoover alerted Attorney General Kennedy, in what appears to be veiled blackmail, to the contents of a file relating to a court settlement of a lawsuit brought by a woman who had allegedly been engaged to marry John F. Kennedy in 1951—"Files Disclose Letter on Kennedy," "J. Edgar's Private Files," NYT, Dec. 15, 1977; "J.F.K. and the Mobsters' Moll," *Time,* Dec. 29, 1975; "A Shadow over Camelot," *Newsweek,* Dec. 29, 1975.

32 Church, Book III, p. 346.

33 In an executive order exempting Hoover, then sixty-nine, from compulsory retirement at seventy, Johnson hailed him as "a quiet, humble and magnificent public servant . . . a hero to millions of citizens and an anathema to all evil men"—"Johnson Hails Hoover Service, Waives Compulsory Retirement," NYT, May 9, 1964.

34 "Fund Official Attacks F.B.I. Chief on Red Legends," NYT, Aug. 7, 1962; "Robert Kennedy Lauds F.B.I. Head," NYT, Aug. 8, 1962; "Shop Talk at Thirty," by Robert I. Brown, *Editor & Publisher,* Sept. 15, 1962.

35 Katzenbach tried without success to require Hoover to route memos to the White House through his office. Tom Wicker, "Nobody Dares to Pick His Successor," *Life,* April 9, 1971; "Whoever Runs It, F.B.I. Faces Problem of Political Control," NYT, March 26, 1973.

36 See the following stories from the *New York Times:* "Rightists Oppose Pact with Soviet," Aug. 19, 1965; "Rusk Hints Hoover Assents on Consuls," Jan. 21, 1967; "Rusk Renews Plea for Consular Pact," Jan. 24, 1967; "Senate Unit Asks Hoover to Appear," Jan. 26, 1967; "Dirksen Reports Soviet Lobbying," Jan. 27, 1967; "Morton Endorses Consular Treaty," Feb. 1, 1967; "Dirksen Relenting on Consular Pact," Feb. 7, 1967; Editorials: "Clear It with Hoover," Jan. 23, 1967, and "The Consular Treaty," Jan. 31, 1967; see also Drew Pearson columns, Jan. 30, 1967, Feb. 3, 1967.

37 "Mao's Red Shadow, China in the Eyes of the F.B.I. Director," NYT, Aug. 17, 1971.

38 Guest column for Victor Riesel, St. Louis *Globe-Democrat,* July 20, 1962.

39 James Boyd, *Above the Law, The Rise and Fall of Senator Thomas J. Dodd* (NAL, 1968), pp. 109–110, 151–152, 161–162.

40 Demaris, p. 172.

41 See "FBI Data and Congress," Washington *Sunday Star,* April 28, 1957, and below, Chapter 11.

42 *Annual Report of the Committee on Un-American Activities* (1947), p. 1. The committee (Senate and House) publications under Hoover's by-line are listed in Appendix II under the heading "Additional Pamphlets."

43 "Files Show F.B.I. Rift with Warren Panel," NYT, Jan. 19, 1978.

44 "Secrecy and Abuse of Power," NYT, Feb. 14, 1977.

45 As of 1971, twenty-eight Bureau agents were assigned as investigators to the staff of the House Appropriations Committee whose chief investigator was, for a number of years, Paul J. Mohr, an agent on leave and brother of John P. Mohr, Hoover's assistant for administration and third in the FBI hierarchy. When Mohr returned to the Bureau in May 1971, he was replaced by another agent, Walter Pincus—"The FBI's Budget Watchdogs," *N.Y. Post,* June 14, 1971; "F.B.I. Agents Vital to a House Panel," NYT, April 25, 1971. Congress as a whole approved nineteen of the agency's last twenty-one budget estimates exactly as submitted— "Secrecy and Abuse of Power," NYT, Feb. 14, 1977. On two occasions, Hoover was given a larger appropriation than he requested— Walter Pincus, "The Bureau's Budget: A Source of Power," in Watters and Gillers, eds., p. 65.

46 "FBI's Hoover Scores Ramsey Clark, RFK," Washington *Post,* Nov. 17, 1970; "Hoover Reported Describing Clark as Jellyfish," NYT, Nov. 17, 1970.

47 "FBI Surveillance," CR, April 19, 1971, p. 10650; May 19, 15762, 15763, vol. 117. The Nixon White House denounced the Muskie charges as "blatantly political" and an attempt to create "a feeling of fear and intimidation"—"Muskie Is Accused of Creating Fear," Washington *Post,* April 17, 1971.

48 The Boggs speech (15½ columns long)

appeared in the *Congressional Record*
for April 22, 1971, pp. 11561–11566, Vol.
117. For background and supplementary
accounts see: "Boggs, Charging
Wiretapping, Bids Hoover Resign,"
NYT, April 6, 1971; "Boggs Sees Peril
to U.S. from F.B.I.," NYT, April 7,
1971; "Boggs to Assert a Tap Was
Found," NYT, April 22, 1971; "FBI
Obtained Phone Call List, Boggs Says,"
L.A. *Times,* April 20, 1971; "What's
Bugging Boggs," *Newsweek,* April 19,
1971. The White House, the Justice
Department, and the FBI denied that
congressmen's phones had ever been
tapped—"Hill Taps Denied by U.S.,"
Washington *Post,* April 7, 1971.

49 "Bugging of Dowdy by FBI Revealed,"
Washington *Post,* April 17, 1971; "FBI
Is Said to Bug a House Member,"
NYT, April 16, 1971; "Kleindienst
Assails Boggs; Invites Inquiry into
FBI," NYT, April 8, 1971; "Kleindienst
Modifies Suggestion Congress
Investigate the F.B.I.," NYT, April 9,
1971.

50 Senator McGovern's statements and
Record insertions on the subject of the
FBI and Hoover include the following
major items:

1. *Nov. 17, 1970.* McGovern statement
in Senate deplores Hoover's attack on
Attorneys General Ramsey Clark and
Robert F. Kennedy—CR, Vol. 116,
pp. 37642–37643.

2. *Feb. 1, 1971.* "FBI Agent's Dismissal
Calls for Investigation." McGovern
outlines Shaw case and McGovern's
actions on his behalf, inserting a L.A.
Times article, correspondence
between McGovern and Hoover,
McGovern letter to Mitchell, and
Shaw's letter to his professor in the
Record. McGovern asks Senate
Subcommittee on Administrative
Practice to investigate circumstances
surrounding the termination of Agent
Shaw's service—CR, Vol. 117, pp.
1195–1201.

3. *Feb. 10, 1971.* McGovern statement
in Senate accuses Hoover of
contempt of Congress for sending
details of his position on the Shaw
case to an Atlanta newspaper while
refusing a Senate investigating
committee the same information on

the grounds that the matter was
before the courts—CR, Vol. 117, pp.
2507–2508.

4. *March 1, 1971.* "FBI Review
Needed." Unsigned letter from ten
special agents of the FBI concurring
in McGovern's call for a review of
Hoover's administration, McGovern's
response to the letter, and a letter
from John Jay Law Club also calling
for an investigation of the treatment
of Agent Shaw—CR, Vol. 117, pp.
4414–4415.

5. *March 3, 1971.* Letter from the
president of the John Jay College of
Criminal Justice to Attorney General
Mitchell contesting Hoover's position
on the Shaw case—CR, Vol. 117, pp.
4815–4816.

6. *March 8, 1971.* "Top Hoover Aides
Defend Their Boss." Letter from
twenty-one upper-echelon
administrators of the FBI attacking
McGovern for releasing the unsigned
letter—CR, Vol. 117, pp. 5367–5372.

7. *April 1, 1971.* Two letters from
Assistant Director William C.
Sullivan—CR, Vol. 117, p. 9230.

8. *April 19, 1971.* McGovern statement
delivered at Lewis-St. Francis College
in Lockport, Illinois, accusing FBI of
attempting to "destroy the career" of
a TWA pilot, Captain Cook, who
had been critical of Bureau actions in
New York during the hijacking of a
TWA plane to Rome, inserted into
Record on April 22, 1971, by
Representative Abner Mikva—CR,
Vol. 117, pp. 11,612–11,615.

9. *May 10, 1971.* McGovern statement
that he has received evidence that
Hoover acted illegally in seeking to
discredit a TWA pilot who criticized
Hoover.

10. *July 21, 1971.* Friends of the FBI
(Efrem Zimbalist, Jr., Honorary
Chairman) charges that Hoover was
"being subjected to the degradation
of a vicious partisan attack by
self-serving politicians, their
supporting media and certain radical
elements that ultimately seek the
destruction of all law and order in
the United States"—CR, Vol. 117, p.
26388.

[51] "FBI Clerks Rejoining Class after AU Apology to Hoover," Washington *Post,* Nov. 16, 1970; "Forced Out of FBI, 2 Peace Backers Say," L.A. *Times,* April 8, 1971. Hoover's puritanical sex, dress, and political standards of staff behavior produced extensive publicity. See, for example, "Ousted F.B.I. Aide Sues Hoover," NYT, April 2, 1971; "F.B.I. Turnover High for Capital," NYT, April 24, 1971; "U.S. Aide Says F.B.I. Barred Promotion," L.A. *Times,* April 22, 1971; "2 Women Sue FBI on Jobs as Agents," Washington *Post,* Aug. 5, 1971; Jack Anderson columns, Aug. 12, 1971 (ban on long hair and sideburns), and Sept. 13, 1971 (after-hours romance).

[52] Statement of Attorney General Mitchell, April 15, 1971; Attorney General Mitchell's address to Kentucky Bar Association, April 23, 1971; "President Says Hoover Is Victim of Unfair Attack," NYT, April 17, 1971; "Agnew Calls Hoover's Critics Politically Motivated," NYT, April 27, 1971. The Nixon White House discontent with Hoover, largely the result of his reluctance to take the risks demanded of him, is elaborated in John D. Ehrlichman's Watergate testimony— Book 6, pp. 2531, 2605-2606, 2625-2629. See also "Nixon Dilemma over Hoover," Washington *Post,* April 5, 1971, and "J. Edgar's Boss," Washington *Post,* June 5, 1971, columns by Rowland Evans and Robert Novak; "Capital Playing New Guessing Game: Who Will Succeed J. Edgar Hoover?", NYT, May 14, 1971.

[53] "Nixon Sees End of Permissiveness Era," NYT, June 1, 1971.

[54] CR, pp. 10486, 12715, 10058-10060, Vol. 117. Prior to May 10, many voices were heard in support of the FBI and Hoover, including that of Majority Leader Mike Mansfield, who deprecated the charges, voiced confidence in Hoover, and questioned the need for a congressional investigation—"Mansfield Backs Hoover and F.B.I.: Ridicules Critics," NYT, April 16, 1971. Detailed supporting statements came from Hoover's conservative champions both before and after the May 10 special tribute. The most noteworthy of the former is a speech (CR, April 30, 1971,

12886, Vol. 117) by Indiana Congressman William Bray, which was drafted by the Bureau, charging that the "smear campaign" against the FBI "is an incredibly accurate replay of exactly what went on 30 years ago" when Communists plotted to discredit the FBI. On May 19, another member of the congressional palace guard, Congressman John Ashbrook, weighed in with an eleven-column speech on "The FBI and Its Detractors," CR, pp. 15761-15765, Vol. 117.

[55] See "Hoover at 75: Mr. FBI and His G-Men," *Congressional Quarterly,* Dec. 22, 1969, reprinted in CR, Jan. 20, 1970, pp. A96-105.

[56] *The Fabulous Century, Sixty Years of American Life,* Vol. IV (Time-Life, 1930-1940), p. 113.

[57] "1959 Search of Room of a Woman Is Reported," NYT, July 22, 1975.

[58] CR, May 28, 1968, p. 15298, Vol. 114.

[59] Harvey column, "God Help Us Without J.E.H.," Norwalk *Hour,* April 25, 1963.

[60] See, for example, "F.B.I. Investigated Hong Kong Woman Friend of Nixon in '60's to Determine If She Was Foreign Agent," NYT, June 22, 1976. The FBI, it is alleged, opened a file on JFK beginning in World War II when he was a naval lieutenant, because he was dating a woman suspected of being a Nazi agent. Hoover is supposed to have sent the file to the White House, first in 1959 and again in 1971—in both cases for possible use by Richard Nixon in political campaigns—"Hoover's Kennedy File," *Newsweek,* Dec. 29, 1975.

[61] One folder in the Director's OC files consists of Washington field office letters from 1958 to 1965 describing, in the language of a Department of Justice summary, "general immoral or criminal activities on the part of diplomats, Government employees, politicians, sport figures, socially prominent persons, Senators and Congressmen."

[62] Biddle, *In Brief Authority,* pp. 258-259.

[63] The assignment to collect dirt on authors of books critical of the Warren Commission Report—there were seven in all—came directly from the Johnson White House, and the Bureau's memoranda were transmitted to Marvin

Watson, LBJ's personal assistant, without the knowledge of the Attorney General—Vol. 6, pp. 82, 511; "Did FBI Spy on JFK Probe Foes?", *N.Y. Post,* Jan. 21, 1975.

64 Church, Vol. 6, p. 477.

65 OC File Summaries; Testimony of Attorney General Edward H. Levi in *Hearings on FBI Oversight* (1975), Subcommittee on Civil and Constitutional Rights of House Committee on the Judiciary, pp. 8–10.

66 "Hoover Mad Man, Ex-F.B.I. Aide Says," Boston *Globe,* May 16, 1973; see also to the same effect, *Pike Hearings (Hearings of House Select Committee on Intelligence),* Part 3, p. 1068 (testimony of Arthur Murtagh).

67 "Files from Hoover to Backers Reported," NYT, Feb. 25, 1974. Both Rooney and the Bureau denied the charges in the 1974 story that information had been supplied about Eikenberry. The limited Bureau involvement in the Eikenberry campaign is described in "Memo Shows Rep. Rooney Got Data from F.B.I. on '68 Opponent," NYT, June 2, 1978. That Eikenberry's broader allegations of Bureau investigations and the release of a dossier to Rooney dealing with his personal life not limited to "public record" material may have been well founded is suggested by the practice of relaying requests and instructions of this sensitive sort by telephone rather than in writing.

68 Samuel Stouffer, *Communism, Conformity and Civil Liberties* (Doubleday, 1955), pp. 330–331.

69 Letter to Frank H. Capell's *Herald of Freedom,* Sept. 11, 1963; letter of Jan. 23, 1963, reprinted in *Vigilante,* Jan. 23, 1962; William J. Gill, *The Ordeal of Otto Otepka* (Arlington House, 1969), p. 4. Both Capell and his lawyer were

wiretapped shortly after the receipt of Hoover's warm letter of reassurance (see Chapter 7).

70 See Lowenthal and Guterman, p. 118.

71 T. W. Adorno, *et al.,* p. 239.

72 Ollestad, p. 239.

73 For a perceptive analysis of the authoritarian as prophet, see Lester G. Crocker, *Jean Jacques Rousseau, The Prophetic Voice* (Macmillan, 1973), pp. 189–196. Also useful is Fred Greenstein, *Personality and Politics* (University of Chicago Press, 1969).

74 Murphy, *The Commissioner* (Simon and Schuster, 1978), p. 90; Demaris, p. 142; Jack Anderson (with Les Whitten) column, Jan. 5, 1977: "Files Show Rift with Warren Panel," NYT, Jan. 14, 1978.

75 "Hoover Assailed on Jenkins Case," NYT, Oct. 28, 1964.

76 Guthman, *We Band of Brothers* (Harper and Row, 1964), p. 280 (after text, p. 230, "White House").
   An illuminating description of Hoover's campaign to discredit Attorney General Kennedy by feeding an all-too-receptive President Johnson invented tales of Kennedy's disloyalty appears in Schlesinger, *Robert F. Kennedy and His Times,* pp. 628–630.

77 The "notorious liar" interview is described in "Hoover Assails Warren Findings," NYT, Nov. 19, 1964; for the subsequent address and its emendation see "Hoover Pledges Impartial F.B.I.," NYT, Nov. 25, 1964; "J. Edgar Hoover—Man and Legend," NYT, Dec. 6, 1964.

78 Quoted by Christopher Lydon in Hoover's obituary, NYT, May 3, 1972.

79 Memo from Executive Conference to Clyde Tolson, June 24, 1971.

80 Schott, pp. 149–150, 166, 183.

81 Lifton, p. 93.

5. The Bureau in Action

1 *GAO Report* (1976), pp. 3, 13–15, 35, 44–45.

2 See *ibid.,* p. 35.

3 FBI headquarters letters of Jan. 30, 1967, and July 23, 1968, quoted in *ibid.,* pp. 50–52.

4 Church, Book II, pp. 6–7.

5 The chart is adapted from one that appears in *GAO Report* (1976) at p. 107.

6 "F.B.I. Once Honored Its 'Bag Jobs,' " NYT, May 1, 1976; "F.B.I. Sought Cash Awards for Team of Agents That Broke into Socialist Group's Offices Here in '64–'65," NYT, June 28, 1976.

7 Church, Book III, p. 360.

8 Statement of William Gardner before the Senate Appropriations Subcommittee on

State, Justice, Commerce and the Judiciary, April 28, 1978; "Behind the FBI Indictments," *Justice Department Watch* (Spring 1978).

9 The SWP program was disclosed in 400 pages of FBI documents turned over in its damage suit and is summarized in "F.B.I. Burglarized Leftist Offices Here 92 Times in 1960–66, Official Files Show," NYT, March 29, 1976; "F.B.I. Is Linked to Thefts of Socialist Workers Reports Last Year," NYT, June 27, 1976.

10 "Burglaries by F.B.I. Conceded by Kelley," NYT, July 15, 1975; "Burglaries by F.B.I. as Late as 1972–73 Conceded by Kelley," NYT, July 1, 1975; "Kelley 'Deceived' On F.B.I. Break-Ins," NYT, Aug. 9, 1975. Some break-ins occurred even after Kelley took office. "Ex-F.B.I. Informant Says Agents Ordered 2 Oregon Break-Ins in '74," NYT, Sept. 15, 1976; "F.B.I. Linked to East Side Break-In Months after Kelley Took Office," NYT, Sept. 29, 1976; "U.S. Uncovers Evidence Indicating an F.B.I. Break-In in Upstate Town," NYT, Oct. 1, 1976; "F.B.I.'s Break-In Ban Reported Violated," NYT, Oct. 21, 1976; "Details on Illegal Break-ins Provided to Justice Dept.", NYT, Jan. 27, 1979.

11 The discussion of informers is based, in addition to the sources specifically cited, on a study of court and legislative records (including, most recently, Church, Book III, pp. 225, 227; Book II, pp. 178, 192–197; Vol. 6, pp. 109–158; *Pike Hearings* (Part 3, pp. 1050–1052), research by the author for use in preparing cross-examination and appellate briefs on behalf of clients and interviews with surfaced informers and their agent-handlers. The text distils the author's writings on the subject, which include "Political Informers," in Watters and Gillers, pp. 338–369; "The Informer," *Nation*, April 10, 1954; "Spies on Campus," *Playboy* (March 1968), reprinted in *Voices of Concern* (Harcourt Brace Jovanovich, 1971); "Theory and Practice of American Political Intelligence," *New York Review of Books*, April 22, 1971, reprinted in Skolnick and Curry,

"Crisis in American Institutions" (3d ed. 1976); "Confession of an FBI Informer," *Harpers* (December 1972) "Provocateur as Folk Hero," *Civil Liberties* (September 1971); "Hoover's Legacy," *Nation*, June 1, 1974; "Political Intelligence: Cameras, Informers and Files," *Civil Liberties Review* (April–May 1976), based on a paper prepared for the Chief Justice Earl Warren Conference on Advocacy, 1974, sponsored by the Roscoe Pound-American Trial Lawyers Foundation.

12 Examples of informers who engaged in illegal or provocative activities with either prior knowledge or subsequent approval of their agent-handlers are William O'Neal (Ch. 6), Charles Grimm, Jr. (interview with NET reporter, Paul Jacobs); David Sannes (interviews with author and Paul Jacobs; affidavit submitted in Seattle Seven conspiracy case, April 2, 1971); Horace L. Parker (trial transcript in Seattle Seven conspiracy case at pp. 1566–1567; 1648); Richard T. Cooper, "Undercover Weatherman: Informant Tells of Supplying Explosives to Revolutionaries, L. A. *Times,* reported in CR, Jan. 2, 1971, p. 44799, Vol. 116; Jeffrey Paul Desmond (affidavit in *U.S.* v. *Tissot et al.,* July 12, 1971; interviews with Paul Jacobs and Seattle *Post-Intelligencer* reporter, "(P. O. Bombing Figure Claims He Was Acting as Informer," Seattle *Post-Intelligencer* July 22, 1971); T. Tongyai (Tommy the Traveler, *Civil Liberties,* supra); Howard Godfrey (Ch. 12); and Robert Hardy (*Pike Hearings,* Part 3, pp. 1050–1052). See also, A. Karmen, "Agents Provocateurs in the Contemporary U.S. Leftist Movement," in C. Reasons, *The Criminologist: Crime and the Criminal* (Goodyear, 1974), pp. 209–226; Gary T. Marx, "Thoughts on a Neglected Category of Social Movement Participants: *The Agent Provocateur and Informant,"* paper delivered at American Sociological Association meeting, New Orleans, 1972; Paul Jacobs, "Informers —the Enemy Within," *Ramparts,* August–September, 1973; footnote 11 supra, and note at p. 181, ch. 6.

13 "Webster, FBI Aides Differ on Number of Informants," May 7, 1978, Washington *Post;* "Dispute FBI Totals on Spies in U.S.," May 7, 1978, Chicago *Tribune;* "Domestic Spies for FBI Exceed Total Webster Publicly Acknowledged," May 7, 1978, Washington *Star.*

14 "Hoover Says Reds Exploit Negroes," NYT, April 22, 1964.

15 *GAO Report* (1976), p. 60.

16 Documents dealing with the FBI's surveillance of the women's movement are described in Letty C. Pogrebin, "The FBI Was Watching You," *MS.* (June 1977).

17 *GAO Report* (1976), pp. 51–52.

18 *Ibid.,* p. 57.

19 CBS, "Under Surveillance," Dec. 23, 1971.

20 "FBI Informer Confesses," *Daily Rag,* Oct. 12, 19, 1973; Tim Butz and John B. Hayes, "Biography of an Informant," *WIN* Magazine, March 14, 21, 28, 1974; "Informers Spied on D.C. Activists," Washington *Star,* Oct. 7, 1963; "Informers for Police Exposed," Washington *Post,* Oct. 7, 1963.

21 The discussion in the text of campus surveillance is based on legislative hearings and court records, interviews with campus targets, informers, and college administrators. In addition to my articles in *Playboy, Civil Liberties, New York Review of Books* and *Harpers,* cited earlier, see William T. Divale (with James Joseph), *I Lived Inside the Campus Revolution* (Cowles Book Co., 1970); "Big Man on the Campus: Police Undercover Agent," NYT, March 29, 1971; L. McDonald, "A Profile of Two Friends," *Civil Liberties,* November 1974; "The Changeling," *Hard Times,* Sept. 29–Oct. 26, 1969; Report of the President's Committee on Student Unrest (Scranton Commission) (September 1971), and the Media papers, the most important of which are reprinted in *WIN* Magazine, March 1, 15, 1972.

22 *Connecticut Bar Journal,* Vol. 40 (1966), pp. 752–757; Vol. 41 (1967), pp. 164–167.

23 The role of the Army in campus surveillance is documented in *Ervin Hearings* (1971), pp. 319, 325–326, 328–329, 531–569, 959, 990–1021, and described in NBC, "First Tuesday," Dec. 30, 1971, and "CBS Reports," Jan. 1, 1971.

24 Church, Vol. 6., pp. 409–411. For the history and development of the FBI's custodial detention program, see *ibid.,* pp. 412–427, 645–668. It is discussed in Church, Book III, pp. 412–414, 442–447, 542–548; Book II, pp. 54–56; *GAO Report* (1976), pp. 66–75, Robert J. Goldstein, "The FBI's Forty Year Plot," *Nation,* July 1, 1978, and "An American Gulag: The Story of Summary Arrest and Emergency Detention of Political Dissidents in the United States," *Columbia Human Rights Law Review* (Fall 1978); see also Caroline Ross and Ken Lawrence, "J. Edgar Hoover's Detention Plan," American Friends Service Committee Program on Government Surveillance and Citizens Rights (1978).

25 Church, Book III, p. 542.

26 *Ibid.,* p. 547; Book II, p. 126.

27 FBI filing practices are discussed in Church, Book II, pp. 253–264. See also L. Patrick Gray III, *Confirmation Hearings* (1973), pp. 151–183, 404–408, 466, 476, 478; *Ervin Hearings* (1971), pp. 492, 530; A. Theoharis, "Double-Entry Intelligence Files," *Nation,* Oct. 22, 1977; John Rosenberg, "Catch in the Information Act," *Nation,* Feb. 4, 1978; "The FBI Would Shred the Past," *Nation,* June 3, 1978; "Prying Open the Files," *Newsweek,* Feb. 2, 1976. The FBI's sabotage of the FOIPA is discussed in "FBI Agents Rap Policy of Burning Files; Link it to Public Access Acts," *Wall Street Journal,* Sept. 27, 1978.

28 Church, Vol. 2, pp. 115, 117.

29 "New Director Says Nixon Wants Non-Political F.B.I.," NYT, May 4, 1972; "The FBI's New Chief: There Are No Secret Files," *Newsweek,* May 15, 1972.

30 "F.B.I. File Issue Revived by Nixon," NYT, Oct. 27, 1954.

31 CR, June 1, 1976, pp. 16070–71, Vol. 122; "Bell Urged to Move Against F.B.I. Aide," NYT, May 10, 1976.

6. Aggressive Intelligence

[1] Quoted in Donner, "Theory and Practice of American Political Intelligence," *New York Review of Books,* April 22, 1971.

[2] Church, Book III, pp. 16–27; Church, Vol. 6, pp. 372–394.

[3] Frederick Pollock and Frederic William Maitland, *History of English Law* (Cambridge University Press, 1952), Vol. II, p. 449.

[4] Demaris, p. 317.

[5] *Memoirs of Chief Justice Earl Warren* (Doubleday, 1977), pp. 5–7.

[6] "Overseeing the Secret Services," *New Republic,* Dec. 7, 1974.

[7] Church, Book III, p. 73.

[8] An edited version was made public with deletions allegedly to protect the national security. But this was a pretext to justify suppressing embarrassing portions of the report, which confined its criticism to the observation that COINTELPRO actions in "isolated instances" involved practices that "can only be considered abhorrent to a free society." Saxbe's public statement on releasing the bowdlerized report was equally emollient.

[9] Church, Vol. 6, pp. 70–71; CRCR, *Hearings,* pp. 10–11, 44.

[10] Church, Book III, pp. 6–7.

[11] "The Movement in a New Era of Repression," *Berkeley Journal of Sociology,* Vol. 16 (1971), pp. 1–14.

[12] Press releases of remarks by FBI Director Kelley, Dec. 7, 1973, and Nov. 18, 1974. See also CBS Reports, "Inside the FBI," Jan. 26, 1976.

[13] "Light on the Dark Side of Hoover's F.B.I.," NYT, Nov. 24, 1974.

[14] Church, Vol. 6, pp. 992–995.

[15] The discussion of the FBI's COINTELPRO actions in this chapter is based on documents from the following sources: Church Committee releases (only a small portion of which were printed), FOIPA releases to individuals and groups who were targeted by COINTELPRO actions; documents turned over to plaintiffs in damage suits; and a mass of COINTELPRO memoranda made public by the FBI in November 1977. In addition, I cite more accessible printed sources such as legislative hearings and reports, periodicals, and newspapers.

[16] CRCR, *Hearings,* pp. 10–11, 13.

[17] Church, Vol. 6, p. 70.

[18] Church, Book III, p. 75.

[19] The Albertson story is recounted in the author's "Let Him Wear a Wolf's Head," *Civil Liberties Review* (April–May 1976). The sources for both the text and the article are documents released under the FOIPA and interviews with Albertson and his widow.

[20] In addition to the COINTELPRO sources cited above, documents specifically relating to the SWP Disruption Program along with commentaries appear in Nelson Blackstock, *COINTELPRO—The FBI's Secret War on Political Freedom* (Monad Press, 1975).

[21] A series of releases by both the Church Committee and the FBI (under the FOIPA) has documented these programs—especially the anti-Klan actions—in great detail. A selection of relevant documents is printed in Vol. 6 of the Church Committee *Hearings* at pp. 378–382, 403–405, 513–527, 679–680. See also Church, Book III, pp. 18–20, 45, 51–52, 66–69.

[22] Ben Haas, *KKK* (Regency Books, 1963), p. 148.

[23] Richard Nixon, "On Going Beyond the Letter of the Law," Washington *Star,* June 5, 1977.

[24] In addition to the released COINTELPRO documents already referred to, the principal sources for the discussion in the text are a number of memoranda in the Director's "Official and Confidential" file released under the FOIPA to the Center for National Security Studies in May 1978. The FBI's operations against Dr. Martin Luther King, Jr., are the subject of a Church Committee case study (Book III, pp. 81–184), as well as of a "Report of the Department of Justice Task Force to Review the Martin Luther King, Jr. Security and Assassination Investigations" (1977), at pp. 113–139, 165–176. An informative report appears in Schlesinger, *Robert F. Kennedy and*

His Times, pp. 343–365. Published documents dealing with the FBI's program against black groups and leaders appear in Church, Vol. 6, pp. 383–392, 398–402, 405–407, 428–433, 440–442, 617–622, 695–698, 767–784, 788–803.

The Black Panther Party (BPP) is the subject of a Church Committee study, "The FBI's Covert Action Program to Destroy the Black Panther Party," Book III, pp. 185–224. Supplemental sources are the records—trial transcripts and exhibits—in the Hampton case *(infra)* and *Black Panther Party et al.* v. *Levi et al.* Civil Action no. 76–2205 (D.C.D.C.). A useful account of the FBI's attack on the Panthers is Lowell Berman and David Weir, "Revolution on Ice," *Rolling Stone,* Sept. 9, 1976.

25 Navasky, pp. 146–147; Church, Book III, pp. 115–117.

26 His name, deleted when the original memo was released, was disclosed by Victor Navasky, editor of *The Nation*—"The FBI's Wildest Dream," *Nation,* June 17, 1978.

27 Hugh Sidey, "L.B.J., Hoover and Personal Spying," *Time,* Feb. 10, 1975; Bill Moyers, *Newsweek,* March 10, 1975.

28 *Time,* "FBI Dirty Tricks," Dec. 5, 1977.

29 Hartford *Courant,* "Parole Court Jails Pardoned Killer," April 30, 1977.

30 The account given here is based primarily on the record in the civil case, *Iberia Hampton et al.* v. *City of Chicago et al.,* No. 70 C1384 (N.D. Ill.), an action for damages brought by the mothers of Fred Hampton and Mark Clark and the seven raid survivors. The 246-page investigative report on the raid by a federal grand jury made public in May 1970 is seriously biased but is illuminating as a record of the collaboration, described in the text, between federal and state officials to suppress the truth. The most useful accounts of the raid are *Search and Destroy,* a Report of an Investigative Commission, headed by Roy Williams and Ramsey Clark (Metropolitan Applied Research Center: New York, 1973); "Fred Hampton: A Case of Political Assassination," *First Principles* (November 1976), and Bo Burlingham,

"The Unquiet Grave of Fred Hampton," *New Times,* May 31, 1974.

31 The account in the text is based on court records and interviews. See also Donner, "Hoover's Legacy," *Nation,* June 1, 1974, and "State's Attorney Blasts Panther Indictments," Baltimore *Afro-American,* May 25, 1971; "Ex-Prosecutor Testifies Panther Witnesses Aided," Baltimore *News American,* June 18, 1971; "Police Admit Paying Witnesses in Panther Slaying Case," Washington *Post,* June 18, 1971; "Turco Trial: 'Agent 94' Testifies," Washington *Post,* June 19, 1971; "Key State Witness's Testimony Stricken in Turco Trial," Baltimore *Sun,* June 23, 1971; "Kebe Faces New Quiz in Turco Trial," Baltimore *News American,* June 22, 1971; "Turco Case: Kebe Withdrawn, Testimony Stricken from Record," Baltimore *Afro-American,* June 26, 1971.

32 See Chapter 10, and Robert Fink, "The Unsolved Break-Ins, 1970–1974," *Rolling Stone,* Oct. 10, 1974.

33 The Ward ambush slaying was first investigated by Richard T. Cooper, whose story "Killing Nags Consciences in Seattle" appeared in the May 2, 1971, L.A. *Times.* Subsequent accounts include Jon R. Waltz, "Staked Out for Slaughter," *Nation,* July 5, 1971; "Coroner's Inquest Released after Dramatic Interruption," Seattle *Post-Intelligencer,* May 23, 1970; "Attorney Seeks Writ to Prosecute Hannah," Seattle *Post-Intelligencer,* June 13, 1970; and Ardie Ivie, "The Killing of Larry Ward—Act II," *Seattle Magazine* (July 1970). See also "Riots, Civil and Criminal Disorders," *Hearings,* Senate Permanent Subcommittee on Investigations (1970), Part 24, p. 5531.

34 In addition to the unpublished sources already referred to, the New Left program is discussed in Church, Book II, pp. 88–90, and documented in Church, Vol. 6, pp. 393, 438, 535, 537, 612, 669, 693.

35 Church, Vol. 6, p. 807; Robert Friedman, "FBI Manipulates the Media," *RIGHTS* (May–June 1977).

36 Church, Vol. 6, pp. 762, 812–813, 814–815, 817; " '70 Effort to Discredit Jane

Fonda Described in Memo," NYT, Dec. 16, 1975.

[37] Church, Vol. 6, p. 792; Chip Berlet, "Media Op," *Public Eye* (April 1978); Mark Ryter, "COINTELPRO: Corrupting American Institutions," *First Principles* (May 1978); "FBI Media 'Friends': What Are They Now?", *The Real Paper*, April 16, 1967;

"WBZ and FBI: A Curious History," Boston *Phoenix*, April 12, 1977.

[38] Church, Vol. 6, pp. 785–787.

[39] *Pike Hearings*, Part 3, pp. 1171–1200; "FBI Checking of Radicals Went on Beyond Deadline," NYT, Oct. 6, 1975; "Enough Is Enough," NYT, Oct. 10, 1975.

[40] Church, Book III, p. 63, n. 225.

7. Intelligence As a Mode of Governance

[1] House Committee on the Judiciary, *Impeachment Hearings*, Statement of Information, Appendix I, 93rd Congress, 2nd Session, 1974.

[2] The subject of electronic surveillance on national security grounds is surveyed in detail by the author in "Electronic Surveillance: The National Security Game," *Civil Liberties Review* (Summer 1975), and by Victor Navasky and Nathan Lewin, "Electronic Surveillance," in Watters and Gillers, eds., pp. 297–337. In addition to the sources specifically cited, the discussion in the text is based on court records and the following legislative hearings: *Warrantless Wiretapping*, Hearings before the Subcommittee on Administrative Practice and Procedure, Constitutional Rights Subcommittee of the Senate Judiciary Committee and the Subcommittee on Surveillance of the Senate Foreign Relations Committee, 93rd Congress, 2nd Session *(Joint Hearings)* (1974); Senate Hearings before Select Committee on Presidential Campaign Activities of 1972, 93rd Congress, 1st Session *(Watergate Hearings)*, and Final Report of Select Committee (1974), pp. 109–111; *Surveillance Technology—1976*, Staff Report of the Subcommittee on Constitutional Rights of the Senate Committee on the Judiciary, 94th Congress, 2nd Session (1976), pp. 403–429; *Surveillance*, Parts 1 and 2, Hearings before the Subcommittee on Courts, Civil Liberties, and the Administration of Justice of the House Committee on the Judiciary, 94th Congress, 1st Session (1975). The following volumes of the Nixon impeachment proceedings contain valuable documentation: Book VII, Part

1; Minority Memorandum on Facts and Law, pp. 55–120; Statement of Information Submitted on Behalf of President Nixon, Book IV, and Transcripts of Eight Recorded Presidential Conversations. A useful Church Committee staff study, "Warrantless FBI Electronic Surveillance," is presented in Book III, pp. 271–353.

[3] The contemporaneous expansion of the 1940 Roosevelt directive is well illustrated by the wiretapping of labor leader Harry Bridges. See Charles Sears, *In the Matter of Harry Renton Bridges, Memorandum of Decision* (1941), pp. 183–184; Charles P. Larrowe, *Harry Bridges* (Lawrence Hill, 1977), pp. 127, 153, 196, 234–237; Biddle, *In Brief Authority*, pp. 166–167; and St. Clair McKelway, "Some Fun with the F.B.I.," *New Yorker*, Oct. 11, 1941. Clark's alteration of the language of the 1940 Roosevelt directive is documented in *Joint Hearings*, p. 70.

[4] In testimony before the Long Committee in 1965, Attorney General Nicholas de B. Katzenbach put it this way: "As I have said repeatedly, once you put a wiretap on or use an illegal device of any kind, the possibilities of prosecution are gone. It is just like a grant of immunity . . . and I have dismissed cases or failed to bring cases within that area [national security] because some of the information did come from wiretaps. But there we feel that the intelligence and preventive aspects outweigh the desirability of prosecution in rare and exceptional instances"—*Invasions of Privacy*, Hearings before the Subcommittee on Administrative Practice and Procedure of the Senate

Committee on the Judiciary, Part 3, p. 1163.

5 The real, more prosaic concern of the Department of Justice is reflected in its petition filed with the Subversive Activities Control Board seeking postponement of its proceeding against an alleged Communist front, the W. E. B. DuBois Clubs of America, until the resolution of its rehearing motion in the Supreme Court. When the Court refused to reconsider its disclosure decision, the Attorney General dropped the SACB case because it had been a target of a national security wiretap. Since the most likely candidates for such front proceedings were wiretap targets, the enforceability of the registration statute was crippled. "Bugs Making SACB Nervous," Washington *Post,* March 25, 1968; "Bugging of Du Bois Clubs Hinted in Justice Department Inquiry," NYT, March 20, 1968. On Mitchell's pressure campaign, see "Ruling Held Bar to Trial of Spies," NYT, May 3, 1968; "Wide Impact Seen in Wiretap Ruling," NYT, March 12, 1969; "Mitchell Hopes High Court Will Reverse Eavesdropping Ruling," NYT, March 19, 1969; "Bugging 'Subversives,' " *New Republic,* July 5, 1966; "Thanks for Small Favors," NYT, March 25, 1969; and "Mitchell Denies Court Tampering," N.Y. *Post,* May 16, 1973.

6 *United States* v. *Smith,* 321 F. Supp. 424.

7 *United States* v. *Donghi,* No. 70 CR-81 (N.D.N.Y.).

8 *United States* v. *United States District Court,* 407 U.S. 297. In a key passage the Court stated: "National Security cases . . . often reflect a convergence of First and Fourth Amendment values not present in cases of 'ordinary' crime. Though the investigative duty of the executive may be stronger in such cases, so also is there greater jeopardy to constitutionally protected speech. . . ."

9 Leaks united three Nixon phobias: the press, betrayal by disloyal insiders, and the never-ending machinations of enemies seeking to undermine his achievements as a world leader. Of the many accounts of his obsession by Nixon's aides, the most graphic, by Charles Colson, appears in

Impeachment Hearings, Book VII, p. 626.

10 See "What Hath Xerox Wrought," *Time,* March 1, 1976.

11 The indictment of Ellsberg is discussed in Chapter 10. His trial is the subject of a book by Peter Schrag. The Plumbers' pursuit of Ellsberg is documented in *Impeachment Hearings,* Book VII, pp. 620–649, 654, 664–727, 898–1030, 1082–1112, 1126–1340, 1392–1414, 1450–1481, 1504–1513, 1830–1837, 1868–1897, 1930–1941, 1948–2090. See also Church, Vol. 6, pp. 486–490.

12 The administration's persecution of Anderson and his suspected source is described in the complaint and record in *Anderson* v. *Nixon et al.,* Civil Action No. 76–1794; *Impeachment Hearings,* Book VII, pp. 864–897; *Gray Confirmation Hearings,* pp. 436–539; Church, Book IV, pp. 133–137; and "Plots to Kill Me," Jack Anderson and Les Whitten column, Nov. 11, 1975.

13 The account that follows is based on the following sources: "Transmittal of Documents from the National Security Council to the Chairman of the Joint Chiefs of Staff," Hearings before the Senate Armed Services Committee, Parts 1–2 (Feb. 6 and 20–21, 1974); Church, Book III, pp. 326–327; *Impeachment Hearings,* Book VII, pp. 1771–1773; "The Pentagon—NSC Spy Mystery: Full Investigation Is Essential," CR, Feb. 5, 1974, pp. S1197–1211; NYT articles by Seymour M. Hersh on the following dates in 1974: Jan. 12, 13, 14, 15, 16, 19, Feb. 1, 2, 3, 6, 8, 10, 11, 12, 18, 20, 21, 24, 24, 26, March 3, 7, 9, and April 26; and related news stories on Jan. 15, Feb. 7, 10, and March 3, 1974, and "The Nixon Watch —Peepers and Creepers," *New Republic,* Jan 26, 1974; "The Yeoman and the Admirals," *New Republic,* March 9, 1974.

14 "The Yeoman and the Admiral," NYT, Feb. 11, 1974.

15 The relationships of the Johnson administration to the FBI, discussed in the text, are documented in Church, Book III, pp. 485–486, 519–520; Church, Vol. 6, pp. 162–164, 166–255, 478–480, 483–484, 495–512. The record of the Johnson administration is

particularly stressed in memos submitted to John Dean by William C. Sullivan in spring 1973 describing the ways in which prior administrations used the FBI for political purposes. While these memos were never made public, they were leaked to the media by Nixon staffers. See "Leaning on the FBI," *Newsweek,* June 25, 1973; "FBI— Past Dirty Tricks," *Time,* Aug. 27, 1973; "Nixon Staff Compiles JFK, LBJ Bugging Files," Dallas *Times Herald,* Jan. 27, 1974. Three accounts based on further investigation (Ronald Kessler, "FBI Tapped King at 1964 Convention," Washington *Post,* Jan. 26, 1975) and personal observation (Bill Moyers, "LBJ and the FBI," *Newsweek,* March 10, 1975; Hugh Sidey, "L.B.J., Hoover and Domestic Spying," *Time,* Feb. 10, 1975) shed additional light on the LBJ record.

[16] Church, Vol. 6, p. 180.

[17] The DeLoach Atlantic City operation is the subject of Church Committee testimony by DeLoach (Church, Vol. 6, pp. 173–189) and documentary exhibits (Church, Vol. 6, pp. 495–510, 623–638. For a detailed description of the political background of the Atlantic City surveillance, see Schlesinger, *Robert F. Kennedy and His Times,* pp. 663–664.

[18] Church, Book III, p. 335.

[19] Church, Vol. 6, pp. 172–173, 177.

[20] *Ibid.,* p. 512.

[21] *Ibid.,* pp. 195, 539.

[22] Congressional admirers paid their respects to the departing DeLoach with twelve columns of *Congressional Record* insertions of press tributes, many by his former clients—CR, June 10, 1970, p. 19899; July 20, p. 24974; July 21, pp. E24974–E24975, Vol. 116.

[23] The right wing was no problem. A corps of conservative journalists was eager to ventilate planted White House tips about Communist plans to take over the anti-war movement. See, for example, David Lawrence, "Role of Communists in the Anti-War Demonstrations," *N.Y. Herald Tribune,* Oct. 19, 1965 ("The American government has strong suspicions that the student demonstrations have been aided, if not instigated, by agents of the

Soviet Union and of Red China in this hemisphere").

[24] Church, Vol. 2, p. 181.

[25] "American Public Should Be Advised if Hanoi Is Behind Peace Demonstrations," CR, Nov. 22, 1967, pp. 33706–33707, Vol. 113; "Rep. Ford Says Johnson Cited Red Protest Role," NYT, March 23, 1967.

[26] "The Dangerous World of Walt Rostow," *Look,* Dec. 12, 1967, and see "Scholar Who's No. 2 at the White House," *Business Week,* March 25, 1967, and William J. Gill, *The Ordeal of Otto Otepka* (Arlington House, 1969), pp. 87–99.

[27] The CIA's studies and reports for the Johnson White House are described in Church, Book III, pp. 696–698, and were released in response to FOIPA requests.

[28] Church, Book III, p. 697.

[29] The Nixon administration's efforts to extend and intensify domestic intelligence coverage and operations centering on the Huston Plan are the subject of Church, Vol. 2 (testimony and documents), Church, Book III, pp. 923–986, and *Impeachment Hearings,* Book VII, pp. 384–607.

[30] Church, Vol. 2, p. 202; Church, Book III, p. 929.

[31] Church, Vol. 2, pp. 287–308, 309–311.

[32] Church, Book III, p. 932.

[33] "U.S. to Tighten Surveillance of Radicals," NYT, April 12, 1970.

[34] *Impeachment Hearings*, Book VII, p. 377.

[35] Church, Book III, p. 956.

[36] Church, Vol. 2, pp. 317–329.

[37] In October 1970 Sullivan in a speech at Williamsburg, Va., broke ranks by deprecating the role of the Communist Party as a factor in American anti-war protest. Enraged, Hoover denounced this line: "How do you expect me to get my appropriations if you keep down-grading the [Communist] Party?" Sullivan sought refuge in the Nixon camp but was ousted by Hoover the following year—Church, Book III, p. 962; "F.B.I. Aide Says Unrest in U.S. Not Caused by Communists," NYT, Oct. 13, 1970; CR, Dec. 17, 1970, pp. 42319–42320, Vol. 116, "Old Left—New Left—What Is Left," reprint of a

speech by Charles Brennan, FBI intelligence executive.

[38] Sources documenting the domestic activities of the CIA discussed in this section include file materials released under the FOIPA Report to the President by the Commission on CIA Activities Within the United States, June 1975 *(Rockefeller Commission Report);* Church, Book III, pp. 681–723; Church, Book II, pp. 96–103, 107–108; *Inquiry into the Alleged Involvement of the Central Intelligence Agency in the Watergate and Ellsberg Matters,* by Special Subcommittee on Intelligence of the House Committee on Armed Services, *Hearings* (1973–1974); *Report* (1973); Watergate Committee, *Final Report,* pp. 37–40, 1115–1116. A ground-breaking account of the Agency's domestic operations is Seymour M. Hersh, "Huge C.I.A. Operation Reported in U.S. Against Anti-war Forces, Other Dissidents in Nixon Years," NYT, Dec. 22, 1974. See also Colby, pp. 313–317, 390–394, and Statements presented Jan. 15, 1975, to Intelligence Subcommittee of Senate Appropriations Committee, reported in full, NYT, Jan. 16, 1975.

[39] HTLINGUAL is described in Church, Vol. 4; Church, Book III, pp. 559–636; Church, Book II, pp. 107–108; *Rockefeller Commission Report,* pp. 101–116, and in the records of two lawsuits—*Driver et al.* v. *Helms et al.* (D.C. R.I.) and *Birnbaum et al.* v. *U.S. (E.D. N.Y.)*—which ultimately resulted in rulings that the program was illegal.

[40] See "C.I.A. Men Opened 3 Senators' Mail and Note to Nixon," NYT, Sept. 25, 1975; "CIA Opened Mail of Humphrey, Nixon, Kennedy," Washington *Post,* Sept. 25, 1975; "Official: CIA Read Mail of Meany, 2 Labor Aides," *N.Y. Post,* Oct. 10, 1975; "Those Secret Letter Openings," *Time,* Oct. 6, 1975.

[41] NSA communications interception programs are the subject of Church Committee Hearings (Vol. 5, testimony and documents) and a staff study (Book III, pp. 733–785). See also David Kahn, "Big Ear or Big Brother," *N.Y. Times Magazine,* May 16, 1976; Morton H. Halperin, "The Most Secret Agents," *New Republic,* July 25, 1975; "Study on

Bugging by NSA Reported," NYT, Oct. 26, 1975; "House Panel Calls for Five Contempt Citations in Inquiry," NYT, Feb. 26, 1976; "No Place to Hide," *Newsweek,* Sept. 8, 1975. Also the testimony of David L. Watters before the Subcommittee on Intelligence and the Rights of Americans, Senate, Select Committee on Intelligence, *Foreign Intelligence Surveillance Act of 1978,* 1978, pp. 178–231.

[42] Church, Book III, p. 750.

[43] Quoted in "CIA Foreign and Domestic Activity," Hearings before Senate Foreign Relations Committee, Jan. 27, 1975. The text of Helms's statement before the Senate Armed Forces Subcommittee on Intelligence defending the CIA against charges of improper domestic activities appears in NYT, Jan. 17, 1975. Helms was subsequently indicted on two misdemeanor counts for a watered-down version of lying— not about the CIA's domestic activities but solely about its activities in Chile. Helms termed his subsequent conviction and punishment, a suspended two-year sentence and a $2000 fine, a "badge of honor"—See Morton H. Halperin, "Did Richard Helms Commit Perjury?", *New Republic,* March 6, 1976, and Richard Harris, "Reflections," *New Yorker,* April 10, 1978, and Powers, p. 305.

[44] See Church, Vol. 2, pp. 52–96; "Illegal Domestic Spying Is Discovered by Helms," NYT, Dec. 25, 1974; "C.I.A. Man Fears Fading of Values," NYT, Dec. 26, 1974; "The Making of a Master Spy," *Time,* Feb. 24, 1975; Seymour M. Hersh, "The Angleton Story," *N.Y. Times Magazine,* June 25, 1978; "Angleton: The Quiet American," *Newsweek,* Jan. 6, 1975; "The Spy Who Came into the Heat," *Time,* Jan. 6, 1975; "The Spy Who Stays Out in the Cold," Boston *Phoenix,* July 29, 1977; Powers, pp. 282–285. Angleton was associated with Sullivan in the drafting of the Huston Plan and shared with him the view that intelligence is an élitist calling, a secular religion whose rituals were not to be profaned by crude requirements of legality or accountability.

[45] From a summary by NYT investigative

reporter Nicholas M. Horrock of the leaked report, NYT, Oct. 7, 1977; see also "U.S. Seeking to Learn How Times Got Data," NYT, March 10, 1978, an account of the Justice Department investigation of the report's release. An earlier investigation by Justice Department prosecutors in the Kearney case had likewise failed to produce support for the Bureau's contention that the Weather Underground fugitives were linked to hostile foreign governments.

46 The text of the report was reprinted in NYT, Sept. 27, 1964.

47 *Rockefeller Commission Report,* p. 118. The Justice Department's information-gathering activities are described in greater detail in Church, Book III, pp. 475–505, and in *Ervin Hearings* (1971), Part I, pp. 867–876 (testimony of Robert Mardian), and HISC, Hearings on "Domestic Intelligence Operations for Internal Security Purposes" (1974), Part I, pp. 3545–3560. All of these accounts of the origin and growth of the Department's intelligence activities tend, following the lead of the Rockefeller Commission, to scapegoat Attorney General Ramsey Clark as the architect of the repressive surveillance

plans of the Nixon era. This thesis is inaccurate: the IDIU under Clark played a limited intelligence role and was not, as the Rockefeller Commission claimed, "secret." These slanted views were picked up by conservative journalists (such as William Safire and Victor Lasky) to document the Nixon administration's *tu quoque* defense to virtually all the charges confronting it —that it had conducted itself no differently than its predecessors. See the author's "Lies in a Bad Cause," *Nation,* Aug. 14, 1976.

48 On the police abuses, including violence spawned by countersubversive agitational and conspiratorial theories, see Jerome H. Skolnick, *The Politics of Protest: A Report to the National Commission on the Causes and Prevention of Violence* (1969), pp. 262–264.

49 "Dissidence Unit Has Dossier [sic] on 14,000," NYT, April 2, 1971.

50 Church, Book III, pp. 502–503, 974–977.

51 Dean memorandum, quoted in Watergate Committee *Final Report,* pp. 5–6.

52 Church, Vol. 2, p. 255. This volume reprints (at pp. 255–271) a number of other documents dealing with the IEC.

8. Military Surveillance of Civilian Politics

1 10 USC 331–334.

2 Defense Department General Counsel Fred Buzhardt admitted that "There is no act that we know of that deals with the subject one way or another, in specific terms"—*Ervin Hearings* (1971), p. 416. Though the Ervin Committee explored a variety of intelligence-related subjects, it focused most intensively on military intelligence. References to the committee's final report will be designated *Report* with an accompanying page reference. *Documentary Analysis* refers to the committee's Documentary Analysis. *Ervin Hearings* (1974) will refer to the Ervin Committee's hearings in April 1974 on "Military Surveillance." A useful staff study of military surveillance of civilians appears in Church, Book III, pp. 785–834.

3 *Ervin Hearings* (1971), pp. 1172–1179.

4 The role of the military intelligence police in World War I is described in Zechariah Chafee's classic analysis, "A Contemporary State Trial," Chap. III of *Freedom of Speech,* pp. 120–160, dealing with Supreme Court Espionage Act case *United States* v. *Abrams.*

5 For the wartime role of the APL, see Jensen *passim.*

6 Hapgood, ed., pp. 107–109; Jaffe, pp. 119–120.

7 "Military Surveillance of Civilians," a statement submitted for the record in *Ervin Hearings* (1974), pp. 169–173.

8 "Ex-agent Says He Bugged Room of Mrs. Roosevelt," NYT, Nov. 1, 1965, an account of an NBC television program "The Big Ear" in which Adams participated. Adams, who became a private investigator in the capital area, also suggested that Army intelligence

might have bugged labor leader Harry Bridges for the FBI (see Chapter 7).

9 For accounts of domestic military intelligence operations against civilians in the late forties and fifties, see *Ervin Hearings* (1971), pp. 1489, 1499, 1502, 1503, 1508, 1511.

10 Army-McCarthy Hearings (1954), Part 20, pp. 749, 761; Part 19, pp. 722, 724, 731, 743. The letter, purportedly signed by J. Edgar Hoover, was widely believed to be a forgery, the work of a McCarthy ally in G-2, fabricated in such a way as to permit the use of material thought to be helpful to the senator but without exposing him to charges of ventilating classified information.

11 The key sources for the discussion in the text of the Army's cold war role are Senator J. William Fulbright's "Memorandum Submitted to Department of Defense on Propaganda Activities of Military Personnel," with attachments, reprinted in CR, Aug. 2, 1961, pp. S13436–13443; Hearings of Special Preparedness Subcommittee of the Senate Committee on the Armed Forces, Parts 1–6 (especially 4 and 5), and Donald Janson and Bernard Eisman, *The Far Right* (McGraw-Hill, 1963), pp. 74–198. See also remarks of Senator Strom Thurmond, "Censoring by the Department of Defense," CR, Sept. 18, 1961, pp. S18770–18781; "The Walker Case Issue: Thurmond's View," *N.Y. Times Magazine,* Jan. 14, 1962; "Military in Politics," *Progressive,* September 1961; "Military Indoctrination of Civilians," *New Republic,* June 26, 1961; "Puzzle of the 'Military Mind,' " *N.Y. Times Magazine,* Nov. 18, 1962; "Juggernaut: The Warfare State," *Nation,* Oct. 28, 1961; and "Trudeau Was Here," *N.Y. Post,* Jan. 1, 1962. The Preparedness Subcommittee's final report quarreled only with the Army's failure to insure "quality control" to screen out "controversial" views or sponsorship, but insisted on the propriety of its role in educating the public to "the threat which the . . . philosophy of communism presents to our way of life"—Report of Special Preparedness Subcommittee, pp. 28–35.

12 Radford on retirement joined the right-wing American Security Council (see Chapter 12), whose membership included such luminaries as General Albert C. Wedemeyer, Lieutenant General Edward M. Almond, Admiral Felix B. Stump, Admiral Ben Moreell, and Rear Admiral Chester Ward—all retired. Further to the right one finds an array of retired officers including Major General Charles A. Willoughby, General Douglas MacArthur's intelligence chief in World War II, Major George Racey Jordan, General Bonner Fellers, Admiral John Crommelin, Generals Stratemeyer, Jr., and Wedemeyer—Mark Sherwin, *The Extremists* (St. Martins, 1963), pp. 220, 153; Janson and Eisman, *op. cit.,* pp. 129–136; Benjamin Epstein and Arnold Forster, *The Radical Right* (Vintage, 1967), p. 211; and Epstein and Forster, *Danger on the Right* (Random House, 1967), pp. 178, 192, 242.

13 *Ervin Hearings* (1971), pp. 1722–1726.

14 The branch is now a "Detachment."

15 "Roger" recalls that much of his time was spent "reading books, smoking, joking, and drinking coffee, but whenever a briefing was scheduled, the commanding officer would bring the generals in or admirals or whoever they were. They'd say, 'This is our operations center and there are eighty phones around the room.' They were automatically snowed, you know. And just before the briefing would start, this major [the commanding officer] would walk around to all of us and say, 'Now, when this general comes in, pick up those papers and look like you're doing something, but make sure that you know what you're picking up so that if you are asked what you're doing, you know what you are doing' "—Interview with the author, June, 1971.

16 *Report,* p. 29.

17 *Ibid.,* p. 30.

18 Sample short and long form reports, as well as daily and weekly summaries, appear in the Ervin Committee's *Documentary Analysis,* pp. 24–30.

19 *Report,* p. 48.

20 A partial listing of these organizations "of intelligence interest" and their corresponding dossier numbers appears

in the USAINTC Information Collection Plan (ICP)—*Report,* pp. 129–130.

21 According to an old hand at Fort Holabird, the repository "is about a quarter of a warehouse and the shelves go up about twelve or fifteen feet, and they're about three feet apart and there are—I really don't know how many shelves there are in there, because it's so massive. An office just outside the double door entrance to the IRR housed the Records Reprocessing Branch (RRB). Two or three ladies sit at this big keyboard and all they have to do now, rather than go through and hand-pick a dossier off the shelf for an authorized requester, is to push a button and this big fork-type thing goes down the aisle, lifts up whatever number of dossier has been punched on the button. It goes directly to that slot, picks that dossier off the shelf, and puts it in a little plastic thing, and it comes back to you already sterile. That's the Army's pride and joy because this is going to speed up the ability to retrieve this information quickly. If new stuff comes in, they just request the dossier, the dossier comes up, they file it in the dossier and the dossier goes right back." This same intelligence officer continues, "I never really understood the workings of the computer, but they were putting all the names of people in the IRR files on massive tapes. They had one big room set aside right outside of IRR, specially built to accommodate the computer. The room had to be air-conditioned, electricity had to be constant, and the computer never stopped, a great source of pride to the intelligence command. When they took someone through there to brief them, they told them, 'This is our computer, we are going to have all of our dossiers computerized' "—Interview with the author, January 7, 1973.

22 *Documentary Analysis,* pp. 39–40.

23 In Captain Christopher Pyle's January 1970 *Washington Review* article on CONUS intelligence, he described a computer card from the file dealing with Arlo Tatum, executive secretary of the Central Committee for Conscientious Objectors, with the sole

entry that Tatum had made a speech at a university on the legal rights of Conscientious Objectors. The fact that this card subsequently disappeared along with a number of other suspicious circumstances led the Ervin Committee to surmise that the biographic file had been heavily edited to eliminate the more embarrassing entries.

24 *Documentary Analysis,* p. 47.

25 *Ibid.,* pp. 51, 69.

26 In addition, the files stored details about subjects' private lives—beliefs, finances, and sexual activities (especially if illicit or unconventional)—*Ervin Hearings* (1971), pp. 265, 266, 296.

27 *Report,* p. 89.

28 *Documentary Analysis,* p. 91.

29 *Ibid.,* p. 50.

30 *Ibid.,* p. 57.

31 For discussions of such needs, see generally Hearings before Special Subcommittee to Inquire into the Capability of the National Guard to Cope with Civil Disturbances, Committee on the Armed Services (1967).

32 See Hearings of House Internal Security Committee (1968), *Subversive Influence in Riots, Looting and Burning,* p. 798, testimony of Adrian H. Jones, a retired lieutenant colonel in the military police corps, military intelligence expert, and industrial security consultant.

33 See, for example, Eleanor Sheldon, *Indicators of Social Change* (Russell Sage Foundation, 1968); Raymond Bauer, ed., *Social Indicators* (M.I.T. Press, 1966); U.S. Department of Health, Education and Welfare, *Toward a Social Report* (Government Printing Office, 1968). In the sixties the Department of Defense turned to social and behavioral scientists for research aid; in 1965 alone, the Department of Defense spent $27.5 million on such research, primarily by outside consultants and "think tanks"— Hearings of the House Committee on Foreign Affairs, "Winning the Cold War: The U.S. Ideological Offensive," Report No. 4, "Behavioral Sciences and the National Security" (1966), p. 97. The use of social science to develop forecasts was dramatized by Project

Camelot. Working through a contractor at American University, the Special Operations Research Office (SORO), the Army launched a study to "predict and influence politically significant aspects of social change in the developing nations of the world"—I. Horowitz, ed., *The Rise and Fall of Project Camelot* (M.I.T. Press, 1967), pp. 4–5. The project was canceled in 1965 in the wake of national and international critical furor.

³⁴ The entire thrust of the Army's post-1967 collection efforts was influenced by the thesis that local unrest was the product of a conspiracy, national in scope. This assumption led to requests for broader-based and speedier reporting. The Fort Holabird researchers were in turn pressured to weave dispersed and seemingly unrelated data into a single conspiratorial pattern. (See, for example, *Ervin Hearings* [1971], p. 1463). While such a procedure may have been ideologically comforting, it submerged the disparities, the peculiarly local components, that social science theory stresses as the key to useful predictions—Bertram M. Gross and Michael Springer, "A New Orientation in American Government," CR, June 20, 1967, pp. S8494, 8495.

³⁵ NBC, "First Tuesday," Dec. 1, 1970. A transcript of the telecast is reproduced in CR, Dec. 10, 1970, pp. S19937–19942.

³⁶ NYT, Jan. 18, 1971.

³⁷ The most detailed account of the military spying at the 1968 conventions is given by investigative reporter Jared Stout, "Military Agents Used at 1968 Conventions," Washington *Star,* Dec. 2, 1970, reprinted in CR, Dec. 2, 1970, pp. S19198–20000. See also Stout, "Big Brother Pentagon—Keeping Tabs on Civilians," *Nation,* Dec. 28, 1970.

³⁸ A spokesman for the Secret Service, which was authorized by Congress to draw aid from the Army in protecting presidential candidates after the assassination of Robert Kennedy, denied having asked for the ASA. However, a former Secret Serviceman who covered the convention said he had been told the ASA was present "to help the Secret Service protect against the use of electronic surveillance against candidates." When ASA's role was uncovered in December 1970, both Ramsey Clark and Clark Clifford (at the time of the conventions Attorney General and Secretary of Defense, respectively) denied knowledge of the ASA role in Chicago. However, two years later, *New York Times* investigative reporter Seymour Hersh reported that he had obtained government documents implicating Clark in the decision to allow the ASA to eavesdrop not only in Chicago but in Miami at the Republican Convention. Hersh also reported he had seen a memo showing that the ASA was authorized by Army Chief of Staff William Westmoreland to institute eavesdropping of the Republican Convention and the Huey Newton trial. The agency had apparently been assigned by Westmoreland's predecessor as Chief of Staff, General Harold K. Johnson, to surveil the 1967 March on the Pentagon, the April 1968 riots in Washington, and the Poor People's March. A secret Army analysis of these activities concluded, according to Hersh, that approval was obtained for these activities from civilian authorities —Seymour Hersh, "Files Disclose More Army Snooping Under Johnson," NYT, Dec. 1, 1972, and Jared Stout, "Military's Spying on Civilians at '68 Conventions Revealed," *Pittsburgh Press,* Dec. 1, 1970.

³⁹ *Ervin Hearings* (1971), p. 440.

⁴⁰ *Ibid.,* pp. 1468–1469.

⁴¹ *Ibid.,* p. 1488.

⁴² *Ibid.,* p. 148.

⁴³ *Ibid.,* p. 337.

⁴⁴ *Ibid.,* pp. 285, 286, 289, 291, 1457, 1486, 1488, 1499.

⁴⁵ *Ibid.,* pp. 219, 291, 1460.

⁴⁶ *Ibid.,* p. 1475.

⁴⁷ *Ibid.,* pp. 1465–1466.

⁴⁸ *Ibid.,* p. 280.

⁴⁹ *Ibid.,* pp. 305–332.

⁵⁰ The ultimate justification for an intelligence operation that is otherwise indefensible is that the agency properly charged with responsibility for it is unprofessional. This was the asserted basis for the resistance by intelligence officers to the demands of their civilian

superiors that the Bureau should do this work.

[51] *Ervin Hearings* (1971), p. 315.

[52] *Ibid.*, pp. 330, 1511. Such over-eagerness inevitably invites hoaxes. In the fall of 1969 activist Tom Hayden announced in a Chicago speech that 400 escaped soldiers from the Fort Carson Stockade were locked in battle with 5th Division infantry troops in Pike National Forest and that only the closeness of tourists in the area had prevented the use of napalm bombs. When the commanding general heard of Hayden's statement, he promptly called the G-2 office for details about the escape—*Ibid.*, p. 330.

[53] *Ibid.*, p. 1490.

[54] *Westmoreland* (I refer in this way to the pages of the *Westmoreland Record*), p. 565.

[55] *Ibid.*, pp. 758, 847–848.

[56] *Ibid.*, pp. 620, 619, 535, 540, 533, 531, 537, 258.

[57] Waltz, "On Being Monitored," *Nation*, Jan. 25, 1971.

[58] *Westmoreland*, p. 536.

[59] *Ibid.*, p. 515.

[60] *Ibid.*, pp. 543–544.

[61] *Ibid.*, p. 555.

[62] *Ibid.*, p. 651.

[63] *Ervin Hearings* (1971), p. 1492.

[64] *Westmoreland*, p. 1057.

[65] *Ervin Hearings* (1971), p. 1493.

[66] *Ibid.*

[67] *Westmoreland*, p. 1062.

[68] The prevailing university policy of requiring a signed release from the individual under inquiry was circumvented "by going to the different campus police departments and requesting that they obtain the information for us in exchange for information that we had that might be of interest to them"—*Ervin Hearings* (1971), p. 495. An agent wrote (*ibid.*, p. 1498): "As a general rule we were in contact with security officials at local colleges from the time of my arrival approximately in 1969; we were instructed by our superiors to be knowledgeable concerning dissenting groups but . . . [this] problem . . . became . . . a concern for groups merely protesting government policy . . . only expressing their beliefs. . . . I should also mention that I knew of

other agents outside Chicago who infiltrated peace groups at different universities to obtain information of the plans of anti-war leaders and their followers."

[69] "Army Spied on Nile Hi," *Skokie Life*, March 18, 1971; *Ervin Hearings* (1971), pp. 1706–1707.

[70] The agents who testified or wrote statements for use by the Ervin Committee had taken debriefing oaths but insisted that none of the material they disclosed was properly classified in the first place.

[71] *Ervin Hearings* (1971), p. 978.

[72] The large-scale defections of intelligence agents are all the more remarkable in view of the traditional special solidarity of intelligence personnel. Like other intelligence agents and officers, former Army intelligence agents have formed their own association, the National Counter-Intelligence Association (NCIA). The NCIA announced in 1970 an investigation to determine whether a lawsuit should be lodged against investigative journalists for "deliberately and falsely cast[ing] [Army intelligence] in the roles of plotters against the people of the United States. . . ."—"Set Probe of Army Snooping," *N.Y. Post*, July 9, 1970.

[73] See *Ervin Hearings* (1971), pp. 1467, 1475, 1476, 1477, 1479, 1491.

[74] "The [recruiting] pamphlet offered fun, travel, adventure, training in a college type atmosphere and possible duty as a civilian investigator. With visions of James Bond flashing through my mind I eagerly accepted the offer"—From the first of a five-part series in the University of Wisconsin *Daily Cardinal*, May 14–20, 1970, summarizing the experiences of an ex-Army intelligence agent.

[75] For a diverting account of pursuit of an actual subject by a team of agents, see Allen Woode, "I Surveilled Civilians for the U.S. Army," *Village Voice*, April 22, 1971. The chase led the agents to a birthday party to which the subject had escorted his daughter. Commenting on their report that nothing suspicious took place, their irritated case officer asked, "So how do you know it was a birthday party and not a meeting of the

Communist infrastructure?" But it would be erroneous to suppose that the instruction was not serious or professional. It covered all phases of combat intelligence and, in the domestic field, included personnel security investigations and a wide spectrum of other forms of counterintelligence security. It was designed to introduce the trainee to every aspect of intelligence work, including such subjects as lock security, photography, audio surveillance, interrogation techniques, and personnel security interviews. Ideological indoctrination included courses in "Totalitarianism vs. Democracy," "Communist Ideology," and "Nightmare in Red: An Introduction to the Soviet State"—See *Daily Cardinal* series cited in note 74.

[76] See "Ex-Army Official Says Unit Spied on Campus in City," NYT, Dec. 23, 1970.

[77] The spectacle of professional soldiers trying to make sense of a world from which they could hardly have been further removed evoked the same mixture of amusement and amazement in CIAB analyst Ralph Stein in the course of "desktop briefing" of officers —*Ervin Hearings* (1971), pp.250–251, 269.

[78] Here is how "Roger" recalls his instructions at OPS IV: "I was told to tell MIG groups to just hide it, get it out of the way, this will all blow over, and I think that's almost a direct quote from my superior at the intelligence command." Field personnel later were formally told to destroy embarrassing documents, but were privately advised to "put them somewhere where they couldn't be found and wait for this type of thing to blow over."

[79] Assistant Defense Secretary Froehlke himself was deceived on his field inspection tours. For example, the video viewer used by 113th MIG, Region 1, usually prominently displayed in the office, was locked up in a vault when Froehlke and his inspection team came through and, on their departure, brought out on display again—*Ervin Hearings* (1971), p. 490.

[80] The view of the brass on the responsibility for the Army's spy program is put forth in a *New York Times* article by Major General Thomas A. Lane, "A Right To Intelligence," Lane said that "the tasks were undertaken reluctantly, only on the direct orders of the President and his civilian Cabinet officers." But as in the case of similar justifications, he did not explain why the civil disturbance mission required the objectionable intelligence program. He added that claims of military invasions of the civilian sphere seemed contrived "in an era when President Johnson could boast that 'not a chicken shed in North Vietnam was bombed' without his permission." The kernel of his argument appears to have been that, since all other phases of the war were under civilian control, the intelligence effort must also have been a civilian initiative. Lane also hinted that former Attorney General Ramsey Clark could support his charges. For reasons that have never been adequately explained, Justice Department officials in the Johnson and Nixon administrations who were mentioned in connection with the military spying issue were never invited to testify before the Ervin Committee. See "Who's The Snoop-in-Chief? Nobody Is Saying," NYT, March 14, 1971, and "Spying on Long-Hairs and Other Dangerous Types," NYT, March 4, 1972.

[81] "Johnson and Clark Linked to Surveillance Planning; Ex-Attorney General Disputes Files on His Role in White House Talk and Changes of Memorandums," NYT, April 17, 1971; "Files Disclose More Army Snooping Under Johnson," NYT, Sept. 1, 1972. These and related charges were leaked by Nixon's civilian officials and the Pentagon in a planned campaign with a dual objective; to transfer blame for the Army's excesses to civilians and at the same time to relieve the Nixon Administration of responsibility. See especially the testimony of Nixon's Defense Secretary Melvin R. Laird, Hearings on the Department of Defense Appropriations for 1972 (March 4, 1971), p. 215.

[82] "Army Spied on 18,000 Civilians in 2-Year Operation," NYT, Jan. 18, 1971.

[83] Exclusive of tactical intelligence in

Vietnam combat operations and of the intelligence activities of the CIA and State Department, the armed services in fiscal year 1970 spent $2.9 billion on intelligence collection and related functions, foreign and domestic. In testimony in March 1970, Assistant Defense Secretary Froehlke indicated that these figures for fiscal year 1971 would be reduced by about $100 million, to $2.8 billion—"Intelligence Costs for Military in '70 Put At $2.9 Billion," NYT, May 20, 1970. The resulting cutback in jobs led to a protest by Army intelligence agents that they were being forced out of undercover work in direct violation of contracts they signed when they enlisted. The men complained at a mass meeting that they had volunteered to serve for four years as opposed to the normal enlistee's three-year tour in combat. The Army replied that the fine

print showed they were guaranteed only an "initial assignment" with the ASA. See UPI story, June 19, 1971, "Army Security Men Protest Cutback."

[84] The electronic devices—sensors, laser beams, computers, relay and read-out capabilities—which came into use in the Vietnam War form an awesome arsenal readily adapted to peacetime surveillance uses. Among the newly developed sensor devices already in use are more than 250 night observation and other types of sensors called, generically, Surveillance, Target Acquisition, and Night Observation (STANO). The STANO items include a searchlight undetectable by the enemy, and chemical and biological "people-sniffing" equipment. Other systems transmit information through "seismic intrusion detecters" signaling the movements of enemy forces.

9. Internal Revenue Service

[1] CR, Oct. 9, 1975, p. E5367.

[2] For a number of years, IRS-instigated non-national security mail covers have exceeded those of all other federal agencies. See submission of Chief Postal Inspector William J. Cotter to House Judiciary Subcommittee on Courts, Civil Liberties and the Administration of Justice, May 20, 1975. In the mid-sixties a Senate committee probe headed by Missouri Senator Edward V. Long laid bare a wide variety of questionable IRS intelligence practices ranging from mail covers to wire tapping. See Long Committee Hearings, *Invasion of Privacy,* Parts 3 and 4 *(Government Agencies),* Subcommittee on Administrative Practice and Procedure, Committee on the Judiciary, U.S. Senate, 1965–66. See also Press Release, "Bugged Conference Rooms," *Long Committee,* Aug. 9, 1965; Fred J. Cook, "Law-Enforcement Underground," *Nation,* Dec. 20, 1965, "I Dreamt I Was a Spy," *New Republic,* June 18, 1966. Highlights of the hearings are described in the following press accounts: "Electronic Spies Shown in Senate," NYT, Feb. 19, 1965; "Don't Talk into Your Martini—

The Olive Is Really a Mike," *N.Y. Herald Tribune,* Feb. 19, 1965; "Tax Chief Admits 6-Year Bugging," NYT, July 13, 1965; "2 Officials Concede U.S. Revenue Men Used Wiretapping," NYT, July 14, 1965; "Tax Agent Called 'Dr. Strangelove,'" NYT, July 21, 1965; "Tax Office Admits Snooping Tactics," NYT, Aug. 9, 1965; "Tax Agent Recalls Phone Booth Tap," NYT, Aug. 10, 1965; "Senator Asks Bankers: Stand Up to IRS Men," *N.Y. Herald Tribune,* Dec. 12, 1965; and "Tax Chief Says Wiretap Use Is Over," NYT, Dec. 15, 1965. A brief summary of testimony before the Long Committee describing some of the agency's abuses appears in Long, *The Intruders* (Praeger, 1966), pp. 113–115.

[3] Treasury Department, Press Service, No. S-613, Feb. 4, 1948.

[4] Mimeographed release by William L. Holland, Ex. Sec. IPR, Oct. 26, 1955.

[5] See *Ervin IRS* (1974), p. 329 (I refer in this way to the Ervin Committee's study, *Political Intelligence in the Internal Revenue Service—The Special Service Staff,* 93rd Congress, 2nd Session).

[6] Thomas Reeves, *Freedom and the Foundation* (Knopf, 1969), p. 236.

7 *Hearings on the Black Panther Party* (1970), House Internal Security Committee, Part 4, p. 5096.

8 *Communist Party* v. *Commissioner of Internal Revenue,* 373 F 2d 682 (App. D.C., 1967).

9 *Lenske* v. *United States,* 383 F 2d 20 (C.A.9, 1967).

10 *Lenske* v. *United States,* 383 F 2d 20 at 27 (C.A.9, 1967).

11 *Ervin IRS* (1974), pp. 21–24, 94–95, 119–120, 172–173.

12 Church, Vol. 3, p. 47.

13 The term was first used by the IRS in the Kennedy administration to designate "organizations seeking to educate the public in controversial fields," and which "direct their efforts toward influencing the beliefs or actions of others with reference to certain predetermined governmental, social or economic ends." See Joint Committee on Internal Revenue Taxation, *Investigation of the Special Service Staff of the Internal Revenue Service,* 94th Congress, 1st Session, 1975 (hereinafter cited as *Jt. Cm. SSS*), p. 101.

14 *Ibid.,* p. 104.

15 Donner, "The Colleges Play Ball," *Nation,* Aug. 11, 1969.

16 This discussion is based on Reese Cleghorn, "When Readers Become Suspect," *South Today* (August 1970); "Freedom in Peril Librarian Warns," NYT, July 1, 1970; "Agents Hunt Subversives by the Book," L.A. *Times,* July 9, 1970; "T-Men's Library Spying Hit," *N.Y. Post,* July 21, 1970; "Head of Treasury Bars Book Search," NYT, July 30, 1970; and "Spies in the Library," NYT, July 31, 1970.

17 *Hearings on Riots, Civil and Criminal Disorders,* Permanent Subcommittee on Investigations of the Committee on Government Operations, Part 19 (1969) (hereinafter cited as *McClellan Hearings*).

18 *Ervin IRS* (1974), pp. 117–118.

19 *Ibid.,* p. 118.

20 The names of organizations are deleted from the document referred to in the text, but the fact that SNCC was the targeted organization is confirmed in a letter from Mitchell Rogovin, then Assistant Attorney General in charge of the Tax Division.

21 *Ervin IRS* (1974), pp. 311–313.

22 *Jt. Cm. SSS,* p. 26.

23 *Jt. Cm. SSS,* pp. 16–17.

24 *Jt. Cm. SSS,* pp. 17–18.

25 However, a wealth of evidence demonstrates that the meeting did take place—See *Jt. Cm. SSS,* pp. 17–18.

26 *Jt. Cm. SSS,* pp. 19–20. The pressure had an oblique effect; Thrower later indicated that he acquiesced in the SSS project to shield himself against pressures on other tax fronts.

27 *Ervin IRS* (1974), pp. 120–127; *Jt. Cm. SSS,* pp. 21–23.

28 The IRS has denied that the White House played a role in the creation of SSS. But an IRS memorandum of July 29, 1969, refers to the fact that, aside from congressional committees, the "highest levels of Government are interested . . . in this extremely important and sensitive matter"—*Ervin IRS* (1974), pp. 326 and 323 (memorandum of July 1, 1969).

29 *Ibid.,* p. 329.

30 *Jt. Cm. SSS,* p. 6.

31 *Jt. Cm. SSS,* p. 6.

32 *Ervin IRS* (1974), p. 12.

33 *Jt. Cm. SSS,* p. 37.

34 *Ervin IRS* (1974), p. 124.

35 *Ibid.,* p. 9.

36 "IRS Team Collects Data on Extremists for Tax Use," NYT, Jan. 13, 1972.

37 *Ervin IRS* (1974), p. 155.

38 *Ibid.,* p. 172.

39 *Ibid.,* pp. 165–168.

40 *Ibid.,* p. 30.

41 *Ibid.,* pp. 2, 176. "Keeping a Little List at the IRS," *Time,* Aug. 13, 1972. Charges of continuing political surveillance have been brought against the IRS despite the Aug. 9 order—See "I.R.S. Accused of Recent Spying," NYT, April 13, 1975.

42 *Ervin IRS* (1974), p. 13; *Jt. Cm SSS,* p. 3.

43 Church, Vol. 3, p. 43.

44 *Ibid.,* p. 42.

45 *Ibid.,* p. 43.

46 *Ervin IRS* (1974), pp. 31–36.

47 *Jt. Cm. SSS,* p. 66.

48 *Jt. Cm. SSS,* pp. 57, 64–65; *Ervin IRS* (1974), pp. 38–39.

49 *Jt. Cm. SSS,* p. 52.

50 The initial disclosures of the SSS files were made by Tax Research Reform Group. The Nader organization filed a lawsuit

under the Freedom of Information Act
and, on Nov. 17, 1974, made public
forty-one IRS memoranda concerning
the SSS. Additional lists of SSS file
subjects were subsequently released in
1974 ("I.R.S. Dept. Watch on
'Subversives,' " NYT, Nov. 18, 1974)
and 1975.

51 *Jt. Cm. SSS,* pp. 73–87.

52 *Jt. Cm. SSS,* p. 95.

53 See *Jt. Cm. SSS,* pp. 57–71.

54 On the operations of the IGRS, see the
IRS publications, *Inspection Report on
Information Gathering Activities,
Jacksonville District,* June 23, 1975;
*Report of Task Force on Intelligence
Gathering and Retrieval Systems,* June
25, 1969; and "Inquiry Reveals I.R.S.
Master List," NYT, June 21, 1975.

55 *Report of Task Force on Intelligence
Gathering and Retrieval Systems,* June
25, 1969, p. 111.

56 *Ibid.,* pp. 6, 38.

57 *Inspection Report on Information Gathering
Activities,* June 23, 1975; *Internal
Revenue Manual,* March 4, 1974, Sec.
9393--3.

58 The memorandum "Intelligence Gathering
and Retreival [sic] System," dated Jan.
18, 1971, was made available in response
to the Freedom of Information Act
request by the Washington-based Public
Citizens Tax Reform Research Group.

59 The principal source for Operation
Leprechaun is the IRS *Inspection
Report on Information Gathering
Activities,* June 23, 1975. The press
accounts referred to in the text
appeared in Philadelphia *Evening
Bulletin,* Jan. 27, 1975, Feb. 4, 1975;
Miami *News,* Feb. 1, 1975; Miami
Herald, March 14, 15, 1975; NYT,
March 15, 1975. Tax Commissioner
Donald Alexander testified about the
project on March 13, 1975, in Hearings
before the Subcommittee on
Governmental Operations and
Individual Rights of the House
Committee on Government Operations.
Additional testimony by Commissioner
Alexander appears in Hearings before
the same subcommittee, as well as the
investigations subcommittee of the
House Ways and Means Committee
and a Consumer Affairs subcommittee
of the House Government Operations

Committee. It is summarized in "I.R.S.
Chief Heard in Spying Inquiry," NYT,
March 27, 1975; "Some in House See a
Cover-Up by I.R.S.," NYT June 25,
1975. See also "Federal Officials Fear
Dispute Over 'Strike Force,' " NYT,
March 26, 1975; "A Miamian Says
I.R.S. Recruited Her to Spy," NYT,
March 15, 1975; "Burglary Is Laid to 2
I.R.S. Agents," NYT, March 23, 1975;
"I.R.S. Study Questions Value of
Undercover Inquiry," NYT, June 25,
1975; "FBI Joins Inquiry on Miami
IRS," Washington *Post,* May 15, 1975;
and "Ex-Candidate Suing I.R.S. in '72
Break-In," NYT, May 14, 1975. A
number of the most important news
stories are collected in "Illegal Spying
by the IRS," CR, March 18, 1975, pp.
H1942–1944. The most useful summaries
of IRS afflictions appear in stories by
Louise Brown in *People and Taxes*—
the publication of the Tax Reform
Research Group—for April, June, and
July 1975.

60 "IRS Trained Its Agents in Drinking,"
NYT, April 14, 1975; "IRS Chief Says
He Halted Liquor Use in Training
Agents Because It Was
'Inappropriate,' " NYT, April 15, 1975;
"Former Agent Says IRS School was
'Amateurish,' " NYT, April 16, 1975.

61 Regulations concerning informer
recruitment, confidentiality, payment,
and security may be found in *Policy
Statement,* pp. 1–190, approved Aug. 9,
1962; Sec. 9370–9373, *Internal Revenue
Manual;* Handbook for Special Agents,
Intelligence Division, Sections 232 23
(1), *Internal Revenue Manual,* 9900;
Internal Revenue Manual Supplement,
June 23, 1975. The most comprehensive
critique of IRS informer abuses appears
in "Internal Audit Report of the
Review of the National Office
Intelligence Division Undercover
Special Agent Program and
Investigative Imprest Fund," May 1,
1975. A GAO report submitted to
Congress on September 1, 1977, on the
IRS's "Controls Over the Use of
Confidential Informants" concluded
that "recent improvements (were) not
adequate." "Informants were sometimes
used in ill-defined and overly broad
intelligence gathering efforts, procedures

for evaluating their information were inadequate and their use was not systematically reviewed by management."

[62] *United States* v. *Jim Garrison et al.,* Criminal Action No. 7—542 Testimony on Sept. 19, 1973, Transcript, p. 132.

[63] *Ibid.,* pp. 146–148.

[64] *Figaro,* Sept. 19, 1973.

[65] "Gervais Forced to Entrap DA," New Orleans *State-Item,* May 23, 1972; "Gervais Details Assertion of Justice Department Deal," New Orleans *State-Item,* May 25, 1972.

[66] "Gervais, Garrison Engage in Verbal Fireworks," New Orleans *Times-Picayune*, Sept. 21, 1973.

[67] "U.S. Drops Case of IRS Chief," *N.Y. Post,* Sept. 29, 1975.

[68] "Justice Department to Investigate the IRS," *People and Taxes* (July 1975); "IRS Investigating Its Use of Informers," NYT, May 15, 1975; "IRS Is Accused of Recent Spying," NYT, April 13, 1975; "At Sea with the IRS," *Newsweek,* Oct. 13, 1975; "IRS Chief Heard on Scofflaws," NYT, Oct. 7, 1975.

[69] *Jt. Cm. SSS,* pp. 20–21.

[70] "Informer Says He Was Part of Coast Plot to Kill Cesar Chavez," NYT, June 2, 1972.

[71] The discussion in the text about Martinez and his career as an ATF informer is based on a series of interviews and a corroborative investigation.

[72] *Watergate Hearings,* Part 3, p. 1338.

[73] *Watergate Hearings,* Part 10, pp. 4114–4118; Part 3, pp. 1338–1345.

[74] Mark J. Green, "Perils of Public Interest Law," *New Republic,* Sept. 20, 1975.

[75] A full account of the controversy may be found in Richard Corrigan, "Tax Report/Public Interest Law Groups Win Tax Battle with IRS over Exemptions, Deductions," *National Journal,* Nov. 21, 1970. See also "Tax Exemptions and 'The Public Good,' " *Non-Profit Report,* October 1970 (no. 10); "IRS to Review Tax Exemptions of Units Engaging in Litigation," NYT, Oct. 9, 1970; "IRS Denies Pressure on Exemptions," Washington *Post,* Oct. 25, 1970; "Rep. Ford Hits IRS Tax Stand," Washington *Post,* Oct. 29, 1970; "Blocking Access to Legal System,"

NYT, Nov. 5, 1970; "IRS Move Stays Ford Fund Grant," NYT, Nov. 9, 1970; "IRS Proposal on Pro-Public Firms Protested by Ex-Government Aides," Washington *Post,* Nov. 20, 1970. The IRS reversal is described in a news release, IR–1078, Nov. 12, 1970, accompanied by guidelines.

[76] *Center on Corporate Responsibility* v. *Schultz,* 368 F. Supp. 863.

[77] Watergate Committee, *Final Report,* pp. 1016–1030. Ehrlichman made no bones about the fact that he wanted a preelection audit for political purposes. *Impeachment Hearings,* Book VIII, pp. 219–220, 235, 337–339; Kalmbach testimony, Book III, pp. 615–617.

[78] In 1961, Tax Commissioner Mortimer Caplin ruled that the IRS must honor an oral request of Carmine Bellino, special consultant to President John F. Kennedy, to inspect tax files—CR (Daily Ed.), April 16, 1970, pp. 12221–12222. This precedent was cited in the Watergate Hearings in defense of the Nixon administration practices. Bellino, then chief Watergate Committee investigator, responded that he had been shown investigative files, not tax returns, and that although a White House consultant at the time, he acted on behalf of Attorney General Kennedy in connection with pending criminal investigation—"Bellino: I Didn't See Returns," *N.Y. Post,* Aug. 1, 1973.

[79] *Impeachment Hearings,* Book VIII, pp. 35–42. Thrower's investigation was conducted by Commissioner Vernon Acree—*Ibid.,* p. 41.

[80] Deposition of Roy Kinsey in Center on Corporate Responsibility lawsuit; "Dean Aide Details Colson IRS Bid," NYT, Aug. 3, 1973.

[81] *Impeachment Hearings,* Book VIII, p. 196.

[82] *Watergate Hearings,* Book 4, pp. 1350–1387, 1409–1411, 1689–1690, 1692–1696.

[83] *Impeachment Hearings,* Book VIII, pp. 72–78.

[84] *Ibid.,* pp. 238–239, 243, 275–276, 279.

[85] *Ibid.,* pp. 333, 334–336, 354, 356; Impeachment Committee Transcripts, pp. 1, 10–11, 15; Dean testimony before House Impeachment Committee,

Testimony of Witness, Book II, pp. 229, 301, 302.

86 *Impeachment Hearings,* Book VIII, p. 368; Impeachment Committee Transcripts, p. 5.

87 *Impeachment Hearings,* Book VIII, p. 199.

88 *Impeachment Hearings,* Book VIII, pp. 171–174; memorandum on Moyers released by Senator Lowell Weicker, April 7, 1974.

89 *Final Report,* Watergate Committee, p. 139.

90 "White House's IRS Tipster Named," *N.Y. Post,* June 8, 1975. This defense, also employed by Colson and Haldeman, appears to have been a prefabricated cover. It was also used to justify access to FBI files.

91 ABC News Close-up, Transcript of Telecast, March 21, 1975, "IRS: A Question of Power," pp. 33–35.

10. Kangaroo Grand Juries

1 See "U.S. to Tighten Surveillance of Radicals," NYT, April 9, 1970.

2 Donner, "Theory and Practice of American Political Intelligence," *New York Review of Books,* April 23, 1971.

3 The sources for the discussion in the text of the transformation of the federal grand jury into an intelligence resource include interviews, court records, and legislative hearings. The use of grand juries for repressive political purposes is an important theme in Hearings before the Subcommittee on Immigration, Citizenship and International Law of the House Judiciary Committee, captioned "Federal Grand Jury" (1976) and "Grand Jury Reform" (Parts 1 and 2, 1977), referred to hereinafter as *Eilberg 1976* and *Eilberg 1977,* respectively. A Senate legislative hearing on proposed grand jury reforms conducted in September 1976 before the Subcommittee on Constitutional Rights of the Senate Judiciary Committee also covers alleged political abuses at pp. 156–218.

Relevant testimony and articles appear in *Eilberg 1976* at pp. 368–376, 419–513, and in *Eilberg 1977,* Part 1, at pp. 17–20, 57–78, 191–192, 691–701, 872–894, 908–922; Part 2, at pp. 1533–1539, 1552–1571. See also the following background articles: Leonard B. Boudin, "The Federal Grand Jury," Vol. 61, *Georgetown Law Journal* (1972); John Conyers, "Grand Jury: The American Inquisition," *Ramparts* (August–September 1975); Paul Cowan, "The New Grand Jury," *N.Y. Times Magazine,* April 29, 1973; Frank Donner and Frank Cerruti, "The Grand Jury Network," *Nation,* Jan. 3, 1972; Frank Donner and Richard Lavine, "From the Watergate Perspective: Kangaroo Grand Juries," *Nation,* Nov. 19, 1973; Eilberg, "Federal Grand Jury: A Misunderstanding," *The Retainer,* Oct. 8, 1976; David Fine, "Federal Grand Jury Investigation of Poltical Dissent," Vol. 7, *Harvard Civil Rights and Civil Liberties Law Review* (1972); Marvin Frankel and Gary Naftalis, "The Grand Jury," *New Leader,* Nov. 10, 1975; Charles Goodell, "Where Did the Grand Jury Go?", *Harper's* (May 1973); Richard Harris, "Taking the Fifth," *New Yorker,* April 5, 12, 19, 1976; Samuel Popkin, "The Scholar Invokes His 'Privilege,'" *Trial;* (January–February 1973); Helene Schwartz, "Demythologizing the Historic Role of the Grand Jury," Vol. 10, *American Criminal Law Review* (1972), p. 701; Isidore Silver, "Not So Grand Jury?" *Commonweal,* Dec. 14, 1973; Fred Solwey, "The Grand Jury and Post-Watergate America," *Trial* (November–December 1974); Michael Tiger and Madeline Levy, "The Grand Jury as the New Inquisition," *Michigan State Bar Journal* (November 1971); Peter Weisman and Andrew Postal, "The First Amendment as a Restraint on the Grand Jury Process," Vol. 10, *American Criminal Law Review* (1972), p. 671; and Barry Winograd and Martin Fassler, "The Political Question," *Trial* (January–February 1973).

4 Quoted in Mary McGrory, "A Smooth Bully," *N.Y. Post,* Dec. 17, 1974; see also "Rival Banquet Protests Law Day Speech by Security Official," NYT, April 28, 1970.

5 A description of the reorganized ISD and

the Special Litigation Section appears in "The Red Squad," *Time,* May 31, 1971.

[6] *Rogers et al.* v. *United States,* 179 F. 2d 559, *aff'd* 340 U.S. 367 (1951) petition for rehearing denied, 341 U.S. 912 (1951); *Patricia Blau* v. *United States,* 180 F. 2d 103 *rev'd* 340 U.S. 159 (1950); *Irving Blau* v. *United States,* 179 F. 2d 559, *rev'd* 340 U.S. 332 (1951); *Bary* v. *United States,* 179 F. 2d 559.

[7] Clark, p. 49.

[8] Senator Kennedy's testimony before House Judiciary Subcommittee No. 1 on "The Fort Worth Five and Grand Jury Abuse" (1973), reprinted in *Eilberg 1977,* pp. 498–513.

[9] Moore's *Federal Practice* (1973), Section 6.02 (1) (b).

[10] Quoted in *Eilberg 1977,* p. 910.

[11] *Wood* v. *Georgia,* 370 U.S. 375; see also Frederick Kuh, "The Grand Jury Presentment," Vol. 55, *Columbia Law Review,* 1103, 1107–1109; "The Grand Jury as an Investigatory Body," Vol. 74, *Harvard Law Review* (1961), p. 590; Note, "The Rights of a Witness Before a Grand Jury," *Duke Law Journal* (1967) pp. 97, 100–101. ". . . [T]he grand jury's most important function became the task of standing 'steadfast between the crown and the people in the defense of liberty of the citizen.'. . . Considered in the light of its history in American law, the more important of the grand jury's roles would appear to be its protective function. In addition to the fact that, at the time the institution was enshrined in the Constitution, English law stressed the protective feature. The placement of the grand jury guarantee in our Bill of Rights as a restraint upon governmental prerogative— accompanied by the guarantees against self-incrimination, double jeopardy and deprivation of due process— convincingly indicates the dominant character of the protective role."

[12] William Campbell, "Eliminate the Grand Jury," *Journal of Criminal Law and Criminology,* (June 1973), pp. 174–182. Grand juries still occasionally rebel against overreaching prosecutors. See "Bingham—Jackson Grand Juror Says the Prosecutor's Tactics Divided Panel," NYT, Oct. 10, 1971. The

mechanics of the takeover of the grand jury have never been better described than in this account:

Though free to take part in the interrogation, the grand jurors must place enormous trust in the prosecutor's guidance. It is he, after all, who tells them what the charge is, who selected the facts for them to hear, who shapes the tone and feel of the entire case. It is the prosecutor alone who has the technical training to understand the legal principles upon which the prosecution rests, where individual liberty begins and ends, the evidential value of available facts and the extent to which notice may be taken of proposed evidence.

In short, the only person who has a clear idea of what is happening in the grand jury room is the public official whom these twenty-three novices are expected to check. So that even if a grand jury were disposed to assert its historic independence in the interest of an individual's liberty, it must, paradoxically, look to the very person whose misconduct they are supposed to guard against for guidance as to when he is acting oppressively.

Actually, the concern of protecting the individual from wrongful prosecution is one about which grand juries in general show little interest. . . .

Thus, when a case is brought into the grand jury room the prevailing feeling is that the prosecutor wouldn't bring it there if he didn't think he could get a conviction. . . . Antel, "The Modern Grand Jury," Vol. 51, *American Bar Association Journal* (1965), p. 154.

[13] Frankel and Naftalis, p. 92.

[14] *In re U.E.,* 111 F. Supp. 858 (S.D.N.Y.). Judge Weinfeld's decision is analyzed in *Eilberg 1977,* pp. 1559–1566.

[15] "Activities of United States Citizens Employed by the United Nations," Subcommittee to Investigate the Administration of the Internal Security Act and Other Internal Security Laws, Jan. 2, 1963.

[16] Goodwin's role and style are described in Lacey Fosburgh, "Who Is Guy Goodwin and Why Are They Saying Those Terrible Things About Him?,"

Juris Doctor (January 1973); Michael Drosnin, "Nixon's Radical Chaser Bags a Whopper," *New Times,* Oct. 18, 1974; Ronald Ostrow, "Have Jury, Will Travel," Washington *Post,* Feb. 11, 1973, and Cowan, *supra.*

[17] See "U.S. Prosecutor on Coast Resigns," NYT, Dec. 18, 1971.

[18] *Briggs et al.* v. *Goodwin,* 569 F. 2d 10 (C.A.D.C., 1977). The Supreme Court denied review in June 1978.

[19] *Eilberg 1977,* pp. 841–871.

[20] *Levinson* v. *Attorney General,* 321 F. Supp. 984 (E.D.Pa., 1970); see also *Eilberg 1977,* p. 1555.

[21] Grand jury proceedings are supposed to be secret but transcripts of questioning have been circulated in three forms: the witness's recollection of the interrogation, copies of the actual proceedings, and transcripts of contempt hearings in which the questions have been set forth. The Tucson interrogations were the subjects of two pamphlets, one the testimony and the other ("With Liberty and Justice for All") dealing with the rights of the witness. The proceedings are discussed in *Eilberg 1977,* pp. 1537 and 1555. Beginning in the late sixties, at least two dozen pamphlets, guides, handbooks, legal summaries, and transcripts were disseminated to prospective New Left witnesses, including a "People's Guide to the Federal Court System," "What You and Your Lawyer Should Do in Exhausting Legal Non-Cooperation," "Talking, Maybe Even Shouting: But We're Not Singing," "It Could Be You!", and "Are You Now or Have You Ever Been?"

[22] Quoted in *Eilberg 1977,* p. 7.

[23] *In re Grand Jury Subpoena of Martin R. Stolar,* Misc., No. 11–118 (S.D.N.Y.).

[24] The pursuit of Bacon by Guy Goodwin described in the text is based on examination of court records, interviews, legislative hearings, and stories in the underground press. For a useful compressed version of the bizarre twists and turns in the Bacon case, see the following NYT news stories: "Girl, 19, Seized as Witness in Bombing of U.S. Capitol," April 29, 1971; "Court Bars Release of Girl Held as Bombing Witness," April 30, 1971; "Girl Is Flown to Seattle for Bombing Inquiry," April 30, 1971; "Radical, Yes, but Violent? Reports Differ," April 30, 1971; "Grand Jury Hears Girl in Bomb Case," May 1, 1971; "Miss Bacon, Before a U.S. Jury, Denies Knowing of Capitol Blast," May 2, 1971; "Witness in Bombing of Capitol Refuses to Answer Questions," May 3, 1971; "Judge Bids Miss Bacon Reply to Questions on Bank Bombing," May 7, 1971; "Miss Bacon Refuses to Answer Questions about Day of Bombing," May 13, 1971; "Warrant Awaits Miss Bacon Here," May 16, 1971; "Bombing Witness Offered Immunity," May 19, 1971; "Miss Bacon Sent to Jail after Balking at Questions," May 20, 1971; "Phase of Capitol Bombing Inquiry Ends," May 22, 1971; "U.S. Court Orders Miss Bacon Freed," June 16, 1971; "Miss Bacon Freed; Posts $1,000 Bond," June 18, 1971; and "Miss Bacon to Face Bomb Charge Here," June 18, 1971.

[25] Quoted in *Eilberg 1977,* pp. 1534–1535.

[26] *Bacon* v. *United States,* 408 U.S. 915; 466 F. 2d 1197 (C.A. 9, 1972).

[27] Transcript of Record, pp. 69–75, *In the Matter of Sylvia Jane Brown,* 465 F. 2d 371 (C.A. 9, 1972); "Barnard Coed Jailed in Seattle for Balking at Jury's Queries," NYT, May 28, 1972.

[28] Statement of Charles Bradley, July 23, 1973, in *U.S.* v. *William Ayers et al.,* U.S. District Court, Eastern District of Michigan, Crim. No. 48104, in support of motion attacking indictment on the ground of abuse of the grand jury process. The discussion on p. 372 in the text of incidents and interrogations linked to the Detroit indictment is similarly based on uncontradicted affidavits submitted in support of the claim that the Detroit indictment was tainted by improprieties.

[29] *Eilberg 1977,* p. 1553, and see Fred J. Cook, "Justice in Gainesville: The Real Conspiracy Exposed," *Nation,* Oct. 1, 1973.

[30] See *Eilberg 1977,* p. 1538.

[31] "Subpoena Linked to Gun Case," NYT, March 14, 1973; see also Senator Edward M. Kennedy, "Statement to the House Judiciary Committee,"

March 13, 1973, Hearings on "Fort
Worth Five and Grand Jury Abuse."

[32] *Impeachment Hearings,* Book VII, pp.
592–609.

[33] See Chapter 7, note 11.

[34] *Impeachment Hearings,* Book VII, pp.
1392–1395.

[35] An illuminating analysis of the indictment
appeared in the *Christian Science
Monitor* for Jan. 15, 1972, "Ellsberg
Case Explained."

[36] *Impeachment Hearings,* Book VII, p. 1476.
The most revealing documentation of
Nixon's almost pathological obsession
with leaks in general and Ellsberg's
conduct in particular is recorded in
Ehrlichman's handwritten notes of
conferences with the President and
others reprinted in *ibid.,* Statement of
Information, Appendix III, pp. 89–249.

[37] "New Pentagon Papers Counts May be
Filed," L.A. *Times,* Aug. 3, 1971.

[38] Statement of Aug. 16, 1971, reprinted in
Los Angeles *Free Press,* Aug. 20, 1971.

[39] Transcript of Colloquy Between Anthony
Russo and David Nissen Outside
Grand Jury Room, Oct. 18, 1971;
Benedict, "Secrecy and the Grand Jury
System, the Indictment of Anthony
Russo," *New Republic,* May 29, 1972,
and *Eilberg 1977,* p. 1536.

[40] "Held 47 Days, Ellsberg Friend Agrees to
Testify and Is Freed," NYT, Oct. 2,
1971.

[41] "Grand Jury Calls Ellsberg's Son," *Boston
After Dark,* Oct. 19, 1971.

[42] The legal documents dealing with Senator
Gravel's attacks on the grand jury,
both for interrogating Rodberg and for
investigating his dissemination of the
Pentagon Papers, are printed in two
lengthy CR inserts, Nov. 22, 1971, pp.
E12541–12611, and April 12, 1972, pp.
E3673–3728; see also "Ellsberg Fishing

Trip Moves to Los Angeles," *Boston
After Dark,* Aug. 10, 1971.

[43] "Foreign Relations Group Yields Ellsberg
Seminar Paper to FBI," NYT, Nov. 4,
1971; "Goldberg Protests the Surrender
of Ellsberg Paper," NYT, Nov. 5, 1971.

[44] Diamond, "Fishing in Ellsberg's Wake,"
MORE (January 1972).

[45] "Investigation: Strictly Academic,"
Newsweek, Nov. 8, 1971; "Scholars
Seeking Right Not to Release Sources,"
NYT, Oct. 25, 1971.

[46] See *Eilberg 1977,* pp. 1568–1569, where
Popkin's courtroom struggles are
summarized. In addition to a series of
NYT news stories during November
1972, the Popkin issue is discussed in
"Secret Documents," *New Republic,*
April 15, 1972; Hentoff, "A Plea to
Academe," *Village Voice,* Dec. 7, 1972;
and in a personal account, Popkin,
supra.

[47] *United States* v. *Briggs,* 514 F. 2d 794
(C.A. 5, 1975). The unindicted
co-conspirator abuse is discussed in
Eilberg 1977, pp. 1562–1563.

[48] The most rewarding description of the
abuse of the grand jury proceedings in
the pursuit of Saxe and Powers is
Harris, *Freedom Spent,* Part Three, pp.
273–378, based on "Taking the Fifth,"
a widely reprinted series of *New Yorker*
articles.

[49] "FALN Grand Juries," *Quash* (newsletter
of the Grand Jury Project,
September–October 1977).

[50] Proposed remedial legislation was
introduced in the 94th Congress by
Congressmen Conyers, Eilberg,
Kastenmeier, and Rangel. A
comprehensive grand jury reform bill
(S. 3405) was introduced in the Senate
on Aug. 14, 1978, by Senator James
Abourezk—CR, pp. S13258–13263.

11. Intelligence as a Mode of Governance—The Role of Congress

[1] The modern countersubversive attainder is
best illustrated by a rider attached to
an appropriation bill by Congress,
invalidated in 1946 by the Supreme
Court, withholding the compensation of
three government employees
condemned as subversive by the Dies
Committee. *U.S.* v. *Lovett,* 328 U.S.
303 (1946); see also *U.S.* v. *Brown,* 381

U.S. 437 (1965). On attainders
generally, see Woodeson, *Law Lectures*
(1792), pp. 653 *ff.*; Miller, *Lectures on
Constitution of the United States* (1893),
p. 584, and David Kairys, "The Bill of
Attainder Clauses and Legislative and
Administrative Suppression of
'Subversives,' " *Columbia Law Review*
(December 1967), Vol. 67, p. 1470.

2 See Donner, "HUAC—From Pillory to Farce," *Nation,* Sept. 3, 1966.

3 *Group Research Report,* Oct. 31, 1973, Aug. 3, 1974; ASC *Washington Report,* September 1973.

4 CR, Jan. 9, 1973, p. 537, Vol. 119. Ichord's "right way" pseudo-libertarianism and professed devotion to "painstaking and thorough" inquiry are celebrated in his foreword to HISC's first *Annual Report* (1970), pp. 1–3. In September 1971 the ACLU jestingly invited him to become a member, noting his self-description as a "civil libertarian" in resisting the proposed repeal of the concentration camp statute. The not overly bright Ichord solemnly rejected the invitation and citing, among others, John Stuart Mill and the Roman historian Livy on the distinction between liberty and license, charged that the ACLU had fallen from true libertarianism into the abyss of "libertinism"—CR, Sept. 28, 1971, p. 33721, Vol. 117. A month later he attacked the Committee for Public Justice for presuming to criticize the FBI. Not, he explained to his colleagues, that the FBI was beyond criticism, but these critics were either subversive, biased, or tainted by "McCarthyism of the left"—CR, Oct. 28, 1971, p. 38091, Vol. 117. p. 10129.

5 Despite the denial by the federal Court of Appeals of a motion for summary reversal of Judge Gesell's injunction, the House nevertheless ordered the printing and dissemination of the report with only fifty-four dissenting votes— HISC *Ann. Rep.* (1970), pp. 182–191. HISC subsequently eliminated eight entries from the list: seven individuals listed only because of their membership in a group seeking the committee's abolition, and the scientist Linus Pauling. The background and history of the controversy are traceable in the following CR entries, Vol. 116: July 15, 1970, p. 24495; Oct. 13, 1970, p. 36606 (reprinting the entire list); Oct. 14, 1970, p. 37112; Oct. 14, 1970, p. 37260; Nov. 17, 1970, p. 37791; Nov. 30, 1970, 39863; Dec. 2, 1970, pp. 39512–39525; Dec. 3, 1970, p. 39859; Dec. 10, 1970, p. 39237; Vol. 117: April 6, 1971, p. 9931; May 27, 1971, p. 17292. One of the plaintiffs in

the suit seeking to enjoin the dissemination of the list, liberal journalist Nat Hentoff, wrote three articles on the issue in his *Village Voice* column for Oct. 22, Nov. 5, and Nov. 19, 1970. The HISC report and its dissemination also offended conservative columnist William F. Buckley, Jr., "A Truly Lousy Job," *N.Y. Post,* Dec. 3, 1970.

6 HUAC/HISC's publications run to 93,902 pages and SISS's to 70,967 pages. To this total must be added the substantial output (an estimated 10,000 pages) of the more than 30 other committees that over the years conducted hearings on aspects of subversion.

7 "McClellan Group Chosen to Make a Study of Riots," NYT, Aug. 2, 1972.

8 "How Riots Are Stirred Up: Interview with Senator McClellan," *U.S. News & World Report,* May 6, 1968, reprinted in CR, May 8, 1968, p. 12346, Vol. 114.

9 *McClellan Hearings,* Part 20, p. 4498.

10 Most of the subpoenaed universities complied with the committee's demands despite the threat to their independence. See Donner, "The Colleges Play Ball," *Nation,* Aug. 11, 1969.

11 The McSurely affair is traced in illuminating detail in Harris, *Freedom Spent,* Part Two, and Walter Goodman, "The Senate v. Alan and Margaret McSurely," *N.Y. Times Magazine,* Jan. 10, 1971. The McSurelys subsequently initiated a civil suit for damages against Senator McClellan and his aides in which, after lengthy litigation, a federal appellate court rejected the defendants' claim of legislative immunity, a ruling the Supreme Court in June 1978 decided not to disturb.

12 House Committee on Internal Security, *Subversive Influences in Riots, Looting and Burning* (1968), Part 4, pp. 1965–1966.

13 *Ibid.,* p. 1858.

14 Paul Scott, "New Left Gets Support," Topeka *Daily Capital,* July 9, 1971; Ronald Koziol, "News Service for Left Wing Underground Papers Probed," Feb. 17, 1970; "Financing the New Left with Episcopal Funds," *Christian Challenge* (June 1971).

[15] CR, Feb. 28, 1974, p. 4842, Vol. 120.

[16] Letter to Congressman Richard Bolling, March 26, 1974, and Press Release, March 27, 1974.

[17] CR, Sept. 30, 1974, pp. 32812–14, Vol. 120; "House to Retain Security Panel," NYT, Oct. 3, 1964; CR, Jan. 14, 1975, p. 22, Vol. 121, "House Democrats Vote Abolition of Panel that Investigated Reds," NYT, Jan. 14, 1975.

[18] CR, March 16, 1970, voi. 116, pp. 7462–7465; Oct. 18, 1972, Vol. 118, pp. 37584–37594; Nov. 8, 1972, p. E9089. Both HISC and SISS routinely used the *Congressional Record* to give broader circulation to their investigations and especially to disseminate lists of names. SISS also made extensive use of leaks to media clients.

[19] Susan Jacoby, "Miami si, Cuba no," *N.Y. Times Magazine,* Sept. 29, 1974.

[20] Jack Anderson column, May 30, 1972; "Midland Hotel Head Links Wiretap Plan to Federal Probers," Chicago *Sun Times,* June 1, 1972; "House Units Bugging Gets Hanrahan Eye," Chicago *Sun Times,* June 6, 1972.

[21] SISS, "Extent of Subversion in New Left," Part 6, pp. 889–890.

[22] See, for example, HISC's *Gun Barrel Politics, 1966–1971* (1971), p. 137.

[23] *SISS Ann. Rep.* (1972), p. 19; chief investigator Alphonse Tarabochia regularly attended and addressed national and area conferences of the Law Enforcement Intelligence Unit (LEIU, discussed below)—*ibid.,* p. 3; "Worst Yet to Come," Chicago *Tribune,* May 7, 1970 (report of Tarabochia address to 400 intelligence agents at 15th annual LEIU conference); SISS Hearings, "Assaults on Law Enforcement Officers," Parts 1–5 (1970).

[24] CR, pp. 13507–13510, Vol. 113; "Eastland on a New Subversive Hunt," NYT, Oct. 29, 1967; *New Politics Wins* (Newsletter of National Conference for New Politics, Nov. 15, 1967); "Senate New Left Inquiry Scored by Anti-war and Rights Leaders," NYT, Oct. 28, 1970.

[25] *Testimony of Gerald Wayne Kirk* (1970), at p. 225. Of the 365 printed pages of hearings, at least 225 are devoted to questions and answers involving identifications of individuals.

[26] *Ibid.,* pp. 41, 65, 135.

[27] "Security Risk Specialist," NYT, Nov. 6, 1963; "Fund with Birch Ties Helped Otepka in State Department Fight by Payment of Legal Fees," NYT, April 16, 1969; "Dirksen Accuses Times of a Smear," NYT, April 16, 1969; "Senate Confirms Otepka for Subversive Activities Control Board," NYT, June 25, 1969; William J. Gill, *The Ordeal of Otto Otepka* (Arlington House, 1969), *passim;* SISS Hearings, *State Department Security* (1963), Parts 2–20, pp. 1–1806 ("The Otepka Case").

[28] *SISS Ann. Rep.* (1973), pp. 12–13, and see "Passport Chief, 72, Told to Retire," NYT, May 29, 1977; Sanford J. Ungar, "J. Edgar Hoover Leaves the State Department," *Foreign Policy* (Fall, 1977).

[29] "Sourwine, Long Foe of Communists, Retires," NYT, Feb. 28, 1975; Jack Anderson column, Feb. 4, 1975.

[30] See Donald J. Kemper, *Decade of Fear* (University of Missouri Press, 1965), pp. 51–73.

[31] A self-described account of Romerstein's early years in the trenches of anti-radicalism appears in CR, Dec. 15, 1977, p. E7451.

[32] The Senate huzzas were led by Florida's Senator Richard Stone who, like Congressman Pepper on the House side, welcomed an opportunity to court his Cuban constituents by hailing SISS as a bulwark against Castro-trained bombers—CR, June 28, 1976, pp. 20964–68, Vol. 122; see also CR, Dec. 12, 1975, p. 40372, Vol. 121 (Senator Jesse Helms). The MacDonald series appears in CR for June 28 (pp. 21074–21075, Vol. 122) and June 30, 1976 (pp. 21778–21779, Vol 122).

[33] "2 Counter-rallies in Philadelphia," NYT, July 5, 1976; Letter of Rev. Paul Mayer, NYT, June 25, 1976.

[34] The HUAC filing and dissemination operation is described in the author's book on HUAC (Chap. 8), Goodman, pp. 374–375, and in greater detail in Nelson, pp. 28–57. The HISC system, which continued the former practices without change, is discussed in CR: March 22, 1973, p. 9014, Vol. 119; April

1, 1974, p. 8930; 9140, Vol 120; Aug. 7,
1974, p. 27269, Vol. 120; Feb. 25, 1975,
p. 4190, Vol. 121.

35 Senate Internal Security Subcommittee,
Ann. Rep. (1972), pp. 4–5.

12. Countersubversive Intelligence in the Private Sector

1 *Post,* p. 80.
2 For further details on Jung, see "Patriotic
Associations as Undercover Agents,"
*Hearings of Subcommittee of Senate
Education and Labor Committee,*
(1935), 74th Congress, 2nd Session, pp.
321–327.
3 U. S. Army, "Memorandum for the
Record," Feb. 22, 1971. The collection
also included a "Rogues' Gallery"
consisting of 1387 photographs of
radicals.
4 "Senate Panel Holds Vast 'Subversives'
File," NYT, Sept. 7, 1971.
5 See "Senator Fisher Charges Use of File
Data," San Diego *Union,* Feb. 18, 1962;
Michael O'Connor, "Subversion Files'
History Related," San Diego *Union,*
Feb. 26, 1962; "Undercover Activists
Claim Stirs Guard Reserve Probe," San
Diego *Union,* March 9, 1962; Richard
Cate Collins, "A Review of the
Activities of Right Wing Data
Organizations," unpublished paper
submitted in political science seminar,
Princeton University, May 15, 1972, pp.
2–4. The entire saga of Van Deman, his
files and the state of California, can be
traced in the San Diego *Union* and the
L.A. *Times* for the spring and summer
of 1962.
6 *THINK* (October 1962), p. 41.
7 Miller, p. 82.
8 From Hartnett's testimony in a successful
libel suit brought by John Henry Faulk
and reproduced in Faulk's book *Fear
on Trial* (Simon and Schuster, 1964), p.
292.
9 See "J. B. Matthews, Leftist Turned
Conservative, Dies," NYT, July 17,
1966.
10 *Dies Committee Hearings,* pp. 818–819.
11 *Group Research Report,* "The Church
League of America," Feb. 11, 1963.
12 Charles R. Baker, "Blacklisting,"
Homefront (March 1969).
13 Edgar C. Bundy, "Special Report to All
CLA Supporters," Aug. 30, 1967.
14 *Group Research Report, op. cit.*
15 "Rightist Group Fights SDS Plan by

Keeping Files on Job Applicants,"
Chicago *Sun Times,* June 8, 1969; see
also "International Symposium on
Communism," sponsored by the CLA,
Chicago, March 10–12, 1967.
16 *Group Research Report,* "American
Security Council," May 25, 1962. See
also Bernard D. Nossiter, "Group
Earmarks $150,000 to Defeat Liberals,"
Washington *Post,* Oct. 26, 1970; Harold
C. Relyea, "The American Security
Council," *Nation,* Jan. 24, 1972, pp.
113–116; "Small Town Is Home for Slick
Band of Right Wing Activists,"
Arizona *Republic,* Feb. 18, 1979.
17 Wallace Turner, "Anti-Communist
Council Prepares a Voting Index on
Congress," NYT, Aug. 17, 1970. See
also Jack E. Ison, "The Security
Officer's Notebook; Research and
Information Centers on Subversive
Activity," *Law and Order* (June 1961).
18 Berkeley Rice, "Degrees in Paranoia; The
Cold War College," *Nation,* Oct. 4,
1971.
19 Michael T. Klare, "The Boom in Private
Police," *Nation,* Nov. 15, 1975.
20 O'Toole, *passim.*
21 Thomas W. Ennis, "Fear of Sabotage
Spurs Industrial Security Drive," NYT,
Oct. 2, 1970. See also Charles D.
Brennan, "Subversion and Security,"
Industrial Security (April 1968), pp.
14–19.
22 Fred J. Cook, "Governor Kirk's Private
Eyes," *Nation,* May 15, 1967, pp.
616–622. Material on the evolution of
Wackenhut can be found in James
Ridgeway, "Spying for Industry," *New
Republic,* May 14, 1966, pp. 10–11, and
Richard Hartzman, "Private Police in
America: The Private Security
Industry," issued by the Project on
Privacy and Data Collection, ACLU,
New York, Aug. 1, 1976.
23 "The Wackenhut Corporation," prospectus
issued by Francis I. duPont, A. C.
Allyn, Inc., April 26, 1966, p. 13.
24 Cook, *op. cit.*
25 Baker, "Blacklisting," *op. cit.*

[26] File material about the Legion of Justice produced in the course of litigation as well as the fruits of further investigations by journalists are summarized in the following press stories: Chicago *Daily News:* "Ex-terrorist Tells CIA Ties," Jan. 21, 1975; "Report Cops Aided 4 Right Wing Raids," April. 8, 1975; "Seizures of Tapes, Files Told," April 8, 1975; "Russ Ballet One Target of Rightists," May 1, 1975; "Police Spies Tied to 2 Gas Bombings," May 1, 1975; "Witness Links Cops to Terror Activities," July 22, 1975; "Working with Legion of Justice," July 22, 1975; "Terrorists' Ties to Cop Spies Told," July 23, 1975; "Spy Figure Told: Talk or Else . . . ", July 24, 1975; "Cop Spying Witness Admits Lies," July 28, 1975; "Links Cops to Source of Tear Gas," July 29, 1975; "Second Witness Ties Terror Group to Military Spy Unit," Aug. 1, 1975; and "Cops 'Encouraged' Terrorist Rampage by Right Wingers," Nov. 10, 1975. Chicago *Tribune:* "Robbery and Other Charges Dropped Against Informer in Police Spy Probe," June 15, 1975; "Testimony of Police Spy Figure Stricken," Aug. 13, 1975. Chicago *Sun Times:* "Harasser of Anti-War Groups Tells of Police Assistance," July 23, 1975; "Hear Cop Planned to Run Rightist Unit," July 30, 1975; and "Right Winger Believes Army Spies Engineered Passport," Aug. 1, 1975. See also, "Chronology—Partial List of Recent Right Wing Terrorists' Activities," *Second City,* April 1979; " 'Z' in Chicago—a Report of the Independent Voters of Illinois" and Report by the Extended March 1975 Cook County Grand Jury on "Improper Police Intelligence Activities," Nov. 9, 1975.

[27] Alan Stang, "The Communist Plot to Kill George Wallace," *American Opinion* (October 1972); "Schwartz Says U.S. Hides Data on Plot to Slay Wallace," NYT, Sept. 15, 1972; Heinan's corroborative version ("Stop the Conspiracy of Silence") appears in *Review of the News,* Sept. 29, 1972, and the SDS response ("2 Scoff at Charge of Link to Bremer") in the *Milwaukee Journal,* Sept. 15, 1972, and ("Heinan Never Graduated from MU") the *Marquette Tribune,* Sept. 20, 1972.

[28] Quoted in "NCLC/U.S. Labor Party," *The Public Eye* (Fall 1977), at p. 18. This detailed documented account is, next to NCLC's own voluminous output, the most rewarding source of information about LaRouche's group. Also useful is Gregory Rose, "The Stormy Life and Times of the NCLC," *National Review,* March 30, 1979. For a more recent account see "U.S. Labor Party: Cult Surrounded by Controversy" and "One Man Leads U.S. Labor Party on Its Erratic Path," *New York Times,* Oct. 7 and Oct. 8, 1979, and "Nazis on the Run," *Our Town,* Sept. 2–Oct. 14, 1979. This last issue in a seven-part series deals with the group's intelligence activities.

[29] The discussion of Ducote's operation is based on the record in the case of the *People of the State of California* v. *Jerome Ducote,* and on interviews by the author with some of the principals. An account of Ducote's activities appears in Warren Hinckle and William Turner, "California's Watergate, or How the Right Tried to Win the West," *New Times,* Aug. 20, 1976.

[30] CR, Aug. 15, 1967, Vol. 113, p. 22701.

[31] The SAO saga is based on the records and briefs in *William Francis Yakopec* v. *People of the State of California, Court of Appeals, State of California, Fourth Appellate District.* Further information is contained in an investigative report based on an interview of a legal investigation with the appellant in the above case, in the FBI file of Peter George Bohmer, and in the interrogatories and responses of former FBI agent Steven Christensen in the case of *People of the State of California* v. *Calvin Fox.* Also useful are issues of *On Target,* publication of the Minutemen Patriotic Party, Committee of Correspondence, 1968–70; Minutemen internal memoranda and report forms, and a special bulletin dated Jan. 1, 1971, "Armageddon Precipitated"; Memorandum submitted by H. Peter Young, attorney, of Venice, Calif., to the Senate Select Committee on Intelligence, June 27, 1975; and the files of the L.A. *Times,* San Diego

Union, and San Diego *Door.* Aspects of the SAO operation are described in Milton Viorst, "FBI Mayhem," *New York Review of Books,* March 18, 1976; Richard Popkin, "The Strange Tale of the Secret Army Organization (USA)," *Ramparts,* (October 1973); and Peter Biskind, "The FBI's Secret Soldiers," *New Times,* Jan 9, 1976.

32 Lowell Bergman and Maxwell Robach, "Nixon's 'Lucky City': C. Arnholt Smith and the San Diego Connection," *Ramparts* (October 1973).

33 In addition to issues of *Information Digest* (hereafter referred to as *ID*), Church League publications, and court records, the principal sources for the discussion in the text of the Reeses are "Information 'Digest,' " *Public Eye* (Fall 1977); "State Police Surveillance," Report of New York State Special Task Force on State Police Non-Criminal Files, September 1977, and Hillel Levin, "Spies as Newsmen: The Information Digest Ploy," *Nation,* Oct. 7, 1978. Mr. Levin also generously made his research materials available to the author.

34 *New York State Legislative Oversight Report,* Feb. 20, 1976, Memorandum to Speaker Stanley Steingut and Assemblyman Mark Siegel from William F. Haddad and Thomas M. Burton, "Re: Sources of State Police Information"; *ID,* Nov. 19, 1971.

35 *ID,* June 17, 1972.

36 "Congressional Aide Spies on Left," *CounterSpy* (Spring 1976), p. 17.

37 *The Iron Fist and the Velvet Glove* (Center for Research on Criminal Justice, 1975), p. 182.

38 "John Rees: His Newsletter Supplied Data on Anti-War Activists," Washington *Post,* June 27, 1976.

39 Script, NBC News, "Utility Security," Dec. 25, 1977. See also "Georgia Utility Kept Files on Critics," Washington *Post,* Nov. 7, 1977.

40 See, for example, CR, Feb. 23, 1956, Vol. 102, pp. 3217–56; Jan. 14, 1958, Vol. 104, pp. 453–6; April 20, 1960, Vol. 106, p. 8362.

41 See "Clipping the Far Out Right Wing," *N.Y. Herald Tribune,* Oct. 4, 1964; "The Invective," *Time,* Jan. 31, 1964; "Pauling Loses Libel Suit Appeal Against News," NYT, July 8, 1964; "The Man Who Defied His Defamers," *N.Y. Herald Tribune,* Feb. 21, 1965; "Yale Professor Sues National Review for Libel," NYT, Aug. 30, 1963; "U.S. Action Asked in Phone 'Libels,' " NYT, Sept. 3, 1965. For a discussion of the inadequacy of libel suits as therapy for the exposé, see Donner, "Beyond Libel," *Nation,* Aug. 26, 1968.

42 See Harold L. Nelson, pp. 12–13, 26, *Doe v. McMillan,* 412 U.S. 306 (1973), and *Hutchinson v. Proxmire and Schwartz,* _____ U.S. _____ 47 Law Week 4827, decided June 26, 1979.

43 See H. Jon Rosenberg and Peter C. Cederberg, eds., *Vigilante Politics* (University of Pennsylvania Press, 1976), *passim,* and "American Vigilantes," *Society,* March/April 1976.

44 Alan Wolfe, "Extralegality and American Power," *Society,* March/April 1976.

Epilogue

1 A perceptive analysis of the new right is Andrew Kopkind, "Cold War II," *New Times,* Oct. 30, 1978, and "America's New Right," *New Times,* Sept. 30, 1977. See also Irving Howe, "The Right Menace," *New Republic,* Sept. 9, 1978; "Is America Turning Right?" *Newsweek,* Nov. 7, 1977; "A Citizen's Guide to the Right Wing," Americans for Democratic Action, 1978; Morton Kondracke, "The Assault on SALT," *New Republic,* Dec. 17, 1977 and "Home for Hardliners," *New Republic,* Feb. 4, 1978.

2 See, for example, M. Stanton Evans, "KGB Working Hard to Gain an Edge on SALT," Norwalk *Hour,* Nov. 18, 1978; Jack Anderson, "Tracing a Bug," N.Y. *Post,* Dec. 11, 1975; "Moscow Press Spies," N.Y. *Post,* July 1, 1975; "Detente Is Said to Give the KGB a Bigger Work Load," NYT, June 2, 1975; "Soviet Intelligence Service Reportedly Intercepts and Records Phone Conversations Within the U.S.," NYT, June 24, 1975.

3 CR, April 8, 1976, pp. 10187–88, Vol. 122; March 9, 1976, p. 5730–31, Vol. 122;

"Buckley Assumes Russians Infiltrate Staff of Congress," NYT, April 29, 1976; "Soviet Spying on Capitol Hill," *Time,* March 22, 1976; John Barron, "Espionage—The Dark Side of Detente," *Reader's Digest,* Jan. 1978; Jack Anderson, "KGB on Capitol Hill," Norwalk *Hour,* June 30, 1975.

4 CR, April 26, 1976, p. 11130, Vol. 122; Oct. 9, 1975, p. 32913, Vol. 121; "Disavowal by Rockefeller Fails to Mollify Jackson," NYT, April 23, 1976; William Safire, "The Sunshine Boys," NYT, May 6, 1976.

5 See for example, Michael Ledeen, "A Mole in Our Midst?," *New York,* Oct. 2, 1978.

6 Judith Coburn, "Jimmy Carter's Tet Offensive," *New Times,* April 17, 1978; "Carter and Aides Press Spy Trial Case That May Test President's Power," NYT, April 16, 1978 and Walter Karp, "Carter's 'Reforms' Restore Secrecy to Surveillance Systems," *Politicks,* April 11, 1978.

7 For example: "Terrorism in America: The Developing Internal Security Crisis," *Backgrounder,* Heritage Foundation, Aug. 7, 1978; Stefan T. Possony, and L. Francis Bouchey, "International Terrorism—The Communist Connection," *American Council for World Freedom,* 1978; Walter Bleiberg, "Terrorist Threat—in This Country Only the Law-Abiding Are Living Dangerously," *Barron's,* April 10, 1978 (reprinted in CR, April 12, 1978, p. E 1850) and Eugene R. Methvin, "The Secret War of Terrorism in U. S.," Atlanta *Constitution,* July 6–10, 1975 (five-part series).

8 M. Stanton Evans, "No Apparatus to Deal with Terrorists," Norwalk *Hour,* Dec.

16, 1978; "FBI Investigating Jones Plot Using Statute on Assassinations," NYT, Nov. 22, 1978.

9 Developments in this area are explored in Tim Butz, "Surveillance of the Anti-Nuke Movement," *Public Eye,* April 1978; Donna Warnock, "Nuclear Power and Civil Liberties, Can We Have Both?" Citizen's Energy Project (1978); and Christine Marwick, "Nuclear Power Critics and the Intelligence Community," *First Principles,* April 1, 1979.

10 A background discussion of the civil liberties issues raised by the campaign against nuclear power appears in John H. Barton, "Intensified Nuclear Safeguards and Civil Liberties," Oct. 31, 1975, Nuclear Regulatory Commission Contract No. AT (49–24) 01190, and Russell W. Ayres, "Policing Plutonium, The Civil Liberties Fall Out," *Harvard Civil Rights/Civil Liberties Review,* Spring, 1975 and Warnock cited above. Spying by utilities is described in Rory O'Connor, "Anti-Nuke Movement Spooked," *Rolling Stone,* June 1, 1978; Richard P. Pollock, "The Shifty Eye of Reddy Kilowatt," *Mother Jones,* May 1978; Bill Richards, "Georgia Utility Kept Files on Critics," Washington *Post,* Nov. 7, 1977; "Nuclear Power and Civil Liberties: Electric Utility Payments to Detective and Investigative Agencies, 1976," *Critical Mass Energy Project,* 1978; "Utilities Generate Sparks by Keeping Close Eye on Critics," *Wall St. Journal,* Jan. 11, 1979, and "Utility Security," *NBC News,* Dec. 25, 1977.

11 Bill Wallace, "California's Own Political Police," *Inquiry,* Feb. 6, 1978.

12 "Police Given 'Spy' Classes at Institute," Washington *Post,* May 14, 1978.

Selected Bibliography

In addition to the sources listed in this Bibliography, the author has made extensive use of documents released under the Freedom of Information and Privacy Acts (FOIPA), some 28,000 pages in all; materials made available in lawsuits brought against intelligence agencies both at the pretrial and trial levels; and personal correspondence with congressional committees, attorneys, informers, and, over the years, a substantial number of targets of surveillance. A wide variety of American Civil Liberties Union (ACLU) file material and surveys conducted by the author through a series of questionnaires has yielded important data. Interviews have also contributed to an understanding of the subject, including sessions with informers, both surfaced and still operative, ex-FBI agents, and surveillance targets. Finally, my own extensive files assembled over a thirty-year period in the course of legal practice have proved invaluable.

The vast periodical literature on surveillance and intelligence is not covered here; however, salient articles are cited in footnote references. *The Public Eye,* a bimonthly publication of the Repression Information Project, produces well-researched articles on the political context of intelligence. Of a number of specialized intelligence newsletters, *First Principles,* a monthly publication of the Center for National Security Studies, is the most useful as a source of developments in the field. With its emergence as a prominent subject of public concern, intelligence has become a journalistic specialty. Investigative reporters for large daily newspapers, such as the *New York Times,* the Washington *Post,* the Los Angeles *Times,* and the Chicago *Sun-Times,* have unearthed and published information that has vastly increased the usable resources in the field.

Books

Abell, Tyler, ed. *Drew Pearson: Diaries 1949–1959.* New York: Holt, Rinehart and Winston, 1974.

Adorno, T. W., Else Frenkel-Brunswik, Daniel J. Levinson, and R. Nevitt Sanford. *The Authoritarian Personality.* New York: Norton, 1950.

Agee, Philip. *Inside the Company: CIA Diary.* New York: Stonehill Publishing Company, 1975.

Allen, Charles R., Jr. *Concentration Camps, U.S.A.* Pamphlet of the Citizens Committee for Constitutional Liberties. New York, 1966.

Allport, Gordon W. *The Nature of Prejudice.* Boston: Beacon Press, 1955.

Alsop, Stewart and Thomas Braden. *Subrosa: The O.S.S. and American Espionage.* New York: Reynal and Hitchcock, 1946.

American Protective League: The Minute Man Division. Seattle: American Protective League, 1918.

Arendt, Hannah. *The Origins of Totalitarianism.* Cleveland: World Publishing, 1951.

Ashmore, Harry S., ed. *The William O. Douglas Inquiry into the State of Individual Freedom.* Boulder, Colo.: Westview Press, 1979.

Bales, James D., ed. *J. Edgar Hoover Speaks Concerning Communism.* Nutley, N.J.: Craig Press, 1951.

Barth, Alan, *Government by Investigation.* New York: Viking Press, 1955.

Belfrage, Cedric. *The American Inquisition 1945–1960.* Indianapolis: Bobbs-Merrill Company, Inc., 1973.

Belknap, Michael. *Cold War Political Justice.* Westport, Conn.: Greenwood Press, 1978.

Bell, Daniel, ed. *New American Right.* New York: Criterion Books, 1955.

——. *The Radical Right.* New York: Anchor Books, 1964.

Bellah, Robert N. *The Broken Covenant.* New York: Seabury Press, 1975.

Bernstein, Barton, ed. *Towards a New Past: Dissenting Essays in American History.* New York: Random House, 1968.

Biddle, Francis. *In Brief Authority.* Garden City, N.Y.: Doubleday, 1962.

——. *The Fear of Freedom.* Garden City, N.Y.: Doubleday, 1951.

Blackstock, Paul W. *Agents of Deceit.* Chicago: Quadrangle, 1966.

Blum, Richard H., ed. *Surveillance and Espionage in a Free Society.* New York: Praeger, 1972.

Bontecou, Eleanor. *The Federal Loyalty-Security Program.* Ithaca, N.Y.: Cornell University Press, 1953.

Borosage, Robert and John D. Marks, eds. *The CIA File.* New York: Grossman Publishers, 1976.

Bunyan, Tony. *The Political Police in Britain.* New York: St. Martin's Press, 1976.

Burns, James MacGregor. *Roosevelt: The Soldier of Freedom.* New York: Harcourt Brace Jovanovich, 1970.

Calomiris, Angela. *Red Masquerade: Undercover for the FBI.* Philadelphia: Lippincott, 1950.

Carr, Robert K. *The House Committee on Un-American Activities, 1945–1950.* Ithaca, N.Y.: Cornell University Press, 1952.

Cash, W. J. *The Mind of the South.* New York: Knopf, 1941.

Caute, David. *The Great Fear: The Anti-Communist Purge Under Truman and Eisenhower.* New York: Simon and Schuster, 1978.

Cave Brown, Anthony. *Bodyguard of Lies.* New York: Harper and Row, 1975.

Center for Research on Criminal Justice. *The Iron Fist and the Velvet Glove: An Analysis of the U.S. Police.* Berkeley, Calif.: Center for Research on Criminal Justice, 1975.

Chafee, Zechariah, Jr. *The Blessings of Liberty.* Philadelphia: Lippincott, 1956.

——. *Free Speech in the United States.* Cambridge: Harvard University Press, 1941.

——. *Freedom of Speech.* New York: Harcourt, Brace and Howe, 1920.

Chapman, Brian. *Police State.* New York: Praeger, 1970.

Chase, Harold W. *Security and Liberty: The Problem of Native Communists, 1947–1955.* Garden City, N.Y.: Doubleday, 1955.

Chevigny, Paul. *Cops and Rebels: A Study of Provocation.* New York: Curtis Books, 1972.

Citizens Research and Investigation Committee. *The Glass House Tapes.* New York: Avon Books, 1973.

Clark, Leroy. *The Grand Jury.* New York: Quadrangle, 1975.

Clark, Ramsey. *Crime in America: Observations on Its Nature, Causes, Prevention and Control.* New York: Pocket Books, 1970.

Clubb, O. Edmund. *The Witness and I.* New York: Columbia University Press, 1974.

Coben, Stanley. *J. Mitchell Palmer: Politician.* New York: Columbia University Press, 1963.

Cogley, John. *Report on Blacklisting.* New York: Fund for the Republic, 1956.

Colby, William and Peter Forbath. *Honorable Men: My Life in the CIA.* New York: Simon and Schuster, 1978.

Collins, F. L. *The FBI in Peace and War.* New York: Ace Books, 1962.

Cook, Fred J. *The FBI Nobody Knows.* New York: Macmillan, 1964.

——. *The Nightmare Decade: The Life and*

Times of Senator Joe McCarthy. New York: Random House, 1971.

Copeland, Miles. *Without Cloak or Dagger.* New York: Simon and Schuster, 1974.

Corson, William R. *The Armies of Ignorance: The Rise of the American Intelligence Empire.* New York: Dial Press, 1977.

Cowan, Paul, Nick Egleson, and Nat Hentoff. *State Secrets: Police Surveillance in America.* New York: Holt, Rinehart and Winston, 1974.

Cummings, Homer and Carl McFarland. *Federal Justice.* New York: Macmillan, 1937.

Dash, Samuel. *The Eavesdroppers.* New York: Da Capo, 1959.

Demaris, Ovid. *The Director: An Oral Biography of J. Edgar Hoover.* New York: Harper and Row, 1975.

de Toledano, Ralph. *J. Edgar Hoover: The Man in His Time.* New Rochelle, N.Y.: Arlington House, 1973.

Diggins, John P. *The American Left in the Twentieth Century.* New York: Harcourt Brace Jovanovich, 1973.

Donner, Frank J. *The Un-Americans.* New York: Ballantine Books, 1961.

Dorsen, Norman and Stephen Gillers. *None of Your Business: Government Secrecy in America.* New York: Viking Press, 1974.

Dulles, Allen. *The Craft of Intelligence.* New York: Harper and Row, 1963.

Elliff, John T. *Crime, Dissent and the Attorney General.* Beverly Hills, Calif.: Sage Publications, 1971.

———. *The Reform of FBI Intelligence Operations.* Princeton, N.J.: Princeton University Press, 1979.

Emerson, Thomas I. *The System of Freedom of Expression.* New York: Random House, 1970.

Fain, Tyrus G., ed. *The Intelligence Community: History, Organization, and Issues.* New York: R.R. Bowker, 1977.

Farago, Ladislas. *The Game of the Foxes.* New York: David McKay, 1971.

Faulk, John Henry. *Fear on Trial.* New York: Simon and Schuster, 1964.

Feurlicht, Roberta Strauss. *America's Reign of Terror.* New York: Random House, 1971.

Ford, Corey. *Donovan of OSS.* Boston: Little, Brown, 1970.

Forman, James. *The Making of Black Revolutionaries.* New York: Macmillan, 1972.

Frankel, Marvin E. and Gary P. Naftalis. *The Grand Jury: An Institution on Trial.* New York: Hill and Wang, 1975.

Fried, Richard M. *Men Against McCarthy.* New York: Columbia University Press, 1976.

Gellhorn, Walter, ed. *The States and Subversion.* Ithaca, N.Y.: Cornell University Press, 1952.

Goldstein, Robert J. *Political Repression in Modern America.* Cambridge/New York: Two Continents, 1978.

Goodman, Walter. *The Committee: The Extraordinary Career of the House Committee on Un-American Activities.* New York: Farrar, Straus and Giroux, 1968.

Griffith, Robert and Athan Theoharis, eds. *The Specter.* New York: Franklin Watts, 1974.

Halberstam, David. *The Best and the Brightest.* New York: Random House, 1972.

Halperin, Morton H., Jerry J. Berman, Robert L. Borosage, and Christine M. Marwick. *The Lawless State: The Crimes of the U.S. Intelligence Agencies.* New York: Penguin Books, 1976.

Halperin, Morton H. and Daniel Hoffman. *Freedom vs. National Security.* New York: Chelsea House, 1977.

———. *Top Secret: National Security and the Right to Know.* Washington, D.C.: New Republic Books, 1977.

Hamby, Alonzo L. *Beyond the New Deal: Harry S. Truman and American Liberalism.* New York: Columbia University Press, 1973.

Hapgood, Norman, ed. *Professional Patriots.* New York: Albert and Charles Boni, 1927.

Harney, Malachi and John C. Cross. *The Informer in Law Enforcement.* Springfield, Ill.: Charles C. Thomas, 1960.

Harper, Alan D. *The Politics of Loyalty: The White House and the Communist Issue, 1946–1952.* Westport, Conn.: Greenwood Press, 1969.

Harris, Richard. *Freedom Spent.* Boston: Little, Brown, 1975.

———. *Justice: The Crisis of Law, Order, and Freedom in America.* New York: E. P. Dutton, 1970.

Hayden, Tom. *Trial.* New York: Holt, Rinehart and Winston, 1970.

Hellman, Lillian. *Scoundrel Time.* Boston: Atlantic-Little, Brown, 1976.

Higham, John. *Strangers in the Land: Patterns of American Nativism, 1860–1925.* New York: Atheneum, 1968.

Hiss, Alger. *In the Court of Public Opinion.* New York: Knopf, 1957.

Hofstadter, Richard. *The Paranoid Style in American Politics and Other Essays.* London: Cape, 1966.

Horan, James D. *The Pinkertons: The Detective Dynasty That Made History.* New York: Crown, 1967.

—— and Howard Swiggett. *The Pinkerton Story.* New York: G. P. Putnam's Sons, 1951.

Hougan, Jim. *Spooks.* New York: Morrow, 1978.

Hyde, H. Montgomery. *Room 3603: The Story of the British Intelligence Center in New York During World War II.* New York: Farrar, Straus, 1963.

Jaffe, Julian F. *Crusade Against Radicalism.* Port Washington, N.Y.: Kennikat Press, 1972.

Jensen, Joan M. *The Price of Vigilance.* Chicago: Rand McNally, 1968.

Jones, Howard Mumford, ed. *Primer of Intellectual Freedom.* Cambridge: Harvard University Press, 1949.

Kampelman, Max. *The Communist Party vs. the C.I.O.* New York: Praeger, 1957.

Kearns, Doris. *Lyndon Johnson and the American Dream.* New York: Harper and Row, 1976.

Kirchheimer, Otto. *Political Justice: The Use of Legal Procedure for Political Ends.* Princeton, N.J.: Princeton University Press, 1961.

Kirkpatrick, Lyman B., Jr. *The U.S. Intelligence Community.* New York: Hill and Wang, 1973.

Lamb, Edward. *No Lamb for Slaughter.* New York: Harcourt Brace and World, 1963.

Latham, Earl. *The Communist Controversy in Washington.* Cambridge: Harvard University Press, 1966.

——, ed. *The Meaning of McCarthyism.* Boston: D. C. Heath, 1965.

Lasch, Christopher. *The New Radicalism in America, 1889–1963.* New York: Vintage, 1965.

Lens, Sidney. *The Futile Crusade: Anti-Communism as an American Credo.* Chicago: Quadrangle, 1964.

Levin, Murray B. *Political Hysteria in America: The Democratic Capacity for Repression.* New York: Basic Books, 1971.

Lifton, Robert Jay. *Revolutionary Immortality.* New York: Vintage, 1968.

Lipset, Seymour Martin and Earl Raab. *The Politics of Unreason: Right-Wing Extremism in America, 1790–1970.* New York: Harper and Row, 1970.

Long, Edward V. *The Intruders: The Invasion of Privacy by Government and Industry.* New York: Praeger, 1966.

Longaker, Richard P. *The Presidency and Individual Liberties.* Ithaca, N.Y.: Cornell University Press, 1961.

Lowenthal, Leo and Norbert Guterman. *Prophets of Deceit.* Palo Alto, Calif.: Pacific Books, 1949.

Lowenthal, Max. *The Federal Bureau of Investigation.* New York: William Sloane Associates, 1950.

Lukas, J. Anthony. *Nightmare: The Underside of the Nixon Years.* New York: Viking Press, 1973.

Lumer, Hyman. *The Professional Informer.* New York: New Century, 1955.

Marchetti, Victor and John D. Marks. *The CIA and the Cult of Intelligence.* New York: Knopf, 1974.

Marks, John D. *The Search for the Manchurian Candidate.* New York: Times Books, 1979.

Masterman, John C. *The Double-Cross System in the War of 1939 to 1945.* New Haven, Conn.: Yale University Press, 1972.

Matusow, Allen J. *Joseph R. McCarthy.* Englewood Cliffs, N.J.: Prentice-Hall, 1970.

Matusow, Harvey. *False Witness.* New York: Cameron and Kahn, 1955.

McAuliffe, Mary S. *Crisis on the Left.* Amherst, Mass.: University of Massachusetts Press, 1978.

McGarvey, Patrick J. *C.I.A.: The Myth and the Madness.* London: Penguin Books, 1973.

Messick, Hank. *John Edgar Hoover.* New York: David McKay, 1972.

Miller, Merle. *The Judges and the Judged.* Garden City, N.Y.: Doubleday, 1952.

Monat, Pawel and John Dille. *Spy in the U.S.* New York: Harper and Row, 1962.

Murray, Robert K. *The Red Scare: A Study in National Hysteria.* Minneapolis: University of Minnesota Press, 1955.

Nash, Jay Robert. *Citizen Hoover.* Chicago: Nelson Hall, 1972.

Navasky, Victor. *Kennedy Justice.* New York: Atheneum, 1971.

Nelson, Harold L. *Libel in News of Congressional Investigating Committees.* Minneapolis: University of Minneapolis Press, 1961.

Nelson, Jack and Jack Bass. *The Orangeburg Massacre.* New York: Ballantine Books, 1970.

Nelson, Jack and Ronald J. Ostrow. *The FBI and the Berrigans.* New York: Coward, McCann and Geoghegan, 1972.

Ogden, Raymond A. *The Dies Committee: A Study of the Special House Committee for the Investigation of Un-American Activities, 1938–1944.* Washington, D.C.: Catholic University of America Press, 1945.

Ollestad, Norman. *Inside the FBI.* New York: Lyle Stuart, 1967.

O'Toole, George. *The Private Sector.* New York: Norton, 1978.

Overstreet, Harry and Bonaro. *The FBI in Our Open Society.* New York: Norton, 1969.

Oxnam, G. Bromley. *I Protest.* New York: Harper, 1954.

Packer, Herbert L. *Ex-Communist Witnesses.* Stanford, Calif.: Stanford University Press, 1962.

Parenti, Michael. *The Anti-Communist Impulse.* New York: Random House, 1969.

Payne, Cril. *Deep Cover.* New York: Newsweek Books, 1979.

Perkus, Cathy, ed. *COINTELPRO: The FBI's Secret War on Political Freedom.* New York: Monad Press, 1975.

Philbrick, Herbert. *I Led Three Lives.* New York: McGraw-Hill, 1953.

Philby, Kim. *My Silent War.* New York: Grove Press, 1968.

Pinkerton, Allan. *The Spy of the Rebellion.* New York: G. W. Carleton, 1886.

——. *Strikers, Communists, Tramps and Detectives.* New York: Arno Press, 1964.

Platt, Anthony M., ed. *The Politics of Riot*

Commissions *1917–1970.* New York: Macmillan, 1971.

Popov, Dusko. *Spy/Counterspy.* New York: Grosset and Dunlap, 1974.

Post, Louis F. *The Deportations Delirium of Nineteen-Twenty.* Chicago: Charles H. Kerr, 1923.

Powers, Thomas. *The Man Who Kept the Secrets.* New York: Alfred A. Knopf, 1979.

Preston, William, Jr. *Aliens and Dissenters: Federal Suppression of Radicals, 1903–1933.* New York: Harper and Row, 1963.

Ransom, Harry Howe. *The Intelligence Establishment.* Cambridge: Harvard University Press, 1970.

Raskin, Marcus. *Notes on the Old System: To Transform American Politics.* New York: David McKay, 1974.

Reynolds, Quentin. *The F.B.I.* New York: Random House, 1963.

Roche, John P. *The Quest for the Dream.* New York: Macmillan, 1963.

Rorty, James and Moshe Decter. *McCarthy and the Communists.* Boston: Beacon Press, 1954.

Rowan, Richard Wilmer. *The Pinkertons: A Detective Dynasty.* Boston: Little, Brown, 1931.

——. *Spy and Counter-Spy: The Development of Modern Espionage.* New York: Viking Press, 1928.

Rule, James B. *Private Lives and Public Surveillance.* New York: Schocken Books, 1974.

Sale, Kirkpatrick. *SDS.* New York: Random House, 1973.

Schlesinger, Arthur M., Jr. *Robert F. Kennedy and His Times.* Boston: Houghton Mifflin, 1978

——. *A Thousand Days.* Boston: Houghton Mifflin, 1965.

Schott, Joseph L. *No Left Turns.* New York: Praeger, 1975.

Schrag, Peter. *Test of Loyalty.* New York: Simon and Schuster, 1974.

Seymour, Whitney North, Jr. *United States Attorney: An Inside View of "Justice" in America under the Nixon Administration.* New York: Morrow, 1975.

Shils, Edward A. *The Torment of Secrecy.* Glencoe, Ill.: The Free Press, 1956.

Skolnick, Jerome H. *The Politics of Protest.* New York: Ballantine Books, 1969.

Smith, R. Harris. *O.S.S.: The Secret Story of America's First Central Intelligence Agency.* New York: Dell, 1973.

Sorensen, Theodore C. *Kennedy.* New York: Harper and Row, 1965.

Spolansky, Jacob. *The Communist Trail in America.* New York: Macmillan, 1951.

Starobin, Joseph. *American Communism in Crisis, 1943–1957.* Cambridge: Harvard University Press, 1972.

Steven, Stewart. *Operation Splinter Factor.* Philadelphia: Lippincott, 1974.

Stevenson, William. *A Man Called Intrepid.* New York: Ballantine Books, 1976.

Sullivan, William C. and Bill Brown. *Bureau: My Thirty Years in Hoover's FBI.* New York: Norton, 1979.

Szulc, Tad. *Compulsive Spy: The Strange Career of E. Howard Hunt.* New York: Viking Press, 1974.

Taylor, Telford. *Grand Inquest: The Story of Congressional Investigations.* New York: Simon and Schuster, 1955.

Theoharis, Athan. *Seeds of Repression: Harry S. Truman and the Origins of McCarthyism.* Chicago: Quadrangle, 1971.

——. *Spying on Americans.* Philadelphia: Temple University Press, 1978.

Thurwald, Jürgen. *Century of the Detective.* New York: Harcourt Brace and World, 1964.

Tully, Andrew. *CIA, The Inside Story.* New York: Morrow, 1970.

Turner, William W. *Hoover's F.B.I.* Los Angeles: Sherbourne Press, 1970.

Ungar, Sanford J. *FBI: An Uncensored Look Behind the Walls.* Boston: Little, Brown, 1975.

Watters, Pat and Stephen Gillers, eds. *Investigating the FBI.* New York: Doubleday, 1973.

Wechsler, James A. *The Age of Suspicion.* New York: Random House, 1953.

Wheeler, S., ed. *On Record: Files and Dossiers in American Life.* New York: Russell Sage Foundation, 1969.

Whitehead, Don. *Attack on Terror: The FBI Against the Ku Klux Klan.* New York: Funk and Wagnalls, 1970.

——. *The FBI Story.* New York: Random House, 1956.

Wilcox, Clair, ed. *Civil Liberties Under Attack.* Philadelphia: University of Pennsylvania Press, 1951.

Wilensky, Harold L. *Organizational Intelligence: Knowledge and Power in Government and Industry.* New York: Basic Books, 1967.

Wise, David. *The American Police State.* New York: Random House, 1975.

——. *The Politics of Lying: Government Deception, Secrecy and Power.* New York: Random House, 1973.

—— and Thomas B. Ross. *The Espionage Establishment.* New York: Random House, 1967.

——. *The Invisible Government.* New York: Vintage Books, 1974.

Wittenberg, Philip, ed. *The Lamont Case: History of a Congressional Investigation.* New York: Horizon Press, 1957.

Wolfe, Alan. *The Seamy Side of Democracy: Repression in America.* New York: David McKay, 1973.

Wright, Richard O., ed. *Whose FBI?* La Salle, Ill.: Open Court, 1974.

Government Publications

Listed below are reports of executive commissions and of the General Accounting Office, followed by congressional hearings and reports on intelligence-related subjects. Additional sources such as the hearings and reports of congressional anti-subversive committees are referred to in the footnotes.

National Advisory Commission on Civil Disorder. *Report of the National Advisory Commission on Civil Disorder.* Washington, D.C.: Government Printing Office, 1968.

National Advisory Committee on Criminal Justice Standards and Goals. *Disorders and Terrorism: Report of the Task Force on Disorders and Terrorism.* Washington, D.C.: Government Printing office, 1976.

National Advisory Committee on Criminal Justice Standards and Goals. *Private Security: Report of the Task Force on Private Security.* Washington, D.C.: Government Printing Office, 1976.

U.S. Commission on CIA Activities within the United States. *Report to the President.* Washington, D.C.: Government Printing Office, 1975.

U.S. Commission on Organization of the Executive Branch of the Government. *Intelligence Activities.* Washington, D.C.: Government Printing Office, 1955.

U.S. Comptroller General. *F.B.I. Domestic Intelligence Operations: An Uncertain Future.* Report to the House Committee on the Judiciary. Washington, D.C.: General Accounting Office, 1977.

——. *F.B.I. Domestic Intelligence Operations —Their Purpose and Scope: Issues that Need to be Resolved.* Report to the House Committee on the Judiciary. Washington, D.C.: General Accounting Office, 1976.

——. *Internal Revenue Service's Controls Over the Use of Confidential Informants: Recent Improvements not Adequate.* Report to the Joint Committee on Taxation. Washington, D.C.: General Accounting Office, 1977.

U.S. Congress. House. Committee on Armed Services. *Inquiry into the Alleged Involvement of the Central Intelligence Agency in the Watergate and Ellsberg Matters.* Hearings, 93th Congress, 1st Session, 1973.

——. House. Committee on Government Operations. *Access to Records.* Hearings, 93rd Congress, 2nd Session, 1974.

——. House. Committee on Government Operations. *Data Processing Management in the Federal Government.* Hearings, 90th Congress, 1st Session, 1967.

——. House. Committee on Government Operations. *Interception of Non-Verbal Communications by Federal Intelligence Agencies.* Hearings, 94th Congress, 1st and 2nd Sessions, 1976.

——. House. Committee on Government Operations. *Operations of the I.R.S.* Oversight Hearings, 94th Congress, 1st Session, 1975, part 1.

——. House. Committee on Government Operations. *Operations of the I.R.S. (Operation Tradewinds, Project Haven, and Narcotic Traffickers Tax Program.)* Oversight Hearings, 94th Congress, 1st Session, 1975.

——. House. Committee on Government Operations. *Privacy and the National Data Bank Concept.* 90th Congress, 2nd Session, 1968. (H. Rpt. #1842).

——. House. Committee on Government Operations. *Special Inquiry on Invasion of Privacy.* Hearings, 89th Congress, 2nd Session, 1965.

——. House. Committee on Government Operations. *The Computer and Invasion of Privacy.* Hearings, 89th Congress, 2nd Session, 1966.

——. House. Committee on Internal Security. *Domestic Intelligence Operations for Internal Security Purposes.* Hearings, 93rd Congress, 2nd Session, 1974, part 1.

——. House. Committee on Internal Security. *Statutory Authority for the FBI's Domestic Intelligence Activities: An Analysis.* Committee Print, 93rd Congress, 1st Session, 1973.

——. House. Committee on Standards of Official Conduct. *Investigation of the Publication of Select Committee on Intelligence Report.* 94th Congress, 2nd Session, 1976.

——. House. Committee on the Judiciary. *FBI Counterintelligence Programs.* Hearings, 93rd Congress, 2nd Session, 1974.

——. House. Committee on the Judiciary. *FBI Oversight.* Hearings, 94th Congress, 1st and 2nd Sessions, 1975, 1976.

——. House. Committee on the Judiciary. *Grand Jury Reform.* Hearings, 95th Congress, 1st Session, 1977, parts 1, 2.

——. House. Committee on the Judiciary. *Impeachment of Richard Nixon, President of the United States.* 93rd Congress, 2nd Session, 1974. (H. Rpt. #93–1305).

——. House. Committee on the Judiciary. *Statement of Information—Books I–VI: Events Following the Watergate Break-In.* Hearings, 93rd Congress, 2nd Session, 1974.

——. House. Committee on the Judiciary. *Statement of Information—Book VIII: Internal Revenue Service.* Hearings, 93rd Congress, 2nd Session, 1974.

——. House. Committee on the Judiciary. *Statement of Information—Book VII: White House Surveillance Activities and Campaign Activities.* Hearings, 93rd Congress, 2nd Session, 1974.

——. House. Committee on the Judiciary. *Statement of Information: Appendix I—*

Presidential Statements on the Watergate Break-In and Its Investigation. Hearings, 93rd Congress, 2nd Session, 1974.

——. House. Committee on the Judiciary. *Statement of Information Submitted on Behalf of President Nixon—Book I: Events Following the Watergate Break-In.* Hearings, 93rd Congress, 2nd Session, 1974.

——. House. Committee on the Judiciary. *Statement of Information Submitted on Behalf of President Nixon—Book IV: White House Surveillance Activities.* Hearings, 93rd Congress, 2nd Session, 1974.

——. House. Committee on the Judiciary. *Surveillance.* Hearings, 94th Congress, 1st Session, 1975.

——. House Committee on the Judiciary. *The Matter of Wiretapping, Electronic Eavesdropping and Other Surveillance.* Hearings, 94th Congress, 1st Session, 1975, parts 1, 2.

——. House. Committee on the Judiciary. *Wiretapping and Electronic Surveillance.* Hearings, 93rd Congress, 2nd Session, 1974.

——. House. Committee on Ways and Means. *IRS Intelligence Operations.* Hearings, 94th Congress, 1st Session, 1975.

——. House. Committee on Ways and Means. *IRS Operations and Taxpayer Assistance.* Hearings, 94th Congress, 1st Session, 1975.

——. House. Select Committee on Intelligence. *U.S. Intelligence Agencies and Activities.* Hearings, 94th Congress, 1st Session, 1975, parts 1–6.

——. House. Select Committee on Intelligence. *Investigation of Publication of Select Committee on Intelligence Report.* Hearings, 94th Congress, 2nd Session, 1976.

——. Joint Committee on Internal Revenue Taxation. *Investigation of the Special Service Staff of the Internal Revenue Service.* 94th Congress, 1st Session, 1975.

——. House. Permanent Select Committee on Intelligence. *The CIA and the Media.* Hearings, 95th Congress, 1st and 2nd Sessions, 1978.

——. House. Permanent Select Committee on Intelligence. *Disclosure of Funds for Intelligence Activities.* Hearings, 95th Congress, 2nd Session, 1978.

U.S. Congress. Senate. Committee on Appropriations. *International Criminal Police Organization (INTERPOL).* Hearings, 94th Congress, 1st Session, 1975.

——. Senate. Committee on Appropriations. *Review of Secret Service Protective Measures.* Hearings, 94th Congress, 1st Session, 1975.

——. Senate. Committee on Armed Services. *Military Cold War Education and Speech Review Policies.* Hearings, 87th Congress, 2nd Session, 1962, parts 1–8.

——. Senate. Committee on Armed Services. *Military Cold War Education and Speech Review Policies.* Report, 87th Congress, 2nd Session, 1962.

——. Senate. Committee on Armed Services. *Nomination of William E. Colby.* Hearings, 94th Congress, 1st Session, 1973.

——. Senate. Committee on Foreign Relations. *CIA Foreign and Domestic Activities.* Hearings, 94th Congress, 1st Session, 1975.

——. Senate. Committee on Foreign Relations. *Dr. Kissinger's Role in Wiretapping.* Hearings, 93rd Congress, 2nd Session, 1974.

——. Senate. Committee on Foreign Relations. *Nomination of Richard Helms to Be Ambassador to Iran and CIA International and Domestic Activities.* Hearings, 93rd Congress, 1st Session, 1973.

——. Senate. Committee on Foreign Relations. *Report on the Inquiry Concerning Dr. Kissinger's Role in Wiretapping, 1969, 1971: Review and Findings.* Committee Print, 93rd Congress, 2nd Session, 1974.

——. Senate. Committee on Government Operations. *Legislative Proposals to Strengthen Congressional Oversight of the Nation's Intelligence Agencies.* Hearings, 93rd Congress, 2nd Session, 1974.

——. Senate. Committee on Government Operations. *Oversight of U.S. Government Intelligence Functions,* Hearings, 94th Congress, 2nd Session, 1976.

——. Senate. Committee on the Judiciary. *Army Surveillance of Civilians: A*

Documentary Analysis. 92nd Congress, 2nd Session, 1972.

——. Senate Committee on the Judiciary. *Computer Privacy.* Hearings, 90th Congress, 1st Session, 1967.

——. Senate. Committee on the Judiciary. *Federal Data Banks, Computers and the Bill of Rights.* Hearings, 92nd Congress, 1st Session, 1971, parts 1, 2.

——. Senate. Committee on the Judiciary. *Government Dossier* Report. 90th Congress, 1st Session, 1967.

——. Senate. Committee on the Judiciary. *Invasions of Privacy. (Government Agencies).* Hearings, 89th Congress, 1st Session, 1965, parts 1, 2.

——. Senate. Committee on the Judiciary. *Invasions of Privacy. (Telephone Systems).* Hearings, 89th Congress, 2nd Session, 1966, part 1.

——. Senate. Committee on the Judiciary. *Louis Patrick Gray III.* Hearings, 93rd Congress, 1st Session, 1973.

——. Senate. Committee on the Judiciary. *Military Surveillance.* Hearings, 93rd Congress, 2nd Session, 1974.

——. Senate. Committee on the Judiciary. *Nomination of Clarence M. Kelley to Be Director of the Federal Bureau of Investigation.* Hearings, 93rd Congress, 1st Session, 1973.

——. Senate. Committee on the Judiciary. *Political Intelligence in the IRS: The Special Service Staff. A Documentary Analysis.* 93rd Congress, 2nd Session, 1974.

——. Senate. Committee on the Judiciary. *Reform of Federal Criminal Laws.* Hearings, 93rd Congress, 1st Session, 1973, parts 1–6.

——. Senate. Committee on the Judiciary. *Report on Military Surveillance of Civilian Politics.* 93rd Congress, 1st Session, 1973.

——. Senate. Committee on the Judiciary. *Right of Privacy Act of 1967.* Hearings, 90th Congress, 1st Session, 1967, parts 1, 2.

——. Senate. Committee on the Judiciary. *Surveillance Technology. Report on Policy and Implications: An Analysis and Compendium of Materials.* 94th Congress, 2nd Session, 1976.

——. Senate. Committee on the Judiciary. *Wiretapping, Eavesdropping and the Bill of Rights.* Hearings, 85th and 86th Congresses, 1958–1960.

——. Senate. Committee on the Judiciary and Committee on Foreign Relations. *Warrantless Wiretapping and Electronic Surveillance—1974.* Joint Hearings, 93rd Congress, 2nd Session, 1974.

——. Senate. Committee on the Judiciary and Committee on Foreign Relations. *Warrantless Wiretapping and Electronics Surveillance: Report.* Committee Print, 94th Congress, 1st Session, 1975.

——. Senate. Select Committee on Intelligence. *Foreign Intelligence Surveillance Act of 1978.* Hearings, 95th Congress, 2nd Session, 1978.

——. Senate. Select Committee on Intelligence. *Whether Disclosure of Funds Authorized for Intelligence is in the Public Interest,* Hearings, 95th Congress, 1st Session, 1977.

——. Senate. Select Committee on Presidential Campaign Activities. *Presidential Campaign Activities of 1972: Watergate and Related Activities, Phase I: Watergate Investigation.* Books 1–9. Hearings, 93rd Congress, 1st Session, 1973.

——. Senate. Select Committee to Study Governmental Operations with Respect to Intelligence Activities. *Alleged Assassination Plots Involving Foreign Leaders,* Interim Report, 94th Congress, 1st Session, 1975.

——. Senate. Select Committee to Study Governmental Operations with Respect to Intelligence Activities. Hearings, 94th Congress, 1st Session, 1975, Vols. 1–7: Vol. 1. *Unauthorized Storage of Toxic Agents,* Vol. 2. *Huston Plan,* Vol. 3. *Internal Revenue Service,* Vol. 4. *Mail Opening,* Vol. 5. *The National Security Agency and Fourth Amendment Rights,* Vol. 6. *Federal Bureau of Investigation,* Vol. 7. *Covert Action.*

——. Senate. Select Committee to Study Governmental Operations with respect to Intelligence Activities. Final Report, 94th Congress, 2nd Session, 1976, Books I—VI: Book I. *Foreign and Military Intelligence,* Book II. *Intelligence Activities and the Rights of Americans,* Book III. *Supplementary Detailed Staff Reports on the Intelligence Activities and the Rights of Americans,* Book IV. *Supplementary Detailed Staff Reports,*

Book V. *Investigation of the Assassination of President John F. Kennedy: Performance of the Intelligence Agencies,* Book VI. *Supplementary Reports on Intelligence Activities.*

——. Senate. Committee on the Judiciary. *FBI Statutory Charter,* Hearings, 95th Congress, 2nd Session, 1978, parts 1–3.

——. Senate. Select Committee on Intelligence and Committee on Human Resources, *Project Mkultra, the CIA's Program of Research in Behavioral Modification,* Joint Hearings, 95th Congress, 1st Session, 1977.

——. Senate. Select Committee on Intelligence, *The Use of Classified Information in Litigation,* Hearings, 95th Congress, 2nd Session, 1978.

——. Senate. Select Committee on Intelligence, *National Security Secrets and the Administration of Justice,* Report, 95th Congress, 2nd Session, 1978.

——. Senate. Select Committee on Intelligence, Annual Report, 96th Congress, 1st Session, 1979.

——. House. Committee on International Relations, *International Terrorism: Legislative Intiatives,* 95th Congress, 2nd Session, 1978.

——. House. Committee on the Judiciary, *Federal Capabilities in Crisis Management and Terrorism,* 95th Congress, 2nd Session, 1978.

——. Senate. Committee on Governmental Affairs, *An Act to Combat International Terrorism,* Hearings, 95th Congress, 2nd Session, 1978.

——. House. Committee on the Judiciary, *Bill of Rights Procedure Act,* 95th Congress, 2nd Session, 1978.

——. House. Committee on Interstate and Foreign Commerce, *Contempt Proceedings Against Patricia Atthowe,* 95th Congress, 2nd Session, 1978.

——. Senate. Select Committee on Intelligence, Annual Report, 95th Congress, 2nd Session, 1978.

Index

A Note on the Type

The text of this book was set in a face called Times Roman, designed by Stanley Morison for The Times *(London), and first introduced by that newspaper in 1932.*

Among typographers and designers of the twentieth century, Stanley Morison has been a strong forming influence, as typographical adviser to the English Monotype Corporation, as a director of two distinguished English publishing houses, and as a writer of sensibility, erudition, and keen practical sense.

Composed, printed, and bound by The Haddon Craftsmen, Inc., Scranton, Pennsylvania.
Designed by Camilla Filancia.